RESEARCH HANDBOOK ON THE HISTORY OF COPYRIGHT LAW

RESEARCH HANDBOOKS IN INTELLECTUAL PROPERTY

Series Editor: Jeremy Phillips, *Intellectual Property Consultant, Olswang, Research Director, Intellectual Property Institute and co-founder, IPKat weblog*

Under the general editorship and direction of Jeremy Phillips comes this important new *Handbook* series of high quality, original reference works that cover the broad pillars of intellectual property law: trademark law, patent law and copyright law – as well as less developed areas, such as geographical indications, and the increasing intersection of intellectual property with other fields. Taking an international and comparative approach, these *Handbooks*, each edited by leading scholars in the respective field, will comprise specially commissioned contributions from a select cast of authors, bringing together renowned figures with up-and-coming younger authors. Each will offer a wide-ranging examination of current issues in intellectual property that is unrivalled in its blend of critical, innovative thinking and substantive analysis, and in its synthesis of contemporary research.

Each *Handbook* will stand alone as an invaluable source of reference for all scholars of intellectual property, as well as for practising lawyers who wish to engage with the discussion of ideas within the field. Whether used as an information resource on key topics, or as a platform for advanced study, these *Handbooks* will become definitive scholarly reference works in intellectual property law.

Titles in the series include:

The Law and Theory of Trade Secrecy
A Handbook of Contemporary Research
Edited by Rochelle C. Dreyfuss and Katherine J. Strandburg

Research Handbook on Intellectual Property Licensing
Edited by Jacques de Werra

Criminal Enforcement of Intellectual Property
A Handbook of Contemporary Research
Edited by Christophe Geiger

Research Handbook on Cross-border Enforcement of Intellectual Property
Edited by Paul Torremans

Research Handbook on Human Rights and Intellectual Property
Edited by Christophe Geiger

International Intellectual Property
A Handbook of Contemporary Research
Edited by Daniel J. Gervais

Indigenous Intellectual Property
A Handbook of Contemporary Research
Edited by Matthew Rimmer

Research Handbook on Intellectual Property and Geographical Indications
Edited by Dev S. Gangjee

Research Handbook on the History of Copyright Law
Edited by Isabella Alexander and H. Tomás Gómez-Arostegui

Research Handbook on the History of Copyright Law

Edited by

Isabella Alexander
University of Technology Sydney, Australia

H. Tomás Gómez-Arostegui
Lewis and Clark Law School, USA

RESEARCH HANDBOOKS IN INTELLECTUAL PROPERTY

Edward Elgar
PUBLISHING

Cheltenham, UK • Northampton, MA, USA

© The Editors and Contributors Severally 2016

All rights reserved. No part of this publication may be reproduced, stored in a retrieval system or transmitted in any form or by any means, electronic, mechanical or photocopying, recording, or otherwise without the prior permission of the publisher.

Published by
Edward Elgar Publishing Limited
The Lypiatts
15 Lansdown Road
Cheltenham
Glos GL50 2JA
UK

Edward Elgar Publishing, Inc.
William Pratt House
9 Dewey Court
Northampton
Massachusetts 01060
USA

A catalogue record for this book
is available from the British Library

Library of Congress Control Number: 2015952679

This book is available electronically in the **Elgar**online
Law subject collection
DOI 10.4337/9781783472406

ISBN 978 1 78347 239 0 (cased)
ISBN 978 1 78347 240 6 (eBook)

Typeset by Columns Design XML Ltd, Reading
Printed and bound in Great Britain by TJ International Ltd, Padstow

PUBLISHER'S NOTE

Every effort has been made to trace all copyright holders but if any have been inadvertently overlooked the publishers will be pleased to make the necessary arrangements at the first opportunity.

We dedicate this book to the memory of our esteemed colleague and friend, Catherine Seville (1963–2016)

Contents

List of contributors	xi
1. Introduction *Isabella Alexander and H. Tomás Gómez-Arostegui*	1

PART I HISTORIOGRAPHY

2. Copyright history in the advocate's arsenal *Barbara Lauriat*	7
3. Law, aesthetics and copyright historiography: A critical reading of the genealogies of Martha Woodmansee and Mark Rose *Kathy Bowrey*	27
4. The 'romantic' author *Martha Woodmansee*	53

PART II UNITED KINGDOM PERSPECTIVES

5. The Stationers' Company in England before 1710 *Ian Gadd*	81
6. The anatomy of copyright law in Scotland before 1710 *Alastair J. Mann*	96
7. Literary property in Scotland in the eighteenth and nineteenth centuries *Hector MacQueen*	119
8. Music copyright in late eighteenth and early nineteenth century Britain *Nancy A. Mace*	139
9. How art was different: Researching the history of artistic copyright *Elena Cooper*	158
10. Determining infringement in the eighteenth and nineteenth centuries in Britain: 'A ticklish job' *Isabella Alexander*	174
11. Equitable infringement remedies before 1800 *H. Tomás Gómez-Arostegui*	195

PART III INTERNATIONAL PERSPECTIVES

12. Proto-property in literary and artistic works: Sixteenth century papal printing privileges *Jane C. Ginsburg*	237
13. British colonial and imperial copyright *Catherine Seville*	268

x *Research handbook on the history of copyright law*

14.	The public international law of copyright and related rights *Sam Ricketson*	288
15.	El Salvador and the internationalisation of copyright *Jose Bellido*	313

PART IV   NATIONAL PERSPECTIVES

16.	United States copyright, 1672–1909 *Oren Bracha*	335
17.	'Cabined, cribbed, confined, bound in': Copyright in the Australian colonies *Catherine Bond*	372
18.	Aspects of French literary property developments in the eighteenth (and nineteenth) centuries *Frédéric Rideau*	391
19.	Codified anxieties: Literary copyright in mid-nineteenth century Spain *Jose Bellido*	423

Bibliography	444
Index	471

Contributors

Isabella Alexander is an Associate Professor in the Faculty of Law at the University of Technology, Sydney, Australia.

Jose Bellido is a Senior Lecturer in Law at the University of Kent, Canterbury, UK.

Catherine Bond is a Senior Lecturer at the Faculty of Law, UNSW Sydney, Australia.

Kathy Bowrey is a Professor at the Faculty of Law, UNSW Sydney, Australia.

Oren Bracha is the Howrey LLP and Arnold, White & Durkee Centennial Professor of Law in the University of Texas School of Law, Austin, Texas USA.

Elena Cooper is Orton Research Fellow in Intellectual Property Law at Trinity Hall, Cambridge, UK and CREATe Postdoctoral Researcher in Copyright Law, History and Policy, at the CREATe Copyright Centre, Glasgow University, UK.

Ian Gadd is Professor of English Literature at Bath Spa University, UK.

Jane C. Ginsburg is the Morton L Janklow Professor of Literary and Artistic Property Law at Columbia University School of Law, New York USA.

H. Tomás Gómez-Arostegui is the Kay Kitagawa & Andy Johnson-Laird IP Faculty Scholar and a Professor of Law at Lewis & Clark Law School in Portland, Oregon USA.

Barbara Lauriat is a Senior Lecturer in Law at King's College London, a Research Fellow of the Oxford Intellectual Property Research Centre, and an Academic Fellow of the Honourable Society of the Inner Temple.

Nancy A. Mace is Professor of English at the US Naval Academy in Annapolis, Maryland USA.

Hector MacQueen is a Scottish Law Commissioner and Professor of Private Law in the School of Law, University of Edinburgh, Scotland, UK.

Alastair J. Mann is a Senior Lecturer in History in the Division of History and Politics, School of Arts and Humanities, at the University of Stirling, Scotland, UK.

Sam Ricketson is Professor of Law, Melbourne Law School, and member of the Victorian Bar, Victoria, Australia.

Frédéric Rideau is a Maître de conferences (Lecturer) in Legal History at the Faculty of Law of the University of Poitiers, France.

Catherine Seville is Reader in Law, University of Cambridge and Director of Studies in Law, Newnham College, Cambridge, UK.

Martha Woodmansee is a Professor of English and of Law at Case Western Reserve University in Cleveland, Ohio USA.

1. Introduction
Isabella Alexander and H. Tomás Gómez-Arostegui

The study of copyright's history dates back almost to the birth of copyright as a statutory construct. First emerging during the common law copyright debates of the eighteenth century, and featuring prominently in the lawyer's texts of the nineteenth century, historical narratives of copyright moved outside the legal academy in the twentieth century to capture the interest of book historians, literary scholars and economic historians. Over the last three decades the interest has grown to the extent that copyright history is clearly a discrete and popular field of academic inquiry, and the tercentenary of the Statute of Anne was celebrated with gusto around the globe in 2009 and 2010 (depending on dating preference). Another key indicator of this flourishing field was the launch, in March 2008, of the *Primary Sources on Copyright (1450–1900)* digital archive, funded by the UK Arts and Humanities Research Council. For seven years, this collection has proven a boon without peer for those already working in the area, and more so for those seeking insight into copyright history but without the time or resources to immerse themselves in the physical archives.

It is therefore an opportune moment to take stock of the field of copyright history, as it stands today, and how it might develop in the future. The Oxford English Dictionary Online defines 'handbook' as follows:

> Originally: a book small enough to be easily portable and intended to be kept close to hand, typically one containing a collection of passages important for reference or a compendium of information on a particular subject, *esp.* a book of religious instruction (now *hist.*). Later also more generally: any book (usually but not necessarily concise) giving information such as facts on a particular subject, guidance in some art or occupation, instructions for operating a machine, or information for tourists.[1]

In compiling this Handbook of Copyright History we have taken this definition seriously. Our brief to contributors was to provide an overview of their particular field of expertise within copyright history, as well as suggestions for future research. The outcome is a book which will, we hope, appeal to 'tourists' in the field – those seeking an accessible summary of the current state of knowledge in the chosen topics – as well as to those seeking reminders and highlighting of key developments, as well as updates of the most recent scholarship.

As historical research of copyright has grown in popularity, it has become subject to some of the inevitable 'turf wars'. In *Piracy*, Adrian Johns is critical of the historical focus on intellectual property law, positing the offence of piracy as being the proper object of historical inquiry, logically prior to the law that is supposed to constitute it.[2]

---

[1] OED Online (3rd edn, OUP 2015) <http://www.oed.com/view/Entry/83815>.
[2] Adrian Johns, *Piracy* (U Chicago Press 2009) 7.

Richard Sher also considers that an 'overemphasis' on the legal regime of copyright mistakenly treats the history of copyright law as synonymous with the history of authorship and authors' rights, and places copyright at the heart of book history, displacing evidence of extra-legal practices and relations.[3] By compiling this handbook we do not seek to exaggerate the role of copyright law in broader social, economic and cultural practices of the book, music and art trades, or the sphere of literary, musical and artistic endeavours, nor do we wish to displace the important role of historical work in adjacent and related fields, all of which add immeasurably to our understanding of these historical periods and cultures. This book is a work of legal history; a work which seeks self-consciously to place the history of law at the centre of its inquiry and to excavate its operation in different fields.

Part I opens with a historiographical perspective on copyright history. Barbara Lauriat examines the ways in which copyright history has been employed in making descriptive arguments about copyright's past with normative force for copyright's future. Copyright history is important, she avers, because it allows us to gain a fuller understanding of how copyright works; moreover, it is just as important to be aware of how copyright history has been *used* because it alerts us to its status as a rhetorical device and allows a critical perspective to be trained on historically founded claims. Kathy Bowrey's contribution takes us beyond the implications that historical interpretations or manipulations may have for lawyers and policy-makers. Using two of the seminal texts in copyright's historiography – Mark Rose's *Authors and Owners*[4] and Martha Woodmansee's *The Author, Art and the Market*[5] – Bowrey's aim is to interrogate critically the disciplinary boundaries of copyright historiography and identify some of the inadequacies and omissions which flow from the lack of interdisciplinary inquiry in the field. Following Bowrey, Martha Woodmansee's chapter draws on her own earlier work to call similarly for greater interdisciplinary reflection on the nature of authorship and how it operates in copyright law. Woodmansee ties the eighteenth century absorption of Romantic ideology into copyright law to two more recent legal disputes of the late twentieth century, arguing that this ideology continues to hold sway today.

Part II of the book examines various perspectives on copyright history in the United Kingdom. Ian Gadd begins by discussing the history of printing rights in England before 1710, which was the year Parliament enacted the Statute of Anne. Principally, he illuminates the key role played by the Company of Stationers in laying the foundations for what would become the statutory law of copyright. Among other things, Gadd traces the beginnings of the Company, the awarding of printing privileges granted by patent and placard, and the role and prominence of the Company's registration system. Alastair Mann and Hector MacQueen next provide a Scottish perspective on developments before and after the watershed date of 1710. Despite the union of the Crowns in 1603 and of the kingdoms themselves in 1707, the approach taken to printing rights in Scotland often differed from that in England. Mann and MacQueen offer a perspective and comparison of the influential Scottish book trade.

---

[3] Richard Sher, *The Enlightenment and the Book* (U Chicago Press 2006) 25.
[4] Mark Rose, *Authors and Owners* (Harvard UP 1993).
[5] Martha Woodmansee, *The Author, Art and the Market* (Columbia UP 1994).

The next two chapters address copyrightable subject matter. Nancy Mace first shepherds us through the development of copyright in musical works in the eighteenth and nineteenth centuries. Using *Bach v Longman* (1777) as a pivot point – the case in which the Court of King's Bench ruled that printed music fell within the ambit of the Statute of Anne – she discusses the state of music as intellectual property before and after the decision, as well as the decision itself. Elena Cooper then turns our focus to artistic copyright, which includes subjects such as engravings, sculptures, paintings and photography. Cooper highlights the ways in which the history of artistic copyright differed from that relating to literature.

Part II closes with chapters written by Isabella Alexander and Tomás Gómez-Arostegui. Both authors examine legal principles arising through the litigation process. Alexander discusses how copyright developed and expanded through the doctrine of infringement. The Statute of Anne was largely silent on what constituted infringement – apart from generally prohibiting 'printing', 'reprinting' and 'importing' of books – and this offered courts a certain flexibility in crafting infringement doctrines that took competing interests into account. Gómez-Arostegui, in turn, addresses the two principal remedies available to copyright and printing-patent holders in the Court of Chancery before the year 1800 – injunctions and a disgorgement of the defendant's profits – and how they were obtained.

Part III shifts the focus to international law. In her chapter, Jane Ginsburg studies the precursor to copyright that existed in the sixteenth century in the form of Papal printing privileges. Ginsburg argues that these early printing privileges demonstrate that over time a sense of entitlement arose in those who petitioned for them, and that increasingly that entitlement was grounded in the act of creation. Next, Catherine Seville covers the international reach and impact of UK copyright law in the colonies and other dominions. Starting from 1710, and concluding with the 1911 Imperial Copyright Act, Seville explores the efforts that were undertaken to protect British authors and publishers from competition abroad. Sam Ricketson takes up the public international law of copyright. His primary purpose is to survey the range of sources that are available for those researching the subject and to suggest some areas that require further study. In the last chapter to this Part, Jose Bellido offers an intriguing story of the role El Salvador played – through the diplomat Torres Caicedo – in the internationalisation of copyright in El Salvador, particularly through the negotiation of bilateral treaties and in the Berne Convention more broadly.

Part IV concludes this volume and covers national perspectives outside the United Kingdom. We begin with the United States. Oren Bracha treats the development of copyright from 1672 through the period just before the Copyright Act of 1909. Starting with colonial precursors, Bracha takes us through the early grants of *ad hoc* printing privileges, state and federal legislation, and the associated judicial developments of the period. Catherine Bond next addresses copyright in the Australian colonies and focuses in particular on the influence of Imperial law on local statutes. She also offers reflections on colonial copyright as an area for ongoing research. In our penultimate chapter, Frédéric Rideau discusses the development of literary property in France in the eighteenth and nineteenth centuries. Among other things, he describes a marked shift from treating copyright as privilege granted as a matter of grace by the Crown to an entitlement in authors as proprietors in their own right. Lastly, Jose Bellido returns to offer another continental example, that of Spain. Bellido describes the circumstances and actions that led to the first Spanish copyright statute in 1847 and how it was influenced by the international market for books.

The huge commercial value and serious implications for cultural policy mean copyright will always be a subject of hot debate, vested interests and ideological contest. Historical interpretation becomes a key rhetorical tool in such debates. A recently published Australian polemical collection on copyright law and the digital world, aimed squarely at the popular market, starkly demonstrates this. Three contributors directly appeal to the Statute of Anne in the course of their arguments about the impact of digitisation on copyright law. Sherman Young, Macquarie University's Pro Vice-Chancellor in Teaching and Learning, whose academic background lies in media and communications, claims that the Statute of Anne 'was devised specifically to balance the competing interests of monopoly rights holders and the wider needs of society.'[6] By contrast, José Borghino, Policy Director of the International Publishers Association, characterises the Statute of Anne as being 'about the individual's ability to exploit and profit from their individual labour',[7] while popular author Linda Jaivan asserts it was introduced 'explicitly to protect the rights of authors.'[8]

The inevitability of such rhetorical appeals makes it all the more important that careful and detailed historical work, closely attentive both to the primary sources and to broader historical, social, cultural and economic contexts, continues to be undertaken and published. This handbook emphasises and continues this scholarly tradition. We would like to thank our distinguished contributors for giving their time to this project and for their patience. It has been a privilege to work with all of them. We look forward to reading their future contributions, and the contributions of those they inspire, in this ever-growing field.

---

[6] Sherman Young, 'A Hack for the Encouragement of Learning' in Phillipa McGuiness (ed) *Copyfight* (NewSouth Publishing 2015) 35, 46.
[7] José Borghino, 'Codified Respect: Copyright as Ethics' in ibid 174, 180.
[8] Linda Jaivan, 'Big Content' in ibid 191, 201.

PART I

HISTORIOGRAPHY

2. Copyright history in the advocate's arsenal
Barbara Lauriat

1. INTRODUCTION

In 1966, Benjamin Kaplan delivered the Carpentier Lectures at Columbia University – the basis for his tour de force *An Unhurried View of Copyright*, in which he succinctly recounted centuries of copyright's history. He began by observing:

> As a veteran listener at many lectures by copyright specialists ... it is almost obligatory for a speaker to begin by invoking the 'communications revolution' of our time, then to pronounce upon the inadequacies of the present copyright act, and finally to encourage all hands to cooperate in getting a Revision Bill passed.[1]

He went on to present a fuller view of the history and development of copyright than had been widely appreciated at the time. He delivered a historical narrative in order to show 'that as things were different in the past, they probably need not be as they are.'[2] The importance of the history of copyright, to Kaplan, was as an aid to questioning the status quo and a caution against unwarranted conservatism when considering copyright reform.

The next communications revolution only three decades later inspired many more lectures along the lines described by Kaplan. But others have followed his lead in looking back at copyright's history, examining the past communications revolutions that have affected the development of the law of copyright and indeed, as Kaplan observed, started the whole enterprise off in the first place.[3]

Using copyright history as the foundation for arguments about the nature and purpose of copyright is not itself a new phenomenon. As early as 1762, the anonymous author of *An Enquiry Into the Origin and Nature of Literary Property* looked back at 'The History of Literary Property', beginning with the wandering bards whose expression was rewarded through hospitality.[4] After reviewing the case of the ancient authors, he noted that following the introduction of printing in England a 'Custom then first arose, by which they claimed the sole Right of multiplying Impressions of their books.'[5] This, in his view, led to authors becoming the desperate slaves of the booksellers, dependent on lump sum payments when they could not wait for royalties

---

[1] Benjamin Kaplan, *An Unhurried View of Copyright* (Columbia UP 1967) 1.
[2] Ibid 124.
[3] Kaplan refers to 'the Gutenberg revolution, which started it all.' ibid.
[4] *An Enquiry into the Nature and Origin of Literary Property* (London 1762), available at Lionel Bently and Martin Kretschmer (eds), Primary Sources on Copyright (1450–1900) <http://copy.law.cam.ac.uk/record/uk_1762a>.
[5] Ibid 19.

and leading to an impoverished national literature. He admitted that some English authors – namely Shakespeare, Otway, and Dryden – might compete with the ancient poets, though he bemoaned the fact that 'they had not Leisure to polish and refine their Works' and 'that their Poverty obliged them to Humour, instead of correcting the Taste of the Public.'[6] He believed copyright was new, not a creature of common law or natural right. 'This therefore is a new Right, arisen within the Time of Memory; but no original incorporeal Right, which is not founded on the agreement of the Parties, can at this Day be created,' he wrote.[7] In arguing against a perpetual right of literary property, he used a historically grounded argument to distinguish literary property from other forms of property arising from natural right.[8]

We see that the history of copyright has been used as a tool in copyright debates throughout the history of copyright. Even now, questions about copyright's Anglo-American common law foundations influence decisions about the limits of protection. The absence of copyright history can also be used; its relative novelty and lack of a Roman law pedigree have also been employed in arguments to question the legitimacy of copyright law or the inevitability of its expansion.[9] Exploring copyright reform attempts from the past may illuminate future discussions by showing us roads not taken.[10] Historical anecdotes may be used rhetorically to argue for or against changes in levels of protection.[11]

This history of copyright occasionally even has doctrinal legal significance. In *Lucasfilm v Ainsworth*, the UK Supreme Court included a description of the history of the aims of early copyright legislation in order to interpret the current statutory categories.[12] Lords Walker and Collins explained that the current legislation could not be understood without reference to its historical antecedents. In looking back to the 1911 Act, they explained,

> it may give the impression of embodying a well-proportioned symmetrical principle providing equal protection to every form of human creativity. Any such impression would be misleading. When the 1911 Act was passed there had already been two centuries of

---

[6] Ibid.
[7] Ibid 21.
[8] Ibid 21, 33.
[9] *Hinton v Donaldson* (Ct Sess 1773) in James Boswell, *The Decision of the Court of Session, Upon the Question of Literary Property* (Edinburgh 1774), available at Bently and Kretschmer (n 4) <http://copy.law.cam.ac.uk/record/uk_1773>.
[10] For example, several works of copyright history have considered the 1878 Royal Commission on Copyright, which heard proposals for replacing copyright with a royalty system. Paul K Saint-Amour, *The Copywrights: Intellectual Property and the Literary Imagination* (Cornell UP 2003) 53–89; Ronan Deazley, (2008) 'Commentary on the Royal Commission's Report on Copyright (1878)' in Bently and Kretschmer (n 4) <http://www.copyrighthistory.org/record/uk_1878>; Barbara Lauriat, 'Revisiting the Royal Commission on Copyright' (2014) 17 JWIP 47.
[11] Eg, Macaulay referring to the case of Milton and Milton's granddaughter in his famous speech discussing proposals for a posthumous term. Thomas Babington Macaulay, *Speech to House of Commons, Feb. 5, 1841*, in *The Works of Lord Macaulay: Speeches, Poems, & Miscellaneous Writings* (1898) 667.
[12] [2011] UKSC 39.

legislative history, starting with the Copyright Act 1709 ('the 1709 Act'), and for most of that time it was the protection of printed words – published literary works – that was the law's principal concern. Moreover the original legislative purpose of laws on literary copyright was the protection of the commercial interests of stationers (the early publishers) and booksellers, and the control of unlicensed (and possibly subversive) publications, rather than the vindication of the legal and moral rights of authors.[13]

And in *Golan v Holder*, the United States Supreme Court considered eighteenth-century sources in determining the implications of common law copyright to the constitutionality of legislation removing copyright works from the public domain.[14] The High Court of Australia referred to the intent behind the Statute of Anne when addressing the originality of factual compilations in *IceTV v Nine Network*.[15]

This chapter explores some of the ways in which copyright history has been used in arguments about copyright law throughout its history. It provides examples of several ways in which copyright history has been used to reflect on copyright, then it focuses on three kinds of historically grounded arguments with normative significance. The 'advocate' of the title does not refer only to advocates practising in a court of law, but also includes academics, philosophers, politicians and others who use historical arguments to advance their cases about the justifications and aims of copyright law. The past 300 years of copyright controversy have revealed three areas of debate where copyright history has repeatedly been used to make fundamental claims about the nature and purpose of copyright: first, the relative newness of copyright protection as a legal and cultural concept; second, the issue of whether there was ever copyright at common law; and third, the original purpose(s) and beneficiaries of copyright legislation.

Analyses of these three debates are interrelated; and one's position on each question may impact upon one's views of the others. Indeed, one often sees them conflated in the literature, but these three questions can and should be separated conceptually. Siva Vaidyanathan, for example, has written of the eighteenth-century copyright controversies, 'Was copyright a product of a statute, and therefore limited to the statutory term, or a right secured by the ill-behaved and ill-defined beast, the common law, and therefore perpetual? In other words, who is copyright for?'[16] Yet, even if copyright is wholly a product of statute, that fact alone does not necessarily tell us anything about the intended beneficiaries of the statutory regime. These contested areas stand as distinct building blocks in larger arguments about the foundational principles of copyright.

The first set of debates is primarily philosophical, going to the issue of whether recognition of some control by a creator of her work has long been a widely accepted norm, which ought to be recognized in our laws (even if it has not always been historically) or whether it is a fairly recent commercial experiment without any connection to overarching moral imperatives. The second set is both doctrinal and

---

[13] Ibid [15].
[14] (2012) 132 S Ct 873.
[15] [2009] HCA 14 [24]–[26].
[16] Siva Vaidyanathan, *Copyrights and Copywrongs: The Rise of Intellectual Property and How it Threatens Creativity* (NYU Press 2003) 41.

philosophical. The questions of whether copyright was ever recognized at common law and whether it persisted in any form once statutory protection came into force has been revisited time and again in the case law, as well as having force in terms of property theory. The third set is both philosophical and practical. The history of copyright is employed to lend force to arguments about what the law was truly meant to achieve and whom the law was originally intended to benefit. Such arguments about the fundamental purpose(s) of copyright can be deeply theoretical or functionally pragmatic. The first and second are closely linked; both involve using the historical record as evidence about the nature of copyright, which in turn, informs questions of whether it is properly deemed a property right. The third is broad in scope and involves using historical sources to advance arguments about the purpose and function of copyright. All three have existed for centuries, remain unresolved, and have force to this day.

Reviewing the ways that copyright history *has* been used can assist us in considering the extent to which it *ought* to be used to inform contemporary debates on copyright law and policy. Kaplan delved into the history in order to challenge complacency with regard to the inevitability and desirability of strong copyright. But the history of copyright can also help us to examine critically the persuasiveness and relevance of historical arguments about copyright when they were made in the past.

2. THE USES OF COPYRIGHT HISTORY

Copyright history, once attended to primarily by literary scholars and book historians, is increasingly of interest to legal scholars and lawyers, as this book itself demonstrates. Aspects of the history of copyright law have been used to further arguments in works of post-structural theory,[17] Marxist historical analysis,[18] and literary scholarship.[19] Unsurprisingly, different disciplines tend to emphasize different aspects of the history and often draw different conclusions.[20] But interdisciplinarity has been one of the great strengths of copyright history. Percy Winfield observed in his introduction to *The Chief Sources of Legal History* that the advantages of a common law legal education can prove a hindrance to historical research. Such training, he noted, is 'apt to narrow the vision and to cramp the hand. The lawyer is too much inclined to throw to one side everything except the formal expression of the law itself … . It neglects the axiom that law expresses the needs of human beings'.[21] As a branch of legal history

---

[17] Most famously, Michel Foucault, 'What is an Author?' (James Venit tr) (1975) 42 Partisan Rev 603.
[18] Eg Bernard Edelman, *Ownership of the Image, Elements of a Marxist Theory of Law* (Routledge 1977); NN Feltes, *Modes of Production of Victorian Novels* (U Chicago Press 1986); NN Feltes, *Literary Capital and the Late Victorian Novel* (U Wisconsin Press 1993).
[19] Eg Martha Woodmansee and Peter Jaszi (eds), *The Construction of Authorship: Textual Appropriation in Law and Literature* (Duke UP 1994); Saint-Amour (n 10).
[20] Kathy Bowrey, 'Who's Writing Copyright's History' (1996) 18 EIPR 322; John Feather, 'The Significance of Copyright History for Publishing History and Historians' in Ronan Deazley, Martin Kretschmer and Lionel Bently (eds), *Privilege and Property: Essays on the History of Copyright* (OpenBook Publishers 2010) 359, 359–60.
[21] Percy Henry Winfield, *The Chief Sources of English Legal History* (B Franklin 1925) 4.

populated with as many literary scholars and historians as lawyers, copyright history is less apt to fall into this trap, as the diversity of sources and methodologies demonstrates.

The history of copyright has always been of interest to those trying to understand the nature of the legal right and has frequently been employed for rhetorical purposes by those seeking to persuade others that their view of copyright is the correct one. The observation that 'historical analysis provides a framework to serve a basis for interpreting and evaluating modern copyright laws' has been to a great degree accepted.[22] But the ways in which copyright history – or perhaps selectively mythologized copyright history – has been employed in disputes about copyright has at times attracted criticism. Thus, the contribution of any historians attempting to compile an accurate narrative of copyright's past is an important one and the critical examination of their methodologies is just as essential.

A few works have considered the rising interdisciplinary field of copyright history and addressed some of the different methodologies used by scholars in examining the history of copyright. In one of these historiographic pieces, Kathy Bowrey has observed that two of the early works of copyright history written from a lawyer's perspective – namely discussions of the early history of copyright in Lyman Ray Patterson's *Copyright in Historical Perspective*[23] and Kaplan's *Unhurried View*[24] – sought to use the history to question current beliefs about the legitimacy and coherence of copyright's legal formulation.[25] These studies presented the history in order that we might not view the system as it stands as an inevitable monolith. Later scholarship went further, aiming to 'de-naturalize' our contemporary understanding of copyright law through sweeping studies of its history, for example, works such as Lionel Bently and Brad Sherman's *The Making of Modern Intellectual Property Law*,[26] and Ronan Deazley's *Rethinking Copyright*.[27] Some are explicitly forward looking in their reasons for examining the historical record. Adrian Johns' book *Piracy* explores the history of intellectual property piracy, with the aim of preparing society for a 'radical reconfiguration of what we now call intellectual property'.[28] He argues that the history suggests such a radical reconfiguration may soon be upon us and that society needs to re-evaluate its approach to piracy – an exercise that he says calls for a 'historical vision'.[29]

The field of copyright history has seen many broad proposals about the nature of modern authorship and revisionist studies questioning the inevitability and desirability of copyright's expansion, but it also encompasses narrow, focused studies of events,

---

[22] Gillian Davies, *Copyright and the Public Interest* (2nd edn, Sweet & Maxwell 2002) 9.
[23] Lyman Ray Patterson, *Copyright in Historical Perspective* (Vanderbilt UP 1968).
[24] Kaplan (n 1).
[25] Bowrey, 'Copyright's History' (n 20).
[26] Brad Sherman and Lionel Bently, *The Making of Modern Intellectual Property Law: The British Experience, 1760–1911* (CUP 1999) 6.
[27] Ronan Deazley, *Rethinking Copyright: History, Theory, Language* (Edward Elgar 2006).
[28] Adrian Johns, *Piracy: The Intellectual Property Wars From Gutenberg to Gates* (U Chicago Press 2009) 15.
[29] Ibid 15, 517–18.

individuals, or subjects of protection.[30] In their introduction to *Privilege and Property: Essays on the History of Copyright*, Deazley, Kretschmer, and Bently suggest that the 'grand theories' about the nature of copyright and authorship 'are being challenged by micro-studies that bring a wider range of methods to bear on a wider range of sources.'[31]

In considering the uses of copyright history, one must distinguish between those works of history that set forth a historical narrative and draw conclusions pertaining to the nature of copyright by analyzing that narrative and those works of legal scholarship where the history serves the broader argument by means of providing an illustrative example or comparison. Many works of contemporary legal scholarship draw on history to support arguments, though they are not themselves engaged in historical research – that is to say, they are not producing original contributions to our knowledge of the past. This is not to suggest that one method is superior to the other, but only that they have to be approached on different terms; the inclusion of historical material or a historical argument in a work does not make it a work of history. James Boyle refers to Thomas Jefferson and Lord Macaulay's views on intellectual property not to clarify the historical record but because he finds aspects of their arguments to be persuasive and applicable to copyright debates today.[32] Historical comparative approaches have also been taken. For example, Ned Snow cites early English case law to show that judges brought fair use principles into their infringement analysis and compares this to the present treatment of fair use in the United States.[33] Dane Ciolino and Erin Donelson cite early British and early American copyright law to demonstrate that strict liability has not always been an essential part of copyright law.[34] Recently, Sir Richard Arnold has reviewed the history of UK copyright reform attempts back to the 1878 Royal Commission on Copyright for comparative purposes – to illustrate some of the inadequacies of more recent government-commissioned inquiries into the intellectual property regime and to bolster his argument for a comprehensive review of UK copyright law.[35]

The popularity of using historical arguments in otherwise non-historical work has, however, occasionally resulted in the proliferation of certain fallacies about the history of copyright. Justin Hughes has taken to task some critics of the 'propertization' of

---

[30] A small selection of examples include: Isabella Alexander, 'Criminalising Copyright: A Story of Publishers, Pirates and Pieces of Eight' (2007) 66 CLJ 625; Lionel Bently, 'Copyright, Translations, and Relations Between Britain and India in the Nineteenth and Early Twentieth Centuries' (2007) 82 Chi-Kent L Rev 1181; Catherine Seville, 'Authors as Copyright Campaigners: Mark Twain's Legacy' (2008) 55 J Copyright Soc'y USA 283; and contributions by Oren Bracha, Friedemann Kawohl, Katie Scott, and Isabella Alexander, in Deazley, Kretschmer, and Bently (n 20).

[31] Deazley and others, *Privilege and Property* (n 20) 20.

[32] James Boyle, *The Public Domain: Enclosing the Commons of the Mind* (Yale UP 2008) 17–41.

[33] Ned Snow, 'The Forgotten Right of Fair Use' (2011) 62 Case W Res L Rev 135, 142–43.

[34] Dane Ciolino and Erin Donelson, 'Questioning Strict Liability in Copyright' (2002) 54 Rutgers L Rev 351, 359–61.

[35] Richard Arnold, 'The Need for a New Copyright Act: A Case Study in Law Reform' (2015) 5 QMJIP 110.

copyright for historically inaccurate statements appearing repeatedly in copyright scholarship, such as the alleged newness of the terms 'piracy' and 'intellectual property'.[36] The propertization critics, in turn, disapprove of certain repeated tropes in copyright narratives – in particular those relating to common law copyright. Deazley, for example, disapproved of the characterization of the holding of *Donaldson v Becket* in the treatise *Copinger and Skone James on Copyright* as stating that the Statute of Anne had superseded the common law copyright in published works but not affected the common law right in unpublished works.[37] He argues instead that the only right in common law was not an intangible property right but a right to divulge flowing from the ownership of the physical manuscript.[38] Thus, the role of the copyright historian may include policing the accuracy of casual rhetorical, anecdotal, and illustrative uses of copyright history in mainstream intellectual property scholarship. It is, however, to those uses of copyright history which speak to arguments about the fundamental nature and purpose of copyright that we turn next.

3. A 'NEW RIGHT'

> The most imposing institutions of mankind are the oldest; and yet so changing is the world, so fluctuating are its needs, so apt to lose inward force, though retaining outward strength, are its best instruments, that we must not expect the oldest institutions to be now the most efficient. We must expect what is venerable to acquire influence because of its inherent dignity; but we must not expect it to use that influence so well as new creations apt for the modern world, instinct with its spirit, and fitting closely to its life.[39]

Bagehot's balanced view of innovative institutions, as described in *The English Constitution*, recognizes the natural tendency to revere the old for withstanding the passage of time, but recalls the advantages of flexibility and efficiency that the new may possess. Whether, from our present standpoint, copyright is 'new' or 'old' may be a matter of opinion. Its relative youth when compared to other areas of law has, however, featured in arguments about its purpose and merits. Some of the arguments about copyright's 'newness' may relate to those for or against a right at common law versus a statutory privilege. A distinction can be made, however, between those historical arguments about the newness of the concept of an intangible right in creative works broadly and those that seek to identify or discredit a common law right.

As noted above, the author of *An Enquiry Into the Nature and Origin of Literary Property* cited its newness as a mark of its suspect nature. 'The Courts have been ever jealous of new Inventions', even of those which are founded on its most unquestioned principles, 'till Experience and length of Time has given them a Sanction,' he warned.[40] Augustine Birrell, however, viewed the advantages of new institutions in much the

---

[36] Justin Hughes, 'Copyright and Incomplete Historiographies: Of Piracy, Propertization, and Thomas Jefferson' (2006) 79 S Cal L Rev 993.
[37] Deazley, *Rethinking Copyright* (n 27) 23–24.
[38] Ibid 18.
[39] Walter Bagehot, *The English Constitution* (1867; Paul Smith ed CUP 2001) 8.
[40] *Enquiry* (n 4) 21.

same way as Bagehot, commenting that 'whatever charm is possessed by the subject of copyright tis largely due to the fact that it is a bundle of ideas and rights of modern origin.'[41] Of course, over 100 years later, some suggest that copyright is getting long in the tooth. In 2013, the US Register of Copyrights stated that the 'law is showing the strain of its age and requires your attention.'[42]

One of the arguments deployed in the eighteenth century was to find, or fail to find, precedent for the protection of literary property or intangible property in Roman law and other ancient sources. There is no evidence that Roman law contained anything resembling copyright law – even defined broadly as a right to prevent creative works from being copied.[43] The author of *An Enquiry Into the Nature and Origin of Literary Property* would have it that the ancient authors were less driven by material gain than later creators: 'the Ancients were smitten with a Love of Glory; if they had a Desire of gain, it was subordinate passion.'[44] Some have claimed that the ancients thought that all creative expression came directly from the gods and so could not conceive of the author gaining a proprietary right.[45] Nevertheless, authority from classic texts was used by Blackstone and others to demonstrate that the concept of a right that vested in an author had ancient precedents. Equally, *lack* of authority from Roman law elsewhere was used to suggest that copyright protection was a recent, statutory invention.

In the collusive lawsuit of *Tonson v Collins*,[46] Blackstone, representing the plaintiff booksellers, used sources as varied as Roman law, Roman literature, Chancery precedents,[47] and Lockean natural rights arguments to make his case for perpetual copyright.[48] He tried to demonstrate the ancient pedigree of literary property, noting that while the 'antient Way' of profiting from creative works was to perform or orate, the 'Sale of Copies, or a Price paid for the Liberty of rehearsing an Author's Works in

---

[41] Augustine Birrell, *Seven Lectures on the Law and History of Copyright in Books* (Cassell 1899) 1.

[42] 'The Register's Call for Updates to US Copyright Law: Hearing Before the Subcommittee on Courts, Intellectual Property, and the Internet of the House Committee on the Judiciary' (20 March 2013), available at <http://copyright.gov/regstat/2013/regstat03202013.html>.

[43] JA Crook, *Law and Life of Rome* (1967) 207, 530 (the ancient Romans had 'no law of patent or copyright' and 'no protection for property in an idea'). See also Ruurd Nauta, *Poetry for Patrons: Literary Communication in the Age of Domitian* (Brill Academic 2000); TP Wiseman, 'Pete Nobiles Amicos: Poets and Patrons in Late Republican Rome' in Barbara K Gold (ed), *Literary and Artistic Patronage in Ancient Rome* 28, 28–31 (U of Texas Press 1982). For a contrasting view, suggesting that Roman law did at least have a notion of trade secrets (usually placed in the category of 'intellectual property'), see Arthur Schiller, 'Trade Secrets and the Roman Law: The *Actio Servi Corrupti*' (1930) 30 Colum L Rev 837. But see Alan Watson's persuasive critique of Schiller's thesis in 'Trade Secrets and Roman Law: The Myth Exploded' (1996) 11 Tul Eur & Civ L F 19.

[44] *Enquiry* (n 4) 17.

[45] Carla Hesse, 'The Rise of Intellectual Property, 700 B.C.–A.D. 2000: An Idea in the Balance' (2002) Daedalus 26, 26, available at <http://www.amacad.org/publications/spring2002/hesse.pdf>.

[46] Mark Rose, *Authors and Owners: The Invention of Copyright* (Harvard UP 1993) 74–78; Ronan Deazley, (2008) 'Commentary on *Tonson v Collins* (1762)' in Bently and Kretschmer (n 4) <http://www.copyrighthistory.org/record/uk_1762>.

[47] See the cases mentioned in 2 Eq Ab 522–24.

[48] *Tonson v Collins* (1761) 1 Bl R 321.

public, are as old as the Establishment of Letters.'[49] Citing examples from the ancient literature, he noted:

> *Terence* sold his *Eunuch* to the Aediles, and was afterwards charged with stealing his Fable from *Menander – Exclamant Furem, non Poetam, Fabulam dedisse*. He sold his *Hecyra* to *Roscius* the Player. *Statius* would have starved, had he not sold his Tragedy of the *Agave* to *Paris*, another Player – *Esurit, intactam Paridi nisi* vendat *Agaven* [the emphasis on the Latin verb *vendat* 'sell' is Blackstone's]. *Juvenal*. These Sales were, and are founded upon natural Justice.[50]

It was these same examples from the classical literature, alongside Blackstone's interpretation of property acquisition by a Roman law principle of accession, which he later cited in his Commentaries as ancient authority for literary property as a legal principle grounded in natural justice.[51] Given Blackstone's influence, these examples would be repeated by later writers trying to piece together the early foundations of copyright.[52]

In the 1773 Scottish case *Hinton v Donaldson*, the newness of the concept of literary property was a central argument.[53] In the words of Lord Monboddo: 'It has been said that literary property is unknown in this country and was not known till of late in England.'[54] The Lord Justice Clerk noted that the great authors of the past, such as Homer and Virgil, had not written with any consciousness of possessing a property right. In contrast to Blackstone's arguments in *Tonson,* Lord Alva used the absence of any recognition of literary property in Roman law to demonstrate that copyright law was a recent legal innovation and could not lay claim to the same heritage as property law as such.[55]

Nineteenth-century works using copyright history tended to focus on the eighteenth-century debates, but occasionally ventured further back in history. Some, like Lowndes, referred back to the same ancient sources as Blackstone. But American publisher George Haven Putnam went back further, attempting to find evidence of a growing conception of property in intellectual productions in ancient civilizations. Putnam, a strong proponent of authors' rights and the Secretary of the American Publishers' Copyright League, which had lobbied for international copyright,[56] explored what he

---

[49] Ibid 323.
[50] Ibid.
[51] 2 Bl Comm 405–06.
[52] Eg JJ Lowndes, *An Historical Sketch of the Law of Copyright* (2nd edn, Saunders and Benning 1842) 1. Lowndes does, however, note that, 'To seek the origin of Copyright in times prior to the invention of Printing, would partake more of curious research than of useful investigation, and would, at best, furnish rather matter of conjecture than of information.' ibid.
[53] *Hinton* (n 9). See Ronan Deazley (2008) 'Commentary on *Hinton v Donaldson* (1773)' in Bently and Kretschmer (n 4) <http://www.copyrighthistory.org/record/uk_1773>. See also Hector MacQueen, 'The War of the Booksellers: Natural Law, Equity, and Literary Property in Eighteenth-Century Scotland' (2014) 35 J Legal Hist 231.
[54] *Hinton* (n 9).
[55] Ibid 31–32.
[56] Catherine Seville, *The Internationalisation of Copyright Law: Books, Buccaneers, and the Black Flag in the Nineteenth Century* (CUP 2006) 35–36.

considered to be evidence of incipient literary property in ancient societies, including Greece, China, Japan, Egypt, Rome, Judaea, and Constantinople.[57] Putnam's book acknowledged that literary property – in the form of a State-recognized right to control particular forms of expression – did not exist in the ancient world and came into being only after the invention of printing. His professed aim was:

> to outline the gradual evolution of the idea that the producer of a literary work, the poet, ποητας, the maker, is entitled to secure from the community not only such laurel-crown of fame as may be adjudged to his work, but also some material compensation proportioned as nearly as may be practicable to the extent of the service rendered by him.[58]

He finishes his study noting that 'property control' could not exist until the invention of the printing press, but that even after the advent of printing, it took 'more than four centuries of further development in national morality' for the recognition of 'International Copyright.'[59]

Birrell also examined the evidence from the ancient world but came to the opposite conclusion to Putnam. He rejected the overly simplistic position that printing was necessary to create a market for copies of literary works and that therefore the ancients could never have conceived of a right to control copying. Citing Putnam, he notes that there 'were books and booksellers, and libraries public and private, bookhunters and bookstalls, in Cappadocia and other places, before Fust and Gutenberg.'[60] But instead of using the historical evidence of ancient book trades as suggestive of the recognition of a nascent conception of literary property, as did Blackstone and Putnam, in Birrell's view, it served as evidence that literary property is entirely a modern invention rather than a natural right that had been implicitly recognized in ancient times and required only the technological innovation of the printing press to be duly enshrined in legal systems.[61] 'It is … a fact of great significance that at no time during the manuscript period was any claim for author's copyright made or asserted,' he writes.[62] The printing press alone was not enough to bring copyright into existence, Birrell suggests – censorship and the monopoly of the booksellers played a role as well.[63]

Christopher May and Susan Sell's *Intellectual Property Rights: A Critical History* looks back over millennia, considering how attitudes in ancient Greece and Rome, and later, in the Middle Ages and the Venetian Republic, about the value of knowledge and creativity contributed to the future commodification of intellectual creations.[64] These earlier historical examples are assembled to support their thesis about the relationship between intellectual property and modern capitalism. According to them 'intellectual

---

[57] GH Putnam, *Authors and Their Public in Ancient Times: A Sketch of Literary Conditions and of the Relations With the Public of Literary Producers, From the Earliest Times to the Invention of Printing* (GP Putnam's Sons 1894).
[58] Ibid vi.
[59] Ibid 296.
[60] Birrell (n 41) 43.
[61] Ibid 47.
[62] Ibid 47–48.
[63] Ibid 51.
[64] Christopher May and Susan Sell, *Intellectual Property Rights: A Critical History* (Lynne Rienner 2006) 43–49.

property is the result of developments in *three* specific social areas: the technological, the legal/political, and the philosophical (as regards the conceptualization of the individual knowledge producer).'[65] In attempting to show how the history of intellectual property has been a 'policy battleground' rather than the reasoned progression of natural justice, they reach back to the ancient world, while explaining that 'the beginning of a recognizable body of intellectual property rights' does not appear until late-fifteenth-century Venice.[66] They do, however, acknowledge that 'condemnation of plagiarism and the acknowledgement of the theft of ideas stretches back to the beginnings of recorded history.'[67] Some scholars question even this. Giancarlo Frosio, for example, rejects contemporary ideas of copying and plagiarism, selectively reviewing the history of creativity from Homer to Coleridge in order to argue for systemic recognition of mass collaborative creativity. He claims, 'For most of human history, the essential nature of creativity was understood to be cumulative and collective.'[68]

The broad consensus, however, seems to be that copyright is new, and that vexation caused by being copied is old, but what this actually tells us about the nature of the legal regime is vigorously debated.

4. COMMON LAW COPYRIGHT

The question of whether copyright is a property right or a statutory privilege was first raised early in the eighteenth century and persists to the present day. As Birrell explained, the debates over whether copyright was the creation of common law went right to the question of whether copyright was to be allowed into the 'sacrosanct circle' of those rights 'recognised, venerated, worshipped, under the word property.'[69] In Britain and America, this issue could not be resolved without reference to a further question: whether the common law recognized literary property. In shaping arguments about the proprietary or non-proprietary nature of copyright, the question of its common law antecedents (if any) are relevant to the debate, just as is the question of its newness in the sweep of human history, described in the previous section. The implications of copyright being recognized as a creature of common law and a property right are potentially both doctrinal and philosophical. The eighteenth-century cases of *Millar v Taylor* and *Donaldson v Becket* turned on the issue. Critics of common law copyright suggest that the proprietary construction would give the right a moral status that it does not deserve.[70]

The implications of the first copyright act, the 1710 Statute of Anne, were contested a short time after the Act was passed. Did the statute simply provide additional

---

[65] Ibid 73.
[66] Ibid 43.
[67] Ibid.
[68] Giancarlo F Frosio, 'Rediscovering Cumulative Creativity From the Oral Formulaic Tradition to the Digital Remix: Can I Get a Witness?' (2014) 13 J Marshall Rev Intell Prop L 341, 390.
[69] Birrell (n 41) 12.
[70] Timothy Brennan, 'Copyright, Property, and the Right to Deny' (1992) 68 Chi-Kent L Rev 675, 682–83.

protection by way of granting access to statutory penalties and forfeitures for a limited term or did it preclude authors from availing themselves of a perpetual common law right to prevent unauthorized publication? Did such a common law right even exist? The remaining uncertainty as to the legal effects of the Statute of Anne led to the eighteenth-century Battle of the Booksellers, the consequences of which have been disputed ever since.

In 1739, Lord Hardwicke granted an injunction until answer to protect Jacob Tonson's right in *Paradise Lost*, which he had acquired in 1683, 72 years after John Milton's initial assignment.[71] Nevertheless, because the decision did not reveal his reasoning, the question of whether there was a common law of copyright and, more importantly, whether the Statute of Anne superseded such rights, remained open. The controversy over the nature of copyright was discussed in journals, law courts, and the political arena. Despite the statute, trade in copyrights continued as if the copyrights were perpetual. A collusive effort in 1761 to decide the issue in favour of the London booksellers failed in *Tonson v Collins*.[72] Then, in 1763, publisher Andrew Millar brought an action in the King's Bench against another bookseller Robert Taylor, who had republished James Thomson's poem *The Seasons*, the copyright of which Millar had purchased in 1729.[73] Millar died before a majority of three judges, led by Lord Mansfield, came to the conclusion that the Statute of Anne did not take away the author's perpetual copyright which existed at common law and had been assigned to Millar.[74] Yates, J dissented, denying any basis for a common law right. On the basis of *Millar*, perpetual copyright was the law of the land in Britain for five years. The matter was not laid to rest, however, and a few years later an action brought against Edinburgh bookseller Alexander Donaldson resulted in the Scottish Court of Session denying the existence of a perpetual right in *Hinton v Donaldson*.[75] Donaldson had also republished *The Seasons*. Thomas Becket and others, who now owned the Thomson copyrights, sought and obtained a perpetual injunction in Chancery, which Donaldson appealed to the House of Lords in 1772, leading to the seminal case of *Donaldson v Becket* in 1774.[76]

Most of the confusion and lack of consensus results from difficulties in interpreting the extent of the holding in *Donaldson*, in which five questions speaking to the nature of copyright protection and the effect of the Statute of Anne were put to the judges in the House of Lords. Lord Mansfield abstained from giving his opinion on the matter so only 11 judges responded to the questions. A majority of the judges identified a common law right that had been superseded by the Statute of Anne. Even so, the Lords were not bound to vote in accordance with the opinions of the judges, and a majority of the Lords determined that the Statute of Anne operated to preclude authors or their publishers from asserting a common law right in literary property. Yet, following the

---

[71] *Tonson v Walker* (1739) (referred to in *Tonson v Walker* (1752) 3 Swanst 672 and *Millar v Taylor* (1769) 4 Burr 2303, 2325).
[72] *Tonson v Collins* (1761) 1 Bl R 301.
[73] *Millar v Taylor* (1769) 4 Burr 2303.
[74] Ibid.
[75] *Hinton* (n 9). See Deazley, 'Commentary on *Hinton*' (n 53).
[76] *Donaldson v Becket* (1774) 4 Burr 2303.

decision, lawyer and layman alike remained unsure whether any vestiges of common law copyright remained – perhaps in regard to unpublished works – and, indeed, whether there had ever been such a thing as common law copyright.[77]

'The common law principles which lie at the root of the law have never been settled,' stated the Royal Commission's Report in 1878, 'the well known cases of Millar vs. Taylor, Donaldson vs. Becket, and Jeffries vs. Boosey, ended in a difference of opinion amongst many of the most eminent judges who have ever sat upon the Bench.'[78] The 1883 first edition of TE Scrutton's *The Laws of Copyright*, which contained his theoretical and historical analysis of the area of law with the aim of reform and codification suggested that the common law right had been vested in authors prior to the Statute of Anne.[79] A 1902 copy of the *Law Times*, however, treated the question as resolved, 'In Scotland, as in England, copyright is of purely statutory *origin*, and the theory of "common law copyright" so pertinaciously asserted in the English courts until finally discredited in Donaldson v Becket ... never received any encouragement from the Court of Sessions.'[80] More recently, Tomás Gómez-Arostegui has articulated the main issue under dispute as being,

> whether in the late 18th century, copyright was a natural or customary property right, protected at common law, or a privilege created solely by statute. These viewpoints compete to set the default basis of the right. The former suggests the principal purpose was to protect authors; the latter indicates it was principally to benefit the public.[81]

The significance of the *Donaldson* holding for establishing the nature and purpose of copyright is indeed the reason why this argument continues to rage on. Once again, however, it is important to distinguish the question of what is the *nature* of the right from the question of what is the *purpose* of the right. The existence at one time of a common law or natural right might well 'suggest' a creator-focused right, and showing that copyright was a purely statutory entitlement might 'suggest' a public interest aim, but neither would constitute conclusive proof of intention.

Several witnesses before the Royal Commission on Copyright in the late 1870s differed profoundly in their views on the historical implications of the Statute of Anne. Composer Charles Henry Purday testified before the Royal Commission that a perpetual property right ought to exist despite the effect of the Statute of Anne.[82] He explained his position more fully in his own book, published in 1877, the same year as his appearance before the Commission.[83]

> There can be no doubt but that the Bench generally considered the Act of Anne did not interfere with the vested rights of authors, especially as the Act was called '*An Act for the*

---

[77] See Deazley, *Rethinking Copyright* (n 27) 26–55, describing how attitudes 'as to the existence of the common law right ... waxed and waned throughout the nineteenth century' 27.
[78] Report of the Royal Commission on Copyright (1878) [c-2036] vii.
[79] TE Scrutton *The Laws of Copyright* (1st edn, John Murray 1883) 91–92.
[80] (18 June 1902) 113 Law Times 197 (emphasis added).
[81] H Tomás Gómez-Arostegui, 'Copyright at Common Law in 1774' (2014) 47 Conn L Rev 1, 4.
[82] Minutes of the Royal Commission on Copyright (1878) [C-2036-1] 195.
[83] CH Purday, *Copyright: A Sketch of its Rise and Progress* (W Reeves 1877).

Encouragement of Learning,' .... Yet by the case of Donaldson and Becket, the House of Lords decided by a majority of six judges against five (Lord Mansfield not voting) that the Act of Anne took away the common-law right, and therefore the term of copyright must in future be subject to the limitation of the statutes. This decision has never been reversed, although admitted to be unjust.[84]

Publisher John Blackwood expressed the view that the Statute of Anne functioned to limit the rights of authors and that the previous right had been perpetual.[85] Civil servant TH Farrer, however, disagreed with the position that a perpetual property right had ever existed. Stating that he had reviewed the history of early copyright as one of State-granted privileges, he asserted that the Statute of Anne had created the right afresh and cautioned that 'those who rest an absolute claim to monopoly on history ought also to be ready to submit it to state control.'[86]

Legal scholars have continued to argue about the result of *Donaldson*, mainly on the issue of whether it held that there had or had not been a common law right.[87] Abrams and Deazley have presented what might be described as a revisionist view of the decision in *Donaldson*, in that they challenge the widely held view that the 1710 Act had superseded a common law right. The thrust of Abrams' argument was much the same as Farrer's in the 1870s – that the Lords had, in fact, held that no common law right had existed and copyright's origins were purely statutory.[88] Deazley took the argument further, claiming that *Donaldson* must be interpreted as holding that there was no common law copyright in unpublished works,[89] despite this having been a generally accepted principle in nineteenth-century Anglo-American law, since unpublished works were not covered by the Statute of Anne.[90] As the copyright scholar Copinger wrote in 1870: 'What amounts to publication sufficient to defeat the common law right is a question of some nicety.'[91] Recently, Gómez-Arostegui has revisited the primary sources and persuasively argued that the original interpretation was probably the correct one.[92] According to his conclusions, while ambiguities in *Donaldson* exist,

---

[84] Ibid 22–23.
[85] Minutes of the Royal Commission on Copyright [C-2036-1] 42.
[86] Ibid 203.
[87] Patterson (n 23); Rose (n 46); Howard Abrams, 'The Historic Foundation of American Copyright Law: Exploding the Myth of Common Law Copyright' (1983) 29 Wayne L Rev 1119; Ronan Deazley, 'The Myth of Copyright at Common Law' (2003) 62 CLJ 106; Ronan Deazley, *On the Origin of the Right to Copy* (Hart Publishing 2004); Gómez-Arostegui (n 81).
[88] Abrams (n 87).
[89] Deazley, *On the Origin of the Right to Copy* (n 87) 191–220.
[90] 'That there is property in the ideas which pass in a man's mind is consistent with all the authorities in English law. Incidental to that right is the right of deciding when and how they shall first be made known to the public. Privacy is a part, and an essential part, of this species of property. In *Millar v. Taylor*, the property which a man had in his unpublished ideas was admitted by all the Judges: *Donaldson v. Beckett*.' *Prince Albert v Strange* (1849) 1 H & Tw 1, 41 ER 1171; In the United States, see *Wheaton v Peters* (1834) 33 US 591, 658.
[91] WA Copinger, *The Law of Copyright in Works of Literature and Art* (Stevens & Haynes 1870) 9.
[92] Gómez-Arostegui (n 81).

we cannot confidently assert that it goes further than saying that *if* there had been a right at common law, the Statute of Anne superseded that right.[93]

Some criticize this prolonged, unresolved debate over the common law right versus statutory right, arguing that establishing lengthy, historically grounded analyses of copyright's common law or statutory nature is normatively insignificant. Andreas Rahmatian has argued that there 'is no difference ... whether copyright is a common law right or a statutory right, these are merely different means of legal form.'[94] He notes that such scholarship seems to forget that a 'common law creature has no more force or permanence since it is as much a legal artifice as a statutory one.'[95] In support of his case, he points to the very fact that the House of Lords could come to the conclusion that copyright was not perpetual, contrary to the earlier holding in *Millar v Taylor*.[96]

Counter to Rahmatian's position are the traditional attitudes of many legal scholars equating common law rights with natural rights. As Bowker wrote of copyright, the 'inherent right of authors is a right at what is called common law – that is, natural or customary law.'[97] Adopting a more positivist view of the common law, however, Rahmatian's argument has some force. Even if Deazley and Abrams were shown to be entirely correct to the extent that common law copyright is a myth that arose from incorrect interpretations of *Donaldson v Becket* and perpetuated throughout the nineteenth and twentieth centuries, one might question whether that ends the debate. When the determination of truth requires complicated interpretation of antiquated procedural rules, the actual reception and subsequent interpretation become as forceful a part of the record over time. The observation of non-lawyer Rose that 'given the way that *Donaldson* came to be understood, perhaps it should be simultaneously regarded as confirming the notion of the author's common-law right put forward by Mansfield and Blackstone', has some resonance, whether one agrees with it or not.[98] We must take Winfield's cautions about the limitations of a lawyer's view of history seriously; popular perceptions of the law may have as much historical significance as what the law, in fact, was.

5. PURPOSE OF COPYRIGHT

As well as being relevant to debates over the nature of copyright – whether it be a property right, natural right and/or statutory privilege – history has informed debates about the essential purpose(s) of copyright law. When addressing the question of what are the appropriate goals of copyright legislation, it can be informative to examine the aims of earlier legislation. Who were the intended beneficiaries of the first copyright

---

[93] Ibid at 45–46.
[94] Andreas Rahmatian, *Copyright and Creativity: The Making of Property Rights in Creative Works* (Edward Elgar 2011) 27.
[95] Ibid.
[96] Ibid.
[97] Richard R Bowker, *Copyright, its History and its Law* (Houghton Mifflin 1912) 5.
[98] Rose (n 46) 112.

regimes? Was copyright originally meant to protect booksellers or authors? Is the public interest paramount or the interest of authors? Copyright history has sought to answer some of these questions, particularly with regard to the Statute of Anne. Conclusions about the aims of early copyright laws are then used to build arguments about whether the purpose of the legal regime has changed over the centuries, as well as lending force to claims that it ought to be refocused in a particular direction. As noted above, arguments about the nature of copyright as a natural or common law right are relevant to the question of its purpose but not necessarily decisive.

The question of whether the Statute of Anne, which gave to authors 'the sole right and liberty of printing books', was for the benefit of booksellers, authors, or the public – framed to solidify entrenched trade interests, rescue starving authors, or achieve lofty goals of public edification – remains highly controversial.[99] As Seville has pointed out, the current disagreements about the purpose of the Statute of Anne, described below, echo those of the nineteenth century.[100]

Earlier legislation protected the *owner* rather than author of a book: for example, the 1662 Licensing Act prohibited 'the printing of any book unless first licensed and entered in the register of the Stationers' Company, and prohibiting also the printing without consent of the owner'.[101] Despite settling the rights on the authors for the first time, it has been suggested that the 1710 Statute was primarily a bill to protect the interests of the printers and booksellers in the absence of the Licensing Acts; the stationers were the driving force behind the statute and their representatives lobbied for amendments to ensure the authors' rights were limited.[102] Certainly, Farrer cautioned the Royal Commission in 1878,

> It must be borne in mind that the monopoly of reproducing books did not take its origin in the modern notion of a private right of property. It was granted as a privilege or monopoly ... No doubt property in copyright had grown up under that system in the hands of printers and publishers, and it was a claim to such property that was partially recognised by the Act of Anne in 1710.[103]

Indeed, Birrell thought the Act 'singularly ill-framed to secure the privilege of the booksellers' and noted that it 'did (and for the first time) confer directly upon authors a qualified and time-limited property in their compilations and productions.'[104] Karl-Nikolaus Peifer, referring to Birrell, identifies the 'tragic side of the well-meant statute' as the fact that 'it interrupted the path to a common law copyright, or in continental-European terms, the legal acknowledgement of the personal interests of the

---

[99] John Feather, 'The Book Trade in Politics: The Making of the Copyright Act of 1710' (1980) 8 Publishing History 19, 36.

[100] Catherine Seville, 'The Statute of Anne: Rhetoric and Reception in the Nineteenth Century' (2010) 47 Hous L Rev 819.

[101] Licensing Act 1662 (13 & 14 Car II c 33).

[102] John Feather, *A History of British Publishing* (Routledge 1988) 36. Mark Rose, however, disagrees with regard to the amendments. Rose (n 46) 45–46, fn 10.

[103] Minutes of the Royal Commission on Copyright [C-2036-1] 203.

[104] Birrell (n 41) 93.

author in his work.'[105] He claims that the Statute of Anne was intended to protect the personal rights of an author and uses this point to argue that 'if we go back to the construction of copyright law as a personal right, many problems of overprotection appear in a new light.'[106] Simon Stern has examined the Statute of Anne and four of the eighteenth century copyright cases (*Burnet v Chetwood*; *Pope v Curll*; *Millar v Taylor*; and *Donaldson v Becket*) identifying their recognition of the dignitary concerns of authors.[107]

In making his case that copyright was originally focused on publishers rather than authors, Patterson depicted the Statute of Anne as a 'trade regulation statute directed to the problem of monopoly in various forms.'[108] David Saunders challenged post-structural narratives of the Act, which identified its purpose as recognizing 'the writer's subjectivity in the work' by instead portraying the Act 'as a trade regulation statute' that 'delineated and attributed the legal capacity to own copyright in a manner designated for the regulation of a specific economic activity – the making and trading of a printed commodity.'[109] The purpose of the legislation was, according to Saunders, to break the monopoly held by the Stationers' Company.[110] May and Sell also view it in terms of trade and commodification; the Act represents a 'significant move into the realm of property in the production of authorial outputs, the clear commodification of literary property.'[111]

Deazley, however, interprets the Statute of Anne as a straightforward bargain for the good of society: authors will receive a limited right in order to encourage them to produce books.[112] He has tried to use the historical record to resituate the focus of copyright from authors to the public interest as the fundamental purpose of the legal regime. Claiming later interpretations of the eighteenth-century copyright disputes are essentially flawed, he argues that the emergence of the Statute of Anne, as well as the decision in *Donaldson*, 'turned primarily upon the same basic impulse ... a desire to encourage and promote the advancement of learning, to nurture a buoyant marketplace of ideas. In all of this, the interests of the public were paramount.'[113] The High Court of Australia appeared to adopt this interpretation in *IceTV v Nine Network*, noting:

> In both its title and opening recitals, the Statute of Anne of 1709 echoed explicitly the emphasis on the practical or utilitarian importance that certain seventeenth century philosophers attached to knowledge and its encouragement in the scheme of human progress. The 'social contract' envisaged by the Statute of Anne, and still underlying the present Act, was that an author could obtain a monopoly, limited in time, in return for making a work available to the reading public.[114]

---

[105] Karl-Nikolaus Peifer, 'The Return of the Commons – Copyright History as a Helpful Source' (2008) IIC 679, 684.
[106] Ibid 687.
[107] Simon Stern, 'From Author's Right to Property Right' (2012) 62 UTLJ 29.
[108] Patterson (n 23) 150.
[109] David Saunders, *Authorship and Copyright* (Routledge 1992) 10, 11.
[110] Ibid.
[111] May and Sell (n 64) 93.
[112] Deazley, *Rethinking Copyright* (n 27) 13–14.
[113] Deazley, *On the Origin of the Right to Copy* (n 87) 216–17.
[114] [2009] HCA 14 [25].

24 *Research handbook on the history of copyright law*

Alexander suggests that Deazley's analysis of the Statute of Anne as a bargain goes too far; the legislative history does not clearly demonstrate the kind of trade-offs between interests that his interpretation requires.[115] In her view, the Act lacks 'any real coherent underlying rationale.'[116] Others have also observed that the Statute of Anne was not framed with a single, clear justification for the rights it granted – it contains traces of a recognition of natural rights, incentivization of creative labour, and public interest.[117] Certainly the universities as an interest group did rather well out of the legislation (and later from the 1775 Universities Act[118]), and their interests cannot be absolutely equated with the interests of the public. Rose admits that the Act 'did not settle the theoretical questions behind the notion of literary property' but does identify its contribution in a cultural transformation from printing matters as being seen as regulation to a shift towards authors' interests and a property right.[119]

Of course, American historical arguments about the original purpose of copyright go beyond the Statute of Anne and take into account the attitudes of the Framers of the US Constitution and broader American values. Neil Netanel, for example, employed historical arguments about copyright's emergence as coinciding with that of a 'democratic, print-mediated public square' in order to support his claims that copyright is best when centred around its ability to further democratic civil society and limited where it has less desirable effects that might thwart such aims.[120] He claimed that for the Framers of the US Constitution 'copyright's importance lay in its structural, as well as production, function. By underwriting a flourishing national market in authors' writings, copyright would help to secure authors' and printers' freedom from the corruptive influence of state, church, and aristocratic patronage.' Vaidyanathan used a historical argument to demonstrate that the US moved closer to a European author-focused philosophy of copyright and away from a focus on the public sphere.[121] He found this shift to be a 'disturbing trend' away from copyright's origins in early America and blames Mark Twain to some extent for popularizing the rhetoric of romantic authorship in relation to copyright.[122] Wendy Gordon has recently used historical arguments about the treatment of published versus unpublished works to question the extent to which the intention of the copyright regime in the US is intended to protect non-creative disseminators of copyright works.[123]

Of course, while establishing the driving forces that led to early legislation or the policy decisions behind significant legal decisions is interesting and informative, it is not entirely clear how much weight the veiled intentions of legislators drafting the first copyright statute or the United States Constitution should have in terms of informing

---

[115] Isabella Alexander, *Copyright Law and the Public Interest* (Hart Publishing 2010) 26.
[116] Ibid.
[117] Davies (n 22) 13–17; May and Sell (n 64) 93.
[118] Universities Act 1775 (15 Geo III c 53).
[119] Rose (n 46) 48.
[120] Neil Netanel, 'Copyright and a Democratic Civil Society' (1996) 106 Yale LJ 283, 352–55.
[121] Vaidyanathan (n 16) 80.
[122] Ibid 77–80.
[123] Wendy Gordon, 'The Core of Copyright: Authors, Not Publishers' (2014) 52 Hous L Rev 213.

our contemporary understanding of the justification(s) for the legal regime. After reviewing treatments of the Statute of Anne over the course of the nineteenth century, Seville concludes the Act 'offers no detailed blueprint to modern legislators and no easy resolution to the continuing challenges faced by those determining copyright policy in a digital world.'[124] Indeed, one may make a case that the purpose or focus of the law has changed over the centuries, but it does not logically follow from that the purpose and focus *ought* to be identical and unchanged today. Understanding the development of copyright law in the past has its own inherent value, but part of that value – as Kaplan understood – may be in freeing us from contemporary expectations and assumptions.

6. CONCLUSION

Historical examples of the recognition of property in intangibles or an acknowledgement of copying as a moral or ethical wrong are used to support copyright as a natural right. Evidence of creativity before the advent of strong copyright protection is cited to suggest it is unnecessary. Episodes from copyright's past, such as its scandalous early association with censorship,[125] are dragged out to challenge copyright's legitimacy. The positions of well-known historical figures are set forth as authoritative statements of the purpose and value of copyright or lack thereof. In common law jurisdictions, the question of whether copyright was originally a creature of common law or wholly one of statute has not been resolved despite about 300 years of argument.

This chapter has provided an overview and classification of historically grounded normative arguments about copyright that appear time and again. The aim is to help in clarifying debates and to aid critical analysis of these arguments when they appear in works of copyright history and elsewhere. It also gently recommends caution when assessing the normative force of such historically grounded arguments. The extent to which historical understandings of copyright can and should have any impact on current legislation and legal interpretation is debatable, particularly where the history itself clearly reveals a profound lack of consensus. Given the difficulties in reaching agreement on some of copyright history's crucial moments, even copyright historians may have some sympathy for Farrer's pragmatic view:

> It is however, quite unnecessary to enter upon a discussion of these abstruse points of history and of jurisprudence. It is quite clear that the law can create and has created a property in a monopoly of this kind; and it is also quite clear that has created and can create a limit to that monopoly. The real question is how to give to authors the amplest encouragement and reward without imposing on the public a higher price or more onerous conditions than are necessary for that purpose.[126]

---

[124] Seville, 'The Statute of Anne' (n 100) 875.
[125] 'But when constructed recklessly, copyright can once again be an instrument of censorship, just as it was before the Statute of Anne.' Vaidyanathan (n 16) 184.
[126] Minutes of the Royal Commission on Copyright [C-2036-1] 203.

The history of the way copyright history has been used throughout copyright's history – despite the several levels of abstraction – helps us to examine critically the persuasiveness and relevance of such historical arguments today. A better understanding of copyright's history can illuminate aspects of currently disputed issues, but it cannot provide a clear solution to all of the law's challenges. This is not to suggest that it is not important to continue delving into the historical record in order to better understand how copyright developed. To the contrary, such scholarly inquiry is valuable for its own sake.

If 'meta' copyright history teaches us one thing it is that the debate over copyright has always encompassed positions across the full range of the spectrum: from advocating strong, perpetual copyright to recommending its abolition. In the days leading up to the meetings of the Royal Commission on Copyright, journalist Edward Dicey described the copyright debates as having all of the requisite elements of a perpetual, irresolvable dispute, namely, 'abstract principles which are incapable of practical application, conflicting interests which cannot all be satisfied in accordance with logical equity, and accepted axioms which cannot be adapted to the circumstances of the case.'[127] While most arguments about the nature and purpose of copyright are situated somewhere in the middle, current and past dissatisfaction with the state of the law may be easily explained by the fact that copyright legislation has always represented a compromise between these two extreme poles of protection rather than the careful balancing act that Farrer recommended and which many copyright scholars find desirable.

---

[127] Edward Dicey, 'The Copyright Question' (1876) 19 Fortnightly Rev 126.

3. Law, aesthetics and copyright historiography: A critical reading of the genealogies of Martha Woodmansee and Mark Rose*
Kathy Bowrey

1. INTRODUCTION

This chapter discusses the importance of Martha Woodmansee's *The Author, Art and the Market*[1] and Mark Rose's *Authors and Owners*[2] to the history of copyright. My ambition is to use these works as a springboard to open up a broader discussion about the disciplinary boundaries of copyright historiography in order to reflect upon some of the reasons for the limited disciplinary exchange between humanities and law in Anglo scholarship.

In detailing late eighteenth century refinements of German aesthetics that come to inform the notion of authorship, Woodmansee shows the importance of understanding the interplay between philosophy, materiality and the law. She shows how the conditions facing authors in literary markets in the late eighteenth century led to a disciplinary exchange that ultimately affected the character of the aesthetic project, the development of copyright law and the cultural reception of the idea of authorship. However Woodmansee's history does not detail how aesthetics came to life within the law.

Whereas Woodmansee offers a genealogy of aesthetics, Rose is interested in setting out the genealogy of the 'author as owner'. Rose chooses the literary property debates that culminate in the leading case of *Donaldson v Becket* (1774),[3] which he argues was key to establishing the notion of the author as proprietor. As philosophy is primarily addressed through the prism of the legal arguments and political advocacy Rose's work is, perhaps, an easier read than Woodmansee for legal scholars. However, using Rose's appropriation of Locke as an example, I argue that Rose's failure to delve more deeply into philosophy and related theories of property leads to an oversimplification of the authorship debate and the role of philosophy within it and the law. Further, notwithstanding that the notion of authorship was discussed so widely and in such detail in the

---

* With thanks to Isabella Alexander, Lionel Bently, Jose Bellido, Tomás Gómez-Arostegui, James Meese and Martha Woodmansee for their discussions and comments; also to Jennifer Kwong for editorial assistance.

[1] The full title is Martha Woodmansee, *The Author, Art and the Market: Rereading the History of Aesthetics* (Columbia UP 1994).

[2] Mark Rose, *Authors and Owners. The Invention of Copyright* (Harvard UP 1993). This book draws upon Mark Rose, 'The Author as Proprietor: Donaldson v. Becket and the Genealogy of Modern Authorship' (1988) 23 Representations 51.

[3] *Donaldson v Becket* (1774) 4 Burr 2408, 98 ER 257.

British literary property debates that 'its normative status was effectively rendered incontestable',[4] *Donaldson v Becket* provided no definitive legal construction of authorship. Nor did it advance legal methodologies that authoritatively relate law and philosophy. This gap remains in place in the twenty-first century.

Woodmansee and Rose were both inspired by Foucault and his observation that 'the coming into being of the notion of the author constitutes the privileged moment of individualization in the history of ideas, knowledge, literature, philosophy, and the sciences'.[5] Both authors have made major contributions that work to demystify authorship by revealing the particular philosophical, historical and material conditions that supported the emergence of copyright. Woodmansee's history reminds us that it was not just the eighteenth and nineteenth century development of aesthetic ideas that supported the development of copyright. There were also cultural and political strategies devised to support reception of the idea of authorship. Yet Anglo copyright history, largely based upon consideration of the significance of the Statute of Anne (1710),[6] as well as related case law and subsequent statutory revision, remains uncomfortable about engaging with the nuances of the philosophical ideas that support new legal claims. There has been comparatively little discussion of the role of strategies and methods that inform and sustain the interplay between law, philosophy and culture or consideration of the way the notion of authorship continued to develop as the marketplace for cultural products matured and copyright was extended to encompass far more than books. Though it is well understood today that copyright is both a legal and a cultural category, the relationship between law and philosophy remains very sketchy in the writing of Anglo copyright history. This chapter concludes with a discussion about why this problem needs to be overcome and why we need to think more productively about copyright's essential connection with philosophy and aesthetics.

2. A GENEALOGY OF AESTHETICS

The full title of Woodmansee's work, *The Author, Art and the Market. Rereading the History of Aesthetics*, simply, if elliptically, defines the scope of her inquiry. The book is first and foremost a contribution to the history of ideas, a critical reading of the genealogy of aesthetics. Woodmansee engages in a contextual reading of eighteenth century German writers, exploring shifts and permeations in metaphysical constructs that came to inform the meaning of authorship and artistic creation. Importantly, she connects the rise of ideas about the nature and significance of art, and the bifurcation of cultural production into high and low art, with discussion of the cultural politics and economics of artistic production associated with the growth of literature markets in the eighteenth century. She highlights the close but problematic relationship between art,

---

[4] Brad Sherman and Lionel Bently, *The Making of Modern Intellectual Property Law: The British Experience 1760–1911* (CUP 1999) 40.

[5] Both works cite as inspiration, Michel Foucault, 'What is an Author?' in Josué V Harari (ed), *Textual Strategies* (Cornell UP 1979) 141–60.

[6] Statute of Anne 1710 (8 Anne c 19).

literature and audiences. In so doing she provides insights into the relatively unexplored slippage familiar to copyright scholars whereby the terms 'author' and 'artist' become somewhat jumbled and used interchangeably, and reminds us that the rise of the author did not necessarily require the relegation of the reader to the status of passive consumer.

A lengthy, descriptive treatment of Woodmansee's book follows. In my experience most legal readers have not read the entire book. Rather, the focus is only on the copyright chapter, first published as a stand-alone article.[7] However it is only by reading the insights into copyright in relation to the other chapters that the full significance of the work, and the philosophical and political ambition of German aesthetic thinkers, can be appreciated.

Chapter One, 'The Interests of Disinterestedness', begins by tracing the arrival and critical reception of the idea of fine art as a coherent category that is defined by the character of the pursuit and the artist's relationship with the world. The basis for the discussion is an original translation of Karl Philipp Moritz's essay, *Toward a Unification of all the Fine Arts and letters under the Concept of Self-Sufficiency* (1785). In seeking to 'unify' the arts Moritz was advocating the radical view that all fine art – poetry, painting, sculpture, architecture, eloquence, dance and music – shared common qualities. This challenged the orthodoxy that art should be appreciated and judged in terms of the utility of a particular medium for imparting distinctive lessons about the human condition, our faculties and our relation to the exterior world, through imitation of nature or God. Moritz argues that fine art, as a distinctive kind of human endeavour, has intrinsic rather than extrinsic worth. Art is defined by its abstract relationship to the world. Art is 'self-sufficient' because it communicates beauty and excellence by offering insights into an interior world. As Moritz put it, fine art is contemplated 'for its own sake', that is, 'disinterestedly'. Achievement in art is where 'we seem to lose ourselves in the beautiful object; and precisely this loss, this forgetfulness of ourselves, is the highest degree of pure and disinterested pleasure which beauty grants us'.[8]

Woodmansee relates the arrival of this modern theorisation of art to developments in late eighteenth century book markets:

> The middle-class reading public in Germany had developed by the last quarter of the century, a voracious appetite for the entire spectrum of light entertainment – from sentimental love stories and novels of education, to tales of ghost-seers and exorcists, and an aggressively escapist literature of adventure and intrigue ... Literary entertainment was becoming an industry.[9]

Yet according to the new aesthetics, the appropriate attitude of the artist toward audiences is one of 'indifference', to sever valuation of a work from consideration of its popular reception. A public that is merely 'diverted', 'moved' or 'stimulated' is suggestive of artistic failure. As Woodmansee explains, Moritz 'inspired a new theory of art in which, as it were, a virtue is made of necessity, and the relative ineffectuality

---

[7] Martha Woodmansee, 'The Genius and the Copyright: Economic and Legal Conditions of the Emergence of the "Author"' (1984) 17 Eighteenth Century Studies 425.
[8] Woodmansee, *The Author, Art and the Market* (n 1) 19.
[9] Ibid 25.

30 *Research handbook on the history of copyright law*

of beautiful art, instead of rendering its value problematic, can be construed as evidence of its very excellence'.[10] This aesthetics sets in train a fractious relationship between the artist and the external world – between art, the market and the reader. And, most relevantly to copyright historians, Woodmansee argues that this tension is further worked out through development of the notion of 'the author' and consideration of the education of the reader.

The construction of authorship is the primary subject of Chapter Two, 'Genius and the Copyright'. Mirroring the previous discussion of the changing status of the artist, this chapter explores how author and text come to be read through appreciation of the genius that forms the work. However in taking up Foucault's challenge of understanding how the modern invention of the author came into being, of 'how the author became individualized in a culture like ours',[11] Woodmansee includes a consideration of the role of law. She argues that German theorists were particularly interested in new theories of authorship including works of English writers, such as Edward Young's *Conjectures on Original Composition* (1759), because of relations in the book publishing industry in Germany. There was an extraordinary demand for reading material that supported the growth of late eighteenth century book markets. This encouraged the adoption of writing as a profession. However there was no legal infrastructure in Germany that recognised a private property right in texts. Texts, like all ideas, were perceived as an embodiment of truth that belonged to the public. Honorariums to authors, like aristocratic patronage, provided symbolic recognition of the importance of particular contributions, but any such fees were discretionary and did not reflect the market value of the works or authorial distinction in creating the work per se. While German book privileges existed, these were merely a right against reprinting and described by Johann Gottlieb Fichte as an 'exception to natural law'.[12] That is, ideas, according to natural law, belonged to the public. There was also an additional limitation with the role of privilege related to the geopolitical nature of Germany at this time. Whereas the United Kingdom had created a common market across England and Scotland subject to the same trade regulations in 1707[13] (around the same time as the passage of the Statute of Anne), eighteenth century Germany was comprised of three hundred independent states. Privileges were limited to the town or municipality in which they were awarded. Thus Woodmansee points out that book privilege lacked both a clear philosophical foundation and the legal institutional support that was present in other jurisdictions such as Great Britain and France[14] in the eighteenth century. In Germany, book privilege was 'not really a law at all but, as the

---

[10] Ibid 22.
[11] Ibid 35.
[12] Ibid 45.
[13] Union with Scotland Act 1706 (6 Anne c 11); Union with England Act 1707 (6 Anne c 7) art iv. See also Allan I Macinnes, *Union and Empire: The Making of the United Kingdom in 1707* (CUP 2007).
[14] French legal recognition of the author is dated by Hesse from six decrees in 1777. Ginsburg also cites decrees of 1791 and 1793. See Carla Hesse, 'Enlightenment Epistemology and the Laws of Authorship in Revolutionary France, 1777–1793' (1990) 30 Representations 109; Jane C Ginsburg, 'A Tale of Two Copyrights: Literary Property in Revolutionary France and America' (1990) 64 Tul L Rev 991.

word itself suggests, a special concession or dispensation conditionally granted to printers or publishers who enjoyed the favour of the court'.[15] Woodmansee argues that the lack of an equivalent to the Statute of Anne stifled the development of the book industry in Germany compared to Britain:

> [E]ighteenth century Germany found itself in a transitional phase between the limited patronage of an aristocratic age and the democratic patronage of the marketplace. With the growth of a middle class, demand for reading material increased steadily, enticing writers to try to earn a livelihood from the sale of their writings to a buying public. But most were doomed to be disappointed for the requisite legal, economic and political arrangements and institutions were not yet in place to support the large number of writers who came forward.[16]

The analysis stresses the importance of linking the success of philosophical developments in aesthetics to engagement with legal, political and social realms: '[I]t is this interplay between legal, economic, and social questions on the one hand and philosophical and aesthetic ones on the other that critical concepts and principles as fundamental as that of authorship received their modern form.'[17] She argues that aesthetics do not develop in disciplinary isolation; theories are not simply a consequence of the autonomous development of philosophical thought; ideas also stem from an 'interplay' with the historical and material conditions of the time. Here philosophical discourse is historicised through relating developments in philosophy with the market and to the law. The author has a presence in all three realms and is a product of the exchange, rather than represented as a philosophical idea developed in disciplinary isolation. Woodmansee argues that the need to improve the material conditions of authors and publishers provided a particular impetus in Germany to carefully re-theorise the properties of 'books'. Numerous theories of authorship were advanced by publishers, lawyers, philosophers and poets. And consequently 'the nature of writing ... [was] completely rethought'.[18]

Ideas of authorship stressed that the text could not be effectively reduced or contained by its physical manifestation. The book communicates to readers more than the ideas it presents or re-presents to the public. For instance, Fichte, developing Young's observations about the nature of genius, argued the printed paper and the content are conceptually distinct. The book can be divided into related parts: 'the *material* [materiell] aspect, the content of the book, the ideas it presents; and ... the *form* of these ideas, the way in which, the combination in which, the phrasing and wording in which they are presented'.[19] Whilst the material aspect, the book as a physical object, is owned by the purchaser and the thoughts or content passes to the reader, 'the *form* in which these ideas are presented, however remains the property of the author eternally'.[20] The author is the creator and owner of 'the form' of thought.

---

[15] Woodmansee, *The Author, Art and the Market* (n 1) 45.
[16] Ibid 41–42.
[17] Ibid 47.
[18] Ibid 49.
[19] Ibid 51.
[20] Ibid.

Fichte's work connects an older tradition of the public domain of ideas with a radical new notion of creation. The idea that *form* is capable of being defined with reference to its creator produces a new kind of intangible property with potentially major ramifications for the respective claims of authors, publishers and the reprint trade. As was commonly acknowledged, the author will draw upon known ideas. Aspects of a published work may already be with the public – effectively beyond private ownership. However, the author needs to consent to the recirculation of the form of his ideas. With a voracious appetite for reading and an interest in education of the emerging middle class, reprints were a major part of the book trade. The development of the notion of authorship provided a foundation for the expansion of the notion of piracy. Unauthorised reprints do not involve theft of the material aspect of the book or the thoughts, but they involve a theft of 'an intellectual creation that owes its individuality solely and exclusively to [the author]'.[21] Accordingly authorial permission is required to print and to reprint, notwithstanding that the ideas expressed within the work may already be circulating in public.

Woodmansee briefly sketches how an idea of individualised authorship creeps into ensuing German literary property regulations helping establish the concept of authorship that is familiar to us today. She argues that the new literary property right led to little change in the financial situation for authors. What it did lead to is a significant reconceptualisation of the act of reading. The act of reading, in permitting 'a revelation of the personality of the author', becomes 'the exploration of the Other'.[22] Buying a book involves the purchase of a right of access to the form of the author's expression – permission to take pleasure and interrogate the text and, through that, connect with the author.

In laying out late eighteenth century German refinements to the concept of authorship, Woodmansee demonstrates how the notion entailed complex metaphysics. It is important for lawyers to grasp that recognition of the genius in authorship is not just about the author and the text. Aesthetics activates a particular theory of cognition – a hierarchical construction that seeks to privilege the 'experience' of the writer over other paths of interpretation of the text, which diminishes consideration of the reader. Woodmansee argues that this development will transform the reading of texts, but not without facing a number of philosophical, cultural and political challenges. The remaining chapters explore broader dissemination and the development of aesthetic theory, the cultural and political ramifications for German society and the take-up of these ideas by the leading English Romantic poets, Wordsworth and Coleridge.

In her elaboration of the development of aesthetic thought, Woodmansee provides little detail about the literary regulations, the nature of the legal order and legal reasoning at this time – the capacity of the law to absorb new thought. Thus whilst her work suggests to copyright readers a path that provides law with a solution to the dilemma of settling the boundaries to the work important to the development of literary property rights, there is no elaboration of how this opportunity is taken up within the

---

[21] Ibid 52.
[22] Ibid 55.

law, and in turn whether the legal elaboration of authorship also then impacts on developments in aesthetics.[23]

Chapter Three, 'Aesthetic Autonomy as a Weapon in Cultural Politics', considers in depth Johann Christoph Friedrich Schiller's *Aesthetic Letters* (c 1790) in the context of wider German debates about the power of poetry, inspired by concern for the terror of post-revolutionary France and the challenge of writing for a society marked by radical divisions between the elite and the masses: 'To Schiller the violent turn of events in France signifies that men are not ready for the freedom they are demanding.'[24] In turn this leads to significant debate about the nature and function of poetry, which is sketched in terms of the critical reception and debate that followed the success of Gottfried August Bürger's popular ballad *Lenore*. There was agreement that simply appealing to a small intellectual elite will do little to impact or improve the education of the masses. Aesthetics needs a broader audience. However as Schiller saw it, in expanding the audience for poetry Bürger 'threatened to render [poetry] even more marginal than it had already become in modern society. ... The immaturity, the deficiency of spirit, the enthusiasm, and the vulgarity that endear Bürger's verse to common readers cannot but "repel" the elite'.[25] Schiller argues that Bürger's egalitarian orientation threatens the 'cause of art'.[26] A solution settled on, to build a bridge between high and low art, was to address the education of readers with Schiller seeking to lead by example.

Broader strategies for improving the art of reading are carefully elaborated in Chapter Four, 'Aesthetics and the Policing of Reading'. So important was the task of educating the middle class and improving their discrimination and taste that some argued for the trade to be regulated to restrict the flow of literature, even though it was the freedom of the press that had helped Luther and Calvin free Germany from 'the scepter of the clerisy'. Nationalising lending libraries was also considered so that appropriate civil servants could be placed in charge of acquisition, in particular with a view to influencing women's reading.[27] It was argued that reading should be taught to the middle classes as an active and reflexive act, rather than left as a form of passive consumption, leading to the production of manuals for instruction in the art of reading. Johann Adam Bergk's *Die Kunst, Bücher zu lesen* (The Art of Reading Books) (1799) addresses the need to instruct the masses in literary taste. It imparts lessons designed 'to make reading a kind of creation in reverse, the object of which is to re-experience what an author originally thought and felt'. His reading strategies 'oppose the "passive receptivity" of the new novel readers'.[28] Drawing upon Immanuel Kant's *Critique of Judgment* (1790) Bergk argues that the author needs to cultivate 'all human faculties and modes of operation – sense, fantasy and imagination, understanding, reason (both

---

[23] There is some take up of this agenda in Martin Kretschmer and Friedemann Kawohl, 'Johann Gottlieb Fichte, and The Trap of Inhalt (Content) and Form: An Information Perspective on Music Copyright' (2009) 12 Information, Communication & Society 41.
[24] Woodmansee, *The Author, Art and the Market* (n 1) 58.
[25] Ibid 73–74.
[26] Ibid 79.
[27] Ibid 91–92.
[28] Ibid 100.

speculative and practical), and judgment (teleological and aesthetic)'.[29] In doing so, reading can provide the knowledge and intellectual skills required so that man can 'fulfill his responsibilities as a human being and citizen'.

In addressing the broader cultural politics of authorship in Chapters Three and Four, Woodmansee reminds copyright scholars that this aesthetics is not about transforming the writer into the author for self-centred reasons. Nor was a transformation sought to benefit publishers. It was not about property or the economic benefits of private rights in a narrow sense, where economy is constructed as a largely self-regulating sphere of private pursuit. There was a much larger social and cultural project in train. The cultural politics of authorship justified a new form of literary property with the hope that, coupled with a broader education about literature and reading, it could resolve the 'literary philandering' of the reading public and, through contributing to a broad education of the middle class, improve the social and political conditions of society. In reading past Chapter Two we learn that authorial rights were simply one part of a much larger ambition, accompanied by other strategies designed to effect a kind of social engineering of the masses designed to discipline consumer taste and ensure that the market better supports 'cultural' products.

Chapter Five, 'Engendering Art', considers the publication, translation and critical reception of Sophie von La Roche's *Fräulein von Sternheim* (1771) to explore the gendered nature of genius. Woodmansee shows how despite the success of women writers in terms of print runs, translations, piracies and fame, women are excluded from the status of genius. Discomfort with the notion of women's full participation in the literary world is indicated by the work being published anonymously, ostensibly without her permission at the instigation of her friend, the writer Christoph Martin Wieland, 'as he could not "resist the urge to present to all the virtuous mothers and charming young daughters of our nation"' a work that seemed to him so well designed to foster wisdom and virtue 'among [their] sex, and even among [his] own'.[30] For her to seek to publish in her own name 'of right' would alienate potential readers. As editor of the volume his preface stresses her personal motivations in writing. She only circulated it to him in order to obtain his opinion on her manner of judging human experience to assist her to refine her wisdom and virtue. He draws attention to perceived 'defects' that one might expect from an amateur production and constructs the book as primarily suited for women readers. Women writers are constructed as 'Other' to genius and their works are relegated to the special category of 'women's literature', clearly constructed as marginal and utilitarian productions rather than works of art. Nonetheless as La Roche's correspondence with her friend Juliet Bondeli reveals, it is worth noting that women did conceive of themselves as authors and discuss claims to genius, well aware that the prescription of gender would prejudice any such recognition. Woodmansee concludes that in terms of broader significance, the gendered construct of genius means that women are erased from the literary canon altogether, failing to be noted in subsequent literature on significant works.

In reminding readers of the gendered qualifications of authorship, this chapter reinforces the importance of considering not just the rationale for authorship, but also

---

[29] Ibid 93.
[30] Ibid 106–07.

its morality[31] and its application and rationalisation in practice. Authorship is more than an aesthetic, but also a cultural and political practice that impacts on our understanding of art and accomplishment across the ages.

The final Chapter Six, 'The Uses of Kant in England', discusses the influence of German aesthetics on William Wordsworth and Samuel Taylor Coleridge, exploring how the English poets faced the challenge of creating works of art for an ill-educated audience. Woodmansee traces shifts in Wordsworth's appraisal of Bürger's *Lenore*. His poem 'overran all Europe, helping more than any other German work of the period ... to call the Romantic movement to life'.[32] Wordsworth initially praises Bürger's sensational 'manner of relating'.[33] Yet after having experienced a frustrating reception for his *Lyrical Ballads*, Wordsworth later shifts to a critique of Bürger and his appeal to the public. By 1815 Wordsworth suggests that the value of significant poetry has no direct or immediate relation to its reception, drawing a distinction between the reading public for whom contempt is shown and 'the PEOPLE, philosophically characterized and to the embodied spirit of their knowledge, so far as it exists and moves, at the present, faithfully supported by its two wings, the past and the future, [to whom] his devout respect, his reverence, is due'.[34] She argues that Wordsworth 'tells a reassuring history of English poetry in which it turns out that all of the great poets from Spenser to Percy met with similar fates during their lifetimes while lesser talents flourished'.[35] Genius will not be recognised by the reading public and the value assigned to a work in the marketplace is not a reflection of artistic worth but grounds to suspect a work's corruption. Woodmansee thus links Wordsworth's journey with Bürger with that of Schiller's, discussed in Chapter Three. Serious writers will struggle 'to compete effectively with an ever growing literature of diversion'.[36]

Coleridge's *On the Principles of Genial Criticism Concerning the Fine Arts* (1814) is similarly compared to Bergk's *Art of Reading* as a manual designed to address the taste of the reading public – to create an audience for 'true art'. However in execution, Coleridge borrows 'surreptitiously, from [Kant's] *Critique of Judgment*'.[37] He also seeks to discount what was then the dominant theory of art in Britain – associationist aesthetics,[38] which constructed the viewer of art empirically, so that 'as their situations differ, so too will the ideas individuals associate with a given object, and hence also will its effect, which is to say, its meaning and value to them. There is thus bound to be an individual element in every act of reception'.[39] To Coleridge, 'a work's associations with things external to it cannot be relevant to appreciation of it as art', for it is the

---

[31] For example, middle class women's reading and writing is conceived of in terms of improving her personal virtue, to benefit her in nurturing her father, husband and children.
[32] Woodmansee, *The Author, Art and the Market* (n 1) 63.
[33] Ibid 113.
[34] Ibid 118.
[35] Ibid 117.
[36] Ibid 118.
[37] Ibid 119.
[38] For a discussion of associationist aesthetics and its connection to romantic thought, see Timothy M Costelloe, *The British Aesthetic Tradition. From Shaftesbury to Wittgenstein* (CUP 2013).
[39] Woodmansee, *The Author, Art and the Market* (n 1) 126–31.

function of art, as Coleridge defines it, to provide '*immediate* pleasure, through the medium of beauty'.[40] Rather than produce practical guidance for reading art,

> [T]he philosophical project that evolves ... places demands on readers that [they] are not equipped to meet. To follow Coleridge down the metaphysical path he pursues there one needs to be versed in philosophy, in particular in the philosophy of art that was being generated in England and on the continent at the beginning of the nineteenth century.[41]

Thus Wordsworth and Coleridge both alienate, rather than satisfactorily relate, the new philosophical insights to the audiences they seek to educate.

Woodmansee concludes with a consideration of Wordsworth's efforts to secure a perpetual copyright for authors to ease the situation for '*difficult* authors'[42] and his rebuttal of strong political and trade opposition to a term extension: 'what we want in these times, and are likely to want still more, is not the circulation of books, but of good books, and above all, the production of works, the authors of which look beyond the passing day, and are desirous of pleasing and instructing future generations'.[43] She argues this was a far more successful political operationalisation of the theory he had advanced in his *Essay* of 1815. The legislative compromise was for a term of 42 years from first publication or, if the author survived that term, the author's life plus seven years.[44] In leaving off at this point Woodmansee makes no comment on the significance of a shift from a philosophical project of winning over an intellectual reading public to one of winning parliamentary votes.[45]

Whilst demonstrating the impact of German aesthetics on key English romantic figures, the book does not seek to advance a genealogy of British authorship or law. This work is left to others to accomplish. Yet it is important for copyright scholars to consider what is given up when legislative solutions are sought without the support of broader social and political strategies to effect the reception of ideas. As Woodmansee explains, the German romantics understood that it was not enough to simply elaborate a new rationality. Effecting social change required attention to the audience and to how they might be led into a sustained engagement with new thought in order to affect prevailing attitudes and behaviours. One of the existing problems with copyright historiography today is the presumption that when ideas are posited by cultural elites and come to circulate in the broader culture they are magically 'taken up' by the public and the law. How does this occur? And how are the 'philosophical' ideas transformed through this engagement? As modern society increasingly pays heed to the rational construction of key public institutions, and in particular, the law, the ability to import aesthetic traditions into the legal order becomes a much more complex problem. This

---

[40] Ibid 139.
[41] Ibid 122.
[42] Ibid 146.
[43] Ibid.
[44] *Copyright Amendment Act 1842* (5 & 6 Vict c 45).
[45] This is explored in Martha Woodmansee, 'The Cultural Work of Copyright: Legislating Authorship in Britain 1837–1842' in Austin Sarat and Thomas R Kearns (eds), *Law in the Domains of Culture* (Michigan UP 1998) 65–96.

concern is taken up further below in relation to seminal work on English literary property advanced by Mark Rose.

3. A GENEALOGY OF AUTHORSHIP

In his 1988 article Mark Rose notes the influence of Woodmansee's work. However whereas Woodmansee's book centres on explication of developments in aesthetics, Rose is primarily interested in the legal-cultural conception of authorship. As such, his work is not primarily an exposition on romantic authorship, but on the genesis of a far more abstract, legally informed construct: the author as proprietor.

The literary property debates of the late eighteenth century form the basis from which he argues this modern notion of the author emerges. The cases[46] settled on the question whether there was a perpetual, common law right of authors and if so, whether this right survived beyond the creation of statutorily limited rights in the Statute of Anne. The ensuing popular debate in the courts and in the surrounding public discourse led to major refinements in the philosophical tenets that, Rose argues, come to support the Anglo idea of authorship. In his 1988 article, Rose defines the notion of the author as proprietor. He argues that 'the author' and 'the literary work' are 'orbiting concepts at the heart of the modern literary system'.[47] There is 'a twin birth' whereby authorship comes to be inextricably tied to the notion of the literary work, each informed and bounded by reference back to the other.

Rose unearths an impressive array of literature that he argues contributes to the invention of the modern idea of authorship. However, in terms of advancing this construct, Rose's article prioritises three main sources that are central to the development of the author as proprietor: the political philosopher, John Locke's *Two Treatises on Government* (1689) and the works of two barristers, William Blackstone's *Commentaries on the Laws of England* (1765–69) and Francis Hargrave's *Argument in Defence of Literary Property* (1774). The book includes a much wider range of cultural references that inform the same idea of authorship, but stripped bare, the argument in the article and the book is essentially the same.

Rose argues that from Locke we come to appreciate 'the axiom that an individual's "person" was his own property. From this it could be demonstrated that through labour an individual might convert the goods of nature into private property'.[48] The statutory limitation on copyright in the Statute of Anne directly undermined the London booksellers' established practice of assigning perpetual copyrights in texts and recognising shares in texts. Accordingly the London booksellers soon attempted to read down the impact of the legislation by establishing an alternate prior right to literary property in the courts. The booksellers championed themselves as the time-honoured guardians of the author, whom, it was claimed, had always 'owned' the text:

---

[46] Most notably *Millar v Taylor* (1769) 4 Burr 2303, 98 ER 201; *Donaldson v Becket* (1774) 4 Burr 2408, 98 ER 257.
[47] Rose, 'The Author as Proprietor' (n 2) 72.
[48] Ibid 56.

38 *Research handbook on the history of copyright law*

> Authors have ever had a property in their Works, founded upon the same fundamental maxims by which Property was originally settled, and hath since been maintained. The Invention of Printing did not destroy this Property of Authors, nor alter it in any Respect, but by rendering it more easy to be invaded.[49]

Rose argues that the Stationers adapted the Lockean discourse for real property to the literary property issue:

> Every man was entitled to the fruits of his labor, they argued, and therefore it was self-evident that authors had an absolute property in their own works. This property was transferred to the bookseller when the copyright was purchased and thereafter it continued perpetually just like any other property right.[50]

He notes Blackstone, counsel in support of perpetual literary property in *Tonson v Collins*[51] and *Millar v Taylor*, further advances the idea that the author has a natural right to his creation. To clarify that the author is not claiming any right to own ideas Rose argues that Blackstone drew upon a reworking of Edward Young's influential *Conjectures on Original Composition* (1759) to introduce the notion that it is the 'style and sentiment are the essentials of a literary composition'.[52] Blackstone then sought to further reinforce this new ownership claim by linking literary property to a right of real property based on occupancy.[53] Blackstone argued that a right to property based on occupancy was supported by Locke's theory and also by the principles of Roman law.[54]

From Hargrave, Rose argues there is a further refinement of Blackstonian authorship that helps determine the boundaries around the authorial right. Readers may form different views about how one identifies style and sentiment. Hargrave creates certainty in the definition of the right by displacing consideration of the literary merits of the work altogether: rather than defining what is owned with reference to the literary

---

[49] Ibid 57.
[50] Ibid.
[51] *Tonson v Collins* (1761) 1 Bl R 321, 96 ER 169.
[52] Rose, 'The Author as Proprietor' (n 2) 63.
[53] Ibid 64.
[54] Blackstone wrote:

There is still another species of property, which, being grounded on labor and invention, is more properly reducible to the head of occupancy than any other; since the right of occupancy itself, (a) is supposed by Mr Locke, and many others, (b) to be founded on the personal labor of the occupant… When a man, by the exertion of his rational powers, has produced an original work, he has clearly a right to dispose of that identical work, as he pleases, and any attempt to take it from him, or vary the disposition he has made of it, is an invasion of his property. Now the identity of a literary composition consists entirely in the sentiment and the language, the same conceptions, clothed in the same words, must necessarily be the same composition and whatever method be taken of conveying that composition to the ear or the eye of another, by recital, by writing, or by printing, in any number of copies or at any period of time, it is always the identical work of the author which is conveyed; and no other man can have a right to convey, or transfer it, without his consent … .

William Blackstone, 'Chapter 26: Of Title to Things Personal by Occupancy' in *Commentaries on the Laws of England, Book 2: The Rights of Things* (Clarendon 1773) s 8.

composition itself, one can determine the distinctiveness of the work with reference to the identity that occupies it. Hargrave:

> Collapse[s] the category of the work into that of the author and his personality ... He has shown the individuality of the work to be identical to that of the author, and in the process the category of the work has dissolved. Interestingly, this action traces in reverse the Lockean notion of the creation of property in which property originates when an individual's person – already understood as a kind of possession – is impressed upon the world through labour.[55]

Compared to Fichte's careful differentiation of the public and private properties of the text, this formulation collapses the need to distinguish ownership of ideas from the expression by focusing more abstractly on the labour and personality presumed to be attendant in the expression of ideas. The author and work are thus as one, and concern for the free circulation of ideas and the reader is displaced.

In focusing on authorship as an outcome of a discourse on property rights Rose follows the legal development of philosophical ideas. However there is little discussion of the way the literary property advocates he selects cherry-pick from a much larger range of traditions, philosophical sources and social influences. In *Authors and Owners* Rose partly justifies some inattentiveness to philosophy by arguing that whilst interested in understanding the relationship between law and aesthetics, he is not interested, in a philosophical sense, in exploring the subjectivity or consciousness of the author. His focus is more narrowly confined to the rise of authorial discourse based on notions of property, originality and personality.[56] Thus his author is neither a philosophical nor legal subject but a hybrid.

In pursuit of this end, other relationships with the text that complicate the claim to the necessity of any such authorial property right or connection are quickly moved over. For example, seventeenth century patents, guild regulation of stationers and printers and, with respect to Milton's assertion of rights to his text, 'propriety' are analysed as pre-modern for lacking the individualised assertion of rights that marks modern authorship. Here he shows that authorship is not a timeless or constant idea. To the genealogy sketched in the article the book adds some earlier sources as the rights of authors and concern for piracy featured in debates about press licensing and censorship around the time of the passage of the Statute of Anne. For example, there is reference to Defoe's thoughts on the paternity of the text: *A Book is the Author's Property, 'tis the Child of his Invention* (1710).[57] Rose argues the rhetoric of paternity helps distance authorial rights from the mechanical rights awarded in patent. He also includes Locke's advocacy in favour of a limited term of literary property, with Locke's intervention in the debate presented as an anti-printer, anti-monopoly advocacy, presumed to be more generally supportive of the development of author as proprietor.

Rose argues that the circulation of these ideas about author's rights around the time of the passing of the Statute of Anne shows that the act was not simply regulation of the printer's right to the copy. Thus whilst it may be true that British (authorial) discourse 'could not have been derived from Romanticism, not least because the latter

---

[55] Rose, 'The Author as Proprietor' (n 2) 73.
[56] Rose, *Authors and Owners* (n 2) 7.
[57] Ibid.

would not emerge as a coherent movement for the best part of a century',[58] Rose argues that at the time of the passage of 'An Act for the Encouragement of Learning, by *Vesting the Copies of Printed Books in the Authors* or Purchasers of such Copies, during the Times therein mentioned', there was already a nascent right of authors, as argued by Defoe, Addison and Locke.[59] His most important insights relate to how this idea of authorship is more fully developed in litigation pursued by authors in the courts in the eighteenth century in Chancery and in the common law courts. Rose argues that the case of *Pope v Curll* (1741)[60] was especially significant because it extended the scope of literary property beyond 'books' to personal letters, where a distinction was made between owning the tangible property in the physical letter and the literary content as a form of intangible property: 'The discourse of literary property was moving away from its old foundation in the materiality of the author's manuscript. In this decision ... not ink and paper but pure signs, separated from any material support, have become the protected property.'[61]

Rose sees legal forums as providing foundational opportunities to advance new ideas that resonate far beyond the walls of the court. Law is thus recognised as a creative force that transforms philosophical ideas. Though he does not discuss it, this observation is perhaps especially apt for a time when law itself is not conceived of as a discrete form of expert knowledge. Lawyers draw upon an array of sources, forms of argument and rhetorical traditions. But as Lobban notes specifically in relation to literary property:

> [E]ach judge often had a different conception of what the common law was about. Probably the best-known example of this in the eighteenth century occurred with *Millar v Taylor* where the judges in turn argued that the law was based on justice, natural law, custom, and convenience. ... [T]his case proved that law was not the simple uncontentious application of doctrine, the articulation of answers from within the law. It showed, rather, that 'the most considerable portion of the whole is composed of determinations and resolutions of the judges, proceeding upon analogy, public policy and natural justice'.[62]

The eighteenth century was also a time for inventing legal ideas of property and exchange to further commercial opportunities in order to free the law from the weight of tradition: 'English jurists were interested in the philosophical investigation of economic change; they were influenced by new insights into the nature of human

---

[58] Anne Barron, 'Copyright Law's Musical Work' (2006) 15 Social and Legal Studies 101, 108.
[59] See also Joseph Loewenstein, *The Author's Due* (Chicago UP 2002) 209–12, 230–32.
[60] *Pope v Curll* (1741) 2 Atk 342, 26 ER 608.
[61] Rose, *Authors and Owners* (n 2) 65.
[62] The quotation is from John Miller, *An Inquiry into the Present State of the Civil Law of England* (John Murray 1825) in Michael Lobban, *The Common Law and English Jurisprudence, 1760–1850* (Clarendon 1991) 81. See also Michael Lobban, 'Custom, Nature and Authority' in David Lemming (ed), *The British and Their Laws in the Eighteenth Century* (Boydell & Brewer 2005) 27–58.

passion, and new arguments about its impact on the social order. Ideas about sentiment, desire and civility informed eighteenth century legal disputes and legal theory.'[63]

It should also be noted that this was a time when law reporting was relatively limited, disorganised and available reports were unreliable.[64] Pamphleteering about the significance of litigation was itself a form of legal education, advancing ideas of the rights of subjects. Ideas about what the law was, and what it should be, were advanced in litigation and in pamphlets about injustices with a view to winning over both lawyerly and broader public opinion. It is thus not surprising that this was a time when new authorial claims could be fruitfully advanced.

However in pursuing his narrative, Rose, an English Professor, glosses over much of the complexity of law and the legal order that complicates the ability to make any certain claims about the impact of new ideas on the trajectory of the law: the different jurisdictions of equity and common law until the late eighteenth century, the importance of procedural rules, particular forms of pleading, imprecise legal categorisations, diverse styles of legal reasoning based on various sources of law and restrictions in available remedies. While new definitions and defences of common law were developed, 'innovations in commercial law, were now, in turn subject to a mounting insistence on the applicability (and desirability) of stable common law procedures and remedies'.[65] A combination of dynamic variables, moving the law to innovation as well as toward establishing certainty and order, complicates both the expression of legal argument and the conclusions that can be drawn about the development of new principles throughout the entire eighteenth century.

My point here is not that fertile exchanges leading to new ideas about the properties in texts were not occurring or that the law was unreceptive to these. Rather the problem is that it is very difficult to make large claims about an isolated case and its role in developing particular 'new' legal precepts given the general messiness of the jurisprudence at this time. And more generally with common law, it is only by subsequent citation as authority that the significance of the decision can be understood, and even then, what the decision stands for often remains subject to much conjecture as the principle is broadened or narrowed or the case distinguished by the facts. Thus *Pope v Curll* may 'advance' a particular idea of an abstract intangible property in a literary text in a loose sense, but it is not clear how this idea sat among other possible interpretations of the issue before the court, such as the court was protecting the confidentiality of the letter writer; that is, protecting the privacy of the person rather than the thing, or as is more likely in the early eighteenth century, that a distinction between the right of persons, property and a notion of propriety was very hard to distinguish.[66]

---

[63] Julia Rudolph, *Common Law and Enlightenment in England, 1689–1750* (Boydell 2013) 259.
[64] See generally Chantal Stebbings (ed), *Law Reporting in Britain: Proceedings of the Eleventh British Legal History Conference* (Hambledon 1995).
[65] Rudolph (n 63) 269.
[66] See Margaret M Radin, *Property and Persuasion. Essays on the History, Theory and Rhetoric of Ownership* (Westview 1994) 58–61.

Similar legal dynamics complicate analysis of *Donaldson v Becket* and its claim to a landmark status in terms of developing the legal foundation of copyright.[67] In failing to identify the fluidity of the legal order and reason, Rose fudges the significance of the events that are claimed to develop the idea of copyright. He argues that although '[t]he London booksellers failed to secure perpetual copyright ... the arguments did develop the representation of the author as a proprietor, and this representation was very widely disseminated'.[68] He goes on to note that, '[T]he Lords' decision did not touch the basic contention that the author had a property in the product of his labour. Neither the representation of the author as a proprietor, nor the representation of the literary work as an object of property was discredited.'[69]

I think this overstates the significance of *Donaldson v Becket* as a legal event, notwithstanding the discourse may have a larger cultural significance. That an idea of the author as proprietor broadly circulates in political and cultural discourse as a consequence of a case does not necessarily advance it ahead of other ideas also in circulation that contest these foundations. As Deazley shows one needs to take care not to be too dismissive of enlightenment ideas and their enduring relevance.[70] Further while Rose's analysis shows the initial interaction between aesthetics and law, he leaves off from how this legal-cultural hybrid notion of authorship is then disseminated and taken up, played with, rejected or transformed within the life of the law. Of necessity his work is confined to a limited time-frame, but if Woodmansee is correct and the English romantics broke with the Germans in seeking to win over the hearts and minds of the reading public at large, settling instead for pressuring Parliament, Rose's work leaves us with the challenge of understanding why a particular idea of the author as proprietor succeeded in the cultural domain over others.

For me the problem with citing *Donaldson v Becket* as 'authority' is that it arrived at a negative definition of literary property. Property did not attach to his 'style and sentiment' in the way Blackstone or Hargrave had suggested because as Lord Camden claimed, the author 'let [the words] fly out in private or public discourse'.[71] But if so, what did the authorial right relate to? The difficulty with this case is that there was no progress in distinguishing what it was in the text that the author legally owned or assigned to another as separate from the paper and print. Indeed, while numerous philosophical conceptions were called upon as 'common sense' by advocates for and against literary property,[72] the collision of ideas was chaotic, with proponents largely talking past each other. *Donaldson v Becket* failed to produce a leading judgment from

---

[67] See Kathy Bowrey and Natalie Fowell, 'Digging up Fragments and Building IP Franchises' (2009) 31 Syd LR 185, 197–200.
[68] Rose, 'The Author as Proprietor' (n 2) 69.
[69] Ibid.
[70] Ronan Deazley, *Rethinking Copyright: History, Theory, Language* (Edward Elgar 2006) 6.
[71] 'The Pleadings of the Counsel before the House of Lords in the Great Cause concerning Literary Property' in Stephen Parks (ed), *The Literary Property Debate: Six Tracts 1764–1774* (Garland 1975) F32.
[72] See generally Kathy Bowrey, 'Chapter Three. Speculative reportings of literary property in the eighteenth and nineteenth centuries', in 'Don't Fence Me In. The Many Histories of Copyright' (SJD Thesis, University of Sydney 1994); Ronan Deazley, *On the Origin of the Right*

which one can derive with any certainty what the term 'author', referred to in the Statute of Anne, meant.[73] As the 1878 Copyright Commission noted:

> The common law principles which lie at the root of the law have never been settled. The well known cases of *Millar v Taylor*, *Donaldson v Becket*, and *Jeffries v Boosey*, ended in a difference of opinion amongst many of the most eminent judges who have ever sat upon the Bench.[74]

The common law left us with the notion of authors as proprietors but without any universal legal endorsement of philosophical criteria by which the nature or limits to which this authorial property could be discerned.

4. THE ABSTRACTION THESIS

For most copyright historians the lack of normative clarity underpinning the late eighteenth century legal construction of authorship does not pose a problem. The current orthodoxy is to say, as Rose more or less does, that British law ultimately resolved the problem in the nineteenth century by recourse to an abstraction. That is to say, historians advance the notion that mental labour could give rise to private property, that the literary work was a thing capable of being privately owned, and thus that there was no need to clarify its precise nature or origins further.[75] This leaves us with a copyright that need not refer to art (in the broad sense) with respect to its function or place in society, the practices and traditions of that form of expression, the genre, kinds of readers etc. Instead copyright simply refers to the author as owner and the copyrighted work (rather than a particular distinctive form of expression) is defined with reference to the fact of authorial creation. Further, it is clear that this circular dynamic worked to support a large number of analogous claims. All kinds of cultural expressions and thus previously distinct rights, such as those awarded to engravings and sculptures, could be seen to be related with painting. But by the mid-nineteenth century the new copyright category of 'fine art' is also more abstract-legal than a romantic concept, and thus also able to incorporate new mediums such as photography even though there remained dispute as to the artistic credentials of the photographer.[76]

---

to Copy. Charting the Movement of Copyright Law in Eighteenth Century Britain, 1695–1775 (Hart Publishing 2004); Barron (n 58) 110–15.

[73] See also Tomás Gómez-Arostegui, 'Copyright at Common Law in 1774' (2014) 47 Conn L Rev 1.

[74] Copyright Commission, Laws and Regulations relating to Home, Colonial and Foreign Copyrights (1878) vii.

[75] In addition to Rose, Barron (n 58), Kretschmer and Kawohl (n 23) and Sherman and Bently (n 4) take this view. It is worth noting that Sherman and Bently argue that the resulting confusion in the law that flowed from the inability of the judges to settle the law's normative foundation was later addressed by a jurisprudential shift to consequential thinking, concern for the costs of not protecting an ownership claim rather than with justifying the grant of the right.

[76] Fine Arts Copyright Act 1862 (5 & 26 Vict c 68). See generally Ronan Deazley, (2008) 'Commentary on *Fine Arts Copyright Act* 1862' in L Bently and M Kretschmer (eds) *Primary Sources on Copyright (1450–1900)*, www.copyrighthistory.org; Kathy Bowrey, 'The World

However, the orthodox view engages in some significant fudging of its own. There are scant details about how the 'abstraction' operates within the body of literary property and related copyright-like laws in the nineteenth century. In other words, the abstraction thesis remains a rather 'abstract' construct itself, entailing another circularity – the abstract notion of the author as proprietor supports an abstract connection with legal rationality. This removes from clear view the reality that there remains a problem with the state of British jurisprudence and the historic disorder of this legal subject matter. It should be remembered that, despite his subsequent influence (especially in the colonies), Blackstone's historicist attempt to produce an order to the law was most soundly criticised in the nineteenth century.[77] And the 'solution' of legal positivism – a legal philosophy designed to overcome history by pretending one can insulate legal rationality from social influence and unwelcome aspects of tradition by reducing consideration to the singular and limited task of tracing an authoritative and narrow line of legal authority – fumbles when the 'leading case' and rather bare copyright legislation endorses no useful criteria to help determine the logic of the right awarded.

Just as importantly, settling on the 'abstraction thesis' distracts our attention from building upon the insights from the humanities that can be drawn from scholars like Woodmansee – that copyright needs to relate to philosophy (amongst other things) – because any sophisticated determination of a copyright claim draws upon ideas about cognition, circulation of knowledge, reception of meaning, the scope for creativity and imagination and identity. Because this 'pre-modern' sensibility is now so far removed from the law the dimension of the problem may be hard for us to grasp.

The following section returns to Locke and offers a reappraisal of the significance of Locke to the authorship debate. In his own time Locke was not recognised as a supporter of a natural right of authors based upon a labour theory of property. This was a later invention. However Blackstone's and others' appropriation of Locke's philosophy is rarely commented on in intellectual property history.[78] Perhaps this is because it is hard to avoid some familiarity with Locke's labour theory of property and his broader political philosophy as part of a liberal education, while today it is far rarer to come across his works on education and philosophy. It is common to reduce Locke's concerns about literary property to his anti-publisher and anti-monopoly views.[79] Though Rose recognises later that Locke was an empiricist philosopher 'who challenged tradition and located personal identity in consciousness' in his *Essay on Human Understanding* (1789),[80] in wanting to avoid discussion of subjectivity he avoids

---

Daguerreotyped – What a Spectacle!' Copyright law, photography and the economic mission of Empire' in Brad Sherman and Leanne Wiseman (eds), *Copyright and the Challenge of the New* (Kluwer 2013) 11.

[77] Bentham described him as 'everything as-it-should-be Blackstone, a muddled and shallow apologist for the status quo'. Wilfrid Prest, *William Blackstone* (OUP 2008) 9. See also Wilfrid Prest, 'Legal History in Australian Law Schools: 1982 and 2005' (2006) 27 Adel L Rev 267.

[78] For example, it is not noted in Peter Drahos, *A Philosophy of Intellectual Property* (Ashgate 1996) 28; Justin Hughes, 'The Philosophy of Intellectual Property' (1988) 77 Geo LJ 287. Barron is a notable exception, Barron (n 58) 111.

[79] Rose, *Authors and Owners* (n 2) 33.

[80] Ibid 127.

consideration of the significance of Locke's enlightenment views on the nature of his support for 'author's property' altogether. This ensures little disruption to his singular push toward a particular construction of authorial property and leads to an oversimplification of the philosophical difficulties being confronted in literary property discourse.

The point of this detour into Locke is not to try to 'reclaim' Locke's rightful place in the history of copyright or to dispute the currency and influence of labour theories of property in the late eighteenth century that supported a range of 'property-like' claims. A reconsideration of the nature of Locke's misgivings about literary property is undertaken in order to remind us of the complexity that sits within the subject matter of copyright that is lost by not taking up more closely the reasons the notion of the author as proprietor was once so controversial – by sitting too comfortably today with the abstract notion of the author as proprietor and ignoring some of the historical reasons 'abstraction' was required. Abstraction is a legal strategy that seeks to paper over conceptual difficulty, to shift the view to a neater 'solution' by selectively retreating from engagement with the larger context of the inquiry.

Locke's theorisation of the problem of literary property reveals a complex enlightenment position that is both supportive of the public domain of ideas and an instrumental (limited) right of authors. However like the judges in *Donaldson v Becket*, Locke too, was unable to create clear boundaries around this authorial property. His empiricism disrupted ascription of a form of subject-hood that could support a natural property right of authors. And the 'pragmatism' commonly ascribed to Anglo copyright, compared to Continental law, could also be attributed in part to this Enlightenment legacy – to a real and genuine epistemological disputation about the nature of the human intelligence, language and identity, as much as to a preference for 'humble', culturally unambitious laws.[81]

5. THE PROPERTIES OF LOCKE'S SELF

According to Locke's episteme the labour theory of property as expounded in his *Two Treatises on Government* cannot be easily transposed to the case for literary property because one does not *labour* on ideas that exist in a literary common. In locating identity in consciousness[82] Locke viewed our knowledge of self as really limited to our self-interested capacity:

> *Self* is that conscious thinking thing (whatever Substance, made up of … it matters not) which is sensible, or conscious of Pleasure and Pain, capable of Happiness or Misery, and is concern'd for it *self,* as far as that consciousness extends.[83]

---

[81] This is discussed in Sherman and Bently (n 4) 216.
[82] '[The] *self* is not determined by Identity … of Substance … but only by Identity of consciousness'. John Locke, *An Essay on Human Understanding*, as quoted in Christopher Fox, *Locke and the Scriblerians: Identity and Consciousness in Early Eighteenth Century Britain* (California UP 1988) 12.
[83] Locke, *An Essay on Human Understanding*, as quoted in Fox (ibid) 12 ('*An Essay*').

According to Joseph Butler's analysis of 1736:

> [Locke's] hasty observations ... when traced and examined to the bottom, amounts, I think, to this: *'That personality is not a permanent, but a transitory thing'*: that it lives and dies, begins and ends continually: that no one can any more remain one and the same person for two moments together, than two successive moments can be one and the same moment: that our substance is continually changing; but whether this be so or not, is, it seems, nothing to the purpose; *since it is not substance, but consciousness alone, which constitutes personality;* which consciousness, being successive, cannot be the same in any two moments, nor consequently the personality constituted by it.[84]

This kind of concern led many to inquire whether this meant that one's soul was divisible, or whether two men could then share the one soul, whether the one man could be different persons, or how the 'same consciousness' survived when a man forgot or fell asleep.[85] Locke's *An Essay* was the source of great confusion and was the subject of much amusement.[86]

6. THE PROPERTY OF LOCKE'S TEXT

Locke's emphasis on the importance of consciousness very much complicates the case for an author's property in the text. Whilst, as Rose claims, it is true Locke was a strong supporter of an author's literary property, he was not at all concerned with defining what it is that the author 'owns' in the text and justifying that as a 'right' with a view to facilitating commodification of literary works. Locke suggested that language does not attest to a common social heritage at all. He argued that language began when Man, with a great variety of thoughts 'all within his own breast, invisible and hidden from others', tried to communicate his ideas to others:

> [I]t was necessary that man should find out some external signs whereby those invisible ideas, which his thoughts were made up of, might be made known to others. For this purpose nothing was so fit, either for plenty or quickness, as those articulate sounds which with so much ease and variety he found himself able to make. Thus we may conceive how words, which were by nature so well adapted to that purpose, came to be made use of by men as the signs of their ideas. ... The use, then, of words is to be sensible marks of ideas, and the ideas they stand for are their proper and immediate signification.[87]

---

[84] As quoted ibid 10.

[85] The theological implications led to Locke being 'almost unanimously condemned in pulpit and pamphlet'. In 1703 there was also meeting of the heads of Oxford to censure Locke's *Essay on Human Understanding* (1689) and to forbid the reading of it. See ibid 124 and 138.

[86] For instance he argued that two men could not have the same soul, because they only had consciousness of their own actions, and ultimately he argued that we would be judged by God on the state of our consciousness, and not on the state of our soul. For further examples, see ibid 29–37.

[87] Locke, *An Essay* as quoted in A Rosen, 'Reconsidering the Idea/Expression Dichotomy' (1992) 26 UBC Law Rev 263, 271.

Law, aesthetics and copyright historiography 47

But as words are signs for invisible ideas that are already formed in the privacy of the mind, this raises the question as to how our nominal descriptions can be comprehended with any accuracy by other members of the linguistic community, all of whom have different consciousnesses based upon different experiences:[88]

> The names of Substances would be much more useful, and Propositions made in them much more certain, were the real Essences of Substances the Ideas of our Minds, which those words signified. [But the real Essences are beyond our perception.] And 'tis for want of those real Essences, that our Words convey so little Knowledge or Certainty in our Discourses about them.[89]

As Jackson explains:

> Under these circumstances, it would seem more accurate to describe a playing child as chasing 'the rolling circle's speed' (choosing two primary qualities: shape and motion), as Gray does in his 'Ode on a Distant Prospect at Eton College,' than to name the inscrutable 'hoop' – and more useful to specify 'the rapid Greek', like Samuel Johnson in 'The Vanity of Human Wishes,' than to identify Alexander the Great.[90]

Locke did not outright reject poetry as engaging in deception and illusion. However, Abrams suggests that in his *Thoughts Concerning Education* he 'does not disguise his contempt for the unprofitableness of a poetic career, either to the poet himself or (by implication) to others'.[91] Locke thought that it was not productive to seek pleasure and delight (ornaments) when information and improvement could be pursued. However, he did not discriminate between kinds of works and kinds of knowledge in the sense that all works merely bring forth signs of phenomenal data:

> The mind in Locke's *Essay* is said to resemble a mirror which fixes the objects it reflects. Or (suggesting the *ut pictura poesis* of the aesthetics of that period) it is a *tabula rasa* on which sensations write or paint themselves. Or (employing the analogy of the *camera obscura,* in which the light, entering through a small aperture, throws an image of the external scene of the wall) external and internal sense are said to be 'the windows by which light is let into this dark room'. ... Alternatively, the mind is a 'waxed tablet' into which sensations, like seals, impress themselves.[92]

---

[88] As Rosen puts it 'In Locke's theory, each person creates his or her own language, with no way of knowing whether or to what extent it coincides with the language spoken by anyone else. This is a Babel of ideolects, not a community of persons speaking the same language'. Ibid 272.

[89] Locke, *An Essay*, as quoted in G Jackson, 'From Essence to Accident: Locke and the Language of Poetry in the Eighteenth Century' in R Ashcraft (ed), *John Locke: Critical Assessments* (Routledge 1991) 254.

[90] Ibid.

[91] MH Abrams, *The Mirror and the Lamp: Romantic Theory and the Critical Tradition* (WW Norton & Co 1953) 300.

[92] Ibid 57. Abrams goes on to note the similarities between Locke's expression and that of Plato and Aristotle. Plato compared sense perception to reflecting images in a mirror, as well as to paintings, the writing of characters in the pages of a book, and the stamping of impressions into a wax plate. Aristotle suggested that the receptions of sense 'must be conceived of as taking place in the way in which a piece of wax takes on the impress of a signet ring without the iron or gold'. Ibid 57.

Thus Locke responds to his friend Molyneux's question whether a man, blind from birth, on regaining his sight would be able to distinguish a cube from a sphere without touching. Locke claims he could not because he would need the tactile experience to understand the corresponding visual imagery.[93] Locke's theory thus challenges claims to the universality of perception.

Locke frequently uses sight as a favoured example and as a metaphor, but unlike the German philosophers that follow him, he does not mean for poetry to become a visual art in the sense that his emphasis is not on pictures of whole objects, but on component ideas.[94] The mind is inertly receptive and to the extent that it orders the sensations it receives, it relies upon common sense. The author does not 'clothe' the idea and deliver its essence into another's mind. The author cannot 'clothe' it and in this way ground an individual right to an expression in his episteme. For this reason attempts to use Locke's theory to justify an author's right with reference to an idea/expression dichotomy in a work, differentiating what it is that is held in common (the idea) and what it is that is private (the author's expression) mistakes his project.[95] The author is incapable of bringing forth any essential meaning – the author can only suggest to us a nominal essence. But we, the reader, are incapable of discerning where the authorial expression starts and ends, or appreciating its meaning in the same way it was understood by the writer.

Locke makes it incredibly difficult to specify what it is that the creator of a text 'owns'. For example, we can name 'Locke' as the author, but we cannot clearly see how the man called Locke, as rational activity, is reproduced in the text. We know little of him. What we know is of the primary qualities he describes, such as bulk, shape and motion that we too can perceive.

So what does Locke's author have a right to?

In the debates concerning the renewal of the licensing laws in the 1690s Locke, along with Addison and Defoe, advocated for the inclusion of a clause stipulating that anyone who printed an author's name on a publication without his permission should be liable to forfeit to the author all copies he had printed.[96] His interest in the question of attribution of authorship was not motivated by a concern that the author be acknowledged – that her/his name be made public. Rather he was more interested in attribution as a question of privacy – one should have a right to control the exposure of what may be understood as her/his consciousness.[97] Thus Locke did not support a perpetual right of authors in a work. The reason for limiting one's rights and relating them to specific editions, leading to the need for permission for reprints, is clear from his own musings on the appropriateness of a second edition of the *Essay*. He wrote to William Molyneux:

---

[93] Jacqueline Lichtenstein, *The Blind Spot: An Essay on the Relations between Painting and Sculpture in the Modern Age* (Chris Miller tr, Getty Research Institute 2008) 45.

[94] Jackson (n 89) 255.

[95] This is discussed in Rosen (n 87) 270–73.

[96] See Raymond Astbury, 'The Renewal of the Licensing Act of 1693 and its Lapse in 1695' (1978) Ser 5, 33 The Library 296, 313.

[97] For his alarm at being attributed as the author of an anonymous work, see Letters No 1268 and 1288 in ES De Beer (ed), *The Correspondence of John Locke,* vol 4 (Clarendon Press 1979) 38, 65.

But now that my notions are got into the world, and have in some measure bustled through the opposition and difficulty they were like to meet with from the receiv'd opinion, and that prepossession which might hinder them from being understood upon a short proposal; I ask you whether it would not be better now to pare off, in a second edition, a great part of that which cannot but appear superfluous to an intelligent and attentive reader. If you are of that mind, I shall beg you to mark to me those passages which you would think fittest to be left out. If there be any thing wherein you think me mistaken, I beg you to deal freely with me, that either I may clear it up for you, or reform it in the next edition. For I flatter myself that I am so sincere a lover of truth, that it is very indifferent to me, so I am possess'd of it, whether it be by my own, or any other's discovery.[98]

Publication was valued by Locke as an agent in the pursuit of truth rather than as a personal or commercial pursuit. In this sense Lord Camden was correct to note in *Donaldson v Becket*, that '[i]t was not for gain, that Bacon, Newton, Milton, Locke instructed and delighted the world.'[99]

For similar reasons he argued against the existence of copyright in the classical works because:

This liberty to any one of printing them is certainly the way to have cheaper and better and tis this which in Holland has produced soe many fair and excellent editions of them. Whilst the printers all strive to out doe an other which has also brought great sums to the trade in Holland. Whilst our Company of Stationers haveing the monopoly here by this act and their patents slubber them over as they can cheapest, soe that there is not a book of them vended beyond seas both for their badness and dearnesse nor will Schollers beyond seas look upon a book of them now printed in London soe ill and false are they ...[100]

He suggested that the protection of contemporary works should be limited to 50 or 70 years after the first printing of the book or the death of the author.[101] But it is always the pursuit of universal truth that Locke celebrates and not the sanctity of any private literary property.

The writer had a right to the profit that accrues from the mass circulation of the work, but this private interest is justified as serving the common interest – by facilitating the pursuit of truth. Or as Locke put it, 'For I count any parcel of this gold not the less to be valued, nor not the less enriching, because I wrought it not out of mine self. I think every one ought to contribute to the common stock.'[102]

The author's property right is instrumental to the cause of enlightenment. And whatever fundamental claim exists to the expression of one's consciousness, this is a matter we cannot identify with any exactness at all. Because of this shadowiness, the value or meaning of the work to the individual author has to be put to one side and any fundamental right to authorial property is correspondingly compromised.

---

[98] Ibid 523.
[99] 'The Pleadings of the Counsel before the House of Lords in the Great Cause concerning Literary Property' in Stephen Parks (ed), *The Literary Property Debate: Six Tracts 1764–1774* (Garland 1975) F34.
[100] 'Documents relating to the termination of the Licensing Act, 1695' in ES De Beer (ed), *The Correspondence of John Locke*, vol 5 (Clarendon Press 1979) 786.
[101] Ibid 791.
[102] Astbury (n 96) 307.

In summing this up, Locke's problem with literary property is based in philosophical objections that confound identification of an author who can communicate meaning to others. Without certainty as to the true nature of knowledge it is difficult to ascribe a text with sufficient stable meaning so that its meaning can be transferred to readers in a transactional sense. Another way of putting this is that we are all readers of the text, which we interpret according to our own experience.[103] But there is simply not a property relation inherent in a text that connects an author to a reader (separable from the material aspects – ink and paper). Additionally whilst seeing the necessity of a market for books, Locke simply has no real interest in the nature of market transactions and in understanding how the economy for books is sustained. His epistemology directs him to far loftier concerns and, again, away from theorising the property *in* books, even though *An Essay* is somewhat obsessively concerned with theorising the properties *of* books and the value of their wider distribution to humanity.

As noted above, Locke's particular contribution to a theory of knowledge caused alarm and amusement in its own time. Contemporary readers may well feel the same. However moving away from the distinctiveness of Locke's philosophical conclusions to consider the broader parameters of his problem with literary property, his work shows that 'settling' the property in the text, defining the boundaries to a private claim, so copyright can then rationally discuss competing claims to own knowledge, requires a theory of cognition and a consideration of the conditions for exchange of knowledge between the writer, the text as object and the reader. If one moves beyond Locke's prioritisation of the value of 'useful' knowledge over other kinds of human capacities and expressions and also includes insights from aesthetics, this detour into philosophy suggests that copyright jurisprudence also requires a way of appreciating the importance of imagination, humour and a wide range of sensual experience, and has to accommodate divergent manners of judging these things.

7. A FOUNDATION ON INTELLECTUAL QUICKSAND?

The orthodoxy remains that the 'author as proprietor' notion/abstraction thesis is the foundation of Anglo copyright. However, it is also generally accepted in copyright scholarship that the legal form that supported the individualisation of ideas is intellectually unstable and essentially bankrupt. It justifies ownership claims with reference to the author in historical and social isolation when ideas (such as authorship) and cultural works more generally generate meaning and value from their mode and manner of circulation and broader engagement with them.

The strength of the author as proprietor idea was that it was especially well suited to the transactional nature of the market. The contract allows for an exchange of 'intangible property' without requiring precision as to its parameters or limits, or in fact without concern for the specifics of copyright law at all.[104] But contract is a remarkably

---

[103] There are similarities here with some of the concerns of post-modern scholarship.
[104] It is not uncommon to find contracts that assign rights that where there is uncertainty that the assignor owns any such right. For an historical example, see Jose Bellido and Kathy Bowrey, 'From An Author's To A Proprietor's Right: Newspaper Copyright & *The Times* (1842–1956)'

crude mechanism that lacks transparency in managing the complex cultural context that this area of law must, of necessity, engage with.

It needs to be recalled that the early German romantic notion of property imagined that literary property law might complicate, rather than advance, the commodification of culture. While one would not suggest adoption of either Locke's or the German romantic formulation of the right as appropriate for today, this earlier period did at least appreciate the broader implications of creating such a right, relating it to a vision of the kind of society and culture they wanted to live in. One may reject the subject position of romantic aesthetics as the foundation for copyright and still reconsider the importance of eighteenth century cultural concerns about art and the market. Complaint about the lack of financial support for the production of 'serious' work, about the cultural knowledge, education and taste of 'users', and questioning if conditions support innovation and creativity or public support for the arts is needed to supplement market dynamics, are core copyright concerns that resonate.

Humanities scholars such as Woodmansee and Rose made a significant contribution to copyright history by linking the law to the larger cultural dialogue that informed it. A consideration of the early history of copyright matters to us today because it shows some of the complexity that was involved in the commodification of ideas for society and the law. Fleshing out the boundaries of the property right with any particular certainty required reference to some kind of philosophy of subject-hood, whilst at the same time still managing some way of determining what is in fact not protected. Woodmansee's work shows that this was exactly what was anticipated as required by the German romantics. Rose's and others' works uncover no comparative British strategizing to effect social and political change through the take up of a particular world view and vision of property on the broader society, even though ideas were effectively disseminated through the publicity related to the literary property litigation in pamphleteering and through lobbying of Parliamentarians.

Rose concludes his book with the claim that Anglo authorship is an 'institution built on intellectual quicksand: the essentially religious concept of originality, the notion that certain extraordinary beings called authors conjure works out of thin air'.[105] However, without there being a coherent order to the law itself in the eighteenth and early nineteenth century, such an 'institution' could not fully come into being. In other words, for the notion of the author as proprietor to succeed in this form, it would have required fidelity to a romantic construct as well as a corresponding legal subjectivity to be integrated into a much larger holistic philosophical and cultural system. Instead what transpired was the legal formulation of the author as proprietor simpliciter, the abstraction. Thus it is no surprise that when the law was challenged to consider the consequence of ownership, that is, what the exclusive right extended to, the law subsequently struggled throughout the nineteenth century with determining what was

---

(2014) 6 JML 180. For a contemporary example, see Kathy Bowrey and Michael Handler, 'Instituting Copyright: Reconciling Copyright Law and Industry Practice in the Buying and Selling of TV Formats' in Kathy Bowrey and Michael Handler (eds), *Law and Creativity in the Age of the Entertainment Franchise* (CUP 2014) 140–69.

[105] Rose, *Authors and Owners* (n 2) 142.

infringement and what was fair use, whether authorship supported rights of dramatization (adaptation), abridgment or translation and, in the twentieth century, with the meaning of 'originality'.

A problem for the law remains. Lacking unequivocal authoritative reference to any particular philosophical concepts, Anglo law is left with a vague celebration of copyright as private property, disconnected from any development of: discourse about why culture matters; material support for artists; the social value of art; the distinctiveness of particular cultural productions and markets; empirical knowledge of trade practice; and the need for linkages between cultural and legal education. We are left with a naked law that struggles to demarcate intelligently infringement, fair dealing, justify distinctions between different kinds of productions and limits to ownership. Woodmansee's and Rose's histories do not celebrate romanticism as the foundation for copyright, but in deconstructing the story of authorship they reveal how copyright law, art and economy were seen as intimately inter-related and how the interplay between these factors affects the kind of society that develops.

In their wake, contemporary critiques – commonly 'cultural readings' from humanities scholars – consider the law contextually and how intellectual property laws affect particular cultural and business practices.[106] In copyright there are also calls for a more 'relational' reading of texts, considering the essential connectedness of the subject positions of author-user-pirate.[107] However, a significant historical challenge remains for any humanities scholarship to impact upon the law because, as a matter of copyright jurisprudence, law's capacity to engage with new ways of thinking is now severely constrained by centuries-old disengagement from aesthetics and from a critical awareness of broader philosophies that explore our ways of knowing, our capacity for judging and the reception of ideas. In reading existing genealogies of aesthetics and of authorship we need to consider far more than what was taken up into the law. We also need to reflect upon what it was that we have lost along the way because it is from here that we will come to better understand some of the major obstacles that now disrupt the capacity for humanities to impact on the law, and that stop the law benefiting from a deeper understanding of the context in which it operates.

---

[106] See for example, Laura J Murray, S Tina Piper and Kirsty Robertson (eds), *Putting Intellectual Property in its Place: Rights Discourses, Creative Labor, and the Everyday* (OUP 2014).

[107] Adrian Johns, *Piracy. The Intellectual Property Wars from Gutenberg to Gates* (Chicago UP 2009); Carys J Craig, *Copyright. Communication & Culture. Toward a Relational Theory of Copyright Law* (Edward Elgar 2011).

4. The 'romantic' author
*Martha Woodmansee**

1. INTRODUCTION

Authorship is one of the central interests of literary scholars. It is an interest we share with lawyers and legal scholars specializing in copyright, for 'authorship' lies at the very center of this body of law. It is the term of art for the diverse modes of creative production that it is the function of copyright to promote. 'Authorship' acquired its legal meaning in the rich interdisciplinary – better, pre-disciplinary – theoretical milieu of the eighteenth and early nineteenth centuries. With the subsequent specialization of the disciplines, however, conversation between legal and literary theory waned, with the result that the two disciplines have since been grappling more or less independently with the same body of ideas. My aim in this chapter is to spur greater interdisciplinary reflection on the nature of authorship. This is important because it is due in significant measure to the antiquated understanding of authorship at the center of copyright that this body of law so often misfires – that it distributes property in ideas in ways that few today accept as fair or rational. I first sketch the history of thinking about authorship, identifying a pre-modern moment extending deep into the eighteenth century and then the Romantic turn that has given us our modern vision thereof. Then, drawing on research undertaken in collaboration with Peter Jaszi, I sketch the absorption of Romantic ideology into British copyright law and subsequent international agreements culminating in the Berne Convention of 1886. Finally, I turn to several contemporary court cases to demonstrate through close rhetorical analysis how Romantic ideology operates in legal practice.

One may lay legal claim to ownership of ideas only insofar as one is an 'author.' What is an author? In the usage that has been absorbed into the law an 'author' is the individual responsible for the production of an 'original' work. Its originality warrants the work's legal protection both in Anglo-American copyright and in European author's rights. While this way of defining authorship may seem straightforward and unproblematic to many lawyers and legal scholars, in literary studies today we view creative work in more 'intertextual' terms – we view it as more dependent on the work of others than such a definition suggests. We may work with stone, in oils on canvas, with pen and paper, or pixels – whatever our medium of preference, we invariably draw on the work of others in our creative activities, if not contemporaries working in close proximity, then those working at some temporal remove, whom we may or may not acknowledge as 'influences.' In other words, our creative work is largely derivative, it is in an important sense collective, corporate, and collaborative.

---

* I would like to thank Kathy Bowrey for her generous advice throughout the drafting of this chapter.

For the better part of human history this derivative aspect of new work was believed to contribute to, if not virtually to constitute the work's value. Writers, like other artisans, considered their task to lie in the re-working of traditional materials according to principles and techniques preserved and handed down to them in rhetoric and poetics. It was only in the course of the eighteenth century, and then primarily in Western Europe, that an alternative vision of creative production focusing on the endowments and accomplishments of the individual genius emerged. In a sharp departure from the self-understanding of writers of previous generations, authors in the new 'Romantic' mode began to view their task to lie in innovation – to lie in breaking with inherited tradition to create something utterly new, unique, in a word, 'original.' Their heroic vision caught on and it mystified the creative process, obscuring the reliance of these writers on the work of others.

First sketched out in Edward Young's path-breaking *Conjectures on Original Composition* (1759), this vision of creative writing was elaborated by a generation of aspiring professional writers across Europe, from Herder and Goethe to Coleridge and Wordsworth, who famously postulated in his *Essay, Supplementary to the Preface* to *Lyrical Ballads* that:

> Of genius the only proof is, the act of doing well what is worthy to be done, and what was never done before: Of genius, in the fine arts, the only infallible sign is the widening the sphere of human sensibility, for the delight, honour, and benefit of human nature. Genius is the introduction of a new element into the intellectual universe: or, if that be not allowed, it is the application of powers to objects on which they had not before been exercised, or the employment of them in such a manner as to produce effects hitherto unknown.[1]

For Wordsworth the genius is someone who does something utterly new, unprecedented, or in the radical formulation he prefers, produces something that never existed before. We owe our modern idea of an author to the reconceptualization of writing set forth in this essay of 1815.[2] That it represents a mystification of an activity that is of necessity rooted in tradition emerges from the burgeoning number of 'new histories' of authorship that have made it their object to explore the manifold social, economic, political, and legal impulses responsible for this development.

2. BEFORE 'AUTHORSHIP'

As we move backward in time, recognition of the tradition-rooted, derivative element in writing becomes ever more pronounced. In the Middle Ages right down through the Renaissance writing derived its value and authority from its affiliation with the texts

---

[1] William Wordsworth, 'Essay, Supplementary to the Preface' in WJB Owen and JW Smyser (eds), *The Prose Works of William Wordsworth* (Clarendon 1974) vol 3, 82.
[2] For a fuller description of this development, see Martha Woodmansee, 'The Genius and the Copyright: Economic and Legal Conditions of the Emergence of the "Author"' (1984) 17 Eighteenth-Century Studies 425, rpt in Martha Woodmansee, *The Author, Art, and the Market* (Columbia UP 1994) 34–55. See also Martha Woodmansee and Peter Jaszi, 'The Law of Texts' (1995) 57 College English 769.

that preceded it, its derivation rather than its deviation from prior texts. For Saint Bonaventure, writing in the thirteenth century, there are four ways of making a book, and none of them involves the kind of individual origination that Wordsworth sought to promote:

> A man might write the works of others, adding and changing nothing, in which case he is simply called a 'scribe' [*scriptor*]. Another writes the work of others with additions which are not his own; and he is called a 'compiler' [*compilator*]. Another writes both others' work and his own, but with others' work in principal place, adding his own for purposes of explanation; and he is called a 'commentator' [*commentator*]. ... Another writes both his own work and others' but with his own work in principal place adding others' for purposes of confirmation; and such a man should be called an 'author' [*auctor*].[3]

While Bonaventure's *auctor* would seem to be making a substantial (original) contribution of his own, he does so as part of an enterprise conceived collaboratively. Nor is this mode of book production privileged over the other three – over transcription, compilation, and commentary.

But it is hardly necessary to go back to the Middle Ages to find so corporate a view of writing, for it was still shared by Samuel Johnson (1709–84). Although official history presents Johnson as the very archetype of the modern author, his energies as a writer went into the full spectrum of activities Bonaventure identifies.[4] The large projects to which he put his name, like the monumental *Dictionary of the English Language* (1755), the edition of *The Plays of William Shakespeare* (1765), and the *Lives of the Poets* (1779–81) were collective and collaborative. The last of these, a series of 'prefaces, biographical and critical,' for a multi-volume collection of England's 'major' modern poets, was – like so much else in the domain we are exploring – the inspiration of the London booksellers. It seems that an Edinburgh publisher had brought out just such a collection. Alarmed by this incursion on their virtual monopoly of the book trade, James Boswell reports in his biography of Johnson (1791), some 40 of London's 'most respectable booksellers,' including in particular 'all the proprietors of copy-right in the various Poets,' met to devise a strategy for countering this 'invasion' of their 'Literary Property.' To their great relief the Edinburgh volumes had been carelessly printed and in a type too small to be read with comfort. So it was agreed 'that an elegant and uniform edition of *The English Poets* should be immediately printed, with a concise account of the life of each author, by Dr. Samuel Johnson.'[5]

The resulting *Lives* contributed decisively to the differentiation of 'authoring' from ordinary literary labor by establishing a pantheon of great authors whose 'works' were intended to be viewed as differing qualitatively from the sea of mere writing. Yet this

---

[3] As quoted by Elizabeth L Eisenstein, *The Printing Press as an Agent of Change* (CUP 1979) vol 1, 121–22.

[4] For a more comprehensive account of Johnson's relevance to our thinking about the essentially collective, corporate, and collaborative nature of writing, see Martha Woodmansee, 'On the Author Effect: Recovering Collectivity' (1992) 10 Cardozo Arts & Ent LJ 279, rpt in Martha Woodmansee and Peter Jaszi (eds), *The Construction of Authorship: Textual Appropriation in Law and Literature* (Duke UP 1994) 15–28.

[5] James Boswell, *Life of Johnson* (RW Chapman ed., OUP 1980) 802.

multi-volume accomplishment was the product not of the solitary originary mode of composition whose myth it helped to foster, but of fruitful collaboration between Johnson, the poets he immortalized, the London booksellers – and countless others. To mention only one instance, Johnson drew freely from others' work for his *Life of Pope*. The account of Pope's personal habits, which constitutes 'one of the most interesting parts of that life,' according to Bertram Davis, was incorporated without acknowledgment from either the *Universal Magazine* for August 1775 or the *Gentleman's Magazine* for September 1775 (it having appeared in both).[6]

But if, to quote Martin Luther, Johnson 'freely received,' freely did he also give. 'Few friends who needed anything written were ever turned away, so long as what they wanted was in a genre in which Johnson felt comfortable' (and during his long career he wrote in more of them than probably any writer before or since).[7] Indeed, even as *Lives* was being planned Johnson was involved in an elaborate ghostwriting exercise to save one of London's most popular preachers, the Reverend William Dodd, from execution. Dodd had been convicted of forgery, 'the most dangerous crime in a commercial country,' according to Boswell, and had appealed to Johnson for help in securing a royal pardon. Although they had barely even met, Johnson threw himself into the effort, 'writing (as if from Dodd) letters to the Lord Chancellor, Henry Bathurst, and to Lord Mansfield, the Chief Justice; a petition from Dodd to the King and another from Mrs Dodd to the Queen; a moving sermon preached by Dodd at the chapel in Newgate Prison … on the text "What must I do to be saved?" and published with the title "The Convict's Address to his Unhappy Brethren"; and several other pieces. …'[8] To no avail. Following a brief, poignant correspondence with Johnson, Dodd was executed on 27 June 1777.

This was no isolated incident. In the eighteenth century it was common for clergymen to 'borrow' sermons from one another[9] – a practice that is likely at least as widespread in today's digital networked era. Johnson, who was no clergyman, carried the practice further, ghostwriting sermons on a large scale: 'I have begun a sermon after dinner, and sent it off by the post that night.'[10] For his 'pulpit discourses,' we learn from his lifelong friend and early biographer John Hawkins, Johnson 'made no scruple of confessing, he was paid … and such was his notion of justice, that having been paid, he considered them so absolutely the property of the purchaser, as to renounce all claim to them. He reckoned that he had written about forty sermons; but, except as to some, knew not in what hands they were – "I have," said he, "been paid for them, and have no

---

[6] Bertram H Davis, *Johnson Before Boswell* (Yale UP 1957) 49. In this connection it is interesting that Boswell feels called upon to defend his hero against imagined allegations of plagiarism: 'The richness of Johnson's fancy, which could supply his page abundantly on all occasions, and the strength of his memory, which at once detected the real owner of any thought, made him less liable to the imputations of plagiarism than, perhaps, any of our writers.' Boswell (n 5) 236.

[7] Paul Fussell, *Samuel Johnson and the Life of Writing* (Harcourt 1971) 39.

[8] Walter Jackson Bate, *Samuel Johnson* (Harcourt 1975) 524. See also Boswell (n 5) 827–35.

[9] Samuel Johnson, *Sermons* in Jean Hagstrum and James Gray (eds), *The Works of Samuel Johnson* (Yale UP 1978) vol 14, xxvii–xxviii.

[10] Ibid xxi.

right to enquire about them.'"[11] His eventual output may have exceeded the number claimed here,[12] but such was Johnson's discretion that only 28 have been identified with sufficient certainty to be included in his collected works.

In addition to letters and sermons, Johnson composed prologues, dedications, and advertisements, proposals, lectures, treatises, and political speeches for others – that is, in their names. So extensive was his ghostwriting that it is still being uncovered today.[13] Indeed, it is the chief object of modern textual scholarship to identify in all this writing those words that originated uniquely with Johnson so that they may be properly credited to him and a definitive oeuvre can be established. I do not wish to suggest that there is anything wrong with such activities, only that they presume a modern, proprietary authorial impulse that Johnson did not himself feel.

Johnson the author in this modern sense is the creation of his biographer James Boswell (1740–95), who, like biographers before and since selected from among the infinite facts of his subject's life to construct a life story in accordance with his own vision.[14] 'Without Boswell,' Alvin Kernan writes, 'Johnson would surely have been an important writer and an interesting, powerful personality, but probably not the literary type that he is, the towering and highly charged image of the first writer in the industrial, democratic, rationalistic age of print.'[15] Yet, having called attention to the crucial role played by Boswell in the making of the modern author, Kernan does not press his advantage, and instead of recreating the master wordsmith for us, he falls in with Romantic biographers from Boswell to Bate to evoke the precursor of Wordsworth. While 'many writers before Johnson may have, certainly did, write greater books,' Kernan observes,

> even the most individualized of them, a Petrarch or a Milton, let alone the anonymous Shakespeare, seem alongside him pale, fading, a few thin lines without much depth, shading, or emotional color. His intense personality, in a way *the first romantic artist*, appears at exactly the right point in literary history in several ways, the kind of poor, strange, troubled person that the print business could attract and use as a Grub Street hack, and, at the same time, the type of individual who needed and could use print to satisfy certain existential needs of his own for bread, for status, for meaning. But it went beyond this, and in the end, out of their own needs, Johnson and Boswell together created a social role that transcended individual needs, giving writers an important social function and making books, even in the vast numbers now produced by the printing press, something more than mere information, amusement, and commodity. Johnson and Boswell, in my opinion, worked in the same general directions in making the writer. ... In the following pages I therefore freely mix

---

[11] Ibid xxii.
[12] Ibid xxiii.
[13] See, for example, Thomas M Curley, 'Johnson's Secret Collaboration' in John J Burke Jr and Donald Kay (eds), *The Unknown Samuel Johnson* (U Wisconsin P 1983) 91–112; Thomas M Curley, 'Johnson's Last Word on Ossian: Ghostwriting for William Shaw' in Jennifer J Carter and Joan H Pittock (eds), *Aberdeen and the Enlightenment* (Aberdeen UP 1987) 375–94.
[14] For an especially illuminating study of the role biography plays in the making of an author, see Margreta De Grazia, *Shakespeare Verbatim* (Clarendon 1991).
[15] Alvin Kernan, *Printing Technology, Letters & Samuel Johnson* (Princeton UP 1987) 107–08.

evidence from the *Life*, from other biographical writings, and from Johnson's own works (italics mine).[16]

Kernan writes as if the author in the modern, Romantic sense were the goal toward which history had always been striving. But as I have tried to suggest, Johnson's life contains another, more collaborative story – for readers disposed to attend.[17]

3. ROMANTIC AUTHORSHIP

The new Romantic construction of authorship is vividly illustrated in William Wordsworth's famous lyric of 1807 which begins 'I wandered lonely as a cloud.' In this poem, commonly known as 'Daffodils,' Wordsworth (1770–1850) presents creative production as a solitary originary process. However the genesis of the poem suggests otherwise. With the publication of the journals of his sister Dorothy it became clear that far from emerging from the operation of solitary imagination on the raw materials of experience 'Daffodils' evolved 'intertextually.' Recording the sights and sounds of an after-dinner walk with William, Dorothy notes in the journal she kept and shared with him:

> When we were in the woods beyond Gowbarrow Park we saw a few daffodils close to the water-side. We fancied that the lake had floated the seeds ashore, and that the little colony had so sprung up. But as we went along there were more and yet more; and at last, under the boughs of the trees, we saw that there was a long belt of them along the shore, about the breadth of a country turnpike road. I never saw daffodils so beautiful. They grew among the mossy stones about and about them; some rested their heads upon these stones as on a pillow for weariness; and the rest tossed and reeled and danced, and seemed as if they verily laughed with the wind, that blew upon them over the lake; they looked so gay, ever glancing, ever changing. This wind blew directly over the lake to them. There was here and there a little knot, and a few stragglers a few yards higher up; but they were so few as not to disturb the simplicity, unity, and life of that one busy highway.[18]

A good deal of both the letter and spirit of this journal entry is assimilated into William's later poem, but without any reference to its author. Dorothy's substantial contribution – indeed, her very participation – has been erased. Her five 'we's' have been replaced by 'I's,' transforming the siblings' collective experience into a solitary one. The resulting poem relates the poet's moving experience of a phenomenon of nature that produces renewed pleasure whenever it is relived in memory:

> I wandered lonely as a cloud
> That floats on high o'er vales and hills,
> When all at once I saw a crowd,
> A host, of golden daffodils;
> Beside the lake, beneath the trees,
> Fluttering and dancing in the breeze.

---

[16] Ibid 114–15.
[17] So substantial is this 'other' Johnson that it proves difficult to identify (a single) one of his 'works' for inclusion in author-driven Brit Lit survey courses.
[18] Dorothy Wordsworth, *The Grasmere Journals* (Pamela Woof ed, OUP 1991) 84–85.

Continuous as the stars that shine
And twinkle on the milky way,
They stretched in never-ending line
Along the margin of a bay:
Ten thousand saw I at a glance,
Tossing their heads in sprightly dance.

The waves beside them danced; but they
Out-did the sparkling waves in glee:
A poet could not but be gay,
In such a jocund company;
I gazed – and gazed – but little thought
What wealth the show to me had brought:

For oft, when on my couch I lie
In vacant or in pensive mood,
They flash upon that inward eye
Which is the bliss of solitude;
And then my heart with pleasure fills,
And dances with the daffodils.[19]

In the poem's final stanza the poet's pleasurable recollection of his experience of the daffodils becomes a metaphor for the poetic process per se, constructing it as an activity not of several minds in collaboration but of a single individual mind in interaction with the natural world. Ironically, the very lines in which this vision is set forth were supplied – as William elsewhere acknowledges – by his wife, Mary Hutchinson: 'They flash upon that inward eye / Which is the bliss of solitude.'[20]

The case of 'Daffodils' illustrates the element of collaboration at the heart of creative production generally even as it dramatizes the process by which such collaboration gets denied. As I noted, we inevitably build on the work of others in our creative activities – if not contemporaries working in close proximity, then those working at some temporal remove. Our collaborations are both synchronic and diachronic, or serial. If we are tempted to deny others' contributions to our work, this is because we remain captivated by the vision of authorship that has come down to us from poets like Wordsworth.

The acquisitiveness that Wordsworth exhibits in the 'Daffodils' episode may surprise readers who know him chiefly as joint author with Samuel Taylor Coleridge of *Lyrical Ballads* (1798), the slim volume that revolutionized English poetry. For *Lyrical Ballads* was a deeply collaborative project – the most famous collaboration in English literature – and it was first published anonymously, as if in acknowledgment of its debt to the English people of the 'middle and lower classes' whom the poets credit in the

---

[19] William Wordsworth, *Poems, In Two Volumes, and Other Poems, 1800–1807* (Jared Curtis ed, Cornell UP 1983) 207–08.
[20] Wordsworth ascribed these lines to Hutchinson in a note dictated to Isabella Fenwick. Ibid 418. On the law's absorption of the type of gender bias that is exhibited in the 'Daffodils' episode, see Kathy Bowrey, 'Copyright, the Paternity of Artistic Works and the Challenge Posed by Postmodern Artists' (1994) 8 IPJ 285.

'Advertisement' at the beginning of the volume for much of the material and especially the style of the poems therein.[21]

However by the time it was completed Wordsworth had asserted 'a strong proprietary interest in the book,' and so completely did he take control of the second edition, Stephen Gill writes, 'that *Lyrical Ballads* 1800 bears only residual marks of the collaborative effort of 1798.'[22] The most striking mark of his assertion of authorial control is the appearance in the new edition of Wordsworth's name on the title page. It appears there alone. In this new edition the short 'Advertisement' has also been expanded into a lengthy 'Preface' containing a defense of the poetics underlying the volume's experimental contents. Coleridge was intimately involved in the conceptualization of this preface, if not directly in its composition, yet the only trace of his input is the attribution to 'a Friend' of certain of the poems contained in the collection, followed by the remark:

> I should not ... have requested this assistance, had I not believed that the poems of my Friend would in a great measure have the same tendency as my own, and that, though there would be found a difference, there would be found no discordance in the colours of our style; as our opinions on the subject of poetry do almost entirely coincide.[23]

The 'Preface' was to be the most substantial and influential statement of his theory of poetry that Wordsworth would produce. It is here that, even as he was effacing the traces of its collaborative provenance, Wordsworth first set forth his vision of *genuine* authorship as a secular priesthood, which sets the poet apart from and above other creative producers. In a new section devoted to the question 'What is a poet?' which he added to the 'Preface' for the third edition of 1802 Wordsworth would elaborate, pronouncing poetry the 'breath and finer spirit of all knowledge,' and the poet,

> the rock of defence of human nature; an upholder and preserver, carrying every where with him relationship and love. In spite of difference of soil and climate, of language and manners, of laws and customs, in spite of things silently gone out of mind and things violently destroyed, the Poet binds together by passion and knowledge the vast empire of human society, as it is spread over the whole earth, and over all time. The objects of the Poet's thoughts are every where; though the eyes and senses of man are, it is true, his favourite guides, yet he will follow wheresoever he can find an atmosphere of sensation in which to

---

[21] William Wordsworth, *Lyrical Ballads, and Other Poems, 1797–1800* (James Butler and Karen Green eds, Cornell UP 1992) 738.
[22] Stephen Gill, *William Wordsworth: A Life* (Clarendon 1989) 184–85.
[23] Wordsworth, *Lyrical Ballads* (n 21) 741–42. On the genesis of the Preface, including Coleridge's involvement, see Mary Moorman, *William Wordsworth: The Early Years* (OUP 1957) 492–96; cf Richard Holmes, *Coleridge: Early Visions* (Viking Penguin 1989) 285:

> Wordsworth, from a position of apparent weakness, had ruthlessly come to dominate the terms of the collaboration. Having used Coleridge – even, one might think, having exploited him – as advisor and editor, drawing him up to the Lakes for that very purpose, he had entirely imposed his own vision of the collection on the final text.

move his wings. Poetry is the first and last of all knowledge – it is as immortal as the heart of man.[24]

These are extravagant claims. At a moment of radical ferment in every domain from the natural sciences to political theory, Wordsworth declares poetry 'the first and last of all knowledge.' This, as Gill observes, 'is more than a declaration of the importance of humane learning, more than an assertion of the imagination against the pressure of a sceptical, scientific, or utilitarian ethos. Wordsworth confers upon the poet the roles of chronicler and preserver, of comforter and moral guide, of prophet and mediator.' To Alexander Pope 'such exalted affirmations would have seemed ravings,' Gill concludes, and Samuel Johnson, 'who defined the poet as "an inventor; an author of fiction; a writer of poems; one who writes in measure," would have thought them nonsense, probably blasphemous nonsense.'[25]

Even as he was articulating this heroic vision of his vocation Wordsworth was systematically erasing the traces of Coleridge's contribution. This peculiar blend of self-aggrandizement and strategic suppression of others characterizes our modern enactments of 'authorship.'

4. AUTHOR EFFECTS

Today this heroic vision of authorship operates in the intellectual property laws of countries around the world to mediate the process by which acts of cultural appropriation yield legal rights in the appropriator, and Romantic poets played a critical practical role in bringing this about. When the first copyright statute, the 1710 Act of Anne, recognized the 'author' as the person in whom textual rights initially vest, this body of law chiefly just served publishers, whose business practice (before and after the legislation) usually involved purchasing writers' manuscripts for a single lump sum. For the first century and a quarter of British copyright the author-figure was, in short, an indistinct one.[26] But it was filled in, with Romantic coloration, during a campaign for copyright law reform – specifically, copyright term extension – which culminated in the British Copyright Act 1842.

---

[24] Wordsworth, *Lyrical Ballads* (n 21) 752–53. At this time, and also in regular consultation with Coleridge, Wordsworth was attempting to articulate these ideas in the long narrative poem that was eventually published as *The Prelude*. Here Wordsworth repeatedly acknowledges his friend's contribution; however he did not publish this poem in his lifetime, but rather instructed that it be released posthumously. By the time it appeared in 1850, the year of Wordsworth's death, Coleridge had been dead for 16 years.

[25] Gill (n 22) 197.

[26] Peter Jaszi and Martha Woodmansee, 'The Ethical Reaches of Authorship' (1996) 95 South Atlantic Quarterly 953, rpt as 'Die globale Dimension des Begriffs der "Autorschaft"' in Fotis Jannidis and others (eds), *Rückkehr des Autors: Zur Erneuerung eines umstrittenen Begriffs* (Max Niemeyer 1999) 391–419; 'Para além da "autoria": A propriedade intellectual na perspectiva global' in Flora Süssekind and Tánia Dias (eds), *A Historiografia Literária e as Técnicas de Escrita: Do Manuscrito ao Hipertexto* (Vieira & Lent 2004) 115–38. See also Peter Jaszi, 'Toward a Theory of Copyright: The Metamorphoses of "Authorship"' (1991) 40 Duke LJ 455.

This campaign, initiated in Parliament by the lawyer-litterateur Thomas Noon Talfourd, was directly inspired by Wordsworth, who had been complaining privately since at least 1808 that the short term of copyright served only the interests of 'the useful drudges in Literature, ... flimsy and shallow writers, whose works are on a level with the taste and knowledge of the age,' while 'men of real power, who go before their age, are deprived of all hope of their families being benefited by their exertions.'[27]

Wordsworth wanted perpetual copyright, but he was practical enough to recognize that this goal presented political problems. So, from 1837, when Talfourd's first bill calling for an expanded copyright term of an author's life plus 60 years post mortem was introduced, Wordsworth was privately and publicly involved in promoting the legislation: he not only coached Talfourd, providing material for his speeches, but personally wrote to dozens of Members of Parliament and other influential acquaintances to drum up support for the legislation, he wrote several anonymous letters to newspapers, organized a campaign of petitions from well-known authors, and ultimately even petitioned Parliament in his own name.

The terms of the eventual 1842 legislation established post-mortem copyright as an author's legacy to the next generation. Its specific provisions are less important in the present context than the rhetoric of the debate leading up to the legislation, which brought to center stage the Romantic author-figure who, in Talfourd's words, 'persevere[s] in his high and holy course, gradually impressing thoughtful minds with the sense of truth made visible in the severest forms of beauty, until he ... create[s] the taste by which he shall be appreciated'.[28] This vision of authorship as a kind of secular prophecy, the product of 'true original genius' operating on the raw materials of experience to create something new and unanticipated, has informed British copyright – and, by extension, that of other English-speaking countries – for the last century and a half.

Similar accounts of originary genius had provided the rationale for authorial entitlement in various Continental legal systems from the late eighteenth century on, and by the middle of the nineteenth century this vision of authorship was also exercising a shaping influence on the European campaign for a comprehensive international law of copyright. As Peter Jaszi has detailed, until at least the first Act of the Berne Convention of 1886 individual authors and authors' organizations took

---

[27] William Wordsworth to Richard Sharp, 27 September 1808, in Ernest de Selincourt and Mary Moorman (eds), *The Letters of William and Dorothy Wordsworth: The Middle Years, 1806–1811* (OUP 1969) 266. For a fuller treatment of this lively author-driven campaign for copyright term extension, including the key role Wordsworth played in it, see Martha Woodmansee, 'The Cultural Work of Copyright: Legislating Authorship in Britain 1837–1842' in Austin Sarat and Thomas R Kearns (eds), *Law in the Domains of Culture* (U Michigan P 1998) 65–96. Cf Woodmansee, *The Author, Art and the Market* (n 2) 111–47.

[28] Thomas Noon Talfourd, 'Speech to the House of Commons' in *Parliamentary Debates* 3rd ser, vol 38, col 877 (18 May 1837). Talfourd is appropriating Wordsworth's assertion in his 1815 *Essay, Supplementary to the Preface* to *Lyrical Ballads* that 'every author, as far as he is great and at the same time *original*, has had the task of *creating* the taste by which he is to be enjoyed: so has it been, so will it continue to be.' Owen and Smyser (n 1) 80 (italics Wordsworth's).

prominent roles in this campaign, and notions of inherent entitlement rooted in the Romantic vision of authorship figured prominently in its rhetoric.[29]

In 1838 Britain's first international copyright legislation was rationalized on the ground that British authors had a right to the same protection abroad that British inventors already enjoyed. It is common knowledge, Poulett Thomson, the Member of Parliament who introduced the bill, observes,

> that works were [being] pirated abroad as soon as they made their appearance at home: that no sooner were productions sent to the press in this country, than the utmost efforts were exerted to purloin proof-sheets for the purpose of sending them to America, France, Belgium, or Germany. Pirated editions were published at once in those countries and circulated over those countries forthwith, by which means the authors were deprived of the fair fruits of their labour – of those legitimate pecuniary rewards for which they were reasonably entitled to look.[30]

The legislation authorized the Crown to enter into agreements with other states for the mutual protection of copyright, and with it Great Britain joined the growing number of European countries that were concluding bilateral copyright treaties with one another – often on terms that varied considerably from one agreement to the next.

The protection that such a network of bilateral treaties could offer authors in countries other than their own was far from comprehensive or systematic. It fell short of being a truly 'universal' scheme, as Sam Ricketson has explained in his history of the Berne Convention,[31] and it was for a universal scheme that authors began to campaign in earnest in the 1850s, commencing with the nongovernmental Brussels Congress on Literary and Artistic Property of 1858, which issued a series of resolutions introduced by the statement: 'The Congress is of the opinion that the principle of international recognition of the property of authors in their literary and artistic works should be enshrined in the laws of all civilized countries'.[32] The clear suggestion is that any country that fails to recognize the rights of authors cannot fairly lay claim to civilization.

This exalted view of authors' rights is further revealed, as Jaszi explains, in the final communiqué of another important international congress held in Paris in 1878 with Victor Hugo in the chair and authors (and publishers) from around the world in attendance.[33] Its first two resolutions read: '1. The right of the author in his work constitutes, not a concession of the law, but one of the forms of property which the legislature must protect. 2. The right of the author, his beneficiaries and legal representatives is perpetual.'[34] In this view copyright is a natural and indefeasible right

---

[29] Jaszi and Woodmansee, 'The Ethical Reaches of Authorship' (n 26) 955.
[30] Poulett Thomson, 'Speech to the House of Commons' in *Parliamentary Debates* 3rd ser, vol 41, col 1098 (20 March 1838). See also James J Barnes, *Authors, Publishers and Politicians: The Quest for an Anglo-American Copyright Agreement, 1815–1854* (Routledge & Kegan Paul 1974).
[31] Sam Ricketson, *The Berne Convention for the Protection of Literary and Artistic Works: 1886–1986* (Kluwer 1987) 39.
[32] Ibid 42.
[33] Jaszi and Woodmansee, 'The Ethical Reaches of Authorship' (n 26) 956.
[34] Ricketson (n 31) 46.

that arises – without intermediation of the state – from the very act of 'authorship' itself. Out of this 1878 congress grew the International Literary Association (later the International Literary and Artistic Association, or ALAI), which would prove to be a powerful voice for 'universal copyright.' Membership was open to literary societies and writers of all nationalities; Hugo initially served as chair, and the association's first 'committee of honor,' nominated in 1879, consisted of Longfellow, Emerson, Tennyson, Trollope, Disraeli, Gladstone, the Emperor of Brazil, de Lesseps, Dostoyevski, Tolstoy, Auerbach, the Prince of Wales, the King of Portugal, and the President of France.[35] Thus began an energetic political and public relations campaign that eight years later, in 1886, produced the first Act of the Berne Convention.

From its inception, Jaszi concludes, the Berne Convention has been more than a treaty in the conventional sense – more, that is, than an agreement through which a group of states acknowledges certain finite obligations among themselves. In the domain of international law the most unusual feature of Berne – and one that it retained in its sixth iteration, the Paris Act 1971 – is the first Article, which provides that signatory countries 'constitute a Union for the protection of the rights of authors in their literary and artistic works.' This legal device makes the Berne Convention an agreement with a cause, so to speak – the cause of promoting and extending authors' rights, however these may be secured in the national laws of countries around the world.[36] By the same token, interests which cannot readily be conceptualized in terms of 'authorship' find no place in the scheme of the Berne Convention.

International copyright has retained this author fixation ever since – despite the fact that even before 1886 the drive for 'universal' copyright had in large measure been co-opted by publishers, for whom a truly international legal regime represented an important precondition for a world market in books.[37] Today the international copyright system is evolving to address their (strictly commercial) concerns about the openness and fairness of the world trading system but, as Jaszi and I have argued, new agreements that treat intellectual property as an international trade issue tend to perpetuate and extend the Romantic values of Berne.[38]

To see how Romantic values operate in legal decision making let us turn to several colorful court cases from the late 1980s–90s.

5. ROGERS V KOONS

In 1987 the 'appropriation artist' Jeff Koons sent a greeting card he had purchased in a gift shop to his workshop in Italy with the instructions that his collaborators there should fashion a three-dimensional sculpture closely resembling the photo reproduced

---

[35] Ibid 48 fn 28.
[36] Ibid 144–46.
[37] On the critical role played by publishers in the internationalization of copyright, see Norman Feltes, *Literary Capital and the Late Victorian Novel* (U Wisconsin P 1994).
[38] Jaszi and Woodmansee, 'The Ethical Reaches of Authorship' (n 26) 957 ff.

on the card.[39] In the black and white photo, by the professional photographer Art Rogers, may be seen a couple holding a litter of German Shepherd puppies (Figure 4.1). The photo had been commissioned by a California couple whose pet had recently given birth to the litter. Subsequently Rogers published the photo, which he titled 'Puppies,' in his column in a local newspaper, he submitted it for exhibition along with some of his other works at the San Francisco Museum of Modern Art, and he licensed it for reproduction by a greeting card company. Jeff Koons's adaptation of the photo, entitled 'String of Puppies,' is life-sized and rendered in polychrome wood (Figure 4.2). It was exhibited along with some 20 other sculptures in Koons's 'Banality Show,' which opened in November 1988 at the Sonnabend Gallery in New York and ran simultaneously at galleries in Chicago and Cologne. Koons had had editions of three of all of the sculptures in the show produced, and the three 'String[s] of Puppies' sold for a total of $367,000. On learning about the show, Art Rogers sued Koons for copyright infringement. A district court ruled with the plaintiff, Rogers, and its ruling was upheld by the Second Circuit Court of Appeals. For artists like Koons – for all creative producers whose objectives require the reworking of preexisting works – this decision was a chilling one.

Figure 4.1

---

[39] My discussion of *Rogers v Koons* is indebted to Peter Jaszi's remarks on the case in 'On the Author Effect: Contemporary Copyright and Collective Creativity' (1992) 10 Cardozo Arts & Ent LJ 293, 305–12; rpt in Woodmansee and Jaszi, *The Construction of Authorship* (n 4) 41–48.

Figure 4.2

Readers of the present volume will be familiar with 'appropriation art' of the kind that interests Koons. As Koons explained to the court, he works 'in an art tradition dating back to the beginning of the twentieth century.' To quote from the case:

> [H]e belongs to the school of American artists who believe the mass production of commodities and media images has caused a deterioration in the quality of society, and this artistic tradition of which he is a member proposes through incorporating these images into works of art to comment critically both on the incorporated object and the political and economic system that created it. These themes, Koons states, draw upon the artistic movements of Cubism and Dadaism, with particular influence attributed to Marcel Duchamp, who in 1913 became the first to incorporate manufactured objects (readymades) into a work of art, directly influencing Koons's work and the work of other contemporary American artists.[40]

As Koons explained to the court, the objective of 'String of Puppies' – as of the 'Banality Show' as a whole in which the sculpture figured – was a particular kind of social criticism that operates through parody. To function, a parody cannot but incorporate the work that it is parodying.

US law recognizes parody as an important mode of criticism and thus in principle considers it a legitimate, or 'fair use'[41] of materials protected by copyright. In the case

---

[40] *Rogers v Koons* 960 F 2d 301, 309 (2d Cir 1992).

[41] From the infancy of copyright, an opportunity for 'fair use' of copyrighted materials has been thought necessary to fulfill copyright's purpose as defined in Art. I, §8, cl. 8 of the US Constitution – ie 'to promote the Progress of Science and useful Arts' – but fair use remained judge-made doctrine until the passage of the Copyright Act of 1976, which states in §107 that 'the fair use of a copyrighted work, including such use by reproduction in copies or

at hand, however, the court is not able to discern a parody. Even granting 'that "String of Puppies" is a satirical critique of our materialistic society,' the court observes, 'it is difficult to discern any parody of the photograph "Puppies" itself ... [T]he essence of Rogers's photograph was copied nearly in toto, much more than would have been necessary even if the sculpture had been a parody of [his] work. In short, it is not really the parody flag that appellants are sailing under, but rather the flag of piracy.'[42]

Let us explore the understanding of creative production, or art, that may have blinded the court to the point of Koons's sculpture. It is already apparent in the 'opinion' at the beginning of the court's decision:

> The key to this copyright infringement suit, brought by a plaintiff photographer against a defendant sculptor and the gallery representing him, is defendants' borrowing of plaintiff's expression of a typical American scene – a smiling husband and wife holding a litter of charming puppies. The copying was so deliberate as to suggest that defendants resolved – so long as they were significant players in the art business, and the copies they produced bettered the price of the copied work by a thousand to one – [that] their piracy of a less well-known artist's work would escape being sullied by an accusation of plagiarism.[43]

In rationalizing its opinion the court relies on biography, selecting from among the available facts of the litigants' lives to cast the conflict not as one of competing cultural workers pursuing different objectives and audiences in entirely different media but rather as a conflict between a pure 'artist' on the one hand and a corrupt 'player in the art business' on the other. Koons suffers in the opinion of the court both because he works collaboratively and because he works mercenarily. '[W]hile pursuing his career as an artist,' the court notes that Koons 'also worked until 1984 as a mutual funds salesman, a registered commodities salesman and broker, and a commodities futures broker.'[44] Then, after turning full time to art, he secured galleries in various parts of the world to 'represent' him and created a workshop system enabling him to send out for execution the works he conceived. In preparation for the 'Banality Show,' we read that 'certain European studios were chosen to execute his porcelain works, other studios chosen for the mirror pieces, and the Demetz Studio, located in the northern hill country town of Ortessi, Italy was selected to carve the wood sculptures.'[45] Koons sent to the latter workshop 'a chart with an enlarged photocopy of [Rogers's] "Puppies" in the center; painting directions were noted in the margin with arrows drawn to various areas of the photograph. The chart noted, "Puppies, painted in shades of blue. Variation of light-to-dark as per photo. Paint realistic as per photo, but in blues[,]" and "Man's hair, white with shades of grey as per black and white photo!"'[46]

---

phonorecords or by any other means ... for purposes such as criticism, comment, news reporting, teaching (including multiple copies for classroom use), scholarship, or research, is not an infringement of copyright.'

[42] *Rogers* (n 40) 311.
[43] Ibid 303.
[44] Ibid 304. On the Romantic roots of this opposition between art and commerce, see Woodmansee, *The Author, Art, and the Market* (n 2) 11–33.
[45] *Rogers* (n 40) 304.
[46] Ibid 305.

68   *Research handbook on the history of copyright law*

There is no sign in the court's opinion of any recognition of the long and venerable history of Koons's utilization of a workshop to execute his sculpture – eg, in the practice of Renaissance sculptors and painters – or indeed of the legitimacy of the kind of intermingling of his own and others' words that Samuel Johnson regularly practiced to such effect.

By contrast with the mercenary division of labor that characterizes Koons's mode of production in the eyes of the court Rogers appears as a Wordsworthian artist whose life and work are fully integrated: '[H]e has a studio and home at Point Reyes, California, where he makes his living by creating, exhibiting, publishing and otherwise making use of his rights in his photographic works.'[47] In addition to working more or less solitarily from his home, Rogers's technique and his imbrication in the economy are also artisanal in the eyes of the court. Thus we read that:

> Substantial creative effort went into both the composition and production of 'Puppies,' a black and white photograph. At the photo session, and later in his lab, Rogers drew on his years of artistic development. He selected the light, the location, the bench on which the [subjects] are seated and the arrangement of the small dogs. He also made creative judgments concerning technical matters with his camera and the use of natural light. He prepared a set of 'contact sheets,' containing 50 different images, from which one was selected.[48]

Rogers's work had been commissioned by the subject of the photo. When he later licensed it for reproduction, this was to a company that produces and sells greeting cards 'with high quality reproductions of photographs by well-respected American photographers including, for example, Ansel Adams.'[49]

The vision of art, then, the vision of 'authorship' that underlies and rationalizes the court's opinion in *Rogers v Koons*, is a distinctly Romantic vision – one in which a solitary individual working at some distance from the commercial nexus applies his imagination, not *intertextually* by reworking preexisting art, but rather directly to the materials of 'nature' to create an 'original' work.

With its sight set on promoting 'originality,' copyright law appears to have forgotten the value, the necessity of collaboration – here, 'serial' collaboration, the kind of successive elaboration of an idea by a series of creative workers that occurs over years or decades. It had once recognized the value of such creative 're-use' – it had envisioned the possibility of 'improving' existing works through redaction, abridgement, or expansion – but the law today is preoccupied chiefly with the potential harm such re-use could do to the economic interests of the author whose work has temporal priority. To rework, or incorporate portions of protected works, it is now necessary to obtain their authors' permission. What are the prospects, however, if the use one envisions is as critical as Koons's? Is it likely that Rogers would have granted Koons permission to parody his 'Puppies'? Possibly – for a fee. But if not, 'Puppies' would be off limits to critique like Koons's for nearly a century. It would also be off limits to

---

[47] Ibid 303.
[48] Ibid 304.
[49] Ibid.

more traditional – that is, more modest and/or more appreciative – uses, because few artists have the means to pay licensing fees or to risk expensive litigation.[50]

I observed that once upon a time the law did recognize the value of creative re-use. Copyright has expanded dramatically both in scope and duration since its origin in 1710 in the British Statute of Anne. Over the 300 years of its existence the trend in this body of law has been toward longer and longer terms of protection for more and more kinds of 'works' against more and more kinds of unauthorized uses. At the time of Anne it was pretty much just unauthorized *reprinting* of *books* that constituted copyright infringement. Copyright was designed to protect the large capital investment of printers in the then nascent book trade. They needed time to recover their investment before another upstart printer stepped in to reprint and undersell them or they could not have afforded to make the investment – they could not have risked getting into, or could not have afforded to stay in publishing. A robust book market was desirable, so the British Parliament stepped in to stimulate its development by giving publishers the incentive of 14 years of protection against reprinting – renewable for another 14 years if the book's author was still living. At this time you could do all manner of other things with the book: you could publish a translation of it, you could adapt it – into, say, a novel or a play – or you could use it to create some other commodity – an engraving, say, or a lady's fan, a doll, or a pin cushion. You just could not *reprint* it until its copyright lapsed. Today much more is protected. Not just books, but all written expression, musical expression, pictorial, graphic, sculptural, audiovisual, cinematic, architectural, choreographic expression – pretty much all expression insofar as it is 'fixed' in some tangible form. All such 'creative' expression is now protected from unauthorized reproduction for the life of its author plus 70 years *post mortem*. This represents quite an increase in the duration of copyright. And its scope has expanded just as significantly. Today translation, most types of adaptation, and an ever-increasing number of other creative – or, as the law terms them, 'derivative' – uses of protected material constitute infringements of an author's copyright. Even re-uses as important to the life of democracy as the kind of substantial quotation needed to write history and biography, or to level social and political criticism – as the case of *Rogers v Koons* suggests. Unless you can afford to pay an attorney to defend you.

The expansion of copyright is now seriously impeding creativity.[51] But its expansiveness is extremely selective. Copyright also denies protection to a whole body of works

---

[50] Koons fared better in *Blanch v Koons* 467 F 3d 244 (2d Cir 2006), an appellate case separated from *Rogers* by 14 years and the landmark US Supreme Court decision in *Campbell v Acuff-Rose* 510 US 569 (1994). Some would argue that the *Blanch* court's foregrounding of 'transformation' in its (fair use) analysis of Koons's debt to Blanch bespeaks a growing grasp of the necessarily derivative element in postmodern creative production (across the spectrum of genres and technologies) if not in creative production more generally. See Peter Jaszi, 'Is There Such a Thing as Postmodern Copyright?' in Mario Biagioli, Peter Jaszi, and Martha Woodmansee (eds), *Making and Unmaking Intellectual Property: Creative Production in Legal and Cultural Perspective* (U Chicago P 2011) 413.

[51] For an accessible exposé of the ways in which copyright is impeding creative production, see Lawrence Lessig, *Free Culture: How Big Media Uses Technology and the Law to Lock Down Culture and Control Creativity* (Penguin 2004).

that many people would wish to see protected. And here again the Romantic vision of creativity at the center of this body of law is a key culprit.

The kinds of collaborative production that are characteristic of many of the world's peoples, especially the collective forms that today are most often found in traditional cultures of the developing world, are invisible to our author-driven legal regime. The international intellectual property system, as I have noted, is no less, indeed, possibly even more author-driven than the body of US law applied in the *Rogers v Koons* decision. This international system's exclusive vision of authorship has moreover been internalized in many developing countries – often as part of their post-colonial legal legacy. So their national law frequently does not recognize their most characteristic and possibly most valuable cultural productions any more than the international copyright system. The result is that their traditional designs, music, stories (folklore), etc. often circulate internationally, becoming subject to appropriation by the culture industries of the developed world. It has become increasingly common to see creative productions that originated in developing countries being appropriated and reprocessed by entrepreneurs in the developed world, only to be sold back – in debased variations and at exorbitant prices – to the very peoples that originated them.

Let me offer a trivial example. Some years ago Peter Jaszi reported noticing in the gift shop of the Museum of African Art in Washington, DC an attractive coffee mug decorated in a characteristic East African motif that included black, highly stylized figures of animals on a red field. The bottom of the mug, he observed, bore two legends: 'Made in South Korea' and '© Smithsonian Institution.' The community in which this imagery originated had taken no part in, and derived no benefit from its commodification. But the Smithsonian, which had employed both Korean production workers and American product designers to produce the mugs, claimed rights in the outcome of their efforts. Our stores are awash in such instances of cultural appropriation.[52] It is not just that the creators or cultural custodians of the imagery and tunes, etc. do not realize any financial benefit from their exploitation, no matter how profitable or widespread. They also have no say – and certainly no veto – over how their cultural heritage is exploited. Thus, for example, it would not be possible for the East African community in which the coffee mug motif originated to prohibit its use on coffee mugs. To accomplish this – or to realize a profit from the motif's exploitation – the community would first have to identify its author. But of course this would probably be impossible. In all likelihood the motif has come down by tradition, that is, it is the result of long-term collective enterprise. However the law does not recognize collective authorship. To qualify for protection under our laws of copyright and author's rights a work must have one or more identifiable (even if anonymous) authors. It must also be new, or original. Thus the creator of the motif in question – assuming one could be found – would have to show how it diverges from, how it transforms the tradition of design on which it draws. But this too would probably be impossible. In a sense this was Koons's dilemma. The law in his case was looking for transformation, and unable to discern any – seeing in his life-sized polychrome wood sculpture only a replication of Rogers's black and white photo, it ruled against him. This is just what would happen

---

[52] For additional examples, see Jaszi and Woodmansee, 'The Ethical Reaches of Authorship' (n 26) 961 ff.

The 'romantic' author 71

if the rights to the African motif in question were to find their way into litigation – except here it would be even more problematic to argue that the offending motif transformed the tradition on which it has drawn because this is generally not an aspiration of traditional artisans. The whole point in the cultures from which such motifs stem is to carry forward inherited tradition.

The apparent incompatibility between traditional culture on the one hand and our intellectual property system on the other has been recognized for some time, and it has also been inching its way up international diplomatic agendas. Quite a lot of thinking is being devoted to the problem. This is very good, but it is doomed to failure, I would suggest, until it faces up to the contradiction inherent in copyright's core concept. Its core concept, 'authorship,' prescribes origination when in fact we are, as it were, always 'cutting and pasting.' To repeat my refrain, we cannot avoid drawing on the work of others in our creative activities. If we are inclined to ignore or deny such influences, this is on account of the Romantic vision of 'genuine' creativity that has dominated European thought for the last 200 years. That is, what would seem to be a necessary feature of our creative activities – their corporate, collective, and collaborative roots – is occluded in our modern European concept of creative production. A genuinely creative producer – an 'author' in the modern sense – is the creator of 'original' works.

Sustained theoretical criticism of its central category, 'authorship,' has been a preoccupation of literary studies for several decades, as has also the recovery of some of the diverse creators and forms of creative production that this category has excluded or marginalized – women (such as Dorothy Wordsworth), non-Europeans, artists working in traditional (and non-traditional) genres, individuals engaged in group or collaborative projects, to name just a few. But the same cannot be said for the law. The 'critique of authorship' that has marked literary studies in the wake of French theory from Barthes to Foucault has yet to affect the law, as we have seen. So when it is faced with anomalies like the intentionally traditional creative production of indigenous communities, it sees only two options: to allow their creations to be plundered, as in the case of the coffee mug motif, or to force them under the protective umbrella of copyright.[53] The consequences of this latter approach are, however, no less problematic than those of the former, as may be seen by examining a 'landmark' Australian case that spearheaded this strategy.

6. *BULUN BULUN*

John Bulun Bulun was a widely recognized painter belonging to the Ganalbingu people who reside in Arnhem Land in the Northern Territory of Australia. In the late 1980s Bulun Bulun's bark painting 'Magpie Geese and Waterlilies at the Waterhole' (Figure 4.3) was reproduced on T-shirts manufactured by Flash Screenprinters (Figure 4.4) for

---

[53] In 2001 the World Intellectual Property Organization established the Intergovernmental Committee on Intellectual Property and Genetic Resources, Traditional Knowledge and Folklore with a view to establishing a new treaty, however there remains no outcome and draft texts do not interfere with mainstream authorial rights.

72 *Research handbook on the history of copyright law*

sale in tourist shops without the painter's permission having been sought. In 1989 Bulun Bulun brought suit for infringement of copyright and breach of fair trade practices, and the manufacturer settled: the offensive T-shirts were withdrawn from the market and substantial damages were paid to Bulun Bulun. Hence we do not have a decision to examine in the sense we did in *Rogers v Koons*, but we do have an article describing the suit, published by Bulun Bulun's attorney, Colin Golvan.[54] Its aim is to

Note: © Johnny Bulun Bulun/Licensed by Viscopy, 2015

Figure 4.3

---

[54] Colin Golvan, 'Aboriginal Art and Copyright: The Case for Johnny Bulun Bulun' (1989) 11 EIPR 346.

'document the approach [he] adopted ... in this "landmark" case of vital importance to Aboriginal artists and artistry.'[55] That is, Golvan is putting his handling of the case forward as a model, and indeed several subsequent Aboriginal infringement suits closely emulate his approach, which, simplifying, reduces to bringing in art historians. He solicits the testimony of experts whose training in art history – arguably the most romantic of disciplines at this juncture – inclined them to 'situate' the artifacts in question in much the same way as the court did Rogers's 'Puppies' photograph, that is, within the modern system of art.

Figure 4.4

One of the experts Golvan quotes in the article, Margaret West, begins her deposition by conceding that the settings in the two bark paintings 'have been painted on numerous occasions by Bulun Bulun himself and his forebears,' but then she goes on to add that they are nevertheless

---

[55] Ibid 347.

74   *Research handbook on the history of copyright law*

> products of considerable skill, and reflect facets of the Applicant's *distinctive styles*. I note, for example, the fineness and detail of the cross-hatching, which is one of the most important features in any Aboriginal bark painting. I also note the particular depiction of the *figures and composition*, which are *unique* to the Applicant. For example, I am not aware of *any other artist* who depicts magpie geese, long-necked turtle and water snake at waterholes in the fashion of the Applicant. I would describe the works as *very decorative, very busy and very nicely composed*. I note that they share a number of important features in common, such as the rarrk, or cross-hatching, the placement of the figures relative to the waterholes, the depiction of large footprints, the depiction of the waterholes, the striping on the magpie geese figures, the depiction of the geese figures in a red ochre, the depiction of the snake figures and the use of leaves. These are all *distinctive features* of the Applicant's work. I would rate the Applicant as amongst the best exponents in his artform just as one might rate a particular Western artist as a leading exponent in his particular artform of, say, sculpture or water-colour painting.[56]

I have added italics to this passage to call attention to the categories the deponent has deployed. They are the categories of art history operating in the romanticizing authorial mode we are familiar with from the *Rogers* court's description of the artistry of Rogers's photographic techniques. The other depositions Golvan quotes in his article take a similar tack. One, by Charles Godjuwa, goes a step farther than West, and in addition to describing Bulun Bulun's style as 'distinctive' – which is to say original – ascribes its originality to the painter's 'intimate' 'personal knowledge' of the subject matter depicted in the bark paintings.[57] This was precisely Wordsworth's claim to greatness – and a basis of his claim to (perpetual) ownership of his verse: that rather than developing intertextually, in contestation with the work of his predecessors, his poems were expressions of his unique, unmediated individual experience.

What then could be wrong with such a strategy? After all, it worked. The pirate T-shirt manufacturer was vanquished – it withdrew the rip-off T-shirts from the market and paid generous damages. To answer this question we need to ask what has been silenced by this winning strategy – what has been lost in this copyright-friendly description of Bulun Bulun's bark painting that his attorney touts as 'open[ing] the way

---

[56] Ibid 349–50.
[57] Bulun Bulun, according to Godjuwa:

> adopts a particularly distinctive approach to the depiction of magpie geese. I know of no other artist who paints these birds as the Applicant does. As it happens, magpie geese are a prized food in the Applicant's area, and the emphasis on the bird by the Applicant is of significance to the area. Included amongst other prominent figures in his work are depictions of the long-necked turtle, flying fox and water snake. I know of no other artist who paints these figures in the manner of the Applicant. I note the particular prominence these figures assume in his work, and, of course, the Applicant's distinctive cross-hatching style. Because of the Applicant's detailed personal knowledge of the country of his tribe, through his hunting and ceremonial experience, he has an intimate understanding of the manner of these creatures, all of which are common to the Applicant's tribal land, as well as of the significance of them as totems in his tribe's dreaming practices. This understanding guides the Applicant in his attention to detail, for which his works are much sought after.

Ibid 350.

for Aboriginal artists to rely on copyright ... to prohibit the unauthorized reproduction of their designs.'[58]

To answer this question let us turn to a subsequent suit in which Bulun Bulun joined forces with fellow painter and clan elder George Milpurrurru and other affected artists to charge a fabric manufacturer with unauthorized reproduction of a number of works including Bulun Bulun's design in 'At the Waterhole,' which had been at issue in his suit against Flash. In this suit too the defendant, R&T Textiles, admitted infringement and withdrew the offending fabric from the market, but the suit nevertheless went to trial because of a communal title claim lodged by the litigants that drew the state into proceedings. Its upshot is that while Bulun Bulun may have held copyright to his paintings in Australian law, in Aboriginal law they belonged to the Ganalbingu people collectively. The Ganalbingu people, Milpurrurru submits, 'are the traditional Aboriginal owners of the corpus of ritual knowledge from which the artistic work is derived, including the subject matter of the artistic work and the artistic work itself.'[59]

The court proceedings contain a long affidavit by Bulun Bulun in support of this charge – one that diverges so sharply from the art historians' account of the process by which his bark paintings came into being that it merits quoting at some length here. Where the art historians focused on *form*, Bulun Bulun focuses on *content*. The water hole referenced in his 'Magpie Geese and Waterlilies at the Waterhole' painting is for Bulun Bulun the source, or 'clan well,' of his lineage – 'the place from which our creator ancestor ... Barnda, or Gumang (long neck tortoise) first emerged from the earth.'

> In the same way my creator ancestor formed the natural landscape and granted it to my human ancestors who in turn handed it to me. My creator ancestor passed on to me the elements for the artworks I produce for sale and ceremony. Barnda not only creates the people and landscape, but our designs and artworks originate from the creative acts of Barnda. They honour and deliberate the deeds of Barnda. This way the spirit and rule of Barnda is kept alive in the land. The land and the legacy of Barnda go hand in hand ... [T]he ownership of land has with it the corresponding obligations to create and foster the artworks, designs, songs and other aspects of ritual and ceremony that go with the land. If the rituals and ceremonies attached to land ownership are not fulfilled, ... then traditional Aboriginal ownership rights lapse. Paintings, for example, are a manifestation of our ancestral past. They were first made in my case by Barnda. Barnda handed the painting to my human ancestors. They have been handed from generation to generation ever since. ... The creation of artworks such as 'At the Waterhole' is part of my responsibility. ... I am permitted by my law to create this artwork, but it is also my duty and responsibility to create such works, as part of my traditional Aboriginal land ownership obligation. A painting such as this ... is part of my bundle of rights in the land and must be produced in accordance with Ganalbingu custom and law.[60]

It would be difficult to imagine a description of a painting that differs more sharply from that of the art historians I have quoted than the one we have here by its creator. Their depositions – in Golvan's winning defense of the work against its unauthorized

---

[58] Ibid 347.
[59] *Bulun Bulun & Anor v R&T Textiles* (1998) 157 ALR 193 (Fed Ct) 197.
[60] Ibid 198.

appropriation for the manufacture of T-shirts – efface pretty much everything that gives the painting its meaning and value to Bulun Bulun. In his eyes it has manifestly sacred meaning and value. He views it moreover as having originated at the behest of his people in strict accordance with rules and techniques preserved and handed down to him in Ganalbingu custom. He is something closer to its midwife than its originator in our modern, Romantic sense, and thus, much as the land itself in his eyes, it belongs to – it is the 'property' of – his people collectively.

The cost, then, of endeavoring to force collective works under the protective umbrella of copyright is very high indeed. Yet at present this submission to cultural imperialism is the only option open to traditional producers because copyright does not recognize collective production.[61] Testing the limits of the law in this regard – testing its capacity to expand to embrace the collective forms of making characteristic of his clan – had been Bulun Bulun's clansman George Milpurrurru's objective in pursuing this suit in court after the initial settlement in favor of Bulun Bulun. But this portion of the suit failed – abysmally. I will conclude with this passage from the decision:

> Section 35(2) of the Copyright Act [of] 1968 provides that the author of an artistic work is the owner of the copyright which subsists by virtue of the Act. That provision effectively precludes any notion of group ownership in an artistic work, unless the artistic work is a 'work of joint authorship'. ... In this case no evidence was led to suggest that anyone other than Mr Bulun Bulun was the creative author of the artistic work. A person who supplies an artistic idea to an artist who then executes the work is not, on that ground alone, a joint author with the artist. ... Joint authorship envisages the contribution of skill and labour to the production of the work itself. ... To conclude that the Ganalbingu People were communal owners of the copyright in the existing work would ignore the provisions of section 8 of the Copyright Act, and involve the creation of rights in indigenous peoples which are not otherwise recognized by the legal system of Australia.[62]

In sum, copyright law requires an 'author' in the Romantic sense we have been investigating – one that has been discredited in literary and cultural theory. As a consequence, this body of law adjudicates arbitrarily – in ways we cannot and should not accept. Greater interdisciplinary and cross-cultural discussion thus seems called for.[63]

---

[61] For a more comprehensive treatment of the dilemma posed by the collective forms of making characteristic of traditional culture, see Jaszi and Woodmansee, 'The Ethical Reaches of Authorship' (n 26) 961 ff; Peter Jaszi and Martha Woodmansee, 'Beyond Authorship: Refiguring Rights in Traditional Culture and Bioknowledge' in Mario Biagioli and Peter Galison (eds), *Scientific Authorship: Credit and Intellectual Property in Science* (Routledge 2003) 195. See also Kathy Bowrey, 'The Outer Limits of Copyright Law – Where Law Meets Philosophy and Culture' (2001) 12 Law and Critique 1.

[62] *Bulun Bulun* (n 59) 205. Compare US law's substitution of the 'inventive or master mind' for the 'author' to rationalize vesting exclusive copyright in a corporation, in *Aalmuhammed v Lee* 202 F 3d 1227 (9th Cir 1999); cf my discussion of the case in Martha Woodmansee, 'Response to David Nimmer' (2001) 38 Hous L Rev 231.

[63] The way was paved in the 1991 launch of a collaborative project sponsored by the Society for Critical Exchange. See <http://www.case.edu/affil/sce/IPCA_main.html?nw_view=1428098017>. Progress is visible in the subsequent emergence of interdisciplinary organizations devoted

But what should be the topic of such discussion? In legal scholarship 'fair use' is often viewed as a corrective to the authorial bias of the law. It is called upon to rebalance rights in the interest of artistic freedom, and other goals. Yet while fair use has been successfully asserted in some cases[64] our examination of *Rogers v Koons* demonstrates that it is also itself informed by a Romantic vision of authorship.

Humanities scholars, such as myself, are sometimes called upon to give expert opinion in suits hinging on fair use. Thus, for example, in the charge by JD Salinger that a 2009 novel *Sixty Years Later Coming Through the Rye* infringed his copyright in *Catcher in the Rye* I and another literary historian and critic Robert Spoo were asked to advise the court on the relationship between the two novels. After studying both carefully I testified that far from being a mere infringing sequel to Salinger's 1951 classic, as charged, *Sixty Years Later* was in my view a sophisticated experimental novel which draws both structurally and thematically on Mary Shelley's *Frankenstein* (1818) to level a devastating critique of both the panoply of values celebrated in Salinger's classic and of Salinger himself.[65] In his testimony Dr. Spoo reached similar conclusions.

It was surprising to see how little our expert opinion mattered. Employed only impressionistically in the defense's litigation strategy, it was seemingly all but discounted by the court, whose opinion projects arresting confidence in the sufficiency of the interpretive skills of 'ordinary' readers (like themselves), however untrained, to make sense of narrative fiction however complex and experimental.

In short, however welcome the law's acknowledgment of its need to draw on external expertise, there remains a problem with its manner of using such expertise to inform its work. Its use is constrained by the legal questions and priorities established by litigation strategies. Interdisciplinary discussion is quite limited, and thus any cross-disciplinary understanding that emerges from the exchange is hard to locate from the traces left behind in the legal record. What is needed is a more encompassing engagement between the law and humanities, not so much to correct or rebalance 'the law gone wrong'[66] in particular cases as to promote a deeper understanding of the history, philosophy, and material foundations of categories like authorship that are so central to how we understand law and culture today.

---

to the study of copyright, such as the International Society for the History and Theory of Intellectual Property <http://www.ishtip.org>.

[64] *Blanch* (n 50); *Cariou v Prince* 714 F 3d 694 (2d Cir 2013); cf *Fairey v Associated Press* No 09-01123 (SDNY 2010).

[65] Declaration of Martha Woodmansee, *Salinger et al v John Doe et al*, 15 June 2009; *Salinger v Colting* 607 F 3d 68 (2d Cir 2010).

[56] *Sun Trust Bank v Houghton Mifflin Co* 268 F 3d 1257 (11th Cir 2001).

PART II

UNITED KINGDOM PERSPECTIVES

5. The Stationers' Company in England before 1710
Ian Gadd

1. INTRODUCTION

Among the provisions of the 1710 Statute of Anne was a requirement that 'the Title to the Copy of such book or books hereafter published shall before such publication be entered in the Register Book of the Company of Stationers in such manner as hath been usual which Register Book shall at all times be kept at the Hall of the said Company'.[1] Mention was also made of the Company's 'Clerk' and 'Warehouse Keeper' and their duties under the Act. No further explanation was given about what the Company was or what it did, or indeed where its hall, let alone its clerk and warehouse keeper, were to be found. Yet its 'Register Book' was identified as the central, and only, record-keeping mechanism for the rights and activities enshrined by the Act. That the 'Company of Stationers' needed no glossing was hardly surprising for a trade and craft body whose membership comprised most, but not all, of London's printers and booksellers; moreover, any member of the London book trade and many of those active outside London, knew exactly where to find the Company's headquarters, and adjacent warehouses, just off Ludgate Hill, west of St Paul's Cathedral. However, neither the Company's size nor prominence fully explains its presence in this statute, because for all that the Statute of Anne may have appeared to be new, many of its provisions were shaped by how the Company and book trade had developed over the previous two centuries. It is the story of the Company of Stationers, its hall, its clerk, its warehouse keeper, and above all its 'register book' that is the focus of this chapter.

2. PRINTING AND PRIVILEGES: THE BOOK TRADE TO 1553

The Company of Stationers – or the Stationers' Company as it is more commonly known – was a London craft guild or 'company'. Its origins can be traced back to 1357, but its formal foundation dates from 1403, when members of the 'misteries' of Textwriters (non-legal scribes) and Limners (who illustrated and illuminated manuscripts) along with those who 'use to bind and sell books' sought permission from the city authorities to band together as a single mistery. By 1417, 'Stationers' appears as part of the organisation's title, and from 1441 onwards it was known solely as the mistery or Company of Stationers.[2] As London custom allowed any citizen to practice virtually any craft or trade regardless of the company to which they belonged, the

---

[1] Act for the Encouragement of Learning 1710 (8 Anne c 19).
[2] Peter WM Blayney, *The Stationers' Company and the Printers of London, 1501–1557* (CUP 2013) 4–19. Most of the detail given in this section is derived from this very important

Stationers' Company never comprised the entirety of the London book trade – nor, for that matter, were all its members active in the book trade – but nonetheless it was the largest single grouping of book producers and booksellers in the city. At this stage, of course, the Company included no printers: printing would not arrive in England until the 1470s, and it was not until 1500 or thereabouts that any printers joined the Stationers' Company.

By the early sixteenth century, the English book trade was already subject to a good deal of regulation, much of it economic. Membership of a London company brought with it particular economic, social, and political benefits but prior to the mid-sixteenth century a printer, unlike a bookseller, bookbinder, or scribe, was not subject to any accompanying regulatory system. A printer who joined the Stationers' Company was expected to obey company and city ordinances regarding labour, prices, and selling practices, as well as abide by general economic and trade-specific legislation, and statutes and proclamations relating to blasphemy and treason. However, the new craft of printing was not yet subject to any direct regulatory control: no London company, for example, had jurisdiction over printing regardless of whether printers were numbered among its members. In fact, during the first half of the sixteenth century, it was more likely for a printer to be a member of another London company than belong to the Stationers' Company.[3]

This relative freedom had important consequences. Printing was more than a new technology. It was a capital-intensive activity that, unlike the production of manuscripts, involved the acquisition of a good deal of specialist equipment before a single sheet could be printed. Crucially, it also differed in its underlying business model. Unlike manuscripts, printed books were not produced in complete units one at a time; instead, a decision had to be taken at the outset about how many copies should be printed, none of which were available for sale before the entire print-run was effectively complete. Producing printed books for sale – or what we would call publishing – involved up-front costs and commercial risks far beyond what a scribal workshop faced, even one that might produce some manuscripts in anticipation of demand. The economics of publishing were not for the faint-hearted. Moreover, as the printed book trade developed, a new risk appeared: someone else publishing someone else's previously published work, and selling it cheaper.[4] It was this that prompted publishers to seek ways of protecting their investments.

In England, that moment was not reached until 1510. As Peter Blayney observes, during the first decade of the sixteenth century:

[t]he demand for books was growing faster than was their output, and no one printer could expect to satisfy it all. It hardly mattered which of them printed which of the books in greatest demand; if 'competing' editions of a steady-selling work happened to appear in the same year, that simply meant that each printer's next edition of it would be somewhat

---

revisionist history that supplants all previous accounts of the development of printing privileges in the sixteenth century.
[3] Ibid 929–32.
[4] Savings could be made by lowering the cost of materials (cheaper paper, narrower margins, smaller type), by not having to pay for the original manuscript, and by not having to spend time readying the manuscript for typesetting.

delayed. Given the close proximity in which they lived and worked it is anyway difficult to doubt that they would sometimes have discussed their plans and negotiated with each other in order to prevent potential clashes of interest. But none of them had ever had the exclusive right to print any work, so we cannot expect them to have behaved as if such rights were the expected norm.[5]

Over the following decade, the principle of protecting one's right to print a particular work was established through a series of royal grants that forbade others from printing named works for a specific period.[6] The first such privilege was issued to the printer, Richard Pynson, most likely in 1510, protecting his right to print the first statute of Henry VIII's reign for a period of two years.[7] In 1512 Thomas Linacre was granted a two-year privilege to protect his new Latin schoolbook; Linacre was the first author, as opposed to a printer, to receive such a privilege but, as Blayney suggests, it was unlikely that such a privilege had been obtained without the involvement of the work's printer (and probable publisher).[8] A third privilege, this time granted to the Oxford printer John Scolar in 1518 by the Chancellor of the University, was narrower in its geographic scope – it only applied to Oxford – but extended the term of protection to seven years. Strikingly, its terms seemed to apply to all subsequent works printed by Scolar and forbade the sale in Oxford of any rival editions printed elsewhere. It proved a crucial precedent: later that year, Pynson appears to have secured a lifetime privilege that protected all his new publications for a period of two years from the date of publication.[9] Similar 'generic' privileges were granted to six further printers and one author during the 1520s. By 1528 almost half of the printers active in England had privileges: in Blayney's words, '[t]he idea of entitlement had arrived – and it was a genie that would never go back into the bottle.'[10] Further privileges followed during the next decade, and by 1538 over a third of all extant books printed during the previous two decades claimed some kind of privileged protection.

As the example of Scolar shows, it was possible for an authority other than the monarch to grant a privilege; in other words, the Crown had no special or exclusive right to bestow grants relating to printing. This may seem self-evident but, over a century later, the idea that there was in fact a 'property' inherent in printing that belonged ultimately to the crown and that it was this 'property' that was granted by a privilege was cited in legal cases. Many scholars have assumed that this concept dated back to the Tudors but, as Blayney has persuasively argued, this was not how it was understood during Henry VIII's reign:

> [a] hitherto-unprinted book ... had no owner at all, and could therefore be printed by anyone. By granting a privilege Henry did not transfer property rights that were otherwise his: he used the prerogative to *forbid* anyone *other* than the grantee to print it for a specific period – after which it returned to the public domain from which he had temporarily removed it.[11]

---

[5] Blayney, *Stationers' Company* (n 2) 109.
[6] Ibid 171–72.
[7] Ibid 160–63.
[8] Ibid 165–66.
[9] Ibid 167–71.
[10] Ibid 233–35, 322–26, 928.
[11] Ibid 170–72.

Privileges were thus no more than temporary commercial monopolies. That many of them were generic – that is, they applied to all new publications by a specific printer – also warns us against seeing 'cum privilegio regali' on the imprint of a sixteenth-century book as an official endorsement. Indeed the risk that some contemporary readers might do just this seems to have prompted a royal proclamation in 1538 that any book bearing that phrase on its title page should add 'ad imprimendum solum' to make it clear that the privilege only concerned the *printing* of the book.[12] The *content* of books was instead regulated through a system of pre-publication licensing that owes its origins to papal bulls of 1487 and 1515,[13] and was cited in various forms by ecclesiastical and secular authorities in England from the 1520s onwards; the system, albeit in a more developed form, remained England's primary means for controlling the publication of texts, with some hiatuses, through until the end of the seventeenth century.[14] Privileges, however, were not part of the mechanism of censorship.

During Henry's reign, the majority of privileges issued by the Crown were granted 'by placard' – a relatively simple bureaucratic process that bypassed Chancery (which required more expense).[15] The first privilege to be granted under the great seal as opposed to by placard was issued to Anthony Marler in 1542 for the right to print the English bible: the added authority (and cost) reflected the king's particular interest in the work and may, according to Blayney, have been intended 'to *prevent* publication rather than facilitate it'. The following year, a privilege to the printer Richard Grafton and his associate Edward Whitchurch granted them seven years' protection for any work they published and indefinite protection to any Sarum liturgy published: both the term-limit and specification of genre represented a departure from the usual practice.[16] Under Edward VI, privileges by placard continued to 'significantly outnumber those issued under the great seal', with a much larger number than before being granted to non-printers.[17] As before, some privileges were for specifically named works, but there were also more for *genres* of books: books in Latin, Greek, and Hebrew; all authorized service books; service books for use in Wales and the Marches; liturgies in French for the use of the Channel Isles; primers, psalters, and books of private prayer; and common law books.[18] As privileges began to jostle with one another overlaps became inevitable, such as Richard Tottell's common law book privilege which explicitly excepted certain titles already published, or John Day's privilege for Ponet's *Short Catechism* which originally allowed him to print it also in Latin (thus clashing with Reyner Wolfe's rights as the Royal Typographer for Latin, Greek, and Hebrew). Apparently by way of compensation, Day secured the right to publish the *ABC with the*

---

[12] Ibid 480–87.
[13] Ibid 173–78; R Hirsch, 'Bulla Super Impressione Librorum, 1515' (1973) Gutenberg-Jahrbuch 248.
[14] Most notably 1547–49, 1641–43, and 1685–87.
[15] Blayney, *Stationers' Company* (n 2) 952–59. 'By placard' privileges were issued 'under the sign manual, the privy signet, or more probably both'. ibid 953. Privileges issued under the great seal were enrolled (that is, formally copied) onto the Chancery patent rolls.
[16] Ibid 542–47. Scolar's Oxford privilege was a grant of seven years; the earliest royal example appears to date from 1531. ibid 322–23.
[17] Ibid 721.
[18] Ibid 604, 606–07, 644–46, 649, 628, 734.

Brief Catechism (itself already under privilege) but *only* when annexed to the *Catechism,* a nicety that Day himself failed to observe.[19]

3. THE INCORPORATION OF THE STATIONERS' COMPANY

The impact of Mary's accession to the throne in 1553 on the English book trade was dramatic: within a matter of months, over half of the printers who had been active immediately prior to her accession stopped their presses, including 'the five most prolific printers of Edward's reign, who between them had printed more than 60 percent of the nation's output'.[20] The number of Edwardian privilege-holders also shrank markedly although some key privileges (such as for common law books and books in Latin, Greek and Hebrew) continued; new privileges were issued and existing ones renewed.[21] However, as Blayney has been the first to argue, Mary's reign marked a transformation in the history of what became copyright, by facilitating a remarkably audacious commercial coup on behalf of the Stationers' Company that, while relying on a particular set of contingencies, derived directly from a 'guild' ethos.

Guilds, their ambitions, and their effect on local and national economies has been the subject of scholarly debate ever since Adam Smith condemned them as conspiracies against the public. Guilds, many scholars have argued, prevented economic competition, deterred entrepreneurship and technological innovation, kept prices high, restricted the labour market, and condoned the production and sale of poor quality wares by their members. They were, in economic terms, 'inefficient', 'inflexible', and 'rent-seeking'; in other words, they used their dominant position to exploit customers and to inhibit the activities of craftsmen or tradesmen outside the guild system, and they refused to adapt to changing economic circumstances. They were monopolists by instinct, and they survived for so long not because they were beneficial for the European urban economy, but because they were ruthlessly efficient at protecting and extending their privileged status. Their decline and eventual disappearance by the early nineteenth century was thus an inevitable, and worthy, victory for modern capitalism and the free market.

This critical view of the European guild system represented the economic orthodoxy until relatively recently when some economic historians began to argue that guilds, while not being wholly 'efficient' or 'optimal' organisations, did, on balance make a net social and economic contribution. To quote one leading advocate, Larry Epstein, guilds:

> mediated between members with market power and negotiated with more powerful merchants; they supplied members with financial support and cheap credit; they enforced quality standards and fixed prices ... ; and they protected members from exploitation by opportunistic urban elites. Not least, they sustained systems for the transmission of skills and technical innovation. This functional complexity and flexibility ... explains the extraordinary longevity of the craft guild as an economic organization ... . [B]etween the thirteenth and the eighteenth centuries they offered a superior organizational matrix for the acquisition and

---

[19] Ibid 735–36.
[20] Ibid 757.
[21] Ibid 756–58, 761–62, 824–25.

deployment of skills by most urban artisans working under the prevailing technological, commercial, and political circumstances.[22]

So, while the vast majority of printers and publishers in England prior to the mid-sixteenth century were members of London companies, and so were subject to their individual company regulations regarding training and labour, the craft of printing and by extension the trade of publishing operated outside a corporate framework. Such 'freedom', though, created a problem when it came to seeking protection for one's publications: as no single company 'owned' printing or publishing, no company could protect its members against the activities of those in other companies. Conceivably, a printer or publisher could seek the authority of London's Lord Mayor and Aldermen to protect their publication within the city's jurisdiction as John Scolar did in Oxford but it was much more effective to secure protection from the highest authority in the land, especially once it became possible to gain privileges that protected *all* of one's new publications for a specific period. However, it came at a price – not just literally. The process was complex, costly, and while there was opportunity for objection (as seems to have happened with Nicholas Udall's privilege application in 1550 which was halted presumably for its inclusion of the English Bible),[23] there was no systematic way for the trade to assess the commercial impact of any proposed new privilege. Printers and publishers doubtless learned about each other's privileges through word of mouth, and there were formal mechanisms: the possibly routine verbal announcement of privileges to them as a group, the use of 'cum privilegio' in some form on an imprint, and the full text of the privilege in the work itself (mandatory after 1538).[24] Even so, applicants had either to know in advance of other privileges that theirs might otherwise infringe or to seek out the intervention of senior officers of state to resolve overlaps after the privilege had been granted (as in the cases of Tottell, Day, and Wolfe mentioned above). Moreover, there was no easy mechanism for resolution when it came to the protection of any new work covered by an existing privilege. Disputes would, ultimately, have to lead to proceedings in the Court of Chancery. Finally, such privileges were never perpetual: even if the monarch was feeling generous the term could not usually exceed the recipient's own lifetime, and of course a change of monarch might well require a renewal.

The ideal solution was a system of publishing-only privileges that was operated by trusted members of the book trade; had sufficient authority among the trade as a whole; was reliable, easy, and relatively cheap to use; did not require the display of a statement on an imprint or in the work itself; provided a straightforward means for resolving disagreements; did not interfere with or challenge existing or future Crown privileges; and did not require periodical renewal. It was precisely the kind of trade-specific system that guilds were good at establishing and operating, not least because they

---

[22] SR Epstein, 'Craft Guilds in the Pre-Modern Economy: A Discussion' (2008) 61 Econ Hist Rev 155, 155–56, 172.
[23] Blayney, *Stationers' Company* (n 2) 730.
[24] Ibid 404–5.

provided an established and recognized hierarchy, a dependable record-keeping apparatus, a pre-existing system for arbitrating disputes between members, and a deep-seated ethos of mutual social obligation and equity that sought to balance an individual's commercial autonomy against the trade as a whole. For such a system to work, though, printing and publishing needed to be subject to a single company's jurisdiction.

It was the city's formal recognition of the Stationers' Company in 1403 that founded the organisation, and consequently its jurisdiction extended no further than the city's. For many London companies this was perfectly adequate but, from probably the late fourteenth century, some began seeking incorporation by the Crown. Incorporation was the legal process that created a corporation: it unified a group of individuals into a single, immortal legal entity that could enter into contracts, go to law, own property, and be granted privileges. An incorporated company could thus own a hall more easily, protect its rights at law, and use its own seal to make agreements with individuals or other corporations. It could govern itself without seeking approval at each year's elections from the city authorities, and its ordinances were ratified by the kingdom's chief legal officers (although the expectation was that both the charter and ordinances were approved by the city as well).[25] Finally, and crucially, incorporation provided a company with the opportunity to seek powers that extended beyond the city's boundaries and to define the crafts and trades over which it had jurisdiction: in certain cases such as the Goldsmiths' and Pewterers' companies, incorporation granted them national rights of search and confiscation for substandard wares.[26] For the Stationers' Company, incorporation by the Crown was the only way that it would be able to achieve formal control over printing and publishing.

The Company unsuccessfully sought incorporation in 1542. The charter's provisions are unknown but it is possible that the process was thwarted by other London companies.[27] The fact that London's printers and publishers were scattered among the companies and that many of the most influential and important privilege-holders belonged to companies right at the top of the city's hierarchy meant that any attempt by the Stationers' Company to redefine the jurisdiction regarding printing and publishing was bound to be closely scrutinised, if not opposed. As Blayney has shown in considerable detail, the Reformation, especially under Edward VI, weakened the significance of many of those printers who belonged to the Stationers' Company in favour of religious reformers who were, for the most part, members of other companies.[28] It was only with the accession of the Catholic Mary that the scales tipped sufficiently towards the Stationers' Company to make a renewed attempt at incorporation worthwhile: '[l]eft decisively behind in the race to lead the book-driven Edwardian Reformation, within a month of their 150th anniversary, they suddenly and

---

[25] Ibid 913.
[26] IA Gadd and P Wallis, 'Reaching Beyond the City Wall: London Guilds and National Regulation, 1500–1700' in SR Epstein and M Prak (eds), *Guilds, Innovation and the European Economy 1400–1800* (CUP 2008).
[27] Blayney, *Stationers' Company* (n 2) 514–15; IA Gadd, '"Being like a field": Corporate Identity in the Stationers' Company 1557–1684' (D Phil, University of Oxford 1999) 34.
[28] Blayney, *Stationers' Company* (n 2) 933–34 and *passim*.

88 *Research handbook on the history of copyright law*

unexpectedly found themselves the last printers standing after the Marian purge had culled all the winners.'[29]

The eventual incorporation of the Stationers' Company in May 1557 granted it a near-exclusive national jurisdiction over printing:

> no person within this our realm of England or the dominions of the same shall practise or exercise, by himself or by his subordinates, his servants, or by any other person, the art or mistery of impressing or printing any book or any thing for sale or traffic within this our realm of England or the dominions of the same, unless the same person at the time of his foresaid impressing or printing is or shall be one of the company of the foresaid mistery or art of stationery of the foresaid city, or has licence for it from us or the heirs or successors of us the foresaid queen by letters patent from us or the heirs or successors of us the foresaid queen.[30]

Thus, no one was allowed to set up or operate a printing press anywhere in England unless either they were a member of the Stationers' Company or they held a privilege direct from the Crown. This near-monopolisation of printing in effect restricted printing to London for almost 140 years, excepting only the two universities who had their own privileges for printing. However, as the phrase 'for sale or traffic' implies this was not merely about printing. While the charter did not explicitly grant the Company's members a near-exclusive right to publish any new work that was not covered by an existing privilege, it did make it impossible to publish without engaging with a member of the Stationers' Company unless one was, or contracted directly with, an existing privilege-holder. By transforming the Company into a kind of privilege-holder in its own right, the charter enabled the Company to develop its own system for managing publishing rights of its members: the so-called Stationers' Register.

4. THE STATIONERS' REGISTER

Central to this system was the concept of 'copy'. An entry in the Stationers' records that can be almost certainly dated to immediately after the Company was incorporated notes a substantial fine of 20 shillings imposed on one of its most senior members 'for printing of a breafe Cronacle co[n]trary to o[u]r orden[an]c[es] before he ded presente the Copye to the wardyns'.[31] These ordinances were brand-new and although they do not survive we know that the specific ordinance that had been breached here stipulated 'That no Man shall print any Book unless the Copy be first assigned by the Master and the Wardens of the Company of Stationers'.[32] While the precise procedure, fees, and wording did not stabilise for a number of decades, the primary principle remained unchanged throughout the period covered by this chapter: any member wishing to publish a work had to visit Stationers' Hall to seek the permission of the Company's

---

[29] Ibid 922.
[30] Ibid 1025.
[31] Ibid 859–63.
[32] Quoted by the House of Lords when they summoned the Stationers' Company to present its charter and ordinances to them in 1641. 4 HLJ 182.

senior officers, who would assess whether the work in question was likely to affect adversely any other member's existing publication. This was purely a commercial decision and hence was entirely separate from the system of licensing; the publisher was expected to seek suitable 'authority' for his work prior to publishing and the officers had no power to judge a work's contents, although in many cases they made their permission to publish explicitly conditional on the publisher securing a licence. This permission to publish (which, confusingly, was called 'licence' by the Company) in turn granted the publisher the Company's protection over his work; should any other member publish the same work without his permission or publish something that threatened his publication rights, he could appeal direct to the Company's governing body. These rights applied only to printing and not any other form of reproduction, and they were enforceable only within the Company's membership although, in certain cases, publishers who were members of other London companies were tacitly allowed to use the Register. The process of approval required only a signature from an officer on the relevant manuscript and the payment of a fee; the formal written 'entrance' of that permission in the Stationers' records (the 'Register') by the Company's clerk was not obligatory (which is why so many published works do not appear in the Register) but had the advantage that the publisher was not depending solely on the memory of the officers or his retention of the original signed manuscript to defend his rights. For the first 25 years of the system's operation, such permission was also conditional on the actual publication of the work; after that, the act of permission itself granted the recipient immediate protection. These publishing rights – or 'copy' – were initially understood to last for an individual's lifetime, although by the early seventeenth century, they were considered to be perpetual and hence could be bequeathed or transferred to any other member without limitation.[33]

The Stationers' Register did not stop all 'piracy' – that is, the printing of another publisher's copy without permission – but it did provide a ready mechanism for restitution should the 'pirate' in question be a member of the Company. For 'piracies' by individuals outside London, however, it was wholly ineffectual. For example in 1585 the Oxford printer, Joseph Barnes, republished without permission *A Booke of Christian Exercise Appertaining to Resolution*, which had been entered in the Register by the London bookseller John Wight the year before. Despite the work being 'the most vendible Copye that happened in our Companie theis manie yeeres', Wight could not appeal to the Company's officers as Barnes was not a member and instead had to resort to sending his son to Oxford to buy up the whole edition and to extract a promise from Barnes not to publish any future editions – which Barnes promptly broke.[34] Barnes, though, was an exception – a printer who was not based in London or a member of the Stationers' Company – and even he came to see the advantages of a

---

[33] PWM Blayney, 'The Publication of Playbooks' in JD Cox and DS Kastan (eds), *A New History of Early English Drama* (Columbia UP 1997) 389–405; Gadd, 'Corporate Identity' (n 27) 180–81; remarks made by Blayney at Mapping the British Book Trades Workshop, Oxford May 2014.

[34] E Arber (ed), *A Transcript of the Registers of the Company of Stationers 1554–1640 AD* (1875–94) vol 2, 435, 793.

system that was recognised in effect by the whole of the London book trade, and duly apprenticed his son to the Company, primarily it seems to gain access to the Register.[35]

At this stage, it was not yet known as the 'Register'. The Company talks of the 'Book of copies', the 'clerk's books', the 'hall book', the 'book of entrances for the clerk', and the 'entry book of copies', and the earliest references to a 'register' date from 1599 ('Registrum Copiarum') and 1605 ('Register of Copies'). Nonetheless its growing importance for the Company and the trade can be seen in its increasing prominence amongst the Company's records. Prior to 1571 entrances were recorded in a single volume alongside apprenticeships, freedoms, fines, and other financial information; in 1576 a new volume was begun only for entrances and membership; and from 1595 onwards, entrances were maintained as a wholly independent record. Apart from an archival gap between 1571 and 1576, the Register runs without a break from 1557 to the twentieth century.[36]

In 1591 the Company granted the University of Cambridge some very limited rights of entrance, and seven years later it tightened up its procedures so that members could not enter works on behalf of others.[37] The Register was not in any way a public document (only the clerk and the officers had access) but it was well enough known by 1621 for an author to request that entrances of his works be 'quite razed out of your Register' and so be understood 'to bee wholelie and solelie at mine owne disposing, for the reprinting, and in euerie other respect'.[38] The Star Chamber decrees concerning printing in 1637 required that no book should be printed without it being authorized (ie licensed) *and* entered into the 'Registers Booke [*sic*] of the Company of Stationers'; the requirement to register also appears in the 1662 'Printing Act' which reinstated the system of pre-publication licensing following the restoration of the monarchy.[39] In 1684 the Company secured a new but ultimately short-lived royal charter that explicitly gave royal endorsement to what it called 'a *publick Register*' and confirmed that all entrances were duly protected from any unauthorized republication anywhere in the kingdom.[40] The Register also seems to have become a model for protecting publishing rights. Entries were made in the Register in the mid-seventeenth century that recognized the prior rights to 'copy' of works published in Oxford and not previously entered, while records survive of 'copy' assignments made between authors and the University of Oxford in the 1660s and 1670s. The 1662 Printing Act acknowledged that

---

[35] Ibid 195, 238, 730, vol 3, 642, 644–47, 652–54, 656–59, 663; WA Jackson (ed), *Records of the Court of the Stationers' Company 1602 to 1640* (Bibliographical Society 1957) 109.

[36] R Myers, *The Stationers' Company Archive 1554–1984* (St Paul's Bibliographies 1990) 21–30, xxxi. The Register up to 1710 has been transcribed in Arber and Eyre.

[37] WW Greg and E Boswell (eds), *Records of the Court of the Stationers' Company 1576 to 1602 from Register B* (Bibliographical Society 1930) 39–40, 59.

[38] Bodleian Library, MS Bodley 313, ff 66ᵛ–67ʳ.

[39] *A decree of Starre-Chamber concerning Printing* (1637) sig B2ʳ ⁻ᵛ; An Act for Preventing Abuses in Printing 1662, s 3 (13 & 14 Car II c 33). The act echoed many of the same provisions given in the 1637 decree.

[40] *The Charter and Grants of the Company of Stationers of the City of London, Now in Force, Containing a plain and rational Account of the Freemen's Rights and Privileges* (1741) 21–23. The charter was revoked in 1690. Gadd, 'Corporate Identity' (n 27) 49–59.

the universities might maintain their own registers: such files of 'copies' survive at Cambridge and Oxford for 1656–92 and 1672–6 respectively.[41]

From the outset, a 'copy' clearly had commercial value as it protected one's publication from unauthorised reprinting; for a 'vendible Copy' (to adopt the phrase used during Wight's dispute with Barnes), that value was enhanced because of the likely long-term future returns from new editions. Consequently, and especially once 'copies' were considered perpetual, a separate market for 'copies' developed. They could be leased, mortgaged, sub-divided, bought, sold, and bequeathed, and it became possible to develop one's career primarily through the acquisition and management of 'copies': as the 1684 charter noted many of the Company's members 'have great Part of their *Estates* in *Books* and *Copies*'.[42] Some of these transactions are noted in the Register itself and others are recorded in the minutes of the Company's governing body but much, if not most, of the activity relating to copies took place outwith the Company's records. In many cases, the evidence can only be deduced from changes to imprints as books were republished but there is some evidence of formal transfers: such as, for example, the sale of 380 'copies' owned by Richard Bentley in 1698, or the almost 450 'copies' purchased by Jacob Tonson, jnr, in 1707 and 1709.[43]

The Register's authority was thus fundamental to the operation of a system of 'copies' upon which much of the wealth of the trade depended: hence the Register's inclusion in the 1637 decrees, the 1662 Act, the 1684 charter, and, of course, the 1710 Copyright Act. Such citations strengthened the Register's importance, which doubtless explains why the Company were keen to promote it. However, in each case the ultimate sanctioning body was external to the Company: Star Chamber and the High Commission in 1637, Parliament in 1662 and 1710, and the Crown in 1684. Consequently when Star Chamber and the High Commission were abolished by Parliament in 1641 as part of its attempt to roll back the royal prerogative, or when the Printing Act of 1662 lapsed in 1679 and again in 1695, the authority of the Register suffered.[44] A petition of 1643 urging the reinstatement of many of the same provisions that had been included in the 1637 decrees, cast the Register as the guarantor not only of trade stability but also of learning itself:

> [the] propriety of Copies ... [is] a necessary right to Stationers; without which they cannot at all subsist ... . A well regulated propriety of Copies amongst Stationers, makes Printing flourish, and Books more plentifull and cheap; whereas Community ... brings in confusion,

---

[41] Arber (n 34) vol 4, 421; GEB Eyre (ed), *A Transcript of the Registers of the Company of Stationers from 1640–1708 A.D.* (1913–14) vol 1, 41, 221, 256, 264, 269, vol 2, 306; S Gibson and J Johnson (eds), *The First Minute Book of the Delegates of the Oxford University Press 1668–1756* (Clarendon Press 1943) 6, 10; All Souls College, Oxford, MS 238, f 522^r; Oxford University Archives, SP/D/1/6; D McKitterick, *A History of Cambridge University Press* (CUP 1992) vol 1, 261, 307; Oxford University Archives, SEP/P/17b/4b.

[42] *Charter and Grants* (n 40) 22.

[43] G Mandelbrote, 'Richard Bentley's Copies: The Ownership of Copyrights in the late 17th Century' in A Hunt, G Mandelbrote and A Shell (eds), *The Book Trade and its Customers 1450–1900: Historical Essays for Robin Myers* (St Paul's Bibliographies 1997); Bodleian Library, MS Charters Surrey c.1 (84); Folger Shakespeare Library, MS S.a. 160.

[44] The pre-publication licensing system and the restrictions regarding the location and size of the printing trade were also, in effect, swept away by these events.

and many other disorders both to the damage of the State and the Company of Stationers also … this confusion will hinder many men from Printing at all, to the great obstruction of Learning the Printing of Pamphlets is now the utmost ambition of Stationers in *England* … . Community of Copies destroyes that Commerce among Stationers … it's a great discouragement to the Authors of Books also … many Families have now their Lively-hoods by Assignments of Copies, some Orphans and Widows have no other Legacies and Dowries to depend upon … [Thus] the whole Company … has drooped and grown poor.[45]

This explicit linking of the Register with learning and the encouragement of authors in many ways anticipates the wording of the 1710 Act.

The impact of the lapsing of the Printing Act in 1695 on the Register is also very marked. In the days before the lapsing, there was a flurry of entries followed by a sudden decline: within five years, the number of entries being made per year dropped to a mere handful. The Register's uncertain status and future prompted the book trade to explore different ways of protecting their rights. Some returned to seeking royal licences, others established copy-owning 'congers' or partnerships of booksellers 'who put in Joynt Stocks for the Buying and Printing of Copies, and Trading for their common Advantage'.[46] Traditionally, disputes over copy-ownership were arbitrated by the Company's own governing body; however, cases were now also being brought in Chancery and even in the Court of Exchequer.[47] The documented transfers of 'copies' noted above in connection with Bentley and Tonson also suggest a concern that ownership rights might need to be put on a more official legal footing.

5. PRIVILEGES, COPIES, AND 1710

One of the last entries entered prior to the lapsing of the Printing Act in 1695 was made by Benjamin Tooke 'in trust for ye p[ar]tn[e]rs of ye English Stock'.[48] The English Stock was the Company's own joint-stock company, established by privileges granted in 1603 and 1616 for the sole right to print 'psalters[,] psalms[,] prymers, Almanack[es] & other book[es]' in perpetuity.[49] Following a 1583 investigation by the Privy Council into the concentration of printing privileges in the hands of a very small book-trade elite, a number of the privilege holders agreed to yield 'somewhat of that w[hi]ch they

---

[45] *To the High Court of Parliament: The Humble Remonstrance of the Company of Stationers* (1643) sig A3ᵛ–A4ʳ. Parliament duly obliged. CH Firth and RS Rait (eds), *Acts and Ordinances of the Interregnum, 1642–1660* (Professional Books Ltd 1982), vol 1, 184–87.

[46] S Rogers, 'The Uses of Royal Licences for Printing in England, 1695–1760: A Bibliography' (2000) 7th ser, 1 The Library 150; N Hodgson and C Blagden (eds), *The Notebook of Thomas Bennet and Henry Clements (1686–1719)* (Oxford Bibliographical Society 1956) 85–86.

[47] H Tomás Gómez-Arostegui, 'The Untold Story of the First Copyright Suit under the Statute of Anne in 1710' (2010) 25 Berkeley Tech LJ 1247, 1255–56.

[48] Eyre (n 41) vol 3, 457–61.

[49] Greg and Boswell (n 37) 94; Arber (n 34) vol 3, 42–44, 679–82.

have in right for the releife of the poore' of the Stationers' Company.[50] The grants of the early seventeenth century consolidated those privileges but they also ensured that they were now held by the Company – or rather Company members who were shareholders of the Stock – in perpetuity. The English Stock, which endured until the twentieth century, transformed the Company economically, socially, and politically: it improved the Company's finances considerably (allowing it, for example, to move to substantially larger premises in the early seventeenth century) and provided regular work for poorer printers as well as an important source of welfare. However, the combination of regular dividends and a limited number of available shares increased social inequality within the Company itself, with the Company's senior members so closely involved with the oversight of a major printing privilege that the Company's own strategic priorities shifted too. Thus, when the trade's privilege holders were again the subject of criticism in the 1640s, it quickly developed into a struggle over the political accountability of the Company's elite.[51] The protection of the English Stock became an increasing priority for the Company's officers, leading it not only to defend its rights at law on many occasions during the seventeenth and eighteenth centuries but also to make a series of financial agreements with the universities of Oxford and Cambridge, both of which held printing privileges that, in principle, allowed them to print any work. In return for an annual payment (which by the 1760s represented their largest single source of income), the universities agreed not to print works belonging to the English Stock as well certain works belonging to the royal printer and the privilege-holder for law books.[52]

When in the 1690s the first serious political campaign was mounted against the terms of 1662 Printing Act, the English Stock was a particular target for criticism. The 1662 Act had been initially enacted for only two years, but had been regularly renewed; although it lapsed in 1679, it had been re-enacted again in 1685.[53] Its renewal in 1692 took place amid some controversy, with its second reading only passing the Commons by 19 votes, and there was further heated debate in the run-up to the renewal date of 1695, with John Locke himself an instrumental agent in the Act's eventual lapsing.[54]

---

[50] WW Greg (ed), *A Companion to Arber, Being a Calendar of Documents in Edward Arber's Transcript* (Clarendon Press 1967) 18–33, 125, 128, 136–37; Arber (n 34) vol 1, 114–16, 144, vol 2, 786–89.

[51] C Blagden, 'The Stationers' Company in the Civil War Period' (1958) 5th ser, 13 The Library 1.

[52] I Gadd, 'The Press and the London Book Trade' in I Gadd (ed), *The History of Oxford University Press, Volume I: Beginnings to 1780* (OUP 2013).

[53] The 1662 statute (13 & 14 Car 2, c 33) is variously known as the 'Printing Act' or 'Licensing Act'. Renewals: 16 Car 2 c 8; 16 & 17 Car 2 c 7; 17 Car 2 c 4; 1 Jac 2 c 17, s 15; 4 & 5 W & M c 24, s 14. The 1679–85 lapsing coincided with a period of acute political crisis, from the Popish Plot through to the death of Charles II and the accession of James II.

[54] G Kemp and J McElligott (eds), *Censorship and the Press, 1580–1720* (Pickering & Chatto 2009) vol 3, 347; M Treadwell, '1695–1995: Some Tercentenary Thoughts on the Freedoms of the Press' (1996) 7 Harvard Library Bulletin 3; R Astbury, 'The Renewal of the Licensing Act in 1693 and its Lapse in 1695' (1978) 5th ser, 33 The Library 296; M Treadwell, 'The Stationers and the Printing Acts at the end of the Seventeenth Century' in J Barnard, DF McKenzie and M Bell (eds), *The Cambridge History of the Book in Britain: Volume IV 1557–1695* (CUP 2002).

Scholars have for the most part seen the debate in terms of censorship as the Act had perpetuated the system of pre-print licensing instituted back in the early sixteenth century. Much, though, was made at the time of the Act's protection of privileged printing which, critics argued, raised prices and impoverished non-privileged members of the trade.[55] Specific mention was made of the Company's monopoly over classical authors: as Locke remarked, "'tis very absurd & ridiculous yt anyone now living should pretend to have a propriety in or a pow[e]r: to dispose of ye proprietie of any copies or writeings of Authors who lived before printing was known & used in Europe'.[56] The Company recognised that the future of both the Register and the English Stock were at stake. The Company appointed its own committee 'to consult about getting the Act for Printing revived', it drew up its own proposals for presentation to the Commons, and presented a petition urging that the question of 'their Property' be recognized by the proposed new Act. A decision to add *salvo iure cuiuscumque* ('reserving the rights of all others') to all entries in the Stationers' Register in March 1695 suggests that the Company was bracing itself for a change in the legal status of its copies.[57] In mid-April the Company was summoned to present its charters, patents, and court minutes between 1679 and 1682 (the period after the previous lapsing of the Act) as well as the Register itself. By the end of April with the new bill still in committee and the prorogation of Parliament imminent, the Company fretted over its rights to the works covered by the English Stock patents, and it was this that prompted Tooke's entry of all of the Stock's titles into the Register only days before the Act finally lapsed, suggesting that the Company had more faith in the future of Register than the English Stock patent.[58]

The next 15 years were a time of considerable uncertainty for the trade as far as the preservation of their rights to 'copies' were concerned. Neither of the two bills that were considered during 1695 made any mention of the Stationers' Company, its Register, or the English Stock; if anything, the ambition was for the registration of copy-ownership to be swept away entirely.[59] New bills were proposed over the following years, but very few even made it to a second reading. Regular petitions from the Company and senior members of the trade stressed the need to preserve the 'copy' system, while the printers urged that the size of the printing workforce be strictly limited. Debates in Parliament and among pamphleteers focused instead primarily on the question of licensing and press regulation. However, the debate began to be reframed in terms that strikingly echoed the Company's 1643 petition. Daniel Defoe's *An Essay on the Regulation of the Press* (1704), argued that it should be a legal requirement for the names of the author, printer, and publisher to appear on every title

---

[55] Kemp and McElligott (n 54) vol 3, 351–56, 417–24.

[56] Ibid vol 3, 421.

[57] 11 HCJ 200, 228, 288; Stationers' Company, London, Court Book F, ff 214^r, 216^v, 217^v, 218^v. Such caveats appear periodically in the Register from the 1590s onwards: see, for example, Arber (n 34) vol 2, 651, vol 3, 394, vol 4, 207. Their frequency increased between the 1640s and 1670s: between July 1671 and April 1672, for example, they appear against practically every entry. The precise purpose of these caveats has yet to be investigated. Despite the order of March 1695 no caveats are noted after December 1694. Eyre (n 41) vol 3, 449.

[58] Stationers' Company, London, Court Book F, f 221^v; Eyre (n 41) vol 3, 458–61.

[59] J Feather, 'The Book Trade in Politics: The Making of the Copyright Act of 1710' (1980) 8 Publishing History 21.

page: such a practice would not only 'put a Stop to a certain sort of Thieving which is now in full practice in *England* ... viz. some Printers and Booksellers printing copies none of their own' but it would also protect authors and encourage learning. Three years later, 13 senior members of the Company and the book trade petitioned Parliament in similar terms: a statutory system of 'literary property' would benefit the trade, authors, and scholarship.

The resulting bill did not proceed very far but the groundwork it seems was laid. When a new bill was proposed early in 1710 that outlined such a system, the Company moved swiftly to assert its own priorities. A series of trade petitions were presented to Parliament, all of but one of which stressed the importance of preserving the rights to 'copies'; moreover these petitions argued that copy-ownership was underwritten by common law and that 'copies' were perpetual. The bill was duly revised to downplay the rights of authors and to give greater legal weight to the trade's ownership of copies, although instead of perpetual 'copyright', the term for existing works was set at 21 years. The Register was added as the primary mechanism for recording ownership, and the Company was to handle the distribution of deposit copies for all new publications to nine libraries. (This was not a new provision: the idea that copies of every new publication be deposited in major libraries dated back to an agreement between the Company and the Bodleian Library made in 1610, and the procedure had been enshrined in both the 1637 decrees and the 1662 Printing Act, although the 1710 Act increased the number of receiving libraries.)[60] The Company promptly established a committee to consider how to handle these various procedures, and agreed that it and the English Stock should bear the cost of supporting the bill through to enactment.[61]

In many ways, then, the Act of 1710 represented a major success for the Company and the book trade. It placed the Company, its procedures, and above all its Register at the centre of a 'new' system of 'literary property' that, in effect, was a continuation of its existing practices. The Company's English Stock privileges were wholly unaffected. The statute may have stipulated that existing 'copies' could only last for a further 21 years and that the Register should be accessible to outsiders but neither was honoured in practice. Publishers continued to enter titles in much the same way that they had done in previous years. However, although the 'copy' remained fundamental to the economy of the book trade, the practices developed outside of the Company following the lapsing of the Act in 1695 endured. The frequency of entrances in the Register dropped away markedly from 1715 and instead 'copies' were increasingly established, managed, and sold outside the Register. The Act of 1710 may have saved the Stationers' Register but it was no longer as central a record for the book trade as it had been 150 years earlier.

---

[60] Gadd, 'Corporate Identity' (n 27) 155–57.
[61] Feather (n 59) 29–37.

6. The anatomy of copyright law in Scotland before 1710

Alastair J. Mann

1. BEGINNING OF THE END – THE END OF THE BEGINNING

In 1707, when Scotland joined with England in parliamentary union, a partnership was joined both political and economic. Setting aside a few temporary taxation exemptions for Scotland, economic union with England meant a shared currency, common weights and measures and standardised customs and duties, but more significantly, as confirmed in article IV of the Treaty of Union, 'full freedom and intercourse of trade'.[1] Scotland had helped create the largest free trade area in western Christendom. While one of the temporary exemptions agreed for Scotland was from English duties on stamped paper, a brief advantage for the book trade in the north, the regulation of that trade and of copyright was unmentioned; by omission, the *status quo ante* would prevail. Given the depredations of Anglo-Scottish copyright litigation from *Tonson v Walker* in 1739 to the more 'infamous' *Donaldson v Becket* in 1774 perhaps it is as well that such a topic was set aside.[2] Such controversy might have delayed a vital treaty that for many secured religion and security. The Statute of Anne of 1710 was intended, of course, to fill the regulatory void, yet by then that void had become a vacuum with the demise of the Scottish Privy Council in 1708, as well as pressure from an English book trade

---

[1] KM Brown and others, *The Records of the Parliaments of Scotland* ('*RPS*') (University of St Andrews, National Records of Scotland 2008–15), <www.rps.ac.uk> (all following *RPS* references accessed on 15 March 2015); *RPS*, 1706/10/257 'Act ratifying and approving the treaty of union of the two kingdoms of Scotland and England' as approved 16 January 1707.

[2] Alastair J Mann, '"A Mongrel of Early Modern Copyright": Scotland in European Perspective' in Ronan Deazley, Martin Kretschmer and Lionel Bently (eds), *Privilege and Property: Essay on the History of Copyright* (OpenBook Publishers 2010) 65. There are many accounts of this, but for a sharp, recent rendering from a Scottish perspective, see Warren McDougall, 'Copyrights and Scottishness' in Stephen W Brown and Warren McDougall (eds), *The Edinburgh History of the Book in Scotland, volume 2: Enlightenment and Expansion, 1707–1800* (EUP 2012) 23; Warren McDougall, 'Copyright Litigation in the Court of Session, 1738–1749 and the Rise of the Scottish Book Trade' (1988) 5 Transactions Edinburgh Bibliographical Soc'y 2. See also Richard B Sher, 'Corporatism and Consensus in the Late Eighteenth-Century Book Trade: The Edinburgh Booksellers' Society in Comparative Perspective' (1998) 1 Book History 32; Richard S Tompson, 'Scottish Judges and the Birth of British Copyright' (1992) Jur Rev 18; Hector L MacQueen, *Copyright, Competition and Industrial Design* (2nd edn, EUP 1995) 1–6. For English accounts, see John Feather, 'The Publishers and the Pirates: British Copyright Law in Theory and Practise, 1710–1775' (1987) 22 Publishing History 5; John Feather, *A History of British Book Publishing* (2nd edn, Routledge 2006) 76–83; John Feather, *Publishing, Piracy and Politics: An Historical Study of Copyright in Britain* (Mansell 1994) 64–96.

smarting at the opportunism of Scottish books entering the English market. In fact the Scottish Privy Council had enormous significance for the history of copyright in early modern Scotland. Although secured in the Treaty of Union it became the victim of administrative impotence during the brief Jacobite invasion scare of 1708, and also was the target of opposition Scottish politicians who wished to deliver a lethal blow to the patronage network of those in power. Thereafter Scottish copyright traditions were unleashed on perplexed English lawyers and their courts, though ultimately to the benefit of book commerce broadly and of authors who saw the recognition of their rights over those of book trade copyright holders.

2. LEGAL TRADITION

Both the curious transition period from 1707 to 1710 – a 'clumsy book trade engagement and marriage' – and the history of Scottish early modern copyright for the two centuries before, require much more extensive research. Existing historiography remains thin on the ground.[3] Comparisons with England and the emphasis on the eighteenth century 'battle of the booksellers', have unfortunately narrowed the focus, even though Anglo-Scottish comparative study is a necessity. In many respects Scotland's copyright foundations were built from European not 'British' materials and this is exemplified by Scots law. Early training in the law was encouraged by Scottish legislation in the 1490s that declared that the eldest sons of men of means must familiarize themselves with Latin and law, and by the commencement of legal training at Aberdeen's King's College in the sixteenth century. Nevertheless, the tradition was for Scottish students to travel not to England but to the Continent to learn law, in particular to Leiden and Utrecht in Holland. Even after Scotland's first chair in law was introduced at Edinburgh University in 1707, a pattern of post-graduate study overseas was retained. Anglo-Scottish educational interaction had been limited since the thirteenth and fourteenth century Scottish Wars of Independence, and even after general Protestant amity broke out in the sixteenth century, confessional differences were often a barrier to Scots being educated in the southern kingdom. As a result of these cultural dynamics, Scottish lawyers become conversant with the law of Rome and conflated this with Scotland's own legal codes, as confirmed in *Regium Majestatum*, a Glanville-based legal manual in widespread use from the late medieval period, to produce the fundamentals of Scots law.[4]

Three aspects arising from this emphasis are pertinent to the legal and philosophical attitudes to pre-modern Scottish copyright before 1710. Firstly, the influence of Roman

---

[3] For general surveys of Scotland, see Alastair J Mann, *The Scottish Book Trade 1500 to 1720: Print Commerce and Print Control in Early Modern Scotland* (Tuckwell Press 2000) ch 4; Alastair J Mann, 'Scottish Copyright Before the Statute of 1710' (2000) Jur Rev 11; Mann, 'A Mongrel of Early Modern Copyright' (n 2) 51–65; and for quote at 65. The only previous survey is WJ Couper, 'Copyright in Scotland before 1709' (1931) 9 Records of the Glasgow Bibliographical Soc'y 42; but see also, generally, Dr John Lee, *Memorial for the Bible Societies in Scotland* (Edin Bible Soc'y 1824).

[4] *RPS*, A1496/6/4 (13 June 1496).

law gave Scottish jurists a passion for codification. This is seen in a sequence of early modern and modern legal treatises, notably Sir Thomas Craig's *Jus Feudale* (1603), James Dalrymple, Viscount Stair's *Institutions of the Law of Scotland* (1681) and later George Joseph Bell's *Principles of the Law of Scotland* (1829). Secondly, although both Scots law and Roman law accepted the theory of 'incorporeal' rights, as seen in Justinian's *Institutes, 'de rebus incorporalibis'*, such as, for example, in noble titles without necessarily a territorial basis, Scots interpretation appeared to abrogate the concept of 'incorporeal' property in creations or inventions. That is to say, for such 'property' to have a secure legal basis it had to have physical form. Thus an author's manuscript or a printed book was legal property, but not the text or its ideas. In addition, it was only illegal to 'copy' such intellectual or commercial property if a successful application was made to the appropriate licensing authority for a copyright licence or commercial patent. Thirdly, Scots law, in theory at least, was grounded on social law and the application of 'evident utility', which interestingly is a phrase found in article XVIII of the Treaty of Union on 'the laws concerning regulation of trade'. These elements came together in a balancing of public interest and private right which saw limitations placed on the duration and extent of copyright protection in early modern Scotland. In contrast, under English law before 1710, with its less codified, common law and more statute-focused basis, the author created property when he wrote a text, and English common law confirmed perpetual copyright as long as no statute qualified that right.[5]

In Scotland, however, 'reasonableness' was the test through 'evident utility'. There are many cases where 'reasonableness' was the deciding factor in Scottish court judgments over copyright, and more especially before the Privy Council of Scotland. The most well known and striking of such cases arose in 1614 and concerned Andrew Hart (fl. 1589–1621), the great Edinburgh printer-bookseller of the first half of the seventeenth century. This occurred when Hart was at the height of his commercial success. The same year he published John Napier's famous mathematical text *Mirifici Logarithmorum Canonis Descriptio* which was read throughout Europe. Hart not only printed books but was also the largest Scottish book importer before the Restoration of 1660. He had an exotic background as a committed Presbyterian and acted as an English spy before the Union of the Crowns of 1603. In June 1614, and for a considerable sum, Hart purchased from King James VI and I (r. 1567–1625) the exclusive right to print overseas and import books into Scotland. This move led to protests from Hart's co-religionists, the Presbyterian Edinburgh booksellers James Cathkin (fl. 1601–31) and Richard Lawson (fl. 1603–22), and the then king's printer Thomas Finlason (fl. 1602–27). In a subsequent judgment on the matter, the Privy Council ruled against Hart in spite of the fact that he came to the hearing armed with a letter from the king demanding the right be confirmed 'without onye delay or impediment'. The council's judgment is a statement about liberty of trade, of executive independence from Crown action and of a late renaissance commitment to literate society:

---

[5] *RPS*, 1706/10/257; JB Moyle (trs), *The Institutes of Justinian* (Clarendon Press 1913) bk II, 2, 'Of incorporeal things'; Mann, *Scottish Book Trade* (n 3) 96–7; Mann, 'Scottish Copyright' (n 3) 13; MacQueen, *Copyright, Competition and Industrial Design* (n 2) 1–7.

The freedom, liberty and privilege of printing, importing and selling of all such books and volumes, which are allowed and not forbidden, ought to be free to all His Majesty's subjects and not conferred and given to any one person without great hurt and prejudice to the country, because every such private freedom, liberty and privilege is not only a monopoly of evil consequence and example, but will give occasion to alter and raise, heighten and change the prices of all books and volumes at the appetite and discretion of the person and persons in whose favour the privilege shall happen to be conferred, and for this reason the said Lords ordain the gift and privilege purchased by the said Andrew Hart from the king to be halted, and in no way to be passed or expedited.[6]

The rejection of this privilege clearly illustrates executive views on the licensing of the press and copyright, the council being the very agency that granted copyright in Scotland. In spite of some further Crown-supported pressure to secure restrictive monopolies for the post of Scottish king's printer in the 1670s, this philosophy would be reflected in the views of the Scottish Parliament in the 1670s and 1680s and also the Scottish courts.

3. 'PARTICULAR' COPYRIGHTS: ENGLAND AND SCOTLAND

Given the political instability of the age, it is obvious that for the governments of early modern England and Scotland the main purpose of regulation was censorship not copyright. However, frequently these different pillars of print control came together. In England, between 1566 and 1695, most books had to be licensed jointly by a government licenser with a warden of the Stationers' Company (established by royal charter in 1557) before they could be published; they were then recorded in the Stationers' Register, as 'entered for ... copy' of the particular book. The owner of the right to 'copy' was always the printer or bookseller who was entering the book for publication and the author was seldom even mentioned.[7] In spite of English book traders and the Stationers' Company setting up a Society of Stationers in Edinburgh in the late 1630s, a venture disrupted by the Scottish Covenanting rebellion and English Civil War and abandoned in the 1660s, and also incomplete plans by the Scottish king's printer Andrew Anderson to set up an exclusive Edinburgh society in the early 1670s,

---

[6] John Hill Brown and others (eds), *Register of the Privy Council of Scotland, 1545–1691* ('*RPCS*') (Scottish Record Office 1877–1933) i, 10, 827–28; AJ Mann, 'Hart, Andro (*b.* in or before 1566, *d.* 1621)', *Oxford Dictionary of National Biography* (OUP 2004–15); online edn, Jan 2008 <http://www.oxforddnb.com/view/article/12470> accessed 15 March 2015. Text modernised by the author.

[7] Feather, *History of British Book Publishing* (n 2) 21; Lyman Ray Patterson, *Copyright in Historical Perspective* (Vanderbilt UP 1968) 78–113; Mark Rose, *Authors and Owners: The Invention of Copyright* (HUP 1993) 1–12; Alastair J Mann, '"Some Property is Theft": Copyright Law and Illegal Activity in Early Modern Scotland' in Robin Myers, Michael Harris and Giles Mandelbrote (eds), *Against the Law: Crime, Sharp Practice and the Control of Print* (Oak Knoll Press and British Library 2004) 31–32. The first formal use of 'copy right' does not appear in the Company records until 1678, when it appeared in one of the Company's bylaws that prohibited members from suing in the regular courts for copyright infringement. *The Orders, Rules, and Ordinances, Ordained, Devised, and Made by the ... Stationers* (1692) 1, 20 (3 Jan 1677/8).

no Scottish equivalent of the London Stationers' Company was ever established in the Scottish capital.[8] This was a key difference in the regulation of the press and of the system of copyright registration and licensing. Both the smaller scale of the Scottish press and the medieval tradition of burghs having equal status and rights to develop commerce independently prevented the permanent formation of a centralising society that might have acted as an intermediary between the Crown and copyright holders.

Scotland's first statute that forbade unlicensed printing was to arrive in early 1552, as Protestant ideas and printings began to threaten the established order of the Church of Rome. The act 'Anent printaris' therefore prescribed that the 'ordinarie', that is the local bishop, took responsibility for licensing.[9] This was a typical legislative measure and the most common method of preventive or *a priori* censorship in early modern Europe, although clearly an author, printer or publisher of seditious material was unlikely to submit his manuscript for the censor's approval. It is for this reason that licensing was far more significant to the 'legitimate' press and became a systemic support for copyright regulation.

From the Scottish Reformation of 1560, secular crown officials and councillors rather than clergy took on the role of censors, where necessary, and also for licensing and so copyright. In sixteenth and seventeenth century Scotland, therefore, copyrights for printings sprung directly from patents granted by the Crown and continued so throughout the period, when in England this practice declined, though never entirely, as registration with the Stationers' Company offered a secure means of establishing copyright protection. Meanwhile, the typical Scottish licensee was granted the 'power', 'licence', 'liberty' or 'privilege' to 'print, reprint, vend, sell and import' but not specifically 'to copy'.[10] Individual Scottish book licences granted by the Crown, or its representatives, usually the Privy Council, were for a limited number of years, either a specific period or the lifetime of the licence holder. Essentially like France, Spain and the Low Countries there was no Scottish notion of perpetual copyright; on the other hand, the Stationers' Company, English booksellers and even some English authors continued to claim perpetual copyright until it was quashed in the House of Lords in 1774.

William Lily's Grammar, written in 1513 and first published in final form in 1542, is an extreme example of English perpetual copyright. It became a prescribed text in English schools for the next 200 years and as late as the early eighteenth century Thomas Longman acquired the profitable patent. The first Scottish 'particular' copyright is of similar vintage and stemmed from the patent granted to the printer Thomas Davidson (fl.c.1532–42) in 1541 to print for six years the Acts of the Scottish Parliament. This was followed in 1559 by the remarkable 11-volume, and ten-year multi-title patent granted to the author and grammarian William Niddrie. This was a bold attempt at a school-book publishing programme which did not survive the hiatus of the Scottish Reformation the following year. Nevertheless, these copyrights confirm

---

[8] *RPCS*, iii, 3, 423–25; Mann, *Scottish Book Trade* (n 3) 117.
[9] *RPS*, A1552/2/26 (February 1551/2).
[10] Scottish patents for books used some or all of the terms 'power', 'licence', 'liberty' or 'privilege' with some additional variations such as 'sole liberty'. 'Privilege' and 'licence' were the most common.

that from the onset Scottish authors were considered on a par with any other copyright holders in Scotland.[11] Also, the contrast between Niddrie (term limited) and Lily (endlessly transferrable and so unlimited) could not be starker and the test of 'reasonableness' hangs in the air.

That the English book trade got away with monopolistic tendencies may seem a surprise given the resentments that monopolies created in the late sixteenth and early seventeenth centuries. This perhaps signifies the special status sometimes attributed to intellectual property: it also had some impact on the Scottish book trade. Two types of copyright existed in early modern England, the 'printing patent', that is those copyrights granted by the sovereign, and after 1557 the Stationers' copyright; essentially the former public and the latter private. Taking the second of these first, from the 1580s onwards Stationer's guild members began a process of transfer and purchase of copyrights which facilitated their accumulation in the hands of a small group of wealthy copy holders. This process was intensified after the Union of the Crowns in 1603 as James VI and I responded to parliamentary anxiety over monopolies by inadvertently making them worse as far as the English book trade was concerned. James recalled and gifted to the Stationers' Company 'for the benefit of the pouer of the same' the valuable patents already granted to John and Richard Day (for primers and psalters) and to James Roberts and Richard Watkins (for almanacs and prognostications) and these patents became the legal basis for the 'English Stock', as it was known, and reenergised the frantic buying and selling of copies within the Company, concentrating patents into even fewer hands, in a narrowing 'collective monopoly' or oligarchy. Some years after, fear over monopoly trading culminated in the English Statute of Monopolies of 1624 where the Westminster Parliament limited to fixed periods patents in industrial processes and inventions. Books were excluded and of course the statute did not apply in Scotland. There, however, the terms of industrial patents and copyrights in any case shadowed each other, even though monopolies were also subjected to greater scrutiny in this period. With King James's approval the Scottish Privy Council set up a commission of grievances over monopolies in 1623, and later that year when a Standing Commission of Manufactories was established to monitor such monopolies, copyrights were not considered. In 1641 the Scottish Parliament halted some major monopolies, including those for tobacco, leather, pearling and armoury 'because of the great hurt inflated on the lieges by monopolies, all patents purchased for the benefit of particular persons in prejudice of the public', but again, like England, books were not on the agenda.[12] The entire process of monopoly review and copyright trading in the Stationers' Company emphasised the increasingly perpetual nature of their copyrights compared to the fixed periods for industrial processes in both kingdoms and of copyrights in Scotland. If these nations'

---

[11] *Registrum Secreti Sigilli regum Scotorum: Register of the Privy Seal of Scotland* (printed series) ('*RSS*') (HM General Register House, 1908–82); *RSS*, ii, 653, no 4335; *RSS*, v, pt 1, 143–44, no 658; Mann, 'Copyright Law and Illegal Activity' (n 7) 32; Feather, *History of British Book Publishing* (n 2) 21.

[12] *RPCS*, i, 13, 219–22, 299–302, 240; *RPS*, 1641/8/192; Mann, 'Copyright Law and Illegal Activity' (n 7) 34.

copyright systems were fairly similar in the mid-sixteenth century, by 1600 they were drifting further apart.

The initial similarity between these copyright regimes needs some emphasis, however. Licences granted by the English Crown, or the 'printing patent' continued throughout the early modern period in parallel with the Stationers' copyright. The first of these was granted by Henry VIII to John Rastell in 1512 for printing Thomas Linacre's Latin grammar *Progymnasmata grammatices vulgaria* (c.1515), a text actually in English. In Scotland meanwhile, the first royal patent was that given by King James IV (r.1488–1513) to Scotland's first printers Walter Chepman and Andro Myllar in 1507. The chief reason for granting this patent was to print a new national breviary, the *Breviarium Aberdonense* (1510), compiled by William Elphinstone, bishop of Aberdeen and founder of King's College Aberdeen. This text was prescribed to replace 'Sarum use', the Salisbury breviary which was the standard liturgy to this point. The patent was though a general gift listing the right to print statutes, histories and chronicles as well as the breviary, and not strictly a copyright for a single act or acts of publication, unlike Davidson's of 1541 or Niddrie's of 1559. Nevertheless, it is important to note that these two Scottish types correspond to English equivalents, the Chepman and Myllar licence – 'general', for life and containing generic classes of books, and the Davidson variety – 'particular' and limited in time, in England typically to licences of seven to ten years and in Scotland to six to ten years but gravitating towards a standard period of 19 years.[13]

Thus, before the Stationers' Company was well established the practicalities of copyright in England and Scotland were not too dissimilar. Indeed, such was the similarity that various English printers had since the 1580s operated in Edinburgh out of commercial opportunism or through political exile. In the reign of Charles I (r.1625–49) the Stationers of London reached deep into Scotland's public copyright regime. The so-called 'Scotch Patent', as it was known in London, was acquired as part of Miles Flesher's Stationers' Company monopoly which he built up from 1617 to 1638. This included a share in the office of Scottish royal printer which he obtained in 1632 with his partner Robert Young, the printer of the controversial Prayer Book which sparked the Covenanting rebellion against King Charles. Ironically, Flesher had his dividend suspended by the Stationers in 1634 as a punishment for importing into England psalms produced at his Edinburgh press.[14] These Englishmen lingered in Edinburgh until the late 1660s by which time the impracticality of controlling a press

---

[13] Patterson, *Copyright* (n 7) 86–87; *RSS*, i, 223 no 1546; Robert Dickson and John Philip Edmond, *Annals of Scottish Printing* (MacMillan and Bowes 1890) 7–8; National Records of Scotland ('NRS'), Privy Seal Manuscript Registers ('PS') PS.1.3, 129; *RSS*, 2, p 653, no 4335; Peter WM Blayney, *The Stationers' Company and the Printers of London* (CUP 2013) vol 1, 166–67.

[14] Cyprian Blagden, *The Stationers Company, 1403–1959* (George Allen & Unwin 1960) 138–45; Mann, *Scottish Book Trade* (n 3) 117. For reflections on the wide historiography on the Stationers' Company, see Robin Myers and Michael Harris (eds), *The Stationers' Company and the Book Trade, 1550–1990* (St Pauls 1997); Robin Myers, *The Stationers' Company Archive: An Account of the Records, 1554–1984* (St Pauls 1990) xv–xvi; Robin Myers (ed), *The Stationers' Company: A History of the Later Years, 1800–2000* (Worshipful Company of Stationers and Newspaper Makers 2001) 247–48; Deazley, *Privilege and Property* (n 2) 14.

from the distance of London had them withdraw and a new king's printer patent, with what a contemporary described as 'exorbitant clauses', was then awarded to the Glasgow printer Andrew Anderson in 1671.[15]

4. REGULATION AND DEVOLUTION

Anderson's general patent was given under Scotland's Great Seal in 1671 and ratified by the Scottish Parliament in 1672, which suggests a fragmented system of regulation. In fact senior government appointments and noble titles were confirmed through both these mechanisms conflating royal wishes with political and public affirmation. Confirmation of particular copyrights was another matter entirely, however. Scottish copyright from 1507 to 1710 depended on government copyright underpinned by royal prerogative. This was the case whether licences were granted by the monarch or his or her representatives, 'the king in council' or the 'king in parliament', or passing the great or privy seals. The Privy Council was the main licensing authority in the period, although there were changes in the systems of regulation. Until about 1610 copyright licences for individual books were confirmed by the royal Privy Seal, but after then and particularly from the 1660s, publishing privileges were confirmed by act of Privy Council. Thus the Privy Seal confirmed in 1599 to the bookbinder John Gibson a seven-year licence to sell an edition of the psalms printed in Middelburg, and in 1602 that the sons of the printer Robert Smyth, Robert and David, were granted 25-year licences to print a range of texts, including 'Catechisms, the plane donat ... the celect and familiar epissillis of Cecero ... the second Rudiments of Dunber, [and] the psalmes of Buchanane'.[16] Subsequently, the likes of the authors David Wedderburne and Andrew Brown, for respectively a 25-year licence for a new grammar in 1632 and a 19-year licence for Brown's medical volume *A Vindicatorie Schedule about the New Cure of Feavers* in 1691, were derived from acts of council. This is not about the king residing in London, and in any case there are exceptions to the chronology. After 1610 or so the Privy Seal was still employed when the monarch had a personal interest in the copyright, as in the 21-year privilege granted for the catechism *God and the King* in 1616, a pet project of King James given its focus on obedience and royal prerogative, and the 31-year licence to Sir William Alexander (c.1567–1640) to publish in 1627 an 'official' edition of *The Psalms of David* which Alexander translated with the help of King James. Later in the century, the ten-year licence granted to the geographer-royal Robert Sibbald (1641–1722) in 1682 for his *Scotia Antiqua* and *Scotia Moderna*, which was subsequently published in one volume entitled *Scotia Illustrata* in 1684, was confirmed via the Privy Seal.[17] In the seventeenth century, however, ordinary book patents followed other types of patent in the general administrative shift as a patent in brewing in 1594 was licensed under the Privy Seal whereas that in glass-making in

---

[15] John Lauder of Fountainhall, *The Decisions of the Lords of Council and Session from June 6th 1678 to July 30th 1712* (Hamilton and Balfour 1759–61) vol 1, 205.

[16] NRS, PS.1.71, f 451; PS.1.73, f 8.

[17] *RPCS*, ii, 4, 500–01; iii, 16, 443–4; NRS, PS.1.85, 254r–247v; PS.1.100, f 305; PS.3.3, ff 450–51; *RPCS*, iii, 38, 423.

1662 was under act of Privy Council.[18] This was yet another example of Scottish licensers seeing books as commercial properties to be handled like any other.

Nevertheless, an evolving sense of literary property was also becoming evident and in a manner parallel with the book markets of England and of Holland. Copyright began to be seen more as personal property rather than a gift from the Crown. This is seen in the surviving registers of the Privy Council which from the 1670s reveal that almost all book licences were enacted and recorded in decreta registers (private business) with only national publishing concerns, such as Wedderburne's new national grammar in 1632, the winner of a remarkable national 'battle of the grammars' competition, being considered public business for recording in the Privy Council's acta registers. After a spell of elite recording in acta in the Restoration period, such as the licence granted to the partners Swinton, Glen and Brown to print in three simultaneous printings *The Law and Customs of Scotland in Matters Criminal* (1678) by the Lord Advocate Sir George Mackenzie of Rosehaugh (1636–91), when we reach the 1690s all copyrights are recorded in decreta.[19] Commercial exploitation and literary property come together in what was now accepted as a private right.

This process of private and disposable printed property was further emphasised during the seventeenth century as copy holding was traded in terms not too dissimilar to London. One of the best examples of this behaviour is found in the career of Thomas Finlason, the former Dundee merchant and the last of the royal printers in Edinburgh to be gifted the position for life. Interestingly before he acquired the royal patent in 1612, and succeeded Robert Charteris (fl.1600–10), Finlason set about from 1602 to 1611 buying up the copyrights of other Edinburgh printers. These included 16 copyrights from Robert Smyth (fl. 1582–1602), purchasing his privileges, stock and equipment from Smyth's widow in October 1602 and setting up his press; nine in 1606 from the son of John Gibson (fl. 1580–1600), royal bookbinder, some of which originally came into the hands of Alexander Arbuthnet (fl. 1575–85), co-printer of Scotland's first domestic Bible, in the late 1570s, then passed to George Young, archdeacon of St Andrews in 1585, then to the bookseller Gilbert Masterton (fl.1587–99) to 1587, and finally to be acquired by Gibson in 1589. It seems at each stage in the chain the copyrights increased in value. Finlason then registered some of his own copyrights in 1611. By the time he became king's printer he owned some of the most profitable copyrights in early modern Scotland, including *Dunbar's Rudiments*, George Buchanan's *Psalms*, 'Blind Hary's' *The Wallace* and *The Works of Sir David Lindsay*, along with a range of classical and vernacular works. In Scottish terms this was an impressive accumulation of copyrights and a clear competitive advantage even before he became king's printer. He also acquired the privileges and materials of the Englishman Robert Waldegrave (fl. 1590–1604), the former 'Martin Mar-prelate' puritan printer who fled England to Scottish exile, became printer to James VI, produced the king's own works, and followed him to London in 1603 only to die soon

---

[18] For a more extended list, see *RSS*, viii, 70, no 414 (coal-mine pumps); PS.1.66, ff 107ᵛ–108ʳ (brewing); *RPCS*, i, 12, 106 (soap-making); iii, 1, 155 (glass-making).

[19] *RPCS,* ii, 4, 168–69 and 500–01; *RPCS*, iii, 5, 218–19; Mann, 'Scottish Copyright' (n 3) 15.

after. Finlason acquired Waldegrave's stock and copyrights from his grieving widow, a common enough event in the career of this remarkable commercial vulture.[20]

Given that the main copyright agency in Scotland was the Crown, working through its executive arm the Privy Council, we have the impression of a highly centralised copyright regime. Nevertheless, there were other mechanisms through which copyright could be confirmed. Copyright was sometimes devolved to local agencies and in a manner not too dissimilar to the Stationers' Company. Edinburgh, or a society of its major book traders, never gained a regulatory supremacy over the remainder of the kingdom, as did London of course, and although printing did not commence in Aberdeen, Glasgow and Dundee until 1622, 1638 and 1703 respectively, no centralised limitation was placed on the proliferation of presses. Local town councils were authorised, as with any other commercial activity, to license and manage their local presses.[21] These burgesses took responsibility to employ town printers, to supervise the appointment of college printers, not always the same as the former, and to license and censor the local press output. This local press control was occasionally ratified by the government, and at times by a variety of supplementary authorities. In 1634, for example, Charles I confirmed the power of the masters of the Old College of Aberdeen to censor the output of the local press, and 50 years later the Privy Council ruled that the Aberdeen, Glasgow and Edinburgh presses could not operate without license 'from the Bishop of the dioces for any thing in divinitie' and without reference to the appropriate medical, legal and, if necessary Privy Council authorities, for specific genre. These were measures driven as much by censorship as by copyright and qualitative considerations. Copyright was also a factor, however. After the Restoration the 'printing burghs' gave local copyright protection for a variety of burgh almanacs, diurnals, newssheets and newspapers, such as Aberdeen Town Council's licensing and protection of the Aberdeen almanac from the 1660s.[22]

'Local copyright', therefore, existed on a private basis by authority of the magistrates of burgh corporations. Often this merely represented a licence to print rather than a specific term, yet it was copyright nevertheless. Many local printings were in any case either ephemeral or of insufficient value to necessitate a proprietary approach. Almanacs and newspapers were, though, considered the most valuable properties,

---

[20] Harry G Aldis, 'Thomas Finlason and his Press. With a Handlist of his Books' *Papers of the Edinburgh Bibliographical Society, 1890–95* (1896) vol 1, no 20. To trace this complex series of acquisitions see the patents listed in Mann, *Scottish Book Trade* (n 3) 235–43. For a summary of Waldegrave's career, see KS van Eerde, 'Robert Waldegrave: The Printer as Agent and Link Between Sixteenth-Century England and Scotland' (1981) 34(1) Renaissance Quarterly 40; Alastair J Mann, 'Waldegrave, Robert (*c*.1554–1603/4)', *ODNB*, <http://www.oxforddnb.com/view/article/28441> accessed 18 March 2015, and a forthcoming detailed study by Rebecca Emmett based on 'Networks of print, patronage and religion in England and Scotland, 1580–1604: the career of Robert Waldegrave', PhD, Plymouth, 2013.

[21] For the establishing of these burgh presses, see Mann, *Scottish Book Trade* (n 3) 7–12.

[22] John Stuart (ed), *Extracts from the Records of the Burgh of Aberdeen* ('*ABR*') (Scottish Burgh Record Soc'y 1871–2) vol 1, 245–46; JP Edmond, *The Aberdeen Printers, 1620 to 1736* (J & JP Edmond & Spark 1884–86) xiv, xxxi; J MacLehose, *The Glasgow University Press, 1638–1931* (MacLehose 1931) 61; Mann, *Scottish Book Trade* (n 3) 102–03.

especially from the Restoration. The Privy Council granted licences for local newssheets or diurnals, as well as newspapers, such as the patent for a weekly diurnal awarded to the Edinburgh news editor and postmaster Robert Mein in 1661, and that to the news publisher James Donaldson for the *Edinburgh Gazette* in 1699, Scotland's first regular newspaper with some longevity. Nevertheless, local licensing in this field could arise when the central authorities were 'distracted' or slow to respond. In 1657, for example, during the licensing uncertainties of the Cromwellian period, Aberdeen council licensed the town printer John Forbes to produce a weekly diurnal 'for the use of the inhabitants'. Also, in the early eighteenth century the Edinburgh town council found it necessary to license newspapers during the two-year hiatus between 1708 and 1710, including the *Scots Postman* to David Fearn (1709) and the *Edinburgh Courant* to the ubiquitous English propagandist Daniel Defoe (1710).[23]

Of even greater commercial value than newspapers, before the *Edinburgh Gazette* and those that followed on, were the burgh almanacs, printed annually but to very large print runs of up to 50,000. The magistrates of Edinburgh, Glasgow and Aberdeen each licensed burgh printers to produce their respective almanacs and took considerable steps to protect the local monopoly and rights beyond the city boundaries. In October 1667 the chapman Alexander Gray was found to be selling 'alien' almanacs in Aberdeen. When the burgh printer, John Forbes, the elder (fl. 1656–75), protested over this the council took action to safeguard the 'Aberdeen almanac' within the burgh, censuring Gray and prohibiting the sale of all except the Forbes edition within the burgh. Also, in November 1684, the Edinburgh magistrates took action to protect from counterfeit editions the Edinburgh almanac written by the mathematician James Paterson.[24]

The one body not yet considered that occasionally granted a copyright was the Scottish Parliament itself. As with the government on a day-to-day basis, it mostly regulated censorship providing a legislative framework for censors, yet it also ratified the general gifts to king's printers, and authorised and licensed the more prestigious or national publishing activity. This included prescribed national publications such as the Directory of Public Worship introduced by the Covenanters in 1645 and even prestigious legal texts as in 1633, when Parliament, in the presence of Charles I, agreed that Robert Craig, son to jurist Sir Thomas Craig (1538–1606), be licensed for 21 years to print in three volumes his father's great treatise on Scottish land law *Jus Feudale*. A committee appointed to oversee the printing was headed by Charles I's Lord Advocate, Thomas Hope of Craighall (c.1586–1643), himself a significant published jurist. This publishing venture was of long duration and the first printing did not appear until the

---

[23] *RPCS*, iii, 1, 115; NRS, Manuscript Privy Council Registers, PC.2, 28, ff 366ʳ–366ᵛ; *ABR*, 2, 165–66 (29 July 1657); JD Marwick, M Wood and H Armet (eds), *Extracts from the Records of the Burgh of Edinburgh* ('*EBR*') (1573–1718) (Oliver and Boyd 1867–1967) vol 13, 183 (1 February 1710); Couper, 'Copyright in Scotland before 1709' (n 3) 46.

[24] Aberdeen Council Records ('ACR') 55, ff 66–67; *EBR*, xi, 128; Edmond, *Aberdeen Printers* (n 22) xlv (30 October 1667). For an excellent summary of Scottish almanacs, see William R McDonald, 'Scottish Seventeenth-Century Almanacs' (1966) 4 The Bibliotheck 257.

Edinburgh edition of 1655.[25] Until then Craig's book circulated in numerous manuscript copies showing that to the legal profession manuscript circulation was of great significance well into the Restoration period. No evidence has yet been found of a debate over manuscript copyright.

The London Stationers' Company is remarkable for its record keeping but the same cannot be said of the recording of copyrights in Scotland. Historians have to dig deep into the many volumes of state and local records. Nevertheless, there is evidence that a procedure of maintaining a register of patented books occurred sporadically, even though such registers remain lost to us. In July 1574, during the regency of James Douglas, earl of Morton, when James VI was eight years old and at a time when Scotland's press output was small, an act of Privy Council was passed charging that no book should be printed without license of the chancellor and commissioners to be chosen by the Privy Council. It was also agreed:

> that ther be a register keippit be the Secretar, or his deput, of the licences, and privilegeis to be granted for eschewing of confusion, and that the libertie of the prenting of ane thing be not given to twa Personis at anis.[26]

Over a century later when in 1695 a committee of the Privy Council was considering means to better control and regulate the printing and sale of books, it was ordained that each bookseller of Edinburgh should be compelled to deliver up for approval by the Council exact catalogues of stock to be sold. The clerks of the Council were ordered to keep a list of approved booksellers and their stock.[27] Many of these booksellers would also have been the major copy holders of the time, but again no register of book traders and their stocks has been found. We might ask how such administrative tasks could have been carried out without some form of register and the circumstantial evidence for its existence is compelling.

5. AN ANATOMY OF 'PARTICULAR' COPY PATENTS

In early modern Scotland, copyright patents were normally granted in response to applications from potential licensees and generally these requests came in the form of petitions. To begin with these petitions addressed one of the most fundamental aspects of copyright protection, the term. Other factors such as the scope and width of the right granted and the penalties and compensations for breaches were also of huge significance. As noted above, English copyright tended to extend for seven to ten years under the printing patent, and in perpetuity for those rights registered with the Stationers' Company. Throughout the period French, German and Italian publishers were often granted short licences of less than five years' duration, France lengthening to ten years in 1700, although the relevant authorities were generally prepared to extend privileges

---

[25] *RPS*, 1645/1/65 (6 February 1645); *RPS*, 1633/6/65 (28 June 1633); Mann, *Scottish Book Trade* (n 3) 50; James Maidment (ed), *States Papers and Miscellaneous Correspondence of Thomas Earl of Melrose* (Abbotsford Club 1837) vol 1, 43–44 and 84–85.
[26] *RPCS*, i, 2, 387; Couper, 'Copyright in Scotland before 1709' (n 3) 57.
[27] NRS, PC.1.51, ff 20, 28.

after rights expired. Meanwhile, Dutch copyright tended to be for longer periods of 15–25 years. In Scotland, by 1670, the standard term of copyright for 'particular' works, whether granted to an author, printer, or licensee, was 19 years, a term closer to Dutch than English or French norms.[28] The reasons for this specific duration are unclear. The granting of gifts, rights and patents for the period of 19 years goes back to at least the 1580s. There are many examples: under the Privy Seal we find tacks (leases) granted in 1583, appointments to Crown offices in 1588, and a monopoly for paper making in 1590, all for 19 years. Commercial patents for processes and inventions were actually more commonly 21 years from 1600 to 1660, but the Scottish Parliament's 1661 Act for Erecting of Manufactories provided 19 years of tax exemptions, and certainly by the 1690s 19-year patents were the norm, including a curious grant in 1699 to James Donaldson, editor of the *Edinburgh Gazette*, for a brass block process for printing burial letters.[29] Indeed, in spite of the fact that book copyright terms could extend from as little as six years to the 31 years granted to Sir William Alexander for the Psalms in 1627, a consistent and logical approach was taken to the terms granted depending on the circumstances of publication. Reprints, perceived as inferior 'intellectual property', were granted shorter copyright durations. The standard term for reprints was 11 years from the 1670s. The Edinburgh printers George Swintoun and James Glen were granted 11-year licences in 1617 to reprint William Guthrie's popular *Christian Interest* and the many sermons of the minister Andrew Gray. Fully revised editions received a full-term copyright, however, as with terms given to the grammarian James Kirkwood for the new editions of his grammar and vocabulary published in the 1690s.[30]

For specific reason, some new titles also became subject to reduced terms of copyright. Before the 1590s the government awarded short licences to printers such as Robert Lekpreuik (fl. 1561–74) and Alexander Arbuthnet (fl. 1575–85) for fear that important scripture and liturgical printing would not be carried out. The 20-year licence given to Lekpreuik in 1568 for printing the Geneva Bible, a task he never began, was a salutary warning of the dangers of granting long licences that produced no results, and thereafter short licences of seven or ten years were given for printing Bibles, psalms, and catechisms, notwithstanding the generic rights of the king's printer.[31] Shorter licences were also granted for some works of public utility, such as the ten-year copyright awarded in 1624 to the author and Edinburgh burgess Alexander Hunter for his *Treatise on measurement*, a guide to agriculture and commerce described in the patent as 'for the benefit of the haill realme', and five-year licence to the printer John Reid to publish Thomas Livingstone's guide to military discipline *Exercise of the*

---

[28] Lucien Febvre and Henri-Jean Martin, *The Coming of the Book: The Impact of Printing, 1450–1800* (David Gerard tr, Geoffrey Nowell-Smith and David Wootton eds, NLB 1976) 241; Elizabeth Armstrong, *Before Copyright, The French Book-Privilege System, 1498–1526* (CUP 1990) 16–17; PG Hoftijzer, *Engelse boekverkopers bij de beurs: De geschiedenis van de Amsterdamse boekhandels Bruyning en Swart*, (APA-Holland University Press 1987) 108.

[29] *RSS*, viii, 257–58, no 1577 and 379–80, no 2204; NRS, PS.1.57, f 77; PS.1.61, f 84ᵛ; PS.1.63, f 103ᵛ; PC.2.27, ff 201ʳ–202ʳ; *RPS*, 1661/1/344.

[30] NRS, PS.1,100, 305; *RPCS*, iii, 3, 306; *RPCS*, iii, 4, 292 and 5, 268; NAS, PC.2, 26, f 47ᵛ. Mann, *Scottish Book Trade* (n 3) 104–14.

[31] *RSS*, vi, 53, no 230; *RSS*, vii, 333–4.

foot ... and exercise of the Dragoons in 1693.[32] This level of public concern did not stretch to school books as seen in the copyright for the prescribed national grammars of Alexander Hume (1611) and David Wedderburne (1632) with terms of 20 and 21 years respectively. Translations were often subject to shorter licences, such as Sir James Turner's *Historicall and Politicall Observations on the War with Hungary*, licensed for ten years in 1669. Translations appear to have had less value as literary property. As for the more ephemeral works, copyright for which was rarely worth seeking, the briefest of licences could follow. Such was the case in 1696 when George Mosman (fl. 1685–1707), printer to the General Assembly of the Church of Scotland, was granted by the Privy Council a one-year licence to the sensational *A true relation of an apparitioune*, an account by Alexander Telfer of the haunting of a house in Kirkcudbright.[33]

Some aspects of copyright protection, in terminology and breadth of right, remained virtually unchanged throughout the period. One of the first 'particularised' or private copyrights, that given to William Niddrie in 1559, granted him and 'his factouris and assignais, to have onlie the prenting of the saidis volumes' and that no subjects, printers and booksellers 'should tak upoun hand to prent, sell, caus be prentit or sald [them] within this realm'. In one respect the terms of Niddrie's copyright are unique in Scottish publishing history. During the licence of ten years, copyright was assured for all other volumes 'that it sal happin him be author or sett furth during the said space', a rather open-ended arrangement explained by the fact that his books represented an official and agreed curriculum. In other respects, however, the terminology is as familiar by 1700, with some evolutionary developments. Thomas Bassandyne (fl. c.1564–77) and Arbuthnet's Bible licence of 1576 is the first to clearly prohibit other book traders from importing competing editions.[34] Subsequently, such protection became a standard addition to the discharge to print, reprint, vend or sell, regardless of the likelihood of foreign competition. Bibles at least always offered that possibility from the presses of Holland and England after the Reformation. Meanwhile, there is no evidence that export rights were ever requested or granted in any copyright.

The multi-title, 11-book patent granted to the Edinburgh printer Robert Smyth in 1599 is the first to indicate monitoring and searching options for a licensee. Yet the 1627 patent awarded to Sir William Alexander for the new Metric Psalms provided a more impressive list of supervisory and policing powers. As an influential courtier, co-author with the late King James and by then also Secretary of State, Alexander was given the right, if contraveners were found, 'to sell, bartar and dispose thairvpoune' and to confiscate 'haill workis, tooles and instruments' as well as the offending books. Sheriffs, justices of the peace, bailiffs and constables were to assist him in the policing effort. Smyth's powers were paltry in comparison.[35] The most comprehensive protections were given to copyright on official business. Nonetheless, it was not until the great 41-year monopoly granted to Andrew Anderson in 1671, on his appointment as

---

[32] *RPCS*, i, 13, 418–19; NRS, PC.2.24, ff 244^v–245^r.
[33] *RPCS*, i, 9, 275; *RPCS*, ii, 4, 500–01; *RPCS*, iii, 2, 602, 593; NRS, PC.2.26, ff 90^v–91^r.
[34] *RSS*, v, pt 1, 143–44; *RSS*, vii, 12, 94, no 642; NRS, PS.1, 43, f 103^r.
[35] NRS, PS.1.71, 86; PS.1.100, 305. For a list of the titles in Smyth's patents, see Mann, *Scottish Book Trade* (n 3) 239–40.

king's printer, that such powers became controversial and the subject of frequent litigation.[36] As policing copyright was at the behest of the copy holder, this placed the advantage with the wealthier, royal printers, and especially with Agnes Campbell (fl. 1676–1717), Anderson's widow, who succeeded him in 1676 and was extraordinarily litigious. James Watson, the younger (fl. 1695–1722), Edinburgh printer and bitter rival of Campbell, records in his *History of the Art of Printing* (1713), the first history of printing in the British Isles, that in 1688 Campbell fell 'tooth and nail' upon those who breached her privileges.[37]

Other aspects of Scottish rights granted are also noteworthy. Sometimes exclusive rights were moderated in some respect. For example, it was made clear that the licensing of Wedderburne's national grammar did not prevent masters of schools using other grammars if they wished. Also, while the bookseller Gilbert Dick's 1618 patent for two 'official' catechisms was the first to add the right to 'distribute throughout the realme', we see an extra 'right' stemming from a desire for satisfactory performance in liturgical publishing. This attitude was replicated when Robert Young was awarded the printing rights to the controversial Service Book of 1637.[38] Conversely, some copyrights obtained in the 1670s and 1680s only refer to the right to print, confirming not only the more extensive bookselling network throughout Scotland but also that behind the scenes authors were making contracts directly with printers.

A further sophistication is found in the extension of rights to heirs as well as assignees. Assignees were, of course, recognised in the earliest copyright patents. Meanwhile, heirs were first mentioned in the copyrights granted to the king's bookbinder John Gibson in 1599, and the first royal appointment declaring likewise was that of Walter Finlason when he became king's printer in 1628. Finlason succeeded his father, although not as of right. Thereafter, the right of heirs is more commonly declared, although by the 1680s there is a greater tendency to accept the right of authors' heirs rather than those of printers, at least in grants for 'particular' copyrights. Thus the translator Robert Kirk (1684), and author George Dallas (1695) have copyrights secured for their heirs. Nevertheless, some copy holders, such as the law publisher and bookseller John Vallange, secured impressively comprehensive copyrights with rights conferred on heirs, co-partners and assignees.[39]

---

[36] *RPS*, 1672/6/158 (11 Sept 1672). This relates to the ratification by Parliament of the Anderson patent. It was granted under the Scottish Great Seal in May 1671 but was not recorded in the register. For a detailed account of the subsequent disputes, see Alastair Mann, 'Book Commerce, Litigation and the Art of Monopoly: The Case of Agnes Campbell, Royal Printer, 1676–1712' (1998) 18 Scottish Economic and Social History 132, 136–39.

[37] James Watson, *A History of the Art of Printing* (Watson 1713) 16; John Lauder of Fountainhall, *Historical Notices of Scottish Affairs* (Constable 1848) vol 2, 866; Fountainhall, *Decisions* (n 15) vol 1, 494; NAS, PS, 1, 71, 86. Although Watson's is the first history of printing in the British Isles it is based on Jean de la Caille's *Historie de L'imprimerie* (1689).

[38] *RPCS*, ii, 4, 168–69, 500–01; *RPCS*, i, 11, 30–31, 643–44; Mann, *Scottish Book Trade* (n 3) 39–40, 107. Wedderburne's rights in terms of exclusivity were reduced in June 1632 from the original rights of 1631.

[39] NRS, PS.1.71, f 47^r; PS.1.101, f 120; Lee, *Memorial for the Bible Societies* (n 3) appendix, xii, xxii; *RPCS*, iii, 8, 414; NRS, PC.2.25, f 155^v; PC.2.27, ff 248^r–249^r.

Redress or compensation for a breach of copyrights was suggested from the advent of the press in Scotland but it was not until the 1565 copyright granted to Robert Lekpreuik for Acts of Parliament and the Psalms of David that we find the first mention of confiscation of offending stock for 'particular' licences. The first generic licence, the patent of Chepman and Myllar of 1507, warned that forbidden trafficking of printings within the gift would result in 'escheting of the buiks'.[40] This sanction was added to almost every copyright patent down to 1710. From the 1560s fines were also introduced, though always in addition to confiscation, and ranged from £200 to £2,000 scots. With the larger fines half of the sum could be allocated to the Crown or even in some cases to the poor. Imprisonment was not felt an appropriate sanction for abusers of private copyrights – a relatively minor offence. The only instance of a particular licence threatening prison can be found, not too surprisingly, in the terms of the royal grant to Sir William Alexander for the 'new' Psalms of David (1627). Imprisonment was nevertheless an element in some copyright disputes, yet these cases always arose over the rights of the king's printer, notably in 1677 when the Glasgow printer Robert Sanders, the elder (fl. 1661–94), was accused of breaching the general copyright of Agnes Campbell. The breach, according to the pursuer's charge, involved a range of 'New Testament and psalm books ... grammars ... many thousands of catechisms ... [and numerous] books of divinity and school books', all of which were subject to the royal gift. However, the main reason for Sanders' spell in prison was his failure to attend part of the hearing, make his oath before the Council and accept its best efforts at arbitration. In other words, as reflected in the Alexander case, the closer you got to the king and government the greater the sanction for a breach of copyright, or of course contempt.[41]

Assessing the scale, frequency and recipients of such copyrights provides some idea of their pervasiveness and a hint to the respect in which the system was held. As the table in the appendix shows from the 1540s to 1708 some 188 book titles were provided with particular copyright protection by way of over 90 patents.[42] Unsurprisingly there is a considerable expansion in patents granted as publishing activity increased from the 1670s. For probably political reasons, as no doubt also record keeping omission, there are no recipients in the years 1687–90, as the Revolution built, a Catholic press hovered in Edinburgh and then the Revolution came. The 1650s were also empty as not only was a recession in the general book trade evident but Edinburgh printers, such as Englishman Evan Tyler, began to register books with the Stationers' Company. In his case he even departed for London in 1652.

Clearly this number of copyrights represents a small proportion of all printing in Scotland during this period. This figure of particular grants excludes all generic privileges through the Scottish 'printing patent', as well as local licences not ratified by

---

[40] *RSS*, v, pt1, 564, no 1987; *RSS*, i, 223, no 1546; Dickson and Edmond, *Annals of Scottish Printing* (n 13) 7–8.

[41] *RPCS*, iii, v, 141–42; NAS, PS.1.100, f 305; Mann, *Scottish Book Trade* (n 3) 108–09; Mann, 'Agnes Campbell' (n 36) 142. Campbell's claim of £20,000 of damages, opportunistically half to the Crown, was rejected.

[42] A list of 'Particular' copyrights so far discovered can be found in Mann, *Scottish Book Trade* (n 3) 235–52.

the Crown. Also, many printings were too ephemeral or insignificant as literary property to warrant protection in any case. The fee payable when applying for a patent was also a disincentive in such cases. Some copyrights are, however, clearly missing. For example, there appears to be no official record of the 'particular' copyrights acquired separately by Alexander Arbuthnet and Robert Waldegrave, which were later bought by Finlason in 1604 and 1606 respectively, neither of which can be accounted for by the gift of king's printer held by both. There are other more blatant examples: no recorded copyrights for Andrew Hart and Henry Charteris (c.1568–99), neither of whom was king's printer and both of whom were among Scotland's most successful and original printer/publishers. In spite of this, some interesting observations can be made, not least of which is that authors were the recipients of many copyrights – in fact 46 per cent of recorded recipients were authors, a proportion which increased throughout the period. In Scotland, authors became more important as copy holders than printers. There are also indications that copyright protection was reasonably effective in Scotland by the late seventeenth century, and not so inferior to the more formal English system, given estimates that perhaps 40 or 50 per cent of all English printings were not registered with the Stationers' Company.[43]

6. THE 'PRINTING PATENT' AND LITIGATION

The most valuable monopolies available to Scottish book traders of early modern Scotland were those associated with royal appointments. These provided wide generic copyrights. The most significant of these appointments was the king's or queen's printer, the 'printing patent', which always remained at the behest of the Crown and never became subjected, by sale and mortgage, to endless co-partnerships as did the equivalent in England. A continuous line of king's printers for Scotland existed from the 1560s with less certain continuity from 1507 until then. Also, in its handling of this position and associated prerogatives the Crown was not always a benevolent force as far as the freedom to print unhindered by restrictive rights to copy was concerned. Early royal appointments, unlike particular copyrights, were for life, but it was only with the appointment of Walter Finlason as king's printer in 1628 that heirs and assignees were recognised. Nonetheless, for this and subsequent appointments all royal printer gifts were for a set period of years. Co-partnerships, hereditary rights and the involvement of assignees were only possible after such positions were limited to a fixed period, a key contrast with England.[44]

The attitudes of royal printers, nevertheless, bring into sharp focus the proprietorial view of copyright before 1710: it increasingly became the concern of courts and of lawyers. Certainly 200 years before, the courts, in the form of the Privy Council, took action in 1509 and 1510 to protect the privileges and copyrights of Walter Chepman

---

[43] AW Pollard, 'Some Notes on the History of Copyright in England, 1662–1774' (1922) The Library (4th ser) 99; Feather, *Publishing, Piracy and Politics* (n 2) 27.
[44] NAS, PS.1,101, 120. For a summary of the history of the privileges of Scottish royal printers, see Mann, *Scottish Book Trade* (n 3) 114–22.

concerning the new *Brevarium Aberdonense*. Chepman issued a complaint that booksellers had been illegally importing England's 'Salisbury use', and the Council issued a warning to a group of merchants to immediately halt such trade in favour of Elphinstone's text. The legal complexities increased markedly from the Restoration. The wide supervisory and generalised copyrights granted in 1671 by Charles II (r. 1649–85) and his senior minister the Duke of Lauderdale to Andrew Anderson, royal printer 1671–76, and subsequently inherited of course by his widow Agnes Campbell, were the cause of major disputes in the book trade of Scotland in the 1670s and 1680s. Anderson, his partners and assignees were not only 'his Majesties ... onlie sole and principall printer', with rights to print all Bibles, liturgy and school books, but they were also 'Masters, Directors and Regulators of his Majesties office of Printing', with powers to police imports, prevent printers setting up presses who had not served apprenticeships, and could, subject to the Privy Council, 'seclude and debarr all others [of the] freedoms and immunities' of trade. The ruling against Hart in 1614 (as noted above) was temporarily forgotten.[45] Then arose James VII and II's appointment in 1686 of the Catholic James Watson, senior (fl. 1685–87), to the anomalous post of 'household printer' existing concurrently with that of king's printer, and with a monopoly over all almanacs, even those already in print. This created much consternation in the trade and especially for Agnes Campbell. Nonetheless, the courts showed a remarkable degree of independence in the face of much irrational exercise of royal prerogative. While the Revolution of 1688/9 took care of the post of 'household printer' and James VII (r. 1685–88), the Privy Council gradually reduced the sweeping copyrights of Campbell and her supervisory role over the Scottish press, taking it back in stages by 1681 to the privileges enjoyed by Evan Tyler in 1641. Campbell's policing prerogatives were no longer to extend to imports from England, unless specifically in competition with her own existing Bible printings and her apparent power to prevent competing presses from opening was rescinded. Campbell's appeal to the lords of session in the winter of 1682–83 failed and her weak argument for the status quo, that 'one press [was] sufficient' for official documents, was seen by the investigating committee as acting, like her old patent, 'to restrain the liberty of printing too much'.[46] The fact that George I (r. 1714–27) made the absurd appointment of John Baskett, English royal printer, and Robert Freebairn as sole printers to the King in Scotland in 1714, in spite of a valid 1711 warrant that existed in the names of Freebairn, Baskett and James Watson, the younger, confirms the continued and irrational Crown interference. This case *Watson, the younger v Freebairn, Baskett and Campbell* (1713–18) reached the Court of Session, which from the 1680s began to take over competence for book trade disputes from an over-stretched Privy Council. Eventually the House of Lords gave its judgment in 1718 in favour of the 1711 gift. Farce continued to dog the

[45] *RPS*, 1672/6/158; Lee, *Memorials for the Bible Societies* (n 3), appendix no xxix, 56–61; Dickson and Edmond, *Annals of Scottish Printing* (n 13) 84–85; Mann, *Scottish Book Trade* (n 3) 129–30.
[46] Fountainhall, *Historical Notices* (n 37) vol 1, 311, 393; *RPCS*, iii, 7, 257, 12, 460–61; NRS, Registrum magni sigilli, Register of the Great Seal of Scotland manuscript registers (paper register) ('RMS') C3/10 no 343; Lee, *Memorials for the Bible Societies* (n 3) 146; Mann, 'Copyright and Illegal Activity' (n 7) 44–46. For the appeal by Campbell which was concluded in January 1683, see Fountainhall, *Decisions* (n 15) vol 1, 205, 424.

affair when Robert Freebairn became printer to the Old Pretender in the Jacobite rebellion of 1715, and subsequently was forfeited his share of the gift.[47]

Disputes about copyright privileges in the late seventeenth century centred around two main classes of books: Bibles and almanacs. The most prestigious and lucrative rights for religious publishing were of course those connected to the 'Bible patent'. But while it was regarded as one of the duties of the royal printer to deliver printed Bibles to the nation, both the government and the Church of Scotland were more concerned with issues of supply, and occasionally textual and production quality, than the preservation of restrictive copyrights. The early modern Scottish book trade, let alone a single royal printer, was never able to meet the demand for scripture in this period. Therefore, as seen in various Privy Council rulings in the 1670s and 1680s, the Bible rights of the royal printer only protected those editions and formats that he or she could keep in print.[48] Nevertheless, Bible imports from England were also a threat to the royal Bible patent. Campbell regularly complained to the Privy Council over these incursions. In 1688 she seized octavo Bibles at Leith which had been imported from London by the Edinburgh bookseller Alexander Ogston (fl. 1680–90). Ogston was well connected to the legal profession, having received his burgess ticket free in 1680 on the recommendation of the College of Justice and the Lord Advocate, Sir George Mackenzie of Rosehaugh. Regardless, Campbell won the day. The lawyer Sir John Lauder was left to reflect on the meanness of her octavo that was shown to the court to justify her entirely legal actions.[49] Ironically her Edinburgh press printed a counterfeit London Bible in 1707 looking to take advantage of the trade opportunities that the Union provided.[50]

The disputes over almanacs were even more complicated given that the presses of Aberdeen, Glasgow and Edinburgh were all involved. From a commercial point of view these small, annual, 16-page, octavo booklets, selling for only 4d, were the most valuable publishing properties in the late seventeenth century. They carried advertising, a reflection of their mass circulation and linking them to the newspaper revolution that began at the turn of the century. The earliest known almanacs out of Scotland's three printing burghs were Aberdeen (1623), Edinburgh (1632) and Glasgow (1661).[51] In 1682 and 1683, Robert Sanders of Glasgow and Agnes Campbell each produced separate counterfeit editions of the highly successful 'Aberdeen Almanac'. This Aberdeen edition, compiled with the help of the mathematicians at King's College, had become the market leader since the 1660s. The most infamous case arose in 1684, in which year Forbes, the younger (fl. 1662–1704), with the support of the magistrates of

---

[47] NRS, Privy Seal Registers, PS.3/4, 248; *RPCS*, iii, 13, xx; RMS, C3/15 no 388; NAS, Court of Session Papers, Productions and Processes CS29/ box 436.1 (Mackenzie); WJ Couper 'The Pretender's Printer: Robert Freebairn' (1917) 15 Scottish Historical Review 106. For a full account of the Watson legal battle, see Mann, 'Agnes Campbell' (n 36) 140–41.

[48] For such licences, see *RSS*, vii, 94, no 642; NAS. PS.1.43, f 103r; *RSS*, vi, 53, no 230.

[49] Watson, *History of the Art of Printing* (n 37) 16; *EBR*, x, 392; Fountainhall, *Decisions* (n 15) vol 1, 496; Fountainhall, *Historical Notices* (n 37) vol 2, 866.

[50] For a discussion of this Bible counterfeit, see Mann, 'Copyright Law and Illegal Activity' (n 7) 52–54.

[51] McDonald, 'Scottish Seventeenth-Century Almanacs' (n 24) 257–322; Mann, *Scottish Book Trade* (n 3) 15–16, 103–04; Mann, 'Agnes Campbell' (n 36) 143–45.

Aberdeen, prosecuted Sanders and Campbell before the Privy Council in Edinburgh. After the case was referred to a committee it ruled in favour of Forbes and Aberdeen. He won his case in law because he was 'in use and possession of printing yeirly ane almanack as printer of the toun and coledge of Aberdein', and therefore his copyright was sustained. Aberdeen's copyright had also been breached. Sanders had attempted to forge the city arms of Aberdeen which always adorned the almanac, and therefore his offence was viewed as especially devious. Unfortunately for Forbes the drip, drip of counterfeit editions continued over this highly profitable genre. Some consolation was gained by the fact that Campbell also produced various counterfeit editions of Forbes's main competition, the Edinburgh almanac of James Paterson, the authorised Edinburgh edition licensed by the capital from 1684.[52]

7. CONCLUSION: A SYSTEM OF REPUTE

We might ask if authors and printers adhered to and respected the copyright regime of early modern Scotland – some case studies provide clues. The publishing history of *The Works of Sir David Lindsay*, the early sixteenth century Scottish poet and dramatist (c.1486–1555) is such a case study with a patent history that began in 1590.[53] Although Henry Charteris published the first extant edition in 1568, and commissioned reprints in 1570s and 1580s, the first copyright was granted to the king's bookbinder John Gibson in 1590. Following Gibson's death, his son sold the right to Thomas Finlason in March 1606, which was confirmed in a copyright patent of that year. This period was for 25 years, thus taking us to 1631. In fact, the printed editions provide a bemusing picture in relation to the right to copy. First, Charteris printed two editions in the 1590s, when Gibson possessed the copyright and must have done so under agreement with the latter. Subsequently, during the confused six years between the death of Gibson in 1600, and the sale of his rights by his son to Thomas Finlason, Charteris's son Robert printed two editions, one under licence from the heirs of Gibson and one suspiciously anonymous. Finlason then printed his one and only edition in 1610 and, thereafter, during Finlason's life, all editions came from the press of Andrew Hart, who must also have made an agreement with the licence holder. On the death of Finlason in 1628, whose rights were left in the hands of his son Walter, the Aberdeen printer Edward Raban took the opportunity to print his own edition of Lindsay. The heirs of Andrew Hart printed one more edition, in 1630, before the 25-year patent expired. After this date a free-for-all ensued from the print centres of Scotland.

Lindsay was long dead, but what of a living author seeking to protect literary property? The actions of schoolmaster James Kirkwood echoes typical copyright concerns. The history of grammar licensing and regulation in Scotland shows that the authorities did not take a consistent line in the licensing of school grammars. Prescription under James VI and I, with a set national grammar, was followed by recommendation under Charles I and then scholastic freedom under Charles II,

---

[52] Mann, 'Copyright Law and Illegal Activity' (n 7) 47–52.
[53] For a more detailed account of what follows, see Mann, *Scottish Book Trade* (n 3) 110.

although protecting copyright was no less important.[54] Kirkwood's grammar, published in three parts from 1674 to 1676, was subject to pirating, abridgement and copyright abuse in spite of the nineteen-year licence granted to him in 1674. He was so concerned that he delivered a supplication to the Privy Council in 1677 requesting a revised copyright with more rigorous punishments for abusers. That year he was granted fresh copyrights of 19 years for a one-volume edition of his *Grammatica Facilis* and also for his *Rhetoricae Compendium*, each with the penalty of the very large fines of 2,000 merks (or £1,300) for pirates. Later, as the copyright terms were due to expire, Kirkwood was granted in 1695 new 19-year licences for revised editions of both his grammar and his vocabulary. These were clearly new editions as the standard period for reprints was 11 years. But the fact that no subsequent Kirkwood copyright breach is mentioned in the Council records before 1708 suggests these measures were effective. Being caught pirating such works could be potentially disastrous for printers, a clear deterrent. The penalties protecting Kirkwood's copyrights, which were so severe he may have had friends in high places, declare that contraveners 'make up whatever loss and damage [he] may sustain', as well as confiscation of the offending printed stock and the fine.[55] The proof being in the pudding, these details confirm, then, a pragmatic and practical approach to copyright. Printers both respected literary property, and sold and acquired copyrights, yet also they exploited commercial opportunities when they presented themselves. Furthermore, the copyright for a deceased author was less likely to be policed with rigour.

The legal profession of pre-Union Scotland was clearly at the heart of copyright regulation, interpretation and litigation but also central to an expanding culture of authorship which intensified in the course of the seventeenth century. Evidence for this is widespread, and yet the sense of detail and purposefulness is confirmed in an agreement of 1681 between Sir James Dalrymple of Stair (1619–95), President of the Court of Session, and Agnes Campbell herself, over the printing of Stair's *Institutions of the Law of Scotland* (1681). This agreement was made the month before a successful application for copyright by the author. Stair was contracted to deliver up his manuscript to Campbell, to give the text only to her and to allow her exclusive reprint rights. Meanwhile, Campbell agreed to print the text in English roman, 'conform to the printed sheet subscribed by both parties', to print six sheets per hour and to deliver out no copies without approval. Written copies and printed copies were to be kept 'under lock and key' under penalty. A number of copies were to be delivered for the author's use, half well bound in leather, the other half gilded, and 'so soon as the samen are presented whensoever [Stair] shall call for the samen under the pain of 400 pounds scots money as the Liquidate pryce thairof by consent'.[56] Finally, the printer had to agree to use the privilege, not print the book abroad and not allow others to produce it on her behalf. Printer and author content, publication soon arrived and the law of contract and of copyright came together to produce a highlight of publishing in early modern Scotland and evidence of a broadly fit for purpose copyright system before the Act of Anne of 1710. Yet this is an impression to be challenged or endorsed by future

---

54   For grammar publishing, see Mann, *Scottish Book Trade* (n 3) 153–54.
55   *RPCS*, iii, 4, 292; *RPCS*, iii, 5, 211 and 268; NAS, PC2/26, 47v.
56   NRS, PS.3.3, ff 336–37; NRS, Earl of Stair Papers, GD/135/2762/2.

research. The manuscript registers of the Privy Seal from the late sixteenth century which record early copyrights, and the vast Court of Session records from the seventeenth century, where judgments on book trade cases became a growing competence, require exhumation and analysis. Contracts like that of Dalrymple and Campbell must exist in estate papers and amongst the volumes of deeds in the National Records of Scotland in Edinburgh. Scotland's copyright historiography of the early modern period may be a callow youth but it need not always be so.

118 *Research handbook on the history of copyright law*

APPENDIX

Table 6A.1 Number of 'particular' copyright grants in Scotland, 1540–1708

Decades	Patents	Titles	Authors	Printers/Booksellers	Licensees	Editors
1540s	1	1	–	1	–	–
1550s	1	11	1	–	–	–
1560s	4	5	–	3	1	–
1570s	5	16	–	3	2	–
1580s	1	3	–	1	–	–
1590s	4	18	–	3	1	–
1600s	4	26	1	2	1	–
1610s	7	13	1	5	1	–
1620s	3	3	2	–	1	–
1630s	3	3	2	–	1	–
1640s	1	3	3	–	–	–
1650s	–	–	–	–	–	–
1660s	7	7	2	2	2	1
1670s	11	14	6	4	1	–
1680s	16	23	15	1	–	–
1690s	16	27	4	7	4	1
1700s	9	14	5	3	–	1
Totals	94	188	43	34	15	3
%	100		46	36	16	2

7. Literary property in Scotland in the eighteenth and nineteenth centuries

Hector MacQueen

1. INTRODUCTION

Since the Statute of Anne in 1710, copyright legislation enacted in the United Kingdom has applied throughout the United Kingdom. But prior to the Copyright Act 1911 none of that legislation purported to be a complete statement of the relevant law. Issues thus arose about the relationship between the statutory provisions and the rest of the quite distinct laws respectively applying in the different jurisdictions within the United Kingdom. Unlike English law, Scots law had been much influenced by Roman or Civil law before 1710, and although after the Anglo-Scottish Union of 1707 its long-established court system became subject in civil matters to an appeal to the House of Lords in London, this alone did not change the law and its culture. The Statute of Anne was itself very largely a product of the 1707 Union, but for the remainder of the eighteenth century and into the early years of the nineteenth its accommodation with the pre-existing law presented a challenge for Scottish lawyers. This was at both practical and theoretical levels, most notably illustrated by the great case of *Hinton v Donaldson* in 1773. The challenge was further complicated by awareness of similar struggles taking place in English law, along with doubts about the solutions produced by the English courts. By the mid-nineteenth century, however, Scottish lawyers seem in general to have become much more willing to be led by the analyses and outcomes emerging from England on these questions, and any notions of a distinct approach could not survive the increasingly comprehensive legislation produced by the Westminster Parliament for the whole country.

2. THE 1707 UNION AND THE STATUTE OF ANNE

The 1603 Union of the Crowns of England and Scotland in the person of King James VI and I left in place two separate kingdoms, each under a Crown which simply happened both to be held by the same person for the next century. But the 1707 Anglo-Scottish Union created a single United Kingdom and Crown of Great Britain, a single Parliament, and the legal framework for a single market with full freedom of trade between Scotland and England. But this single market was not thought to require general unification of the distinct laws and legal systems of England and Scotland. In particular, under Article XVIII of the Union agreement Scots law itself was to 'remain in the same force as before', albeit 'alterable by the Parliament of Great-Britain'. The article also sought to regulate the parliamentary power to alter Scots law: only with 'the Laws which concern public Right, Policy, and civil Government' might the object of

120 *Research handbook on the history of copyright law*

the change be to make the law 'the same throughout the whole United Kingdom', whereas 'no Alteration [might] be made in Laws which concern private Right, except for evident Utility of the Subjects within Scotland'.[1]

The Statute of Anne 1710 was an early manifestation of the power of the Parliament of Great Britain under Article XVIII. Before the 1707 Union the Scottish Privy Council provided both the granting body to which application for printing privileges was made by either publisher or author, and the forum in which disputes about the scope of the privileges were determined.[2] This system was however undermined immediately after the Union, when the Scottish Privy Council was abolished by statute from 1 May 1708.[3] In England there had effectively been no system since 1695.[4] The Statute of Anne accordingly introduced a new scheme for the whole kingdom, probably as a matter of 'public right' in Scotland. The Statute declared that an author or a bookseller had 'the sole liberty' of publishing a book for a period of 14 years from first publication, with authors (but not booksellers) being entitled to a further 14 years of exclusive right after the expiry of the initial period of protection. The Statute further provided penal monetary sanctions for infringement of these exclusive rights, half payable to the Crown and the other half to the plaintiff, so long as, prior to publication, the title to the book was registered at Stationers Hall (the headquarters of the London booksellers' guild, near St Paul's Cathedral). The Act thus required registration only for the enforceability of its penalties for infringement, not for the author or bookseller's exclusive right. What was therefore left unclear was whether the Statute actually conferred this exclusivity, or rather merely recognized and then in some respects confined it. Scottish distinctiveness was provided for in the Statute: in particular, the Court of Session was given jurisdiction 'if any person or persons incur the penalties contained in this Act, in that part of Great Britain called Scotland'.

3. PLACING LITERARY PROPERTY IN THE FRAMEWORK OF SCOTS LAW

As literary property grew in practical significance in the first half of the eighteenth century, so writers on Scots law were compelled to put these rights within the general structures of their expositions. These were of course usually based on Civilian systematics, while copyright was generally yoked together with patents.[5] In 1751 Andrew McDouall (soon to go on the bench as Lord Bankton) placed a brief discussion

---

[1] For discussion of the meanings of public and private right, see JD Ford, 'The Legal Provisions in the Acts of Union' (2007) 66 CLJ 106, 108–18; John W Cairns, 'The Origins of the Edinburgh Law School: the Union of 1707 and the Regius Chair' (2007) 11 Edin LR 300, 313–26.
[2] See generally Alastair Mann's contribution to this volume in Chapter 6.
[3] Union with Scotland (Amendment) Act 1707, s 1 (6 Anne c 40).
[4] Ronan Deazley, *On the Origin of the Right to Copy* (Hart Publishing 2004) ch 1.
[5] On Scots patent law, see Hector MacQueen, 'Intellectual Property and the Common Law in Scotland c1700–c1850' in Catherine W Ng, Lionel Bently and Giuseppina D'Agostino (eds), *The Common Law of Intellectual Property: Essays in Honour of Professor David Vaver* (Hart Publishing 2010) 21.

of the two rights in his chapter on 'Permutation and Sale', referring to them as 'exclusive privileges' limiting the general freedom of commerce along with rules privileging markets and fairs and criminal provisions on selling of counterfeit drink and the use of false weights and measures. He also noted that grants to 'the inventors of new manufactures, or authors of books, securing to them the sole benefit of the same', did not fall foul of the common law's prohibition on monopolies, being 'in vertue of statute' (presumably the Statute of Monopolies and the Statute of Anne respectively, although Bankton does not name them specifically) and 'limited to a certain period of years, after which they determine'.[6] His judicial colleague Henry Home, Lord Kames likewise treated patents and copyright as an aspect of the regulation of commerce in his *Principles of Equity*, first published in 1760,[7] observing that the only lawful monopolies were those granted for the public good. Patents for inventions and copyright for books, 'limited to a time certain', were examples: 'the profit made in that period is a spur to invention: people are not hurt by such a monopoly, being deprived of no privilege enjoyed by them before the monopoly took place; and after expiry of the time limited, all are benefited without distinction.'[8]

Later writers discussed copyright and patents, not in conjunction with market regulation, but rather as part of the law of real rights, or property (using that word in a very broad generic sense).[9] The concept of 'exclusive privilege', mentioned by Bankton, began to develop as a form of real right.[10] Lecturing on jurisprudence at Glasgow University in the 1760s, Adam Smith analyzed the four real rights of the Civil Law (Property [ie, in its more precise meaning of Ownership], Servitude, Pledge and Inheritance), and argued that the last of these could only be considered as a distinct real right in the context where the heir was preparing to take up his right following the death of the previous proprietor, since his privilege to inherit excluded the right of any others who would be heirs after him. On this analogy, 'all other exclusive priviledges have the same title, and appear evidently as well as it to be real rights'.[11] Some exclusive privileges, such as inheritance, were founded on natural reason, but 'the greatest part ... are the creatures of the civil constitutions of the country'; and amongst them were to be placed patents for inventions and copyright.[12]

---

[6] Andrew McDouall Lord Bankton, *An Institute of the Laws of Scotland* (1751–53) bk I, tit xix, s 11. I have used the three-volume facsimile reprint produced by the Stair Society, vols 41–43, between 1993 and 1995.

[7] Henry Home, Lord Kames, *Principles of Equity* (3rd edn, Edinburgh 1778) vol 2, bk II, s 3. There are at least three modern reprints of this edition. See Hector MacQueen, 'The War of the Booksellers: Natural Law, Equity and Literary Property in Eighteenth-Century Scotland' (2014) 35 J Legal Hist 231, 239 fn 37.

[8] Kames (n 7) vol 2, 99.

[9] For the doctrine of real rights in Scots law at this time, see Baron David Hume, *Lectures 1786–1822* (Stair Society, 1939–58) vol 2, 2–3.

[10] See further Gillian Black, 'Exclusive Privilege: Adam Smith, John Millar, and the Creation of a New Right' in Ross G Anderson, James Chalmers and John MacLeod (eds), *Glasgow Tercentenary Essays: 300 Years of the School of Law* (Avizandum 2014) 20–52.

[11] Adam Smith, *Lectures on Jurisprudence* (OUP 1979) 82.

[12] Ibid 82–83.

David Hume, Professor of Scots Law at Edinburgh 1786–1822, in his lectures likewise categorized copyright and patents as 'instances of the real right of Exclusive Privilege', which he seems to have conceived of as an 'exclusive title ... to perform a certain operation ... for and within a certain territory of land, and to draw the profit attached to that operation'. Any other person presuming to perform the operation was guilty of 'usurpation ... infringement of the exclusive privilege', and the holder was entitled to vindication, meaning that the right was 'thus marked with all the characters of a proper legitimate and real right'.[13] Other examples included the trading monopolies and privileges of royal burghs, merchant guilds and craft incorporations.

George Joseph Bell, Hume's successor in the Edinburgh Chair from 1822 to 1837, also treated copyrights and patents as real rights, or as 'estates available to creditors',[14] but more or less abandoned the concept of 'exclusive privilege' in favour of seeing the rights as property, albeit in a somewhat opaque passage suggesting that the right of ownership was less than full-blown:

> The right to enjoy the benefit of a useful invention, or literary composition, seems to rest securely on the great foundation on which property depends; namely, occupancy, with skill, labour, expense and intellectual exertion, employed in the acquisition of production. But a more narrow view has been taken of this matter, and instead of considering the invention or the composition as itself the subject of property, it has been held that, as the purchase of the individual machine, or book gives the power of imitating or of copying it, either such copy or the original may be sold, and so copies multiplied to make gain. With this view, in the case of discoveries in the useful arts, concurs the interest which the public has to prevent the undue raising of prices, and restraining of industry and improvement, according to the caprice or self-interest of monopolists. The Legislature has therefore interposed, on the one hand to secure for a certain but limited time, to the authors of useful inventions, or of literary compositions, a monopoly of sale and profit; and on the other to protect the interests of the public.[15]

The *inter vivos* transferability of patents and copyrights was also a significant point of difference from many of the other forms of exclusive privilege mentioned by Smith and Hume. Hume and Bell both clearly, and without much discussion, also considered patents and copyrights to be incorporeal rights. Hume raised, without answering, the question of whether the rights were to be considered as heritable rather than moveable rights;[16] ie, as rights that on death passed to the holder's heir-at-law rather than to that part of the deceased's estate administered by executors which could be bequeathed by will. In 1832 John Shank More, an advocate later to be Bell's successor in the Scots

---

[13] Hume (n 9) vol 4, 38.

[14] GJ Bell, *Commentaries on the Mercantile Jurisprudence of Scotland* (7th edn 1870) vol 1, 103. The 7th edition has been used, since it reprints the text of the 5th edition of 1835, the last produced by Bell himself. The work first began to be published in 1800.

[15] GJ Bell, *Principles of the Law of Scotland* (1st edn 1829; 4th edn (the last produced by Bell) 1839) s 1348. Bell's *Commentaries* refers to the 'exclusive privilege of patent or copyright' in a sub-heading. Bell, *Commentaries* (n 14) 120. Bell's *Principles* reached a 10th and final edition in 1900.

[16] Hume (n 9) vol 4, 565.

Law Chair at Edinburgh, argued that the rights were heritable,[17] his approach being based on the heritability of rights (such as pensions and annuities) with a tract of future time – 'rights of such a nature that they cannot be at once paid or fulfilled by the debtor, but continue for a number of years, and carry a yearly profit to the creditor while they subsist, without any relation to any capital sum or stock'[18] – and the fit between this definition and patents and copyrights. Bell appeared to accept the analogy in his *Commentaries*.[19] But the analysis was not consistently maintained throughout his writings, for his *Principles* brought the substantive treatment of the rights under the general heading 'Property in moveables' and a further sub-heading 'Of incorporeal moveable subjects'. The debate ended when copyrights were declared to be moveable property by the Copyright Act 1842.[20]

4. LITERARY PROPERTY AND EQUITABLE REMEDIES IN SCOTLAND

A requirement of registration far away in London might have made life more difficult for Scottish publishers and authors, but in practice Scottish publications seem to have been frequently entered in the register at Stationers Hall throughout the eighteenth century. The barrier of distance was thus not insuperable for Scots, at least for those with resources and good prospects of literary success.[21] In the mid-eighteenth century, however, London and Scottish booksellers fell into conflict over a number of issues about literary property. The conflict has become known as 'The Battle of the Booksellers'; but in some ways it was more like a war, lasting for over 30 years and involving not just court battles but other forms of struggle.[22]

The issues arose from the making and sale in Scotland by its booksellers of cheap reprints of works with subsisting registrations in Stationers Hall, along with the export of these reprints to England and, indeed, to North America and Continental Europe.[23]

---

[17] JS More, *Notes on Stair* (1832) cxli (Note R(4)).
[18] The definition of John Erskine, *An Institute of the Law of Scotland* (many editions 1773–1871) bk II, tit ii, s 6. I have used the facsimile reprint of the first edition produced by the Edinburgh Legal Education Trust (2014).
[19] Bell, *Commentaries* (n 14) vol 1, 110–11. See also his *Principles*: Bell, *Principles* (n 15) s 1480.
[20] Section 25.
[21] Alastair Mann, *The Scottish Book Trade 1500–1720* (Tuckwell 2000) 123–24; RB Sher, *The Enlightenment and the Book: Scottish Authors and their Publishers in Eighteenth-Century Britain, Ireland, and America* (Chicago UP 2006) 243–44; Warren McDougall, 'Copyright Litigation in the Court of Session, 1738–1749, and the Rise of the Scottish Book Trade' (1987) 5 Edin Bibliographical Society Transactions 2, 26–29.
[22] But McDougall, 'Copyright Litigation' (n 21) 22–29, highlights the considerable degree of business co-operation that also existed between the Scottish and the London booksellers. See further Sher, *Enlightenment and the Book* (n 21) 265–326.
[23] See McDougall, 'Copyright Litigation' (n 21) 14–22, on the overseas markets into which Scottish booksellers were making inroads by the 1740s, including imports as well as exports. See further on the US market later in the eighteenth century Sher, *Enlightenment and the Book* (n 21) chs 8 and 9.

The London booksellers first began to take legal action against such reprints in the late 1730s.[24] The initial question to be debated in the campaign was whether the Statute's very limited sanctions against infringement – forfeiture of the infringing publications and payment of one penny for every infringing sheet, with only half the money going to the person suing – could be supplemented by other remedies available generally from the courts. After some equivocation, the answer given to this question by the Court of Session differed fundamentally from that of the English judiciary.

Well before 1740, the Court of Chancery in England decided that, provided the party bringing the action first waived his claim to the penalties provided by the Statute of Anne, it could grant the equitable remedies of injunctions (orders prohibiting the continuation of infringing activities) and requiring infringers to hand their profits over to the right-holders by way of damages.[25] The basis of Chancery's jurisdiction in these cases received little discussion although it was suggested that at least an accounting of profits was implicitly authorized by the Statute of Anne or a natural incident of granting injunctive relief.[26] The London booksellers certainly saw far greater practical utility in the equitable remedies of the injunction and account of profits than in those provided by the Statute, and neither defendants nor the Chancery judges chose to place too many doctrinal difficulties in their path.

The Scottish judges, on the other hand, after some wavering, ultimately refused in 1748 to allow the supplementation of the Statute of Anne in this way in *Midwinter v Hamilton*.[27] The case, which began in 1743, involved a number of leading London booksellers (including Daniel Midwinter but with the group actually being led by Andrew Millar), as well as an even larger number of Edinburgh and Glasgow booksellers (including Gavin Hamilton amongst other prominent names[28]). The London booksellers' claim was for the penalties in the Statute of Anne plus damages and an accounting of profits, with the latter remedies being justified on the basis that the statutory ones 'were being found attended with such Difficulties, that in no one instance… have the same ever been prosecuted or recovered'.[29] Although the pleadings made reference to Chancery's use of the equitable remedy of the injunction, at this stage the Court of Session does not seem to have much developed what would become its equivalent remedy of 'suspension and interdict' as a preventative measure against prospective or ongoing wrongdoing of all kinds. While the remedy of suspension was

---

[24] See McDougall, 'Copyright Litigation' (n 21) 2–9.
[25] See Deazley, *Right to Copy* (n 4) 57–69, 137–38.
[26] See Tomás Gómez-Arostegui's contribution to this volume at Chapter 11. See also Deazley, *Right to Copy* (n 4) 61–62, 64–65; H Tomás Gómez-Arostegui, 'What History Teaches us About Copyright Injunctions and the Inadequate-Remedy-at-Law Requirement' (2008) 81 S Cal L Rev 1197, 1233.
[27] *Midwinter v Hamilton* (1748) Mor 8295; McDougall, 'Copyright Litigation' (n 21) 5–8; RS Tompson, 'Scottish Judges and the Birth of British Copyright' (1992) Jur Rev 18, 19–22; M Rose, *Authors and Owners: The Invention of Copyright* (HUP 1993) 69–71; Deazley, *Right to Copy* (n 4) 116–32. Note also Bankton, *Institute* (n 6) bk I, tit xix, s 12.
[28] On Hamilton, see Warren McDougall, 'Hamilton, Gavin (1704–1767)', ODNB, <http://www.oxforddnb.com/view/article/65019>.
[29] Information for Daniel Midwinter, 30 November 1744, quoted Deazley, *Right to Copy* (n 4) 117.

long established, it had hitherto been largely confined to preventing the enforcement of wrongfully obtained court decrees.[30] It may be no more than coincidence that not long after *Midwinter v Hamilton* Lord Bankton declared in his *Institute* that '… the Court of Session puts a stop to the unwarrantable encroachments upon any man's property or possession, by suspending the operation till the matter be cognosced'.[31] This certainly pointed to a means of preventing infringing activity in relation to literary property rights.

An appeal to the House of Lords against the Court of Session's refusal to grant the London booksellers a remedy in *Midwinter v Hamilton* failed in 1751, not by upholding the court below, but through a technical finding that the action 'was improperly and inconsistently brought'. The appellant booksellers had illegitimately cumulated non-statutory with statutory remedies (recall here that in Chancery the plaintiff had to waive the statutory penalties in order to gain the protection of the court), as well as suing several defenders in one action when the points at issue against each were about separate and distinct books and rights therein. The case was remitted back to the Court of Session, but no further litigation ensued there.[32]

The pleadings for the London booksellers in *Midwinter v Hamilton* noted that 'the Court of Session in Scotland [is] a mixt Jurisdiction of Law and Equity'.[33] There was no formal division of legal and equitable jurisdictions in Scotland, but this did not disable the court from fashioning a remedy to meet a situation where otherwise injustice might result from the strict application of the law. That the Court of Session administered law and equity together in its procedures was well established, and no doubt the London booksellers sought to invoke that power. This may also explain, at least in part, the waverings of the court before it reached its final decision. Towards the end of the seventeenth century, the position, and its limits, had been explained by the institutional writer Viscount Stair (in his time Lord President of the Court of Session) in terms of the *nobile officium* of a superior or sovereign court in contrast with the mere *officium ordinarium* (or *mercenarium*) of the inferior courts:

> … [I]n new cases, there is necessity of new cures, which must be supplied by the Lords, who are authorized for that effect by the institution of the College of Justice. … [I]n many cases, it is necessary wherein they may have recourse from strict law to equity, even in the matter of judgment; and in more cases they may recede from the ordinary form and manner of probation, whereof there are many instances commonly known.[34]

---

[30] See eg James Dalrymple, Viscount Stair, *Institutions of the Law of Scotland* (many editions, 1681–1981) bk IV, 52 (I have used the 6th and latest edition by DM Walker for EUP); W Forbes, *Institutes of the Law of Scotland* (1722–30, facsimile reprint Edinburgh Legal Education Trust, 2012) 445–46; and the cases reported in WM Morison, *The decisions of the Court of Session, from its institution until the separation of the Court into two divisions in the year 1808, digested under proper heads, in the form of a dictionary* (1801–11), sv 'Suspension'.

[31] Bankton, *Institute* (n 6) bk IV, tit 38, s 20.

[32] *Midwinter v Kincaid* (1751) 1 Pat App 488; see further Rose, *Authors and Owners* (n 27) 70–71; Deazley, *Right to Copy* (n 4) 130–32.

[33] The pleadings in *Midwinter v Hamilton* are here quoted from Deazley, *Right to Copy* (n 4) 117.

[34] Stair, *Institutions* (n 30) bk IV, tit iii, s 1.

Stair acknowledged that matters were differently arranged in England, with the courts of common law disabled from the administration of equity by the existence of a distinct court for the purpose. But England was exceptional: 'Other nations do not divide the jurisdiction of their courts, but supply the cases of equity and conscience, by the noble office of their supreme ordinary courts, as we do.'[35] Passages similar to these remarks of Stair can be found in later institutional writings, especially those of Bankton and John Erskine (Professor of Scots Law at Edinburgh University 1737–65), both of whom wrote during the course of events between *Midwinter v Hamilton* and *Hinton v Donaldson*.[36]

Why did the Court of Session not follow the example of the Court of Chancery when it clearly had the power to do so and when, perhaps, there might have been thought to be, in Stair's language, a 'necessity for new cures' to meet a new case? At least one reason was the far more vigorous debate on the matter in the Scottish compared to the English court. Proceedings in Edinburgh lasted for five years. Among counsel for the Scottish booksellers was the formidable Henry Home, later Lord Kames, a leading figure in the Scottish Enlightenment. His arguments in *Midwinter* seem essentially to have been, first, that the pursuers' right depended entirely upon the Statute of Anne, not on any pre-existing right, and could not be extended beyond what the legislation laid down; second, that the statutory right was at best analogous with property; and, third, consequentialist or *reductio ad absurdum* reasoning that if authors had rights beyond the Statute, why should this not also apply to inventors who had not taken out letters patent?[37]

Kames referred to his past triumph at the bar in his *Principles of Equity*, implicitly criticizing the handling of the Statute of Anne by the English equity courts when he argued that 'monopolies or personal privileges cannot be extended by a court of equity; because that court may prevent mischief, but has no power to do any act for enriching any person, or making him *locupletior*, as termed in the Roman law.'[38] The context in which Kames made his criticism was a discussion of the court's equitable powers in relation to statutes 'preventative of wrong or mischief'. He distinguished between such statutes and those directed to the 'positive good of the whole society, or of some part', in that with the latter the court had no power to 'supply' answers to any defects in them: 'it belongs to the legislature only to make laws or regulations for promoting good positively'.[39] The Statute of Anne was clearly such a piece of legislation in Kames' view. In another chapter on the '[p]owers of a court of equity to remedy what is imperfect in common law with respect to statutes', he drew another distinction, between statutes prohibiting 'noxious evils' absolutely (which courts might use all means within their powers to enforce as well as the statutory penalty), and those regarding 'slighter evils, to repress which no other means are intended to be applied but

---

[35] Ibid.
[36] Bankton, *Institute* (n 6) bk IV, tit vii, ss 23–28; Erskine, *Institute* (n 18) bk I, tit iii, s 22. Note also Forbes, *Institutes* (n 30) 420.
[37] See Deazley, *Right to Copy* (n 4) 117–18, 120–22, 125–27, for Home's arguments.
[38] Henry Home, Lord Kames, *Principles of Equity* (Edinburgh 1760) 185. This statement, or something close to it, reappears in subsequent editions. See Henry Home, Lord Kames, *Principles of Equity* (2nd edn, Edinburgh 1767) 265–66; Kames (n 7) vol 2, 126.
[39] Kames (n 7) vol 2, 116.

a pecuniary penalty only'.[40] The Statute of Anne, he said, plainly belonged in this second class.[41]

The significance of Kames' remark about Chancery's role in the copyright debate is thus that, while in general he favoured the expansion of the equitable aspects of the Court of Session's jurisdiction, he also thought that equity should operate within certain limits. Equity was not simply a matter of doing justice between individuals coming before the court; it needed to be reduced to a rational system of rules as far as possible without, however, depriving it of its flexibility and responsiveness to injustice. Above all, perhaps, equity had to yield to utility, or the greater good of society as a whole.[42]

After their disappointment in *Midwinter v Hamilton*, the London booksellers seem to have abandoned the tactic of suing in Scotland, choosing rather to mount actions in the English courts against those English provincial booksellers who also sold the cheap Scottish reprints.[43] There was however something of a revival of litigation in Scotland in the later 1760s. In August 1767 John Almon, a London bookseller, published a summary of the speeches of the Lords of Session in a notorious cause of the time, with an introductory preface by a barrister at law. Subsequently two editions of this book were re-published in Edinburgh, one by Messrs Robertson and Ruddiman, the other by Robert Fleming. Almon presented a petition to the sheriff of Edinburgh 'to prohibit the sale of these editions and to grant warrants for searching the houses, warehouses, and shops of the defendants, that none of the copies on hand, or in the possession of the defendants, might be sold'.[44] The sheriff granted the orders sought: 'the defendants afterwards came before the Court of Session, where Mr Almon met them with actions, &c. At length, the sale of both publications being entirely prohibited, the matter was allowed to drop, the defendants paying all expenses.'[45] The case provides a striking example of an inferior court granting what was in effect an interdict with discovery attached, with the process apparently being approved by the Court of Session. It seems too that the court's power to compel a defender to 'cease and desist' from wrongful activity in general, and not just the enforcement of wrongly granted court orders, had become much more fully accepted than quarter of a century before. Erskine observed that 'suspension is a process authorised by law for putting a stop, not only to execution of iniquitous decrees, but to all encroachments either on property or possession, and in general to every unlawful proceeding.'[46] This final phrase extended the remedy even further than Bankton's protection against encroachments upon property or possession 20 years before.

---

[40] Ibid vol 1, 339, 350.
[41] Ibid vol 1, 350.
[42] On Kames' approach to equity, see A Rahmatian, *Lord Kames: Legal and Social Theorist* (EUP 2015), chapter VIII and literature there cited.
[43] McDougall, 'Copyright Litigation' (n 21) 9; John Feather, *Publishing, Piracy and Politics: An Historical Study of Copyright in Britain* (London 1994) 83.
[44] Anon, *Memoirs of a Late Eminent Bookseller* (1790) 52.
[45] Ibid 52–53. I owe this reference to Tomás Gómez-Arostegui. Note also RC Cole (ed), *The General Correspondence of James Boswell 1766–1769,* 2 vols (EUP and Yale UP, 1993–97) vol 1, 192, 197–98, 201, 235, vol 2, 7 fn 7.
[46] Erskine, *Institute* (n 18) bk IV, tit iii, s 20.

5. *HINTON v DONALDSON* (1773)

On 27 July 1773 the Court of Session in Edinburgh decided the case of *Hinton v Donaldson and others*.[47] It was about *The New History of the Holy Bible*, a well-known and popular book by the Reverend Thomas Stackhouse (1681/2–1752) first published in London and registered at Stationers Hall in 1733. Although the statutory term had therefore expired in 1761, the pursuer, John Hinton, a highly successful and prominent bookseller based in London, claimed continuing, common law, rights in the book.[48] Stackhouse had sold the rights in his *History* to the publisher, Stephen Austen, in 1740. Austen died in 1750, bequeathing the rights to his widow, Elizabeth;[49] and her subsequent marriage with Hinton transferred them to him. The defenders – Alexander Donaldson, John Wood and James Meurose – were all Scottish booksellers, based in Edinburgh or (in the case of Meurose) Kilmarnock. Donaldson was the major figure amongst them: commercially active in London as well as Edinburgh in reprinting works whose registration at Stationers Hall had expired, and a vigorous critic and competitor of the London booksellers.[50]

Hinton claimed that the defenders had each printed, published and sold editions of Stackhouse's *History* without his permission, so infringing his exclusive common law rights. The remedies he sought were, first, an order against the defenders 'to cease and desist from all further, printing, publishing or selling' of the Stackhouse book; second, delivery up of the already printed but unsold copies (amounting, it was claimed, to some 10,000 in number); third, a sum of £1-10/- for each copy sold and each copy less than the 10,000 of which delivery up was sought; and damages for the invasion of the pursuer's property. But, in a bold decision, nine out of ten Court of Session judges altogether held that literary property, or copyright, had no existence in relation to published works except under the Statute of Anne and that, accordingly, Hinton had no remedy. There was no such thing as copyright at common law in Scotland. The court refused to follow *Millar v Taylor*, the contrary decision handed down for England in 1769 by the Court of King's Bench.[51] Since the pursuer had no rights, there was no need to discuss the competence of the remedies he sought, or to make comparisons with the English position. Seven months later, this Scottish decision was instrumental in persuading the House of Lords in *Donaldson v Becket*, decided on 22 February 1774,

---

[47] *Hinton v Donaldson* (1773) Mor 8307; more fully at 5 Br Supp 508. The bundle of papers forming the process in the case is held in the National Records of Scotland (NRS), call number CS 231/H/2/4.

[48] John Raven, *The Business of Books: Booksellers and the English Book Trade 1450–1850* (Yale UP 2007) 190, 217.

[49] Austen's will is available online from The National Archives, Kew: see <http://discovery.nationalarchives.gov.uk/SearchUI/Details?uri=D537815>. An extract copy is included in the bundle of papers forming the process in *Hinton v Donaldson* (n 47).

[50] For Donaldson's career see JJ Caudle and RB Sher, 'Donaldson, Alexander (*bap.* 1727, *d.* 1794)', ODNB, <http://www.oxforddnb.com/view/article/64278>. See eg, his pamphlet, *Some Thoughts on the State of Literary Property, Humbly Submitted to the Consideration of the Public* (1764). Note also A Donaldson, 'Petition', in *Petitions and Papers Relating to the Bill of the Booksellers now before the House of Commons* (1774) 10.

[51] *Millar v Taylor* (1769) 4 Burr 2303.

to overturn the previous English approach.[52] Alexander Donaldson was also to the fore in this second case, first as losing defendant and then as triumphant appellant.

Hinton v Donaldson had begun in the Outer House in July 1771.[53] Thereafter counsel on each side submitted printed 'informations' dated 2 January 1773 which appeared on the Inner House rolls on 12 January.[54] Meantime, during 1772 a number of other Court of Session actions were raised by London booksellers against Edinburgh counterparts in respect of various alleged infringements of the Statute of Anne.[55] In London, the Court of Chancery granted a perpetual injunction in *Becket v Donaldson* in November 1772, with Donaldson lodging his appeal to the House of Lords the following month.[56]

The oral debate on the written pleadings in *Hinton v Donaldson* began before 11 of the 13 Inner House judges on Tuesday 20 July 1773, and lasted for the rest of the week. The parties were represented by some of the cream of the contemporary Scottish bar. Three counsel spoke on each side. All of Hinton's advocates would later go on to the Court of Session bench.[57] Alexander Donaldson and his colleagues were represented by John MacLaurin (later raised to the bench as Lord Dreghorn), a future Lord President in Ilay Campbell, and James Boswell (never a judge, but already well known as an author himself, albeit only later famous as biographer, diarist and letter-writer). More importantly in the context of 1773, Boswell and MacLaurin were friends of Donaldson and he had previously published works by both men. While with Boswell the publication was of poetry rather than law, MacLaurin was the author of a pamphlet first produced by Donaldson in 1767, entitled *Considerations on the Origin and Nature of Literary Property, wherein that species of property is clearly proved to subsist for no longer than the terms fixed by the statute 8vo Anne.* This may perhaps have been in anticipation of or a response to the Almon case in Edinburgh Sheriff Court the same

---

[52] *Donaldson v Becket* (1774) 4 Burr 2408, 2 Bro PC 129. See further H Tomás Gómez-Arostegui, 'Copyright at Common Law in 1774' (2014) 47 Conn L Rev 1.

[53] The procedure can be followed through the bundle of papers in the process preserved in the National Records of Scotland (above, note 47). See further MacQueen 'War of the Booksellers' (n 7) 243–244.

[54] The 'informations' in this and other cases are now held in the collections of Session Papers in the Advocates Library (ALSP) and the Signet Library (SLSP). See further Angus Stewart QC 'The Session Papers in the Advocates Library' in Hector L MacQueen (ed), *Miscellany Four* (Stair Society vol 49, 2002) 199. For Session Papers in *Hinton v Donaldson* see ALSP, Pitfour Collection, vol 54, no 9, Arniston Collection, vol 3, no 17, and Campbell Collection, vol 23, nos 8–9; SLSP, vols 176 (no 2), 347 (no 1a), and 591 (no 16). The informations in *Hinton v Donaldson* are reprinted as items B and D in S Pratt (ed), *The Literary Property Debate: Six Tracts, 1764–1774* (Garland 1974).

[55] Deazley, *Right to Copy* (n 4) 180–82. The processes can be found in the NRS, call numbers CS237/D/3/12 (*Edward Dilly and Charles Dilly and attorney v Gordon*, 1772); CS237/D/3/15/1 (*Edward Dilly and Charles Dilly and attorney v Anderson*, 1772); CS237/D/3/15/2 (*Donald White and Company v Donald*, 1772, but no process now, ie, wanting – see CS237/MISC/1/34 however); CS237/G/2/31 (*William Griffin and attorney v McPherson*, 1772); CS229/IJ/1/55 (*William Johnston and attorney v Robertson and others*, 1772). See also CS16/1/152 and 154 (Manuscript General Minute Book, Court of Session, for Jun 1772–Jul 1773, 2 vols).

[56] Deazley, *Right to Copy* (n 4) 191–92.

[57] MacQueen, 'War of the Booksellers' (n 7) 245–46.

year. The title manifests the pamphlet's support for Donaldson's position on literary property.[58] It was reprinted in 1768 along with an appendix containing 'a letter to Robert Taylor, bookseller, in Berwick', Taylor being also the printer on this occasion. He was further the defendant in the crucial English case of *Millar v Taylor*, which would not be decided until 20 April 1769. Donaldson's immediate response to *Millar v Taylor*, another pamphlet dated 8 May 1769 which argued once more the case against any literary property beyond the Statute of Anne, and was very likely produced with the assistance of MacLaurin and, perhaps, other friends of Donaldson at the Scottish bar.[59]

Ilay Campbell, the author of the closely reasoned written informations for the Donaldson side, had, rather remarkably, already appeared for Hinton on the other side when the case was in the Outer House in 1771. Then he had been responsible for the written answers to a memorial of preliminary points for Donaldson. But later in 1771 Campbell wrote another information, this time for an Edinburgh printer defending an action brought against him for unauthorized republication of a book, *The Rudiments of the Latin Tongue*. It had never been registered at Stationers Hall despite a patent for its printing having been obtained in 1756 by the author (the Jacobite Latinist Thomas Ruddiman, who was himself a printer as well as librarian of the Advocates Library 1730–52).[60] The patent had expired by the time of the action, which was accordingly based on a common law right of literary property. The apparent change of mind involved in Campbell's arguing against the common law right in the Ruddiman case may have prompted his subsequent switch to Donaldson's side.[61] It is not known, unfortunately, how this case was finally decided; perhaps it, and the other actions raised by the London booksellers in the course of 1772, were sisted (suspended) to await the outcome in *Hinton v Donaldson*.

We have for the eighteenth century an unusually large amount of detail about the judges' opinions in *Hinton v Donaldson* primarily because James Boswell took the trouble to gather and publish them in full text in a booklet of not quite 40 pages. There may have been an unanticipated delay in publication because Boswell spent the period between mid-August and late October 1773 on tour in the post-Culloden Highlands and Islands of Scotland with Dr Samuel Johnson. The case report eventually appeared early in 1774, 'printed by James Donaldson, for Alexander Donaldson, and sold at his Shop,

---

[58] In an unreported case of 1788 Lord Dreghorn refused interdict against piracy of a published account of a sensational trial which had, however, not been registered at Stationers Hall. See John P Grant, 'Pronounced for Doom: Deacon William Brodie' in John P Grant and Elaine E Sutherland (eds), *Pronounced for Doom: Early Scots Law Tales* (Avizandum 2013) 2 fn 1.

[59] *A Letter from a Gentleman in Edinburgh, to his Friend in London; concerning Literary Property* (1769). The pamphlet is signed by 'A Reader of Books' but is generally attributed to Donaldson.

[60] ALSP, Arniston Collection, vol 3, no 16. See further AP Woolrich, 'Ruddiman, Thomas (1674–1757)', ODNB <http://www.oxforddnb.com/view/article/24249>. The case also raises the intriguing question of how many other such individual printing patents were still being granted in favour of works not registered at Stationers Hall.

[61] The information written by Campbell in the Ruddiman case and that for the pursuer (written by David Rae, making the same arguments as he would later make for the pursuer in *Hinton v Donaldson*) can be found in ALSP, Arniston Collection, vol 3, no 16.

No 48 St Paul's Churchyard, London, and Edinburgh; and by all the Booksellers in Scotland'. Thus, despite the delay, the publication was not simply the product of a successful advocate's vanity. It was clearly part of Donaldson's preparation for his appeal to the House of Lords in *Donaldson v Becket*, providing material that could be laid before the court to show the Scottish judges' reasoning on the general question to be determined.[62] The accuracy of Boswell's record can be confirmed from other contemporary notes of the judges' opinions taken by Ilay Campbell and one of the judges (Lord Hailes).[63]

These materials all show that much in the judges' arguments flowed from the powerful Civilian influence on Scottish legal thinking. For the Scots lawyer the 'common law' was closely linked to European ideas of the *ius commune* as the *ius gentium*, Roman law and, ultimately, the *ius naturale*. Natural law was not something separate from, but was rather the foundation of Scots law. Its content was to be determined by looking at what men in general understood and accepted as well as the laws of other peoples and nations – the *ius gentium*. For this purpose the law of England could of course be considered, but if that law was the only system to recognize a right of literary property outside statutory provision or the grant of a special privilege, then it was not very powerful support for the existence of such a right in Scots law. Certainly the mere fact that the English courts had held that such a right existed was not decisive for the Scottish courts. The absence of any previous reference to such a right in Roman or Scots law was also evidence that it was not a natural right, readily comprehended by all.[64]

The judges were probably also influenced by restrictive notions of the role of equity in Scots law. In the later seventeenth century Stair had argued in Aristotleian mode that equity, in the sense of the equality of persons, was part of the law of nature and thus informed the whole of the law, rather than being only a means of moderating the rigour of strict law.[65] Hence equity, 'as the first and universal law', was the recourse when other more formal sources – ancient custom, statutes and recent custom in the practice of the court – ran out. This was tempered, however, by 'expediency, whereby laws are drawn in consequence *ad similes casus*'.[66] The writers of the eighteenth century modified Stair's bold approach significantly, especially in relation to the equitable extension of statute.[67] We have already noted Kames' argument on this point in *Principles of Equity*, directly addressing the interpretation of the Statute of Anne.[68]

---

[62] Tompson, 'Scottish Judges' (n 27) 29; Rose, *Authors and Owners* (n 27) 95–96.

[63] See Sir David Dalrymple, Lord Hailes, *Decisions of the Lords of Council and Session from 1766 to 1791, selected from the original MSS by M P Brown, Esq, Advocate*, 2 vols (1826) vol 1, 535–43. The notes taken by Ilay Campbell as the judges delivered their opinions can be found on the covers of the informations at ALSP, Campbell Collection (ie, his own collection of Session Papers), vol 2, 3, nos 8–9.

[64] MacQueen, 'War of the Booksellers' (n 7) 249.

[65] Stair, *Institutions* (n 30) bk I, tit i, s 6.

[66] Ibid bk I, tit i, ss 15 & 16.

[67] See for the dilution of Stair's ideas Forbes, *Institutes* (n 30), Preliminary Dissertation concerning Law in General and the Several Kinds of it; Bankton, *Institute* (n 6) bk I, tit 1; Erskine, *Institute* (n 18) bk I, tit 1.

[68] See above text accompanying notes 37–42.

132 *Research handbook on the history of copyright law*

Bankton stated that only the legislature itself had the power to moderate the rigour of a statute with considerations of equity,[69] while Erskine thought 'correctory' statutes fell to be strictly interpreted[70] and added, in a passage clearly applicable to the Statute of Anne:

> Laws which carry a dispensation or privilege to particular persons or societies receive a strict interpretation; because, though they are profitable to the grantee, they derogate from the general law, and most commonly imply a burden upon the rest of the community; for which reason they reach no further than to the person or society privileged.[71]

While neither pleadings nor judgments in *Hinton v Donaldson* make direct reference to these issues, a number of the judges clearly took a strict approach in order to determine that the legislation showed no recognition of any rights in authors beyond its own terms.[72] A further point of significance in the *Hinton* opinions can be more readily identified as a result of our earlier discussion of the real right of property – outright ownership – and the different real right of exclusive privilege. Several of the judges referred to the distinction in denying the existence of rights of literary property beyond the statutory privileges.[73] A final important feature of the opinions, however, is that most of the judges were careful to distinguish between unpublished and published books. With the former, they were much more ready to recognize the existence of a general property right.[74]

6. UNPUBLISHED WORKS

The questions raised in *Hinton v Donaldson* about unpublished works quickly became a matter for decision in the Court of Session in relation to the rather special problem of private correspondence.[75] In *Dodsley v MacFarquhar*[76] in 1775, letters written by the Earl of Chesterfield to his son were, after the death of the two men, sold by the son's widow to a London publisher (Dodsley) who published them with the consent of the Earl's executors. Prior to giving that consent, however, the executors had obtained from the Lord Chancellor in England an injunction against publication. The book was registered in Stationers Hall. Dodsley's complaint in the Court of Session was that

---

[69] Bankton, *Institute* (n 6) bk I, tit 1, s 64.
[70] Erskine, *Institute* (n 18) bk I, tit 1, s 53.
[71] Ibid bk I, tit 1, s 55.
[72] MacQueen, 'War of the Booksellers' (n 7) 248.
[73] Ibid 250–51.
[74] Ibid 252.
[75] For insightful discussion of contemporary social attitudes towards personal correspondence see Katrina Williamson, 'The Emergence of Privacy: Letters, Journals and Domestic Writing' in Ian Brown, Thomas Clancy, Susan Manning and Murray Pittock (eds), *The Edinburgh History of Scottish Literature: Enlightenment, Britain and Empire (1707–1918)* (EUP 2006).
[76] (1775) Mor 8308; more fully at ibid, Literary Property, Appendix, 1. The case received extensive coverage in contemporary English as well as Scottish newspapers, information for which I am grateful to Tomás Gómez-Arostegui (personal communication on file with me).

several Edinburgh booksellers, including Colin MacFarquhar as well as, inevitably, Alexander Donaldson, had without authority imported copies from England and also published reprints. Several copies of the printed pleadings survive, and one bears handwritten notes of the court's opinions.[77] The publishers, who also produced an opinion in their favour by John Dunning of the Middle Temple, 'one of the ablest barristers of the time',[78] were held entitled to an interdict. The court rejected contrary arguments that the Statute of Anne conferred no express right upon an author's representatives after his death, and that neither the recipient nor his widow had such rights of property in the letters as would enable them to publish. While the son and then the widow might own the manuscripts, a prohibition of publication was at least implied; and some of the letters expressly stated that they should remain secret. With regard to this latter point, the court seems to have accepted the counter-argument that it was for the sender's representatives to take the point about obligations of secrecy, not those who sought to give the material further public circulation. But the court did not rely upon any notion that the sender retained a right of property in the letters, whether in reference to the original manuscripts or their content. An appeal to the House of Lords was contemplated but eventually not pursued.[79]

Dodsley v MacFarquhar seems to have been relatively little noticed at first, being only briefly reported in Lord Woodhouselee's supplementary volumes (published in 1797) to Kames' Folio Dictionary, from whence it was copied into the collection of reports known as Morison's Dictionary published between 1801 and 1804.[80] The much fuller report produced in the 'Literary Property' appendix to Morison's Dictionary published in 1808 was presumably the result of the research on the case carried out for the next major case, *Cadell and Davies v Stewart*, decided in 1804.[81] Six years after the death of the poet Robert Burns in 1796, a Glasgow publisher projected the publication of a volume of his letters to Agnes McLehose, a close friend whom he addressed as 'Clarinda' (dubbing himself 'Sylvander'). Clarinda, the publisher claimed, consented to

---

[77] ALSP Campbell Collection vol 76, no 8; SLSP vols 166, no 7 and 347, no 2 (the last having the MS notes of the judges' opinions).

[78] ADM Forte, 'Opinions by "Eminent English Counsel": Their Use in Insurance Cases before the Court of Session in the Late Eighteenth and Early Nineteenth Centuries' (1995) Jur Rev 345, 360. On the practice of obtaining English counsel's opinions for use in Scottish cases at this time see further MacQueen, 'War of the Booksellers' (n 7) 244.

[79] Parliamentary Archives, HL/PO/JO/10/3/268/10. I owe this reference to Tomás Gómez-Arostegui.

[80] See *Folio Dictionary* vol 3 (1797) 388. On Woodhouselee's contribution to the *Folio Dictionary* reports series, see David M Walker, *The Scottish Jurists* (W Green 1985) 224; and on the publication of Morison's Dictionary and its appendices see Kenneth Reid, 'A Note on Law Reporting' in Kenneth Reid and Reinhard Zimmermann (eds), *A History of Private Law in Scotland* (2 vols, OUP 2000) vol 1, liv–lxi, lvi.

[81] *Cadell and Davies v Stewart* (1804) Mor, Literary Property, Appendix, 13. See further ALSP, vol 52 (Hume Collection) no 6; vol 65 (Blair Collection) no 13; vol 114 (Campbell Collection) nos 2–3; and Faculty Collection February 1804–July 1804, no 166. See also Hector L MacQueen, 'Ae Fond Kiss: A Private Matter?' in Andrew Burrows, David Johnston and Reinhard Zimmermann (eds), *Judge and Jurist: Essays in Memory of Lord Rodger of Earlsferry* (OUP 2013).

the publication.[82] London and Edinburgh booksellers who had acquired rights to all Burns' works and also had with the concurrence of the Burns family successfully sought interdict to stop the publication. Their argument, put forward by George Joseph Bell advocate, and based on English authorities such as *Pope v Curll*[83] and *Duke of Queensberry v Shebbeare*,[84] was that an addressee such as Clarinda acquired only a limited property right in a letter, with no right to use it in any other way than as manuscript. No reconciliation was attempted between this limited property right and the traditional Scots law view of ownership as the most absolute of all rights, capable of being vested in only one person at a time except in the case of co-ownership where property is held in common by more than one person. But, crucially, the concurrence of the Burns family also enabled further arguments, based on their interest in preventing injury to Burns' character and reputation. On the other side, counsel argued that the recipient had full and unfettered property in the letters, and even if their publication was detrimental to Burns' reputation, that could not restrict the owner's, ie, Clarinda's, legal use of her property. Breach of confidence was an argument of morality, not law: 'whoever intrusts any secret, or makes any communication to another, commits himself in some measure to the discretion of his friend, and he can never hope, by means of a suspension and interdict, to prevent him from telling the secret.'[85]

The judges' opinions can be gleaned from notes taken at the time they were handed down.[86] The property arguments in relation to the letters on both sides were clearly rejected. The report in Morison's Dictionary correctly noted 'little difference of opinion upon the Bench' and summarized the 'ground upon which the Court seemed to pronounce the decision' as follows:

> That the communication in letters is always made under the implied confidence that they shall not be published without the consent of the writer, and that the representatives of Burns had a sufficient interest, for the vindication of his literary character, to restrain this publication.[87]

Discussing these cases alongside the English authorities in his lectures, Hume observed that 'it seems obvious that letters are written and conveyed under the implied condition of not being published without the consent of the writer, who in that respect has certainly no intention of transferring the property of what he writes'.[88] Bell also argued that English law was different from Scots law in denying the right to publish letters: 'In England, it is on the ground of property alone; in Scotland, on the ground chiefly of a just and expedient interference for the protection of reputation.'[89] The argument was reiterated in more detail in Bell's *Commentaries*:

---

[82] Doubt as to the reality of her consent emerges from the pleadings for Cadell and Davies as found in the Session Papers, but the court did not need to make any findings on the matter.
[83] *Pope v Curll* (1741) 2 Atk 342.
[84] *Duke of Queensberry v Shebbeare* (1758) 2 Eden 329.
[85] *Cadell and Davies v Stewart* (1804) Mor, Literary Property, Appendix, 16.
[86] See MacQueen, 'Ae Fond Kiss' (n 81) 479–80, 483–85.
[87] *Cadell and Davies v Stewart* (1804) Mor, Literary Property, Appendix, 16.
[88] Hume (n 9) vol 4, 68.
[89] Bell, *Principles* (n 15) s 1356.

In Scotland, the Court of Session is held to have jurisdiction, by interdict, to protect not property merely, but reputation, and even private feelings, from outrage and invasion. ... By the publication of such effusions, confidential, careless, unthinking of consequences, a man may be wounded in the tenderest part; his literary reputation hurt; his character traduced. It is, accordingly, the understood or implied condition of the communication, the implied limitation of the right conferred, that such communications are not to be published.[90]

In this passage, incidentally, the remedy of interdict is once more extended in scope, from the protection of property on to personality rights. Bell also noted that 'doubts seem to be entertained in England, whether letters falling into the hands of the assignees of bankrupts could be secured from publication by injunction'. 'With us,' he wrote, 'I think, there would be no such doubt.'[91] But Bell limited this personality right analysis to correspondence; otherwise 'unpublished compositions are property at common law; and the publication of them is an invasion of the rights of the owner'.[92]

The Scottish courts nonetheless maintained their refusal to extend protection beyond the Statute of Anne until 1811,[93] when the House of Lords in *Cadell and Davies v Robertson*, a Scottish appeal about the rights in a book of Burns' poetry not registered at Stationers Hall, overturned the view of the Court of Session that no action was competent in such a case.[94] Lord Chancellor Eldon observed that the Statute was 'uniformly administered ... in this country',[95] and cited the 1798 King's Bench decision in *Beckford v Hood*[96] as deciding that unregistered authors nevertheless had exclusive rights to publish, and their publishers could obtain injunctions and damages for infringement. Eldon added:

The judges in Scotland say truly, that they ought not to decide as the judges in England decide, unless they decide rightly and according to the law of Scotland. On the other hand, we may say, that if the judges in Scotland have not decided right, they are not to be followed; and in my own view, they have misunderstood the meaning of the statute in this instance.[97]

The significance of this was a holding that the Statute simply recognized a right of authors existing antecedent to registration in Stationers Hall, which merely conferred a right to particular remedies in relation to that right. It was presumably by way of silent comment on this passage that its reporter provided as an appendix the text of the judicial opinions in *Hinton v Donaldson*. But that case actually also recognized a

---

[90] Bell, *Commentaries* (n 14) vol 1, 111–12.
[91] Ibid 112. See also ibid 114, for more expansive use of interdict in Scotland than would be possible with injunctions in England.
[92] Bell, *Principles* (n 15) s 1356.
[93] See *Payne and Cadell v Anderson and Robertson* (1787) Mor 8312 (where however interdict and damages were granted on the basis that the defenders had committed the wrong (*crimen falsi*) of counterfeiting the pursuers' book.
[94] *Cadell and Davies v Robertson* (1811) 5 Pat 453. The reversed Court of Session decision is at (1804) Mor, Literary Property, Appendix, 16. For the pleadings in the Court of Session, see ALSP, vol 52 (Hume Collection), no 5 (also with MS notes of the judicial opinions). Note that Bell was counsel for the pursuers in the Court of Session.
[95] (1811) 5 Pat at 504.
[96] *Beckford v Hood* (1798) 7 D & E 620.
[97] (1811) 5 Pat at 504.

136   *Research handbook on the history of copyright law*

pre-publication right in authors, without defining what happened to it upon publication, still less the effect of non-registration thereafter. The decision in the *Robertson* case was thus not utterly irreconcilable with *Hinton*, and Bell's general view not without Scottish authority either.

7.   TO THE COPYRIGHT ACT 1911

There is little to say about how the Scottish courts handled statutory copyright in the remainder of the nineteenth century. They accepted that the right was not dependent upon the literary or artistic quality or aesthetic merit of a work. In *Alexander v Mackenzie*,[98] for example, copyright was held to exist in a collection of conveyancing styles, while similar decisions were reached with regard to a list of imports and exports called the 'Clyde Bill of Entry',[99] a trade price list,[100] and a railway timetable.[101] The extension of the copyright term by the Copyright Act 1842 came just in time to preserve the copyright in the works of Sir Walter Scott which would be successfully defended in *Black v Murray* in 1870, a year prior to an exhibition marking the centenary of Scott's birth.[102]

The limited case law of the period on unpublished works and correspondence tended to bear out Bell's distinction between an author's right of property in an unpublished work and a letter-writer's entitlement to control publication to protect reputation. An 1855 jury case held the writer of a letter to a newspaper editor for publication entitled to withdraw it before publication, albeit without reference to Bell.[103] In 1881 the Court of Session discharged an interdict against publication of personal correspondence (while noting that there might be a remedy after publication if injury was caused thereby); but the judges, although thinking the rules the same in England and Scotland, cited Bell and were clear that there was no property, literary or otherwise, in the letters.[104] Four years later, however, in the great case of *Caird v Sime*,[105] which concerned the unauthorized publication of the lecture notes of the Professor of Moral Philosophy at Glasgow University, the judges of the Whole Court of Session were virtually unanimous in declaring that the author of an unpublished work had a right of property in his work, citing mainly English authorities on the matter. This view was upheld in the House of Lords, where the leading speech was given by the Scottish Law Lord, Watson.[106] All were clear, however, that this property right was not copyright, and that it ceased upon publication. The Copyright Act 1911 swept any lingering debate

---

[98]   (1847) 9 D 748.
[99]   *Maclean v Moody* (1858) 20 D 1154.
[100] *Harpers v Barry Henry* (1892) 20 R 133.
[101] *Leslie v Young* (1893) 21 R (HL) 57.
[102] Catherine Seville, *Literary Copyright Reform in Early Victorian England* (CUP 1999) 194–95; *Black v Murray* (1870) 9 M 341.
[103] *Davis v Miller and Fairly* (1855) 17 D 1166.
[104] *White v Dickson* (1881) 8 R 896.
[105] *Caird v Sime* (1885) 13 R 23.
[106] *Caird v Sime* (1887) 14 R (HL) 37.

away with its abolition of the requirement of registration at Stationers Hall and its inclusion of unpublished works in general within the copyright umbrella.

8. CONCLUSION: WORK TO BE DONE

The account just given of the post-1707 history of copyright in Scotland draws heavily on recently published detailed research on the leading cases of *Hinton v Donaldson* and *Cadell and Davies v Stewart*.[107] Similar research is under way upon other such cases, notably *Dodsley v MacFarquhar* and *Cadell and Davies v Robertson*. All these cases were however already relatively well known because they appear in the printed law reports. The research has incidentally shown that the mid-eighteenth century saw many other, not necessarily reported, cases on the subject, suggesting that deeper research in unpublished court records and archives will be well worthwhile.[108] Litigation however shows us only literary property issues in dispute; it tells us much less about the law as the basis for arrangements between authors and their publishers. The subject has been touched upon from time to time in histories of publishing,[109] and also in the biographies of notable authors such as the philosopher David Hume (uncle of the law professor cited several times in this chapter) and the poet and novelist Sir Walter Scott.[110] No doubt, therefore, much more can be learned from further investigation in publishers' archives and collections of authors' private papers, not to mention evidence about readership of what authors and publishers actually produced.[111] Study to date seems also to be dominated by the book, with the publication of personal correspondence emerging as a further important issue in the latter part of the eighteenth century. But little, if anything, has been said about music, art and drama, despite a distinctive and thriving Scottish culture in all these domains in the nineteenth as well as the

---

[107] See above notes 5, 7, 81. See further for an account highlighting the patriotic dimension of the story, Warren McDougall, 'Copyright and Scottishness' in Stephen Brown and Warren McDougall (eds), *The Edinburgh History of the Book in Scotland volume 2: Enlightenment and Expansion 1707–1800* (EUP 2012) 23.

[108] See eg, notes 44, 45, 58 and 60 above. A good starting point for further work is the 'Literary Property' section and appendix in Morison's Dictionary, accessible via the Scottish Legal History section of Hein Online. The indexes to the Session Papers in the Advocates and especially the Signet Libraries, Edinburgh, provide the next port of call. The Signet indexes are available online: search archive.org for the author 'WSSociety'.

[109] See eg, Stephen Brown and Warren McDougall (n 107); Bill Bell (ed), *The Edinburgh History of the Book in Scotland vol 3: Ambition and Industry 1800–1880* (EUP 2007).

[110] See eg EC Mossner, *The Life of David Hume* (2nd edn, Clarendon Press 1980) 312–16; Jane Millgate, *Scott's Last Edition: A Study in Publishing History* (EUP 1987).

[111] See Mark R M Townsley, *Reading the Scottish Enlightenment: Books and their Readers in Provincial Scotland, 1750-1820* (Brill 2010); Vivienne Dunstan, 'Book Ownership in late Eighteenth-century Scotland: a Local Case Study of Dumfriesshire Inventories' (2012) 91 Scottish Historical Review 265.

eighteenth centuries.[112] For the nineteenth century in general, perhaps, the story to be told will be one of a Scotland increasingly embedded in a United Kingdom and indeed imperial world, but the study of which is capable nevertheless of tempering undue Anglo-centricity in British copyright history.

---

[112] For useful introductions to these fields, see Duncan MacMillan, *Scottish Art 1460–2000* (Mainstream 2000); Miles Glendinning, Ranald MacInnes and Aonghas MacKechnie, *A History of Scottish Architecture: From the Renaissance to the Present Day* (EUP 2002); Sara Stevenson and A D Morrison-Low, *Scottish Photography: The First Thirty Years* (National Museums Scotland 2015); John Purser, *Scotland's Music: A History of the Traditional and Classical Music of Scotland from Early Times to the Present Day* (Mainstream 2007); Ian Brown (ed), *The Edinburgh Companion to Scottish Drama* (EUP 2011).

8. Music copyright in late eighteenth and early nineteenth century Britain

*Nancy A. Mace**

1. INTRODUCTION

The history of English music copyright in the late eighteenth and early nineteenth centuries is distinct from that of letterpress books because of music's status as intellectual property and the processes by which music was reproduced during this period. Unlike books printed from moveable type, which were considered a valuable market commodity almost from the invention of the printing press and led to the 1710 Act of Anne, music was largely regarded as ephemera, whose value was so limited that it did not initially warrant protection as intellectual property. However, with the rise of the middle class by the late eighteenth century, the demand for printed music increased, prompting composers and music sellers to attempt to control what had become a profitable commodity.[1] Thus, the latter half of the eighteenth and early years of the nineteenth centuries are significant in the history of music copyright because during that period members of the music trade and their legal representatives considered many of the issues still central to modern concepts of music as intellectual property.[2]

As important as musical compositions became in the late eighteenth century, however, individuals involved in the music trade and the courts recognized that laws designed to protect rights in printed books did not easily apply to music. The 1710 Act of Anne did not specifically mention music under the types of publications it covered. In addition, because music was printed from pewter plates rather than moveable type, it more closely resembled engravings, covered by the 1735 Engraving Act. Furthermore, since musical notation was a form of universal language, not limited to a single nation, laws dealing with publication in foreign languages were not readily applicable to printed musical compositions. Finally, the very nature of musical editions suggested

---

* Note on sources: Sources that begin with C (Chancery), E (Exchequer) and KB (King's Bench) are stored in the National Archives of the United Kingdom in Kew, England. The British Library is abbreviated as BL.

[1] During the eighteenth and nineteenth centuries, the term *publisher* referred to individuals who sold books and music, whereas members of the trade who purchased copyrights and arranged for works to be printed and sold were called *music sellers*. This terminology is similar to that used in the book trade, where a publisher was an individual who sold books, whereas a bookseller acquired copyrights and handled the printing and selling of books. Other members of the music trade were engravers and printers.

[2] In the eighteenth and early nineteenth centuries, performance right was not an issue. For a discussion of the rare instances in which the subject arose, see John Small, 'The Development of Music Copyright' in Michael Kassler (ed), *The Music Trade in Georgian England* (Ashgate 2011) 233, 381–83.

that they were not comparable to books, for many musical pieces required only one or two sheets, unlike books composed of many pages, and music sellers often sold the same work in a wide variety of formats.

The history of music copyright at this time falls into three distinct periods, the first two divided by the landmark decision in *Bach v Longman & Lukey* (1777), when Justice Mansfield ruled that music was a type of writing governed by the Act of Anne (1710), England's first copyright law of the modern era. The third period is bounded by the Copyright Act of 1842, the first major revision of English copyright law. Thus, this chapter treats the state of music as intellectual property before the *Bach* decision, examines the ruling itself, and explores the issues left unsettled after this landmark case.

2. THE PERIOD BEFORE *BACH v LONGMAN*

Given the difficulties of applying the existing law to music in the period before 1777, both composers and music sellers resorted to various strategies in order to control the dissemination of musical compositions.[3] In advertisements, notices attached to music publications and lawsuits, they justified their assertions of exclusive rights in different ways. William Tans'ur (1706–83), a musician and engraver, claimed protection under the 1735 Engraving Copyright Act by citing the law in a notice included in his *Royal Psalmodist Compleat* (1745, 1748), warning individuals not to copy or engrave any part of his work. However clever this stratagem, no one ever fully tested it in the law courts, nor did others routinely adopt it, primarily because of the difficulties in applying the law to music. After all, the 1735 Act required that the engraver also be the inventor, or author, of the print, who would in this case have to be the composer. Second, a publication line invoking the Engraving Copyright Act had to appear on each print or plate, not just the title page, which was commonly not the practice with music.[4]

Another way in which composers and occasionally music sellers tried to prevent unauthorized editions was to obtain a royal privilege from the Crown granting them exclusive rights to musical compositions. Some covered single compositions, while others included a few or all of a composer's works. David Hunter, John Small, and Shef Rogers have identified at least 40 such privileges from the early eighteenth century

---

[3] For full discussions of their efforts, see the following: David Hunter, 'Music Copyright in Britain to 1800' (1986) 67 Music & Letters 269, 269–79; Michael W Carroll, 'The Struggle for Music Copyright' (2005) 57 Fla L Rev 907, 920–43; Small, 'The Development of Music Copyright' (n 2) 256–329.

[4] For a full discussion of Tans'ur and his attempt to apply the law to music, see Hunter 'Music Copyright' (n 3) 278; David Hunter, 'Copyright Protection for Engravings and Maps in Eighteenth-Century Britain' (1987) 7 The Library (6th ser) 128, 142–43. Small, 'The Development of Music Copyright' (n 2) 300–01, also briefly discusses the Tans'ur case. In his bill of complaint against Henry Roberts and John Johnson in 1741, Thomas Augustine Arne invoked the Engraving Act as one basis for his action against these music sellers. For a full account see Ronald J Rabin and Steven Zohn, 'Arne, Handel, Walsh, and Music as Intellectual Property: Two Eighteenth-Century Lawsuits' (1995) 120 J of the Royal Musical Association 112, 117–25, 135–40. The bill and answer for the suit are C11/2260/7.

until around 1770.[5] Privilege holders used these grants to guard against unauthorized printing in two ways. First, composers issued warnings in newspapers and on title pages to discourage dishonest music printers. For example, Thomas Augustine Arne, who was diligent in protecting his compositions, placed at least two notices in the London *Daily Post* in 1741, reminding readers of his royal license and warning potential pirates that he would prosecute them according to law.[6] Second, they cited these privileges in lawsuits filed in Chancery after an unauthorized reprint appeared. In 1741 Arne invoked his privilege along with the 1710 Statute and the Engraving Act of 1735 when he sued the music sellers Henry Roberts and John Johnson for printing and selling unauthorized editions of his compositions.[7] He sought an injunction to prevent them from continuing to issue the works. As the answers of Roberts and Johnson demonstrated, defendants usually challenged the validity of such privileges. Finally in 1775, the Court of Common Pleas lent significant support to such arguments when it voided the patent for almanacs in *Stationers v Carnan*.[8] Thus, like the Engraving Copyright Act, the royal privilege did not prove an effective defense against unauthorized publications.

As the Arne case demonstrates, some litigants did attempt to apply the 1710 copyright statute to musical compositions. In 1769 Isaac Bickerstaffe filed two suits in Chancery against the music engravers Henry Roberts and Henry Fought for printing songs from *The Padlock* (1769). Although Bickerstaffe wrote the libretto, Charles Dibdin, who composed the music, had sold him the rights to it, making Bickerstaffe the proprietor of the music as well as the words. While he did not specifically mention the Act of Anne in his bills of complaint, he alluded to it in his final request to the court when he said that he was 'waiving all penalties incurred… for any Offence or Offences

---

[5] Hunter, 'Music Copyright' (n 3) 277–78; Shef Rogers, 'The Use of Royal Licenses for Printing in England, 1695–1760: A Bibliography' (2000) 1 The Library (7th ser) 133; Small, 'The Development of Music Copyright' (n 2) 276–93 discusses the use of such privileges extensively.

[6] *London Daily Post* (9 March 1741), (24 May 1741). John Worgan, who composed popular songs for Vauxhall Gardens, published a similar notice in 1755, reminding readers that he, too, had obtained a royal license. John Worgan, *Public Advertiser* (26 June 1755). The texts of these notices appear in John A Parkinson, 'Pirates and Publishers' (1972) 58 Performing Right Journal 20, 20–22.

[7] For a discussion of this litigation, see Rabin and Zohn (n 4) 117–25, 135–40. The bill and answer for this suit are C11/2260/7. As in many such cases, the paper trail ended after the initial pleadings, so we do not know whether the case was ever resolved or if the parties came to some private agreement. In 1771 John Pyle, as executor for the estate of the music seller John Walsh, Jr, filed two bills of complaint against the notorious music pirate Robert Falkener, invoking the privilege granted to Walsh in 1760 for printing Handel's music. In his amended bill he added works by the composers Arne and Maurice Greene and the librettist Isaac Bickerstaffe. His grounds for claiming exclusive rights to these works were copyright assignments signed by the respective individuals; thus, his bill implied that music was protected by common law. While the suit was eventually decided in Pyle's favor, Lord Chancellor Apsley did not produce written reasons for his decision. A full discussion of the case appears in Rabin and Zohn (n 4) 125–33, 140–45. The bills and answers are C12/2082/42.

[8] For a general discussion of royal privileges and the *Carnan* litigation as related to printing, see Cyprian Blagden, 'Thomas Carnan and the Almanack Monopoly' (1969) 14 Studies in Bibliography 23.

committed by him against any Act or Acts of Parliament,' suggesting, as did many plaintiffs suing over copyright infringement in equity courts, that he did not seek the statutory remedies to which he might be entitled under the 1710 law. Unfortunately, we do not know how these cases were resolved since they did not progress beyond the initial pleadings; like many such actions, the parties may have settled their differences out of court. In addition to these Chancery suits, Bickerstaffe placed several newspaper notices warning members of the music trade that he would prosecute anyone printing unauthorized editions of the songs from this popular entertainment.[9]

Given the difficulty of applying these strategies, scholars have, not surprisingly, found very few copyright suits filed before 1777 involving music, and, of those, the plaintiffs may have justified their claims for copyright protection because the reprints included unauthorized reproductions of text, specifically covered by the Act of Anne, virtually ignoring the musical notes. For example, in 1765 the librettist Isaac Bickerstaffe sued the music printer Henry Thorowgood for supposedly pirating the music from *The Maid of the Mill*, a musical entertainment for which Bickerstaffe had written the libretto. Bickerstaffe claimed that he had written the music and had adapted the airs for the German flute. He accused Thorowgood of producing an unauthorized edition of the favorite songs from the entertainment copied from this version. As Thorowgood noted in his answer, however, Bickerstaffe himself was not a composer but an author; in fact, Bickerstaffe did not have the rights to the music, since it was written by over 20 different composers and was very likely printed without their consent. Consequently, Thorowgood asserted his right to print his edition. Thus, as in most cases, we cannot clearly determine if the plaintiff's claims relied on an unauthorized reprint of the text rather than the music.[10]

---

[9] The suits are C12/1026/2 and C12/1026/3. Bickerstaffe's suit against Fought went no further than the bill of complaint; his action against Roberts produced a single affidavit from Bickerstaffe and the music seller John Johnson (C31/173/70). A discussion of these suits and Bickerstaffe's advertisements about *The Padlock* appear in Small, 'The Development of Music Copyright' (n 2) 321–23, and Carroll (n 3) 940–41.

[10] The bill and answer are E112/1569, no 730. Although Small states that Bickerstaffe registered the music with the Stationers on 31 January 1765, the entry reveals that the entry was for the text, not the music since the other individuals listed with Bickerstaffe (John Newberry, William Nicoll, William Griffin, Robert Baldwin, Thomas Caslon, Thomas Lowndes and Thomas Becket) were all booksellers rather than members of the music trade: Small, 'The Development of Music Copyright' (n 2) 320–21. A copy of the edition produced is BL 841.b.49. Entries did not always specify that the parties were registering a libretto alone or the music. However, I do not know of any instance in which a bookseller entered music with the Stationers during this period. The following also involved music to varying extents: *Geminiani v Walsh* (ca 1731 or 1732), discussed briefly in Rabin and Zohn (n 4), 112–13, which according to accounts, was settled out of court; *Thomas Holt v Thomas Lowe and Thomas Augustine Arne* (1752) E112/1223, no 2965, discussed in full by Judith Milhous and Robert D Hume, 'Librettist versus Composer: The Property Rights to Arne's *Henry and Emma* and *Don Saverio*' (1997) 122 J of the Royal Musical Association 52, which seems to have gone no further than the pleadings. While Carroll also cites *Gay v Read* (1728) as another action over music, this suit was almost certainly over the text of the ballad opera rather than the music since all of the defendants against whom John Gay filed his suit were not music but booksellers, demonstrating that he sued over unauthorized editions of the letterpress rather than printings of the songs from the ballad

Although some scholars have argued that music sellers were ambivalent or hostile to the idea of applying the Act of Anne to musical compositions, the position of the music trade before 1777 is not completely clear because the evidence is scarce.[11] In fact, some documents suggest that, like composers, music sellers were just as concerned about maintaining their exclusive rights to popular musical works. In 1772 the music seller John Johnson sued the music printer Robert Falkener for unauthorized reprints of popular tunes from *The Jubilee* (1769); like Bickerstaffe earlier, Johnson implied that his basis for bringing the suit was the 1710 Act because he waived any penalties he might receive as a result of any Act of Parliament.[12] Although Falkener did not file an answer, on 4 March 1772, the court issued an injunction prohibiting the defendant from printing or selling any more copies of the disputed songs.[13] In addition to this lawsuit, Johnson and other music sellers published notices in the newspapers warning their competitors that they would prosecute members of the trade who produced unauthorized editions of works owned by them.[14]

Another indication of music sellers' interest in maintaining their rights to copies was their attempt to reach an agreement about reprinting popular songs. Hitherto unknown to scholars, the arrangement suggests that music sellers had formed themselves into an association to control printing since the courts had not proven effective in protecting their rights. The primary source of information about these agreements is an Exchequer suit filed by James Longman and Francis Fane Broderip against the music seller Samuel Babb in July 1783 for producing unauthorized editions of several works owned by them. Although in his answer Babb admitted that he had printed and sold some of the songs in books of instruction for the German flute, he defended his action by describing two agreements made among music sellers. Depositions taken in the case confirmed his story and offered additional details about these arrangements.[15] According to these documents, sometime around December, 1769, an association of music sellers executed a signed document, agreeing that they would not violate each others' copyrights for one year. After that time the owners would permit other music sellers to insert their songs in books of instruction 'by way of example' without considering the practice a violation of copyright.[16] The only problem with this agreement was the

---

opera. See Carroll (n 3) 935–36; James R Sutherland, '"Polly" Among the Pirates' (1942) 37 Mod Lang Rev 291.

[11] For the supposed ambivalence of the trade to the Act of Anne, see Hunter, 'Music Copyright' (n 3) 276–77; Carroll (n 3) 930–34.

[12] The suit is C12/439/38.

[13] The order is C33/437, f 180.

[14] See, for example, notices quoted by Small 'The Development of Music Copyright' (n 2) 321–23, 330–32.

[15] The bill and answer are E112/1691, no 3460. The depositions are E133/82/26. Among other deponents, Peter Thompson testified that the agreement was signed by 'a Company or Society of Sellers of Music and Musical Compositions.' While he gave the date of the agreement as 1769, other witnesses placed it at 1772.

[16] John Johnson called for just such an agreement in the *Public Advertiser* for 24 September 1769, when he said, 'it is wished that the Dealers in Music would appoint a Place of Meeting to consider of Means to put their Property on a more permanent Footing than it is at present.' See a reference to this advertisement in Small, 'The Development of Music Copyright' (n 2) 322; he mistakenly gives the date of the advertisement as 23 instead of 24 September.

imprecise meaning of the term 'books of instruction,' since some members of the trade interpreted the term loosely, including any music compilation, whether intended as a teaching manual or not. In fact, Babb and several deponents noted that, like their competitors, Longman and Broderip used the terms of this agreement to reprint songs owned by others both in book form and as sheet music. This arrangement seems to have been in force until the early 1780s, when the group also decided to end the common practice of producing for customers handwritten copies of others' music.[17] Thus, despite the scarcity of litigation, the existing evidence indicates that even before the 1777 Bach decision, music sellers were attempting through the courts and through various written agreements to control the dissemination of music purchased by them.

3. BACH v LONGMAN

Although some rulings had suggested that the 1710 copyright law might be applicable in respect to music, the decision in *Johann Christian Bach v James Longman & Charles Lukey*, filed originally in 1773, resolved the question of music's status under the Act of Anne.[18] Because of its profound effect on music copyright, the case is worth reviewing in some detail. In December, 1763 the composer Johann Christian Bach obtained a royal privilege giving him exclusive rights over his own compositions for 14 years.[19] On 18 March 1773, Bach filed a bill of complaint in Chancery against the music seller James Longman and his partner at that time, Charles Lukey, accusing them of printing and selling two of his works, composed in 1769, without his permission. Although he cited his privilege as one reason for his suit, he also argued that he

---

[17] Charles Rennett later confirmed the existence of this arrangement in his 1784 litigation against James Longman and Francis Fane Broderip (E112/1702, no 3728). In his defense, Rennett mentioned the 1769 agreement, but he admitted that he had not been able to obtain a complete list of the participants when he had asked Longman and Broderip for such a document in writing. From his comments and from the depositions in the Babb case, we can safely identify some members of the association: Longman and Broderip, John Preston, Samuel, Ann, and Peter Thompson, and probably Samuel Babb. These names represented some of the most important music sellers in this period, and clearly they were joined by other prominent members of the profession.

[18] *Bach v Longman* (1777) 2 Cowp 623, 98 ER 1274, 1275. Detailed discussions of the case appear in the following: John Small, 'J C Bach goes to Law' (1985) 126 Musical Times 526, 526–29; Hunter (n 3) 278–80; Rabin and Zohn (n 4) 115–16; Ann Van Allen-Russell, '"For Instruments Not Intended": The Second J C Bach Lawsuit' (2002) 83 Music & Letters 3; Carroll (n 3) 942–45; Small, 'The Development of Music Copyright' (n 2) 329–70. Transcriptions of many of the original documents appear in Ann van Allen-Russell, 'Documents Relating to *Bach vs. Longman and Lukey*' in Ernest Warburton (ed), *Sources and Documents* in *The Collected Works of Johann Christian Bach, 1735–1782*, vol 48, part 2 (Garland 1999), 556, 557–82. Gwyn Walters, 'The Booksellers in 1759 and 1774: The Battle for Literary Property' (1974) 29 The Library (5th ser) 287, 304 mentions quite briefly the petition that Bach filed in the deliberations in Commons over the booksellers' petition for perpetual copyright, and Carroll (n 3) 944, fn 237 quotes the wording of Bach and Abel's petition to the 1774 committee considering revisions to the 1710 copyright law.

[19] The warrant appears in SP44/375, f 398–99.

deserved protection under the Statute of Anne.[20] Even though five days after the bill was filed Bach obtained a preliminary injunction from the court restraining Longman and Lukey from printing or selling any more copies until the court issued an order to the contrary, presumably after the defendants had answered the plaintiff's bill, he persisted in his efforts until he obtained a final decision and thereby set a precedent.[21]

During the course of this lawsuit, several events occurred that affected the proceedings and led Bach to ask for a ruling on the question of whether music was a type of writing governed by the Act of Anne. First was the House of Lords decision in *Donaldson v Becket* (22 February 1774), when they ruled that exclusive rights were limited to the 28 years specified in the Copyright Act of 1710. As a result, the booksellers, who regarded their copyrights as perpetual, asked the House of Commons for relief. Among the petitions submitted to the committee assigned to consider the issue was that of Bach and Charles Frederick Abel, who asked the committee on their own behalf and that of other composers that it consider the question of music's status under the Act of Anne.[22] Unfortunately for Bach, Abel and other interested parties in the musical world, the committee refused to take the opinion of counsel on the issue. Then in 1775 the decision in *Stationers v Carnan* undermined the validity of Bach's privilege by affirming that the Crown only had a right to grant printing monopolies in limited cases; presumably music was not in this limited category. Thus, Bach was forced to press in the courts his argument that the Statute of Anne governed music. The case finally came before the Lord Chancellor in May 1776, when Bach's counsel argued that music was a form of writing covered by the Act of Anne. The court referred the question to King's Bench. On 16 June 1777 the full King's Bench certified to the Court of Chancery that music was protected by the Copyright Act. Consequently, when on 8 July 1777 the Court of Chancery heard the case again, it decided in Bach's favor.[23] In spite of the small financial award the composer received, the decision had far-reaching implications, for it established music's status as intellectual property protected by copyright law.

---

[20] These details are given in C12/71/22.
[21] The order, dated 23 March 1773, is C33/439, f 185.
[22] Dated 15 March 1774. Carroll (n 3) 944, fn 237, quotes the text of this petition. For a complete account of the petition and the committee's response, see Small, 'J C Bach goes to Law' (n 18) 528; Small, 'Development of Music Copyright' (n 2) 349–53. This was not the first time that music's status under the Act was considered by Parliament. In fact, clause 23 of a bill proposed in 1737 as a revision to the 1710 copyright law, stated 'That this Act shall extend, and be construed and taken to extend, to the Author or Authors of any Book or Books of Musick, or any Composition in Musick whatsoever, whether printed or engraved.' Unfortunately, this bill did not become law because it never passed the House of Lords. For the text, see *An Act for the Encouragement of Learning* (Draft), London (1737), Lionel Bently and Martin Kretschmer (eds), Primary Sources on Copyright (1450–1900), <http://www.copyrighthistory.org> accessed 1 January 2015. (Original is BL 357.c.7.(41)).
[23] The Judges' Certificate, dated 27 July 1777, detailing the ruling in King's Bench is C38/668. According to the Master's Report filed 5 April 1778, Bach was awarded £4 3-½d, representing the profits the music sellers had earned from sales of the disputed composition, and the 200 copies still remaining unsold. In addition, Bach received £72 14s 11d, his court costs. C38/675.

4. THE PERIOD AFTER THE *BACH* DECISION

This ruling had a profound effect on the music trade in two ways. First, music sellers and later composers increasingly registered musical works with the Stationers' Company in order to protect their property. Before 1775, only 53 pieces appeared in the entry books; from 1776–1800, 2,764 musical compositions were registered, representing almost a third of all books entered.[24] The decision also led to a flurry of litigation as music sellers used the law both to protect monopolies and intimidate their competition. These suits raised important issues about the application of the Act of Anne to music that the *Bach* decision did not settle.

The first individual to repeatedly use this ruling against the competition was Charles Rennett (1736–87), an attorney who practiced in the King's Bench. Rennett had extensive connections in the music trade and the theatrical world; in fact, one of his daughters married the singer Charles Dignum, and his will noted that at his death he possessed several musical instruments.[25] At least one individual testified that, in addition to his legal credentials, Rennett was a Doctor of Music.[26] Thus, he was uniquely suited to play an important role in the development of music copyright after the *Bach* decision. He had the legal training necessary to recognize ambiguities in the copyright law, particularly as it applied to music. In addition, he had musical training and knew composers, musicians, and theatre managers, enabling him easily to obtain copyrights and find clients to represent.

In 1778 Rennett established a foothold in the music trade when he became the silent partner of the music seller John Welcker, who had recently gone bankrupt. At the sale of Welcker's stock in trade, held 6 July 1780, Rennett bought approximately 22 works owned by Welcker, and he later purchased additional compositions directly from composers like Johann Christian Bach, John Garth, and Charles Dibdin. He then used his legal knowledge to intimidate his competitors in the music trade by threatening to sue them for pirating works that he owned. Some music sellers avoided litigation by

---

[24] For this account of music registrations, see Nancy A Mace, 'The Market for Music in the Late Eighteenth Century and the Entry Books of the Stationers' Company' (2009) 10 The Library (7th ser) 157.

[25] The source for his birthdate is E133/82/27, dated 1781, where Rennett gave his age as 45. His death on 3 August (his last name was misspelled as 'Rennet') was announced in the *Times* (London, 8 August 1787) 4. One of the obvious problems in assessing Rennett's importance was the various ways in which his name is misspelled, which have often been perpetuated in modern accounts. For example, see the *Times* (London, 13 December 1785) 3, where his name appeared as 'Kennett.' In Frank Kidson, *British Music Publishers, Printers and Engravers* (Blom 1967) 38, under Joseph Dale, his name, based on manuscript transcription, is 'Charles Bennett'. Robert Fahrner, *The Theatre Career of Charles Dibdin the Elder (1745–1814)* (Peter Lang 1989) 111, mentions letters written by Dibdin to one 'Kennett.' From the context in each reference, the individual named is clearly Charles Rennett. For evidence of his daughter's marriage to Charles Dignum, see the letter in the Hampshire Record Office dated 26 May 1788 (1M44/103/8). Rennett's will, dated 1787, is PROB 11/1156, ff 241–46.

[26] In a deposition given on behalf of James Longman and Francis Fane Broderip, John Jeanes, one of their employees, called Rennett a 'Doctor of Music.' E133/104/67.

paying Rennett for what he claimed were unauthorized reprints.[27] Beginning in 1780 Rennett filed suits in the Court of Exchequer against others who denied his claims, initiating 11 suits in his name over the next five years.[28] At the end of 1780, after Rennett filed his first bill of complaint against the music sellers James Longman and Francis Fane Broderip, he stayed his suit when they agreed to employ him as their attorney.[29] As a result, in their name he initiated another ten copyright suits in the Exchequer, costing the music sellers several hundred pounds in legal fees.[30] By 1784, however, Longman and Broderip, concerned about the expense of such litigation, the waste of their time, and the bad will it generated with others in the trade, ordered Rennett to discontinue his efforts on their behalf.[31] Rennett, therefore, broke off his association with them and filed suit once again.

In addition to their lengthy dispute with their attorney, however, Longman & Broderip were either plaintiffs or defendants in at least seven further equity suits over copyright from 1784 to 1791 besides their litigation against Rennett.[32] Thus far,

[27] For example, the music sellers Thomas Cahusac, John Preston, and John Fentum each paid Rennett four or five guineas for the rights to reprint music purchased by Rennett from Charles Dibdin. E112/1702, no 3728; E112/1756, nos 5276, 5277. A notation by William Forster's attorney James Mainstone indicates that the music seller consulted him about Rennett's demand for compensation. BL Egerton MS 2380, f 13.

[28] The bills are the following: *Rennett v Schearer and Bland* (1782) E112/1681, no 3196; *Rennett v Holland* (1783) E112/1684, no 3271; *Rennett v Freeman & Cooper* (1783) E112/1697, no 3590; *Rennett v Napier* (1783) E112/1697, no 3598; *Rennett v Haxby* (1783) E112/1697, no 3601; *Rennett v Nicolai* (1782) E112/1697, no 3619; *Rennett v Thompsons* (1785) E112/1705, no 3808; *Rennett v Haxby* (1785) E112/1718, no 4152; *Rennett v Longman & Broderip* (1785) E112/1758, no 5276; *Rennett v Longman & Broderip* (1784) E112/1758, no 5277; *Rennett v Kerpen, Freeman, and Cooper* (1780) E112/1809, no 7081.

[29] An account of their arrangement appeared in Rennett's answer to Longman & Broderip's bill of complaint against him (E112/1702, no 3728) and in his amended and supplemental bills of complaint against them (E112/1758, nos 5276 and 5277). A fuller account of their dealings appears in Nancy A Mace, 'Charles Rennett and the London Music-Sellers in the 1780s: Testing the Ownership of Reversionary Copyrights' (2004) 129 J of the Royal Musical Association 1, 6–10.

[30] The suits almost certainly filed on their behalf by Rennett were the following: *Longman & Broderip v Fielding* (1783) E112/1684, no 3268; *Longman & Broderip v Sibbald* (1783) E112/1690, no 3450; *Longman & Broderip v Fielding, Harrison & Drury* (1784) E112/1690, no 3452; *Longman & Broderip v Williams* (1783) E112/1691, no 3456; *Longman & Broderip v Bland* (1783) E112/1691, no 3457; *Longman & Broderip v Babb* (1783) E112/1691, no 3460; *Longman & Broderip v Massey* (1783) E112/1691, no 3461; *Longman & Broderip v Haxby* (1783) E112/1691, no 3462; *Longman & Broderip v Roome* (1783) E112/1691, no 3466; *Longman & Broderip v Wilks* (1783) E112/1708, no 3895. The wording of these bills of complaint is virtually identical.

[31] A sign of their strained relations with other music sellers is the receipt given in 1782 by James Nares to the music seller John Preston, stating, 'I James Nares of James Street Westminster, do promise to indemnify M\(^r\) Preston from any Charges that may arise from any Suite in Law, brought on him by Mess\(^{rs}\) Longman and Broadrip[*sic*], on Account of his selling the Book, entitled, a Concise, & easy Treatise on Singing.' Receipts of Preston and Company from 1780 through the 1800s, BL Add MS 63814.

[32] The bills and answers are as follows: *Babb v Longman & Broderip* (1784) E112/1705, no 3821; *Forster v Longman & Broderip* (1788) E112/1724, no 4329; *Longman & Broderip v*

148   *Research handbook on the history of copyright law*

scholars have only found two other music copyright suits for this time period in which neither Rennett nor Longman & Broderip were parties.[33] One significant fact about these suits is that, in nearly every case, both the plaintiffs and the defendants were music sellers, not composers. Thus, even though the landmark decision about music's status as intellectual property was the result of actions filed by composers, the beneficiaries of the decision were predominantly the members of the music trade. Given the expenses involved in equity suits, this turn of events is not surprising since music sellers had the financial resources to pursue a claim until they were granted an injunction. Most composers did not have sufficient funds to carry on what could become a complicated and lengthy undertaking.

In fact, Rennett took advantage of the composer Charles Dibdin's financial problems to acquire the reversionary rights to several popular musical entertainments written by the composer in the late 1760s. The 1710 Statute of Anne granted authors an initial right of 14 years, which would be extended for another term of the same length if the author or composer were still living at the end of the first period. Even though this provision implied that an author could take back and presumably resell his copyright to a new owner, members of both the book and music trades assumed that the receipts composers signed documenting the copyright purchase included all 28 years of copyright protection to which a composer was entitled. Thus, the wording of such documents was intentionally vague, for they often stated that the composer was signing over all his 'right, title, and interest' to the work in question. When Dibdin, constantly short of funds, approached Longman and Broderip, suggesting that they pay him for the reversionary rights to several works they owned, the music sellers asked Rennett, then their legal representative, to obtain an expert opinion about the validity of Dibdin's claim. Although Charles Ambler, a noted jurist, suggested that Dibdin might very well have a case, Rennett advised the partners that they need not worry about the composer's request. Shortly after Rennett terminated his association with Longman and Broderip, he offered to purchase Dibdin's reversionary rights for himself, in part to test whether the composer had the right to resell his compositions when the first 14 years of copyright protection had expired.[34] If Rennett had succeeded in his effort, the results would have been devastating to members of both the book and music trades since it would have reduced the time period a music seller could claim a monopoly over a piece of music without additional payments to the author or composer. However, without hearing any evidence from Longman and Broderip or explaining its reasons, the court on 12 December 1785 sided with the music sellers, dismissing Rennett's suit.

While this ruling suggested that the court was skeptical about Rennett's claims, this issue resurfaced in the early nineteenth century as part of two lawsuits. In the first, the composer Francis Latour filed an action in the Court of King's Bench against the music

---

Forster (1791) E112/1746, no 4924; *Skillern v Longman & Broderip* (1792) C12/185/34; *Storace v Longman & Broderip* (1788) C12/618/12; *Storace v Longman & Broderip* (1789) C12/623/35; *Longman & Broderip v Storace* (1788) C12/1703/11.

[33]   Both suits were filed in Chancery: *Napier v Holland* (1783) C12/2411/17; *Thompsons v Harrison and Drury* (1783) C12/2135/50.

[34]   The details of this case and its ramifications appear in Mace, 'Charles Rennett and the London Music-Sellers' (n 29).

sellers Anne Bland and E Weller for printing and selling his sonata *Le Retour de Windsor*, composed in 1801, after the first 14 years of the copyright had expired.[35] Although he admitted that he had sold his work to the music sellers in 1801, Latour argued that the receipt he had signed conveying the copyright to them only granted them permission to print and sell the work for 14 years. In their response Bland and Weller maintained, like most music sellers in such cases, that purchasers assumed from long-standing practice that a composer or author conveyed all his rights, including the reversion, to the music seller when he executed an assignment.

On 13 June 1818, Justice Abbott ruled that Latour's receipt did not constitute an adequate assignment of the copyright to Bland and Weller because it had not been witnessed as required by the statute. Soon after, the jury returned a verdict in favor of the composer for £100. Notably, Justice Abbott observed that the question remained open whether an author or composer could take back his rights after the first 14 years, noting that an author or composer making such a case might have a valid claim. At the same time, however, he tacitly acknowledged the validity of the music sellers' claims by instructing Latour to convey his reversionary copyright to Bland and Weller: an ambiguous ruling at best.

As a result of this decision, Johann Baptist Cramer in 1818 tried to reclaim 32 of his compositions composed from 1798 to 1811 and originally sold to Robert Birchall. When Birchall had purchased the copyrights, Cramer signed receipts that used the words 'sole copyright.' Consequently, Birchall believed that these receipts and others like them gave him a monopoly over these works for both the initial and reversionary terms granted by the 1710 Act; however, Cramer did not agree, for around the time the first term was about to expire he signed a contract with Samuel Chappell, promising to assign his reversionary rights to him on the condition that Latour's suit against Weller succeeded.

Birchall almost certainly learned about the outcome of *Latour v Weller* shortly after the trial because a full account of it appeared in the *Times* of London two days after the trial. He also knew of the association among Cramer, Latour and Chappell, who were at one time partners in a music-selling firm. Consequently, even though Birchall held written receipts for Cramer's copyrights, he commissioned Christopher Lonsdale to obtain from the composer formal conveyances that stated more explicitly which rights the composer granted to the music seller. When Cramer refused, Birchall filed suit in Chancery against the composer and Samuel Chappell. As proof of his ownership, he produced the receipts, quoting them verbatim in his bill of complaint, filed in 1819. His position was that the receipts proved the composer had in fact transferred both terms of copyright to him. On 18 January, the court heard Birchall's request for an injunction, which it granted to him, restraining Cramer from disposing of his copyrights to Chappell.[36]

---

[35] *Latour v Bland and Another* (1818) 2 Stark 382, 171 ER 679. The documents in the suit are KB122/995, rot 2049, KB122/997, rot 837, and KB125/218. An account of the hearing in this case appeared in the *Times* (London, 15 June 1818) 3.

[36] The suit is C13/1704/16. The account of the hearing at which the injunction was issued is C33/654, f 229. Subsequent orders are C33/657, f 1288, C33/658, f 1619 and C33/659, f 1959.

150 *Research handbook on the history of copyright law*

Although Birchall had effectively won his case since the proceedings went no further than this ruling, the lawsuits and the instability of the copyright law clearly made both Birchall and his successors aware that they needed to revise the wording of assignments made by composers. Consequently, Birchall required many composers to sign receipts that included the words 'absolute sale of all my Copyright and Interest present & future vested and contingent or otherwise.' This phrase clearly demonstrated that the composer was signing over all his rights to Birchall & Company, no matter what the terms of the existing copyright law.[37]

Yet another issue that surfaced in the litigation of the late eighteenth and early nineteenth centuries was the relationship of the words of a song to the musical notes. The librettist of a musical entertainment customarily sold his copyright to a bookseller, who brought out an edition of the entertainment's text without the music. At the same time, the composer sold the music for the songs to a music seller, who produced an edition of the score that often included the words even though he had not purchased the rights to them. In fact, copyright assignments usually did not specify whether the sale involved both the words and the music or the music alone. Although most booksellers tolerated this practice without complaint, several legal actions during this period raised the issue. In 1783 James Harrison and Thomas Drury advertised that they were about to reprint Thomas Augustine Arne's opera *Artaxerxes* over several numbers of the *New Musical Magazine*. Unfortunately, the Thompsons still owned the copyright to the music of this work. Consequently, in November of that year, shortly after the first number of the magazine appeared reproducing some music from *Artaxerxes*, the music sellers sued Harrison and Drury in Chancery for breach of copyright, asking that the court grant them an injunction to restrain the defendants from printing and selling any more of the opera.

In their answer, however, Harrison and Drury claimed that the copyrights of the words and music were separate. Exploiting the vague wording of the copyright assignment, which mentioned 'the Score and all the different Parts Vocal and Instrumental of the Music,' they argued that the Thompsons did not have title to the words of *Artaxerxes*. They revealed that they had spoken to Arne's son Michael, his father's executor, who claimed the 'Literary part of the said Opera as his property.' In fact, he had assured Harrison and Drury that he would 'never consent that these Defendants should be disturbed either in Law or Equity for printing the Words of the said Opera.' While conceding that the Thompsons might own the rights to the music, then, they maintained that Michael Arne was the sole proprietor of the words and that he had granted them the right to reproduce the opera's libretto. Although this argument seemed tenuous because Arne wrote both the words and the music, the partners raised a troubling issue. In fact, Harrison and Drury thought it sufficiently important that they repeated their information about Michael Arne's supposed rights two more times in their answer.[38]

---

[37] See receipts in *Musical & Dramatic Curiosities Exhibited by C Lonsdale*. Newberry Library Vault Case MS folio V 209.52 ('*Lonsdale Receipts*').

[38] For a full discussion of this suit, see Nancy A Mace, 'Litigating the *Musical Magazine*: The Definition of British Music Copyright in the 1780s' (1999) 2 Book History 122. The bill and answer are C12/2135/50.

To reinforce this argument about the separation of the words and the music, Harrison and Drury also explored more fully the relationship between musical and literary property. They stated, 'all the purchasors of Music only have the Literary part through Courtesy and that the words of all operas and so forth form an Independent Work and are sold to a different person.' When a music seller printed the words with the music, then, he was only borrowing the words in order to 'render his Music Compleat.' Otherwise, they reasoned, no bookseller would ever purchase the words to an opera, for he would have no financial advantage in doing so. In this case, however, Arne was the sole author of both the words and music to *Artaxerxes*, suggesting that he could have transferred his rights to both in a single sale. Although their argument was questionable, then, because of Arne's dual authorship, the booksellers had raised a valid issue by contending that the words and the music were separate properties that could be owned by different individuals.[39] They also implied that the rights of booksellers to the words were superior to those of the music sellers who owned the music, since they ignored the fact that, even if they did have permission to reprint the words, the Thompsons were still the proprietors of the music to *Artaxerxes*.

A third topic raised in litigation related to the status of musical adaptations, common in the eighteenth and nineteenth centuries since music sellers frequently issued new arrangements of popular music from public venues because customers wanted versions adapted for such instruments they played in the home as pianoforte, violin, and flute. Consequently, disputes arose when a music seller printed an adaptation of a work owned by a competitor. The resulting litigation raised some troubling questions about the relationship between the original work and those derived from it. For example, could music sellers regard such arrangements as new works, suggesting that they were not unauthorized reprints of the music on which they were based, or were they simply mechanical reproductions of the original, in effect extensions of that musical composition in regard to their importance as intellectual property? Furthermore, how much of a composition had to be different from others to be classified as a unique work, making it eligible for separate copyright protection?

The answer that emerged from lawsuits and copyright receipts during the late eighteenth and early nineteenth centuries is decidedly ambiguous. Music sellers recognized that the marketability of a new arrangement depended on the popularity of the work from which it was taken, acknowledging the symbiotic relationship between the adaptation and the original. At the same time, copyright receipts suggest that they regarded many adaptations as original works eligible for their own protection because they asked composers who adapted such works to convey their rights in these arrangements to them. Lawsuits directly involving composers as litigants or witnesses

---

[39] This issue also arose in 1788 when Stephen Storace sued Longman & Broderip for pirating one of his songs. For a full account of the suit, see Curtis Price, Judith Milhous and Robert D Hume, *Italian Opera in Late Eighteenth-Century London. Volume I. The King's Theatre, Haymarket 1778–1791* (OUP 1995) 388–93; Jane Girdham, *English Opera in Late Eighteenth-Century London. Stephen Storace at Drury Lane* (OUP 1997) 89–92. In this instance, the rights to the music were awarded to Stephen Storace, and those of the words to Longman & Broderip. See the registration in the Stationers' entry books dated 31 December 1787.

indicate that they, too, regarded adaptations as original works worthy of their own copyright protection.

Because they could have used the status of new arrangements as a pretext for litigation, the silence of parties like Rennett and Longman & Broderip on this subject suggests that many in the trade regarded adaptations as at least a grey area in terms of intellectual property. In fact, music sellers employed various strategies to avoid the issue altogether. First, they selected works that had fallen out of copyright; that is, those that were more than 28 years old. Another approach was to adapt traditional English, Scottish or Irish tunes, for they were in the public domain and free for all to reprint. Finally, music sellers often commissioned adaptations of music by nonresident foreign composers whose work had appeared on the Continent but had not been printed in English editions.

One case that highlights music sellers' ambivalent attitude to this issue is that concerning the ballet *La Belle Laitière*, written by Daniel Steibelt, which the music seller Robert Birchall purchased from the composer in 1805, when Steibelt signed over his 'sole copyright' for £100. The music seller first printed and sold the work as arranged for the pianoforte with an accompaniment for the harp done by the composer himself. Later he commissioned Francis Latour to adapt favorite airs from the ballet as duets for two performers on the pianoforte, which he registered with the Stationers on 31 January 1812. By printing an arrangement of a work he already owned, then, Birchall, like many of his competitors, avoided any copyright conflict with the original. However, on 14 March that same year Birchall sued the music seller Charles Wheatstone in Chancery for printing and selling pieces from the ballet adapted for pianoforte, harp or flute in dance collections he produced. In his bill of complaint Birchall established his ownership by right of purchase from Steibelt and demonstrated that the notes of Wheatstone's dance arrangement were virtually identical to the editions printed by his firm.[40] This example illustrates the complex nature of the relationship between an original work and adaptations based on it. Birchall's action in commissioning more than a single adaptation and registering the work with the Stationers suggests, on the one hand, that he did consider arrangements done for other instruments as separate works worthy of their own copyright. However, he was quick to challenge the right of a competitor to market his own adaptations, revealing that, at the same time, he regarded the music to this piece, and presumably others, as an extension of the original composition governed by the copyright assignment made by Steibelt to him in 1805.

Litigation involving composers as defendants or witnesses suggests that they, too, looked on arrangements of others' works as new compositions. For example, in 1782 Charles Rennett sued the composer Valentino Nicolai for selling in London his own edition of four sonatas originally part of his Opus 3, whose copyright Rennett had purchased in 1780. While she was on the Continent, Nicolai's wife had arranged for these pieces to be adapted with a harp accompaniment and printed in Paris. In his defense, Nicolai argued that these adaptations were original pieces, not governed by Rennett's copyright; he stated that they were 'a different and distinct work and

---

[40] The bill is C13/523/17. The receipt signed by Steibelt is in *Lonsdale Receipts* (n 37) f 33ᵛ.

composition.'[41] Later Joseph Haydn indicated that he, too, regarded new arrangements of his works as original pieces when in 1791 he testified as part of the dispute between Longman & Broderip and William Forster over several of his compositions. In his deposition, Haydn stated that although he had written the work sold in London as *A favorite Overture in all its parts composed by Giuseppe Haydn of Vienna and published by his authority*, he considered Charles Frederic Horn's adaptation for the pianoforte or harpsichord with an accompaniment for a violin a different composition, not of his making, implying, then, that it was worthy of separate copyright protection.[42]

The Haydn case raises yet another issue involving music that distinguishes it from letterpress editions: the status of compositions written by foreign composers. On the one hand, evidence from the entry books of the Stationers' Company indicates that nonresident foreigners could sell exclusive rights to their compositions to British music sellers. Of the 124 foreign composers whose work appeared in the Stationers' Entry Books from 1751–1800, 44 (or 35 percent) were not known to have ever visited England.[43] As the dispute between Longman and Forster revealed, however, printing foreign compositions could prove a risky undertaking. In 1786 Longman and Broderip bought the rights to several compositions by Joseph Haydn originally owned and printed by the music seller Artaria of Vienna. Believing that this purchase entitled them to exclusive copyright in England, they brought out their own edition of these works. In the same year William Forster obtained the copyright of these same works directly from Haydn, bringing out his own edition of these compositions. Consequently, the music sellers sued each other in Exchequer, each side claiming that it had the exclusive right to print and sell these works in England. When Haydn gave his deposition, he admitted that he routinely sold the copyright to same composition to music sellers in different countries, for he believed that he was granting them permission to sell the work only in their country. After all, at this time international copyright did not exist.[44]

---

[41] The bills and answers are E112/1697, no 3619.

[42] The deposition is E133/54/55. For a full account of this litigation, see Nancy A Mace, 'Haydn and the London Music Sellers: Forster v. Longman & Broderip' (1996) 77 Music & Letters 527. William Lockhart discusses later litigation involving keyboard arrangements in 1835, 1847 and 1867–68, in 'Trial by Ear: Legal Attitudes to Keyboard Arrangement in Nineteenth-Century Britain' (2012) 93 Music & Letters 191.

[43] For a discussion of the issue, see Small, 'Development of Music Copyright' (n 2) 383–86, where he briefly summarizes various suits involving the works of nonresident foreign composers. For music registrations of works by foreign musicians, see Mace, 'The Market for Music' (n 24) 168–69.

[44] For a full account of the cases, see Mace, 'Haydn and the London Music Sellers' (n 42) 527–41. Haydn's deposition, where he admitted his common practice is E133/54/54. Haydn was not the only composer to sell the same composition to music sellers in different countries. Frederick Kalkbrenner admitted to a similar practice in 1819, writing to Charles Guichard's lawyer that he had only sold the music seller the copyright for his compositions in England, reserving for himself the right to print or sell the work to other music sellers in France and Germany. See *Guichard v Kalkbrenner* (1819) C13/2883/42. Kalkbrenner's sale of another work to music sellers in different countries was also the focus of *Clementi v Walker* (1824) 2 B & C 861, 107 ER 601. See also David Rowland, 'Clementi as Publisher' in Michael Kassler (ed), *The Music Trade in Georgian England* (Ashgate 2011) 159, 171–72.

154 *Research handbook on the history of copyright law*

Unfortunately, the suits never came to a final hearing, so we do not know how the court might have ruled in this instance.

Another difficulty with foreign music involved the status of compositions first appearing in printed editions on the Continent. This question became the focus of a series of Chancery actions involving the British music seller Charles Guichard and the composer Frederick Kalkbrenner, lasting from 1819 to 1831. In 1815 Kalkbrenner sold a set of waltzes and a concertante to Guichard, who printed the concertante and registered it with the Stationers on 12 August 1815. He accused Kalkbrenner of arranging to have the concertante printed in France and imported to England, thereby violating his copyright. Guichard charged that Kalkbrenner had tried to mask his action by calling the work *Septuor* with a title page that imitated his own edition of the work. Consequently, Guichard accused the composer of fraud as well as piracy and asked the court for an injunction restraining Kalkbrenner from selling any more copies in England; in addition, he wanted the composer to account for those that he had already sold. In his answer Kalkbrenner, like many defendants, maintained that the work printed by Sieber in Paris for sale in France under the title *Septuor* was a similar but distinct composition from the concertante printed by Guichard. He also argued that, even if the works were essentially the same, he had the right to have foreign editions printed since he had only sold Guichard exclusive rights in England, which did not extend to foreign countries.[45] Despite his assertions, however, the court granted Guichard's petition, ordering Kalkbrenner to execute a proper conveyance of the copyright to Guichard. Kalkbrenner did so on 4 May 1820.[46]

Unfortunately for Guichard, his action in 1819 did not stop supposedly unauthorized editions of the concertante. Consequently, in 1830 he again turned to Chancery when he sued several music sellers, among whom were Georgiana Goulding, Thomas D'Almaine, Nicholas Mori, and the firm of Clementi, Collard, and Collard, for bringing out their own editions of the concertante, which they had entitled *The Charms of Berlin – Fantasia for the Piano Forte Op. 70*. As proof of his ownership, Guichard produced the 1820 assignment from Kalkbrenner. He maintained that in all its essentials the work contained parts that were identical to the concertante printed by him. As he did in 1819, Guichard asked the court to grant an injunction and require the defendants to account for all sales of the spurious edition. In his answer, dated 14 February 1831, Mori, the only defendant who responded to the charges, argued that the work printed and sold by him was not the same as the concertante even though it contained 'some few bars or trifling portions' of the other composition. Furthermore, he related that a work entitled *Septuor*, very much like the concertante, was first printed in Paris by Sieber, who had purchased the composition from Kalkbrenner after the composer had performed it in France. In fact, on 26 November 1814, Sieber entered the composition in the Dépôt in Paris in order to secure his copyright. Very soon afterwards he exported copies of the work to England, where it was sold as early as December 1814. Because the work as written was too long and difficult for amateurs, however, Kalkbrenner, then in Berlin, took a portion of the piece and added a new introduction

---

[45] The bill and answer are C13/2883/42.
[46] Although the original order does not exist, this information appears in *Guichard v Nicholas Mori* (1830) C13/2936/3.

and parts for the pianoforte, thereby producing a separate composition, which he entitled *The Charms of Berlin*. After this piece appeared in Berlin (1824), many copies circulated in Europe, including England. Thus, the defendants' challenge to Guichard's claim rested on several points. First, the work appeared first in Paris, making it part of the public domain when music sellers printed it later in England. Second, *The Charms of Berlin* was not identical to the concertante; even if it shared some notes, they were not sufficient to make it the same composition as the work owned by Guichard. Nevertheless, Guichard's threat of litigation was sufficient to prompt Mori to withdraw *The Charms of Berlin* from sale.[47]

At first, the court sided with the plaintiff, granting him initial injunctions against the defendants. However, once Mori answered Guichard's bill, it dissolved the injunction and refused to reinstate it even when the Solicitor General appeared on Guichard's behalf. As the newspaper accounts of the hearing reported, the judges ruled in this way because the defendants had proven that Sieber printed and sold *Septuor* in 1814, which was at least six months before Guichard bought the work from Kalkbrenner and almost six years before Kalkbrenner legally conveyed the work to Guichard. Consequently, the court demonstrated that once a musical work had been printed and sold on the Continent, it was considered *publici juris* (in the public domain), confirming the attitude long held by members of the music trade. Thus, no English music seller could claim exclusive right to the work, and anyone could reprint the composition in England without being accused of violating copyright. In its decision, the court did not expressly address the other issue raised by the suit: whether the concertante, *Septuor*, and *The Charms of Berlin* had sufficient similarities to be considered identical compositions subject to a single copyright. However, its ruling suggested that they did consider that at least the concertante and *Septuor* shared enough notes to be effectively the same piece.[48]

---

[47] *Guichard v Mori* (1831) 2 Coop T Cott 216, 47 ER 1134. The actions are *Guichard v Mori* (1830) C13/2936/3; *Guichard v Clementi, Collard and Collard* (1830) C13/2370/43; *Guichard v Goulding and D'Almaine* (1830) C13/2934/8. Only Mori answered Guichard's bill of complaint.

[48] The final orders in the case are C33/810, f 996 (21 March 1831) and C33/811, f 1478 (5 May 1831), when Guichard acknowledged defeat by asking that his bill of complaint be dismissed. Reports of the hearing when the Solicitor General asked that the injunction be reinstated appeared in *The Morning Chronicle* and *Times of London* for 23 March 1831. In the case of *Clementi v Walker* (1824) 2 B & C 861, 107 E R 601 similar issues were raised involving other compositions by Frederick Kalkbrenner. Here Kalkbrenner sold the work entitled *Vive Henri Quatre* to Clementi and Company in 1814 but did not execute a written assignment to them. In 1815 Pleyel of Paris printed the work, after depositing a copy at the Depôt on 17 June 1814 to register his copyright in France. Purchasing a copy of the Paris edition in 1818, the English music seller Walker printed and sold his own edition of the work in London. Finally in 1822 Kalkbrenner executed a written assignment to Clementi and Company. Because the work had first appeared in Paris and Walker's edition came out before Clementi had a written conveyance, the court ruled that the music as printed in England was in the public domain; consequently, neither Clementi nor Kalkbrenner could claim an exclusive right in England. Another important case is *D'Almaine v Boosey* (1835) 1 Y & C Ex 288, 160 ER 117. For a discussion of this case and additional treatment of some of these issues, see Small, 'Development of Music Copyright' (n 2) 383–86.

156 *Research handbook on the history of copyright law*

One final issue that resurfaced continually in court documents was the question of whether sheet music, which often comprised only a single page, was actually the same as a printed book. Even though the Mansfield decision in *Bach v Longman* appeared to have established that copyright law covered musical writings, no matter what the length, defendants throughout the late eighteenth and early nineteenth centuries persisted in raising this objection when they answered suits over unauthorized reprints. For example, in *Whitaker v Hime* (1815), tried in the Court of Exchequer, Dublin, the defendant's counsel argued that Whitaker was not entitled to sue for copyright infringement because the works involved were only single sheets and, therefore, ineligible for protection because they were not books. However, the court did not agree and ruled in favor of the plaintiff.[49]

5. CONCLUSION

As this brief overview demonstrates, the eighteenth and early nineteenth centuries are fundamental to our understanding of music as intellectual property, for during that period printed music, particularly in England, became a sufficiently valuable commodity that composers and members of the music trade for the first time attempted to apply copyright laws written for letterpress books to musical compositions. Although some of the issues considered by the courts, including the very application of copyright law to music, are not relevant to modern discussions about music as intellectual property, various points raised in litigation are the subject of debate today. For instance, courts still struggle to determine whether particular pieces contain sufficient similarities to regard them as identical compositions and consider the relationship of original compositions to new arrangements. Therefore, the developing concept of music copyright in the eighteenth and nineteenth centuries demonstrates the complexities of determining music's nature as intellectual property and the problems of differentiating one musical work from another, suggesting that further research in this period is both worthwhile and necessary. In particular, searches of documents from the common law courts may yield more evidence about litigation over music copyrights both before and after the *Bach* decision, and a more thorough search for additional equity suits before 1777 may expand our understanding of music's status as intellectual property in the first 75 years of the eighteenth century. Furthermore, newspapers from the period are a largely untapped source of information, both for their accounts of important suits and advertisements from music sellers and composers both asserting their rights to works and announcing litigation either intended or filed. Because these newspaper resources,

---

[49] A full account of this trial appears in *Musical Copyright. Proceedings on a Trial Before The Hon Baron George, in the Court of Exchequer, Dublin, May 18th, 1815: in the Cause, Whitaker versus Hime. To which are subjoined, Observations on the Extraordinary Defence made by Mr Serjeant Joy, Counsel for the Defendant by Leigh Hunt, Esq* (Rowland Hunter 1816). My thanks to Tomás Gómez-Arostegui for pointing out this case. This issue also appeared in the 1803 King's Bench suit involving Humphrey Hime and Joseph Dale. For an account of this suit and *Clementi v Goulding* (1809), see Small, 'Development of Music Copyright' (n 2) 380–81; Michael Kassler, 'Earl Stanhope's "Letter Music"' in Michael Kassler (ed), *The Music Trade in Georgian England* (Ashgate 2011) 389, 417–18.

now widely available online, can be searched by keyword, locating such material is now more possible than ever. While much work has been done on music copyright in this period, then, several avenues of research still remain to be explored.

9. How art was different: Researching the history of artistic copyright

Elena Cooper

1. INTRODUCTION

Over a decade ago, Kathy Bowrey surveyed the literature on the history of copyright and concluded that it had 'overwhelmingly' concerned 'literature and not art'.[1] Since Bowrey's observation, a number of pieces of research have been published concerning particular developments in artistic copyright, such as the immediate background to the statutory protection of engravings in Britain in 1735 and paintings in the UK in 1862.[2] However, it remains the case that copyright history scholarship, particularly that setting out the broad parameters of its relation to ideas of authorship and the public interest, primarily concerns literature.[3]

This chapter uncovers some of the significant ways in which the history of UK copyright concerning art was distinct from that relating to literature. The chapter begins with a review of the existing publications in the field, foregrounding the similarities and differences they note with contemporaneous developments in literary copyright, to the codification of copyright by the Copyright Act 1911.[4] It then illustrates how artistic copyright was historically understood to be different by setting out some of the assumptions that underpinned the debate of copyright in a period so far neglected by existing publications: the late nineteenth century. At this time, artistic copyright was regulated by a series of subject specific statutes, passed during the course of the eighteenth and nineteenth centuries, concerning engraving,[5]

---

[1] Kathy Bowrey, 'Who's Painting Copyright's History' in Daniel McClean and Karsten Schubert (eds), *Dear Images: Art, Copyright and Culture* (Ridinghouse RCA 2002) 257, 257.

[2] See, for example, the commentaries by Ronan Deazley published as part of the *Primary Sources* project and the essay by Lionel Bently in the *Dear Images* collection, cited below at nn 18 and 49.

[3] See eg Isabella Alexander, *Copyright Law and the Public Interest in the Nineteenth Century* (Hart Publishing 2010); Ronan Deazley, *On the Origin of the Right to Copy: Charting the Movement of Copyright Law in Eighteenth-Century Britain (1695–1775)* (Hart Publishing 2004); H Tomás Gómez-Arostegui, 'Copyright at Common Law in 1774' (2014) 47 Conn L Rev 1; Mark Rose, *Authors and Owners: The Invention of Copyright* (HUP 1993); Martha Woodmansee and Peter Jaszi, *The Construction of Authorship: Textual Appropriation in Law and Literature* (Duke UP 1994).

[4] 1 & 2 Geo V c 46 (1911).

[5] An Act for the Encouragement of the Arts of designing, engraving and etching historical and other Prints, by Vesting the Properties thereof in the Inventors and Engravers during the Time therein mentioned 1735 (8 Geo II c 13); An Act to amend and render more effectual an Act made in the eighth Year of the Reign of King George the Second, for Encouragement of the Arts

sculpture,[6] painting, drawing and photography.[7] These subject specific Acts, which existed alongside separate legislation protecting 'books',[8] remained in force until their repeal and replacement by the Copyright Act 1911,[9] which was premised on the general principle of the application of a single set of rules to all copyright subject matter.[10] As we will see, the rules contained in the subject specific statutes often involved a conscious departure from the rules protecting literary copyright on account of perceived differences between literature and art.

The late nineteenth century was a time of intense debate about reforming the existing copyright statutes, and the notion that art should be treated differently was articulated even in contexts where the desirability of a single copyright code had been acknowledged. These differences, and their justifications, are discussed with a view to casting light on the contingency of copyright history; from the standpoint of the late nineteenth century, it was far from clear that a single codifying regime premised on the application of the same rules to both art and literature would be passed, as was enacted in 1911. Further, that art was understood to be distinct suggests that the significant gaps in the existing literature are worthy of attention by scholars, as they promise to provide new dimensions to copyright history.

2. ARTISTIC COPYRIGHT: THE STORY SO FAR

The early history of artistic copyright in the jurisdictions comprising the UK remains obscure. While work has been done on the protection of printed texts through printing privileges from the 1500s (explored by Ian Gadd in his contribution to this volume), scholars have yet to consider to what extent privileges protected the printed image and whether this offers a contrasting perspective on copyright history.[11] Art historian Katie Scott argues that this is the case as regards the contemporaneous position in France. One of the earliest privileges granted in France for an image is thought to date from 1608, regarding Francois Quesnel's *Map of Paris*, and in her chapter in the *Privilege*

---

of Designing, Engraving and Etching, Historical and other Prints 1767 (7 Geo III c 38); An Act for effectually securing the property of prints to inventers and engravers, by enabling them to sue for and recover penalties in certain cases 1777 (17 Geo III c57); An Act to extend the protection of copyright in prints to Ireland 1836 (6 & 7 Will IV c 59); International Copyright Act 1852 (5 & 16 Vict c 12) s 14 (hereafter 'the Engraving Acts').

[6] An Act for Encouraging the Art of Making New Models and Casts of Busts, and other things therein mentioned 1798 (38 Geo III c 71); An Act to amend and render more effectual an Act of his present Majesty, for encouraging the Art of making new Models and Casts of Busts 1814 (54 Geo III c 56) (hereafter 'the Sculpture Copyright Acts').

[7] The Fine Arts Copyright Act 1862 (25 & 26 Vict c 68).

[8] Literary Copyright Act 1842 (5 & 6 Vict c 45).

[9] This was subject to a few exceptions. For example, the 1911 Act did not repeal section 7 and section 8 of the Fine Arts Copyright Act 1862 and the Musical Copyright Act 1906 (6 Edw 7 c 36).

[10] For the policy in 1911, see further text to n 83 below.

[11] Examples of such privileges granted in the 1600s, applying to maps, are given by David Hunter, see 'Copyright Protection for Engravings and Maps in Eighteenth-Century Britain' (1987) 6th ser, 9 The Library 128, 146.

and Property anthology, Scott refers to this and other examples to show how in France the printed image made a 'telling contribution to the formulation of the legal forerunner of modern copyright'.[12] Analysing 'property' as a 'boundary object' that sits at the intersection of different discourses (law, economics, politics, aesthetics), Scott argues that property relations implicit in the 'truth' depicted by printed images such as maps and views of towns, actively contributed to the redefinition of the notion of property denoted by the privilege system.[13] Art was a 'participant' in shaping privilege as a modern form of private property, for example through the manner in which the image was described in the legal documentation; art was not the 'passive recipient' of a system established by reference to literary texts. In this context, Scott makes the more general observation that the 'extension of the law of copyright by analogy to new cultural domains always involves a change; a challenge or revision by medium of the principles of the legal right.'[14] It remains to be seen whether similar observations can be made about contemporaneous developments in the jurisdictions comprising the UK. Scholars have instead focussed on the immediate background to the subject specific statutes passed during the course of the eighteenth and nineteenth centuries, concerning engraving, sculpture, painting and photography. The literature concerning these areas is now considered in turn.

2.1 Engraving

An instance of a 'revision' of principles as copyright was extended to new subject matter is provided by research into the immediate background to the earliest legal development in artistic copyright to be considered by existing scholarship: the Engraving Act 1735, which was the first British copyright statute to concern subject matter other than literary works.[15] As a number of scholars have noted,[16] the 1735 Act was passed in response to lobbying efforts by artist William Hogarth, in addition, as David Hunter notes in his reappraisal of the campaign, to a 'diverse group' of other artists.[17] In his commentary on the 1735 Act published as part of the *Primary Sources on Copyright History* resource, Ronan Deazley argues that the legal significance of the

---

[12] Katie Scott, 'Maps, Views and Ornament: Visualising Property in Art and Law: The Case of Pre-modern France' in Ronan Deazley, Martin Kretschmer and Lionel Bently (eds), *Privilege and Property: Essays on the History of Copyright* (OpenBook Publishers 2010) 255, 256.

[13] Ibid 257.

[14] Ibid 276.

[15] See n 5 above. Note that there was some protection for artistic works under literary copyright legislation passed in the nineteenth century. The Literary Copyright Act 1842, defined 'book' to include a 'map, chart or plan separately published' (s 2). Further, the courts considered that protection of a 'book' extended to 'illustrations and designs' forming part of a book. See *Bogue v Houlston* (1852) 5 De G & Sm 267; *Maple & Co v Junior Army and Navy Stores* [1882] 21 Ch D 369. This aspect of the 1842 Act is yet to be considered by scholars.

[16] For example, see the following art historical works: R Paulson, *Hogarth: His Life, Art and Times* vol I (Yale UP 1971) 347; Matthew Hargraves, *Candidates for Fame: The Society of Artists of Great Britain 1760–1791* (Yale UP 2005) 49.

[17] Hunter (n 11) 129–30 considers the campaign to have been 'more than a protective, self-serving move by a single faction'; 'Hogarth was neither solitary nor unsupported', the campaign also being backed by artists who moved in different circles to Hogarth such as George

debates preceding this measure was a shift away from the regulation of the physical object, as had been the case in the debates preceding the Statute of Anne concerning books, to the protection of the engraved image as an intangible work.[18] Mark Rose, who also makes this point in a short article in *The Information Society*, claims this to be 'the earliest explicit recognition of the immateriality of the commodity created by intellectual property law'.[19] The distinction between work and physical object was first articulated by the artists themselves in petitioning Parliament: a copier did not 'steal the very Paper' but rather 'he steals ... every Thing that made the Paper valuable', that is, the application of the artist's skill. In this way, '[e]very one has undoubtedly an equal Right to every Subject'; what was protected was the artist's particular 'design', which was akin to handwriting, that is 'the Manner, Distances and Shape of the Strokes which compose the Letters.'[20] According to Deazley, this petition also illustrates a second way in which the 1735 Act differed from the previous legislation on literary copyright: unlike the Statute of Anne where the printsellers adopted the figure of the author as a 'stalking horse' for their own interests,[21] the claim to copyright was now formulated by artists themselves, in opposition to unauthorised copying by printsellers.[22] As Rose argues, the 1735 Act was 'in that sense an author's law'.[23]

The 1735 Act only provided protection for prints that were engraved and designed by the same artist,[24] which reflected the practice adopted by William Hogarth, but left the majority of engravings unprotected as these reproduced the paintings of others.[25] Mark Rose argues that this was a deliberate omission; Hogarth sought an Act that would

---

Vertue and Joseph Goupy. Matthew Hargraves considers this to have been a 'short term alliance', Hargraves (n 16) 50.

[18] Ronan Deazley, 'Engravers' Copyright Act (1735)' in Lionel Bently and Martin Kretschmer (eds), Primary Sources on Copyright (1450–1900) <http://www.copyrighthistory.org>. This argument is also made by Deazley in the brief consideration of the Engraving Act 1735 in his monograph. Deazley, *Origin* (n 3) 88–94.

[19] Mark Rose, 'Technology in 1735: The Engraver's Act' (2005) 21 The Information Society 63, 63.

[20] Deazley, 'Engravers' Copyright' (n 18) s 3, citing *The Case of Designers, Engravers, Etchers &c. stated In a Letter to a member of Parliament*, Lincoln's Inn Library, MP 102, f 125, available as document 1735_a, in Primary Sources (n 18). Deazley also argues that the provisions of the 1735 Act gave further formal recognition to the distinction between physical object and intangible work; a purchaser of the engraved plates could only use them to reproduce the image if they were purchased 'from the original proprietors.' Deazley, 'Engravers' Copyright' (n 18) s 4.

[21] This argument regarding literary copyright is made by Peter Jaszi, 'Toward a Theory of Copyright: The Metamorphoses of "Authorship"' (1991) 413 Duke LJ 455, 500.

[22] This aspect of the campaign culminating in the Engraving Act 1735 is also noted by Hunter (n 11) 132–33, in considering how the history of engraving copyright provides 'instructive contrasts with the Act of Anne'. Ibid 129.

[23] Rose, 'Technology' (n 19) 63.

[24] The exception here was express protection granted to John Pine's intended engraving 'copied from several Pieces of Tapestry in the House of Lords and His Majesty's Wardrobe' concerning the Spanish Invasion of 1588. See Deazley, 'Engravers' Copyright' (n 18) s 4.

[25] Hunter states that it was 'chiefly Hogarth himself who benefitted' from the 1735 Act. Hunter (n 11) 140. See also the comments of Hargraves (n 16) 49, who describes Hogarth as 'almost the sole beneficiary' of the 1735 Act.

protect 'a creative artist – an author – rather than a mere craftsman'. Copyright was therefore a matter of status and recognition, as well as profit.[26] The lack of protection for reproductive engraving became a source of dissatisfaction on the part of some who had petitioned for the 1735 Act, such as George Vertue.[27] As art historian Matthew Hargraves explains, in his monograph *Candidates for Fame*, the result was a campaign for legislative reform, commenced in 1761 by the Society of Artists,[28] culminating in the passage of the Engraving Act 1767.[29] Hargraves considers the significance of the measure in terms of the Society's institutional history. He argues that the campaign culminating in the 1767 Act indicated that the Society faced a 'contradictory set of impulses'; it sponsored a measure protecting reproductive engraving, at the very time that the position of engravers within the Society was being marginalised through the 'emerging hierarchy' between the 'liberal' and 'mechanic' arts.[30] The legal significance of this measure is yet to be considered by copyright historians. The only example to date is a short section of a longer article by Lionel Bently. Tracing copyright's expansion since the eighteenth century to the present day, Bently notes the significance of the 1767 Act as the first instance of legislation extending the term of copyright protection.[31]

Hargraves provides some details about the Bill's drafting history, pointing to the existence of rich original archival material that would be worthy of review by copyright historians. From Hargraves' account we know that the Society of Artists was advised by Serjeant William Whitaker, a public figure of some prominence[32] and a draft Bill, containing Whitaker's amendments survives at the Royal Academy of Arts archive.[33] In particular, this shows that the Society also sought protection for sculptors, but these clauses were removed by Whitaker in the drafting process, his marginal note indicating that he thought it 'altogether Improper in this Bill' and therefore a source of objection to the Bill as a whole.[34] Accordingly, the 1767 Act was limited to engraving. The 1767 Act was followed by two further Acts, also concerning engraving only, passed in 1777 and 1836 providing for the recovery of damages by a special action on the case and protection in Ireland.[35] These Acts have also so far received little attention by legal

---

[26] Rose, 'Technology' (n 19) 64.
[27] Hargraves (n 16) 49.
[28] Ibid. The Society of Artists was established in the early 1760s with a view to organising regular art exhibitions, and remained active until its dissolution in 1791. It is not to be confused with the Society of Arts, Manufactures and Commerce (known today as the Royal Society of Arts), founded in 1754, which played a prominent role in the campaign culminating in the Fine Arts Copyright Act 1862.
[29] See n 5.
[30] Hargraves (n 16) 45, 61.
[31] Lionel Bently, 'R v. The Author: From Death Penalty to Community Service' (2008) 32 Colum J L & Arts, 1, 64–65. As Bently explains, the 1767 Act extended the term of protection under the 1735 Act, from 14 years from publication to 28 years from publication. Engraving Act 1767 s 7.
[32] Hargraves (n 16) 51, 58.
[33] See Draft Bill, SA/23/1, Royal Academy of Arts Archive, London.
[34] Hargraves (n 16) 59.
[35] See n 5.

scholars, Hunter touching only briefly on the background to the 1777 Act.[36] As with the 1767 Act, these statutes merit further research. For example, Hunter notes that early drafts of the 1777 Act included later abandoned clauses concerning false attribution, which had no precedent in the existing literary copyright statutes.[37]

2.2 Sculpture

That clauses protecting sculpture were considered as early as the 1760s is of particular interest to copyright historians, the history of sculpture copyright having been little considered by scholars. The existing literature consists of two pieces that focus on the immediate background to the first Act to protect sculpture: the Sculpture Copyright Act 1798.[38] Art historian Holger Hoock, as part of his history of the Royal Academy of Arts, considers the place of the 1798 Act within the cultural politics of the time; the Act was sponsored, in part, by the Royal Academy of Arts, which was at this time gaining increasing influence over government policies relating to the arts, as part of a new balance of power between art and state that emerged at the turn to the nineteenth century.[39] At the same time, Hoock's account suggests that to portray the 1798 Act, as has been done by the Court of Appeal in recent times, as 'clearly concerned to identify sculpture as an artistic work',[40] is misguided; the Bill, though sponsored by the Royal Academy, was 'an outside initiative', instigated by a leading modeller of animals, George Garrard, whose commercial concerns resulted in the Bill being also backed by a 'very different' institution: the Board of Agriculture that sought to promote and protect 'correct models of the most approved breeds of cattle' with a view to improving British stock.[41]

The second piece to consider the 1798 Act, Ronan Deazley's commentary which forms part of the *Primary Sources* resource, concerns its legal significance.[42] Deazley argues that while the legislation in many respects followed the form of the Engraving Act 1735, for example in its distinction between the physical object and the intangible work, it was the first instance in which copyright was extended to a medium other than print and therefore prepared the ground for the emergence of 'modern image of copyright as concerned with the promotion of art and literature.'[43] Beyond the drafting

---

[36] Hunter provides a brief outline of the immediate background to the 1777 Act: it originated with a petition of 11 engravers comprising William Woollett and John Boydell among others. See Hunter (n 11) 144–45.
[37] Ibid.
[38] See n 6 above. This was repealed and replaced by a new Sculpture Copyright Act in 1814, passed to correct drafting errors that came to light in the case of *Gahagan v Cooper* (1811) 3 Camp 111. See further, Ronan Deazley, 'Commentary on the Models and Busts Act 1798' in Bently and Kretschmer (n 18) s 6.
[39] Holger Hoock, *The King's Artists: The Royal Academy of Arts and the Politics of British Culture 1760–1840* (OUP 2003) 232.
[40] *Lucasfilm v Ainsworth* [2010] EWCA Civ 1328 [70] (Jacob LJ), referring to the legislative history of the Sculpture Copyright Act 1814 (n 6).
[41] Hoock (n 39) 248–51, 249.
[42] Deazley, 'Models and Busts' (n 38).
[43] Ibid ss 1 and 6.

issues with the 1798 Act, brought to light in *Gahagan v Cooper* and corrected by the legislature in 1814,[44] the history of the application of the Sculpture Copyright Acts is yet to be investigated. As well as the context and historical significance of cases decided under the Act, two of which have been considered by the courts in more recent times,[45] further research might consider the history and implications of sections 6 and 7 of the Designs Act 1850, which allowed for the recovery of remedies, in particular penalties under the Designs Act 1842,[46] in respect of sculptures falling under the Sculpture Copyright Acts which were also registered with the Designs Registry.[47]

2.3 Painting

The modern image of copyright law, encompassing literature and art generally, forms an important context for existing scholarship seeking to explain the history of painting copyright. While the Engraving Copyright Acts provided some residual protection for painters,[48] copyright subsisted in the print and not the painting; it was therefore not an infringement to copy from the painting itself.[49] An Act providing for the subsistence of copyright in painting was not passed until 1862: the Fine Arts Copyright Act.[50] So far, three pieces of scholarship have considered the protection of painting in 1862. Lionel Bently and Brad Sherman, in part of a chapter of their monograph on the history of intellectual property more generally, *The Making of Modern Intellectual Property Law*, argue that the framework for bilateral copyright treaties set down by the International Copyright Act 1844, by drawing its ambit as relating to 'works of art' generally, provided a model for what domestic law should be. This, they argue, was an important context for the protection of painting in 1862.[51] In a further publication, an essay contained in the *Dear Images* collection, Bently explains the protection of painting in 1862 by reference to the convergence of the modern image of copyright with the widespread acceptance of the aesthetic equivalence of painting and writing; painting ought to be put in the 'same category' as literature for copyright purposes, because both were 'the emanations or expressions of the ideas of a creator'.[52] This set the parameters for thinking about the painters' claims and Bently explores a particular development that instigated these: the destabilising impact of photographic copying on the existing commercial relations between painters and engravers.[53]

---

[44] *Gahagan* (n 38). Deazley, 'Models and Busts' (n 38) s 6.
[45] *Caproni v Alberti* (1891) 65 LT 785 and *Britain v Hanks* (1902) 86 LT 765, considered by the Court of Appeal in *Lucasfilm* (n 40), in interpreting the UK's category of 'sculpture'.
[46] Ornamental Designs Act 1842 (5 & 6 Vict c 45).
[47] Copyright of Designs Act 1850 (14 Vict c 104).
[48] The 1767 Act vested copyright *inter alia* in persons who 'from his own work, design or invention, shall cause or procure' an engraving. See Engraving Act 1767, s 1.
[49] *De Berenger v Wheble* (1819) 2 Stark 548; 171 ER 732, discussed by Lionel Bently, 'Art and the Making of Modern Copyright Law' in McClean and Schubert (n 1) 331, 338–39.
[50] See n 7.
[51] Brad Sherman and Lionel Bently, *The Making of Modern Intellectual Property Law: The British Experience, 1760–1911* (CUP 1999) 119–28.
[52] Bently, 'Art and the Making' (n 49) 332.
[53] Ibid 337.

Ronan Deazley draws on these two works in an essay in the *Privilege and Property* anthology, which traces the progress of the various Bills through Parliament in 1862.[54] Amongst other things, Deazley speculates whether the residual protection of painters through the Engraving Acts and commercial practice, might explain why painting copyright was not introduced until 1862, despite it being encompassed by the 'image' of copyright since at least, as Bently and Sherman argue, the International Copyright Act of 1844.[55] As the introductory essay in the same anthology observes, this illustrates how copyright law should be understood as 'only one mechanism' by which proprietary relationships are articulated.[56] Deazley's work also draws attention to a number of innovations contained in the 1862 Act: de-coupling the copyright term from publication,[57] the provision of an 'early forerunner' to today's 'moral rights',[58] as well as the first instance of a statutory criterion of 'originality'.[59] These provisions, combined with the radical nature of early proposals for copyright protection neither subject to formalities nor qualification criteria, lead Deazley to note the ways in which the debates on artistic copyright were distinct. As he concludes, 'what was being proposed was, by no means, a mechanistic expansion of the existing principles and doctrine of copyright law to a new category of subject matter'.[60]

2.4 Photography

The 1862 Act was also the first Act expressly to protect subject matter that fell outside the 'modern image' of copyright: photographs. A number of scholars have focussed on aspects of the history of photographic copyright that suggest it was a challenge for copyright law. Art historian Anne McCauley, in relating the background to the 1862 Act, argues that the tendency to denigrate photography as 'merely mechanical' and to assume that art is instead concerned with 'human qualities' marked debates about its legal status.[61] Ronan Deazley also draws attention to the challenge that photography posed for copyright principles, in exploring the parliamentary debates of 1862 in his essay which forms part of the *Privilege and Property* collection,[62] as well as his short

---

[54] Ronan Deazley, 'Breaking the Mould? The Radical Nature of the Fine Arts Copyright Bill 1862' in Deazley, Kretschmer and Bently (n 12) ch 11. This largely reproduces the commentary published by Deazley as part of the *Primary Sources* resource: Ronan Deazley, 'Commentary on Fine Arts Copyright Act 1862' in Bently and Kretschmer (n 18).
[55] Deazley, 'Breaking the Mould' (n 54) 290–91.
[56] Martin Kretschmer, with Lionel Bently and Ronan Deazley, 'The History of Copyright History: Notes from an Emerging Discipline' in Deazley, Kretschmer and Bently (n 12) 1, 6.
[57] Fine Arts Copyright Act 1862, s 1. The term was the life of the author and seven years thereafter.
[58] Ibid s 7.
[59] Ibid s 1.
[60] Deazley, 'Breaking the Mould' (n 54) 318.
[61] Anne McCauley, '"Merely Mechanical": On the Origins of Photographic Copyright in France and Great Britain' (2008) 31(1) Art History 57.
[62] Deazley, 'Breaking the Mould' (n 54) 304–06.

article in *History of Photography*, providing an analysis of the key cases and attempts at legislative reform in the period from 1857 to the modern day.[63]

Two other scholars explore the challenge posed by photography for copyright through analogies with more recent developments in literary copyright. Kathy Bowrey compares aspects of the history of photographic copyright (the ruling in *Nottage v Jackson* in 1883[64] and subsequent statutory provisions on photographic copyright contained in the Australian Copyright Act 1905[65] and Copyright Act 1911) to more recent challenges regarding the protection of computer programs; photography was considered to lack an 'original expression' which, Bowrey argues, was a prerequisite for copyright protection.[66] Justin Hughes, in an article that considers the parliamentary debates of 1862 alongside nineteenth century US case law on photographic copyright, claims that photography was 'the technological development that posed the most serious challenge to copyright's theoretical structure in the nineteenth century' because 'it challenged our understanding of creativity'.[67] As 'compilations of fact', Hughes argues that the difficulties surrounding the protection of photographs 'is really the same problem' as that posed by copyright protection for databases.[68]

The scholarship about photographic copyright noted so far is premised on the conclusion that copyright principles were challenged by photography. This can be contrasted to the position taken by John Tagg in *The Burden of Representation* and Paul Hirst in his introduction to Bernard Edelman's work on the history of French photographic copyright. They argue that, unlike Edelman's account of the history of French law, photography posed no challenge for UK copyright: UK copyright would not have needed to construct the photograph as the creation of the mental labour of a creative subject as a pre-requisite for protection, as was necessary in France; UK copyright is rooted in a long tradition characterised by a 'non-reference to creativity'[69] as distinct from the author's right tradition of continental Europe.[70] The position taken by Tagg and Hirst ultimately reflects different assumptions about the category of UK copyright in the nineteenth century, to those taken, for example by Kathy Bowrey and Justin Hughes.[71] That a diversity of position is taken on this point, suggests the history of the concept of artistic copyright more generally to be worthy of more rigorous historical interrogation.

---

[63] Ronan Deazley, 'Struggling with Authority: The Photograph in British Legal History' (2003) 27 History of Photography 236.
[64] (1882–83) LR 11 QBD 627.
[65] Copyright Act 1905 (No 25).
[66] Kathy Bowrey, 'Copyright, Photography and Computer Works – The Fiction of an Original Expression' (1995) 18 UNSW LJ 278.
[67] Justin Hughes, 'The Photographer's Copyright: Photograph as Art, Photograph as Database' (2012) 25(2) Harv J L & Tech 327, 341. On the history of photographic copyright in the USA, see also Christine Haight Farley, 'The Lingering Effects of Copyright's Response to the Invention of Photography' (2004) 65 U Pitt L Rev 385; Jane Gaines, *Contested Culture: The Image, The Voice and the Law* (British Film Institute 1992).
[68] Hughes (n 67) 342.
[69] Paul Hirst, 'Introduction' in B. Edelman, *Ownership of the Image* (Routledge & Kegan Paul Ltd 1979) 17.
[70] John Tagg, *The Burden of Representation* (Macmillan 1988) 115–16. Hirst (n 69) 15–17.
[71] See text to n 67 above.

Finally, also on the subject of the history of photographic copyright in the nineteenth century, are two further pieces that raise the question of the law's relationship to broader instrumental policies concerning photography. In an article in *Intellectual Property Quarterly*, Deazley contextualises the debate over copyright protection for photographs in 1862, as well as the later ruling in *Graves' Case* (where a photograph of an engraving of a painting was held to be 'original' under the 1862 Act)[72] with the South Kensington Museum's short-lived experiment in issuing copies of works of art to the public in the early 1860s.[73] For Deazley, this case study raises broader issues regarding the control over the use of publicly owned works of art. Deazley's discussion of the South Kensington Museum's activities raises the question of to what extent there were instrumental policies at work in the protection of photography in 1862. Such issues are explored by Kathy Bowrey, in an essay entitled *'The World Daguerreotyped: What a Spectacle?'* where she considers the broader implications of copyright policies concerning photography for the more general politics of the visual image of the time.[74] Bowrey situates copyright debates over both the 1862 Act, as well as colonial copyright legislation introduced by Victoria thereafter,[75] in the context of policies pursued by the Imperial government in promoting a public visual imagination in seeing the world as 'Empire'.[76] For Bowrey, the 1862 Act is not just a story about private property rights, but also concerns instrumental government policies promoting particular kinds of image.[77]

Bowrey's work also draws attention to another significant difference between artistic and literary copyright in the nineteenth century: the approach taken by the subject specific statutes to its application through the territories of the British Empire. Whereas the Literary Copyright Act 1842 conferred copyright throughout the Empire to works first published in the UK,[78] the Engraving Acts, Sculpture Copyright Acts and the Fine Arts Copyright Act 1862 were applied to the UK only, leaving the colonies to local colonial law.[79] While UK legislation, such as the Fine Arts Copyright Act 1862, was sometimes used as a model by the legislatures of the self-governing dominions, there were examples of diversity in the treatment of artistic copyright, some of which are considered briefly in the closing chapter of *The Common Law of Intellectual Property*

---

[72] (1868–69) LR 4 QB 715.
[73] Ronan Deazley, 'Photography, Copyright and the South Kensington Experiment' (2010) IPQ 293.
[74] Kathy Bowrey, '"The World Daguerreotyped: What a Spectacle!" Copyright Law, Photography and the Economic Mission of Empire' in Brad Sherman and Leanne Wiseman (eds) *Copyright and the Challenge of the New* (Wolters Kluwer 2012) 11.
[75] Copyright Act 1869 (33 Vict 350).
[76] Bowrey, 'World Daguerreotyped' (n 74) 11.
[77] Ibid 12.
[78] *Routledge v Low* (1868) LR 3 HL 100; Literary Copyright Act 1842, s 3.
[79] *Graves v Gorrie* [1903] AC 496. The fact that the 1862 Act applied to the UK only was recognised long before this ruling. See eg Reginald Winslow, *The Law of Artistic Copyright* (William Clowes 1889) 92. The Engraving Acts were also limited to the UK's territory, only applying to prints which were engraved, etched, drawn or designed in the UK. See ibid.

by Catherine Ng, Lionel Bently and Giuseppina D'Agostino.[80] Apart from the essay by Bowrey, which draws attention to the ways in which the artistic copyright statute passed in Victoria related to local cultural politics,[81] this dimension to the history of artistic copyright is yet to be explored in any detail.

2.5 The Copyright Act 1911

The subject specific statutes considered in the literature reviewed so far, together with those protecting other copyright subject matter, were repealed and replaced by the Copyright Act 1911.[82] This was rooted in the general principle of the application of identical principles to all classes of copyright work, including literature and art. As Sydney Buxton, President of the Board of Trade, explained to the House of Commons in 1911, on the Bill's second reading:

> ... the object of the Bill is to bring the same terms and the same obligations and same remedies and same advantages to all [the] various classes of works, and bring them as far as possible under a uniform and simple process ...[83]

The artistic copyright dimension to the debates preceding the 1911 Act have so far not been considered by scholars, the main published work on the 1911 Act instead concerning the implications of that Act for literature and music.[84] Art is a subject deserving further consideration. For example, new artistic subject matter was introduced for the first time in 1911: 'works of artistic craftsmanship' and 'architectural works of art'.[85] The history of these categories is yet to be considered and raises interesting questions: why was architecture not protected until 1911 despite, as Deazley notes in considering the lobbying efforts of the Royal Academy of Arts in relation to the Sculpture Copyright Act 1798, its long acceptance as one of the 'central pillars' of the 'polite arts'?[86] Further, what was the impetus behind the protection of works of artistic craftsmanship, at a time when art historians have shown the Arts and Crafts movement to be in decline?[87] Furthermore, as the pieces by Deazley and Bently on the 1862 Act have noted, the nineteenth century developments in artistic copyright generally, in particular the debates and provisions of the 1862 Act, laid the groundwork for many of the rules adopted by the 1911 Act.[88] These points, some of which are explored in the next section of this chapter, suggest a consideration of the debates concerning artistic copyright culminating in the 1911 Act, may also be of significance to copyright history more generally.

---

[80] Catherine Ng, Lionel Bently and Giuseppina D'Agostino (eds), *The Common Law of Intellectual Property*, (Hart Publishing 2010) 413–14.
[81] Bowrey, 'World Daguerreotyped' (n 74) 32.
[82] There were some exceptions. See n 9 above.
[83] HC Deb vol 23 col 2592 (7 April 1911).
[84] Alexander (n 3) ch 7.
[85] Copyright Act 1911 s 35(1).
[86] Deazley, 'Models and Busts' (n 38) s 3.
[87] Art historians have argued this to be in decline by 1910. See E Cumming and W Kaplan, *The Arts and Crafts Movement* (Thames & Hudson 1991) 206.
[88] Bently, 'Art and the Making' (n 49) 344; Deazley, 'Breaking the Mould' (n 54) 319.

3. HOW ART WAS DIFFERENT: PERSPECTIVES FROM THE LATE NINETEENTH CENTURY

While significant gaps in scholarship remain, the story of the history of artistic copyright told so far suggests that this is a subject offering contrasting perspectives from the contemporaneous history of literary copyright. In the remainder of this chapter, a further aspect of this is explored: how, in late nineteenth century debates, the rules appropriate for regulating artistic copyright were understood to be different to those suitable for literature. As we have seen, existing scholarship has noted the ways in which the Fine Arts Copyright Act 1862 contained important innovations for copyright law, such as the first statutory criteria of originality and 'early forerunners' to moral rights,[89] as well as drawing attention to the difference between literary and artistic copyright as regards copyright policy in the colonies.[90] In this section we look at other ways in which, in the late nineteenth century, artistic copyright was thought to demand different treatment to literature.

3.1 Term and Qualification

An important way in which nineteenth century debates considered literary and artistic copyright to be different concerned the appropriateness of utilising 'publication' in determining qualification and the term of protection. 'Publication' was central to the rules of literary copyright: the Literary Copyright Act 1842 only protected works first published in the UK,[91] with the term of protection lasting for the life of the author plus seven years, or 42 years from first publication, whichever was longer.[92] Further, foreign authors would only qualify for such protection, if they first published their work in England while being resident there.[93] By contrast, in nineteenth century debates on artistic copyright, 'publication' was thought to be problematic because of difficulties in its application to painting. In particular, publication of a painting was thought to be difficult to prove, for example because of the difficulty in ascertaining when a painting was finished.[94] The Fine Arts Copyright Act 1862 departed from the form of the Engraving and Sculpture Copyright Acts, both of which contained rules of term and qualification based on publication;[95] the 1862 Act instead provided for protection

---

[89] See Ronan Deazley's work, discussed at text to nn 57–60.
[90] See Kathy Bowrey's work, discussed at text to n 81.
[91] *Routledge v Low* (1868) LR 3 HL 100; Literary Copyright Act 1842, s 3.
[92] Literary Copyright Act 1842, s 3.
[93] *Jeffreys v Boosey* (1854) 4 HLC 815. See further Alexander (n 3) 100–05.
[94] Copyright Commission: The Royal Commissions and the Report of the Commissioners; PP 1878 C-2036, C-2036-1 XXIV 163, 253, [92]. TE Scrutton, giving evidence to the Select Committee of the House of Lords in 1898: Report of the Select Committee on the Copyright Bill (HL) and the Copyright (Amendment) Bill (HL); PP 1898 (189) at Q3621.
[95] The term of protection for engravings was 28 years from first publication (Engraving Act 1767, s 7). Sculptures were protected for 14 years from publication, with the possibility of a second 14-year term if the author was still alive at the expiry of the initial term (Sculpture Copyright Act 1814, ss 2, 6).

commencing on creation of the work, with publication irrelevant to rules of qualification and term.[96] By the late nineteenth century, it was accepted that copyright law was in need of far-reaching reform; copyright was, as the Royal Commission reported in 1878, 'wholly destitute of any sort of arrangement, incomplete, [and] often obscure'.[97] In a more general reforming context, proposals were put forward to simplify the law of copyright, and this raised the question of whether a single regime could apply to artistic and literary subject matter. The inappropriateness of applying well-established literary copyright rules utilising 'publication' to artistic copyright was frequently cited as a reason why this would not be possible. As the Royal Academy of Arts spokesman, Henry Tanworth Wells RA, expressed in giving evidence to the Royal Commission on this issue, 'the two things', literature and art, 'are so different that a uniform treatment cannot be adopted with justice to both sides.'[98]

3.2 Registration and Ownership

On two other issues, artistic copyright was considered to require different treatment to literature, so as to accommodate the interests of the purchasers of works of art, in particular in relation to painting. First, as regards registration, the approach contained in the Literary Copyright Act 1842, where registration was merely a necessary pre-requisite for the commencement of infringement proceedings,[99] was not followed by the Fine Arts Copyright Act 1862. The 1862 Act provided for registration (at Stationers Hall) in a manner similar to literary copyright, but registration was instead a condition precedent to the subsistence of copyright, such that 'no Action shall be sustainable nor any Penalty recoverable in respect of anything done before registration'.[100] This provision was introduced after Lord Overstone, who was also an art collector,[101] expressed concern in the debate of the Bill in the House of Lords, as to how artistic copyright would impact on the interests of purchasers of paintings; by making registration a condition precedent to copyright, the purchasers of paintings would be able easily to ascertain copyright ownership, and therefore guard against the

---

[96] Fine Arts Copyright Act 1862 s 1. Accordingly, unlike literary copyright, unpublished paintings were protected both by statute and the common law protecting unpublished works. For the meaning of 'publication' under the common law in respect of painting see *Turner v Robinson* (1860) LR 10 Ch 121.

[97] Copyright Commission (n 94) [7].

[98] Copyright Commission (n 94) Q2999. See also the evidence of Edwin Bale, the spokesperson of the Artistic Copyright Society, who expressed in relation the use of 'publication' in a codifying proposal: 'the endeavour to make works of art come under the same rules as a book is … the great blot on this Bill'. See House of Lords Select Committee 1898 (n 94) Q2789.

[99] Catherine Seville, *Literary Copyright Reform in Early Victorian England: The Framing of the 1842 Copyright Act* (CUP 1999) 237, noting *Warne v Lawrence* (1886) 54 LT 371.

[100] Fine Arts Copyright Act 1862 s 4. The rules regulating *inter alia* the keeping of the register, its inspection, the making of false entries and the expunging and varying of entries, were those set out in the Literary Copyright Act 1842 Act: s 5.

[101] D P O'Brien, *The Correspondence of Lord Overstone,* vol I (CUP 1971) 33. 'Lord Overstone and Art' *The Times* (London, 29 November 1883) 2.

position where an innocent purchaser bought a copy, which was later 'seized and suppressed' as infringing.[102]

The interests of purchasers of works of art also resulted in very different debates in artistic, as opposed to literary copyright, as regards the rules of copyright ownership. Unlike the position in literary copyright, where the author would own copyright unless it was assigned,[103] the concerns of purchasers and commissioners of art works resulted in a convoluted copyright ownership clause in the Fine Arts Copyright Act 1862. The author was the first owner, subject to two provisos: first copyright would lapse on first sale of *inter alia* a painting unless reserved in writing by either artist or purchaser, and second, the commissioner would own copyright where a work was commissioned 'for good or valuable consideration'.[104] While it was generally accepted, in debates later in the nineteenth century, that this provision required reform, the first proviso often leaving paintings completely unprotected by copyright, the interests of collectors continued to complicate discussions on this issue in the late nineteenth century. Reporting in 1878, the Royal Commission stated that the question of ownership of artistic copyright was 'the most difficult question' which it had to consider.[105] While it acknowledged that the artists had been unanimous in their submissions that artistic copyright should follow literary copyright, in being first owned by the author, and only divested if assigned in writing, it was of the view that purchasers and commissioners generally assumed that they would acquire copyright.[106] Commissioners expected to own copyright on account of the private nature of the subject matter of commissioned works, particularly in the case of portraits,[107] and purchasers generally sought copyright ownership to guard against the production of replicas by the same artist that would damage a work's economic value, at that time determined by its uniqueness.[108] Accordingly, the Royal Commission proposed that the purchaser or the person for whom it was painted, should be the first owner of copyright in a painting, and that subsequently copyright ownership should follow the ownership of the picture.[109] In the decades that followed, the Royal Academy of Arts accepted a compromise position: that artists' ownership of copyright would be accompanied by a special clause protecting the interests of purchasers and commissioners, by preventing the artist from producing replicas. A clause along these lines appeared in the Artistic Copyright Bill of 1882, prepared by the Society of Social Science on the instructions of Royal Academy.[110] A later proposal, was put forward by the Royal Academy of Arts representative, the lawyer Thomas Edward Scrutton, in 1900: the commissioner would

---

[102] Parl Deb Vol 166 col 2013 (22 May 1862).
[103] Literary Copyright Act 1842, s 3. Special rules applied to encyclopaedias, reviews, magazines and periodical works, as well as works published in a series of parts: s 18.
[104] Fine Arts Copyright Act 1862, s 1.
[105] Royal Commission (n 94) [101], xix.
[106] Ibid [104]–[105], [112], xix–xx.
[107] Ibid, for example the evidence of painter Thomas Faed RA at Q3495–3505.
[108] Ibid [116] and, for example, DR Blaine, *Artistic Copyright: Report prepared at the request of the Committee appointed by the Society of Arts* (Society of Arts 1858) 8 [II]: 'Much of the *conventional* value of a picture depends upon its being *unique*.' Emphasis as original.
[109] Ibid [115].
[110] Copyright (Works of Fine Art, etc) Bill, cl 7; PP 1882 Bill 119.

be given the same rights and remedies against the artist (and other third parties), as the copyright owner, for a period of the life of the commissioner or twenty years from the completion of the work, whichever was longer.[111] This was a dimension to the debates concerning artistic copyright absent from those concerning literature.

3.3 Infringement

Under the Literary Copyright Act 1842, a key consideration in determining infringement was whether the unauthorised use damaged the copyright owner; did the defendant's use compete unfairly with the original work?[112] Artistic copyright raised the question of whether infringement should encompass reproduction in different media, even in circumstances where there was no evidence of harm on the part of the original author. This was raised in particular in relation to the question of whether copyright in sculptures, that is, works in three dimensions, should be infringed by photographic reproduction in two dimensions. The majority report of the Royal Commission noted the 'considerable business' in the sale of photographic copies of sculpture, yet the evidence from sculptors was that this was far from harmful; rather it was 'an advert in a sculptor's favour'.[113] In the copyright debates of the late nineteenth century, this point was thought to be unclear under the existing Sculpture Copyright Acts,[114] but it was generally accepted that it was a point on which change was required: the sculptor was entitled to 'reap the benefits' of the 'money value' in reproductions, even in the absence of harm.[115] In this way, artistic copyright reform was thought to demand a departure from the established principles that guided the courts in considering infringement of literary copyright.

4. CONCLUSION

As these examples show, it was a premise of much debate in the late nineteenth century that art demanded different rules from those applicable to literary copyright. Not only did the subject specific statute passed at this time, the Fine Arts Copyright Act 1862, consciously depart from established literary copyright principles, but also, it was frequently articulated, in nineteenth century debates thereafter, that art should be treated differently from literature. This illustrates the contingency of the approach of

---

[111] Report on the Select Committee on the Copyright Bill [HL] and the Copyright (Artistic) Bill [HL] together with the Proceedings of the Committee, Minutes of Evidence and Appendix; PP 1900 (193), 61, Q791.

[112] Alexander (n 3) 182, 189.

[113] Copyright Commission (n 94) [97]–[98]. See also the evidence of sculptor Thomas Woolner RA at Q4056, Q4077–83 and Q4096–7.

[114] See, for example, the evidence given in 1900 by barrister Thomas Edward Scrutton and solicitor Herbert Bentwich, at n 111 above, Q889 and Q1088–1089. Under the Fine Arts Copyright Act 1862, there was authority that a living picture imitating a painting was not a copy: *Hanfstaengl v Empire Palace* [1894] 2 Ch 1; *Hanfstaengl v Baines* [1895] AC 20.

[115] See the evidence of sculptor William Reynolds-Stephens, giving evidence in 1909: Report of the Committee on the Law of Copyright; PP 1909 Cd 4976, at Q2206 and Q2285–92.

the Copyright Act 1911; from the vantage point of the late nineteenth century, the passage of an Act premised on uniformity of treatment to all copyright subject matter, was far from a foregone conclusion.[116]

Further, as existing scholarship by Lionel Bently notes, in many respects nineteenth century artistic copyright can be seen as preparing the ground for the rules that were to be corner-stones of twentieth century copyright law.[117] For example, the term of copyright was to be determined by reference to the life of the author only, and not a fixed period from publication[118] and infringement would encompass reproductions in different media.[119] Nineteenth century debates also foreshadowed exceptions to the principle of uniformity of treatment contained in the 1911 Act. For instance, one of the few exceptions to the general rule of first ownership by the author, was in respect of portraits produced on commission; as we saw, this was accepted in late nineteenth century debates as a paradigmatic case where copyright ownership by the artist was complicated by other interests in the physical object.[120] On other issues, however, the nineteenth century debates were of little relevance to the position in 1911 and beyond. For example, as regards registration, domestic debates were overtaken by the international position; the Berne Convention, as revised in Berlin in 1908, obliged signatories to grant copyright protection without the exercise of any formalities.[121] This is not to suggest that on these points the history of artistic copyright is not worthy of further research. As noted above, so far as scholarship setting out the broad parameters of thinking regarding copyright history, the nature of the category of copyright and its relation to concepts of authorship and public interest, concern literature. A full exploration of the reasons for the differences in all these rules may provide fresh perspectives on these larger debates. Artistic copyright, therefore, is a subject that merits further attention.

---

[116] The reasons that explain this are yet to be fully investigated. One change that facilitated the principle of uniform treatment in 1911 is developments in international copyright. For example, the Berne Convention as revised in 1908, provided that the term of protection 'shall include the life of the author and fifty years after his death' (art 7). Therefore by 1911, a term commencing on creation was an international standard applicable to all copyright works.
[117] Bently, 'Art and the Making' (n 49) 344.
[118] Copyright Act 1911 s 3. This was in line with the international standard set out in the first multilateral copyright treaty: the Berne Convention Art 7, Berne Convention as revised at the Berlin Conference 1908.
[119] Bently, 'Art and the Making' (n 49) 344.
[120] Copyright Act 1911, s 5(1).
[121] Art 4 Berne Convention, as revised in Berlin in 1908.

10. Determining infringement in the eighteenth and nineteenth centuries in Britain: 'A ticklish job'
*Isabella Alexander**

1. INTRODUCTION

The 1710 Statute of Anne[1] is a convenient, if potentially misleading, starting point for copyright histories. Convenient, because it marks the beginning of copyright as a statutory right allowing authors some measure of control over products of the mind; misleading, because it does so only in retrospect. As Lionel Bently has observed, 'Had anyone celebrated the passage of the Act in April 1710 by declaring "this is the world's first copyright Act," the chances are that few, if any, would have understood what that meant.'[2] At the time it was passed, the Statute of Anne was a narrowly conceived measure aimed at regulation of the book trade. It did not immediately establish a discrete area of law; indeed it had almost no immediate impact on the book trade's commercial practices.[3] It is only when viewed over a much longer duration that it can be seen to provide the backdrop to the development of many of the features of the area of law which we identify today as copyright law.[4]

The most frequently examined effect of the Statute has been the debates it engendered over common law copyright.[5] However, as the writer, translator, inventor, editor and serial literary squabbler William Kenrick wrote after the decision in

---

* With thanks to Kathy Bowrey, Tomás Gómez-Arostegui and Jill McKeough for comments on earlier drafts. Note on Sources: Sources that begin with C (Chancery) are stored in the National Archives of the United Kingdom in Kew, England. The British Library is abbreviated as BL. The quote in the title is from Augustine Birrell, who writes: 'The task of disentangling pirated matter from that which is either original or common property is also a ticklish job'. Augustine Birrell, *Seven Lectures on the Law and History of Copyright in Books* (Cassell & Co Ltd 1899) 176.

[1] *An Act for the Encouragement of learning by Vesting the Copies of Printed Books in the Authors or Purchasers of such Copies during the Times Therein mentioned* 1710 (8 Anne c 19).

[2] Lionel Bently, 'Introduction to Part I: The History of Copyright' in Lionel Bently, Uma Suthersanen and Paul Torremans (eds), *Global Copyright: Three Hundred Years Since the Statute of Anne, from 1709 to Cyberspace* (Edward Elgar 2010) 9.

[3] Michael F Suarez, SJ, 'To What Degree did the Statute of Anne (8 Anne c.19, [1709]) affect Commercial Practices of the Book Trade in Eighteenth-century England? Some Provisional Answers about Copyright, Chiefly from Bibliography and Book History' in Bently, Suthersanen and Torremans (n 2) 54–69.

[4] For further discussion of the role of the Statute of Anne, see William Cornish, 'The Statute of Anne 1709–10' in Bently, Suthersanen and Torremans (n 2) 14; Ronan Deazley, 'What's new about the Statute of Anne? Or six observations in search of an act' in Bently, Suthersanen and Torremans (n 2) 26.

[5] See, in this volume, Barbara Lauriat, 'Copyright History in the Advocate's Arsenal'.

Donaldson v Becket:[6] 'It is to little purpose to determine whether literary property be temporary or perpetual, unless the nature of that property be also precisely determined.'[7] Determining the nature of this property in terms of drawing definite distinctions between it and other areas of law now falling within the umbrella of 'intellectual property' (patents, trade marks, designs) took, according to Bently and Sherman, until the middle of the nineteenth century;[8] Richardson and Thomas (who also include personality rights in their survey of intellectual property rights) appear to suggest this process remains incomplete.[9]

However, it was the boundaries *within* copyright to which Kenrick was referring, and it is those boundaries with which this chapter is concerned. William Cornish has written of Victorian copyright law that '[i]n a variety of interstitial ways … the judges, with some crucial help from the legislature, filled out the capacious body of the copyright idea so as to make it a useful basis for the often harrowing, often aggressive, business of taking publishing risks.'[10] A growing body of scholarship is shedding light on some of these 'interstitial' developments in different ways, examining them in greater detail than hitherto and attempting to place them more securely in their historical contexts. Much of this scholarship emanates from lawyers, or legal historians, rather than historians of other hues, although there are some exceptions.[11] This is not surprising. We would expect lawyers to be more concerned with developments in doctrine, and perhaps more interested in their nuances because, as Michael Lobban has pointed out, this is 'the history of the legal doctrines whose contemporary manifestations they (or their colleagues) also teach.'[12]

Key aspects of copyright's development and the settling of boundaries within which it operates include the subject matter it covers – that is, what separates copyright from other areas of IP, as well as what remains essentially unprotectable – and the scope of protection granted. The latter is largely determined by the law of infringement, meaning how one establishes that one's rights have been violated, as well as any exceptions or defences which might operate in favour of the potential violator. The history of both subject matter and infringement during the eighteenth and nineteenth centuries (and indeed into the twentieth and twenty-first) is largely a narrative of expansion. In 1710 copyright was a narrow right to print and re-print books; by 1911,

---

[6] (1774) 2 Bro PC (2nd edn) 129, 1 ER 837.

[7] William Kenrick, *An Address to the Artists and Manufacturers of Great Britain Respecting an Application to Parliament for the farther Encouragement of New Discoveries and Inventions in the Useful Arts* (London 1774) 65.

[8] Brad Sherman and Lionel Bently, *The Making of Modern Intellectual Property Law* (CUP 1999).

[9] Megan Richardson and Julian Thomas, *Fashioning Intellectual Property: Exhibition, Advertising and the Press 1789–1918* (CUP 2012).

[10] William Cornish, 'Part Five: Personality Rights and Intellectual Property' in William Cornish and others (eds), *The Oxford History of the Laws of England, Volume XIII 1820–1914: Fields of Development* (OUP 2010) 907.

[11] See eg Adrian Johns, *Piracy: The Intellectual Property Wars from Gutenberg to Gates* (University of Chicago Press 2010); William St Clair, *The Reading Nation in the Romantic Period* (CUP 2007).

[12] Michael Lobban, 'The Varieties of Legal History' (2012) 5 Clio@Thémis 1, 3.

176 *Research handbook on the history of copyright law*

the year of the Imperial Copyright Act,[13] it covered engravings, plays, artistic works, photographs, architecture, music, sound recordings and films. In terms of infringement, it evolved over the same period to cover non-verbatim reprints, such as abridgments, translations, dramatisations and performances, as well as preventing copying more than an 'insubstantial' part, unless for a specific purpose deemed to be acceptable.

Anyone seeking a succinct overview of the development of copyright law during the nineteenth century could hardly do better than William Cornish's comprehensive and deftly drawn survey of Victorian copyright law in Part Five, II, of *The Oxford History of the Laws of England*.[14] This chapter will focus solely on the law of infringement during the eighteenth and nineteenth centuries. It begins by sketching in broad outline the story, so far, of copyright's expansion in relation to infringement, and then turns to examine the growing field of academic commentary on this particular aspect of copyright history.

2. OVERVIEW OF THE LEGAL DEVELOPMENT OF INFRINGEMENT OVER 200 YEARS

Today, in common law countries such as the United Kingdom, the United States and Australia, copyright is defined as consisting of a number of exclusive rights held by the copyright owner. Infringement arises when someone carries out one of the exclusive rights without obtaining the copyright owner's permission, in relation to a substantial part of the particular work in question, unless the act falls within one of the legislative exceptions.

This settled state of the law is far removed from the original envisioning of infringement under the Statute of Anne, and has come about over the intervening 200-odd years largely through judicial determinations but also through legislative involvement at various intervals. The Statute of Anne contained no detailed provisions regarding infringement; it prohibited the printing, re-printing and importing of books,[15] but its drafters appear to have given no thought to what would happen if something other than a verbatim copy of the entire book was made. It is therefore somewhat ironic that the very first suit brought under the statute, *Tonson v Baker*, should have involved partial copying.[16] Tomás Gómez-Arostegui's careful excavation of the case, including the books involved, reveals that Baker had copied only parts of Tonson's *Tryal of Dr Henry Sacheverell*. However, Tonson argued, correctly, that Baker's book was the

---

[13] 1 & 2 Geo V c 46.
[14] Cornish and others, *Oxford History* (n 10).
[15] 8 Anne c 19 s 1.
[16] See H Tomás Gómez-Arostegui, 'The Untold Story of the First Copyright Suit Under the Statute of Anne in 1710' (2010) 25 Berkeley Tech LJ 1247. A case immediately prior to the Statute of Anne also involved partial copying and the two books in question were referred to a master in ordinary to compare whether they were the same or not: *Wellington v Levi* (1708/9) C33/312, f 205^{r-v}. See further, in this volume, H Tomás Gómez-Arostegui, 'Equitable Infringement Remedies before 1800' at 202, 208–9.

'Same in Substance & Effect as that printed by and for your Orator'[17] and that any alterations Baker made were done to 'elude and Evade' the Statute of Anne.[18]

However, the issue was squarely raised a decade later in *Burnet v Chetwood*,[19] which involved a translation from the Latin of Dr Thomas Burnet's *Archaeologica Philosophica*. The defendant's counsel made this very point, arguing that:

> A translation of a book was not within the intent of the act, which being intended to encourage learning by giving the advantage of the book to the author, could be intended only to restrain the mechanical art of printing, and that others should not pirate the copy and gain an advantage to themselves by reprinting it; but not to hinder a translation of a book into another language, which in some respects might be called a different book.[20]

The plaintiff succeeded in this case but the injunction was granted on the basis that the work was contrary to religion and morality.[21]

When the London booksellers petitioned Parliament for new legislation in 1737, their proposed Bill sought to include the copying of 'any sheet' of a book within the Statute's prohibition, as well as preventing the printing of abridgments and translations of a book within three years of first publication, and seeking to regulate the printing of books with alterations, additions and notes.[22] The Bill did not succeed and in 1739 two cases were brought before Lord Hardwicke LC in the Court of Chancery on the same day. *Austen v Cave*[23] and *Hitch v Langley*[24] both involved partial copying. In the former, Edward Cave had reprinted large parts of a book of sermons in his popular publication *The Gentleman's Magazine*; in the latter, the architectural writer Batty Langley was accused of copying sections of a book by the prominent architect James Gibbs in his own publication. Neither case proceeded to a decree, and nor did a similar case brought before Chancery the following year.[25] However, in the next case to come before Lord Hardwicke, he did issue a decree and it was reported. The case, known as

---

[17] Gómez-Arostegui (n 16) 1312.
[18] Ibid 1313.
[19] (1720) 2 Mer 441, 35 ER 1008.
[20] (1720) 2 Mer 441, 441; 35 ER 1008, 1008–09.
[21] For further discussion on the history of the principle of denying copyright protection to immoral works, see Isabella Alexander, *Copyright and the Public Interest in the Nineteenth Century* (Hart Publishing 2010) ch 3; Isabella Alexander, 'The Lord Chancellor, the Poets and the Courtesan: Public Morality and Copyright Law in the Early Nineteenth Century' in Andrew Lewis, Paul Brand and Paul Mitchell (eds), *Law in the City: Proceedings of the 17th British Legal History Conference, London, 2005* (Four Courts Press 2007) 230. See also James R Alexander, 'Evil Angel Eulogy: Reflections on the Passing of the Obscenity Defences in Copyright' (2013) 20 J Intell Prop L 209.
[22] A Bill for the better Encouragement of Learning by the more effectual Securing the Copies of printed Books to the Authors or Purchasers of such Copies, during the Times therein to be mentioned (1737) BL BS 68/16(1), 1737.
[23] *Austen v Cave* (1739) 2 Eq Ca Abr 522, 523; 22 ER 440, 411; C11/1552/3, m 1; C33/371, f 493r.
[24] *Hitch v Langley* (1739) 2 Eq Ca Abr 522, 522; 22 ER 440, 440; C11/1559/23, m 1; C33/371, f 493r.
[25] *Read v Hodges* (1740) C11/583/36, m 1; C33/374, ff 153v, 250v, 255v, 275v–276r.

178 *Research handbook on the history of copyright law*

Gyles v Wilcox,[26] involved Sir Matthew Hale's *Pleas of the Crown*, or *Historia Placitorum Coronae*. The defendant argued he was not reprinting but making an abridgment and Lord Hardwicke accepted that a 'fair abridgment' would not fall within the scope of the Statute of Anne.[27] Subsequent judges followed this approach, and the principle emerged that a 'fair abridgment' would not amount to infringement.[28]

Not all defendants, however, could successfully frame their partial copying as a 'fair abridgment' and the courts had to develop different ways of dealing with such cases. Some of the argument as well as the judges' decisions and speeches in the common-law copyright cases of *Millar v Taylor*[29] and *Donaldson v Becket*[30] paid attention to the legal difficulties such behaviour occasioned. As Lord Camden rhetorically complained to the House of Lords in the latter case:

> Then what Part of the Work is exempt from this desultory Claim? Does it lie in the Sentiments, the Language, and Style, or the Paper? If in the Sentiments, or Language, no one can translate or abridge them. Locke's Essays might perhaps be put into other Expressions, or newly methodised, and all the original System and Ideas be retained. Then Questions shew how the Argument counter-acts itself, how the Subject of it shifts, and become public in one Sense and private in another: and they are all new to the Common Law; which leaves us perfectly in the Dark about their Solution?[31]

Building on the 'fair abridgment' principle, subsequent courts suggested that any person who created a 'new work' when copying from an existing one would not be liable for infringement.[32] In such cases, judges made frequent reference to concepts such as labour, industry and expense, which emphasised the relative investment made by plaintiff and defendant in the works in question.[33] Following on from the acceptance that abridgments and new works were 'fair uses' of a copyright work came new assertions by defendants that other types of copying would be permissible. Quotation

---

[26] (1740) 2 Atk 141, 26 ER 489; Barn Ch 368, 27 ER 682; 2 Eq Ca Abr 697, 22 ER 586; C33/375, ff 274ᵛ–275ᵛ.
[27] 2 Atk 141, 143; 26 ER 489, 490; Barn Ch 368, 369; 27 ER 682, 682.
[28] See *Tonson v Walker* (1752) 3 Swanst 672, 36 ER 1017; *Dodsley v Kinnersley* (1761) Amb 403, 27 ER 270; *Strahan v Newbery* (1774) Lofft 775, 98 ER 913.
[29] (1769) 4 Burr 2303, 98 ER 201.
[30] (1774) 2 Bro PC (2nd edn) 129, 1 ER 837.
[31] *The Cases of the Appellants and Respondents in the Cause of Literary Property, Before the House of Lords* (London 1774), reprinted in S Parks (ed), *The Literary Property Debate: Six Tracts 1764–1774* (Garland Publishing 1975) 46.
[32] See eg *Sayre v Moore* (1785) 1 East 361n, 102 ER 139n; *Cary v Kearsley* (1802) 4 Esp 168, 170 ER 679; *Longman v Winchester* (1809) 16 Ves Jr 269, 33 ER 987; *Wilkins v Aikin* (1810) 17 Ves Jr 422, 34 ER 163.
[33] For example, in *Longman v Winchester*, Lord Eldon LC observed: 'I have said nothing that has a tendency to prevent any person from giving to the public a work of this kind; if it is the fair fruit of original labour: the subject being open to all the world; but if is a mere copy of an original work, this Court will interpose against that invasion of copyright.' (1809) 16 Ves Jr 269, 272; 33 ER 987, 988.

was frequently accepted to be non-infringing,[34] as was 'illustration'[35] and extracts for the purpose of criticism.[36]

At the same time, a second approach was emerging which focussed on the damage or prejudice that might be caused to the original work by copying, with Lord Ellenborough commenting in *Roworth v Wilkes*: 'the question is, whether the defendant's publication would serve as a substitute for [the plaintiff's publication].'[37] In *Bramwell v Halcomb*, Lord Cottenham enunciated for the first time the principle that the infringement inquiry must be a fact-dependent exercise focussing on the amount and nature of what was copied, famously stating:

> When it comes to a question of quantity, it must be very vague. One writer might take all the vital part of another's book, though it might be but a small proportion of the book in quantity. It is not only quantity but value that is always looked to. It is useless to refer to any particular cases as to quantity.[38]

When Thomas Noon Talfourd campaigned to reform copyright law in the late 1830s, he put forward several versions of clauses clarifying the nature of infringement. Infringement was expressly stated to include printing 'any portion of a Book' and various exceptions including bona fide extracts for the purposes of criticism, observation or argument, translations and abridgments were drafted.[39] None of the clauses on infringement, however, survived the Bill's final passage through the House of Lords and in the latter half of the century infringement continued to be developed by the courts of law and equity.

As increasing numbers of cases were brought before the courts during this period, some of the principles developed in the eighteenth century and earlier part of the nineteenth century became accepted as key elements of copyright doctrine, such as the threshold of 'substantial taking'. Others, however, began to change. The idea that abridgments were an acceptable form of copying began to lose ground. As early as 1844, Knight Bruce V-C stated that he was 'not aware that one man had the right to abridge the works of another'.[40] Later cases began to circumscribe the principle's operation or criticise it in *obiter dicta*,[41] and the treatise writers also began to

---

[34] See *Wilkins v Aikin* (1810) 17 Ves Jr 422, 424; 34 ER 163, 164; *Mawman v Tegg* (1826) 2 Russ 385, 38 ER 380.

[35] *Wilkins v Aikin* (1810) 17 Ves Jr 422, 425; 34 ER 163, 164; *Campbell v Scott* (1842) 11 Sim 31, 37; 59 ER 784, 787.

[36] *Bell v Whitehead* (1839) 8 LJ (Ch) 141, 142; 3 Jur 68, 68.

[37] (1807) 1 Camp 94, 98; 107 ER 889, 890. See also *Sweet v Shaw* (1839) 3 Jur 217; *Lewis v Fullarton* (1839) 2 Beav 6, 48 ER 1080.

[38] *Bramwell v Halcomb* (1836) 3 My & Cr 737, 40 ER 1110. Lord Cottenham reiterated the approach in *Saunders v Smith* (1838) 3 My & Cr 711, 40 ER 1100.

[39] Alexander, *Public Interest* (n 21) 190–95; Catherine Seville, *Literary Copyright Reform in Early Victorian England* (CUP 1999) 238–47.

[40] *Dickens v Lee* (1844) 8 Jur 183.

[41] In *Sweet v Benning* (1855) 16 CB 459, 139 ER 838, the court was divided as to whether the partial copying amounted to infringement and Cresswell J in particular was unhappy in having to conclude that such a 'useful and meritorious' work should amount to piracy, ibid 491, 139 ER 851. See also *Tinsley v Lacy* (1863) 1 H & M 747, 754; 71 ER 327, 330.

demonstrate their antipathy towards abridgments.[42] As the fair abridgment principle began to fall out of favour with courts and commentators, so too did the new work principle. While some judges continued to refuse to find in favour of plaintiffs where the defendant's work demonstrated that labour had been applied to the copied materials to create a new work,[43] increasingly courts placed greater emphasis on the prejudice that the copied work might cause to the original.[44]

Alongside the emphasis on damage or prejudice, there emerged a growing number of cases which emphasised that defendants should not be permitted to appropriate the labour expended by the plaintiff. As Hall V-C noted in *Hogg v Scott*:

> the true principle in all these cases is, that the Defendant is not at liberty to use or avail himself of the labour which the Plaintiff has been at for the purpose of protecting his work – that is, in fact, merely to take away the result of another man's labour, or, in other words, his property.[45]

In these cases, infringement appeared more like a question of unjust enrichment or misappropriation than a breach of specific rights. Yet another approach taken by courts during this time was to continue the tendency identified in the earlier period of categorising certain types of use as permissible. Criticism, review, quotation, comment and illustration were all referred to at different times and almost interchangeably by different judges as being legitimate purposes for copying.[46]

There was, however, one area in which the new work principle did continue to be accepted in the latter part of the nineteenth century; this was when the work was transformed into something totally new, as in the case of dramatisations of novels.[47] Translations were likewise thought to escape liability, although no cases came before

---

[42] See WA Copinger, *The Law of Copyright* (1st edn, Stevens & Haynes 1870) 36; TE Scrutton, *The Laws of Copyright* (1st edn, J Murray 1883) 42.

[43] *Spiers v Brown* (1857–58) 6 WR 352. In *Sweet v Benning* (1855) 16 CB 459, 482, Jervis CJ recognised that a new work would not infringe where its maker had applied 'the exertion and skill of his own brain ... dressing it up in his own language', that had not occurred in the case before him.

[44] *Bohn v Bogue* (1847) 10 Jur 420, 421; *Scott v Stanford* (1866–67) LR 3 Eq 718, 723; *Bradbury v Hotten* (1872) LR 8 Exch 1; *Ager v Peninsular and Oriental Steam Navigation Company* (1884) LR 26 Ch 637.

[45] *Hogg v Scott* (1874) 18 LR (eq) 444, 445. See also *Maple & Co v Junior Army and Navy Stores* (1882) 21 Ch D 368, 379; *Ager v Peninsular and Oriental Steam Navigation Company* (1884) LR 26 Ch 637,642; *Weatherby v International Horse Agency* [1910] 2 Ch 297.

[46] For example, in *Maxwell v Somerton* (1874) 30 LT (NS) 11, the Vice-Chancellor referred to extracts for the purpose of criticising or reviewing. In *Walter v Steinkopf* [1892] 3 Ch 489, 494, North J noted legitimate extracts might have been made to criticise the article in question. In *Sweet v Benning* (1855) 16 CB 459, 139 ER 838, Jervis CJ referred to 'the fair right of extract which the law allows for the purpose of comment, criticism or illustration' (16 CB 459, 481; 139 ER 838, 847), while Cresswell J referred to 'a fair and legitimate use of another's work for the purpose of extract, or comment, or illustration' (16 CB 459, 488; 139 ER 838, 850). See also *Black v Murray* (1870) 9 Court Sess Cas (3rd ser) 341, 348, 356.

[47] *Reade v Conquest (No 1)* (1861) 9 CB (NS) 755, 142 ER 297; *Reade v Conquest (No 2)* (1862) 11 CB (NS) 479, 142 ER 883; *Toole v Young* (1874) LR 9 QB 523.

the courts in England after the 1814 case of *Wyatt v Barnard*.[48] New transformative technologies raised similar issues and were treated the same way. In *Boosey v Whight* (1900), the sellers of perforated rolls of paper for use in the new mechanical musical instrument known as the Aeolian were found not to have infringed the copyright in the sheet music for the same songs,[49] and several years later the same reasoning meant that the makers of gramophones escaped copyright infringement as well.[50] Interestingly, this reasoning was not applied to cases involving the reproduction of dramatic works on cinematographic film. In *Karno v Pathé Frères*, Jelf J said in *obiter dicta* that a sketch protected as a dramatic work could not be reproduced cinematographically as this would be a representation within the meaning of the Dramatic Copyright Act 1833.[51]

The growing number of copyright cases coming before the courts in the second half of the nineteenth century largely failed to produce coherent or consistent doctrines of infringement. Different courts and different judges (or sometimes the same court or judge, at different times) would apply one or more different approaches, depending on the particular facts before them. The treatise writers of the period also took a variety of approaches to infringement, sometimes within the same publication. In the first edition of his influential treatise, published in 1870, Walter Copinger noted that:

> to be a piracy it is not necessary that the latter work should be a substitute for the original composition ... The inquiry in most cases, is not, whether the defendant has used the thoughts, conceptions, information and discoveries promulgated by the original, but whether his composition may be considered a *new work*, requiring invention, learning, and judgment, or only a mere transcript of the whole or parts of the original, with mere colourable alterations.[52]

However, in his second edition he retained this statement but inserted a comment on the previous page that '[t]he main point must always be what effect will the extracts have upon the original work – how far they will supply its place or injure its sale.'[53] While the two statements are not irreconcilable, the new priority given to market effect demonstrates a shift in emphasis in relation to what amounts to infringement.

Thomas Scrutton considered that infringement ought to arise 'Whenever a substantial part of an author's copyright work is reproduced without his consent or in conjunction with other matter, whether by the same or a different channel to the original, so as to tend to damage the sale of such original work.'[54] However, in practical terms he noted it was difficult to draw the line between what was and was not infringement, concluding, 'we can only say that any direct reproduction of the author's material which tends to supersede, or act as a substitute for, the original work, is an

---

[48] *Wyatt v Barnard* (1814) 4 V & B 77, 35 ER 408.
[49] *Boosey v Whight* [1900] 1 Ch 122.
[50] *Newmark v The National Phonograph Company* (1907) 23 TLR 439; *Monckton v The Gramophone Company Limited* (1912) 28 TLR 205.
[51] *Karno v Pathé Frères* (1908) 99 LT 114. See also *Glenville and Another v The Selig Polyscope Company and Another, The Times* (London, 20 July 1911) 3g.
[52] Copinger, *The Law of Copyright* (n 42) 86–87.
[53] Copinger, *The Law of Copyright* (2nd edn, Stevens & Haynes 1881) 174–75.
[54] Scrutton (n 42) 52–53.

infringement of his copyright, but that moderate quotation for the purpose of fair review or criticism is not such a reproduction.'[55]

The lack of clarity on the law of infringement might have suggested this was an area ripe for legislative codification. However, the Royal Copyright Commission of 1875–78 was reluctant to get involved. In its Report it observed that issues surrounding what is a 'fair use' of the works of other authors was one that could only be decided by the courts and 'no principle which we can lay down, or which could be defined by the Legislature, could govern all cases that could occur.'[56] The Commission did, however, think that the law should be amended to make it clear abridgments could not be made without the consent of the copyright owner and that the right to dramatise a novel should be reserved to the author as well.[57]

Despite the extensive recommendations made by the Royal Copyright Commission for the reform of copyright law more generally, no legislation was introduced in response. Following the Berne Convention of 1886, and more importantly the Berlin Revision of 1908, it became imperative that new copyright legislation be introduced. The first change was to pass an Act which, among other things, allowed foreign copyright owners to prevent English translations of their works being made without their consent, although if no authorised translation appeared within ten years the right ceased.[58] More significant changes came in the 1911 Imperial Copyright Act.[59] Clause 1 of the Act began by providing that the owner's exclusive right would cover acts done to the whole of a work or to a 'substantial part thereof'.[60] It went on to provide that the exclusive right included the right to produce, reproduce, perform or publish translations, the right to convert a novel or other non-dramatic work into a dramatic work and vice versa, and to make a record, perforated roll or cinematograph film of any literary, dramatic or artistic work.[61] In this way the legislation clearly pushed back the boundaries of infringement by drawing into the scope of owner's rights the acts of translation, performance, dramatisation and mechanical reproduction.

The Act's second clause defined infringement for the first time, providing that it would arise when any person does anything 'the sole right of which to do is by this Act conferred on the owner of the copyright'. It went on to list the acts that would *not* amount to infringement, the first of which was 'Any fair dealing with any work for the purposes of private study, research, criticism, review, or newspaper summary.'[62] Viscount Haldane, who had introduced the Bill into the House of Lords, stated that 'the principle of fair dealing is a principle which the Courts have applied with greatest care … All that is done here is to make a plain declaration of what the law is and to put all

---

[55] Ibid 43.
[56] John James Robert (Lord) Manners, 'Royal Commission on Laws and Regulations relating to Home, Colonial and Foreign Copyrights' C (2nd ser) 2036 (1878) xv, xvi.
[57] Ibid xv.
[58] An Act to amend the Law respecting International and Colonial Copyright 1886 (49 & 50 Vict c 39) s 5.
[59] An Act to amend and consolidate the Law relating to Copyright (Copyright Act) 1911 (1 & 2 Geo V c 46).
[60] Copyright Act 1911, s 1(2).
[61] Ibid.
[62] Copyright Act 1911, s 2(1)(i).

copyright works under the same wording'.[63] A confidential memorandum from the Board of Trade also noted that the provisions in the 1911 Bill 'substantially reproduce[d] the existing law'.[64]

In addition to this first clause, five further categories of non-infringing acts were added. Subsection (ii) related to artistic works, and provided it would not be an infringement for an artist, who was not the work's owner to use models, sketches etc made for the purpose of the work, as long as he did not reproduce its 'main design'. The third exception was making paintings, drawings, engravings and photography of works of sculpture or artistic craftsmanship in public places, or architectural works. The fourth specific exception related to the use of extracts in collections of works for use in schools, the fifth allowed public lectures to be published unless expressly prohibited, and the sixth allowed the reading or recitation in public of a reasonable extract of a permitted work.[65]

No mention is made of abridgments or new works as either infringement or exception. The Gorell Committee, which had been given the task of assessing the extent to which British law complied with the Berlin Revision and any necessary alterations, had determined that the law in this area was settled: 'According to British law, the presence of additions, however, ingenious or novel, will not remove the taint of piracy, if any substantial feature or part of the original work has been copied.'[66] There was some intimation that the Committee might be overstating the clarity of British law on the question, as the Report did add, 'But see the cases of *Wilkins v Aikin* ... and *Spiers v Brown*'.[67] However, the failure to include such acts as exceptions in clause 2 meant that they effectively became infringements.

Of course, even after the passing of the Imperial Copyright Act in Britain, and its subsequent adoption in the Dominions, the common law continued to play a key role in how infringement was perceived and applied. However, the form of codification set that development on a new course. From that point on the rights of copyright owners to cover all uses of works, limited only by certain specific categories of permissible behaviour, meant that the question asked of infringement was no longer 'what is protected?' but 'what is allowed?'

3. DOCTRINAL HISTORIES OF INFRINGEMENT

Having provided a 'broad-brush' overview it is time to turn from the hedgehog's perspective to that of the fox (to employ a metaphor made popular amongst copyright

---

[63] Parl Deb HL, vol 10, col 117 (14 November 1911).
[64] BT 209/474.
[65] Copyright Act 1911, s 2(1)(ii)–(vi).
[66] Report of the Committee on the Law of Copyright (Cd 4976, 1910) (Gorell Committee) 22.
[67] Ibid 22.

lawyers by Lord Hoffmann[68]) and start to consider some of the implications of an examination of the law of infringement for our understanding of copyright law and whether the narrative I have just presented is as smooth and seamless as it might appear. Over the past decade, legal scholars have begun to excavate the history of the common law development of infringement. Most of these histories, which fall largely into the category of 'internal history', have focussed on the emergence of the fair dealing exceptions. Some of the earliest pieces provide a brief overview of some of the older cases as a precursor to making an argument about the present-day law.[69] In so doing they make some sweeping claims about fair dealing, such as Puri's allegation that the concept of fair dealing 'has been applied from times immemorial',[70] or Patry's assertion that between 1740 and 1830 the judges had developed 'a relatively cohesive set of principles governing the uses of a first author's work by a subsequent author without the former's consent.'[71]

Responding to calls in several Commonwealth jurisdictions to jettison the current fair dealing exceptions in favour of a fair use defence like that of the United States, Robert Burrell analyses carefully the early English case law.[72] He observes that the dominant history of the evolution of fair dealing places the judiciary in the role of public interest protector with their decisions reining in an overly broad right granted by the Statute of Anne. However, he suggests that the early cases are better seen as placing limits on judicial expansion of a *narrow* right merely to control reprinting. On this reading, the cases which narrow the fair abridgment or new work approaches appear to be extending the rights of owners rather than limiting a broad, judicially created exception. Going on to consider the fair dealing provisions enacted the Copyright Act 1911, he observes that the evidence suggests that there was no intention to alter the common law so as to restrict the scope of copyright exceptions, although that was in fact the result.[73]

Melissa de Zwart also takes a tour through the historical cases relating to abridgments and extracts with the aim of asserting the continuing importance of fair dealing in the current digital environment.[74] She selects a number of English cases from the mid-eighteenth to the mid-nineteenth century and then considers some of the US cases in the late nineteenth and early twentieth centuries. According to her analysis, the cases reveal that there is no generally accepted role served by fair dealing and:

---

[68] *Designers Guild Ltd v Russell Williams (Textiles) Ltd* [2001] All ER 700, 706. The quote is adapted from an essay by Isaiah Berlin, who adopts Archilocus' saying 'The fox knows many things but the hedgehog knows one big thing' to describe different kinds of writers and thinkers.

[69] See David Vaver, 'Abridgments and Abstracts: Copyright Implications' [1995] EIPR 225, 225–27; David Bradshaw, 'Copyright, Fair Dealing and the Mandy Allwood Case: The Court of Appeal gets the max out of a multiple pregnancy opportunity' (1999) 10(5) Ent LR 125, 131–32.

[70] W Puri, 'Fair Dealing with Copyright Material in Australia and New Zealand' (1983) Vict U Well L Rev 277, 290.

[71] William Patry, *The Fair Use Privilege in Copyright Law* (2nd edn, BNA Books 1995) 3.

[72] Robert Burrell, 'Reining in Copyright Law: Is Fair Use the Answer?' [2001] IPQ 361.

[73] Ibid 368–74.

[74] Melissa De Zwart, 'A Historical Analysis of the Birth of Fair Dealing and Fair Use: Lessons for the Digital Age' [2007] IPQ 60.

the most certain principle that can be extracted from the early history of copyright and fair dealing is that, gradually, any use of material protected by copyright came to be seen as an incursion upon the rights of the owner and such incursions would only be justified where there was an overwhelming interest in the public interest in freedom of communication.[75]

In this formulation she seeks to defend fair dealing and fair use against the argument that it emerged in response to market failure and is no longer required for that purpose.[76]

Jane Ginsburg is also interested in the historical development of the law of infringement in her article on the public domain in early copyright law, as part of her investigation into 'the respective domains of author and public at copyright's inception.'[77] Ginsburg reads the fair abridgment cases alongside some of the other early cases on the scope of copyright protection to emphasise the role that authorial labour played in the courts' reasoning in infringement cases. She suggests that abridgers were not considered to infringe because they had their own claim to be authors and thus the courts were presented not with one property owner under attack by a prospective user, but a conflict between two property owners, both of whose claims arose out of the labour, 'invention, learning and judgment' expended on the work.[78]

Kathy Bowrey's 2010 chapter takes a somewhat different approach.[79] The impetus for her piece is to respond to recent Australian cases relating to copyright in works of fact and information in which the courts made reference to nineteenth century cases. Rather than attempting to locate the origins of fair use and tracking its development over the eighteenth and nineteenth centuries, she emphasises both the complexity of the law as well as the advantages of past approaches which have since been lost. In so doing, she shines a light on the considerable difficulties associated with deploying historical precedent in present-day cases. Bowrey's important insight is to observe that in the nineteenth century, unlike today, originality was not solely an issue relating to subsistence but frequently formed part of the infringement inquiry as the early courts attempted to weigh up both the plaintiff's and the defendant's claims to originality to determine the outcome. She concludes, therefore, that considerations as to the public interest were able to inform decisions as to whether to protect an author's private right, but that the Copyright Act 1911 changed this. While it seems clear its drafters were not seeking to alter the law of infringement, the statement that copyright subsists in every *original* work meant that originality became a question of subsistence and the defendant's claims were shifted to the enumerated defences.

My own earlier work on the law of infringement is also concerned with investigating the extent to which concerns relating to the public interest influenced the development

---

[75] Ibid 90.
[76] Ibid 63.
[77] Jane C Ginsburg, '"Une Chose Publique?" The Author's Domain and the Public Domain in Early British, French and US Copyright Law' [2006] CLJ 636, 637.
[78] Ibid 648.
[79] Kathy Bowrey, 'On Clarifying the Role of Originality and Fair Use in Nineteenth Century UK Jurisprudence: Appreciating the "humble grey which emerges as the result of long controversy"' in Catherine W Ng, Lionel Bently and Giuseppina D'Agostino (eds), *The Common Law of Intellectual Property* (Hart Publishing 2010) 45.

of infringement doctrines (forming, as it did, a chapter in a book devoted to excavating the role of the public interest in copyright law).[80] While I agree with Bowrey that in some cases courts took into account the social purposes or public interest aspects of copyright, my concern is the broader question of whether the public interest can be said to be a dominant factor in the shaping of the common law of infringement and I conclude it cannot be so. Instead, as described above, I trace a number of different approaches taken by the courts and conclude that if any overarching force emerges to shape the law it is that the courts were most concerned with regulating the competing claims of commercial competitors appearing before them. Sometimes this would involve considerations of public interest which might weigh in favour of a defendant bringing something new and useful into the marketplace, as in the early cases involving abridgments and new works, or indeed as in the later case of *Walter v Lane*.[81] However, while public interest considerations may have played a role in some cases, particularly the cases involving factual works noted by Bowrey, there were many other cases where they did not and the public interest cannot be characterised as a driving force in shaping the law of infringement in the period up to 1911.

A more recent article by Alexandra Sims also describes some of the early infringement cases, tracing a line of authority which begins with the fair abridgment cases and develops into fair dealing. It is entitled 'fair dealing's prehistory', as it ends in 1911 and a second article describes later developments. Sims argues that in 'creating the first fair dealing exception, the right to abridge, the courts were simply following the practices of the book trade at the time.'[82] This is an important point to which I shall return below. Her reading of the cases leads her to suggest that over time the courts placed less emphasis on trade practice in the case of abridgment, while still recognising other practices like quotation and review.

Matthew Sag also employs the term 'pre-history' in the title of his article, which asserts the importance of going back to the early English cases in order to obtain a fuller understanding of the US doctrine of fair use.[83] While being critical of those scholars who see *Folsom v Marsh*[84] as the first fair use case, his choice of title likewise relegates the English cases to a place of secondary importance. Sag's other motivation is to react to an argument made by Oren Bracha that *Folsom v Marsh* marked a pivotal moment of transformation in US copyright law, when copyright law changed from being a narrow right to control only near verbatim reproduction to a more general right over an abstract 'work'.[85] Sag contends that the English law prior to *Folsom v Marsh* was not so limited, deploying the statements made by courts in the early cases such as *Gyles v Wilcox* to argue that the judges were already expanding on the narrow statutory language of the Statute of Anne. He then goes on to pull out from later judgments a series of statements which demonstrate the courts applying similar reasoning in making

---

[80]   Alexander, *Public Interest* (n 21) ch 6.
[81]   *Walter v Lane* [1900] AC 539. See discussion in Bowrey (n 79) 60–62 and Alexander, *Public Interest* (n 21) 209–12.
[82]   Alexandra Sims, 'Appellations of Piracy: Fair Dealing's Prehistory' (2011) 1 IPQ 3, 27.
[83]   Matthew Sag, 'The Prehistory of Fair Use' (2010) 76 Brook L Rev 1371.
[84]   (1841) 9 F Cas 342 (CCD Mass 1841).
[85]   Sag (n 83) 1378.

decisions on infringement to that which is found in contemporary fair use cases: a case-by-case analysis approach, the amount copied, market effect and transformative use. A further objective is that, in response to those who agitate for narrowing fair use, Sag claims his history reveals that 'copyright owners' rights have been subject to and defined by the public's fair use rights since the beginnings of statutory copyright.'[86] His final argument, that *Folsom* departs from the earlier English cases in its recognition that derivatives are inherently valuable, is problematic. Even the quotes he has selected in his early Part II suggest that the English courts were similarly aware of this and sought to foster such works.[87]

Sag, like Bowrey, deals with the reception of English common law in former British colonies, emphasising the importance of understanding earlier English jurisprudence when considering the law's development. Both Australia and the US drew on the early cases – although in significantly different ways given they formed a body of binding precedent in Australia until the 1970s and 1980s. Bowrey explicitly identifies some of the difficulties that are entailed by the deploying of precedents as though they were representative of a unitary common law within and between jurisdictions, particularly in the light of the scholarly neglect of Australian colonial legal history. Although it goes beyond the scope of her chapter, Bowrey recognises the need for greater attention to be paid to Australia's 'legal distinctiveness'.[88] US scholars have the opposite problem, which Sag seeks to redress in his article asserting the importance of early English law in American legal development. His article raises an equally interesting but unanswered question: if English and American law were so similar in 1841, why are they so different now?

The works just described have left us with a far more detailed picture of doctrinal development of the law of infringement over the eighteenth and nineteenth centuries. They draw out key threads of legal development and offer persuasive explanations of what the courts were doing, or not doing, as they approached the cases brought before them. They describe the subject matter of the law and how it changed but they can only offer limited perspectives on other questions, like why it changed and what were its effects. This is not a criticism, because they are not designed to do so. However, other histories are emerging which do seek to understand legal developments in their social, cultural or political contexts and offer some answers to the causal questions often asked by historians. It is to these histories which we now turn.

4. HISTORY BEYOND THE REPORTED CASES

The early principle which held that a fair abridgment would not amount to infringement has been subjected to considerable attention by the scholars referred to above, as seemingly providing the foundation for the notion that some uses of copyright works are acceptable. As noted above, Sims suggests that in allowing abridgments and other

---

[86] Ibid 1410.
[87] See, for example, the statement of Lord Hardwicke LC in *Gyles v Wilcox* extracted at ibid 1390.
[88] Bowrey (n 79) 53.

extracts the courts were following the practices of the trade.[89] But, even if that is what motivated the courts, is it correct that this was indeed trade practice? In a short article discussing the law of abridgments in 1995, David Vaver comments that '[e]ven after the first Copyright Act of 1710, British publishers frequently abridged one another's works without thinking to ask permission.'[90] Ronan Deazley picks up on two assumptions in this statement: that the practice of abridgments was widespread in the early eighteenth century and that the Statute of Anne might have had some bearing on this.[91] He points out that these assumptions are at odds with the argument of William St Clair that there had been a clamp down on the production of anthologies, abridgments and adaptations between 1600 and 1774 and thus that the Statute of Anne had no significance in relation to them.[92]

Deazley points out the weaknesses in the evidence St Clair provides for his allegations and goes on to uncover a large number of examples of abridged texts being published during the period. Combining a close reading of the arguments made in *Gyles v Wilcox* with evidence provided by printing privileges issued prior to and during the reign of Queen Anne, he is able to build an argument that suggests that it was the intention neither of the legislature, nor of the judges, to place limits on the production of abridgments.

Further enlightenment is thrown on the subject by a recent article by Jordan Howell, whose research into the abridgments of *Robinson Crusoe* emphasises that '[c]ontrary to the modern perception that abridgements are low-brow substitutes for the original texts, earlier readers regarded abridgement as a valued literary practice that improved upon source texts by trimming and updating language to appeal to a broader audience.'[93] Nonetheless, he also seeks to know why, '[g]iven the manifest value of the narrative as a literary commodity', Defoe's publishers were not taking the abridgers to court under the Statute of Anne. While several commentators have referred to William Taylor's well-known threat to take legal action against Thomas Cox for his 1719 abridgment, assuming that a yet-to-be uncovered action took place, Howell argues that no such action was ever brought for the simple reason that the parties resolved their differences privately.[94]

This followed the well-established practice of the Court of Assistants of the Stationers discouraging contentious proceedings in favour of payment of 'acknowledgement fees' – an early form of royalty or even compulsory licence. While authors and publishers welcomed authorised abridgements, over whose outcome they could exert some kind of control, they were less pleased by unauthorised ones, especially where they were done poorly. However, the Court of Assistants was not interested in punishing abridgers, merely requiring them to pay the acknowledgement fee. By the 1720s, the court ordered that only the most serious cases should go to the courts of law,

---

[89] Sims (n 82) 27.
[90] Vaver (n 69) 225.
[91] Ronan Deazley, 'The Statute of Anne and the Great Abridgment Swindle' (2010) 47 Hous L R 793, 798.
[92] St Clair (n 11) 486.
[93] Jordan Howell, 'Eighteenth Century Abridgments of *Robinson Crusoe*' (2014) 15 The Library (7th ser) 292, 293.
[94] Ibid 310. Although note that Howell provides no evidence for this assertion.

referring all others to be heard by the Master Warden and Court of Assistants. Howell concludes that '[t]he court did not intend to establish rules to prevent, prohibit, or to otherwise discourage the printing, selling and distribution of abridgements',[95] although it could equally be argued that they were seeking (as they themselves stated) to save their members 'the trouble and Charge of going to Law.'[96] Howell suggests that acknowledgement fees thus became one of the prices of production which were further subsumed into the operation of the powerful congers.

Howell's research into the operation of the book trade presents a third interpretation of the operation of copyright law and abridgments which falls between the argument that the Statute of Anne presumptively covered them and the argument it failed to do so, either because they had always been accepted or in order to encourage their production. Rather, a greater understanding of how individual traders operated and the way that the law was applied on the ground allows us to view the Statute of Anne as demonstrating the legislature's reluctance to step into a space regulated more or less satisfactorily by the customs of the trade.

What, however, of the courts? While the proprietors of *Robinson Crusoe* might not have wished to bring proceedings to a court of law or equity, it was the case that as the century wore on some booksellers (some of whom were proprietors and/or abridgers of *Crusoe*) did wish to chance their arm at law or equity. Moreover, the proposals in the draft bills of the 1730s to include abridgment and partial taking among the rights of the copyright owner likewise suggest that not everybody was always happy with leaving such matters to tradition. If we are more attentive to the nature of eighteenth century bookselling as a highly competitive activity, which involved both cooperation and rivalry, it becomes more likely that, as I have argued in an earlier work,[97] the booksellers saw the legislature and the Court of Chancery as potential tools in their commercial armoury which could be employed to gain an advantage over competitors. The Statute of Anne may not have set out to change the customs of the time, it may indeed have aimed *not* to do so, but it nonetheless provided a new legal framework which offered new opportunities to astute commercial players.

Milsom has famously adopted a highly instrumentalist approach to the role of lawyers in creating the common law, writing:

> All the lawyer can do for one hit by a rule is to look for a way round it, make a distinction, bring some new idea to bear. If he succeeds, the rule is formally unimpaired. If the route that the special facts of his client's case enabled him to take can be used by others, the result may be reversed but the rule remains. Even when it is abolished or forgotten, its shape will be seen in the twisting route by which it was circumvented. And the ideas he has imported will prove their own strength. The first resort to them may have been artificial; but their natural

---

[95] Ibid 313.
[96] *Records of the Worshipful Company of Stationers, Court Book H*, 126–27, cited by Howell, ibid 313.
[97] Isabella Alexander, 'All Change for the Digital Economy: Copyright and Business Models in the Early Eighteenth Century' (2010) 25 Berkeley Tech LJ 1351.

properties will assert themselves, and consequences may follow as far-reaching as the ecological disturbances produced by alien animals or plants.[98]

Mark Leeming's[99] detailed examination of the litigation over Hawkesworth's *Voyages* seems to bear this out, in its emphasis on the role played by chancery practice and procedure in shaping particular disputes which themselves go on to shape the law.[100] However, Milsom's client-focussed lawyer cannot be the entire story. What of the 'ideas' themselves? Why do some of them capture the imagination of the deciding bench while others fail to do so, or fail to do so initially only to find favour years later?

In a recent article, I examined a series of cases relating to road books which came before the courts towards the end of the eighteenth and start of the nineteenth centuries.[101] Examining these cases in the context of the broader historical context in which road books were made and became valuable reveals a number of interesting facets of how laws evolve. As in the case of abridgments discussed above, map and book sellers had been producing such works for many years before the Statute of Anne arrived and both counsel and court experienced some difficulty in determining whether and how the statute might apply to works which were both highly derivative (all being largely based on Ogilby's *Britannia* produced a century earlier) and purporting to represent 'facts'. Following this close examination I conclude that at the start of the nineteenth century, 'fair use' was not seen as an exception to infringement but its corollary – a use could be fair, in which case it was no infringement, or unfair, in which case it was piratical and against the law. Moreover, I suggest that the courts in deciding such cases were attuned to both the value of the information involved as well as to the need to provide rules that were flexible enough to protect them against those seeking solely to benefit from another's efforts but would allow genuine competition, dissemination and improvement.

This is a finding which emphasises another factor influencing the law's development: the nature of the works involved in the particular cases which came before the courts, which in turn determined the particular ideas at stake. Writing at the end of the nineteenth century, Augustine Birrell lamented the 'literary insignificance' of the books which had been the subject of copyright infringement litigation:

> The big authors and big books stand majestically on one side – the combatants are all small fry. The question of literary larceny is chiefly illustrated by disputes between book-makers and rival proprietors of works of reference, sea charts, Patte[r]son's "Roads", the antiquities of *Magna Græcia*, rival encyclopædias, gazetteers, guide books, cookery books, law reports,

---

[98] SFC Milsom, *Historical Foundations of the Common Law* (2nd edn, Butterworths 1981) 6.
[99] Now Justice of the Supreme Court of NSW.
[100] Mark Leeming, 'Hawkesworth's *Voyages*: The First "Australian" Copyright Litigation' (2014) 9 Aust J Leg Hist 159.
[101] Isabella Alexander, '"Manacles Upon Science": Re-evaluating Copyright in Informational Works in Light of 18th Century Case Law' (2014) 38 MULR 317. For a more detailed focus on the map trade and these cases, see Isabella Alexander, 'The Legal Journey of *Paterson's Roads*' (2015) 67 Imago Mundi 12.

post office and trade directories, illustrated catalogues of furniture, statistical returns, French and German dictionaries, Poole's farce, "Who's Who?" Brewer's "Guide to Science".[102]

However, to complain about the nature of works involved in such litigation overlooks this as a factor of significance. Works of information (as we would call them today) were not just valuable commercial commodities in late eighteenth and early nineteenth century Britain. They were also products and vehicles of Enlightenment philosophy. As Richard Yeo has noted of eighteenth century encyclopaedias, '[they] were a practical embodiment of the notion that that knowledge should be accessible to a wide public and, as such, their purpose was not just to collate knowledge used by elites, but to facilitate conversation and communication.'[103]

That the courts were not immune from the spread of such ideas throughout society can be seen in Lord Ellenborough CJ's famous statement in *Cary v Kearsley*: 'while I shall think myself bound to secure every man in the enjoyment of his copyright, one must not put manacles upon science'.[104] Similar echoes can be found in the statement of Lord Mansfield CJ in *Sayre v Moore*:

> The rule of decision in this case is a matter of great consequence to the country. In deciding we must take care to guard against two extremes equally prejudicial; the one, that men of ability, who have employed their time for the service of the community, may not be deprived of their just merits, and the reward of their ingenuity and labour; the other, that the world may not be deprived of improvements, nor the progress of the arts be retarded.[105]

In particular, encyclopaedias, or dictionaries of arts and sciences as they were sometimes called, were seen as a special case in the courts and outside them. As Ephraim Chambers, whose *Cyclopaedia* was one of the earliest and most popular of these dictionaries, explained in his Preface:

> I come like an Heir to a large Patrimony, gradually raised by the Industry, and Endeavours of a long Race of Ancestors. What the *French Academists, the Jesuits de Trevoux, Daviler, Chomel, Savary, Cbauvin, Harris, Wolsius*, and many more have done, has been subservient to my Purposes. To say nothing of a numerous Class of particular Dictionaries which contributed their Share; Lexicons on almost every Subject, from Medicine and Law, down to Heraldry and the Manage.
>
> Yet this is but a Part. I am far from having contented myself to take what was ready procured; but have augmented it with a large Accession from other Quarters. No part of the Commonwealth of Learning, but has been trafficked to on this Occasion. Recourse has been had to the Originals themselves on the several Arts; and, not to mention what small Matters could be furnished de *proprio penu*, the Reader will here have Extracts and Accounts from a great Number of Authors of all Kinds, either overlooked by former Dictionarists, or not then extant, and a Multitude of Improvements in the Several Arts, especially of Natural Knowledge, made in these last Years.[106]

---

[102] Birrell (n *) 171.
[103] Richard Yeo, *Encyclopaedic Visions: Scientific Dictionaries and Enlightenment Culture* (CUP 2001) 12.
[104] *Cary v Kearsley* (1802) 4 Esp 168, 170; 170 ER 679, 680.
[105] *Sayre v Moore* (1785) 1 East 361n, 362n; 102 ER 139n, 140n.
[106] Ephraim Chambers, *Cyclopaedia, or an Universal Dictionary of Arts and Sciences*, vol 1 (London 1728) i.

Chambers went on to explain that 'the chief Difficulty lay in the Form; in the Order, and OEconomy of the Work' and so emphasised that this was the unique contribution of his own work over previous ones, explaining 'Accordingly, we see nothing like a Whole in what they have done: And hence, such Materials as they did afford for the present Work, generally needed further Preparation, ere they became fit for our Purpose; which was as different from theirs, as a System from a Cento.'[107]

When works such as encyclopaedias, dictionaries and other fact-based compilations came before the courts in cases of alleged copying, the courts accepted such arguments up to a point, but in practice they were rarely successful. In 1783 the rapidly rising bookseller John Murray brought an action against the owners of the *Encyclopaedia Britannica*, the second edition of which published large portions of two works by Gilbert Stuart that Murray had recently published. Murray was successful in this case, in which more than a third of Stuart's works had been copied.[108] While the proprietors of *Encyclopaedia Britannica* argued that finding infringement in such a case would be 'exploded by daily usage in the publication or magazines, reviews, annual registers and other periodical miscellanies which would not exist without the unrestrained freedom of borrowing select passages from all such treatises as excite curiosity', the court thought that in no previous case 'was there a greater infringement of literary property than that which occurs here.'[109]

The proprietor of the *Encyclopaedia Londinensis* was similarly defeated before the Court of the King's Bench when he copied 75 pages of a treatise on fencing. His counsel had argued that 'in a dictionary of all arts and sciences the compiler was justified in taking larger extracts than in another work of the same description with that copied' because 'the public were thus benefited'.[110] Lord Ellenborough agreed that such a compilation might be treated differently but considered that 'there must be certain limits fixed to its transcripts; it must not be allowed to sweep up all modern works; or an Encyclopaedia would be a recipe for completely breaking down literary property.'[111]

In a later case involving allegations of copying articles from the *Encyclopaedia Metropolitana* into the *London Encyclopaedia* the compiler and editor both gave evidence that they had been under the impression that it was perfectly acceptable and within the law to compile and abridge from other such dictionaries of arts and sciences.[112] Lord Eldon LC accepted the earlier statements of Lord Mansfield and Lord Ellenborough that it was not necessary only to consider whether matter had been copied but whether 'the party meant to give to the public what might be fairly called a new work'.[113] But noting it was difficult for a court of equity to make such an assessment he directed the case to go before a master to ascertain what exactly had

---

[107] Ibid i.
[108] See discussion in William Zachs, *The First John Murray and the Late 18th Century London Book Trade* (OUP 1998) 181–91.
[109] *Decisions of the Court of Sessions, from November 1781 to August 1787, Collected by Alexander Law, William Steuart, and Robert Craigie, Esqrs* (Edinburgh 1792) 341.
[110] *Roworth v Wilkes* (1807) 1 Camp 94, 96–97; 170 ER 889, 890.
[111] Ibid 98.
[112] *Mawman v Tegg* (1826) 2 Russ 385, 396; 38 ER 380, 385.
[113] Ibid 401, 387.

been copied. In the end, however, the matter was settled by the defendant paying 'a considerable sum of money' to the plaintiffs.[114]

The role played by Enlightenment philosophy in shaping the doctrines of copyright law is one worth exploring in more detail, if only because a direct link between the Statute of Anne and that school of thought is so often assumed.[115] However, the brief discussion above demonstrates that it did not map easily or directly on to judicial decisions. Barbara Lauriat makes a similar point in her research into the Royal Copyright Commission of 1878.[116] Turning to a different influential idea in mid-to-late nineteenth century society, she questions whether free trade doctrine could be said to exert any influence on copyright law. Lauriat notes that the 'widespread influence of free trade doctrine in the mid-nineteenth century cannot easily be overstated.'[117] Notwithstanding its pervasiveness, it is difficult to track its effect on copyright law policy for the simple reason that free trade beliefs could be just as easily used to support copyright as they could to critique it.

Yet another approach in copyright history to uncovering greater evidence of causal relationships can be found in the growing body of work that focuses on the contribution of individuals to copyright doctrine. Noteworthy examples include Catherine Seville's work on Edward Bulwer Lytton's role in bringing about the Dramatic Copyright Act of 1832 as well as agitating for the copyright of English authors to be recognised in the United States,[118] and the focus of Deazley and Adrian Johns on Samuel Egerton Brydges and the legal deposit debates.[119] Most relevant for the purposes of this chapter, however, is Barbara Lauriat's fascinating investigation of the role played by Charles Reade in shaping dramatic copyright law in the latter half of the nineteenth century.[120] Reade, along with his fellow authors and dramatists Anthony Trollope, Dion Boucicault, John Hollingshead and others, was intimately involved in seeking to mould the law as it related to translations, dramatisation of novels and international copyright in

---

[114] Ibid 405.

[115] See, for example, the comment of the French CJ, Crennan and Kiefel JJ of the High Court of Australia in *IceTV Pty Ltd v Nine Network Pty Limited* [2009] HCA 14, (2009) 239 CLR 458 [25], that:

> In its title and opening recitals, the Statute of Anne of 1709 echoed explicitly the emphasis on the practical or utilitarian importance that certain seventeenth century philosophers attached to knowledge and its encouragement in the scheme of human progress. The 'social contract' envisaged by the Statute of Anne, and still underlying the present Act, was that an author could obtain a monopoly, limited in time, in return for making a work available to the reading public.

[116] Barbara Lauriat, 'Free Trade in Books: The 1878 Royal Commission on Copyright' (2014) J Copyright Soc'y USA 635, 636.

[117] Ibid 2.

[118] Catherine Seville, 'Edward Bulwer Lytton Dreams of Copyright: "It might make me a rich man"' in Frances O'Gorman, *Victorian Literature and Finance* (OUP 2007) 55.

[119] Ronan Deazley, 'The Life of an Author: Samuel Egerton Brydges and the Copyright Act 1814' (2006) 23 Ga St U L Rev 809; Johns (n 11) ch 9.

[120] Barbara Lauriat, 'Charles Reade's Role in the Drama of Victorian Dramatic Copyright' (2009) 33 Colum J L & Arts 1.

the image of his ideals of literary property, notwithstanding his completely contradictory behaviour in relation to it.[121] Despite his vocal agitation for the rights of novelists not to have their novels dramatised without permission, Reade himself made an unauthorised dramatisation of his friend Trollope's novel, *Ralph the Heir*. Lauriat's article does not simply emphasise the point that laws are made by human actors, nor does it merely provide more evidence of the various roles played by authors and other creators in shaping copyright law; it also describes the complex interactions between people and laws, reminding us they are not always unidirectional, as well as aptly illustrating how much social behaviour takes place outside, parallel to, or in direct contravention of, legal regulation.

5. CONCLUSION

Taking a long-term view of the law of infringement over 200 years following the passing of the Statute of Anne gives us a story of copyright expanding from a limited right to print, reprint and import books to a far broader right covering both partial and transformative taking. When the reported cases of the eighteenth and nineteenth centuries are examined closely for what they can tell us about the early law on infringement, a picture emerges which is far from providing a straightforward narrative of evolution towards a fixed and certain doctrine, nor do they demonstrate consistent application of particular ideas, theories or principles. But recognising that the law is more complex and less coherent than a lawyer seeking precedent for a proposition might wish it to be does not mean it is without value. Rather, this examination allows us to observe the judicial officers at work in fleshing out a statute with meaningful context and shaping the law on the basis of the disputes brought before the courts. The very silence of the Statute of Anne on what would amount to infringement allowed a certain flexibility in weighing up competing interests and claims that subsequent developments have obscured and perhaps destroyed.

Moreover, once the view is shortened in time, narrowed in scope but broadened in the perspective, a new picture comes into focus, which goes beyond the legal forces at work in shaping the law of copyright. Internal histories of the development of legal doctrine can tell us something about why the law developed as it did, but they are not the full story. To achieve this, we need to go beyond the pleadings, writs and judgments, to find the humans behind them, the economic forces at work on them, the ideas and ideologies encircling them, the nature of the systems (Parliamentary, guild-based, the common law) in which they are embedded and their roles in that system. The nature of the physical items in question are also revealed to be relevant – are they books or something else? What kind of book – educational, geographical, literary, critical? Every history which casts a spotlight on any of these factors contributes something further to our understanding of copyright law.

---

[121] On this point see also Robert Macfarlane, *Original Copy* (OUP 2007) 130–57.

11. Equitable infringement remedies before 1800
H. Tomás Gómez-Arostegui*

1. INTRODUCTION

The tail that wags the dog. Nowadays, that is how we often refer to the law of remedies in copyright cases. This is not surprising given that the availability *vel non* of certain remedies, such as injunctive relief and statutory damages (in the United States), often drives whether a copyright holder sues. In this chapter, I review the remedies that were available to copyright and printing-patent holders in the Court of Chancery in England before 1800. Although the Court of Exchequer also heard printing disputes on its equity side, the Chancery served as the chief venue for these disputes and was the principal court of equity in England.

The history of this field is interesting for its own sake. But it also happens that in the United States early equity practice remains doctrinally relevant, despite the partial merger of law and equity in 1938. The US Supreme Court continues to rely on eighteenth-century English cases at common law and in equity in deciding whether litigants have a right to a jury trial on copyright remedies and in setting the default equitable remedial powers of the federal courts.[1] The court has also reaffirmed the historical distinction between legal and equitable defences in copyright suits.[2] In short, as Samuel Bray has noted in his recent study of the Supreme Court's remedies

---

* Thanks to Isabella Alexander, Lionel Bently, Sean Bottomley, Hamilton Bryson, John Gordan, Liz Hore, Lydia Loren, Hector MacQueen, and James Oldham for their comments on earlier versions of this chapter or for otherwise assisting in its preparation, and to Isabella for also providing copies of some of the sources cited herein. Any errors are mine alone. Research at institutions in Great Britain and elsewhere was made possible by a gift from Kay Kitagawa and Andy Johnson-Laird. I thank them for their very generous support. Sources that begin with C (Chancery) or KB (King's Bench) are stored in the National Archives of the United Kingdom in Kew, England. Other depositories are abbreviated as follows: Bodl=Bodleian Library; BL=British Library; HLS=Harvard Law School; IT=Inner Temple Library; LI=Lincoln's Inn Library; LMA=London Metropolitan Archives; SJC=St John's College Cambridge; and SCA= Stationers' Company Archive. In manuscript sources, I have left the spelling unchanged but have silently expanded abbreviations. Unless stated otherwise, all cases cited in this chapter are from the Court of Chancery. Dates occurring on or before 2 September 1752 are not converted to the Gregorian Calendar. Moreover, as is customary, when an event falls between 1 January and 24 March, inclusive, prior to 1752, the year is given with a slash mark, eg 24 March 1711/2, but 25 March 1712. Documents reproduced in the Appendix appear with the kind permission of the London Metropolitan Archives.

[1] *Feltner v Columbia Pictures Television, Inc* 523 US 340 (1998); *Grupo Mexicano de Desarrollo SA v Alliance Bond Fund, Inc* 527 US 308 (1999).

[2] *Petrella v Metro-Goldwyn-Mayer, Inc* 134 S Ct 1962 (2014).

jurisprudence, the court has, 'with vigor', insisted 'on the historic division between law and equity.'[3]

In this chapter, I treat the two principal forms of equitable relief: injunctions and the disgorgement of a defendant's profits. I have written on both areas before,[4] albeit on the latter only briefly. This chapter supplements my prior work and draws on newly discovered manuscript sources. Throughout this chapter, I highlight a few areas of equity practice in printing disputes that require further study. In a future publication, I plan to discuss the remedies available to right holders at law.

Because few practice manuals before 1800 expressly address equity practice in printing disputes, I have had to base my findings in large part on the cases themselves. Fortunately, the Chancery offers us a few hundred such cases before 1800. (Most are unpublished.) Accordingly, unless stated otherwise in the text or the margin, every case cited in this chapter involved the infringement of a copyright or a printing patent.

2. INJUNCTIONS

For most litigants before the year 1800, the *sine qua non* of a copyright or printing-patent suit was the injunction. Early on, the Court of Chancery granted injunctions in printing disputes based on its inherent authority and without express statutory authorization. Indeed, it was not until 1819 in the US,[5] and 1862 in the UK,[6] that statutes expressly empowered courts to grant injunctive relief in printing suits. The sections below discuss the first known injunction, the various categories of injunctions that were available, the process for obtaining them, and how strong a case had to be on the merits.

2.1 The Earliest Injunction

It is difficult to state definitively when the first injunction issued in a case involving a copyright or other exclusive printing right. Many early manuscript records remain

---

[3] Samuel Bray, 'The Supreme Court and the New Equity' (2015) 68 Vand L Rev 997, 1000.

[4] H Tomás Gómez-Arostegui, 'What History Teaches Us About Copyright Injunctions and the Inadequate-Remedy-at-Law Requirement' (2008) 81 S Cal L Rev 1197, 1221–50; H Tomás Gómez-Arostegui, 'Prospective Compensation in Lieu of a Final Injunction in Patent and Copyright Cases' (2010) 78 Fordham L Rev 1661, 1701–07. For work on equitable remedies in suits involving patents of invention, which largely tracks the procedures used in copyright suits, see Sean Bottomley, 'Patent Cases in the Court of Chancery, 1714–58' (2014) 35 J Legal Hist 27; Sean Bottomley, *The British Patent System During the Industrial Revolution, 1700–1852* (CUP 2014) 105–42.

[5] Act of 15 Feb 1819, 3 Stat 481. The Judiciary Act of 1801, which lasted only until July 1802, empowered circuit courts to grant 'writs of injunction to stay waste … on any judgment rendered by such circuit court, upon the like terms and conditions as such writs may be now granted, by the justices of the Supreme Court of the United States.' Act of 13 Feb 1801, s 18, 2 Stat 89, repealed by Act of 8 Mar 1802, s 1, 2 Stat 132.

[6] Fine Arts Act 1862, s 9 (25 & 26 Vict c 68). See also Imperial Copyright Act 1911, s 6(1).

unexamined, and the order and decree books of the Court of Chancery before 1544 have not survived. Nevertheless, until an earlier record reveals itself, the honour in England must go to *Wolfe v Payne*, a case filed in the Court of Chancery in 1563/4 to enforce a printing patent. The plaintiff, Reyner Wolfe, held a life appointment to the office of the King's Printer in Latin, Greek, and Hebrew, which among other things gave him the exclusive right to print Latin grammars.[7] Richard Payne and a few others infringed the patent by printing a Latin accidence, a component of grammar books. The Lord Keeper, Nicholas Bacon, enjoined the defendants from printing, uttering, or selling their book, or causing the same to be done, until the case could be heard. This was, essentially, a preliminary or interim injunction. Given its historical significance, the relevant order bears reproducing in full:

> The said Richard Payne and [*blank*] Marshe have this daye made their apparannce before the L. keper of the great seale of Englande and are ordered to make answere to the bill of the plaintiff by saturdaye next, and the said Richard Payne hath undertaken that the said [defendant] Howe who hath not appeared shall also make his answere by the same daye / And yt is ordered by the said L. keper that neither the said Richard Payne nor [*blank*] Marshe nor any of them shall hereafter printe or cause to be prynted any accydences to the preiudice of the priviledge graunted to the plaintiff nor shall in any wyse utter or sell anye of the accidences allreadie printed by them or by their meanes or consent nor shall any wayes be aydinge assisting or consentinge to any person for the printinge of the same untill suche tyme as the cause in questyon shall be hearde, and theruppon other order taken therin by the said L. keper / And it is further ordered that all other accidences not sould or uttred shall be by them retayned and be forthcomynge to be ordered as upon the hearing of the matter shall be thought mete, And besydes that the said Richard and [*blank*] shall be answerable for the said accidences alredye solde and uttred as this court shall adiudge / for the better performance of this order aforesaid The said Richard Payne and [*blank*] Marshe are enioyned by the said L. keper in the somme of CC^{li} [200 pounds] to observe and kepe the same./[8]

2.2 The Categories of Injunctions

Generally speaking, before 1800, the Court of Chancery in England granted four categories of injunctions in copyright and printing-patent disputes: (1) injunctions until answer; (2) injunctions until a trial of the cause in the Chancery – known as a 'hearing'; (3) injunctions until a trial or other adjudication of the cause in a court of common law or other forum; and (4) perpetual injunctions at the conclusion of the case.

2.2.1 Injunctions until answer

The first type of injunction was designed to last until the defendant filed a 'full and perfect' answer; that is to say, an answer that responded to all the material allegations of the bill of complaint. It has no precise modern-day equivalent, but it is somewhat similar to temporary restraining orders in the US and without-notice injunctions in the

---

[7] Patent of Reginald (Reyner) Wolfe as King's Printer in Latin, &c (1547) C66/805, m 50. His patent was strengthened in 1558. (1558) C66/937, m 14.
[8] *Wolfe v Payne* (1563/4) C33/30, f 143^v. The court later referred the case to arbitration with the consent of the parties. (1565) C33/32, f 256^v.

198 *Research handbook on the history of copyright law*

UK. The affinity stems from the fact the court often (though not always) granted these injunctions *ex parte* and could, if warranted, convert them into injunctions that lasted until the hearing.

Claimants would request injunctions until answer after filing a bill of complaint or an amended bill of complaint that added new defendants. Barring exceptional circumstances, requests would be made by 'motion', which at the time meant an oral motion made in court, as opposed to one made in writing in a 'petition'. In my review of nearly 100 injunctions until answer, only two were granted on petition. In one suit, the injunction was to last for only three days until the plaintiff could move orally in court.[9] In the other, the court granted an injunction following a petition made during the long vacation after Trinity term, but it did so only after both sides had attended the Lord Chancellor at his home to present their arguments.[10] The preference for motions stems from an early rule of court which stated that no 'injunction of any nature shall be granted, revived, dissolved, or stayed, upon any private petition.'[11] Although later softened a bit, the general principle remained.[12]

2.2.1.1 Two types Injunctions until answer came in two varieties – those granted as a matter of course and those granted on the merits. As to the first, the court would grant an injunction as a matter of course, on a mere motion by the plaintiff, if the defendant was in contempt for failing to appear in court within certain time limits in response to a *subpoena ad respondendum* or for appearing on time but then failing to file an answer to the complaint within the time required. Outside of contempt, an of-course injunction could issue if the defendant appeared on time but sought a *dedimus potestatem* to answer in the country or otherwise sought an extension of time to respond.[13] Because the time limits to appear and answer were, as Lord Hardwicke candidly described them in 1750, 'very short',[14] and many infringing defendants were in no mood to respond in a hurry, of-course injunctions were fairly common before 1730. They run the gamut: the defendant failed to appear,[15] appeared but departed without answering,[16] craved a

---

[9]   *Tonson v Clifton* (1722) C33/340, ff 30ʳ, 33ᵛ.
[10] *Nicol v Kearsley* (1784) C33/462, f 461ʳ, 2 Dick 645, 645.
[11] Orders of Lord Chancellor Bacon, ca 1618/9, No 20, in John Beames (ed), *The General Orders of the High Court of Chancery* (London 1815) 12.
[12] Orders of Lord Chancellor Clarendon, 1661, Petitions, in Beames (n 11) 214–15. See also *Mason v Murray* (1777) 2 Dick 536, 536 (citing Lord Bacon's ordinance).
[13] William Bohun, *Cursus Cancellariæ* (Savoy 1715) 441; Joseph Harrison, *The Accomplish'd Practiser in the High Court of Chancery* (3rd edn, Savoy 1750) vol 1, 207–09; Notes on Chancery Practice, IT Mitford MS 79, p 17 (ca 1775); [Richard Boote], *The Solicitor's Practice in the High Court of Chancery Epitomized* (5th edn, London 1782) 25.
[14] *Travers v Lord Stafford* (1750) 2 Ves Jr 19, 21 (surety).
[15] Eg *Stationers v Boddington* (1682) C33/260, ff 37ᵛ, 136ᵛ; *Baskett v Farley* (1721) C33/337, ff 42ᵛ, 44ᵛ.
[16] Eg *Stationers v Hartley* (1684) C33/262, ff 465ʳ, 522ᵛ; *Webb v Rose* (1729) C33/354, f 22ᵛ. For an example of a note used by counsel to argue for an injunction on this ground, and the order granting the injunction, see *Stationers v Edwards* (1696) Case, SCA Series II, Box A1; *Stationers v Edwards* (1696) C33/286, ff 505ᵛ–506ʳ.

dedimus potestatem,[17] sought additional time to respond to the complaint,[18] or some combination of the four grounds.[19]

Injunctions granted as a matter of course were nearly always obtained *ex parte* because, as a general rule, a claimant was not required to notify defendants of such a motion, nor were defendants permitted to oppose it:

> Sometimes a Motion is of Course (that is) where by a standing Rule, or the known Course of the Court the Thing desired is to be granted without hearing the Party; and in these there needs no Notice of the Motion to the other Side, nor ought their Council to oppose 'em.[20]

Nevertheless, it appears that plaintiffs sometimes provided notice,[21] and on rare occasions defence counsel even appeared at the argument.[22]

If the plaintiff sought an injunction until answer before the expiration of the aforementioned time limits, the plaintiff would have to address the merits of the case on the motion and submit proof, by means of a certificate obtained from the Six Clerk's Office, that the plaintiff had filed a bill of complaint.[23] This was sometimes called moving 'specially' or on a 'special' motion.[24] The tactic became nearly universal in printing cases after 1730, as claimants more often moved on or within days of filing their complaints. Additionally, nothing prevented a claimant from moving on the merits even after the time limits had expired.

Addressing the 'merits' ordinarily meant alleging by sworn affidavit – in support of the allegations of the bill of complaint,[25] which was not a sworn document – that the plaintiff held the copyright or printing patent at issue and that the defendant was infringing it. Lord Mansfield, Chief Justice of the Court of King's Bench, described the practice in 1761 as follows:

---

[17] Eg *Baskett v Gray* (1719) C33/331, f 427^r; *Baskett v Akenhead* (1725) C33/343, f 273^r.
[18] Eg *Herringman v Clerke* (1681/2) C33/257, ff 213^v, 216^v; *Baskett v How* (1716) C33/327, f 2^v.
[19] Eg *Stationers v Beard* (1682) C33/258, ff 588^v, 621^v.
[20] Bohun (n 13) 423. See also Boote (n 13) 21.
[21] Eg *Pawlett v Braddyll* (1685) C33/264, f 479^r, C41/25, Trin No 80; *Bill v Bradford* (1699) C33/291, f 411^v; *Baskett v Akenhead* (1725) C33/343, f 273^r.
[22] Eg *Stationers v Braddyll* (1681/2) C33/258, f 152^r.
[23] Starting in 1701, orders on merit motions began to include language acknowledging that the plaintiff had submitted proof, by certificate, of having filed a bill of complaint. Eg *Pawlett v Minshall* (1701) C33/298, f 121^r; *Meredith v Wellington* (1701) C33/298, f 117^r. The proof was not gratuitous, as minutes demonstrate the certificates were required. *Atkins v Smith* (20 Nov 1701) C37/702 (before staying a plaintiff on a defendant's cross-bill, the Master of the Rolls stated that the defendant 'must produce a certificate telling the Court of the Defendants \X/ [cross] Bill fyled').
[24] Eg *Travers v Lord Stafford* (1750) Amb 104, 104–05 (surety); *Strathmore v Bowes* (1786) 2 Dick 673, 673–74 (statement of John Dickens, Deputy Registrar, in a case involving waste).
[25] See Harrison (n 13) vol 1, 54 ('[G]enerally where any motion … is made that is not of course, an *affidavit* of the facts alledged is necessary.'); *Anonymous* (1711) BL Hargrave MS 80 (reading affidavits supporting allegations of the bill on a request to enjoin execution of a judgment at law), printed in WH Bryson, *Reports of Cases in the Court of Chancery from the Time of Lord Harcourt (1710–1714)* (Dog Ear Publishing 2014) 136.

[In the Court of Chancery,] [i]njunctions that [a]re granted upon the filing the Bill[,] that does not go of course, because the Judge that grants it hears an affidavit of the Foundation of the Property & a certificate of the Bill being filed[.] That is till Answer[.][26]

The use of merit affidavits seems to have first arisen in the late seventeenth century,[27] but they do not appear in earnest until the early eighteenth century.[28] All told, I have encountered just over 60 injunctions granted on merit affidavits before 1800. There undoubtedly are more.

Affidavits were often quite detailed, and it was not uncommon for a plaintiff to submit more than one to obtain an injunction.[29] Determining whether the court 'read' affidavits – the literal parlance used to indicate a court had considered them – is not difficult, so long as one has access to the manuscript records of the court. The order granting the injunction usually summarizes the affidavits that were read, if any, and identifies the affiants. The draft minutes of proceedings are sometimes fuller, and they should also be consulted if one is to be absolutely certain. In some cases, the affidavits themselves survive, either in their original loose paper form, as copied in the affidavit register of the Chancery, or both.

Occasionally, the court granted an injunction on the merits without affidavits. According to practice manuals, the court could do so if it was, by other means, 'pretty well satisfied' that the injunction should issue.[30] To be sure, those manuals were speaking of injunctions in cases of waste, not printing disputes. But I have unearthed a few examples of merit injunctions granted with limited or no affidavits in printing cases – albeit only during the turn of the eighteenth century.[31]

Injunctions on the merits were often granted *ex parte*, but this was not always so because in some instances notice was required and in others the plaintiff voluntarily provided it. Clear statements on notice requirements are not easy to come by. Some practice manuals state, without referring to printing disputes in particular, that motions

---

[26] *Tonson v Collins* (1761) BL Add MS 36201, ff 53^r, 84^r (KB). See also *Mackenzie v Robertson* (1771) Information for John Mackenzie (Ct Sess) 26 (quoting the opinion of Charles Yorke that 'an injunction ... may be moved on the usual affidavits (of property, and the piratical publishing and vending) immediately after the bill filed.'). For an example of notes a barrister used at argument to obtain an injunction on the merits, along with the order in the case, see *Stationers v Carnan* (1773) Brief, SCA Series I, Box D; *Stationers v Carnan* (1773) C33/442, f 7^r.

[27] Eg *Norton v Lee* (1681) C33/258, ff 117^r, 96^r.

[28] Eg *Wellington v Levi* (1708/9) C33/312, f 205^{r-v}; *Tonson v Baker* (1710) C33/314, f 375^v, C37/726; *Tonson v Clifton* (1722) C33/340, f 33^v; *Stationers v Baddham* (1723) C33/342, f 23^{r-v}; *Stationers v Farley* (1725/6) C33/346, ff 131^v–132^r.

[29] Eg *Gay v Walker* (1729) C41/44, Pas No 572, C41/44, Trin Nos 46–48; *Eyre v Walker* (1735) C41/49, Trin Nos 556 & 557; *Walthoe v Walker* (1736/7) C41/49, Hil Nos 96 & 97. For an example of two affiants submitting a single affidavit, see *Bach v Longman* (1773) C31/188, Pas No 80.

[30] Bohun (n 13) 450. See also Harrison (n 13) vol 1, 207.

[31] Eg *Chiswell v Lee* (1681) C33/257, f 174^v; *Stationers v Lee* (1681) C33/258, f 96^v; *Pawlett v Minshall* (1701) C33/298, f 121^r; *Meredith v Wellington* (1701) C33/298, f 117^r; *Stationers v Farley* (1702) C33/300, f 3^r.

for injunctions 'upon the Merits' required notice.[32] But statements like this most likely related solely to injunctions sought on the merits *until the hearing* of the cause, a type of injunction I discuss below in Part 2.2.2. In 1750, the Court of Chancery declared, albeit in a case not involving copyrights, that notice was generally required if a plaintiff moved for an injunction until answer *after* a defendant had appeared.[33] Examples of this type of notice do appear in printing disputes.[34] The clearest pronouncement we have is on motions made *before* a defendant appeared, and it comes from a litigant in a printing-patent dispute in 1804. In an appeal to the House of Lords, from a decision of the Chancery, the appellant represented that making and granting merit motions without notice before appearance was 'agreeable to the usual practice of the Court in such cases'.[35]

Regardless of whether notice was required or not, it is clear that defendants sometimes received it. It is not uncommon to find defence counsel appearing and opposing merit motions in printing disputes,[36] and even offering counter affidavits.[37] Moreover, oppositions at this stage may have happened more often than the court orders reveal. I know of an instance where an order fails to mention that defence counsel appeared at the argument, but a newspaper report of the same proceeding demonstrates that counsel did appear and vigorously opposed an injunction until answer.[38] A systematic review of the records, including the underlying draft minutes of the court, might reveal additional discrepancies.

I mention the rules on notice and opposition because scholars today often assume that all injunctions until answer, including those granted on the merits, were always sought and obtained *ex parte*. One must consult all the available records – both manuscript and printed – to be certain.

It is hard to know how often the court prodded plaintiff's counsel in open court on *ex parte* merit motions. We lack a critical mass of manuscript and printed reports of these types of proceedings in printing disputes. Nevertheless, there are some hints of rigour

---

[32] Eg *Praxis Almæ Curiæ Cancellariæ* (London 1694) vol 1, 40.
[33] *Marasca v Boyton* (1750) C33/396, f 35^v, 2 Ves Sr 112, 112. See also *Harrison v Cockerell* (1817) 3 Mer 1, 2.
[34] Eg *Sheridan v Falkener* (1776) C33/446, f 302^{r-v}, Gazetteer and New Daily Advertiser, 4 May 1776, p 3; *Mason v Murray* (1777) C33/448, f 152^{r-v}; *Burke v Owen* (1796) C33/496, f 9^r; *Faden v Stockdale* (1797) C33/496, f 321^v. See also *Baskett v Cunningham* (1762) Solicitor's Bill Book, LMA CLC/B/136/MS18744/002, pp 220, 222 ('Drawing Notice of Motion for Injunction Copy and Service on Clerk in Court for such Defendants as had appeared.').
[35] *Richardson v Universities of Oxford & Cambridge* (ca 1804) Case of the Appellants (HL) 3. For the underlying injunction until answer, see *Universities of Oxford & Cambridge v Richardson* (1802) C33/518, ff 119^v–120^r.
[36] Eg *Chiswell v Lee* (1681) C33/257, f 174^v; *Norton v Lee* (1681) C33/258, f 117^r; *Stationers v Lee* (1681) C33/258, f 96^v; *Stationers v Bradford* (1698) C33/292, f 224^r; *Stationers v Partridge* (1709) C33/312, f 363^r; *Knaplock v Curll* (1721/2) C33/337, f 117^v; *Macklin v Richardson* (1766) C33/426, f 249^r; *Lowndes v Harrop* (1768) C33/430, f 352^{r-v}; *Coleman v Wheble* (1778) C33/449, f 186^{r-v}; *Thompson v Harrison* (1783) C33/462, f 9^{r-v}; *Faden v Stockdale* (1797) C33/496, f 321^v.
[37] Eg *Cary v Faden* (1799) 5 Ves Jr 24, 26, C31/294, Mich No 138.
[38] Compare *Rippon v Crosby* (1795) C33/491, f 500^{r-v}, with *Rippon v Crosby* (1795) Morning Post, 31 July 1795, p 1.

before granting an injunction until answer, such as the court asking counsel for precedent,[39] stating that it was already aware of precedent,[40] reading the preface of a plaintiff's work,[41] or examining a defendant's work.[42] Thus, it would be wrong to assume that the Chancery always rubber-stamped *ex parte* requests. The court could and sometimes did raise issues *sua sponte*.

* * *

Appendix A to this chapter reproduces a solicitor's bill book in a printing-patent dispute from 1764 in which the plaintiff sought an injunction until answer on the merits. It is one of several I have found. The bill book lists the tasks performed before filing the suit and through obtaining the injunction, along with the associated costs and fees.

2.2.1.2 Two forms An injunction until answer, once granted, issued in one of two principal forms. The least common form was to grant the injunction *nisi causa*. That is to say, the court would conditionally grant the injunction by stating that it would go into effect unless (*nisi*) the defendant appeared by a certain date and showed cause (*causa*) against it. The following example comes from an order dated 24 February 1708/9:

> [The plaintiff has requested an injunction to last] untill the said Defendant shall Answer the plaintiffs Bill & this Court take other order to the contrary[,] Which his Lordship held reasonable and doth order the same accordingly unless the said Defendant having notice hereof shall at the last General Seale [9 March 1708/9] Shew unto this Court good Cause to the contrary/[43]

By granting the injunction *nisi causa*, the court enabled a defendant – who might not have received notice of the original motion and was thus unable to prevent the order from issuing at the outset – to appear and prevent the injunction from going into effect. It also seems that, in theory, this approach would have permitted a defendant to challenge the order before filing an answer, something that was not regularly permitted until Lord Eldon's time.[44] Unfortunately, the theory is difficult to confirm. I have seen the form used in four cases and in only one did a defendant attempt to show cause, and that occurred on the same day the defendant filed an answer and demurrer.[45] In any case, if the defendant was able to show cause on the basis of affidavits or a deficiency

---

[39] Eg *Bell v Walker* (1785) C33/463, ff 411ᵛ–412ʳ, 1 Bro CC 451, 452; *Gee v Pritchard* (1818) C33/646, f 1819ᵛ, 2 Swanst 402, 406, Times, 18 July 1818, p 3.
[40] Eg *Burke v Owen* (1797) C33/496, f 128ʳ⁻ᵛ, Staffordshire Advertiser, 18 Feb 1797, p 2.
[41] Eg *Cullen v Lowndes* (1771) C33/437, f 16ʳ.
[42] Eg *Butterworth v Robinson* (1801) C33/512, f 136ʳ, 5 Ves Jr 709, 709.
[43] *Wellington v Levi* (1708/9) C33/312, f 205ʳ⁻ᵛ. See also eg *Pawlett v Braddyll* (1685) C33/264, f 479ʳ; *Webb v Rose* (1729) C33/354, f 22ᵛ; *Gilliver v Watson* (1729) C33/351, ff 280ᵛ–281ʳ, C37/1194 (*semble* – the injunction was not expressly stated to last 'until answer').
[44] See n 53 below.
[45] *Gilliver v Watson* (3 June 1729) C37/1194, C11/2581/36, m 2.

in the plaintiff's case, the court would cancel the injunction.[46] If the defendant failed to appear to challenge the order, it was incumbent upon the plaintiff to move to make the injunction 'absolute', meaning no longer conditional. Such a motion was granted as a matter of course, so long as the plaintiff submitted an affidavit averring that he had served the *nisi* order to the other side.[47]

I should note that in two of the four cases I have encountered, the minutes indicate that the court stated during argument that the defendant should 'stay' the printing, publishing, or vending of the allegedly infringing book in the 'mean time',[48] meaning until the date set for the argument on showing cause. This appears to have been an informal request because in neither case did the statement appear in the court's order, and, thus, the defendant could not be in contempt for disobeying it.[49] It was not until the defendant in one of the two cases asked for additional time to show cause that the stay appeared in an order.[50]

Much more common was for the court to simply order the injunction until answer without any conditional language. Nearly all of the cases take this approach. For example:

> Itt was prayed that an Injunction may be awarded to Stay the Defendant … untill the Defendant shall directly answer the plaintiffs bill & this Court take other order to the Contrary[,] Which this Court held reasonable & doth order the same[.][51]

If the above approach was taken, or the conditional injunction mentioned previously was made absolute, then the injunction would by its terms last until the defendant – sometimes all the defendants if there was more than one[52] – put in a full and perfect answer and the court took other order to the contrary. The first step, of course, was actually to file an answer.[53] In some cases this never happened because the defendants

---

[46] cf *Gilliver v Watson* (6 June 1729) C37/1198, LI Misc MS 13, p 57, Bodl Viner MS 38, f 197ʳ, 2 Eq Ab 522, 522 (dissolving injunction).

[47] Eg *Pawlett v Braddyll* (1685) C33/264, f 491ᵛ; *Wellington v Levi* (1708/9) C33/312, f 457ʳ; *Webb v Rose* (1729) C33/354, f 33ʳ.

[48] *Gilliver v Watson* (19 May 1729) C37/1192, C37/1194; *Pawlett v Braddyll* (25 June 1685) C37/416 (stating more ambiguously: 'stay meane', which probably meant stay the printing in the mean time, but could have also meant stay the injunction in the mean time).

[49] See *Anonymous* (1679) HLS MS 1105, p 37, Freem Ch 46, 46 ('[I]t is no order till it is drawn up and passed by the Register, for the Registers minutes are only a warrant for an order, and no order.'). See also John Wyatt, *The Practical Register in Chancery* (London 1800) 297.

[50] *Gilliver v Watson* (1729) C33/351, f 284ᵛ.

[51] *Stationers v Farley* (1725/6) C33/346, ff 131ᵛ–132ʳ.

[52] Bohun (n 13) 442; Harrison (n 13) vol 1, 210–11; Wilmot Parker, *An Analysis of the Practice of the Court of Chancery* (London 1794) 48. See also Gorges E Howard, *A Supplement to the Rules and Practice of the High Court of Chancery in Ireland* (Dublin 1774) 74. But see eg *Hawkesworth v Parkinson* (1773) C33/439, f 256ʳ (dissolving the injunction as to a defendant who answered).

[53] It was not until Lord Eldon's time that injunctions until answer issued in printing cases in the disjunctive: until answer *or* other order to the contrary. Eg *Gee v Pritchard* (1818) C33/646, f 1819ᵛ. A disjunctive order, such as this, permitted a defendant to move to dissolve the injunction on affidavits and without having to first file an answer. See Robert Henley Eden, *A Treatise on the Law of Injunctions* (London 1821) 325–26.

simply acquiesced, thereby making the injunction *de facto* perpetual. In *Tonson v Walker*, for example, the court enjoined the defendants from printing, publishing, or selling John Milton's *Paradise Lost* 'untill the said Defendants shall fully answer the plaintiffs bill and this Court take other order to the Contrary[.]'[54] None of the defendants filed an answer. Eleven years later, in an argument in another case, William Murray (while in practice and before being ennobled as Lord Mansfield) correctly noted that the injunction was still in effect: 'The Property of *Milton*'s *Paradise Lost* … is [still] protected by [an] Injunction[] at this Day.'[55]

More commonly, defendants did file an answer. Then, if a defendant wished to dissolve the injunction – which he often did – he would move in court to do so. An affirmative motion was required to induce the court to order 'the contrary', that is to say, to dissolve the injunction.[56] Typically, the defendant would argue that he had submitted a full and perfect answer that denied the 'whole equity' (ie, the overall merits) of the complaint. If the plaintiff had obtained the injunction as a matter of course because the defendant was in contempt for failing to appear or answer, the defendant would also have to 'clear' his contempt,[57] before the court would entertain his motion, which among other things might entail paying the costs of the coercive process.[58] Of course, a defendant might choose not to dissolve the injunction, in which case the injunction would continue indefinitely, including until the hearing of the cause.[59]

A motion to dissolve could occur in one of two ways.[60] First, the defendant could provide notice to the plaintiff and move on the merits to dissolve the injunction absolutely.[61] This was sometimes called moving to dissolve in the 'first instance'[62] and rarely occurred in printing cases. Second, and much more common, the defendant could move without notice, and as a matter of course, to dissolve the injunction *nisi causa*; this meant the injunction would be dissolved unless the plaintiff, being served

---

[54] *Tonson v Walker* (1739) C33/372, f 208ᵛ.
[55] *Millar v Kincaid* (ca 1749/50) Case of the Appellants (HL) 3.
[56] See *Robinson v Lord Byron* (1788) 2 Dick 703, 705 (statement of John Dickens, Deputy Registrar, in a case involving waste).
[57] Eg *Stationers v Courtnay* (1682) C33/260, f 37ᵛ; *Bill v Bradford* (1699) C33/291, f 411ᵛ; *Baskett v Mist* (1717/8) C33/329, f 204ʳ; *Baskett v Farley* (1721) C33/337, f 44ᵛ; *Webb v Rose* (1729) C33/354, f 22ᵛ.
[58] Harrison (n 13) vol 1, 210. See also *Hall v Darney* (1756) 1 Dick 289, 289 (non-printing case).
[59] Eg *Gay v Walker* (1729–37) C33/351, f 305ʳ, C33/369, ff 315ᵛ–316ᵛ; *Bach v Longman* (1773–77) C33/439, f 185ʳ, C33/447, ff 582ᵛ–583ʳ.
[60] See generally Roger North and Francis North, Chancery, SJC James MS 613(3), p 8 (ca 1726, but based on notes of Francis North ca 1682–85, printed in Roger North, *The Life of the Lord Keeper North* (Mary Chan ed, Edwin Mellen Press 1995) 326.
[61] Eg *Mount v Fenner* (1732) C33/358, f 383ʳ, 2 Dick 793, 793, C33/358, f 395ʳ⁻ᵛ, 2 Dick 676, 676. For an example outside the printing context, see *Norton v Aylett* (1749) C33/392, f 318, printed in Henry Wilmot Seton, *Forms of Decrees in Equity* (London 1830) 314.
[62] *Strathmore v Bowes* (1786) 1 Cox Eq Cas 263, 263 (waste).

with the order *nisi*, showed cause on a certain day to continue the injunction.[63] The following order dated 27 June 1738 illustrates the latter approach:

> Now upon Motion this day made unto this Court by Mr Mills being of the Defendants Counsel[,] It was alleged that the Defendants have since put in a full and perfect answer to the plaintiffs Bill and thereby denyed the whole Equity thereof and therefore It was prayed that the said Injunction may be dissolved[,] which is Ordered accordingly unless the plaintiffs[,] their Clerke in Court having Notice hereof[,] shall on the last Generall Seal [25 July 1738] Shew unto this Court good Cause to the Contrary.[64]

2.2.1.3 Two causes   When faced with the prospect that an injunction would soon dissolve, plaintiffs had two options for showing cause to continue it. The first was to except to the answer on the ground that it was not full and perfect.[65] The purpose of such a move was to continue the injunction until such time as a 'further answer' could be submitted to correct the deficiencies. The process for extending the injunction in this fashion was convoluted. First, the plaintiff would file exceptions to the answer. The court would then send the complaint, answer, and exceptions to one of the 11 masters of the Court of Chancery to review and report on whether the answer was in fact full and perfect. In the mean time, the injunction would continue according to the terms and conditions ordered by the court.[66] Some orders, for example, required the plaintiff to obtain the master's report within four days,[67] while others imposed no express time limits.[68] Failure to obtain a report on time would result in the injunction being dissolved *nisi causa* on the motion of the defendant, or automatically and absolutely without motion, depending on the court's schedule and inclination.[69] Ultimately, if the master timely reported the answer insufficient, the injunction would continue until a further answer came in, after which the whole process might repeat itself on the further answer.[70] If the master reported the answer sufficient, however, the court would dissolve the injunction. As before, the injunction might dissolve automatically and

---

[63] *The Solicitor's Compleat Guide in the Practice of the High Court of Chancery* (London 1776) vol 2, 503; eg *Chiswell v Lee* (1681) C33/257, f 168r; *Wellington v Levi* (1709) C33/312, f 554v, C33/314, f 121r–v; *Baskett v Salmon* (1724) C33/341, f 272v; *Cogan v Cave* (1743) C33/379, f 547r; *Lintot v Owen* (1760) C33/416, f 144r; *Whiston v Donaldson* (1771) C33/436, f 331v; *Clarke v Cock* (1798) C33/501, f 733v.
[64] *Gyles v Barlow* (1738) C33/369, f 621r.
[65] Parker (n 52) 48.
[66] Bohun (n 13) 449; Notes on Chancery Practice, IT Mitford MS 78, p 80 (ca 1775).
[67] Eg *Wellington v Levi* (1709) C33/312, f 425v; *Read v Hodges* (1740) C33/374, ff 275v–276r; *Strahan v Newbery* (1774) C33/442, f 129r. The parties could agree to have the master backdate a report, if necessary, to comply with a time limit. Parker (n 52) 15.
[68] Eg *Norton v Lee* (1681) C33/258, f 68v; *Rippon v Crosby* (1795) C33/494, f 105r.
[69] Harrison (n 13) vol 1, 212; Jeffrey Gilbert, *The History and Practice of the High Court of Chancery* (Savoy 1758) 196–97.
[70] Eg *Norton v Lee* (1681) C33/258, ff 64v, 68v, 79r; *Strahan v Newbery* (1774) C33/442, ff 129r, 131r.

absolutely without the need of a motion,[71] or the defendant might be required to move to dissolve it *nisi causa*.[72]

The aforementioned time limits and automatic dissolutions, when utilized, served to prevent plaintiffs from abusing the exceptions process. An affidavit in a copyright suit from 1681 attests to the potential for misuse:

> John Phillipps of Blackfryers gentleman maketh oath that about the first or second of the instant December the plaintiff comeing to this deponents house & discourseing of the Bill he had Exhibited into this Court against the Defendants[,] this deponent told the said plaintiff he was informed that the Defendants would putt in such an Answer as should admit of noe Exception to which the plaintiff replyed that he would never leave makeing Exceptions to the end he might Continue the Injunction in this Cause or used words to the very same effect & added farther that he he [*sic*] hoped to have the Defendants all in Jayle or words to that purpose[.][73]

Continuing the injunction was not, of course, the only reason for excepting to an answer. Obtaining a full answer was crucial for the hearing of the cause. When the answer was sworn to by the defendant, which was the usual course, it functioned as the principal method for obtaining testimony from the defendant. Additionally, a full answer set forth which allegations the defendant admitted and which were contested.

The second option for continuing an injunction was to show cause on the merits.[74] Showing cause in this manner differed from excepting in two ways. Most obviously, it sought to extend the injunction on the merits of the case, rather than on a procedural failing of the defendant. But more importantly, successfully arguing the merits converted the injunction until answer into an injunction until the 'hearing' of the cause in the Chancery – the court's equivalent of a trial.[75] I will say more about showing cause on the merits in the section that follows.

The decision whether to show cause with exceptions or on the merits was usually left to the plaintiff. But by the mid-eighteenth century, if not earlier, if a plaintiff sought an extension of time in which to show cause, he or she would have to show it on the merits.[76] Of course, once the court rejected a request to continue an injunction on exceptions – because the defendant's answer was full and perfect – the only method to proceed further would be on the merits.[77] And if in rejecting the exceptions the court

---

[71] Eg *Read v Hodges* (1740) C33/374, f 299^{r-v}. See also *Hutchinson v Markham* (1817) 2 Madd 355, 355 (referring to this practice).
[72] Bohun (n 13) 449; Gilbert (n 69) 197–98.
[73] *Chiswell v Lee* (1681) C41/23, Mich No 463.
[74] Parker (n 52) 48.
[75] Robert Hinde, *The Modern Practice of the High Court of Chancery* (London 1785) 598.
[76] Eg *Stationers v Carnan* (1774) C33/442, f 136^v; *Strahan v Newbery* (1774) C33/442, f 179^v. For non-printing cases, see *Pinheiro v Porter* (1738) 3 Swanst 362, 362 fn (a); *Pearson v Dennis* (1747) C33/390, f 17, printed in Seton (n 61) 297.
[77] Gilbert (n 69) 197–98; [Samuel Turner], *Costs in the Court of Chancery* (2nd edn, London 1795) 162–63.

had already dissolved the injunction absolutely, the plaintiff would have to move to *revive* the injunction and extend it to the hearing.[78]

This brings us to our second category of injunctions.

2.2.2 Injunctions until the hearing

Injunctions until the hearing were akin to present-day preliminary or interim injunctions, and there were two ways to request one. The first and most common method was as part of an effort to continue an injunction that had previously been granted until answer – the process I described in the preceding section. The second method was to ask for the injunction *ab initio*. That is to say, a plaintiff could omit a request for an injunction until answer and instead ask for an injunction until the hearing. Naturally, this happened most often when the plaintiff first moved for an injunction after the defendant had filed an answer.[79] Regardless of the approach taken, requests for injunctions until the hearing always required notice to the other side,[80] and the court never granted them as a matter of course.[81] Claimants always had to request and obtain this type of injunction on the merits of the case.

If a prior injunction until answer had been granted as a matter of course, or the plaintiff was moving *ab initio* for an injunction until the hearing, then the plaintiff had the option of submitting sworn affidavits (having not previously done so) attesting that he owned the copyright or patent at issue and that the defendant was infringing it.[82] It was also possible for a plaintiff to submit no affidavits on the motion and instead rely on the admissions of an answer to support an injunction.[83] If a prior injunction until answer had already been obtained on the merits, the plaintiff could rely on the previous

---

[78] Eg *Read v Hodges* (1740) C33/374, f 299[r–v]. cf *Peyto v Hudson* (1754) 3 Swanst 364, 364 (declining to revive an injunction that enjoined execution of a judgment at law, after execution had occurred).

[79] Eg *Stationers v Harris* (1708) C33/310, f 490[r]; *Norton v Hazard* (1713/4) C33/322, ff 155[r], 235[v], C37/707; *Tonson v Walker* (1752) C33/398, f 322[r]. Other variations appear. In one case, the court granted an injunction until the hearing against a defendant who had already answered, but an injunction until answer against one who had not. *Motte v Faulkner* (1735) C33/366, f 18[r]. And in another suit, the court held over a motion for an injunction until answer until after the answer came in, which then resulted in the court granting an injunction until the hearing. *Thompson v Stanhope* (1774) C33/442, f 149[r], Amb 737, 740. Something similar occurred in a suit where the defendants answered before an intended motion for an injunction until answer could be argued, which ultimately resulted in the plaintiffs moving for an injunction until the hearing. *Baskett v Cunningham* (1762) C33/417, ff 165[v], 337[v]–338[r], 1 Bl R 370, 371, 2 Eden 137, 138. I know of only one instance before 1800 where a plaintiff sought and obtained an injunction until the hearing *before* the defendants had answered. *Wolfe v Payne* (1563/4) C33/30, f 143[v]. See the text to n 8 for the order in *Wolfe*.

[80] Hinde (n 75) 583; Parker (n 52) 48.

[81] *Potter v Chapman* (1750) Amb 98, 99 (treasury appointment).

[82] Eg *Tonson v Walker* (1752) C33/398, f 322[r], BL Add MS 36065, ff 15[r], 25[v]. See also *Charlton v Poulter* (1753) 19 Ves Jr 148 fn 70, IT Mitford MS 46, f 192[v] (partnership).

[83] Eg *Stationers v Harris* (1708) C33/310, f 490[r]; *Baskett v Cunningham* (1762) C33/417, ff 337[v]–338[r].

showing by affidavit or submit additional supporting affidavits.[84] And again, the plaintiff could also or entirely rely on admissions in the answer. In any case, the court would consider the defendant's sworn answer, which effectively functioned as an opposition, and the oral arguments of counsel on each side.[85] Occasionally, the court would also consider affidavits submitted by or on behalf of the defendants.[86]

If the plaintiff showed cause on the merits, even in the face of the defendant's answer, affidavits (if any), and arguments, the court would 'allow' the cause and continue, revive, or grant an injunction until the hearing. Consider the following example:

> Now upon opening of the Matter this present day unto this Court by Mr Fazakerley & Mr Browning being of the plaintiffs Counsel who came to shew Cause against the … Order [dissolving the injunction *nisi causa*] & alleadged [a number of matters regarding the plaintiff's title and the defendant's infringement, including] [t]hat the Defendants by their Answer admit the plaintiffs Title to the said Manuscript Treatise but that the book printed by them is an Abridgment there of which they Insist they have a right to print …. Whereupon & upon hearing of Mr Attorney Generall & Mr Mills of Counsel with the Defendants[,] Answer read & what was Alleged on both sides[,] This Court doth allow the Cause now shewn & doth Order that the said Injunction [until answer] be continued untill the hearing of the Cause which the plaintiff is to Speed/[87]

In some cases, of course, the plaintiff failed to show cause because he did not appear at the argument as required[88] or because the court 'disallowed' the cause on the merits.[89] Either way, the court would dissolve the injunction absolutely.

The Court of Chancery sometimes sought assistance from a master in ordinary to determine whether to grant or continue an injunction until the hearing. As Lord Chancellor Thurlow stated in 1785: 'It is not true, as had been urged, that the Court must determine upon the answer of the Defendant. I might refer it to the Master to see whether the work complained of is an original work or not'.[90] In essence, the court sometimes tasked a master with comparing and contrasting the plaintiff's and defendant's works. In *Wellington v Levi*, for instance, the order stated:

---

[84] Eg *Gibbs v Cole* (1734) C33/361, f 338^r, 1 Dick 64, 64, BL Hargrave MS 464, f 89^r. See also *Packington v Packington* (1745) 1 Dick 101, 102 (waste); *Isaac v Humpage* (1792) 3 Bro CC 463, 464–65 (bill for services).

[85] See William Blackstone, *Commentaries on the Laws of England* (Oxford 1768) vol 3, 443. For an example of notes a barrister used to argue cause to continue an injunction until the hearing, see *Macklin v Richardson* (1766) Brief for Charles Yorke, Attorney General, BL Add MS 36193, f 237^r. For the order, see *Macklin v Richardson* (1766) C33/426, ff 281^v–282^r.

[86] Eg *Tonson v Walker* (1752) C33/398, f 322^r.

[87] *Gyles v Barlow* (1738) C33/369, ff 610^v–611^r. See also eg *Atkins v Keeble* (1681/2) C33/257, f 269^r; *Gibbs v Cole* (1734) C33/361, f 338^r; *Baskett v Bentham* (1742/3) C33/379, f 322^r; *Duke of Queensberry v Shebbeare* (1758) C33/409, f 477^v; *Whiston v Donaldson* (1771) C33/436, f 331^v.

[88] Eg *Millar v Donaldson* (1766) C33/426, f 245^r.

[89] Eg *Lintot v Owen* (1760) C33/416, ff 16^v–17^r; *Millar v Donaldson* (1765) C33/428, f 418^v, 2 Eden 327, 328; *Osborne v Donaldson* (1765) C33/428, f 418^{r-v}, 2 Eden 327, 328; *Hawkesworth v Parkinson* (1773) C33/439, f 304^v; *Clarke v Cock* (1798) C33/501, f 732^r.

[90] *Nicol v Stockdale* (1785) 3 Swanst 687, 689.

This Court doth Order that it be referred to Mr. Fallowes one [of the masters of this Court] to examine into the matter and to see whether the Grammer intitled Claudius Mauger's French Grammer and the Grammer intitled the Royall French Grammer by which one may in a short time attaine the French Tongue in perfection be one and the same Booke and whether they matterially differr or not[.] And the plaintiff is to procure the sayd Master to make his Report by the first Seal after Xmas[.][91]

Other orders were similar. By way of example, one Lord Chancellor ordered that the master was to 'see whether the said Books or works so published by the defendant are in any and what respect different from the Book or work published by the plaintiff'.[92] And in a suit involving an engraving, the court ordered the master to determine whether the defendant's work was 'of the same size & scale & has the same Marginal Notes & Directions or Instructions & is in all respects the same' as the engraving published by the plaintiff.[93] Another asked the master to assess whether the 'Book published by the defendants is a fair abridgement'.[94]

The reports, once returned, were fairly succinct, and ultimately, the court was free to accept or reject them. In *Carnan v Paterson*, for example, the Master of the Rolls followed the report of a master who had examined two books about the roads of Great Britain. As Isabella Alexander has explained,[95] the master found that the two books were not exactly the same in that the plaintiff's book solely contained written descriptions of the roads while the defendant's book contained not only written descriptions but engraved maps of the roads as well. As to the written descriptions, the master noted that there were many small differences, additions, corrections, and variations but that the 'said Roads [were] in Substance nearly the same[.]'[96] On this basis, the Master of the Rolls granted an injunction until the hearing, but only insofar as the written descriptions of the roads.[97] Later, the Lord Chancellor, on a motion to dissolve the injunction, was not as confident as the Master of the Rolls about the merits of the case, and he dissolved the injunction and ordered the master to compare the books once more. This time, the charge was to determine whether the defendant's book was 'so essentially different from the … [plaintiff's] as to render the former a new and original Composition in any and what Part.'[98] Ultimately, the master thought that the book was original,[99] but the court later sent the case to the master a third time for more analysis.[100]

* * *

---

[91] *Wellington v Levi* (1709) C33/314, ff 54^v–55^r.
[92] *Trusler v Cummings* (1773) C33/440, f 284^r. See also eg *Bell v Walker* (1785) C33/463, f 475^v, 1 Bro CC (4th edn) 451, 452 fn (2); *Carnan v Paterson* (1785) C33/463, f 696^{r-v}; *Sael v Leadbeater* (1799) 4 Ves Jr 681, 681.
[93] *Jefferys v Bowles* (1770) C33/433, f 267^v.
[94] *Strahan v Newbery* (1774) C33/442, f 179^v.
[95] Isabella Alexander, '"Manacles Upon Science": Re-Evaluating Copyright in Informational Works in Light of 18th Century Case Law' (2014) 38 MULR 1, 19–21.
[96] *Carnan v Paterson* (29 May 1786) C38/728.
[97] *Carnan v Paterson* (1786) C33/465, ff 449^v–450^r, 2 Bro CC 80, 84–85.
[98] *Carnan v Paterson* (1786) C33/467, f 23^v, 1 Cox Eq Cas 283, 285.
[99] *Carnan v Paterson* (19 May 1787) C38/736.
[100] *Carnan v Paterson* (1787) C33/467, ff 617^v–618^r.

210   *Research handbook on the history of copyright law*

Appendix B to this chapter reproduces a solicitor's bill book from a copyright suit in 1741 – the well-known and important case of *Pope v Curll* – in which the plaintiff sought and obtained an injunction until the hearing. As before, the bill book lists the tasks the plaintiff's solicitor performed before filing the lawsuit and through obtaining the injunction, along with some of the associated costs and fees.

2.2.3 Injunctions granted at the hearing

Eventually, if the parties pursued the matter beyond an interlocutory injunction, they could conduct additional discovery and the suit would reach a hearing. A detailed description of a hearing in Chancery is beyond the scope of this chapter, but suffice it to say that it effectively was a bench trial decided on written proofs – namely, sworn answers, depositions (meaning oral answers provided on oath and memorialized in writing by a court agent in response to written interrogatories), and documentary evidence (such as indentures, deeds poll, receipts, letters patent, newspaper advertisements, and the like). As one commentator summarized the process in 1782:

> The method of *hearing* is thus: The parties appearing, one of the [plaintiff's] jun[ior] counsel opens the bill, and then one of the deft's opens the answer, then plt's sen[ior] counsel states the case and matter in issue, and briefly touches on the proofs; then they proceed to read [the proofs], first plt's side, then deft's, the counsel on both sides debating the matter, plt's counsel concluding the arguments; then the court pronounces the decree, the minutes of which are taken down, and frequently read in court by the register.[101]

At the conclusion of the hearing, the court could grant one of two types of injunction. The first was another interlocutory injunction designed to last while the case was referred to another court or forum for further adjudication. The second was a perpetual injunction at the conclusion of the case. I treat each of these in the sections that follow.

2.2.3.1 Injunctions pending adjudication in another forum   During the hearing, the court sometimes discovered an issue that required further attention, such as the validity or ownership of a copyright in a work, the validity of a printing patent, or the meaning of a statutory provision. In these instances, the Chancery could, if it elected to do so, refer the matter to one of the common-law courts – the Court of King's Bench or the Court of Common Pleas – and while the case was pending there continue an injunction in the mean time.[102] Once returned, the Chancery would hold another hearing on the

---

[101]   Boote (n 13) 18. See also Charles Barton, *An Historical Treatise of a Suit in Equity* (London 1796) 187–88.

[102]   Occasionally, the court might send a case to law before the hearing. Most of the very few instances I have encountered were on a plaintiff's attempt, after the defendant had answered, to show cause on the merits to convert an injunction until answer into an injunction until the hearing. It seems likely that in these instances the parties were prepared to proceed to the hearing on the bill and answer alone – without the need for additional discovery – and thus rather than waiting until the hearing to send the parties to law, the parties agreed to go immediately. Eg *Rippon v Crosby* (1796) C33/494, f 202^v; *Beckford v Hood* (1797) C33/497, f 583^{r-v}, C33/500, f 33^r. cf also *Grierson v Jackson* (1794) 1 Ridg L & S 304 (Ch Ir) 311 (stating that sending a case to law could occur only at the hearing, unless the parties consented); *Horton v Maltby* (1783) LI Hill MS 18, pp 148, 149 (arg) (noting the consent of the parties in a case

'equity reserved'. One issue that requires further study, and which is beyond the scope of this chapter, is when (if ever) the Chancery was *obligated* to send a case to law. That is a topic I plan to address in a future work.[103] In any case, referrals, and the injunctions that often accompanied them, could occur in a number of ways, depending on whether the issue was one of law, fact, or both.

Where the disputed issue was strictly legal, the Chancery usually took one of two routes in sending a case to law. The first was to order the plaintiff to file an action in the King's Bench or Common Pleas upon narrowed facts, and for the defendant to then demur or plea, and, if the latter, for the plaintiff to then demur to the defendant's plea, thereby putting the legal question in issue without requiring a jury trial.[104] In two companion cases in 1682/3, for example, the court ordered the parties as follows:

> [The plaintiffs are to bring actions] against the Defendant for Importing into England from partes beyond the seas & vending in England of Twelve Bibles twelve New Testaments 12 bookes of Common prayer & also 12 books of psalmes in metre Imprinted in partes beyond the seas in the English Tongue knowing them to be there Imprinted without Lycense[,] ... to which action ... the said Defendant shall forthwith name his Attorny & by pleading shall confess the [aforesaid] .... Whereby the Kings prerogative & his Grant to the plaintiffs [of certain printing patents] ... be good or no shalbe made the only point of law to be there insisted upon & all matters of fact & other matters whatsoever to be admitted in order to the bringing only of the aforesaid matter in law in Judgment & after Judgment to resort back to this Court for further direction[.][105]

A much more common way to send strictly legal issues to the law courts was on a 'case stated', meaning a statement of facts stipulated by the parties with the assistance of a master in Chancery (if needed).[106] Extant copies of the statements of facts, called

---

involving a patent of invention). In another case, the court sent the parties to law during an argument over exceptions to an answer. *Stationers v Parker* (1696/7) C33/288, f 202[r].

[103] For a general discussion of the matter, particularly as it relates to resolving issues of fact, see Edmund Robert Daniell, *A Treatise on the Practice of the High Court of Chancery* (London 1840) vol 2, 727–62; John H Langbein, 'Fact Finding in the English Court of Chancery: A Rebuttal' (1974) 83 Yale LJ 1620; Michael RT Macnair, *The Law of Proof in Early Modern Equity* (Duncker and Humblot 1999) 276–89; James Oldham, 'On the Question of a Complexity Exception to the Seventh Amendment Guarantee of Trial by Jury' (2010) 71 Ohio St LJ 1031, 1333–38.

[104] A demurrer admitted the facts alleged by the other side but argued that they were not legally cognizable. A plea admitted the facts alleged by the other side and alleged additional facts.

[105] *Hills v Wright & Stationers v Wright* (1682/3) C33/259, ff 313[v]–314[r]; see also *Hills v Wright* (1683/4 judg) KB27/2028, rot 98 (KB); *Stationers v Wright* (1683/4 judg) KB27/2028, rot 100 (KB). In another suit, the Chancery was not as explicit in requiring the parties to descend the pleadings to an issue of 'law', but the numerous admissions required by the court resulted in as much. *Hills v University of Oxford* (1684) C33/263, ff 766[v]–767[r]; *Hills v Parker* (1684/5 issue) KB27/2040, rot 699 (KB).

[106] Eg *Atkins v Roper* (1668) C33/229, f 700[v]; *Stationers v Partridge* (1710/11) C33/316, f 525[r–v]; *Baskett v Bentham* (1743/4) BL Add MS 36054, f 72[v]; *Millar v Taylor* (1765) C33/426, ff 68[v]–69[r]; *Bathurst v Donaldson* (1767) C33/429, ff 546[v]–547[v]; *Stationers v Carnan* (1774) C33/442, ff 188[r]–189[r]; *Bach v Longman* (1776) C33/445, ff 683[v]–684[r].

'cases', are scarce in printing disputes, but I have encountered a few.[107] The court receiving the request would hear argument on the stipulated case – without the need for the plaintiff to file an action at law or the need for a jury trial – and then issue a 'certificate' that answered the questions of law that the Chancery had submitted.[108] Charles Ambler, a regular practitioner in Chancery, described the process in 1775:

> [B]y the Consent of all parties all the facts are admitted and then a Case is sent to the Court of Common Pleas upon those facts[,] which are admitted[,] to know what the Law is resulting from those facts – The Court of Common Pleas ... certifie[s] what in their opinion is the Law ....[109]

Certificates were usually very short because the King's Bench and Common Pleas would answer the question or questions without providing any reasoning.[110]

If the Chancery thought a case involved a factual dispute, the court could direct the plaintiff to bring an action in the King's Bench or Common Pleas for a jury trial at *nisi prius* before a single judge, with the parties to descend the pleadings to an issue of fact. If an issue of fact alone was involved, then the case would usually return to the Chancery soon after the verdict. If an important and anticipated legal question also needed resolution,[111] the verdict would then be followed by an argument decided at the 'Bar' by all the judges of the particular court. The mixed scenario – which was designed to resolve both facts and law – was the more complicated of the two, and so I should say a bit more about it.

To begin the process, the plaintiff would usually file an action for trespass upon the case in the King's Bench (or less often in the Common Pleas), and the defendant would plead the 'general issue' by pleading *non culpabilis* (not guilty). This general denial placed upon the jury the responsibility to resolve the contested facts. Of course, not all facts would necessarily be contested, and sometimes the Court of Chancery ordered a defendant to admit certain facts during the jury trial. For example, the Chancery might order a defendant to concede that he had sold one of the allegedly infringing books within the statute of limitations.[112] After the trial, there were two principal ways to bring the jury's verdict to the Bar of the court for its resolution of the legal issue.

First, the jury might issue a special verdict, meaning that the facts as found by the jury would be stated at large in the 'record' (ie, the plea roll). The court would then address the legal issues on the facts as found. As one practice manual described it:

---

[107] Eg *Baskett v University of Cambridge* (ca 1744–58) Case, BL Add MS 36203, f 129[r] (KB); *Stationers v Carnan* (ca 1774) Case, SCA Series I, Box D8 (CP).

[108] Eg *Bach v Longman* (16 June 1777) Certificate, C38/668.

[109] *Stationers v Carnan* (1775) SCA Series I, Box D3, p 3 (Ambler arg).

[110] Eg *Baskett v University of Cambridge* (1758) 2 Burr 661 (KB) 664; *Stationers v Carnan* (1775) 2 Bl R 1004 (CP) 1009. For a brief time, the King's Bench under Lord Mansfield declared in the King's Bench the reasons underlying its certificate. CHS Fifoot, *Lord Mansfield* (OUP 1936) 57–58, 231–32.

[111] Eg *Millar v Taylor* (1766) C33/426, f 325[r]; *Millar v Donaldson* (1767) C33/428, f 397[r–v].

[112] Eg *Beckford v Hood* (1797) C33/500, f 33[r]; *Faden v Stockdale* (1798) C33/504, ff 107[v]–108[r].

[I]t has become the practice for the jury, when they have any doubt as to the matter of law, to find a *special* verdict, stating the facts, and referring the law arising thereon to the decision of the court; by concluding conditionally, that if upon the whole matter alledged, the court shall be of opinion, that the plaintiff had cause of action, they then find for the plaintiff; if otherwise, then for the defendant.[113]

Another option was for the jury to return a general verdict for the plaintiff, subject to the opinion of the court on a 'special case' drawn up by counsel. The special case laid out the facts on which the court was to make its ruling on the law.[114] This second approach had the advantage of being speedier and less expensive, but the disadvantage of not being appealable on a writ of error to a higher court.[115]

When the Court of Chancery referred a case to law via an action, as opposed to on a case stated, the court often imposed a time limit for the plaintiff to proceed at law, with the penalty for default being that any previously granted injunction would lapse. In one suit, for instance, the Lord Keeper ordered the plaintiff to bring an action in the King's Bench the 'sitting after this terme' and that, 'unless hindred by the defendants', failing to do so would result in a prior injunction being discharged.[116] In another case, the court ordered the plaintiff to file his action within three months, and that in 'default' thereof, the 'Injunction is to stand absolutely dissolved without further Motion.'[117] And at other times, the court would 'retain' the bill of complaint for 12 months, and order that if the plaintiff did not file his action and try the case within that time the Chancery would dismiss the plaintiff's suit.[118]

Before moving to our next category of injunction, I should mention one other type of referral. Apart from sending a case to law, it was also possible for the Chancery to refer a case to arbitration. This occurred in *Gyles v Barlow* in 1740/1, where the chief issue at the hearing was whether the defendants' book was a fair abridgment. At first, the Lord Chancellor contemplated sending the underlying issue of fact to a master in ordinary, who he hoped would be assisted by two experts agreed to by the parties.[119]

---

[113] William Tidd, *The Practice of the Court of King's Bench* (2nd edn, London 1799) vol 2, 799; eg *Millar v Taylor* (1769) 4 Burr 2303 (KB) 2306; *Millar v Taylor* (1769 judg) KB122/338, rot 372 (KB).

[114] Tidd (n 113) vol 2, 801–02; eg *Beckford v Hood* (1798) 7 D & E 620 (KB) 621; *Beckford v Hood* (1798) Special Case, LI Dampier MS LPB 222 (KB). For more on this procedure during Lord Mansfield's tenure on the King's Bench, see James Oldham, *The Mansfield Manuscripts and the Growth of English Law in the Eighteenth Century* (North Carolina UP 1992) vol 1, 101 fn 179, 131–33; James Oldham, 'The Seventh Amendment Right to Jury Trial: Late-Eighteenth-Century Practice Reconsidered' in Katherine O'Donovan and Gerry R Rubin (eds), *Human Rights and Legal History: Essays in Honour of Brian Simpson* (OUP 2000) 225, 231, 233, 235.

[115] Tidd (n 113) vol 2, 801–02. By the late eighteenth century, it became possible to convert a special case into a special verdict to enable a writ. Eg *University of Cambridge v Bryer* (1812) 16 East 317 (KB) 317, 334. See also *Boulton v Bull* (1795) 2 H Bl 463 (CP) 500 (patent of invention).

[116] *Stationers v Parker* (1696/7) C33/288, f 202^r.

[117] *Beckford v Hood* (1797) C33/500, f 33^r. See also eg *Rippon v Crosby* (1796) C33/494, f 202^v.

[118] Eg *Millar v Donaldson* (1767) C33/428, f 397^{r-v}; *Faden v Stockdale* (1798) C33/504, ff 107^v–108^r.

[119] *Gyles v Barlow* sub nom *Gyles v Wilcox* (1740/1) Barn Ch 368, 369–70, 2 Atk 141, 144.

But after the parties nominated the experts, the court reconsidered the matter and, with the consent of the litigants, opted to have the two experts arbitrate and settle 'all Matters in difference between the said partys'.[120] The court also ordered that a previously granted injunction 'be continued in the mean time.'[121]

2.2.3.2 Perpetual injunctions In cases where the Chancery at the hearing did not feel the need to refer the case to another court or where the case came back from a referral in a manner favourable to the plaintiff, the court might grant a fourth type of injunction: a 'perpetual' injunction. Today we more commonly refer to this as a permanent or final injunction. Relative to the number of printing suits filed, final injunctions were uncommon in the long eighteenth century because defendants often acquiesced to interlocutory injunctions. Nevertheless, the absolute number of final injunctions is respectable, and I have encountered many of them in the long eighteenth century.[122] I should note that while many decrees expressly use the word 'perpetual', others do not, and it remains a matter of dispute, particularly before the year 1774, whether the appearance of the word in a decree always meant that the court intended for the injunction to last in perpetuity.[123]

Even though the Chancery usually granted a perpetual injunction only after the plaintiff had prevailed during one or more of the adjudications mentioned above, it was not unheard of for the court to grant a perpetual injunction at the outset of a lawsuit. In *Hills v Lee*, the King's Printer sued several defendants for printing and importing from Holland the statutes of the realm and English Bibles, contrary to the plaintiffs' patent. Within days of the complaint, Lord Chancellor Nottingham granted an injunction until answer as to the infringing Bibles,[124] just as one might expect. But rather than do the same for the statute books, he instead granted a perpetual injunction. The order stated that it was a 'mattre of great concerne to the publique to have the Statutes of this Nacion printed in a fforeign Nation which by some Leaves [ie, pages] now produced in Court appeared to be full of Errors'.[125] I hesitate to call this order unique, as similar orders might later turn up, but it may very well be.

---

[120] *Gyles v Barlow* sub nom *Gyles v Wilcocks* (1740/1) C33/375, ff 274^v–275^v.

[121] Ibid. See also *Gyles v Barlow* sub nom *Gyles v Wilcocks* (1740/1) 3 Atk 269, 269; *Giles v Barlow* (1740/1) BL Add MS 36050, f 108^r.

[122] Eg *Hills v Wright* (1683/4) C33/261, ff 282^v–283^r; *Stationers v Wright* (1683/4) C33/262, f 260^{r-v}; *Baskett v Parsons* (1718) C33/329, ff 418^v–419^r; *Knaplock v Curll* (1722) C33/339, f 12^{r-v}, C78/1934, No 2, Bodl Viner MS 38, f 143^r, 2 Eq Ab 523, 524; *Webb v Rose* (1732–33) C33/358, ff 308^v–309^r, C33/362, f 55^{r-v}; *Gibbs v Cole* (1735/6) C33/365, f 222^{r-v}; *Gay v Walker* sub nom *Baller v Watson* (1737) C33/369, ff 315^v–316^v; *Manby v Owen* (1758) C33/410, f 396^{r-v}; *Millar v Taylor* (1765) C33/426, f 60^{r-v}; *Nicoll v Simpson* (1768) C33/430, ff 251^v–252^v; *Millar v Taylor* sub nom *Grant v Taylor* (1770) C33/433, ff 413^r–414^r; *Macklin v Richardson* (1770) C33/436, ff 35^v–36^r, Amb 694, 697; *Becket v Donaldson* (1772) C33/439, ff 26^r–27^r; *Pyle v Falkener* (1774) C33/442, ff 309^v–311^r; *Bach v Longman* (1777) C33/447, ff 582^v–583^r; *Mason v Murray* (1779) C33/452, ff 486^r–487^r; *Beckford v Hood* (1798) C33/500, f 504^{r-v}.

[123] See Ronan Deazley, *On the Origin of the Right to Copy* (Hart Publishing 2004) 62–65.

[124] *Hills v Lee* sub nom *Newcombe v Lee* (1681) C33/258, f 80^v.

[125] Ibid f 116^v.

2.3 The Merits Required

The grounds on which the various types of injunctions could be granted, denied, or dissolved are legion. An in-depth exposition of all the possible grounds is beyond the scope of this chapter, and I have, in any event, treated many of them earlier in this work and elsewhere.[126] Instead, in this part, I discuss the threshold showing required on the merits to obtain an injunction. By the merits, I principally mean whether the printing patent or copyright at issue was valid, whether the plaintiff owned the right, and whether the defendant infringed it. Interlocutory injunctions could of course die on the merits because of these defects in a plaintiff's right[127] or chain of title.[128] And records also demonstrate that requests for final injunctions likewise failed because of the absence of a valid copyright or patent right[129] or the lack of infringement.[130]

How strong did a plaintiff's case have to be on the merits to receive an *interlocutory* injunction? It is difficult to know for certain. The standard may have varied over time and it appears to have sometimes depended on the Lord Chancellor, Lord Keeper, or Master of the Rolls in office. Remarkably, even judges from the same period did not always agree on the prevailing standard, as is evident from several opinions in the related copyright cases of *Millar v Taylor* and *Donaldson v Becket*. There, the judges had to assess, in deciding a matter of common law, how much precedential value to assign to interlocutory injunctions granted in the Court of Chancery – namely, injunctions until answer and injunctions until the hearing. Two perspectives emerged. Representing one side, Justice Willes stated:

> *Injunctions* to stay *printing* or the *Sale* of Books printed, are in the Nature of Injunctions to stay *Waste* : They never are granted, but upon a clear Right. If moved for, upon filing the Bill; the *Right* must appear clearly, by Affidavits : If continued, after the Answer put in; the *Right* must be clearly admitted by the Answer, or not denied. [¶] Where the Plaintiff's Right is *questioned* and *doubtful*, an Injunction is *improper*; because *no Reparation* can be made to the Defendant for the Damage he sustains from the Injunction ....[131]

Chief Justice Mansfield of the King's Bench, who had practised extensively in the Court of Chancery before becoming a judge, concurred:

> [Injunctions until answer] *never* [are] granted upon Motion, *unless* the *legal Property* of the Plaintiff be *made out*; nor continued after Answer, *unless* it still *remains clear*, allowing all the Defendant has said. ... [¶] The Court of Chancery *never* grant[s] Injunctions in Cases of this Kind, where there is any *Doubt*.[132]

---

[126] See Gómez-Arostegui, 'What History Teaches' (n 4) 1233–47.
[127] Eg *Dodsley v Kinnersley* (1761) Amb 403, 403; *Millar v Taylor* (1766) C33/426, f 325ʳ.
[128] Eg *Gilliver v Watson* (1729) LI Misc MS 13, p 57, Bodl Viner MS 38, f 197ʳ, 2 Eq Ab 522, 522.
[129] Eg *Pyle v Falkener* (1774) C33/442, ff 309ᵛ–311ʳ; *Stationers v Carnan* (1775) C33/444, ff 321ᵛ, 427ʳ–428ᵛ.
[130] Eg *Dodsley v Kinnersley* (1761) Amb 403, 405–06, IT Misc MS 196, p 353.
[131] *Millar v Taylor* (1769) 4 Burr 2303 (KB) 2324.
[132] Ibid 2400. See also ibid 2352 (Aston J) ('It is most certain, that an Injunction in Nature of an *Injunction to stay Waste*, never is *continued to the Hearing*, where the Court is not strongly

216 *Research handbook on the history of copyright law*

On the other side were pronouncements from Lord Camden, who had served as Lord Chancellor from 1766 to 1770, and Chief Justice De Grey of the Common Pleas. Lord Camden stated that interlocutory injunctions could be granted where the right was 'not clear, but doubtful', so long as there was a 'shewing [of] a reasonable pretense of title'.[133] He also stated that his predecessor 'Lord Northington granted them on the idea of a doubtful title; [and] I continued the practice upon the same foundation; and so did the present Chancellor [Lord Apsley].'[134] Chief Justice De Grey agreed: 'To obtain such an injunction, it is by no means necessary that the plaintiff should make out a clear indisputable title. It may be granted on a reasonable pretense, and a doubtful right, before the hearing of the cause.'[135]

The only other direct pronouncement we have on the matter before 1800 comes from Lord Hardwicke in 1752. In deciding whether to grant an injunction until the hearing on a possible common-law copyright, the Lord Chancellor stated:

[I]f the case is doubtful, that may be a ground to grant an injunction until the matter can be considered at the hearing; thus in waste, not a clear right, but probability of right, may be, and is, a ground for an injunction.[136]

In sum, it appears that before 1800 some judges thought that a plaintiff had only to show a reasonable or probable case, while others thought the case had to be clear. Unfortunately, apart from outright pronouncements like the foregoing, it is all but impossible to glean the required threshold from case outcomes. Many granted injunctions were clearly warranted, thus satisfying both standards. Additionally, judges applying the same standard might reach different conclusions, even when reviewing the very same case. In *Millar v Taylor*, the Court of Chancery sent a case to law to determine whether a perpetual common-law copyright existed in published works. Baron Smythe of the Court of Exchequer, who was sitting by designation, continued a previously granted injunction in the meantime, thus suggesting that he believed it at least probable that such a right existed, a view he later confirmed in another case.[137]

---

of Opinion with the Plaintiff'.). For cases on waste, see *Attorney General v Doughty* (1752) 2 Ves Sr 453, 453 (Lord Hardwicke LC) (suggesting that the standard requires a 'plain' case to obtain an injunction until answer); *Field v Jackson* (1782) 2 Dick 599, 600 (Lord Thurlow LC) (stating that 'I am far from thinking, that when a right is doubtful, the Court will grant an injunction').
[133] *Donaldson v Becket* (1774) Morning Chronicle, 24 Feb 1774, p 2 (HL).
[134] Ibid.
[135] Ibid 23 Feb 1774, p 2.
[136] *Tonson v Walker* (1752) 3 Swanst 672, 679; accord *Tonson v Walker* (1752) BL Hargrave MS 470, p 287. For sources supporting this view on the waste of estates, see *Lord Orrery v Newton* (1744) Ridg temp H 252, 253 ('reasonable evidence'); Harrison (n 13) vol 1, 207 ('probability'); *Attorney General v Duplesses* (1751) LI Misc MS 177, p 295 (Exch) ('Attorney General put Cases of Injunctions founded on possibilitys of Title, And at last the Court Ordered an Injunction ....'); Hinde (n 75) 587 ('[The] Court will grant injunction to stay waste, as soon as same is begun, or to prevent the same, if reasonable ground be shewn to apprehend [as much]'.).
[137] *Millar v Taylor* (1765) C33/426, ff 68^v–69^r. For the later case, see *Donaldson v Becket* (1774) 4 Burr 2408 (HL) 2416 (Smythe CB).

But six months later, Lord Camden, the newly appointed Lord Chancellor, granted a petition for rehearing and dissolved the injunction.[138] We know from other proceedings that he not only thought that the right was not clear, but also that it was not even reasonable.[139]

If we are permitted to look a little beyond 1800, we do encounter other pronouncements that relate to interlocutory injunctions. In a case involving a printing patent, Lord Eldon described a standard that seemed most akin to the more lenient one described by some of his predecessors: '[T]his Court has lately said, [in cases involving patents of invention, that] possession [of a patent] under a colour of title is ground enough to enjoin, and to continue the injunction, till it shall be proved at law [in the Courts of King's Bench or Common Pleas]'.[140] Applying the standard to printing patents, Lord Eldon continued a previously granted injunction to the hearing despite harbouring doubts about the plaintiff's right to sue.[141] The defendant appealed to the House of Lords, arguing in part that it was

> contrary to the settled practice of the Court of Chancery, to grant an injunction, of this nature, except where the title of the party, applying for it, is too clear to admit of doubt; or where it has been previously established in a court of law; or where it stands upon the foundation of long and uninterrupted possession.[142]

The plaintiffs responded that '[t]here are several Instances, especially in Cases of Patents for Inventions, of granting Injunctions pending Litigation, and during some Uncertainty attached to the Plaintiff's Title'.[143] Ultimately, the House of Lords affirmed, thus suggesting that it had rejected the defendant's argument.[144]

How strong did the case have to be to obtain a *final* injunction? Success on the merits – either at an initial hearing or on the equity reserved after a referral to another forum – generally entitled a plaintiff to a final injunction. Take, for example, *Hills v Lee*, a case decided in 1683/4 involving the validity of the patent to print Bibles. After the plaintiffs returned victorious from the Court of King's Bench, where the Chancery had referred a legal issue, the Lord Keeper decreed as follows:

---

[138] *Millar v Taylor* (1766) C28/8, ff 84ᵛ–85ʳ, C33/426, f 325ʳ.
[139] *Donaldson v Becket* (1774) Morning Chronicle, 24 Feb 1774, p 2 and 25 Feb 1774, p 2 (HL) (Lord Camden).
[140] *Universities of Oxford & Cambridge v Richardson* (1802) 6 Ves Jr 689, 707. For a discussion of the more rigorous standard adopted in Scotland for patents of invention, see Bottomley, *British Patent System* (n 4) 140.
[141] *Universities of Oxford & Cambridge v Richardson* (1802) C33/518, ff 287ᵛ–288ᵛ, 6 Ves Jr 689, 703–14.
[142] *Richardson v Universities of Oxford & Cambridge* (ca 1804) Case of the Appellants (HL) 4.
[143] *Richardson v Universities of Oxford & Cambridge* (ca 1804) Case of the Respondents (HL) 4.
[144] *Richardson v Universities of Oxford & Cambridge* (1804) 44 HLJ 528 (HL). For more on interpreting judicial decisions of the House of Lords, see H Tomás Gómez-Arostegui, 'Copyright at Common Law in 1774' (2014) 47 Conn L Rev 1, 12–16, 34–38.

This Court declared that where it appeared to the Court that there was a right as it doth in this Case[,] the Law having determined the same for the plaintiff[,] Itt was Naturall for the Court to give releife for the same in specie[,] And doth therefore thinck fitt & soe orders and decrees that the Injunction \formerly granted in this Cause ... be made perpetuall/ ....[145]

Nearly 100 years later, albeit in a case decided in the Court of Exchequer, Chief Baron Skynner similarly stated at a hearing that it was 'a matter of form to direct the continuance of the injunction'.[146]

But the foregoing simply invites the question: How strong did a case have to be at the hearing to succeed on the merits? The query is not so easily answered. With respect to issues of fact – be it facts alone or 'mixed' issues of fact and law, as they were sometimes called[147] – it is difficult to determine what standard of proof prevailed before 1800. Today, we think of a party having to prove the facts by a preponderance of the evidence or the balance of probabilities, and there certainly are hints of such a standard in the eighteenth century.[148] But this is an area that requires further study because the only direct pronouncements I have encountered on the matter appear to have required something more rigorous.

Take, for example, *Whittingham v Wooler*. There, the Master of the Rolls had to decide whether a defendant's periodical had infringed the plaintiff's work or was merely a fair abridgment. At the hearing, the court stated that '[y]ou must show that the work is invaded when you come to ask for a final decree'[149] and that '[t]o support a decree for a perpetual injunction, the Court requires that there shall be nothing like doubt in the case.'[150] Having compared the works, the court ruled that there was no infringement and dismissed the suit.[151]

A similarly rigorous standard also appeared in the context of the validity of a printing patent in *Hills v Lee*, a case sometimes captioned as *Hills v Wright*, and which I have already discussed twice. There, the plaintiffs sought a perpetual injunction to prevent the defendants from printing and importing Bibles, with the principal issue being whether the plaintiffs' patent for printing Bibles was valid. With the case approaching a hearing, the court stated that it could not grant an 'injunction' – by which it meant a perpetual injunction – unless the right was 'plain'.[152] The Lord

---

[145] *Hills v Lee* sub nom *Hills v Wright* (1683/4) C33/261, ff 282^v–283^r.
[146] *Eyre v Carnan* (1781) 5 Bacon Abr (5th edn) 597 (Exch) 600.
[147] See generally *Whitmore v Rook* (1756) 1 Keny 345 (KB) 347; *Tindal v Brown* (1786) 1 D & E 167 (KB) 168–69; *Johnstone v Sutton* (1786) 1 D & E 493 (Exch Chamber) 545.
[148] See generally Macnair (n 103) 263–66; John Leubsdorf, 'Preponderance of the Evidence: Some History' (2014) Rutgers Research Paper Series No 149, <http://ssrn.com/abstract=2466127>.
[149] *Whittingham v Wooler* (1817) Times, 10 Dec 1817, p 3.
[150] *Whittingham v Wooler* (1817) 2 Swanst 428, 431, C33/648, f 141^r.
[151] Ibid. See also George Jeremy, *A Treatise on the Equity Jurisdiction of the High Court of Chancery* (London 1828) 326 (citing *Whittingham* and opining that '[i]f ... the cause should be brought to a hearing, the court will then, if the plaintiff's case be relieved of all doubt, grant a perpetual injunction'.). cf *Macklin v Richardson* (1770) Amb 694, 697 (remarking on a decree that the successful plaintiff had a 'Strong case.').
[152] *Hills v Lee* sub nom *Anonymous* (1682/3) 1 Vern 120, 120.

Keeper acknowledged that the House of Lords had upheld a different printing patent in another case, but stated that, 'yet[,] that is not exactly the same Case with this, tho' near it.'[153] Ultimately, because the validity of the Bible patent was not 'plain', the court stated that the plaintiffs were free to bring what action they pleased at common law to test their patent.[154] Later, the court ordered the plaintiffs to bring the action,[155] during which time an interlocutory injunction remained in place.[156] It was only after the King's Bench held the patent valid, that the Court of Chancery decreed in favour of the plaintiffs.[157]

The most lenient expression of the standard comes from a case where the doubt arose not on an issue of fact, or even a mixed issue of fact and law, but on the law governing the dispute. In *Blackwell v Harper*, a case brought under the Engraving Act of 1735, Lord Chancellor Hardwicke had to determine the effect of certain statutory formalities – namely, a requirement that the name of the proprietor and date of first publication appear on each engraving plate and every print.[158] Failing to comply with the formalities carried two possible consequences. The first was that certain remedies would no longer be available to the plaintiffs. More draconian was the second – the suit could not proceed at all because the formalities were necessary to secure the copyright itself. Ultimately, the court took the first approach and granted the plaintiffs a perpetual injunction, while refusing to award any form of pecuniary relief. Lord Hardwicke ruled for the plaintiffs despite being uncertain about whether he had interpreted the statute correctly. He stated that his 'construction' was not a 'clear

---

[153] Ibid.
[154] Ibid; *Hills v Wright* (18 Jan 1682/3) C37/363.
[155] *Hills v Wright* (1682/3) C33/259, ff 313ᵛ–314ʳ. See the text to n 105.
[156] *Hills v Wright* (21 Feb 1682/3) C37/373. Previously, I was of the view that the court's statement that the right be 'plain' before an injunction could issue referred to the standard for obtaining an injunction while the case was *pending at law*. I also believed that the court had *not* continued the injunction while the case was sent to law because the order referring it did not expressly enjoin the defendant (even though the order did not expressly dissolve a prior injunction either). Gómez-Arostegui, 'What History Teaches' (n 4) 1237. But I have since discovered draft minutes of the proceeding which demonstrate that a previously granted injunction remained in place. *Hills v Wright* (21 Feb 1682/3) C37/373. Contrast this with a similar case, also brought on a printing patent, where the order sending the case to law expressly dissolved a previously granted injunction. *Hills v University of Oxford* (1684) C33/263, ff 766ᵛ–767ʳ, 1 Vern 275, 276. The latter case posed more difficulty because the University of Oxford also held a printing patent.
[157] See the text to n 145. See also *Eyre v Carnan* (1781) LI Misc MS 92, pp 49, 51 (Exch) (Skynner CB) (stating in a case involving the validity of the patent to print the Book of Common Prayer that 'Courts of Equity never proceed in such cases, to decree accounts, but on *clear & undoubted* rights'). cf Gilbert (n 69) 194–95 ('There is another injunction, called a perpetual injunction for quieting a man in the possession of his estate; this is generally ... upon a plain equitable title'.).
[158] Engraving Copyright Act 1735, s 1 (8 Geo II c 13).

220 *Research handbook on the history of copyright law*

case'[159] or 'so certain',[160] but was instead 'doubtful',[161] and that 'other Judges might be of a contrary Opinion.'[162]

* * *

This is, unfortunately, all the space that we have to dedicate to injunctive relief. But I hope that this review, particularly when read in combination with my prior work on injunction practice, offers helpful guidance on the subject. It is now time to turn to disgorgement – the principal way in which the Court of Chancery awarded monetary relief in printing disputes before 1800. This is an area where, regrettably, there are fewer records. As a consequence, less can be said about it.

3. DISGORGEMENT OF PROFITS

Although an accounting and disgorgement of a defendant's profits had existed as part of the writ of account in courts of common law long before 1800, the common-law writ appears never to have played a role in infringement disputes. Perhaps it had to do with the limited scenarios in which the writ was available – namely, cases involving guardians, bailiffs, or receivers – or the more cumbersome processes that sometimes attended it.[163] Instead, right holders pursued the remedy in equity. Courts granted this relief without express statutory authority, as the first statutes to mention it did not arise until near the turn of the twentieth century.[164]

3.1 The Earliest Disgorgement Order

Thanks to the work of Ronan Deazley,[165] we now know that the first instance of disgorgement likely arose in *Gay v Walker*, a case filed in 1729.[166] The plaintiff John

---

[159] *Blackwell v Harper* (1740), printed in KL Perrin (ed), *Sir Dudley Ryder, Ryder Shorthand Documents* (1973) s 10, p 7.
[160] *Blackwell v Harper* (1740) 2 Atk 93, 96.
[161] Ibid.
[162] *Blackwell v Harper* (1740) Barn Ch 210, 214. Lord Hardwicke was right to doubt himself because the common-law courts later ruled that the formalities were necessary to obtain the copyright in an engraving. Eg *Sayer v Dicey* (1770) 3 Wils KB 60 (CP) 61; *Bell v Wenman* (1781) LI Hill MS 13, p 508, LI Hill MS 20, pp 71, 73–74 (CP); *Hooper v Hogg* (1788) London Chronicle, 17 Apr 1788, p 374 (KB).
[163] See generally John Mitford, *A Treatise on the Pleadings in Suits in the Court of Chancery by English Bill* (2nd edn, London 1787) 109–10; Jeremy (n 151) 504–05.
[164] The first statute was the Fine Arts Act 1862, s 9 (25 & 26 Vict c 68). More widespread recognition came about in the UK in the Imperial Copyright Act 1911, s 6. The US added the remedy to its statutory scheme in 1909. Copyright Act 1909, s 25, 35 Stat 1075.
[165] Deazley (n 123) 62–69.
[166] *Gay v Walker* (1729) C12/1817/67. For more on the background of the dispute, see James R Sutherland, '"Polly" Among the Pirates' (1942) 37 Mod Lang Rev 291; Michael F Suarez, 'To What Degree Did the Statute of Anne (8 Anne, c. 19, [1709]) Affect Commercial Practices in Eighteenth-Century England?' in Lionel Bently, Uma Suthersanen and Paul Torremans (eds), *Global Copyright* (Edward Elgar 2010) 54.

Gay, author of the opera *Polly*, sued a printer and a host of others for infringing his copyright. After obtaining an injunction until answer,[167] the case proceeded for several years, partly because it was difficult to obtain answers from the numerous defendants. All the while, the injunction until answer remained in place. Gay died in 1732, after which the suit was revived by his sisters and administrators Catherine Baller and Joanna Fortescue. The suit eventually reached a hearing in 1737. There, the plaintiffs requested that the interlocutory injunction be made perpetual and, more importantly, that the defendants account for and disgorge any profits they had made. As was customary, the court considered the defendants' answers and other written proofs, which in this instance included depositions along with a newspaper advertisement promoting the defendant's book. It also considered what was alleged and admitted by counsel on each side. Defence counsel conceded, for example, that the estate held a copyright in the work: '[T]he plaintiff has proved the necessary Registers to make out Mr. Gay's title.'[168] After apparently having no trouble finding that the defendants had infringed, Lord Chancellor Hardwicke granted the relief sought. The order states in relevant part:

> His Lordshipp doth think fit and so Orders and Decrees That the Injunction formerly granted in this Cause to stay the Defendants from printing publishing and Vending the said Book be perpetual and It is further Ordered and Decreed That It be referred to Master Eld one [of the masters of this court] to take an Accountt against the severall Defendants (Except the Defendant Walker against whom the plaintiff now Waives any Accountt) of the profits of the books mentioned in the Bill printed published or sold by the said Defendants or any of them without the Consent of the plaintiff Intestate or of some person claiming under him[,] for Discovery whereof the said Defendants accounting are upon Oath to produce before the said Master all books Papers and writings which they have in their Custody or power relating thereto and are to be Examined on Interrogatoryes as the said Master shall direct in the taking of which Accountt the said Master is to make unto the said Defendants all just allowances and what upon the said Accountt shall be formed due from the severall Defendants after all just allowances deducted[.] It is Ordered and Decreed That the said Defendants [except Walker] ... do respectively pay the same to the Plaintiff as the said Master shall Direct[.] And It is further Ordered That the said Master do tax the plaintiff the Costs of the Suite hitherto which is to be paid to him by the said Defendants Except the Defendant Walker[,] and his Lordshipp doth Reserve the Costs of the Account untill after the said Master shall have made his Report.[169]

Although *Gay* appears to offer the first such order, I should note that other cases suggest that disgorgement may have been available in some printing disputes before 1737. Take, for example, *Wolfe v Payne*, which I have already discussed. There, the Lord Keeper indicated that if the case reached a hearing the defendant would be answerable for the infringing books 'alredye solde and uttred as this court shall

---

[167] *Gay v Walker* (1729) C33/351, f 305ʳ.
[168] *Gay v Walker* sub nom *Baller v Walker* (1737) BL Add MS 36046, f 19ʳ.
[169] *Gay v Walker* sub nom *Baller v Watson* (1737) C33/369, ff 315ᵛ–316ᵛ. It is sometimes said that Lord Chancellor Talbot presided at the hearing, eg *Blackwell v Harper* (1740) 2 Atk 93, 93, but this is incorrect. Lord Talbot died on 14 February 1736/7, Lord Hardwicke received the Great Seal on 21 February 1736/7, and the hearing in *Gay* occurred on 6 December 1737.

adiudge[.]'[170] The court may have had disgorgement in mind.[171] And in *Baskett v Parsons*, a case involving the patent of the King's Printer for printing Bibles in English, the King's Printer waived an account of profits despite prevailing at the hearing and obtaining a perpetual injunction. This suggests the remedy was thought to be available in 1718.[172] Nevertheless, unless further study sheds more light on the matter, *Gay* must still hold the title for the first printing suit to actually order the disgorgement of a defendant's profits.

3.2 The Legal Basis for the Award

Neither the order nor the few reports of *Gay* explain the legal basis for the award. For that we can only guess, but we do have compelling guidance from a case brought three years later under the Engraving Act of 1735.[173] In *Blackwell v Harper*, Lord Hardwicke stated that the Engraving Act implicitly authorized an account of profits because it contained a provision permitting a court to order a defendant to forfeit a penalty of 5 shillings per infringing print, the infringing plates, and the prints themselves. '[A]n Account of the profits', he stated, 'is founded on the forfeiture Clause only [of the Act] & this Court in Conformity to that directs such an Account because the Court will never decree a forfeiture'.[174] The Statute of Anne of 1710, which governed literary property, contained similar penalties and forfeitures,[175] and thus in *Gay* Lord Hardwicke probably believed that his award of profits was 'founded' on the similar clause contained in the 1710 statute. I should stress that in *Blackwell* the Lord Chancellor did not believe that the Engraving Act expressly empowered him to award profits. Indeed, he recognized that the statute called for penalties and forfeitures, something the Chancery would 'never decree'. Similarly, the statutory monetary penalties at least could only be recovered, by their terms, in a 'court[] of record',[176] which the Chancery, when sitting in equity, was most certainly not.[177]

Although the Engraving Act did not expressly address accountings, Lord Hardwicke sought to adhere to the Act. After stating that the account was founded on the 'forfeiture Clause', the Lord Chancellor denied an award of profits in *Blackwell* partly because the plaintiffs had not complied with certain statutory formalities, formalities the Lord Chancellor believed were necessary to recover the statutory penalties and forfeitures of the Act. Whereas the statute required that the name of the proprietor and

---

[170] *Wolfe v Payne* (1563/4) C33/30, f 143ᵛ. See also the text to n 8.
[171] cf WJ Jones, *The Elizabethan Court of Chancery* (Clarendon Press 1967) 459 (citing two 1580 cases where the defendant had already committed waste, and where the court appointed a commission to 'recompense the rightful owner, while the court in the interim sequestered the profits.').
[172] *Baskett v Parsons* (1718) C33/329, ff 418ᵛ–419ʳ.
[173] Engraving Copyright Act 1735, s 1 (8 Geo II c 13).
[174] *Blackwell v Harper* (1740) BL Hargrave MS 412, ff 130ᵛ, 132ʳ.
[175] Statute of Anne 1710, s 1 (8 Anne c 19).
[176] Engraving Copyright Act 1735, s 1 (8 Geo II c 13).
[177] See generally H Tomás Gómez-Arostegui, 'The Untold Story of the First Copyright Suit Under the Statute of Anne in 1710' (2010) 25 Berkeley Tech LJ 1247, 1331–38.

date of first publication appear on each engraving plate and every print,[178] only the name had appeared in *Blackwell*. Lord Hardwicke stated:

> But as To an Account of the profits[,] It will be very hard to involve the Publisher in an Account of them without his having notice of the Time of Publication – And an Account of the profits is founded on the forfeiture Clause only & this Court in Conformity to that directs such an Account because the Court will never decree a forfeiture & will have the proper allowances made – As therefore ... [the plaintiff] has not entitled her self to the Penalty [under the Engraving Act] I will not direct any Account of the Profits.[179]

Lord Hardwicke also stated that he was inclined to deny the account on two other grounds. First, as I have previously noted, he was unsure whether the formalities were also necessary to secure the copyright itself.[180] And second, 'the Profits [were] ... so extremely small.'[181]

Notably, the Lord Chancellor acknowledged his decision in *Gay*, where he had granted an award of profits. But he pointed out that the defendants there ultimately admitted that the plaintiff had complied with the formalities of the 1710 statute.[182] Interestingly, Lord Hardwicke thought there was something special about granting retrospective monetary relief because, in the end, he granted a perpetual injunction in *Blackwell* despite that remedy having no express statutory basis either.[183]

Lord Hardwicke was not the only Chancellor to question his authority to disgorge a defendant's profits. Indeed, some judges were even more categorical. Before Lord Hardwicke, Lord Chancellor Cowper expressly rejected a prayer for profits in 1710. The details of the underlying suit, *Horne v Baker*, may be found elsewhere.[184] Suffice it to say, the plaintiff sued for copyright infringement before the enactment of the Statute of Anne, and claimed to hold a common-law copyright in his work.[185] The defendant demurred to the complaint on various grounds on 9 January 1709/10,[186] but the argument on the demurrer did not occur until 10 May 1710, which was after the Statute of Anne had entered into force. Among other things, Lord Cowper preemptively rejected the prayer for profits:

> To make the defendant account for the proffits of what he has sold, is going too far; for the injury that the plaintiff has susteined ought to be the measure of the damage, & not the proffit, which the defendant has made.

---

[178] Engraving Copyright Act 1735, s 1 (8 Geo II c 13).
[179] *Blackwell v Harper* (1740) BL Hargrave MS 412, ff 130ᵛ, 131ᵛ–132ʳ. For an identical manuscript report, see BL Add MS 36015, p 248. cf *Blackwell v Harper* (1740) LI Hill MS 5, pp 39, 40 ('He decreed a perpetual Injunction but would not order an Account because it did not appear by the Bill when the Plaintiffs property first arose.').
[180] *Blackwell v Harper* (1740) 2 Atk 93, 96; accord *Blackwell v Harper* (1740), printed in Perrin (n 159) s 10, p 7. See also text to n 162.
[181] *Blackwell v Harper* (1740) Barn Ch 210, 214. See also *Whittingham v Wooler* (1817) 2 Swanst 428, 430 (declining to award profits where the profits were small).
[182] *Blackwell v Harper* (1740) 2 Atk 93, 96.
[183] Ibid.
[184] Gómez-Arostegui, 'Untold Story' (n 177) 1299–309.
[185] *Horne v Baker* (1709) C5/290/70, m 1.
[186] Ibid m 2.

...

> I am not willing to carry this matter so far, especially now the late act of parliament [ie, the Statute of Anne] has given another remedy in respect of the property in Coppies of Books.[187]

Despite the foregoing, it eventually came to be accepted that the court could exercise an inherent power to award profits, even when the copyright holder had not complied with the statutory formalities of the Statute of Anne.[188] This shift in thinking may have come about in part because the foregoing cases were unknown or disregarded. *Horne* and some of the reasoning in *Blackwell* appeared in manuscript reports alone, which naturally did not circulate as widely as reports that were published in print. It is also possible that a printed decision from Lord Hardwicke that dealt not with copyrights, but the cutting down of trees, came to influence thinking on the matter after 1768. In that context, Lord Hardwicke offered the following explanation for disgorging a defendant's profits on a decree: 'Where the bill is for an injunction, and waste has been already committed, the court, to prevent a double suit,' meaning a suit in equity for prospective relief and an action at law for retrospective relief, 'will decree an account, and satisfaction for what is past'.[189] He further stated: 'This is a general principle to prevent suits[;] and as some Decree must be made[,] [t]he Court will make a Compleat one.'[190]

In 1798, the King's Bench in *Beckford v Hood* effectively sanctioned an award of profits, even where a copyright holder had never registered a work at all. The case began in the Court of Chancery, where the copyright holder sought injunctive relief and a disgorgement of the defendant's profits.[191] After granting an interlocutory injunction, the court sent the parties to law to determine whether the plaintiff could maintain a suit against the defendant despite not having registered the work under the Statute of Anne.[192] The action in the King's Bench was to be brought 'for the profits arising from the sale' of the defendant's edition.[193] In the King's Bench the question was reformulated to concern ordinary damages, and the Bench held that an aggrieved party could bring an action under the Statute of Anne, despite not registering a work, and could also recover ordinary damages even though the statute did not expressly provide for

---

[187] *Horne v Baker* (1710) LI Misc MS 10, p 1; accord *Horne v Baker* (1710) HLS MS 1169(b), p 154.
[188] Eg *Nicoll v Simpson* (1768) C33/430, ff 251^v–252^v (disgorging profits despite the fact the copyright holder registered late).
[189] *Jesus College v Bloome* (1745) 3 Atk 262, 262.
[190] *Jesus College v Bloome* (1745) BL Add MS 36017, pp 121, 123. Although the court decided *Jesus College* in 1745, the account of the case in Atkyns's reports did not appear in print until 1768. For later printing disputes citing *Jesus College* as a ground for awarding profits, see *Universities of Oxford & Cambridge v Richardson* (1802) 6 Ves Jr 689, 700–01; *Grierson v Eyre* (1804) 9 Ves Jr 341, 346. cf also *Bacon v Jones* (1839) 4 My & Cr 433, 435 (citing *Jesus College* in a case involving a patent of invention).
[191] *Beckford v Hood* (1797) C12/670/33, m 1.
[192] *Beckford v Hood* (1797) C33/497, f 583^{r-v}.
[193] *Beckford v Hood* (1797) C33/500, f 33^r.

such relief.[194] Soon after, the plaintiff returned to the Chancery on the equity reserved to obtain the defendant's profits instead.[195]

3.3 The Standard for Obtaining Profits

As I have explained elsewhere,[196] after 1737, it became usual for a claimant who succeeded on the merits to obtain an award of profits at the hearing. Barring a problem like that presented in *Blackwell*, all that seems to have been required was that the plaintiff seek and obtain a perpetual injunction. The number of cases awarding disgorgement is not extensive, however, partly because so few cases ever reached a hearing. As Justice Willes stated in *Millar v Taylor*: 'Few Bills against Pirates of Books are ever brought to a Hearing. If the Defendant acquiesces under [an interlocutory] Injunction, it is seldom worth the Plaintiff's while to proceed for an Account [and disgorgement of profits]; the Sale of the Edition being stopped.'[197] Making the number even smaller is the fact that a plaintiff could elect at the hearing to waive an award of profits, as occurred in *Baskett* and (partly) in *Gay*.[198] Nonetheless, I have encountered several decrees, in addition to the cases I have already mentioned, granting a disgorgement of the defendant's ill-gotten gains alongside a perpetual injunction. They include cases for infringement of the Statute of Anne,[199] common-law copyrights in published works,[200] common-law copyrights in unpublished works,[201] and printing patents.[202]

3.4 The Process for Assessing Profits

Unfortunately, we do not at present know much about the method of assessing the profits earned from infringement. For one, I have yet to encounter a manuscript report of proceedings before a master in such a case. Also hampering our understanding is the meagre number of records from the Court of Chancery itself. As previously mentioned, few copyright cases reached a decree. And of those that did, records that must have at one time existed are sometimes no longer extant. In other instances there are no records because the parties stipulated the amount of profits[203] or otherwise took it upon themselves to settle the account without the aid of a master. Nevertheless, broad outlines of the process are visible and they reveal nothing unusual or surprising.

---

[194] *Beckford v Hood* (1798) 7 D & E 620 (KB).
[195] *Beckford v Hood* (1798) C33/500, f 504^{r-v}.
[196] Gómez-Arostegui, 'Prospective Compensation' (n 4) 1701–07.
[197] *Millar v Taylor* (1769) 4 Burr 2303 (KB) 2324.
[198] *Baskett v Parsons* (1718) C33/329, ff 418^v–419^r; *Gay v Walker* sub nom *Baller v Watson* (1737) C33/369, ff 315^v–316^v. See also eg *Dodsley v Kinnersley* (1761) Amb 403, 403.
[199] Eg *Millar v Taylor* (1765) C33/426, f 60^{r-v}; *Bach v Longman* (1777) C33/447, ff 582^v–583^r.
[200] Eg *Becket v Donaldson* (1772) C33/439, ff 26^r–27^r.
[201] Eg *Macklin v Richardson* (1770) C33/436, ff 35^v–36^r.
[202] Eg *Pyle v Falkener* (1774) C33/442, ff 309^v–311^r.
[203] Eg *Mason v Murray* (1779) C33/452, ff 486^r–487^r.

As the decrees indicate, the usual approach was to examine the account, not at the hearing, but afterward.[204] The master was permitted to assess the defendant's profits down to the time of the proceedings before him, rather than being limited to the profits earned before the filing of the complaint.[205] In most cases, this liberal practice of assessment was unnecessary, given that interlocutory injunctions were nearly always in place. We also know that additional discovery, beyond what was produced for the preceding hearing of the cause, might be necessary to conduct the accounting properly. In such a case, if the witnesses necessary for the account were in 'town', meaning London, the master would attend to the matter himself. But if they were in the 'country' an appointed commission might take the account.[206]

One example of additional discovery survives in a set of interrogatories and responses taken in 1766 before Thomas Cuddon, one of the masters of the Court of Chancery. The questions and answers together are too lengthy to reproduce here, but I will print the former to give a sense of the inquiry:

> 1.st Interrogatory. Whether or not have you printed Published or Sold or Caused to be printed published or sold any Copy or Copies of two Volumes of Poems in the pleadings in this Cause mentioned to be wrote by Edward Young LL:D. deceased late Rector of Wellwyn in the County of Hertford without the Consent of the said Doctor Young or of any person Claiming under him[.] If yea[,] whether or not was or were the Copy or Copies of the said two Volumes of Poems so by you printed Published or Sold or Caused to be printed published or sold bound together in One Volume[.] If yea[,] how many Copies of the said two Volumes so bound together in One Volume as aforesaid have you at any time or times and when Vended and Sold or Caused to be Vended or Sold to any and what person and persons and whom by name and where such person or persons live or may be found and at [illegible] for what price or Sum of Money did you Vend and Sell or Cause to be Vended and Sold each of the said Copies respectively to the best of your Knowledge Remembrance and belief. Declare

> 2.d What Sum or Sums of Money did you really and truly lay out and Expend on Printing Binding and Publishing of the Several Copies of the said two Volumes of Poems in the first Interrogatory mentioned and inquired after so Bound up in One Volume as Aforesaid by you Printed Published or Sold and what was the true and Real prime Costs of each of the said Copies so by you Vended and Sold or Caused to be Vended and Sold and what profit did you receive or was you intitled to receive by the Sale of each of the said Copies so by you Vended or Sold or Caused to be Vended or Sold as Aforesaid and how much in the whole to the best of your Knowledge Remembrance and belief. Declare[207]

Following discovery it was then incumbent upon the master to issue a written report to the court. I have not unearthed the report in the aforementioned case, but another survives from a companion case filed against the same defendant for infringing a different work. The report is not lengthy, it spans only one page, but it nevertheless offers some insight into the process. The master stated in relevant part:

---

[204] See Harrison (n 13) vol 2, 6–7.
[205] I have found no printing disputes in which the court has expressly stated this rule. But for cases in other areas, see *Carleton v Brightwell* (1728) 2 P Wms 462, 463; *Archbishop of York v Stapleton* (1740/1) 2 Atk 136, 137; *Bulstrode v Bradley* (1747) 3 Atk 582, 582.
[206] Bohun (n 13) 341–42, 427.
[207] *Millar v Taylor* (1766) C111/166 (involving *The Complaint*).

... I [John Eames] have been attended by the Solicitors on both sides. And the said Defendant having been examined on Interrogatories exhibited before me touching the said Account[,] I find that on the 26.th Day of November 1768 he printed five hundred compleat Copies of the said Poems, & [sent 66 copies to certain booksellers and printers in Scotland in exchange for other books and otherwise sold 14,] ... printed under the Title of Thompson's Works; which said Copies so exchanged & sold amounted together to eighty Copies and that the clear Profits by him the said Defendant received by the Sale of the said Books in Exchange for the said eighty Copies amounted to the Sum of two pounds. – And I further find that the said Defendant did publish & sell one hundred and ten Copies of the said Poems which [were printed by, and which] he got in Exchange for other Books from[,] Alexander Donaldson of the City of Edinburgh ... bound in one Volume[.] And that the clear profits by him received by the Sale of the one hundred and ten Copies ... as aforesaid amounted to the Sum of two pounds fifteen shillings. Which said several Sums of two pounds and two pounds fifteen shillings making together the Sum of four pounds fifteen Shillings[,] I find to be the whole of the Moneys received by the said Defendant on the Account aforesaid and the same is to be paid to the said plaintiffs pursuant to the Directions of the said Decree which I humbly certify to this Honourable Court.[208]

Unless a party excepted to the report, it appears the Court of Chancery would usually confirm the award. This happened, for example, in the foregoing case.[209]

4. CONCLUSION

This chapter has offered an account of the two principal forms of relief available in the Court of Chancery before 1800. Despite what we presently know about equity practice in printing cases, there is still much we can learn. I have, in the preceding pages, highlighted a few areas that might benefit from more study, particularly by resort to analogous procedures and manuscript sources. Additional research may lead us to glean more about the notice requirements for injunctions until answer, the rigour of the review undertaken by judges on *ex parte* motions, the merit thresholds for injunctive relief, and the process for calculating profits.

---

[208] *Millar v Taylor* sub nom *Grant v Taylor* (8 Feb 1772) C38/638 (involving *The Seasons*). This accounting followed the famous ruling in *Millar v Taylor* (1769) 4 Burr 2303 (KB). For another example of an accounting of profits, see *Bach v Longman* (1 Apr 1778) C38/675.

[209] *Millar v Taylor* sub nom *Grant v Taylor* (1772) C33/437, f 161^r.

APPENDIX A: TASKS AND COSTS THROUGH AN INJUNCTION UNTIL ANSWER

Baskett v Lewis
Solicitor's Bill Book
LMA CLC/B/136/MS18744/003

[p 70]

Messieurs Baskett Mount & Page[210] to
Godfrey Kettle[211]

Baskett & others }
 against } In Chancery
Lewis & Pottinger }

Trinity Vacation 1764

	Taking Instructions to Draw Bill against the Defendants the Printer & Publisher of a pirated Edition of the Common prayer	–	6	8[212]
	Attending at several places to learn Lewis's Christian Name	–	6	8
	Drawing Bill folios 82 and Copy	2	1	–
	paid Mr Comyn[213] to peruse and Settle the same	2	2	–
	Attending him	–	6	8
	Gave his Clerk	–	2	6
Augst 30	Attending Mr Comyns in Lincolns Inn being sent for	–	6	8
Sept^r	Attending Mr Cornish[214] several times on Mr Comyns queries and attending Mr Comyns again thereon	–	6	8
	Gave Mr Comyns Clerk bringing home the Draft of the Bill	–	2	6
	Carryed over	6	1	4

---

[210] Mark Baskett, John Mount, and Thomas Page, partners in the Office of the King's Printer.
[211] Solicitor on Basinghall Street.
[212] Pounds, shillings, and pence.
[213] Stephen Comyn of Lincoln's Inn and the Inner Temple (formerly of Gray's Inn), called to the bar on 13 November 1735.
[214] John Cornish, an employee of the plaintiffs.

[p 71]

	Brought over	6	1	4
Ingrossing the Bill		1	6	8
paid for parchment and Stamps 2 Skins		–	6	6
paid filing[215]		–	5	4
paid for subpoena		–	4	6
Service on both Defendants		–	10	–
Paid Mr York[216] a retaining Fee		1	1	–
Attending him		–	6	8
Gave his Clerk		–	2	6

Michaelmas Term 1764

Attending to Buy two of the Books of the Defendants in Order to prove the same	–	6	8
paid at Lewis's 0 4 0 at Pottingers – 3 6	–	7	6
Drawing affidavit thereof and Ingrossing paper and Stamps	–	5	–
paid Oath	–	1	–
paid filing and Duty	–	5	6
paid for Six Clerks Certificate of Bill filed	–	2	6
Abbreviating the Bill folios 82	–	13	8
Drawing Notice of Motion for Injunction Copy and Service	–	2	–
Drawing and Ingrossing Affidavit thereof paper and Stamps	–	5	–
paid Oath and filing	–	5	3
Drawing Mr Cornish affidavit in Support of the Motion and Ingrossing folios 7 and Duty	–	7	5

---

[215] For the bill of complaint, see *Baskett v Lewis* (1764) C12/2383/11.
[216] Charles Yorke of Lincoln's Inn (formerly of the Middle Temple), called to the bar on 4 February 1745/6, and Solicitor General (1756–62), Attorney General (1762–63 and 1765–66), and later Lord Chancellor (1770) for a few days before his death; was to be ennobled as Lord Morden.

	Attending to Settle and afterwards to Swear the same		– 6 8	
	paid Oath and filing		– 10 4	
	paid Six Clerks Certificate of Bill filed		– 2 6	
	Three fair Copies of the Brief for Council folios 3 each		1 2 6	
	Drawing Additional Brief by way of Instructions to Council upon the Motion		– 6 8	
	Three fair Copies thereof and of the Notice of Motion to Annex to the Briefs		– 6 –	
	Ditto of Mr Cornishes Affidavit		– 3 6	
	paid Mr Yorke with his Brief	3 3 –		
	Attending him	– 6 8		
	Gave his Clerk	– 2 6		
		⎯⎯⎯	3 12 2	
		Carried over	19 16 4	

[p 72]

		Brought over	19 16 4	
	Mr Comyn	2 2 –		
	Attending him	– 6 8		
	Gave his Clerk	– 2 6		
		⎯⎯⎯	2 11 2	
	Mr Hett[217]	2 2 –		
	Attending him	– 6 8		
		⎯⎯⎯	2 8 8	
Nov[r] 22	Attending at Westminster when the Motion was made and the Injunction ordered		– 6 8	
	paid Coach hire from Temple Bar		– 1 –	
	paid Register for the Order		– 18 –	

---

[217] John Hett of the Inner Temple, called to the bar on 12 June 1752, and later a master in ordinary in the Court of Chancery (1775–90).

23	Attending Register to pass the same	–	6	8
	paid Entring and Expedition[218]	–	4	6
27	paid for Special Injunction Docketts Duty	1	7	–
	Two copies and Service on the Defendants	–	15	–
	Letters and porters	–	2	–
	Term Fee Clerk in Court & Sollicitor	–	10	–
	27th November 1765			

Received this per Mr   29   7   0
John Cornish GK [Godfrey Kettle]

---

[218] For the entered order, see *Baskett v Lewis* (1764) C33/423, ff 5ᵛ–6ʳ.

APPENDIX B: TASKS AND COSTS THROUGH AN INJUNCTION UNTIL THE HEARING

Pope v Curll
Solicitor's Bill Book
LMA CLC/B/136/MS18744/001

[p 493]

Alexander Pope Esquire
                Debtor [to] Nathaniel Cole[219]

[*blank*] }
against } In Chancery
Curll }

Trinity Term 1741[220]

Drawing Bill in Chancery against Edmund Curll for Pyrating the Edition of Letters between Mr Pope & Dean Swift & Copy to Settle			
Drawing Mr Popes Affidavit to indentifye the Letters & Copy to Settle			
Attending Mr Pope [*blank*] Hours to Settle the Bill & Affidavit	–	6	8
Copy of the Bill as Setled by Mr Pope for Mr Murray[221] to Settle			
Copy of Mr Popes Affidavit for Mr Murray			
Attending Mr Murray thereon	–	6	8
Ingrossing the Bill			
Parchment & Stamps			
Ingrossing Mr Popes Affidavit			
Paid Duty & Oath	–	2	1
Paid Clerk in Court filing[222]	–	5	4

---

[219] Solicitor on Basinghall Street and a member and the clerk of the Company of Stationers.

[220] Many entries have no costs or fees associated with them. It is unclear why, although in some instances it appears that it was done as a courtesy to the plaintiff Alexander Pope.

[221] William Murray of Lincoln's Inn, called to the bar on 23 November 1730, and later Solicitor General (1742–54), Attorney General (1754–56), and Chief Justice of the Court of King's Bench (1756–88); ennobled as Lord Mansfield (1756–76) and as the Earl of Mansfield (1776–93).

[222] For the bill of complaint, see *Pope v Curll* (1741) C11/1569/29, m 1.

Drawing & Ingrossing Thomas Prichards[223] Affidavit of buying the Book			
Paid Duty & Oath			
For Copy Mr Popes Affidavit to File & Duty			
Paid filing it			
For Copy Thomas Pritchards Affidavit to file & Duty			
Paid filing thereof			
Paid for Six Clerks Certificate of Bill being filed	–	2	6
Paid Mr Attorney General[224] a retaining fee	1	1	–

[p 494]

	Brought over	[blank]	
Attending him thereon	–	6	8
Paid his Clerk	–	2	6
Attending the Court at Westminster on the Motion for an Injunction	–	6	8
Paid the Register Drawing up the Order & Expedition	–	18	–
Paid Entring Ditto & Expedition[225]	–	4	–
Paid for Injunction & Subpoena	1	10	–
Copy Injunction to Serve			
Service of Injunction & Subpoena			
Paid for Office Copy of Curlls Answer folios 13[226]	–	10	10
Upon Curlls Notice of Motion to Dissolve the Injunction – Drawing Brief of Bill & Answer			
For three fair Copys of the Brief for Council			
For three fair Copys of Mr Popes Affidavit for Council			

---

[223] Likely working for or with Nathaniel Cole; also a member of the Company of Stationers.

[224] Dudley Ryder of the Middle Temple, called to the bar on 8 May 1719, and Solicitor General (1733–37), Attorney General (1737–54), and later Chief Justice of the Court of King's Bench (1754–56).

[225] For the entered order, see *Pope v Curll* (1741) C33/376, f 350ᵛ.

[226] For Curll's answer, see *Pope v Curll* (1741) C11/1569/29, m 2.

For three fair Copys of Thomas Pritchards Affidavit for Ditto			
Attending Mr Attorney General Mr Noel[227] and Mr Murray with their Briefs who all refused their Fees	–	6	8
Attending the Court at Westminster on the Motion when Lord Chancellor Ordered the Injunction to Stand till the hearing of the Cause[228]	–	6	8
Term fee Clerk & Sollicitor	–	10	–

---

[227] William Noel of the Inner Temple, called to the bar on 25 June 1721, and later a Justice of the Court of Common Pleas (1757–62).

[228] For the ruling, see *Pope v Curll* (1741) 2 Atk 342, 342–43.

PART III

INTERNATIONAL PERSPECTIVES

12. Proto-property in literary and artistic works: Sixteenth century papal printing privileges
Jane C. Ginsburg[*]

INTRODUCTION

This Study endeavors to reconstruct the Vatican's precursor system of copyright, and the author's place in it, inferred from examination of over 500 privileges and petitions and related documents – almost all unpublished – in the Vatican Secret Archives. The typical account of the precopyright world of printing privileges, particularly in Venice, France and England, portrays a system primarily designed to promote investment in the material and labor of producing and disseminating books; protecting or rewarding authorship was at most an ancillary objective.[1] As the former Register of Copyrights

---

[*] This study commenced during a Michael Sovern Fellowship at the American Academy in Rome and has continued through several stays there as a Visiting Scholar and as Scholar in Residence. I am very grateful to the Academy's Directors, Prof. Carmela Franklin and her successors Prof. Christopher Celenza and Prof. Kim Bowes, to Assistant Librarian Denise Gavio, to Assistant Director for Operations Pina Pasquantonio, and to Executive Secretary Gianpaolo Battaglia. Much appreciation also goes to the staffs of the Vatican Secret Archives and of the Vatican Library, and to Dr. Paolo Vian, Director of its manuscript division. Special gratitude to Prof. Christopher Witcombe, whose earlier work on Papal privileges charted my initial path, and whose extraordinary generosity in sharing his notes from the Vatican Secret Archives further enriched this account. For assistance with translation of Latin documents, I am indebted to 2008–09 Rome Prize winners Prof. Eric Bianchi and Prof. Patricia Larash, and to a team of Columbia Law School students (Ella Aiken '11, Matthew Birkhold '14, Jack Browning '13, Nicholas Flath '11, Catherine Kim '15, James Klugman '12, Katherine Mackey '14, Deborah Sohn '12, Denise Sohn '12, Johan Tatoy '13, Prateek Vasireddy '15, and Michael Zaken '14). Thanks for comments and assistance to Prof. Robert Darnton, Prof. Hanoch Dagan, Dr. Dirk Imhof, Prof. Evelyn Lincoln, Prof. Laura Moscati, Prof. Neil Netanel, Prof. Laurent Pfister, Prof. Lisa Pon, George Spera, Prof. Elissa Weaver, Prof. Steven Wilf, and to fellow ASVat researcher Dom. Paolo Fusar Imperatore (*il mio angelo custode*). The study has also benefitted from the observations of participants in faculty seminars at Columbia Law School, at the University of Connecticut Law School, in Professor Lisa Pon's seminar in the art history department at Southern Methodist University, at a seminar organized by Edwige Keller-Rahbé of the Faculté des lettres, sciences et art, Groupe renaissance et age classique, of l'Université de Lyon 2, and at a copyright history workshop organized by Professors Robert Brauneis and Tomás Gómez-Arostegui at George Washington University Law School.

A more fully-referenced version of this chapter, including the original Latin or Italian text of the excerpts from privileges and petitions here quoted in my English translations, as well as a complete Appendix summarizing all the privileges and petitions found, and providing bibliographic information, appears in 36 Colum. J L. & the Arts 345 (2013).

[1] *See, e.g.*, Elizabeth Armstrong, Before Copyright: The French Book-privilege System 1498–1526 (1990); Andrew Pettegree, The Book in the Renaissance 163 (2010)

Barbara Ringer put it: 'The author was the forgotten figure in th[e] drama [of the origins of copyright], which was played out during the 16th and 17th centuries in England, France and other Western European countries ... .'[2]

The sixteenth-century Papal privileges found in the Archives, however, prompt some rethinking of that story because the majority of these privileges were awarded to authors, and even where a printer received a privilege for a work of a living author, the petition increasingly asserted the author's endorsement of the application. The predominance of authors might prompt the conclusion that the Papal privilege system more closely resembled modern copyright than printer-centered systems. That said, it would be inaccurate and anachronistic to claim that authorship supplied *the* basis for the grant of a Papal privilege. Nonetheless, a sufficient number of petitions and privileges invoke the author's creativity that one may cautiously suggest that authorship afforded *a* ground for bestowing exclusive rights.

The Study proceeds as follows: first, a description of the sources consulted and methodology employed; second, an account of the system of Papal printing privileges derived from the petitions for and grants of printing monopolies; third, an examination of the justifications for Papal printing monopolies and the inferences appropriately drawn regarding the role of authors in the Papal privilege system. A few disclaimers: based in primary sources, this Study does not attempt extensive examination of the broader social and economic setting in which the Papacy granted printing privileges. Nor does it delve deeply into the history of the Roman or Italian book trade. Italian book historians have provided the wider context,[3] though they also acknowledge that little has been known about the Roman printing privileges.[4]

Finally, a word about the title, 'Proto-property in literary and artistic works.' It is inspired in part by the French term for copyright, 'propriété littéraire et artistique.' The French Code of Intellectual Property, expressing the predominant (at least Continental) view, emphasizes that copyright is an 'exclusive incorporeal right of property' which authors enjoy in their works 'from the sole fact of their creation.'[5] While printing

---

('The privilege was far more frequently granted to the printer or the publisher than to the author.'); Edward S. Rogers, *Some Historical Matter Concerning Literary Property*, 7 MICH. L. REV. 101, 102 (1908) ('The purpose of these privileges could not have been to encourage authorship. They were almost invariably given to printers and were apparently for the purpose of encouraging printing by eliminating competition, and thus making it more profitable.').

[2] BARBARA RINGER, THE DEMONOLOGY OF COPYRIGHT 7–8 (1974).

[3] Representative works are cited in the Bibliography at the end of this book.

[4] *See, e.g.*, ANGELA NUOVO & CHRISTIAN COPPENS, I GIOLITO E LA STAMPA NELL'ITALIA DEL XVI SECOLO 211 n.184 (2005) (stating there is no systematic study of Papal privileges after 1527); *id.* at 204 n.141; *see also* ARMSTRONG, *supra* note 1, at 13 ('To my knowledge, there exists as yet no general and systematic study of papal book-privileges in this period.').

[5] C. DE LA PROPRIETÉ INTELLECTUELLE art. L. 111-1 (Fr.). The current French law reiterates art. 1 of the 1957 copyright law. For an earlier expression of the same principle from the first international copyright treaty, see the Convention between Austria and the Kingdom of Sardinia (1840), the first article of which declared that works of authorship 'constitute a property which belongs to those who are their authors ... .' On the Austro-Sardinian treaty, see generally Laura Moscati, *Il caso Pomba-Tasso e l'applicazione della prima convenzione internazionale sulla proprietà intellettuale*, *in* MÉLANGES EN L'HONNEUR D'ANNE LEFEBVRE-TEILLARD 747, 754–57 (Bernard d'Alteroche et al. eds., 2009).

privileges, Papal or otherwise, established certain exclusive rights for a certain period, to call these rights 'property' in the sense of modern 'literary property' would be both anachronistic and overstated.[6] The sixteenth-century sovereign *granted* exclusive rights as a 'special grace'; rights did not *arise* from the act of creation, nor was the work's creator necessarily the first beneficiary of any printing monopoly. That said, I believe that examination of the Papal privileges demonstrates, over the course of the sixteenth century, a growing sense of entitlement on the part of those who petitioned for privileges, and an increasing grounding of that entitlement in the creative act. Hence the prefix 'Proto-,' suggesting a partly formed precursor to our current concepts. Nonetheless, I emphasize the 'partly,' and caution against characterizing the system of Papal printing privileges simply as a kind of *droit d'auteur avant la lettre*. For example, as we will see, ensuring the integrity of text and images preoccupied both popes and petitioners, but often for reasons far from the core of contemporary *droit moral*, rooted as the sixteenth-century objective was in fidelity to Counter Reformation Catholic doctrine,[7] rather than in respect for the personality of the author.[8]

I. SOURCES AND METHODOLOGY

A. Documents

Almost all documents studied are located in the Vatican Secret Archives (ASVat), in compendia of sixteenth-century Papal secretarial letters (*brevi*). These are, in effect,

---

[6] Papal privileges shared many attributes of property, including alienability, descendability and (limited) exclusivity, but the basis of the property right differed markedly from *literary* property as we have known it since the eighteenth century.

[7] *See, e.g.*, Sec. Brev. Rev. 293 F 113 (Mar. 6, 1600) (Giulio Calvi) (discussed *infra* Part II.H).

[8] Another reason it may be hazardous to speculate that authors are more central to the Papal privileges than to privileges elsewhere concerns the difficulty of comparing Papal and Venetian privileges. While the proportion of author-recipients of Papal privileges is significantly greater than for Venetian privileges, the data sets do not align. My study covers principally 1509–1605; the principal studies excerpting or reproducing the texts of the Venetian privileges begin in the fifteenth century, but end around 1536. *See* CARLO CASTELLANI, LA STAMPA IN VENEZIA DALLA SUA ORIGINE ALLA MORTE DI ALDO MANUZIO SENIORE (1889); CHRISTOPHER L.C.E. WITCOMBE, COPYRIGHT IN THE RENAISSANCE: PRINTS AND THE PRIVILEGIO IN SIXTEENTH-CENTURY VENICE AND ROME (2003) (discussing later sixteenth-century Venetian privileges, but only concerning prints and engravings); Carlo Castellani, *I Privilegi di Stampa e la proprieta' letteraria in Venezia dalla introduzione della stampa nella città*, 36 ARCHIVIO VENETO 127–39 (1888); Rinaldo Fulin, *Primi privilegi di stampa in Venezia*, 1 ARCHIVIO VENETO 160–64 (1871); Rinaldo Fulin, *Documenti per servire alla Storia della tipografia Veneziana*, 23 ARCHIVIO VENETO 84–212 (1882). According to Angela Nuovo and Christian Coppens, there currently exists no systematic study of sixteenth-century Venetian privileges. *See* NUOVO & COPPENS, *supra* note 4, at 183 n.42, 211 n.184.

Republishing classical authors may have dominated the early years of publishing, but later on publishing shifted to new works both because of a dwindling supply of long-dead authors and because of the role of new works in propagating the Counter Reformation.

copies (of varying degrees of legibility) for the secretarial files, the originals having been sent to the recipients. The principal relevant collections are volumes XXXIX–LXII in the *Armarium* series (ARM), and volumes 11–399 of the *Registra Brevium* (Sec. Brev. Reg.).[9] I have now found approximately 500 privileges and petitions (*suppliche*) and related documents, of which less than 20 percent have previously been reported; less than 10 percent of the Papal *brevi* and/or petitions have been published either in whole or in part in secondary sources.[10] With very rare exceptions, all of the documents are handwritten.[11] Additional documents studied are in the archives of the Plantin Moretus Museum in Antwerp.[12] The privileges are in Latin, and most of the petitions are in Italian, although some are in Latin. More than half of the privileges found in the Archives were granted to authors or their heirs rather than to printers. This Study employs the term 'printer' to cover both those who physically printed books (referred to in the documents variously as *stampatore*, *impressore* and *tipografo*) and the publisher-booksellers (*libraro*, *bibliopola*), who played an editorial role and either hired artisans to print, or exercised that function themselves as well. In any event, in sixteenth-century Rome the difference between printers and booksellers was not always clear,[13] and privileges were awarded both *Bibliopolae* and *Typographis*. I have identified over 231 privileges (approximately 52 percent) as awarded to authors; over 180 (approximately 41 percent) were awarded to printers, including licenses to print missals and breviaries. (I have classified approximately 30 recipients of privileges, such as religious congregations or foreign sovereigns, neither as author nor as printer.) Of over 100 petitions: more than half were made by or on behalf of authors or their heirs,

---

[9] See generally INDICE DEI FONDI E RELATIVE MEZZI DI DESCRIZIONE E RICERCA DELL'ARCHIVIO SEGRETO VATICANO (2013).

[10] One of the principal works on the Vatican privileges remains Pierina Fontana, *Inizi della proprietà letteraria nello stato pontefico: Saggio di documenti dell'Archivio Vaticano*, in 3 ACCADEMIE E BIBLIOTECHE D'ITALIA 204 (1929–30). Fontana reproduces facsimiles and partial transcriptions of several privileges accorded during the first half of the sixteenth century. *See id.* See generally WITCOMBE, *supra* note 8 (referencing petitions and privileges, particularly for engravers, and including some partial transcriptions). For further references see Bibliography.

[11] I have found only two instances of a printed text, in both cases a copy of the privilege as printed in a book was cut from the book and pasted into the *breve* with modifications made to correspond to the new grantee. *See* ARM XL v 46 f. 174 (No. 297) (June 26, 1533) (printed privilege to Melchiore Sessa for poetry of Lodovico Martelli (1499–1527), which appears to be a recycling of 1531 privilege to Antonio Blado for Machiavelli's works. That privilege is published in a 1532 Venetian edition of Machiavelli's work. *See Antonio Blado's Privilege for Machiavelli's Works, Vatican (1531)*, PRIMARY SOURCES ON COPYRIGHT (L. Bently & M. Kretschmer eds.), http://www.copyrighthistory.org/record/i_1531; Sec. Brev. Reg. 339 F pg. ins. between 45–46 (Nov. 5, 1603) (to printer Giovanni Tallini for Summa of St Raymond. Printed privilege recycled from book published by Franzini heirs with privilege from Sec. Brev. Reg. 290 F 107 (Dec. 14, 1599) (to printers for Commentary on St. Luke by the Cardinal of Toledo)).

[12] These documents are labeled MPM Arch.

[13] *See, e.g.*, MASSIMO CERESA, UNA STAMPERIA NELLA ROMA DEL PRIMO SEICENTO: ANNALI TIPOGRAFICI DI GUGLIELMO FACCIOTTI ED EREDI (1592–1640) 37 (2000) ('It is not always easy separately to identify and distinguish the publishing enterprise from the functional and commercial endeavors of the printer and the bookseller.'); IAN MACLEAN, SCHOLARSHIP, COMMERCE, RELIGION: THE LEARNED BOOK IN THE AGE OF CONFESSIONS, 1560–1630, at 101–02 (2012) (describing the conflation of roles of printers, publishers and booksellers).

and slightly less than half by or on behalf of printers. (This breakdown does not include petitioners, such as religious orders, seeking rights to distribute a category of works that I have called 'Tridentine works': missals, breviaries and similar works of uniform liturgical content intended for broad dissemination across the Catholic world.)[14]

B. Methodology for Finding Privileges and Petitions

Most of the petitions and privileges not only are unpublished, they also have not been cataloged. Locating them has required consulting the eighteenth-century handwritten indexes that list *brevi* for each papacy, and cross-referencing to the volumes of sixteenth-century collected letters. Listings consulted included those labeled 'de non imprimen' (or 'de non imprimendo'); 'indultum super impressione'; 'bibliopola'; 'impressore'; 'privilegium ad X annos.' For the Sec. Brev. Reg. series, covering Pius V through Clement VIII (1566–1605), indexes 748–759 are organized chronologically by year and month, and sometimes alphabetically by diocese, and often provide both volume and page references. For Julius II through Pius IV (1503–1565), indexes 290–315 and 734–738 are organized chronologically by year and month, but most do not specifically refer to a volume of ARM. Concordance listings pasted into the front of the indexes or kept by employees of Vatican Archives lead to the probable volume of ARM; the *brevi* for each month in that collection were reviewed in search (not always successful) for the ones identified in the indexes. Petitions accompanying the privileges have not always been preserved; for only about 25 percent of the privileges did I also find the petitions, most of them corresponding to the papacy of Clement VIII (1592–1605). Secretarial copies from this period occasionally include annotations on the back of the document summarizing the nature and basis of the request, even where the original petition is no longer included in the file.

On finding a *breve* or at least an index listing, I crossreferenced it with the database of the *Istituto Centrale per il catalogo unico delle biblioteche italiane e per le*

---

[14] Liturgical works published between 1567 and 1624 are often referred to as 'Tridentine,' although the Council of Trent 'specifically mandated only revision of the missal and breviary of the Roman Rite. Its intention was to eliminate superstitions, redundancies, scribal errors, and other inappropriate elements that had crept into the texts over the course of time. Once those revisions got under way, they led to revisions of other texts such as the Martyrology, the Pontifical, and the Ritual.' JOHN W. O'MALLEY, TRENT: WHAT HAPPENED AT THE COUNCIL 268 (2013).

In addition, I have found one instance of a privilege to print breviaries granted to the Pope's medical doctor as a reward for services apparently unrelated either to printing or to religious activities. *See* Sec. Brev. Reg. 183 F 504 (Sept. 25, 1591) (to Rodolfo Silvestri). Since Papal privileges in Tridentine works were much sought-after, see *infra* notes 36–39 and accompanying text, it would appear that the grant was expected to generate a handsome compensation. Silvestri two years later succeeded publisher Paolo Blado in the office of papal printer, see DOMENICO BERNONI, DEI TORRESANI, BLADO E RAGAZZONI, CELEBRI STAMPATORI A VENEZIA E ROMA NEL XV E XVI SECOLO : COGLI ELENCHI ANNOTATI DELLE RISPETTIVE EDIZIONI 248 (1890). The EDIT 16 database (*infra*, note 15), however, lists Silvestri not as a printer or publisher, but as the author of one work, an updated version of a medical book (CNCA 2214; CNCE 9473).

informazioni bibliografiche (EDIT 16 database)[15] to ascertain if a book had been printed and whether the book was in the Vatican Library (BAVat).[16] If so, I consulted the book at the Vatican Library to see if it referred to or reproduced a Papal privilege.

In the absence of a comprehensive or systematic source of information identifying sixteenth-century Papal printing privileges, one cannot ascertain what proportion of the universe of sixteenth-century Papal privileges the documents found in the Vatican Archives reflect, or, for that matter, what proportion of books published in Italy – or just in Rome – received Papal privileges.[17] Bibliographic records, such as those contained in the SHORT-TITLE CATALOGUE OF BOOKS PRINTED IN ITALY AND OF ITALIAN BOOKS PRINTED IN OTHER COUNTRIES FROM 1465 TO 1600 NOW IN THE BRITISH MUSEUM (created in 1958) do not indicate whether the book had a privilege. Some studies cataloging particular sixteenth-century Italian printers' outputs do show whether books claimed Papal privileges, and on the basis of these listings, one may speculate that less than one-third of the publications received Papal privileges.[18] However, these catalogues generally do not indicate whether the initial grantee was an author, printer or bookseller. Thus, while these bibliographical sources account for some Papal privileges not found in the records of *brevi*, thus augmenting the overall number of identified sixteenth-century Papal printing privileges, their general failure to disclose these privileges' initial beneficiaries makes it difficult to assess whether the author-dominant proportion of privileges found in the Archives is representative of the wider universe.[19]

---

[15] EDIT 16 Database, Istituto Centrale per il catalogo unico delle biblioteche italiane e per le informazioni bibliografiche – Laboratorio per la bibliografia retrospettiva, http://edit16.iccu.sbn.it/web_iccu/imain.htm.

[16] *Printed Books*, VATICAN LIBR., http://opac.vatlib.it/iguana/www.main.cls?sUrl=home PRINT.

[17] *See* NUOVO & COPPENS, *supra* note 4, at 204 (pointing out that there are many more books and prints in circulation mentioning privileges than there are privileges found in archives).

[18] *See* Bibliography (listing sources containing or mentioning Papal privileges). Estimating on the basis of prior bibliographic studies the overall percentage of published books that received Papal privileges is hazardous because some printer-publishers seem to have obtained privileges more often than others, and not all such printers worked exclusively in Rome. For example, one of the printers who most frequently acquired Papal privileges, Michele Tramezzino, worked primarily in Venice; approximately 70 percent of books and maps published by the Tramezzino brothers acquired Papal – as well as Venetian – privileges.

[19] In the scanned images in the EDIT 16 database, reference to a privilege did not always identify the granting authority; '*cum privilegio*' or '*con privilegio*' could refer to a variety of sovereigns within or without Italy. Nor does the simple mention '*cum privilegio*' reveal who applied for or initially received the privilege.

II. SYNTHESIS OF THE SYSTEM: PERSONS, WORKS AND RIGHTS PROTECTED

A. Process of Obtaining Vatican Printing Privileges[20]

Before a book could obtain a privilege, its author or printer was first obliged to apply to the Papal censorship authorities, principally the Master of the Sacred Palace and, later in the sixteenth century, the Congregations of the Inquisition and of the Index, for a license to print.[21] The '*licenza dei superiori*' or '*superiorum permissu*' enabled the book to be published at all; the '*privilegio*' entitled its holder to the exclusive right to publish and sell the work, usually for a period of ten years, potentially renewable.

To obtain a privilege, the petitioner would apply to the Apostolic Secretary or the Secretary of Latin Briefs. Some of the petitions were made by, or were accompanied by the endorsement of, a well-connected ecclesiastical or other patron.[22] Many petitioners assert that the Master of the Sacred Palace has already approved the work, or that they are applying for the privilege conditional on the approval of the Master of the Sacred Palace. In some instances, the petitioners urge a rapid grant of the privilege because the books have already been printed, and await only the addition of the notice of privilege before they are distributed.[23]

---

[20] See generally THOMAS FRENZ, I DOCUMENTI PONTIFICI NEL MEDIOEVO E NELL'ETÀ MODERNA 71–91 (2d ed. 1998); WITCOMBE, supra note 8, at xxix–xxxi.

[21] Many of the privileges pose the condition precedent of censorship approval. *See also* Sec. Brev. Reg. 39 F 237 (June 1, 1576) (to printer Dionisio Zanchio for works of Polidoro Vergilio, now that they have been 'purged' of heretical material and approved by the Congregation of the Index). On Papal censorship and printing in Rome, see, e.g., Gigliola Fragnito, *The Central and Peripheral Organization of Censorship, in* GIGLIOLA FRAGNITO, ed., CHURCH CENSORSHIP AND CULTURE IN EARLY MODERN ITALY 13 (2001); MACLEAN, *supra* note 13, at 153–55; Maria Grazia Blasio, *Privilegi e licenze di stampa a Roma fra Quattro e Cinquecento*, 90 LA BIBLIOFILIA 147, 154–59 (1988).

[22] For petitions by or invoking patrons, see, for example, Arm XL v 49 F 204rv (n 235) (Dec. 5, 1534) (petition of the humanist and Bishop Claudio Tolomei on behalf of his relative Mariano Lenzi); Sec. Brev. Reg. 199 F 172r (Jan. 26, 1593) (Cardinal Cinzio Aldobrandini on behalf of painter Cesare Ripa); Sec. Brev. Reg. 239 FF 382 rv, 383r (petition), 389v, 390rv (May 26, 1596) (petition of Fra Giovannni Baptista Cavoto invoking Cardinal Aldobrandini); Sec. Brev. Reg. 289 FF 179r, 179av (Nov. 29, 1599) (petition by Cardinal Roberto Bellarmino vouching for doctrinal fidelity of book by Jerónimo Gracián de la Madre de Dios); Sec. Brev. Reg. 303 FF 390 rv, 391r (petition), 392v, 393rv (Dec. 16, 1600) (Cardinal Aldobrandini on behalf of printer Antonio Franzini); *see also* Sec. Brev. Reg. 122 F 529 (second petition of Martin Zuria) (Sept. 3, 1586) (referring to perceived obstructionism by the Cardinal Secretary of Papal *brevi*, and asking for another cardinal's intervention to resolve the impasse).

[23] *See, e.g.*, Sec. Brev. Reg. 277 F 296 (petition) (Dec. 30, 1598) (Ulisse Aldovrandi requests that his privilege be expedited so that he can have the mention 'Cum privilegio' printed in the book); Sec. Brev. Reg. 266 F 51 (petition) (Jan. 5, 1598) (Orazio Torsellini asks for privilege to be granted as soon as possible so that publication is not held up; in published volume of Torsellini's *Lauretanae Historiae* the privilege is dated January 5, 1598, though the date on the frontispiece is 1597, and says 'Cum privilegio summi Pont,' with approbations of the Cardinal of Loreto and the General of the Jesuit order dated, respectively May 8 and October 8,

In addition to potentially delaying publication, seeking a Papal privilege appears to have been expensive.[24] Neither the petitions nor the privileges disclose the fees, although in general a variety of taxes attached to the application and receipt of a *breve*.[25] Some petitions refer obliquely to the cost,[26] and one expresses considerable annoyance at the imposition of a fee from which the petitioning author believed he should have been dispensed.[27]

B. Recipients of Papal Printing Privileges

I have already indicated the breakdown between authors and printers.[28] Because the Pope asserted dominium over all of Christendom, a dominion he enforced through excommunication, applicants for privileges often resided far from the Papal States, in

---

1597. This suggests the book was already printed or at least type-set, and its final assembly and distribution were delayed by late grant of the privilege).

[24] *See, e.g.*, MPM Arch. 102 F 379 (Latin); MPM Arch. 21 F 357 (French) (Jan Moretus paid his cousin Peter Bras SJ for various services on his behalf at the Vatican, including payment of 20 ducats for a privilege to print bibles; the sum was the equivalent of 90 days' wages for an Antwerp printer's craftsman). Elizabeth Armstrong also discusses this point:

> Papal privileges were expensive. When Michael Hummelberg, in Rome, set about obtaining a five-year privilege from Leo X for Froben's edition of the works of St Jerome, prepared by Erasmus, he was told by Roman booksellers whom he consulted that it would cost about thirty gold pieces. Submitting the request to the Pope through a series of highly placed and benevolently disposed intermediaries, he eventually secured the privilege for six ducats. '"No one, believe me," he wrote to Froben, enclosing the document and requesting repayment, "could have obtained it for so little."'

ARMSTRONG, *supra* note 1, at 13 & n.3 (citing A. HORAWICZ, ANALECTEN ZUR GESCHICHTE DES HUMANISMUS IN SCHWABEN 1512–1518, at 217 (1877) (privilege no. xxxviii (Aug. 30, 1516)), and pointing out that '[t]he fee paid by Koberger for the privilege referred to above, n. 1, was in fact thirty florins').

[25] FRENZ, *supra* note 20, at 71–91.

[26] *See, e.g.*, Arm XL 50 F 247, 248r, 249r (first and second petitions) (Feb. 5, 1535) (Tommaso and Benedetto Giunta, Antonio Blado, Antonio Salamanca asking Cardinal Blosio 'that you be willing today at the direction of his Blessedness to take the commission and issue the Breve ...'); Sec. Brev. Reg. 122 F 529 (Sept. 3, 1586) (second petition of Martin Zuria, referring to 'the purchase of the privilege').

[27] Sec. Brev. Reg. 140 F 316r (second petition) (Apr. 22, 1589) (to Gerard Voss for translation of St Ephrem):

> I speak truly and sincerely, if this *motu proprio* [privilege] is not granted and conceded to me in all respects for free, I have decided to entirely cease [the translation entrusted to me by His Holiness] and to suspend the whole thing. Therefore, I would like this matter to be judged appropriately, so that a better resolution will be produced.

[28] *See supra* Part I.A.

such locations as Dalmatia,[29] Poland,[30] Cologne,[31] Ingolstadt (Bavaria),[32] Paris,[33] and Mexico.[34] In addition, it is worth noting that, as the sixteenth century (and the Counter Reformation) progressed, an increasing number of authors receiving privileges were clerics, particularly Jesuits.

C. Works Protected

Of approximately 430 privileges identified,[35] the great majority – approximately 323 – were granted for new works (including new commentaries on religious or literary classics) and another 55 for new editions or translations of older works. Privileges for religious works predominated: 244 privileges, of which approximately 161 were for newly authored works. Of the remaining privileges or licenses for religious works, over half (42) constitute missals, breviaries and other Tridentine works. Printers throughout the Catholic world, perceiving lucrative markets in Tridentine texts,[36] vied for geographically subdivided exclusive rights;[37] but some licenses were granted to foreign sovereigns for their territories.[38] In general, in Rome, as elsewhere throughout the latter half of the sixteenth century, most of the money to be made in printing and publishing came from purveying religious texts.[39]

Among works neither liturgical nor commentaries on biblical, patristic or medieval scholastics' texts, the leading categories include prints of historical or religious

---

[29] *See* Sec. Brev. Reg. 52 F 429 (June 29, 1582) (to local bishop for publication of works regarding the Roman Jubilee for the people living under Ottoman rule).

[30] *See* Sec. Brev. Reg. 220 F 224 (Oct. 29, 1594) (to the Chancellor of Poland to print new and old works at the University of Chelm).

[31] *See* Sec. Brev. Reg. 16 F 222 (July 28, 1571) (to Gervinus Calenius, to print missals and breviaries).

[32] *See, e.g.*, Sec. Brev. Reg. 39 F 298 (Aug. 28, 1576) (to David Sartorius, printer in Ingolstadt, for works of Peter Canisius); Sec. Brev. Reg. 69 F 7 (Jan. 3, 1581) (same grantee, for works of Johan Eck).

[33] *See* Sec. Brev. Reg. 53 F 271 (Nov. 5, 1582) (to Guillaume Chaudière, printer for the University of Paris, for commentaries on the Gospels).

[34] *See* Sec. Brev. Reg. 148 F 148 (Oct. 31, 1589) (to Francisco Beteta, schoolmaster in Tlaxcala for compilation of documents on Mexico).

[35] Identification is approximate because, on the one hand, some privileges cover multiple works and, on the other, index entries for other privileges do not detail the works covered, and the indexed privilege has not been found.

[36] *See, e.g.*, COLIN CLAIR, CHRISTOPHER PLANTIN 87–104 (1987).

[37] *See, e.g.*, Sec. Brev. Reg. 224 F 83, 84r (petition) (Feb. 14, 1595) (Wolfgang Eder, seeking privilege for Bavaria); Sec. Brev. Reg. 318 F 236, 237r (petition) (Feb. 13, 1602) (Jan Keerberg, seeking privilege for Antwerp and other areas formerly within privilege of late Plantin).

[38] *See, e.g.*, Sec. Brev. Reg. 13 F 8v (Jan. 6, 1570) (license to the King of Portugal to print Breviaries for his kingdom). The royal recipients might then designate an exclusive printer. *See, e.g.*, Sec. Brev. Reg. 19 F 441, 442 (petition) (Nov. 15, 1571) (petition names Christopher Plantin as printer of breviaries, missals and other Tridentine works for the Spanish provinces).

[39] *See, e.g.*, KAREN L. BOWEN & DIRK IMHOF, CHRISTOPHER PLANTIN AND ENGRAVED BOOK ILLUSTRATIONS IN SIXTEENTH-CENTURY EUROPE 122–25 (2008); PAUL GRENDLER, THE ROMAN INQUISITION AND THE VENETIAN PRESS, 1540–1605, at 170 (1977).

subjects, architecture, maps and other images (the arrival in Rome of pilgrims and other tourists during jubilee years may account for some of the popularity of these works); works of history, politics and biography, including the lives of saints new and old and Popes; canon law books; contemporary literature (including Ariosto's *Orlando Furioso*[40] and Tasso's *Gerusalemme Liberata*[41]); works about science, mathematics and medicine; educational works, such as grammar books; and works of choral music. These categories of works break down roughly as follows (some overlap, for example a book about the monuments of Rome,[42] would be listed in both the 'tourism' and the 'images' categories):

> Art, architecture, images: 51
> History, biography, geography: 45
> Law: 40
> Science, mathematics and medicine: 34
> Literature: 31
> Classics (including translations, new editions): 20
> Education: 17
> Music: 13
> Tourism: 6

D. Rights Protected

1. Geographic scope

In the sixteenth century, as indeed today, exclusive rights in works of authorship were territorial. Each sovereign's grant of a privilege produced effects only within the borders that sovereign controlled. Sovereigns did, however, grant foreign authors' or printers' petitions for local privileges.[43] Because Papal privileges, by contrast, purported to be multiterritorial, the geographic scope of protection distinguished Papal

---

[40] See ARM XL v 46 F 137 (July 8, 1533) (to heirs of Ariosto).
[41] See Sec. Brev. Reg. 207 F 274 (Sept. 2, 1593) (to publisher, for new edition prepared by author).
[42] See Sec Brev Reg. 126 F 61 (Jan. 7, 1587) (to printer Girolamo Franzini for *Le Cose Maravigliose Dell'Alma Citta Di Roma*).
[43] The French king might grant a privilege in a foreign work, but a work's initial publication abroad without the French privilege would disqualify it from subsequent protection in France, even if the foreign claimant had obtained a privilege from his local authorities in the country of first publication. See Simon Marion, *Plaidoyé second, sur l'impression des œuvres de Seneque, revues & annotées par feu Marc Antoine Muret* (1586), in PLAIDOYEZ DE MON. SIMON MARION, BARON DE DRUY, CI DEVANT ADVOCAT EN PARLEMENT ET DE PRESENT CONSEILLER DU ROY EN SON CONSEIL D'ESTAT ET SON ADVOCAT GENERAL 9 (Paris, Michel Sonius, 1598), *reprinted, translated and available at* http://copy.law.cam.ac.uk/record/f_1586 ('Since [the] death of [the humanist Marc Antoine Muret, commentator on Seneca], his friends in Rome have had printed the edition of Seneca which he annotated, without obtaining the privilege from the King [of France]. This rendered it entirely public, and free to print in this Kingdom, where it can no longer be subject to the privilege …'). Marion addressed his plea on behalf of two Paris printers who sought the annulment of a subsequently granted French privilege on Muret's Seneca; the Parlement of Paris ordered the cancellation of the privilege on March 15, 1586. Roman printer

privileges from those of other sovereigns. The Pope exercised both secular power over the Papal States (in central Italy) and spiritual authority over all Catholic lands. Petitioners from within and without the Papal States requested coverage for all of Italy (to the annoyance of the Venetian Senate[44]) and all lands directly or indirectly subject to the Holy Roman Church. Some privileges, particularly those concerning the distribution of missals and breviaries, are explicitly limited to particular territories outside of Rome.[45] And some grant a subsequent petitioner a more limited geographical area carved out from a prior grant covering all (Catholic) Christendom.[46]

Along with fines and confiscation of the books, the principal sanction for violation of an extraterritorial privilege was the supraterritorial remedy of automatic excommunication,[47] a penalty that petitioners must have considered sufficiently efficacious to warrant the effort and expense of obtaining Papal privileges. Nonetheless, claimants who anticipated that their works would be bestsellers frequently sought, in addition to Papal privileges, multiple privileges from a variety of secular sovereigns, most often Venice, France and several Italian principalities, notably Florence. One particularly vigilant grantee, Francesco Priscianese, author of an Italian-language Latin grammar book, received privileges from multiple sovereigns. He published the full text of the Papal and Imperial privileges in the initial pages of the book, followed by this statement: 'We have also for the said time the fullest privileges from the Most Christian King of France, from the Most Illustrious Venetian Senate, and from Florence, and from Ferrara, and from other Rulers of Italy, which we do not copy out in order not to create a Volume of Privileges.'[48]

Bartolomeo Grassi had obtained a Papal privilege in 1585 for Muret's Commentaries on Seneca. *See* Sec. Brev. Reg. 116 F 20 (Nov. 23, 1585). It is unclear whether the privilege extended beyond the Papal States. The grant reaches 'all and individual Christian faithful, especially book printers and book sellers however named, in our City and its district as well as all our ecclesiastic state and all those directly or indirectly subject to the Holy Roman Church.' Other drafts of the grant specify its application beyond Italy, but that language has been struck out. On the other hand, the draft also strikes out language limiting the privilege to persons 'subject to the temporal dominion' of the church.

[44] *See Motu proprio Controversy, Venice (1596)*, PRIMARY SOURCES ON COPYRIGHT (1450–1900) (L. Bently & M. Kretschmer eds.), http://www.copyrighthistory.org/record/i_1596 (complaining that Venetian booksellers and printers were obtaining Papal privileges, to the detriment of the publishing business in Venice, and ordering the beneficiaries of these privileges to renounce them, on pain of confiscation of books and a ten ducat fine per book). *See generally* NUOVO & COPPENS, *supra* note 4, at 224–26.

[45] *See, e.g.*, Sec. Brev. Reg. 14 F 248 (July 28, 1578) (to Christopher Plantin to print and distribute missals and breviaries in Flanders, parts of Germany and Hungary); *see also* Sec. Brev. Reg. 69 F 2 (Jan. 1, 1581) (to Felice de Zara to arrange for the printing of religious works in the 'Illyrian' – Serbo-Croatian – language and alphabet).

[46] *See, e.g.*, Sec. Brev. Reg. 58 F 216 (Feb. 1, 1584) (granting Lyonnais printer Charles Pesuot a privilege for printing and distributing the works of Peter Canisius in France and Spain, notwithstanding earlier privilege to Bavarian printer David Sartorius, at Sec. Brev. Reg. 39 F 298 (Aug. 28, 1576)).

[47] Remedies are discussed *infra* Part II.G.

[48] FRANCESCO PRISCIANESE, DE PRIMI PRINCIPII DELLA LINGUA ROMANA (Venice 1540), BAVat Stamp.Cappon.IV.373(int.2); Stamp.Cappon.IV.374(int.1). Priscianese's Papal privilege can be found at ARM XLI v 14 F339 (Aug. 27, 1539). *See also* NUOVO & COPPENS, *supra* note

2. Duration

Regarding the duration of exclusive rights, most privileges were granted for a ten-year term effective from issuance or from the date of printing or publication of the work,[49] though a few lasted for 15 or 20 years. A comparison of petitions and privileges shows that some petitioners requested longer terms, but routinely received only ten years.[50] Privileges could be renewed,[51] even after some time had elapsed between the expiration of a prior privilege and the grant of a new term in the same work.[52] It does not seem that a request for a renewal required special justification, nor that it advert to some new contribution by the author or printer.[53] Nor does there appear to have been a limit on the number of renewals sought; some original grantees' heirs sought successive renewals.[54] It is not clear whether a privilege granted by one Pope continued in effect under his successor. Petitions referring to prior privileges suggest some grantees shared this uncertainty.[55]

3. Reproduction, sale and importation

All privileges conferred exclusive rights to reproduce and distribute the work. The specific language forbade third parties from printing, selling, offering for sale or importing the work (or hiring others to engage in these activities) without the express permission of the privilege holder, his grantees, his heirs or successors in title. The importation right would have been particularly significant where a privilege covered a limited territory; even Papal privileges purporting to extend to all Christendom would

---

4, at 225–27 (describing the practice of the publishing house of the Tramezzino brothers to obtain privileges from multiple sovereigns inside and outside Italy).

[49] See, e.g., Sec. Brev. Reg. 218 F 90 (Aug. 18, 1594) (privilege for Vittorio Benacci is for ten years calculated from the date of printing); ARM XLII 37 F 244 (Feb. 13, 1579) (privilege awarded to Anthonie Zandvoort vests for ten years from present date).

[50] See, e.g., Sec. Brev. Reg. 200 F 33 (Feb. 8, 1593) (petition requests 20 years for book on the life of the Virgin; privilege grants ten); Sec. Brev. Reg. 217 F 115 (July 21, 1594) (petition requests 15 years for law book; privilege grants ten); Sec. Brev. Reg. 303 F 390 (Dec. 16, 1600) (petition requests 15 years for work of Cardinal Toledo; privilege grants ten).

[51] See, e.g., ARM XLI v 21 F 458 (July 19, 1541) (renewal by author, the jurist Girolamo Giganti, of the privilege on his treatise on pensions, prior privilege (not referred to in renewal) at ARM XL v 34 F 119 (Nov. 4, 1531); Sec. Brev. Reg. 268 F 134 (Mar. 16, 1598) (heir's renewal of privilege in works of Martin de Azpilcueta); Sec. Brev. Reg. 131 F 155 (Nov. 11, 1587) (to author Francisco Toledo; the petition requests an extension of the privilege, without any particular justification; the ensuing privilege grants a renewal for 20 years, without any particular justification).

[52] See, e.g., Sec. Brev. Reg. 290 F 107, supra note 11; Sec. Brev. Reg. 481 F 427 (July 7, 1612) (renewing Sec. Brev. Reg. 284 F 191 (June 23, 1599); (to printer Giovanni Antonio di Paoli for engravings of images of saints)).

[53] See renewals cited supra notes 51–52.

[54] See, e.g., Sec. Brev. Reg. 688 F 402 (Mar. 23, 1624) (seeking renewed privilege for engravings referenced in Sec. Brev. Reg. 284 F 191 (June 23, 1599) (granting privilege to Giovanni Antonio di Paoli for engravings of images of saints); see also Sec. Brev. Reg. 481 F 427 (July 7, 1612) (renewing privilege in Sec. Brev. Reg. 284 F 191)).

[55] See, e.g., Sec. Brev. Reg. 221 F 98 (Nov. 17, 1594) (petition of Domenico Basa, Vatican printer, to Clement VIII referring to privilege granted his predecessor Paolo Manuzio by Sixtus V).

have lacked effect in jurisdictions whose rulers were Protestant. As a result, recipients of Papal privileges would have sought to prevent the entry into territories covered by the Papal privilege of copies that may have been lawfully printed in a jurisdiction outside the scope of the Papal privilege but which, if allowed into the geographical ambit of the Papal privilege, would compete with the recipient's copies.[56]

4. Adaptations and translations

Privileges also came to cover what we would today call derivative works, specifically abridgements, additions or any other manner of changing the work, and translations.[57] With regard to the last of these prohibitions, earlier privileges granted rights in Latin and Italian vernacular; later in the century, they extended to French, Spanish and often all foreign vernaculars. By the end of the sixteenth-century, coverage of different versions of the work had become a matter of course. It is worth emphasizing this point because some commentators contend that rights over translations, abridgements, alterations, or other variations on a prior protected work represent an expansion of the traditionally narrow confines of Anglo-American copyright law.[58] That critique suggests a distinction between modest judicial adjustment of the scope of copyright to

---

[56] *See, e.g.*, Sec. Brev. Reg. 220 F 72, 73r (petition) (Oct. 10, 1594) (Domenico Tarini of Turin has had printed at his expense by Milanese printer Pacifico da Ponte Bishop Panigarola's Disputations against Calvin, and seeks a seven-year privilege prohibiting others from printing the book 'nor, if the book were printed elsewhere, from selling it.'); Sec. Brev. Reg. 290 F 105, 106r (petition) (Dec. 13, 1599) (Alfonso Ciaccone begs 'that no one in the Papal State may for the next ten years neither print, nor if printed elsewhere sell, the *Lives and Deeds of the Popes up to Pius V*,' written by his uncle); Sec. Brev. Reg. 293 F 113 (Mar. 6, 1600) (Giulio Calvi, having written a commentary on Aquinas, prays 'that for ten years the book may not be printed by others in the Papal State, and if printed in other places, it may not be sold in said State'); Sec. Brev. Reg. 341 F 198 (Jan. 14, 1604) (Ottaviano Faiani, having written a poem on the Passion requests a privilege that no one else may print or sell his work in the Papal State, 'nor introduce copies printed by others in other places outside the said State'); ARM XL 46 F 297 (Dec. 19, 1533) (privilege gives Michael Isengrin and Johann Bebel exclusive right to import copies of the works of Polidoro Vergilio into Basel).

[57] As well as larger or smaller paper formats (e.g., from *quarto* to *ottavo*). For a particularly extensive (but not unrepresentative) example, see Sec. Brev. Reg. 130 F 70 (Aug. 29, 1587) (privilege to Venetian printer Giovanni Giolito Ferrari for a Commentary on the Book of Job):

> We prohibit and forbid that for the next 10 years anyone print or prepare to be printed, the works themselves or another version of them or anything in whole or in part in whatever form or with a change or transposition or even with whatever other additions, scholarly notes, summaries, glossaries and expositions on those materials ventured or these referred and to anything similar, just as in Latin as in Italian or in whatever other language and at the urging of whoever by whatever request, pretext or contrivance without the license and assent of yourself or your heirs.

This privilege is of particular interest because it revokes a privilege previously granted to a printer from Lyon. *See* discussion *infra* Part II.H.

[58] *See, e.g.*, Oren Bracha, *The Ideology of Authorship Revisited: Authors, Markets, and Liberal Values in Early American Copyright*, 118 YALE L.J. 186, 224–26 (2008) (scope of early U.S. copyright limited to full verbatim reproduction); Matthew Sag, *The Prehistory of Fair Use*, 76 BROOK. L. REV. 1371, 1380–87 (2011) (Statute of Anne and case law interpreting it did not

protect against a second-comer's substitution of his version for the underlying work (consonant with constrained contours of copyright) on the one hand,[59] and expansion of copyright scope to cover the full extent of a work's value, including in new non-substitutional markets (marking a radical departure), on the other.[60] Without entering the fraught fray of Anglo-American copyright history, one may nonetheless observe that a fuller 'prehistory' of copyright outside the Anglo-American sphere indicates both a wider scope of exclusive rights than those accounts credit, and a combination of motivations for those broad grants.

As Part II.H will examine further, the expansion of the scope of protection to different versions may reflect three motivations, two market-driven, and the third doctrinal. First, coverage of expanded, abridged, or altered versions may have been a response to the tactics of competitors who sought to evade privileges by introducing changes to the copied work.[61] Second, rights over different formats, additions, deletions and other modifications may betoken market-related concerns beyond preventing unfairly competitive near-identical substitutions. Rather, beyond the defensive function of the broader privilege, vesting the rightholder with these extended prerogatives would enable him to control new markets, for example for versions with added illustrations,[62] as well as for new editions. Similarly, the translation right suggests a capacious view of a work's potential markets: given the broad territory to which a Papal privilege could apply, together with an increase in vernacular literacy, it is understandable that authors or rightholders would wish the privilege to cover multiple languages, even in advance of producing or authorizing a third party's translation. That the Papal privileges did indeed come in effect to reserve to the grantee the control over the foreign language market suggests an entrepreneurial, as well as a defensive, conception of the scope of the privilege. Finally, empowering the privilege-holder to prevent variations on or alterations to the work coincided with the interests of the Church: faithful rendering of the contents, particularly of liturgical and theological works, would have been important to ensure adherence to church strictures.

Turning from the right to control the creation of adaptations to the protection accorded derivative works, there is some ambiguity regarding the scope of the rights in a work that built upon a prior, unprotected, work. Did a privilege in a derivative work,

---

cover translations or abridgements); *but see id.* at 1387–93 (nuancing prior proposition to emphasize freedom of 'fair' abridgements incorporating substantial new authorship).

[59] Sag, *supra* note 58, at 1387–93.
[60] Bracha, *supra* note 58, at 226–28.
[61] *See, e.g.*, Victor Plahte Tschudi, *Ancient Rome in the Age of Copyright: The Privilegio and Printed Reconstructions*, 25 ACTA AD ARCHAEOLOGIAM ET ARTIUM HISTORIAM PERTINENTIA 177, 180–88 (2012); *see also infra* text accompanying note 88 (discussing Tschudi's article). Similar motivations may explain the expansion of the scope of French privileges to cover various kinds of alterations, see LAURENT PFISTER, L'AUTEUR, PROPRIÉTAIRE DE SON OEUVRE: FORMATION DU DROIT D'AUTEUR (XVIE SIÈCLE-1957), Thesis, Strasbourg, 1999, esp. privileges cited at n. 135 (forbidding the printing, sale or distribution 'under pretext of enlargement, correction, change of titles, false marks or otherwise, nor any parts separately, of any kind and manner whatsoever').
[62] Particularly as the technology and business arrangements for printing text and illustrations improved in the course of the sixteenth century. *See, e.g.*, EVELYN LINCOLN, BRILLIANT DISCOURSE, PICTURES AND READERS IN EARLY MODERN ROME (2014).

such as a translation or a commentary on an ancient or biblical text confer any exclusive rights in the underlying work? Although some privileges granted rights over 'annotations' and 'interpretations' or glosses,[63] the coexistence of privileges conceded within the same ten-year period for commentaries on the same classical authors, such as Cicero, or of the same biblical texts,[64] suggests that the privilege holder could prevent annotations of or glosses on the privilege holder's own commentaries, but not on the underlying text that was the object of the commentary. With respect to translations, the petitions evidence some confusion whether a privilege granted the translator exclusive rights to translate the underlying literary work, or only in his particular translation. Thus, in 1604 Cosimo Gaci requested a privilege,[65] as well as a derogation from a ten-year privilege granted only the year before to Francisco Soto,[66] for an Italian translation of works of St. Teresa of Avila. Gaci emphasizes that the translation will be his own, and that Soto has already almost fully sold out his edition. The privilege that issued crosses out the reference to Soto's prior privilege, thus prompting the inference that the Secretary of Latin Briefs did not think it necessary to annul or modify the prior privilege. This may suggest that independently authored translations could each enjoy a privilege, and therefore that the exclusive rights attached only to each grantee's version. The grant three years before Soto's to Venetian bookseller Pietro Fetti and his partners, for Italian translations of the same works,[67] may reinforce this conclusion. However, because Fetti seems never to have published his translation, his privilege would not have entered into force,[68] and neither Soto's petition nor his privilege refer to Fetti.

Other documents also evidence an appreciation of what we would today call the 'new matter' doctrine, codified in U.S. copyright law at 17 U.S.C. § 103(b), and

---

[63] *See, e.g.*, Sec. Brev. Reg. 118 F 120 (Mar. 7, 1586) (to printer Bartolommeo Grassi for an edition of the decisions of the Sacra Romana Rota ecclesiastical court); Sec. Brev. Reg. 179 F 167 (May 15, 1591) (to printer Domenico Basa for Jean Etienne Duranti's work on the rites of the Church); Sec. Brev. Reg. 290 F 105 (Dec. 13, 1599) (to Alfonso Ciaccone for his Lives and Acts of the Popes).

[64] *See, e.g.*, Sec. Brev. Reg. 268 F 132 (Mar. 16, 1598) (to printer Luigi Zannetti for works by other authors on Cicero); Sec. Brev. Reg. 31 F 361 (Aug. 30, 1601) (to Alfonso Chacòn for his commentaries on Cicero); Sec. Brev. Reg. 59 F 511 (July 7, 1584) (to the Monks of Cassino for works on the Psalms); Sec. Brev. Reg. 120 F 70 (Apr. 1, 1586) (to printer Giovanni Osmarino for Francesco Panigarola's commentaries on the Psalms).

[65] Sec. Brev. Reg. 349 F 509 (Sept. 23, 1604).

[66] Sec. Brev. Reg. 336 F 250 (Aug. 23, 1603).

[67] Sec. Brev. Reg. 297 F 274 (July 17, 1600).

[68] *See id.* at 274r (privilege effective 'for ten years calculated from the first printing of the work, provided that the work was approved by the Master of the Sacred Palace beforehand').

Both the Soto and the Gaci translations were published. *See* CAMINO DI PERFETTIONE CHE SCRISSE PER LE SUE MONACHE LA B. MADRE TERESA DI GIESU FONDATRICE DE' FRATI E DELLE MONACHE SCALZE CARMELITANE. TRADOTTO DELLA LINGUA SPAGNUOLA NELLA ITALIANA DA FRANCESCO SOTO SACERDOTE DELLA CONGREGAZIONE DELL'ORATORIO (1603), BAVat R.G. Teol.IV.878; Stamp.De.Luca.IV.5578; IL CAMMINO DI PERFEZIONE, E'L CASTELLO INTERIORE. LIBRI DELLA B.M. TERESA DI GIESU FONDATRICE DEGLI SCALZI CARMELITANI. TRASPORTATI DALLA SPAGNUOLA NELLA LINGUA ITALIANA DAL SIGNOR COSIMO GACI, CANONICO DI SAN LORENZO IN DAMASO (1605), BAVat: R.G.Teol.IV.1494; Stamp.Barb.U.XI.92; Stamp.De. Luca.IV.3943 [also 3944] (1-2). EDIT 16 does not list a Fetti edition. *See* EDIT 16 Database, *supra* note 15.

expressed in the Berne Convention's 'without prejudice' principle respecting derivative works.[69] That is, rights accorded a new work or new additions do not affect the existence or extent of protection for an earlier work incorporated in the new work. Thus, for example, in 1575 Diana Mantuana obtained a privilege covering her engravings of biblical and ancient Roman scenes, as well as her engravings based on works by Daniele da Volterra, Raphael and Michelangelo and 'other very celebrated painters and engravers, and those works to this point not printed, and concerning the printing of which nobody has yet obtained the privilege for their own use.'[70] Because Diana's privilege covers engravings 'printed with the inscription of her name,' it appears to have extended only to her own representations of the prior works, and did not give her sole rights to engrave the particular images by Volterra, Raphael or Michelangelo.

With respect to the underlying works, the formulation of Diana's privilege indicates that exclusive rights could be granted in artists' images; indeed, Roman goldsmith Proto Gaviola de America received a Papal privilege covering the rights to prevent the printing, painting or depicting of his design for wax medallions of the Agnus Dei,[71] and Titian obtained Venetian privileges allowing him to control the publication of engravings based on certain of his paintings.[72] Diana's privilege does not, however, suggest that, absent his own privilege, the artist who originated the image could prevent others from reproducing or obtaining a privilege to reproduce the work in the form of engravings. At least, Diana's privilege does not advert to any authorization from the heirs of Volterra, Raphael or Michelangelo, or any of the other unnamed 'very celebrated painters and engravers' or their heirs. The privilege's absence of reference to the underlying artists' permission could mean that, in the absence of privileges of their own, such permissions were not their province, or instead that even if the unprivileged

---

[69] Berne Convention for the Protection of Literary and Artistic Works art. 2.3, Sept. 9, 1886, *as revised at Paris* July 24, 1971, *and as amended* Sept. 28, 1979, 102 Stat. 2853, 1161 U.N.T.S. 3 ('Translations, adaptations, arrangements of music and other alterations of a literary or artistic work shall be protected as original works *without prejudice to the copyright in the original work*.') (emphasis added).

[70] ARM XLII v 28 F 93 (June 5, 1575). This privilege is referenced in WITCOMBE, *supra* note 8, at 183 n.78, and reproduced in EVELYN LINCOLN, THE INVENTION OF THE ITALIAN RENAISSANCE PRINTMAKER app. B, 189 (2000). Diana's is one of only two privileges I have found that was explicitly granted to a woman. The other, Sec. Brev. Reg. 69 F 254 (July 1, 1581), was granted to Jeanne Giunta 'mulier bibliopola lugdunen' (a woman bookseller of Lyon). The Giunta (or Giunti) were a leading sixteenth-century family of printers, originally from Florence, with branches in Venice and Lyon. Women may have held privileges as the heirs of a named printer; Roman publishing was often a family business, and it was not unusual for widows and/or daughters to succeed their husbands, fathers or brothers. *See, e.g.*, LINCOLN, *supra* note 62, at 16–21 (describing relationships of Roman publishing families). *See also* Archivio di Stato, Inv 113/62 Camerale II Stamperia # 1 F 30 (refers to Portia, the widow of Vatican printer Paolo Blado, as 'stampatrice camerale').

[71] Sec. Brev. Reg. 33 F 176 (July 27, 1584).

[72] *See, e.g.*, WITCOMBE, *supra* note 8, at xix–xxii; Lisa Pon, *Prints and Privileges: Regulating the Image in 16th-Century Italy*, HARV. U. ART MUSEUMS BULL. no. 6, 1998, at 40, 47 (pointing out scholarly disagreement over whether Titian's privileges protected the underlying paintings or only the engravings that Titian authorized be made from the paintings).

artist's accord were relevant to the grant of a privilege over an ensuing engraving, the artists in question had been dead too long (the most recent, Volterra, having died almost ten years before the petition). The latter conclusion, however, seems improbable in light of most privileges' systematic pairing of 'heirs, successors, and grantees' in the scope of the rights accorded petitioners. The inclusion of the heirs, etc. shows that rights, when granted, were descendible. But without a privilege, there may have been no rights to inherit, hence Diana's silence regarding any authorization from the predecessor painters or their heirs.

What if the derivative work were an update of a work by the same author, already covered by a Papal privilege, as frequently occurred with law books? Did the new privilege apply only to the new matter, or did it cover the whole work, thus effectively prolonging the privilege on the prior version? The advocate Prospero Farinacci (who was a leading criminal lawyer and something of a celebrity in his day, having unsuccessfully defended Beatrice Cenci against charges that she murdered her sexually abusive father) wrote several books on criminal law, some of which had multiple editions. In one case, the petition and the privilege specified that it concerned the additions to prior editions.[73] Nonetheless, it is difficult to tell whether, in the case of new editions and updates, the principle limiting exclusive rights to new matter, a fundamental tenet of modern copyright law, was fully recognized by the Vatican in the sixteenth century. That said, the reference in many privileges to the 'not previously published' status of the work or its edition,[74] suggests that the novelty of the creation or its publication were an important, if not necessarily determinative, consideration.

E. Formalities

The privileges indicate two different types of formal requirements, the first concerning evidence of the privilege, the second concerning its transfer from authors to printers or from one printer to another. Regarding proof of the existence of the privilege, by the middle of the sixteenth century, the grants routinely called for publication of the privilege in the book and/or registration of the privilege with a notary public. Enforcing officials were to give the printed or registered copy the same faith and credit as an original. Some privileges further required, 'so that no one may claim ignorance of the privilege,' that copies of the *breve* be posted in the area of the Campo de' Fiori,[75] which

---

[73] *See* Sec. Brev. Reg. 301 F 19 (Oct. 31, 1600).

[74] *See, e.g.*, ARM XXXIX 46 F 305 (Mar. 24, 1526) (to Giovanni Filoteo Achillini for books for students); Sec. Brev. Reg. 47 F 96 (Feb. 11, 1580) (to the printer Pacifico da Ponte for a book on the Italian language); Sec. Brev. Reg. 120 F 261 (June 3, 1586) (to Girolamo Catena for his biography of Pope Pius V); Sec. Brev. Reg. 69 F 8 (Jan. 13, 1591) (to Vincenzo de Franchis for the decisions of the Council of the Kingdom of Naples).

[75] *See, e.g.*, ARM XLII vol. 44 F 248 (Dec. 1580) (to Raffaele Bonello for a book of previously unpublished sermons in Italian); privileges reprinted in Ligorio, Pirro, DELLE ANTICHITA' DI ROMA : NEL QUALE SI TRATTA DE'CIRCI, THEATRI & ANFITHEATRI: CON LE PARADOSSE DEL MEDESIMO AUTTORE, QUAI CONFUTANO LA COMMUNE OPINIONE SOPRA VARI LUOGHI DELLA CITTA' DI ROMA (Venice, Michele Tramezzino, 1553), BAVat: Cicognara.III.3762, Stamp.Barb.O.VI.98, Stamp.Cappon.V.214 (int.3), Stamp.Cappon.V.585(int.2), Stamp.Chig. V.2139; Giovanni Cassiano, OPERA DI GIOVANNI CASSIANO DELLE COSTITVTIONI ET ORIGINE DE

was the neighborhood where most of the Roman printers and booksellers were located.[76]

Throughout the century, published books and prints usually incorporated in the frontispiece the mention 'con [or cum] privilegio' – or, more specifically, 'cum privilegio summi pont' – or similar indication of the provenance of the privilege(s). Many republished the full text of the Papal privilege in the initial inside pages. Sometimes the last pages carried the notice. Some books, particularly in the first half of the century, proclaimed stronger admonitions, warning that the printer or bookseller who violates the privilege will 'incur horrendous and most grave fines, and will be anathema,'[77] or cautioning that 'REMEMBER: NO CRIME WILL GO UNPUNISHED;'[78] or proclaiming this more fulsome warning:

> And that shameless one who will be so bold as to disrespect the authority of those Princes [including the Pope], he shall forthwith not only be deprived of the commerce of Christians and the faithful and subject to maledictions and ecclesiastic censure [references to the sanction of excommunication], but he will also immediately incur monetary penalties as set out in each of the privileges granted by the above-named powers. And to make it even clearer to foreign and far-flung printers and booksellers, so that each one of them shall have no excuse, the two following privileges [one of them Papal] are reprinted below.[79]

MONACHI, ET DE REMEDIJ & CAUSE DE TUTTI LI UITIJ; DOUE SI RECITANO UENTIQUATTRO RAGIONAMENTI DE I NOSTRI ANTIQUI PADRI, NON MENO DOTTI E BELLI, CHE UTILI & NECESARI A' SAPERE (Venice, Michele Tramezzino, 1563), BAVat: R.G.Storia.IV.8001, Stamp.Barb.D.III.64. Stamp.De.Luca.IV.3028.

[76] See, e.g., LINCOLN, supra note 62, at 17–18; CHRISTOPHER WITCOMBE, PRINT PUBLISHING IN SIXTEENTH-CENTURY ROME 61–67 (2008).

[77] Privilege appearing in RAFFAELLO MAFFEI, DE INSTITUTIONE CHRISTIANA AD LEONEM X (Rome, Giacopo Mazzocchio 1518), BAVat: R.I.II.103.

[78] 'MEMOR NULLAM ESSE SCELERUM IMPUNITATEM,' Notice printed in Francesco Minizio Calvo edition of Hippocrates. COI MEDICORUM OMNIUM (1515), BAVat, Stamp.Barb.J.XI.17. Calvo's privileged publications often included dire warnings of this type. See, e.g., PLUTARCHUS CHAERONEUS, DE CURIOSITATE IDEM DE NUGACITATE INTEPRETE IOANNE LAURENTIO VENETO (1524) BAVat: Stamp.Ross.3895(int.1,4), Stamp.Ross.4147(int.3):

> Whoever you are, whether a printer or a bookseller, beware of printing, during the next 10 years anywhere in the world, these little books and whatever others have been first printed or are going to be printed in the book workshop of Francesco Minizio Calvo or beware of selling these books perhaps printed rashly by others. For the protector of good arts, Clement VII Pontifex Maximus, has forbidden this with a most severe edict and whoever does differently, not only does he wish to be punished with 10 gold pieces for each individual volume but also to be deprived from the commerce of Christians and the most important necessities of life.
> Farewell and see to it, lest you unwillingly create distress for yourself, that you remember well that no crime goes unpunished.

[79] Notice appearing in PIETRO BEMBO, DELLA HISTORIA VENITIANA (Venice 1552); Papal privilege granted to Carlo Gualteruzzo, Pietro Bembo's testamentary executor for various works in Latin and Italian, ARM XLI v 40 F 219 (Dec. 3, 1547), BAVat copies at, inter alia R.G.Storia.IV.1035; R.G.Storia.IV.599; R.I.IV.520; Stamp.Ferr. IV.5954; Stamp.Ferr.IV.6521; Stamp.Ross.5015; Stamp. De.Luca.IV.8429.

F. Transfers of Rights

Regarding licenses or transfers of rights covered by the privileges, the Papal grants generally barred third parties from printing or selling the work without the privilege holder's authorization, and frequently required that the authorization be 'express' and/or in writing.[80] Once granted, privileges acquired the attributes of property because they could be inherited and transferred: privileges routinely referred to the grantee's heirs, rightholders and successors in title. Some of the privileges granted to authors specify that the rights may pass to the printer chosen by the author, or that others may not print without the permission of the author and/or the printer chosen by the author.[81] Together with the high proportion of privileges accorded to authors, these provisions thus establish the position of the author as an initial grantee (though not necessarily as the primary initial grantee) of exclusive rights. Moreover, in the course of the sixteenth century, petitions for privileges sought by printers or third parties other than the author or his heirs, or even the texts of the privileges themselves, increasingly advert to authors' or heirs' authorization to the printer to obtain the privilege. Thus, for example, in 1593 the painter Cesare Ripa sought a privilege for an iconology, but before the privilege issued it appears that Ripa authorized the heirs of the printer Giovanni Gioliti to publish the work. The ensuing *breve* grants the privilege to the printer's heirs 'as far as they have the cause of action from the same Cesare.'[82] Similarly, bestselling law book author Prospero Farinacci complied with his printer's behest to accompany the printer's petition with a letter endorsing the latter's request for a privilege on a new edition of Farinacci's treatise on criminal practice.[83]

Printers' invocations of the authors' endorsement contrast with my earlier observations regarding engravings based on underlying artistic images. I surmised that unless an artist already held a privilege in his work, the engraver could freely reproduce the image and obtain a privilege over the reproduction.[84] But it may be possible to reconcile the propositions (other than chronologically). The printers were seeking privileges over the first publication of the literary or artistic work (or its new editions),

---

[80] *See, e.g.*, Sec. Brev. Reg. 69 F 270 (July 15, 1581) (to Marcello Francolini for his book on canonical hours); Sec. Brev. Reg. 120 F 261 (June 3, 1586) (to Girolamo Catena for his Life of Pius V); Sec. Brev. Reg. 305 F 118 (Jan. 3, 1601) (to Antonio Valli da Todi for his book on bird songs).

[81] *See, e.g.*, ARM XLI vol. 21 F 458 (July 19, 1541) (law book on pensions by Girolamo Giganti, privilege granted to author refers to the printer Giganti will have selected; Sec. Brev. Reg. 278 F 103 (Jan. 8, 1599) (to Giovanni Cecca for medical book; the petition requests 'so that no one may print nor have printed a work of mine on certain medical counsels, except for the printer that I shall have chosen for this work').

[82] Sec. Brev. Reg. 199 F 172r (Jan. 26, 1593) (petition seeks privilege for author, Cesare Ripa, but privilege refers to Ripa's grant of printing rights to the heirs of Giovanni Gioliti); *see also* Sec. Brev. Reg. 285 F 86rv, 87 rv (petition) (July 4, 1599) (author, Spanish theologian Pedro Jerónimo Sánchez de Lizarazo, names licensee, Francesco de Heredia, who should have book printed in author's name).

[83] Sec. Brev. Reg. 301 F 19, 20r (petition) (Oct. 31, 1600). To the same effect, see Sec. Brev. Reg. 347 F 12rv (July 1, 1604), discussed *infra* Part II.H.

[84] *Supra* Part II.D.4.

256 *Research handbook on the history of copyright law*

while the engravers were creating adaptations of already disclosed works.[85] While it would be anachronistic to speak of authors' inherent rights in their works – recall that privileges were issued as a 'special grace' and 'favor' of the Pope, and, moreover, that no work could be published without the assent of the censors – there may have been some inchoate concept of what we would today call the 'right of divulgation,' that is, the author's personal right to determine whether and how first to disclose his work to the public.[86]

G. Remedies and Enforcement

Typical remedies included excommunication, confiscation of the infringing books or prints and typefonts or copper plates, and a fine, whose amount increased over the course of the century, with 500 gold ducats becoming the standard sum. Most often, the fine was to be divided between the Apostolic Chamber (the repository of Vatican finances) and the grantee. In many cases, the fine was to be further shared with the accuser (if a person other than the grantee) and the magistrate charged with enforcing the judgment of infringement.

I have so far found little evidence of enforcement of Papal privileges. For example, while the amount of the fine to be levied increased substantially throughout the sixteenth century (ranging from 25 ducats in the 1520s to over 1000 ducats in the 1590s), I have yet uncovered no evidence of their payment.[87] This does not necessarily mean that the privileges either were ineffective (excommunication, being *latae sententiae*, was automatic and self-enforcing), or were not enforced. (Making the judge a beneficiary of a share of the fine probably favored enforcement as well.) Art historian Victor Plahte Tschudi has contended that contemporary printer-engravers' apprehension that privileges would be enforced accounts for the later sixteenth-century practice of evading privileges by altering works copied from prior, privileged engravings, which provoked a broadening of privileges to prohibit modifications of images, leading in turn to variants departing ever more fancifully from the copied source.[88] But sixteenth-century documents attesting to infringement actions or application of remedies for violations of Papal privileges most likely remain to be found. Art historian Michael Bury, writing about a lawsuit between Roman printer Giulio Franceschini and Nicolas van Aelst, a Flemish printseller working in Rome, described it as the 'only example that I have so far discovered of an attempt to defend a privilege [over engravings] in

---

[85] *Cf.* Sec. Brev. Reg. 290 F 269rv, 270r (petition) (Dec. 7, 1599) (Philippe Thomassin seeks transfer of privilege granted to engraver Aliprando Caprioli; petition and privilege advert to petitioner's subrogation to Caprioli heirs' rights).

[86] *Cf.* HORATIO F. BROWN, THE VENETIAN PRINTING PRESS 79–80, 291 (reprint 1969) (1891) (reproducing and discussing a Venetian decree of 1544–1545 that required proof of author's assent to publication before a license to print would be granted).

[87] MICHELE BASSO, I PRIVILEGI E LE CONSUETUDINI DELLA REV.DA FABBRICA DI SAN PIETRO IN VATICANO (SEC. XVI–XX) (1987). Chapter V, 'Le risorse economiche della RFSP,' does not list fines from violations of privileges as a source of revenue. *See id.* Privileges granted during the first part of the sixteenth century often listed the Fabbrica as the beneficiary of the fine.

[88] Tschudi, *supra* note 61, at 177.

Proto-property in literary and artistic works 257

Italy.'[89] According to Bury, van Aelst's unsold copies were confiscated, and the parties eventually settled.

While in that instance the privilege seems to have been enforced at least in part, the slim record is mixed at best.[90] In 1598, Antwerp printer Jan Moretus complained to the court in Brussels that local rival Jan van Keerberghen was printing a folio missal in violation of Moretus' Papal privilege.[91] According to Plantin-Moretus Museum archivist, Dr. Dirk Imhof, the commissioners decided in December 1598 that Moretus could keep his privilege for the printing of liturgical books but that Van Keerberghen could sell the 1000 copies of his missal that he had already printed.[92] In other words, the local authorities recognized the privilege but declined to give it any effect against past acts. With an inventory of 1000 copies he was free to sell off, it is unlikely van Keerberghen would have felt much bite from the threat of future enforcement of the privilege.

Perhaps worse for the practical impact of Papal privileges was the decision of the Parlement de Paris of March 14, 1583, authorizing the University of Paris to print works of Canon Law, notwithstanding a broad Papal privilege accorded to the Popolo Romano publishing house to publish the *Corpus iuris canonici*.[93] Pius V and Gregory XIII had in fact granted control over many Tridentine documents to the Popolo Romano, then the official Vatican printer, so that even where local printers received territorially restricted Papal privileges carved out or subcontracted from the Popolo Romano's,[94] they were required to obtain the master text from the Popolo Romano in order to ensure fidelity to the text.[95] In his plea to the Parlement on behalf of the university, the advocate Simon Marion challenged the authority of the privilege. First,

---

[89] Michael Bury, *Infringing Privileges and Copying in Rome c. 1600*, 22 PRINT Q. 133–38 (2005).

[90] *See, e.g.*, GRENDLER, *supra* note 39, at 179–81 (detailing unsuccessful attempt in 1573 to enforce a Papal privilege in Venice: 'Since the threat of excommunication had little effect, the papacy was forced to ask the civil government to rule against the financial interests of its own subjects.').

[91] *See, e.g.*, MPM Arch. 117 F 677 (1598 draft of letter from Jan Moretus to authorities in Brussels regarding violation of Papal and local privileges in Missals and breviaries). MPM Arch 157 contains documents, principally from 1628 and later, concerning attempts to enforce Papal and other privileges in the Low Countries and Germany.

[92] MPM Arch. 1179 No. 324 (Dec. 4, 1598) (decision by the Council of Brabant regarding the rights in privileges for liturgical books in dispute between Jan Moretus and Jan Van Keerberghen and Martinus Nutius).

[93] The basic privilege for the *Corpus juris canonici* referenced at ASVat Index 313 F 224r (July 1, 1580), Pro impressoribus pontefici in Tipografia Popoli Romani, prohibitio ne X/m alibi imprimant, No. 349, and published in A. Adversi, *Saggio di un catalogo delle edizioni del 'Decretum Gratiani' posteriori al secolo XVI*, in 6 STUDIA GRATIANA 413–26 (1959). The privilege called into question by Marion is probably that of May 7, 1582, which refers to the privilege of July 1, 1580, and which granted rights for France (*in Regno Gallici*), to Domenico Basa and the Lyon printer Guillaume Rouillé. *See* Sec. Brev. Reg. 52 F 310 (May 7, 1582).

[94] *See, e.g.*, Sec. Brev. Reg. 52 F 312 (May 7, 1582) (confirming Popolo Romano's assignment of rights in the *Corpus juris canonici* for Venice to Giorgio Ferrari and Girolamo Franzini).

[95] *See, e.g.*, Sec. Brev. Reg. 153 F 346 (Aug. 22, 1590) (awarding Antwerp printer Joachim Trogensius a privilege for lower Germany and the Flemish provinces to print illustrated versions

he contended that the true purpose of the Papal privilege was to guarantee the accuracy of the text, rather than to grant an economic advantage to its recipient. Accordingly, permitting the very reliable University of Paris to publish the volumes of canon law might conflict with the words of the privilege, but would honor its spirit.[96] Second, and far more contentiously, Marion called into question the Pope's authority to grant printing privileges for territories beyond his secular control. Marion distinguished between the Pope's extraterritorial spiritual authority and his temporal authority, confined to Papal lands:

> Just as the doctrine of divine things is of purely ecclesiastical authority which extends its effects universally over all the earth but without requiring payment, so the Church, under this pretext, cannot arrogate to itself any privilege concerning the printing of books, because that is of purely temporal law, and entirely subject to the police and secular Princes each in his domain, without in this respect the Pope being able, no more than any others, to exceed the limits of his secular and civil dominion.[97]

The spiritual/temporal distinction suited Marion's client, who wished permission to print, but had no interest in the unrestrained competition in printing the law books that would have ensued had the court denied all effect to the privilege.[98] The report of Marion's plea does not recount the reason for the Parlement's permission to the printers of the University of Paris, hence it is not clear whether the permission was granted in faith of the high quality of printing the University was expected to extend, or because Papal privileges were unenforceable in France.

---

of missals, breviaries and the Mass of the Blessed Virgin Mary, but following the models of the Vatican printing office).

[96] Simon Marion, *Plaidoyé premier, Sur l'impression du Droict Canon, reformé de l'authorité de nostre Sainct Pere le Pape Gregoire xiii* (1583), in PLAIDOYEZ DE MON. SIMON MARION, BARON DE DRUY, CI DEVANT ADVOCAT EN PARLEMENT ET DE PRESENT CONSEILLER DU ROY EN SON CONSEIL D'ESTAT ET SON ADVOCAT GENERAL 1 (Paris, Michel Sonius 1598).

[97] *Id.* at 5. On the dispute regarding the *Corpus Iuris Canonici*, see ANNA MARIA GIORGETTI VICHI, ANNALI DELLA STAMPERIA DEL POPOLO ROMANO 41–52 (1959) describing the book market of late 1500s as:

> an international world of printers, booksellers, agents and men of letters, for whom no barriers of nationality existed, so long they shared a common end; but as soon as an individual national interest predominated, they were ready to retreat behind their national borders, and claim the protection of their national courts in order to void agreements concluded with foreigners, or to elude privileges conceded by the authorities of other countries.

[98] While this pleading is known particularly for having asserted 'that the book be freely printed in this city and by its Booksellers,' Marion, *supra* note 96, at 7, one should observe that Marion was not arguing for a true freedom of printing. In the same pleading, Marion specified that 'the true goal of His Holiness is simply that the book be well printed by approved persons.' *Id.* at 5. And in his third pleading (in 1586), in favor of the maintenance of the privilege on missels and breviairies initially accorded Jacques Kerver and subsequently transferred to the *Compagnie des Usages*, Marion emphasized the importance of restraining the freedom of printing in order to ensure fidelity to the text: 'The privileges which were conferred have served as a good remedy to the former evil that these books, previously so coarsely produced, shine again today in all elegance and integrity.' *Id.*

Proto-property in literary and artistic works 259

H. Justifications for Privileges

The most frequent justifications for the grant of a privilege advert to the labor and expense invested in the work, and the fear that, absent exclusive rights, unscrupulous printers will unfairly reap the fruits of the author's or printer's endeavors.[99] In this respect, the Papal privileges resemble their counterparts elsewhere.[100] The second most often-occurring justification urges the public benefit that will flow from the publication of the work; the Papal privilege variant on this general theme emphasized the importance to Catholic doctrine of disseminating the works in question. Of course, works could be published without a privilege, and perhaps would achieve wider distribution if their authors or printers did not assert control over their circulation.[101] Hence the importance of a third justification: the privilege will not only recognize the effort and expense invested in a work, but will reward the care the author or printer have taken to ensure the work's accuracy (and conformity to Church doctrine).[102] For

---

[99] Based on the privileges and petitions (both of which may individually offer multiple justifications), the most frequent justifications, in descending order of occurrence are:

Justification	Author	Printer	Total
Unfair Competition	121	84	205
Public Benefit	83	61	144
Labor and Expense	66	49	115
Accuracy	17	20	37
Creation of New Matter	24	9	33
'Usual' Privilege	17	10	27
Skill/Merit	14	4	18
Consent of Author to Allow Printer to Print Work	4	10	14
Patronage	7	5	12
Expedite	6	3	9
Approval by Censor	5	2	7
Poverty	4	2	6
Scarcity of Copies	0	5	5
Incentive to Produce Future Works	2	2	4
Prior Privilege	0	5	5
Honor	2	1	3
Total	372	272	644

[100] *See, e.g.,* ARMSTRONG, *supra* note 1, at 78–91 (describing sixteenth-century French privileges).
[101] *See* discussion *infra* Part II.H (regarding Sec. Brev. Reg. 53 F 264 (Nov. 20, 1582) (revocation of privilege to Antonio Lilio)).
[102] Concerns for editions' accuracy and conformity to Church doctrine prevailed in the absence of printing privileges as well. For example, when Gregory XIII partially annulled the printing privilege on the Calendar and Martyrology so that copies might be freely printed and distributed outside of Rome, *see* Sec. Brev. Reg. 53 F 264 (Nov. 20, 1582), discussed *infra* Part II.H, he nonetheless required that the works be printed in conformity with the Roman master

example, Martin Zuria, the nephew and literary executor of the Spanish canon lawyer Martin de Azpilcueta, in 1586 requested a worldwide privilege because he would:

> spare no expense or effort so that the said works would emerge well ordered and well printed with summaries, reference numbers, and other diligent emendations as required, and because booksellers intent only on making money do not bestow the care needed for the perfection of the said works and instead print them in any way they please, not without detriment to the public interest.[103]

Or Giulio Calvi, a cleric of Frascati, who sought a privilege for a compendium of excerpts of the writings of St. Thomas Aquinas; his work is 'very useful to the church of God, and because others might publish it with some additions which do not correspond to the sincere and true doctrine of Aquinas, in the way the petitioner has diligently followed it.'[104] While many petitions stress the utility of accurate versions to scholars, popular piety was an important goal as well, hence appeals not only to the works' benefit to 'all Christians,' but also 'to women and ignorant people.'[105]

But increasing the dissemination of works, whether for popular audiences or of works 'necessary to scholars but hard-to-find and then only in inaccurate editions,' requires 'great expense of thousands of ducats, and it is therefore customary in recompense of so much effort and of such a useful undertaking and so that [the petitioners] can promptly embrace and pursue these efforts, they plead that Your Holiness will deign to accord them the grace of a privilege.'[106] This petition makes explicit two additional justifications implicit in the general emphasis on effort and expense: first, that privileges provide a necessary incentive to the creation or dissemination of useful works, and, second, that those who undertake such endeavors expect to receive a privilege. Many petitions refer to 'the usual' privilege, in the 'usual form' or

---

copy. Similarly, the *breve*, issued the same day, ordering the substitution of the new calendar prohibited the continued use of the old calendars, on pain of confiscation and one hundred ducats fine, in order to 'ensure that the use [of the calendar] remained uncorrupted all over the world and purged of faults and errors.' Sec. Brev. Reg. 96 F 304 (Nov. 20, 1582).

[103] Sec. Brev. Reg. 122 F 528 (petition) (Sept. 3, 1586). For other petitions and concomitant privileges stressing the accuracy of the text, see, for example, Sec. Brev. Reg. 140 F 314 (Apr. 22, 1589) (privilege granted to Gerard Voss for his translations and editions of works of St Ephrem):

> [A]s with the volume that has already been published, so with the remainder that will later be brought into the light through you, so that they might be produced altogether free from error; and so that they might not be perverted by error through some sort of malice or negligence, or changed, altered or corrupted by some addition or removal.

[104] Sec. Brev. Reg. 293 F 113 (Mar. 6, 1600) (Giulio Calvi).
[105] Sec. Brev. Reg. 217 F 216 (petition) (July 21, 1594) (petition of Venetian printer Giovanni Varisco for a privilege on printing 'the mass of the most Blessed Madonna as revised according to the second Council of Trent with Latin and vernacular headings for the greater understanding of women and ignorant persons, which will also be useful to all Christians.').
[106] Sec. Brev. Reg. 355 F 2r (petition) (Feb. 20, 1595) (petition of printer Orazio Colutio for works of fifteenth-century Spanish theologian Alonso Tostado).

with 'the usual' remedies.[107] Some petitions seek to bolster their cause by stressing the author's or petitioner's parlous circumstances. A 1599 plea by the nephew of the author of a book of lives of the Popes affords a particularly colorful example, combining pitiful evocations of poverty with incentive arguments:

> Because ... everything has gone to pay the debts which still have not been fully paid; [petitioner] is left with only four old things, which he is unable to sell, [but] by extending to him the said privilege he will republish [his Uncle's works] as they should be, and the privilege will encourage said petitioner to publish his Uncle's other works and thus he will be partly acquitted of the money lent to his Uncle and of the fatal servitude [engendered by these debts].[108]

Many incentive arguments, particularly when made by authors (although also made by printers in similar terms[109]) may still resonate with modern readers, and three are worth quoting in full. In 1601, a scholar, Ferrante Palazzo, requested a privilege for a sacred tract, described as:

---

[107] *See, e.g.*, Arm. XL 49 F 204rv (Dec. 5, 1534) (Bottom document is a petition of Claudio Tolomei on behalf of Mariano Lenzi for his translation from the Hebrew of Judah Leone Abravanel's *Dialogues of Love* (Rome, 1535). Petitioner states that granting a privilege is 'a usual thing which is granted without difficulty'); Sec. Brev. Reg. 140 F 314 (Apr. 22, 1589) (petition of Gerard Voss for his translation of Church Father St. Ephrem, requesting 'the usual remedies'); Sec. Brev. Reg. 216 F 84rv, 85r (petition) (June 18, 1594) (petition of Venetian printer Domenico Nicolini for new privilege on Tommaso Manrique's commentary on Aquinas, for which Manrique had previously received a privilege, 'such grace and privilege which it is usual to be granted in such cases for such works'); Sec. Brev. Reg. 262 F 284r, 285v (petition) (Sept. 13, 1597) (petition of Jeronimo Gracián de la Madre de Dios for his various theological works, 'begs a privilege in the usual form').

[108] Sec. Brev. Reg. 290 F 106r (petition) (Dec. 13, 1599) (petition of Alfonso Chacòn, author's heir); *see also* Sec. Brev. Reg. 124 F 288r (petition) (Oct. 3, 1586) (petition of Francesco Rocchi, miniaturist, seeking authorization to make wax medallions of the Agnus Dei, 'having to support with his labors and art his poor widowed mother who is extremely poor with no [other] help, and with useless grandchildren); Sec Brev 295 F 174r (petition) (May 15, 1600) (Francisco Rodriguez petitioning for privilege in a book he wrote on the Jubilee because, inter alia, 'of being poor, virtuous, and burdened with family, as is expected of those who serve others, I wish to have some earnings from this little book').

[109] Popes early on recognized the broader benefits that might flow from according particular privileges. *See, e.g.*, a 1520 privilege from Leo X, *in* LEONE BATTISTA ALBERTI, DE PRINCIPE (Rome, Etienne Guilleret 1520) (BAVat: Cicognara.V.384):

> Desiring the following, we freely and favorably decree that we favor with papal affection those keen to print and distribute the new books of approved authors for the common use and advantage of literature/scholarship and the state, and grant them a special license, so that they can enjoy the fruit of the labors undertaken and can rouse others like them by their example to make similar things more eagerly.

Individual printers also urged that according them a privilege for a given work would encourage others to undertake similar labors. *See, e.g.*, Sec. Brev. Reg. 208 F 13r (petition) (Oct. 6, 1593) (Giulio Burchioni, a Roman bookseller, seeking a privilege for publishing Vincenzo Cervio's *Il Trinciante* (a book about food and table manners), argues that granting him the privilege will 'encourage others so that they will be willing to expend their efforts in similar and other useful works').

> a work which will be of no small usefulness to clerics of both sexes, and which shows the path of regular religious observance, and of the [Catholic] Reform, so greatly desired and achieved with the great vigilance and solicitude of Your Holiness. And because the petitioner's work was a labor requiring ten years, and so that others do not reap his labors, he humbly begs Your Blessedness to design to grant him a privilege so that for the next ten years no one may print or have printed the said work, neither in the language in which the author will publish it nor in any other language in which it may be translated, without the permission of the author or of his heirs, all of which he will receive through the grace of Your Holiness, and which will encourage him to bring forth other fruits of his labors for the benefit of the public.[110]

Palazzo's public benefit argument very explicitly ties his claim to the advancement of the Counter Reformation. He bases his claim not only on reward for past labors (and fear of their misappropriation), but also on the enhanced likelihood of his creation of future beneficial works, should the Pope reward the current work with a privilege. The scope of the petition is also worth noting, for it anticipates that the work will be translated. While it does not appear that the author has himself translated or authorized foreign language versions, he could well have expected that foreign language versions would be in prospect, particularly given the proclaimed utility of the work to the Counter Reformation, and therefore he wants to ensure that all future translations come within the scope of his grant of exclusive rights. As formulated in the petition, the rights over future translations are part of the author's incentive package.

In 1598, Fabrizio Mordente, a mathematician from Salerno, sought a privilege for his *Propositions of Geometry*:

> It seems appropriate that those who exert themselves in study for the benefit of others shall also be recognized and rewarded for their efforts at least with prerogatives so that these same people will more willingly bind themselves to greater labors and so that others will be inspired to similar efforts. Wherefore Fabrizio Mordente of Salerno, the most devoted petitioner of Your Holiness, having through long study and great effort over many years, devised seven Geometric Propositions with a corollary, which effort will be most useful to scholars of that profession, and desiring to publish his work for the public benefit, most humbly begs Your Holiness to design to extend him the grace of granting him a privilege by Apostolic Letter, so that for ten years no one else, other than this petitioner and those having permission from him, may have the said work printed nor sold in any place in the Papal States, under penalty of 1000 scudi and with such provisions as in similar cases are usually granted, which this petitioner will receive through the most singular grace and clemency of Your Holiness.[111]

Mordente has generalized the public benefit argument from the virtues of his particular work to the stimulating effects that the grant of a privilege to him will have not only on his own future creativity, but also on other authors. His rhetoric mixes entitlement for his own achievements with broader consequentialist contentions – a combination that prefigures modern copyright law's complementary (and sometimes competing) natural rights and utilitarian rationales.

---

[110] Sec. Brev. Reg. 304 F 273r (petition) (Jan. 23, 1601).
[111] Sec. Brev. Reg. 277 F 290r (petition) (Dec. 30, 1598).

More grandly still, in 1593, Florentine painter and engraver Antonio Tempesta sought a privilege for his large-scale map of Rome, which he anticipated would become a bestseller:

> Antonio Tempesta, Florentine painter, having in this city [Rome] sent out for publication a new map of Rome, of which he is not only the creator, but also has designed and engraved it with his own hand, with much personal expense, effort, and care for many years, and fearing that others may usurp this work from him for themselves by copying it, and consequently gather the fruits of his efforts, therefore approaches Your Holiness and humbly requests him to deign to grant him a special privilege as is usually granted to every creator of new works, so that no one in the Papal States may for ten years print, have printed, or have others make the said work, and [further requests] that all other works that the Petitioner shall in the future create or publish with permission of the superiors [Papal censorship authorities] may enjoy the same Privilege as well so that he may with so much greater willingness attend to and labor every day [to create] new things for the utility of all, and for his own honor, because he will receive the singular grace [privilege] from Your Holiness.[112]

Notwithstanding the necessary acknowledgement that all his works must receive the approval of the censors, and his recognition of the nature of a privilege as a 'particular grace' from the sovereign, Tempesta pushes the themes of authorial entitlement and of incentive/public benefit to argue that a privilege should automatically attach to his future works.[113] Moreover, he makes this claim in the name of his honor as an author.

Tempesta's petition may be the most explicit example of authorship-based sixteenth-century assertions of rights in creative works, but it is consistent with an evolution throughout the century toward grounding claims to privileges in authorship rather than

---

[112] Sec. Brev. Reg. 208 F 76r (petition) (Oct. 13, 1593). While Tempesta's map dominated depictions of Rome until the 1748 Nolli map, the 1593 original version and its 1603 revision did not sell as well as Tempesta had expected, perhaps because the map's very large format was ill-suited to the Jubilee tourist market. *See* STEFANO BORSI, ROMA DI SISTO V: LA PIANTA DI ANTONIO TEMPESTA 1593, at 16–20 (Officina Edizioni, Rome, 1986).

[113] The ensuing privilege does in fact grant Tempesta exclusive rights to print and sell, including in greater or lesser sizes and altered form, not only the map of Rome but also to 'maps of this kind that he intends to devise and engrave of other places and cities.' Sec. Brev. Reg. 208 F 74r (Oct. 13, 1593). While grants covering future works seem infrequent, others did receive such prospective rights. *See* Sec. Brev. Reg. 356 F 91 (Oct. 8, 1596) (cited in Eckhard Leuschner, *The Papal Printing Privilege*, 15 Print Q. 359, 365.n.8 (1998) (granting privilege in engraver Francesco Villamena's future production of religious images). By contrast, extensions of the privilege to cover potential future translations were more common. *See* discussion *supra* text accompanying notes 57–62 and 110; *see also* 1547 privilege to Venetian printer Michele Tramezzino for 'various Latin and Italian works not yet printed, the Italian works translated from Latin and Spanish and French, as well as translations to be made from Italian to those languages,' reported in Pier Silverio Leicht, *L'Editore veneziano Michele Tramezzino ed i suoi privilegi*, in MISCELLANEA DI SCRITTI DI BIBLIOGRAFIA ED ERUDIZIONE IN MEMORIA DI LUIGI FERRARI 357, 365 (1952). A similarly worded privilege appears in another work published by Tramezzino. *See* LUCIO FAUNO, DELLE ANTICHITA DELLA CITTA DI ROMA (rev. ed. 1552) ('various works in Latin and Italian the Italian works translated from the Latin and the Spanish, and vice-versa, heretofore not printed'); Sec. Brev. Reg. 126 F 61rv, 62rv, 64rv (Jan. 7, 1587) (to Girolamo Franzini for LE MERAVIGLIE DELL'ALMA CITTA DI ROMA, ('to print the said narrations as aforesaid or in any other language').

merely in the labor of production and dissemination, labor which printers even more than authors might advance to justify their petitions. A comparison of privileges from the first third of the sixteenth century (during the papacies of Leo X and Clement VII) with petitions from the end of that century and the first years of the seventeenth century (still during the papacy of Clement VIII) illustrates the point. In 1520, Leo X granted Rinaldo Gencia a ten-year privilege to publish and sell Leon Battista Alberti's (1404–1472) *De Principe*. The basis of Gencia's claim was that the previously unpublished work had 'come into his hands' ('*ad manus tuas pervenerit*'), and were others to print the work it would harm Gencia.[114] The privilege does not indicate that Gencia holds any title to the work through Alberti's heirs; rather, it appears that however he obtained the work, the act of publishing it is what entitles him to a privilege granting the exclusive rights to print and sell it. Similarly, in 1531, Roman printer Antonio Blado received a ten-year privilege to print and sell the Italian works of Niccolò Macchiavelli (1469–1527), namely *The Prince*, *The History of Florence* and the *Discourses*; the privilege refers to Blado's labor, expense and fear of unfair competition from other printers.[115] A later Papal decree regarding the same works makes clear that Blado's privilege issued without regard to the works' authorship. The second petitioner, Florentine printer Bernardo Giunti, contends that notwithstanding Antonio Blado's privilege, Giunti should be permitted to print and sell the works in Florence because he has 'the will and consent of the descendants of Niccolo Macchiavelli himself, whose consent the said Antonio at no time ever had ….' The Pope agreed to a carve-out from Blado's privilege:

> For which reason you have humbly made supplication to us that we with regard to apostolic benevolence deem it worthy to grant license to you on the basis of the consent of the descendants of the said late Niccolo that his books of Histories and on the Prince and the Discourses be printed in Florence. We, considering it equitable that the books of the said Niccolo be printed both in his Fatherland and also with respect to the will of his descendants, and also attentive to the fact that the said Antonio has up until now been able to sell for the greater part of the country the books of Discourses which he has printed, and having been persuaded by your supplications herein, concede and grant to you that you are free, by the apostolic authority and legal tenor of those present, to print the books of the Histories and on the Prince and Discourses, and to sell them wherever they have been printed and to keep them for sale, freely and with license and without incursion of any penalty.[116]

By contrast, by the end of the sixteenth century, petitions from printers seeking to publish works by living or recently deceased authors advert specifically to the

---

[114] Privilege, in LEONE BATTISTA ALBERTI, DE PRINCIPE (Rome, Etienne Guilleret 1520) (BAVat: Cicognara.V.384).

[115] *Antonio Blado's Privilege for Machiavelli's Works, Vatican (1531)*, supra note 11 (translation of privilege for NICCOLÒ MACHIAVELLI, HISTORIE FIORNTINE (Venice, Antonio Blado 1532)).

[116] Bernardo Giunta's privilege for Machiavelli's works, ARM. 40 v. 37, F. 297rv, doc. nr 573, (Dec. 20, 1531). For a translation and transcription of this privilege, see *Bernardo Giunta's Privilege for Machiavelli's Work, Vatican (1531)*, PRIMARY SOURCES ON COPYRIGHT (L. Bently & M. Kretschmer eds.), http://www.copyrighthistory.org/record/i_1531a.

authorization of the authors or their heirs.[117] Thus, in 1599, engraver Philippe Thomassin petitioned for a new ten-year privilege following the grant of a privilege to engraver Aliprando Capriolo:

> Said Aliprando having died, his heirs sold to the petitioner all the plates and prints engraved and designed [by Aliprando] of the Story of the Marriage of Isaac and Rebecca, engraved in four and half sheets, and subrogated the petitioner in all their claims and actions.[118]

And in 1604, Prospero Farinacci's Venetian printers, seeking a privilege in a new volume of Farinacci's treatise on criminal practice not only state in their petition that the 'author's consent supports' their request,[119] but also solicit from Farinacci a letter of endorsement to accompany their petition. Farinacci wrote:

> The person who delivers this letter will be the agent of the Giunti, printers and booksellers in Venice, who have printed my most recent work. They have petitioned Our Lord [the Pope] for the Privilege and I have been told that their request has been sent to Your Illustriousness [the Cardinal having jurisdiction over the issuance of *brevi*]. I beg that the *Breve* be issued as soon as possible, for which I not only give my consent by this letter but also I would be much obliged [were the *Breve* granted].[120]

Nonetheless, I do not wish to overstate the role of the author relative to that of printers in the sixteenth-century Papal privileges. For one thing, many printers, especially early in the century when much printing activity focused on producing quality editions of classical authors,[121] may have performed tasks we would today consider 'authorial' such as preparing critical editions and translations.[122] Thus, creation and dissemination may not always have been clearly differentiated.[123] For another, while many petitions and privileges stressed the importance of ensuring the integrity of a text, whether a new work or a new edition of a medieval or Patristic author, the frequent advancement of these claims by printers, and the often liturgical nature of the works at issue, belie contentions that concern for authors' reputations underlay the preoccupation with textual fidelity.

Similarly, the one document I have found that addresses authorship attribution should not be construed as an embryonic 'right of paternity.' The right of 'paternity' safeguards

---

[117] See sources cited *supra* Part II.F.
[118] Sec. Brev. Reg. 290 F 270r (petition) (Dec. 7, 1599). The engravings are based on a painting by Baldassare Peruzzi (d. 1537); there is no mention of any authorization by Peruzzi's heirs. *See* discussion *supra* text accompanying notes 70–72.
[119] Sec. Brev. Reg. 347 F 13r (petition from publisher) (July 1, 1604).
[120] *Id.* at 14r.
[121] *See, e.g.*, BROWN, *supra* note 86, at 40–49; MARTIN LOWRY, THE WORLD OF ALDUS MANUTIUS: BUSINESS AND SCHOLARSHIP IN RENAISSANCE VENICE 20–21 (1979).
[122] Remo Franceschelli makes this point, too. 1 REMO FRANCESCHELLI, TRATTATO DI DIRITTO INDUSTRIALE 347 (1960).
[123] For a discussion of different concepts of authorship in sixteenth-century Italy, see, e.g., Evelyn Lincoln, *Invention, Origin, and Dedication: Republishing Women's Prints in Early Modern Italy*, *in* MAKING AND UNMAKING INTELLECTUAL PROPERTY 339 (Mario Biagioli, Peter Jaszi & Martha Woodmansee eds., 2011).

the personality of the author that inheres in his creations;[124] this petition addresses the authoritativeness of the text, not the creative individuality of its author. The name of the previously unknown author of a commentary on the Psalms of David came to light, and the Procurator General of the Carmelite Order, of which the newly identified author, Michele Aiguani (d. c. 1400) had been a member, petitioned both for a privilege over a new edition of the commentary and to prohibit other printers from continuing to publish the commentary as by an unknown author. The petition asserts that such publication 'would thus greatly harm the demonstrated truth.'[125] The ensuing privilege appears to place great value on the 'truth' because the privilege sets a fine of 1000 ducats for unauthorized printing or selling of the new edition, but 2000 ducats for publishing the work without the author's name.

Finally, the few instances of revocation of privileges suggest that Papal policy favored dissemination of accurately printed works, even over the interests of their creators. Most often, the affected persons are both printers: for example, where a later privilege carved out a particular territory from the scope of the prior grant,[126] or where a prior printer's edition was so error-filled that the Pope revoked the privilege and granted the rights to another printer.[127] Two other revocations, however, illustrate the paramount goal of dissemination. In both cases, it appears that the authors were unable to ensure the works' distribution. In 1603, the Pope rescinded a privilege granted to Spanish Dominican theologian and member of the Congregation of the Index, Miguel Llot de Ribera (1555–1607) for his edition of the summa of canon law by St Raymond (b. 1175, canonized 1601). According to the petition, the books were printed but never distributed because the creditor-printers were never paid. One may infer from this statement that the books had been printed at the author's expense, a common practice in Rome.[128] The petitioner, the Duke of Sessa, asserts that a new bookseller has been found to pay off the creditors, take over the stock of books and sell them, but only if Llot's privilege is transferred to the new bookseller, Giovanni Tallini. Sessa therefore prays that the Pope will 'accord him the grace of granting to said bookseller that same privilege annulling that of Padre Llot, with which in that way satisfaction will be given

---

[124] *See generally* STIG STRÖMHOLM, LE DROIT MORAL DE L'AUTEUR EN DROIT ALLEMAND, FRANÇAIS ET SCANDINAVE (1973).

[125] Sec. Brev. Reg. 315 F 282r (petition) (Dec. 20, 1601).

[126] *See* discussion of the Blado and Giunta privileges, *supra* text accompanying notes 111–113; *see also* Sec. Brev. Reg. 58 F 216rv, 217r (Feb. 1, 1584) (to Charles Pesuot bookseller in Lyon, privilege to print works of Peter Canisius SJ, appears to carve France and Spain out of earlier privilege granted to David Sartorius of Ingolstadt, perhaps the privilege at Sec. Brev. Reg. 39 F 298rv (Aug. 28, 1576)).

[127] *See* Sec. Brev. Reg. 130 F 70rv, 71rv (Aug. 29, 1587) (privilege to Venetian printer Giovanni Giolito di Ferrari for a commentary on the Book of Job, revoking earlier one for same work given to Lyon printer Jean Stratius for poor quality of Lyon edition; Giolito's Venice edition of 1587 includes a foreword by Cardinal Carafa referring to improvements in new edition).

[128] *See, e.g.*, BRIAN RICHARDSON, PRINTERS, WRITERS AND READERS IN RENAISSANCE ITALY 58–59 (1999); GIAN LUDOVICO MASETTI ZANNINI, STAMPATORI E LIBRAI A ROMA NELLA SECONDA META' DEL CINQUECENTO 206–08 (1980).

Proto-property in literary and artistic works 267

to said creditors.'[129] And in 1582, Pope Gregory XIII substantially revoked a privilege granted to Antonio Lilio, mathematician, astronomer and co-creator of the Gregorian calendar, because Lilio had not managed to arrange for the calendars, which were used to determine feast days and liturgical events, to be published throughout the lands subject to the Church. The Pope concluded:

> Now having considered the inconvenience and the harm which such prohibitions [on the printing of the calendar and the martyrology, imposed by the prior grant of a privilege] can bring about because of the great difficulty of sending the quantity of calendars and martyrologies that are needed for the most remote provinces, and that Antonio Lilio is unable to make arrangements with foreign printers as quickly as is needed, we of our own motion remove and annul both prohibitions, and we leave it open to all persons outside the city of Rome freely to print and sell the said calendars and martyrologies without incurring any penalty whatsoever, so long as they are printed in a way which does not compete in any way with the copies printed in Rome. And we wish that everyone who is obliged to say the mass may use those calendars thus printed without any fear whatsoever.[130]

Thus, while the Popes recognized that privileges could stimulate creation and dissemination of publicly beneficial works, they also acknowledged that conferring exclusive rights to print and sell works could undermine the Church's interests if the grantees failed in fact to make the works widely available. In this respect, yet another basic theme of copyright law, the tension between private rights and the broader public interest (or, in the most recent parlance, 'access to culture'), finds a Counter Reformation Roman antecedent.

---

[129] Sec. Brev. Reg. 339 F 45r (petition) (Nov. 5, 1603). Tallini did in fact that year publish the Summa of St. Raymond. *See* RAYMUNDUS DE PEÑAFORT, SUMMA S.TI RAYMUNDI DE PENIAFORT DE POENITENTIA ET MATRIMONIO, CUM GLOSSIS IOANNIS DE FRIBURGO (Rome, Giovanni Tallini 1603) (BAVat: R.I.II.862; Stamp.Barb.G.IV.49.).

[130] *See* Sec. Brev. Reg. 53 F 264rv (Nov. 20, 1582).

13. British colonial and imperial copyright
Catherine Seville

1. INTRODUCTION

The stories underlying the history of British colonial copyright are often stirring and surprising. They are not all yet very well known. Though much groundwork has been done, it is pleasing to see new work continuing to emerge. Research into the increasingly accessible but also challenging sources repays the effort, helping to build a more detailed picture of some fascinating interactions. These shed considerable light on the history of copyright, which is valuable in itself. Additionally, such work helps to deepen our understanding of histories of publishing and authorship, of trade conditions and trading relationships – and of colonial relationships with the empire more generally.

2. COPYRIGHT AND FOREIGN REPRINTS: AN OVERVIEW

Intellectual property rights are territorial in nature, operating within the boundaries of the state in which they are granted. But once a stable political environment permits international travel and commerce, the question of international protection soon arises. This is certainly true of books, which are easily transported, widely sought, and potentially very profitable. The attempt to protect British authors and publishers from competition 'beyond the seas' brought unexpectedly tricky consequences which affected the British empire's relationship with its colonies in far wider spheres than that affecting simply copyright.

Foreign 'piracy' of English books was a regular occurrence from the sixteenth century onwards. But as economic markets widened in the nineteenth century, the problem became more pronounced. British books were routinely republished on the Continent, and sold to British travellers and others. When these reprints began to appear in British book shops, in quantities suggesting that they had been deliberately imported, British authors and publishers became seriously concerned.[1] The German publisher, Bernhard Tauchnitz, was unusual in seeking permission and offering payment for inclusion in his famous reprint series *Collection of British Authors*. Most continental publishers saw no need to pay. American publishers also sought to republish British works as soon as they appeared, and though some would pay for early sheets, many did not. Such payments were in any case made as a matter of courtesy, not of right.

---

[1] William Briggs, *The Law of International Copyright* (Stevens & Haynes 1906) 44–48; James J Barnes, *Authors, Publishers and Politicians* (Routledge & Kegan Paul 1974) 95–105.

Wider popular education led to a growing reading public. During the nineteenth century a mass market for books emerged, and the book trade became an increasingly global one. Although there were various rules excluding foreign reprints from Britain (whether by customs regulations or copyright law), there were serious practical difficulties in policing them. This led to increased pressure for vigorous enforcement of the rules, particularly from publishers. But there was also resistance from the consumer. A British traveller returning from the continent with a neat parcel of Tauchnitz editions collected during the trip, would resent very much its seizure at a British port. This was the more true of a British family returning from public service abroad, to be told that their carefully-acquired educational library was subject to destruction. Although there was considerable pressure for change, the forces often were conflicting. With regard to both copyright law and book markets, the move from a national context to an international context – and later a global context – only intensified these challenges.

Talfourd was the first to try to introduce a British system of international copyright, in his 1837 Copyright Bill.[2] His proposal was that authors outside the British dominions would be able to register copyright in their works, if they named a publisher within the British dominions. Publication would have given the foreign author copyright throughout the British dominions, with remedies as for a native author. However, the government thought this a matter not suitable for legislation from the back benches, and Talfourd dropped the clause. A government measure was passed the following year, giving power to negotiate agreements with other countries offering reciprocal copyright protection to British authors.[3] The power was not used until 1846, but slowly a network of bilateral agreements grew within Europe. These delivered some improvement for those to whom they applied, but they were only a qualified success. They offered reciprocal protection, but not harmonisation. There were gaps in the schemes of protection, and often differences of approach. The United Kingdom's copyright law offered less than many continental systems, and it was not easy to reach agreement with the countries whose publishing markets offered the most significant threats to the British book trade.[4]

The 1842 Copyright Act therefore responded to the demands of British authors and publishers for more rigorous measures to punish those importing foreign reprints, whether into Britain or her colonies. This had unexpected practical consequences, which led to a great deal of bad feeling, particularly in the North American colonies. An attempt was made to repair this damage, via the 1847 Foreign Reprints Act. But this in turn had further unanticipated effects, sharply revealed in Canada, which were very problematic in other ways. America's geographical position, the history of her relationship with Britain, and her resolutely protectionist stance, all contributed to the complexity of the situation. The issues smouldered without resolution for decades. When the Berne conference produced a draft of an international copyright union in the 1880s, Britain was put in an uncomfortable position. Although she very much wished

---

[2] Copyright Bill 1837, s 11, Schedule 4. See Catherine Seville, *Literary Copyright Reform in Early Victorian England* (CUP 1999) 237–38.
[3] International Copyright Act 1838 (1 & 2 Vict c 59). Replaced by the International Copyright Act 1844 (5 & 6 Vict c 47).
[4] See Catherine Seville, *The Internationalisation of Copyright Law* (CUP 2006) 23.

to support an international copyright convention, without the support of her colonies – particularly the self-governing dominions – this was politically very challenging. Addressing the necessary questions would inevitably raise simmering constitutional questions, which had proved intractable in the past. In addition, the prospect of any agreement with America regarding international copyright, desirable though that would be, seemed a remote possibility (although this was achieved in 1891).

Britain did in the end sign the Berne Convention for her colonies and possessions, but the route even to that point was tough. The 1908 Berlin revision of Berne created further serious political difficulties. Again, a compromise was reached which allowed Britain to sign the Berlin revision, but it was by no means a complete settlement of the issues. The new convention entailed significant changes to British law. Desirable in many ways though it was to have one single imperial copyright law running throughout Britain and her dominions, the various colonies had good reasons to have positions which were not identical to Britain's. The 1911 Imperial Copyright Act shows clearly the marks of these differences. It is these histories which this chapter explores.

3. BRITISH COLONIAL AND IMPERIAL COPYRIGHT

3.1 The Early British Copyright Acts and their Coverage

The Statute of Anne 1710 did not specify explicitly where it applied, but it was clearly Great Britain.[5] The 1801 Copyright Act extended British copyright law to Ireland, following the 1800 Act of Union. Infringement could be committed in any part of the United Kingdom, or 'in any part of the British Dominions *in Europe*'. Actions could be brought in any court of record where the infringement had occurred.[6] Under the 1814 Copyright Act, in a significant extension, infringement could take place in any part of the United Kingdom of Great Britain and Ireland, including the Isles of Man, Jersey and Guernsey, and now '*any other part* of the British Dominions'.[7] The 1842 Copyright Act carefully defined the British Dominions 'to mean and include all parts of the United Kingdom of Great Britain and Ireland, the island of Jersey and Guernsey, all parts of the East and West Indies, and all the colonies, settlements, and possessions of the Crown which now are or hereafter may be acquired'.[8]

3.2 The 1842 Copyright Act and its Impact on the Colonies

The 1842 Copyright Act brought important changes in domestic copyright law. It also strengthened the sanctions against foreign reprints. No treaties had been signed under

---

[5] Statute of Anne 1710 (8 Anne c 19).
[6] Copyright Act 1801 (41 Geo III c 107) s 1. For the effect on the Irish book trade see Ronan Deazley, 'Commentary on *Copyright Act* 1801' in *Primary Sources on Copyright (1450–1900)*, Lionel Bently & Martin Kretschmer (eds), available at <www.copyrighthistory.org> ('*Primary Sources*').
[7] Copyright Act 1814 (54 Geo III c 156), s 4.
[8] Copyright Act 1842 (5 & 6 Vict c 45), s 2.

the 1838 International Copyright Act, and the efforts to control the import of foreign reprints using existing powers and the various customs acts had not done enough to satisfy the publishing trade. As a result of the new powers, the 1842 Act brought unexpected and momentous consequences for both the book trade and copyright law in the British colonies.

The Act gave protection to works first composed, printed or published in the UK, throughout the British dominions. There were substantial new penalties for importing into the UK, or any other part of the British dominions, copyright books for sale or hire which had been reprinted outside the British dominions.[9] The intention was to clamp down on foreign reprints, whether from continental Europe or America. UK publishers were anxious to protect not only their local market, but also British colonial markets, which they saw as part of their rightful territory. Under the mercantile system, the expectation was that mother country should have the exclusive right to sell products – particularly manufactured goods. However, the practical effect of the 1842 Act on British colonies was significant. The North American possessions in particular were accustomed to plentiful supplies of cheap American reprints of British copyright works. Their particular geographic, economic and political circumstances meant that the new rules bit especially hard. These difficulties, and the failure to address them adequately, led to a deep-seated resentment. This in turn affected profoundly what could be done to change British copyright law, particularly in the international context, for many decades.

The first printing press in what would become British North America arrived in 1751. There were 19 by the end of the Napoleonic Wars. The European population in 1761 was about 76,000, though it had grown to 722,000 by 1821. Literacy rates were low, and the inhabitants were comparatively poor. So in the early decades of the nineteenth century, the local book trade focused on bookselling rather than publishing, and imported much of its stock from Britain and America. Trade expanded as communications improved in the 1830s, and the newspaper press fostered a growing readership. There was a ready supply of cheap American books and newspapers, which often reprinted British copyright works.[10] Canada passed its own local Copyright Act in 1832.[11] The Canadian market was now worth fighting for, and British authors and publishers were keen to reclaim it from the Americans. It was thought that the

---

[9] Copyright Act 1842, s 17. Infringing books were forfeited; they were to be seized and destroyed by customs and excise officers. On conviction by local justices of the peace, the fine was £10, plus double the value of the imported book. £5 of the penalty was to go to the officer who had seized the book, and the rest to the proprietor of the copyright. Pirated copies which escaped this procedure were deemed to be the property of the copyright proprietor, who could sue for recovery, or damages for detention or conversion: Copyright Act 1842, s 23.

[10] See Michael Winship, *American Literary Publication in the Mid-nineteenth Century* (CUP 1995).

[11] 2 Will IV c 53. For detailed work on the history of Canadian Copyright see: Sara Bannerman, *The Struggle for Canadian Copyright* (UBC Press 2013); Pierre-Emmanuel Moyse, 'Colonial Copyright Redux: 1709 v. 1832', in Lionel Bently, Uma Suthersanen, Paul Torremans (eds), *Global Copyright* (Edward Elgar 2010); Pierre-Emmanuel Moyse, 'Canadian Colonial Copyright: The Colony Strikes Back' in Ysolde Gendreau (ed), *An Emerging Intellectual Property Paradigm, Perspectives from Canada* (Edward Elgar 2008).

provisions in the 1842 Act would achieve this. Additionally, the 1842 Customs Act allowed proprietors to prohibit all imports of foreign reprints (not just those for sale or hire) by giving notice in writing to the Commissioners of Customs. These too were subject to seizure and destruction.[12]

Both new Acts took effect in the British colonies on 1 July 1843. William Gladstone, President of the Board of Trade, who had crafted the customs reforms, saw clearly that the British book trade would have to change its habits if it wished to supply Canadian readers. The home market was carefully controlled by the publishers. British customers would pay for high-quality paper and fine bindings. Novels were commonly published first as 'three-deckers' – a luxurious three-volume format, which cost a guinea and a half. A single volume edition usually did not follow for over a year, and even then cost perhaps six shillings. Those unable or unwilling to pay these prices could obtain popular books from circulating libraries and reading clubs, within a short time of publication. Although British books could be sent to Canada, there were significant difficulties. Freight consignment was very slow, and often impossible in winter. Books sent by post were charged at letter rate, making this method prohibitively expensive.

The American alternatives were therefore far more appealing to Canadian customers. Reprints of both classic and new books were available very cheaply. The differences in market prices are striking.[13] The so-called 'mammoth' American newspapers (such as *Brother Jonathan* and the *New World*) cost only a few cents, and would regularly offer entire novels as supplements for 50c or less. Shrewdly, Gladstone warned the leading British publisher John Murray III that the changes to the law would be of little effect unless new and popular British books were made available at an affordable price. If this were to be done, Gladstone predicted 'a great extension of our book-trade as well as much advantage to literature', but otherwise, 'we shall relapse ... into the old state of things: the law will be first evaded and then relaxed.'[14]

Murray, and several other traditional British publishers, did make some effort to fill the lacuna which the ban on foreign reprints was intended to create. By August 1843 Murray had developed a plan for 'Mr Murray's Colonial and Home Library'. The prospectus explained that Parliament had recently ordered the 'rigid and entire exclusion' from the colonies of foreign pirated editions. Murray promised to produce a series of 'attractive and useful works, by approved authors, at a rate which shall place them within reach of the means not only of the colonists, but also of a large portion of the less wealthy classes at home'. It was to be a 'Library for the Empire'.[15] However, the series was not a great success, and was discontinued after only six years. The paternalistic and didactic ambitions of the prospectus were also expressed in the list of

---

[12] 5 & 6 Vict c 47, ss 24–25. See Seville, *Internationalisation* (n 4) 48.

[13] For some examples see the Report of a Select Committee of the Nova Scotia Assembly, 11 March 1845, Appendix A: available in *Colonial Correspondence 1872*: 309, xliii, 277 (a return prepared by the Colonial Office in July 1872 for the House of Commons, which had requested all correspondence with the Canadian Government relating to the Foreign Reprints Act), 4.

[14] Gladstone to John Murray (6 February 1843): Samuel Smiles, *Memoir and Correspondence of the Late John Murray* vol II (Routledge/Thoemmes Press 1977) 501.

[15] Simon Nowell-Smith, *International Copyright Law and the Publisher in the Reign of Queen Victoria* (Clarendon Press 1968) 29–31; Angus Fraser, 'John Murray's Colonial and Home Library' (1997) 91 The Papers of the Bibliographical Society of America 339.

nearly 50 titles published. With a strong bias towards travel and history, less than a third were new titles. The improving tone of the catalogue did not much appeal to Colonial readers, who wanted novelty and light reading. In general, there was little point in British publishers offering comparatively expensive editions of titles which had been widely reprinted and in local circulation for a considerable time. These marketing decisions demonstrate their desire to maintain control of colonial markets. They were reluctant to cede anything to local publishers, and anxious at the prospect of cheap colonial editions returning home to undercut their lucrative British market.[16]

British publishers thus failed to respond to the colonial demand for affordable, appealing reading matter. Additionally, the exclusionary measures proved ineffective. The notification measure in the 1842 Customs Act was intended to prohibit importation of foreign reprints of notified titles throughout the Dominions. Through poor drafting, only importation into the UK was covered. Although this was corrected in 1845, the system was fundamentally unworkable. Copyright proprietors were required to notify the Commissioners of Customs of titles that they wished to be excluded. Consolidated lists were drawn up and circulated to the colonies every three months. In the interim, copies could easily be obtained from America, and it was in practice impossible to tell when a particular copy had arrived in Canada.

3.3 Towards the 1847 Foreign Reprints Act

In Canada, the issues surrounding foreign reprints received attention in various governmental bodies. A Committee of the Canadian House of Commons observed that the import of British books had not increased under the 1842 regime, because the majority of the population could not afford to enjoy 'English books at English prices'. It noted that American reprints were openly sold, and that 'a law so repugnant to public feeling cannot and will not be enforced'. It concluded that American reprints should be freely admissible into the Province.[17] Similar points were made by a Select Committee of Nova Scotia, in a detailed and frank report on the current system. It proposed that the import of American reprints should be allowed on payment of a protective duty. The Board of Trade's initial response was that the policy 'of protecting the authors of this country in their right of property in their own productions' was a principle of justice not expediency. Shortly afterwards, the Lieutenant Governor of New Brunswick wrote to Gladstone (then briefly Colonial Secretary) arguing that British copyright should not extend to the North American Provinces, unless any Provincial legislature chose to adopt it by local Act. Gladstone sent a strongly worded letter to his former colleagues at the Board of Trade. His view was that dissatisfaction in the North American Provinces would increase unless 'vigorous and decided efforts' were made by the publishers to respond to the points made.[18]

The Board of Trade reversed its stance, and proposed that the Colonial legislatures should frame regulations appropriate to local conditions. It expressed a confidence that the colonies would be 'animated by a sense of justice, which will lead them to

---

[16] Barnes, *Authors* (n 1) 142–47.
[17] *Athenaeum*, 16 March 1844, 249.
[18] *Colonial Correspondence 1872* (n 13) 2, 8–10.

co-operate with this country in endeavouring to protect the author from the fraudulent appropriation of the fruits of the labours upon which he is often entirely dependent.' Lord Grey, the then Colonial Secretary, expressed the identical confidence when he wrote to the Governors of the North American colonies shortly afterwards. There was little detail in what was outlined. The local legislatures would be given the 'duty and responsibility' of passing such laws as they deemed proper 'for securing both the rights of authors and the interests of the public'.[19] The 1847 Foreign Reprints Act followed swiftly, and its passage was uncontroversial. It provided that where a British possession had passed an Act 'sufficient for the purpose of securing to British authors reasonable protection within such possession', it could be approved by Order in Council. The Order in Council and the relevant Colonial Act had to be laid before both Houses of Parliament for approval. The normal prohibitions against admission of foreign reprints could then be suspended within the relevant colony. It was fairly obvious from the context and previous correspondence that the Government envisaged a local duty, presumably payable to the copyright proprietor. However, the Imperial Act (which was very brief) did not state this explicitly. A number of colonies did, over time, pass suitable acts as envisaged, which were duly approved.[20]

The Canadian Copyright Act 1847 was passed within a week of the passage of the Foreign Reprints Act, but made no reference to it. It was expressed as an entirely independent measure, which extended the existing local copyright protection to British authors who 'printed and published' their works in the Province.[21] This offered no obvious advantage to British authors, who would already have copyright protection in Canada under the (Imperial) Copyright Act of 1842. The Board of Trade seems not to have spotted the problematic aspects of the Canadian Act, and approved it – though did not organise the necessary Order in Council. The Canadian Government eventually made a formal request for this. Having consulted the London publishers, the Board of Trade refused the request, noting that the effect of the Canadian Act would be to remove existing protection without offering any compensation.[22] In North America acceptable local Acts were passed first by Nova Scotia and New Brunswick (March 1848), then Prince Edward Island (May 1848), Newfoundland (April 1849), and finally Canada (August 1850).

The system proved a fiasco. The various procedures were complicated and burdensome, even for those applying them with goodwill – which many were not. The sums collected were insignificant, and the more so because collection costs were deducted. Official Customs returns in 1856 reported that a total of merely £687 10s 8½d had

---

[19] Ibid 12–14.
[20] A return from the Colonial Office prepared for the House of Commons (25 August 1857) lists the Orders in Council issued, and the due provision made: session II, 303, xxviii, 113. The colonies and possessions listed (by date of the Order) were; New Brunswick, Nova Scotia, Prince Edward Island, Barbados, Bermuda, Bahamas, Newfoundland, St Christopher, Antigua, St Lucia, Canada, British Guiana, St Vincent, Mauritius, Grenada, Jamaica, Cape of Good Hope, Nevis, Natal.
[21] An Act to Extend the Provincial Copyright Act to Persons Resident in the United Kingdom (10 Vict c 28), referring to the Canadian Copyright Act 1832 (2 Will IV c 53).
[22] Barnes, *Authors* (n 1) 149–50.

been collected, in a five-year period.[23] The following year a Parliamentary return showed a similar pattern.[24] In 1858 Canada imposed a protective 10 per cent duty on the import of British books, explicitly exempting American books because they already paid a 12.5 per cent duty under the local act of 1850. Since the underlying prices of American books were so much cheaper than British books, however, the sums payable in duty on American books were tiny. American editions of American and British works poured into Canada, for the use of a growing and enthusiastic Canadian readership. British authors and publishers gained very little in return for the loss of their rights. Canadian publishers were resentful that the financial rewards went largely to the American publishers, as Canadian publishers were still unable to reprint British copyright works without permission. Thus, many of those directly interested in the Canadian book trade were very dissatisfied with the prevailing legal situation. However, wider international considerations – notably the British desire for a copyright treaty with America – prevented any progress towards a resolution of these difficulties for decades. Discontent therefore rumbled on.

3.4 Copyright in the Dominion of Canada

In 1867 Canada became the British Empire's first self-governing dominion. Copyright was stated to be within the legislative authority of the Canadian Parliament.[25] The Crown's function in assenting to enactments of the Dominion Parliament was delegated to the Governor General, though assent could be withheld if legislation conflicted with Imperial law. Such legislation was then reserved for consideration in Westminster. In 1868 a new Canadian Copyright Act was passed, imposing a duty on foreign reprints of British copyright works.[26] Its provisions were essentially the same as before (under the act of 1850), but it was accompanied by a request to extend the 1847 Foreign Reprints Act to cover colonial reprints also. Imperial copyright law, as it stood, prohibited publication in the British Dominions by anyone except the copyright proprietor. The Canadian Minister of Finance, John Rose, sent a memorandum to the Colonial Office, proposing that Canadian publishers be licensed to reprint British copyright works, on payment of a duty for the benefit of the author. He argued that this would benefit not only Canadian publishers and the Canadian reading public, but also British authors.[27] This, in effect, would have amounted to a compulsory licensing scheme.

The Board of Trade's response (to the Colonial Office) indicated a strong reluctance to see any local change to the basic model of copyright, as it would be likely to lead to further fragmentation within the British colonies. The Board of Trade also saw wider and particular dangers if this concession were to be made in Canada. There had been recent efforts to resume negotiations towards an Anglo-American copyright treaty, which, if successful, would secure for British authors the prize of copyright protection in the US. Yet if Canadian publishers were entitled to reprint British works for a

---

[23] See Seville, *Internationalisation* (n 4) 88–89.
[24] *Publishers' Circular* (15 September 1857).
[25] British North America Act 1867, s 91.
[26] Canadian Copyright Act 1868 (31 Vict c 54).
[27] *Colonial Correspondence 1872* (n 13) 8–10.

royalty, cheap Canadian editions were very likely to circulate illegally in the US, competing with and undercutting the legitimate trade. This prospect, it was thought, would deter the US from concluding a treaty at all.[28]

Another important consideration was the recent decision of the House of Lords in *Routledge v Low*.[29] The case concerned the well-known American novelist, Maria Cummins. She had posted the manuscript of her new novel *Haunted Hearts* to her London publishers, Sampson Low. She had then travelled to Canada for the time of publication. The copyright had been assigned to Sampson Low, who published a two-volume edition for 16s. Routledge issued an unauthorised 2s edition. The resulting legal dispute raised important questions concerning the conditions governing entitlement to copyright. The House of Lords ruled that publication had to be in the UK, but that protection extended throughout the British Dominions. An alien friend was entitled to copyright if publishing an original work in the UK, so long as at the time of publication he was residing, however temporarily, somewhere in the British Dominions. It made no difference if the place of residence was in a British colony with an independent legislature (such as Canada), under whose local laws he would have no entitlement to copyright.

The practical consequences of this decision for Canada were significant. Publication in a colony did not give copyright throughout the British dominions, giving authors little reason to publish in Canada, unless they were content to sell to a purely local market. Also, whereas an American author could obtain imperial copyright simply by taking a trip to Canada at the time of publication in the UK, a Canadian publishing in Canada did not obtain imperial copyright. Both of these outcomes were perceived as most inequitable, from a Canadian point of view. The Board of Trade privately admitted the injustice of the prevailing arrangements (both the ineffectiveness of the Foreign Reprints Act, and the local inequalities), but thought it impossible to resolve matters comprehensively and satisfactorily with Canada unless the US could be included in any solution. Its recommendation was that Rose's licensing proposal be rejected, therefore, but that the imbalance regarding place of publication should be addressed promptly.[30]

A similar scheme, privately negotiated, also received serious consideration. In 1869 the British publisher F R Daldy travelled to Canada to discuss with Rose what came to be known as the 'Canadian Proposals'. The plan was to repeal the 1868 Canadian Act authorising the import of foreign reprints. Instead there would be a new act, permitting the reprinting of British copyright works in Canada by licensed printers, on payment of a 10 per cent duty. The scheme was carefully crafted to address the interests of British publishers, in particular by prohibiting the import of these new colonial editions into the UK, whether by post or otherwise. The proposed act would have determined automatically if a copyright treaty were to be concluded between the UK and the US. The Canadian Proposals were discussed at a meeting in London in 1870, attended by many of the leading publishers – including Daldy. Although there was a strand of opinion strongly supportive of the proposals, there was a large majority against the

---

[28] Ibid 16–21. Seville, *Internationalisation* (n 4) 90–91.
[29] (1868) LR 3 HL 100.
[30] Seville, *Internationalisation* (n 4) 93–94.

scheme. The meeting passed two resolutions, which were sent to Gladstone (now Prime Minister). One sought the urgent repeal of the 1847 Foreign Reprints Act. The other emphasised the injustice to colonial authors and publishers which resulted from *Routledge v Low*.[31]

The Board of Trade had already drafted a bill to address the publication point, giving the same rights to all works, whether published in the UK or a colony.[32] The Board of Trade sent the publishers' resolutions to the Colonial Office, noting that their support for the principle of the draft bill would be to some extent dependent on repeal of the 1847 Act. Although acknowledging that there would be fierce opposition from the North American colonies, the Board of Trade nevertheless concluded that it was difficult to defend the continuance of the Act. The Foreign Secretary was careful not to couple the issues explicitly. He wrote to the Governors of colonies asking for their views on the draft Bill. He wrote to the same Governors again the following day, asking whether they had any objection to repeal of the 1847 Act. Most colonies were either content, or explained that so few books of value were published there that they were largely indifferent. The Canadian response stood out therefore: although content with the proposed bill, there would be 'very strong objections' to the repeal of the 1847 Act.[33]

The Canadian printing industry, particularly newspaper publishing, was now thriving. Further expansion into book printing was attractive, so the Canadian focus was on supporting local printing, by permitting licensed reprints. In addition to viewing this as an unwarranted appropriation of their property, British publishers were understandably sceptical of likely compliance in payment of duty. Canadian publishers were becoming increasingly provocative; publishing entire works in newspapers, and claiming the right to do so under the combined authority of section 91 of the 1867 British North America Act and the Canadian Copyright Act. This claim had no legal merit, because the power given to establish local copyright did not affect the prohibition in the 1842 Copyright Act. But there was reluctance to drive home the point by bringing legal action, because of the strength of local feeling. Another notorious case was that of the successful Montreal publisher, John Lovell, who had sought to test the limits of the law in a number of well-publicised cases. In 1871 he built a well-equipped printing factory at Rouses Point, just within the US. In Montreal, he set up the type and stereotyped a number of British copyright works, including Macaulay's *Lays of Ancient Rome*. The plates were taken to Rouses Point, where the editions were printed off. The books were reimported into Canada, where they were bound and sold. Counsel's opinion was sought, but this was not an infringement. Lovell was not 'printing' within the British dominions, for the purposes of section 15 of the 1842 Act. Although section 17 prohibited import for sale, this had been suspended in Canada by Order in Council: the duty imposed by the 1868 Canadian Copyright Act had been deemed to afford sufficient protection to authors for the purposes of the Foreign Reprints Act.[34]

---

[31] Ibid 94–96.
[32] *Colonial Correspondence* (n 13) 41–42.
[33] Seville, *Internationalisation* (n 4) 96–97.
[34] Ibid 98–100.

British publishers and authors were exasperated by the situation, and frustrated by lack of progress towards legislative change – both with Canada and the US. This led to the establishment of the Copyright Association; an association of 'authors, publishers, and others interested in copyright property'. The leading publishers were all involved, including Murray, Longman, Macmillan, Routledge and Daldy. A number of authors were also on its Committee, including Sir Charles Trevelyan. Trevelyan was a senior British civil servant, with considerable experience of colonial administration. He was a close friend of Macaulay's, married to his sister, and after Macaulay's death was responsible for managing his copyrights. He supported the Canadian Proposals, thinking 12½ per cent on actual sales more advantageous than a notional customs duty. Longman was Trevelyan's publisher, as he had been Macaulay's. He was strongly opposed to any compulsory licensing scheme, and was infuriated by Lovell's republication of Macaulay's *Lays*. Trevelyan, however, remained supportive of the Canadian Proposals, which he thought a 'just and liberal offer'. He was critical of the publishers for refusing it, and thought their interests were distinct from those of copyright holders. Longman and Trevelyan both published their letters on the subject.[35]

In 1872 the Canadian Government lost patience, and introduced a bill to allow the reprinting and publication in Canada of British works, by licence of the Governor General. Reprints were to be registered, and would be subject to a 12½ per cent duty. Importation of foreign reprints of such titles into Canada was to be prohibited. The Act was passed by the Canadian Parliament in June. As it clearly conflicted with imperial copyright law, it required the sanction of the British Government.[36] Both the Board of Trade and the Copyright Association worked on a number of alternative draft bills, but there was significant disagreement on their terms. The publishers were willing to see the publication point addressed, but remained hostile to compulsory licensing, particularly if colonial reprints were to be permitted to enter the UK. Sir Thomas Farrer, Permanent Secretary of the Board of Trade, and a believer in cheap books, was more willing to concede a licensing scheme. In July 1873 a draft bill (often referred to as 'Lord Kimberley's Bill'), which would have established an elaborate licensing scheme, was circulated to all colonial Governors for comment. Many colonies remained essentially indifferent to these issues, and it was the Canadian response that seemed likely to be key. This was delayed by a change of government, when John A Macdonald was displaced by the more liberal Alexander Mackenzie as Canadian premier. Eventually, a report arrived which welcomed the publication proposal, but noted the conflicting views and interests with respect to reprints. It also thought the procedures very 'intricate', and likely to lead to litigation. Its conclusion was that the change to the rules on publication was the only one needed urgently.[37]

Although certain Canadian publishers remained aggressively in favour of compulsory licensing of British copyright works, a more moderate group of publishers acknowledged that this would lead to competitive underselling, with little return for any of those interested. After further informal diplomacy, both in Britain and in Canada, the

---

[35] Ibid 99, 102.
[36] See return by the Colonial Office to the House of Commons April 1875: 144, l.1, 635.
[37] All the responses are in C-1067, *Correspondence respecting Colonial Copyright* (1874) xliv, 539. Seville, *Internationalisation* (n 4) 103–106.

bones of a solution were agreed. The 1875 Canadian Copyright Act gave Canadian copyright to works published or produced in Canada, even if previously published elsewhere. Foreign editions of these works could not be imported into Canada. This measure (at least in theory) made local publication more attractive to British authors, but did not allow republication without consent, so did not conflict with imperial copyright. It had been a condition of the diplomatic agreement that Canadian reprints of British works could not be imported into the UK, and this was duly provided for.[38] Nevertheless, it was only a partial solution, if a solution at all. The publication question remained unaddressed, and many Canadians remained dissatisfied that there was no right to republish. There were strands of Canadian opinion arguing that copyright fell within the exclusive powers of the Dominion under the British North America Act, and that the 1875 Act had the effect of repealing the 1842 Copyright Act so far as Canada was concerned. In 1876 the Toronto publishers, Belford Bros, reprinted Samuel Smiles' *Thrift* without permission. A test case was brought by the Copyright Association. The publishers lost, and the Toronto Court of Appeal upheld the first instance decision.[39] Nevertheless, *Smiles v Belford* did not put an end to this debate.

3.5 The Royal Commission on Copyright and Colonial Issues

Many arguments and many people familiar from this earlier history reappeared in the work of the Royal Commission on copyright. It was appointed in 1875, and took an immense amount of evidence during a period of over a year, from May 1876.[40] Trevelyan was the first witness examined, and he returned to his disagreement with Longman regarding the Canadian Proposals. His interest in the supply of cheap books to promote national education dated from his time as a civil servant in India, working with the colonial government. When appointed to the Treasury, he had become aware of the accounts rendered to the Treasury by each colony under the Foreign Reprints Act. Trevelyan had them analysed, and concluded that the system was a 'ludicrous failure'. The sums he received for Macaulay's works (whose copyrights he now owned) were trivial. He was in favour of cheap books, sold as widely as possible. His view was that it did not matter to authors who published their books, and that their interests were different from those of the publishers. He advocated a compulsory licence scheme with a 10 or 12½ per cent royalty, for all of the colonies.[41] Longman was also asked again about the possibilities, and whether, from a public point of view, a compulsory licence scheme would not be an advantage to the people of the colonies. His dry response was: 'I daresay that it would. It would be an advantage if each of them had a leg of mutton given him for nothing.'[42]

---

[38] Canadian Copyright Act 1875 (38 Vict c 88). Approved by 38 & 39 Vict c 53. See also Seville, *Internationalisation* (n 4) 106–09; Bannerman, *Struggle for Canadian Copyright* (n 11) ch 3.
[39] *Smiles v Belford* 1 Upper Canada Reports 436.
[40] *Royal Commission on Copyright: Minutes of Evidence*, London (1878) '*RC-Evidence*'.
[41] Ibid 1–4.
[42] Ibid 25.

Sir Thomas Farrer gave a great deal of evidence, on a number of occasions. Although speaking as Permanent Secretary of the Board of Trade, he clearly had taken a great personal interest in the matter, and had a strong point of view; he was a committed free trader. In his evidence were many examples intended to demonstrate that local reprints were far cheaper than English editions. He also objected strongly to the prohibition on import of reprinted Canadian editions into the UK. Overall, Farrer characterised the accumulated copyright laws as a system of objectionable protectionism which favoured English publishers, but was of doubtful benefit to English authors, and left the English reading public paying a needlessly high price. He favoured a right of republication with a royalty.[43] Although Farrer's views were strongly held and strongly presented, he proved somewhat vulnerable under careful cross-examination from several of the Commissioners (particularly Trollope and Froude). He was on occasion found to be confident rather than perfectly accurate in his answers to questions, and came across as something of a zealot for cheap books.[44] These debates on matters of principle continued in the public press after the Royal Commission had reported.[45]

Colonial copyright was carefully addressed in the Commission's Report. The existing law was described as 'anomalous and unsatisfactory' in important respects. One firm recommendation was that publication anywhere in the dominions should secure copyright throughout the dominions. With regard to more the general problem, it was 'highly desirable that the literature of this country be placed within easy reach of the colonies'.[46] Colonies should remain free to pass local colonial copyright acts if they saw fit. Additionally, however, the Commissioners suggested a licensing scheme which would allow republication subject to a royalty where there was no adequate provision for supply of a particular work in a particular colony.[47] The Commissioners acknowledged the pressure to repeal the Foreign Reprints Act entirely, but felt that this would be unfair to the smaller colonies. The suggestion was that far more stringent procedures be instituted for collection of duties under the Act. Foreign reprints of a particular work would not be permitted to enter a colony where a local edition had been issued under local copyright law, or where there was other adequate provision for supply, or where the proposed new licensing scheme had been invoked for that particular title. This plan would have had the effect of curtailing the breadth of operation of the Foreign Reprints Act very considerably, and also of encouraging copyright owners to consider local reprinting very seriously. Farrer's evidence was scrupulously reviewed, particularly regarding the import of colonial editions into the UK. Nevertheless, the Commissioners were not convinced by his arguments. They felt that their own proposals would better meet the grievances of colonial readers.[48]

Even though the problems and grievances regarding colonial copyright were perfectly apparent, and the need for change was clear, it was in practice extremely difficult

---

[43] Ibid 208–10.
[44] Ibid 260–74, 316–25.
[45] Seville, *Internationalisation* (n 4) 273–75.
[46] C-2036, *Commissioners' Report*, London (1878) '*RC-Report*'. *RC-Report* 182–84.
[47] Methods of doing this had been suggested in Daldy's evidence, for example: *RC-Evidence* (n 40) 54.
[48] *RC-Report* 203–26. Suggestions regarding the formalities of registration and deposit were also made: *RC-Report* (n 46) 227–32.

3.6 The Berne Convention and Beyond

The text of the Berne Convention was finalised at the 1885 Conference. The arrangement was that it would be communicated to the countries of the world, and that the convention would be signed formally at a further conference in September 1886. Amendments to British law were required before the Berne Convention could be signed by her. Many – including the Board of Trade – saw this as an ideal opportunity to overhaul and consolidate the entire copyright system, but the Foreign Office decided that this was too much to take on, particularly given the time constraints.[49] The ambitions of the 1886 International Copyright Bill were, therefore, very limited. The necessary amendments to domestic law were made, and the opportunity was taken to make some quite small but practically significant changes to the position regarding the colonies. The publication rule was finally altered, so that publication anywhere in the dominions brought copyright throughout the empire. Local registration was permitted, and deposit in the UK was no longer required.[50] The bill passed through Parliament without difficulty.

The point of real political delicacy was whether Britain should sign the Berne Convention on behalf of her colonies and possessions. The Foreign Office was very keen that all the colonies should remain under the broad umbrella of imperial copyright, but also emphasised that 'nothing could be further from our wishes than to go beyond the mind of the Colonies themselves in this matter.' The bill had been drafted 'with the utmost desire to meet what we believe to be their requirements and wishes, and to secure their co-operation', but it was made clear that if India or any colony 'should wish to stand aloof' that wish would be complied with. Every colony was therefore asked whether it wished to join the Berne Union, whether it approved of the publication clause, whether it wished to retain legislative power with respect to local copyright, and whether it wished to see a clause which allowed a particular colony to be excepted. All of the responses indicated willingness to join the Union, and Britain was able to sign the Berne Convention for all her colonies and possessions, as the Foreign Office had hoped.[51] The British Government's signature was subject to a protocol reserving the power to announce the denunciation of any of the self-governing colonies. Ratifications were exchanged in September 1887, and the Convention entered into effect on 5 December 1887.

For most colonies, membership of the Berne Union was a positive step which brought much of value, particularly to their authors and copyright holders. Canada's

---

[49] Seville, *Internationalisation* (n 4) 69–71.
[50] International Copyright Act 1886, s 8.
[51] See Foreign Office to Colonial Office, 8 April 1886: *Further Correspondence respecting the formation on an International Copyright Union* (continuing Switzerland No. 1 (1886): C-4606). The responses are here, also. For the context of Canada's assent see Bannerman, *Struggle for Canadian Copyright* (n 11) ch 4.

situation was different. She was now obliged to respect the rights of copyright holders throughout the Berne Union. Yet Canada's geographic neighbour, the US, was under no such obligation. Both US and Canadian publishers were publishing in the same language, for a similar reading public. It was impossible to prevent the flow of cheap American reprints into Canadian territory, and Canadian publishers could not compete on price. Although Canadian authors and publishers now had the advantage of copyright throughout the Berne Union, this did not amount to even remotely equivalent compensation.

Canadian discontent therefore continued to simmer. In 1888 the Canadian Government announced its plans to implement the Berne Convention. The proposal included abandoning the local manufacturing clause, and protest erupted. A Canadian Copyright Association was formed, and in 1889 it submitted a memorial (with 2000 signatories) to the Canadian Privy Council. It expressed the view that bringing Canada within the Berne Union would have 'the most disastrous consequences' for the printing and manufacturing trades, and would deprive the Canadian reading public of access to cheap reprints of British copyright works. It proposed various different changes to the Canadian Copyright Act, including a strict local manufacturing clause, and a compulsory licence scheme covering all works which did not have Canadian copyright. Only those domiciled in Canada or the British possessions, or citizens of countries having an international copyright treaty with the UK, would have been entitled to Canadian copyright.[52] In May 1889 a Canadian Act was passed, very much on these lines.[53] The Act was sent to the Governor-General for assent, accompanied by a long report in support from Sir John Thompson, the Minister of Justice. There was also a request that the British Government should announce Canada's denunciation of the Berne Convention. Copyright had become an issue symbolising Canadian desire for independence, self-determination, and self-governance.[54]

The British Government was dismayed at the prospect of Canada withdrawing from the Berne Union, particularly so soon after its creation. Unwilling to assent to the Act, and unable to find an alternative way forward, the British Government did nothing, hoping that an agreement with America might help resolve the situation. In March 1891 the American Copyright Act was passed, giving American copyright to foreigners from countries offering equivalent privileges, subject to a manufacturing clause. The American President accepted the Prime Minister's assurance that copyright could be obtained by publication anywhere in the British dominions, and the Act came into force as regards Britain on 1 July 1891. However, beneficial as this arrangement was to British copyright holders, in practice, the Canadian book industry remained at a disadvantage. Americans were now entitled to imperial copyright if they published anywhere in the dominions. In contrast, American copyright was granted to foreigners only if the work was manufactured in the US. This further heightened the Canadian publishing industry's competitive disadvantage vis-à-vis the American book trade. In

---

[52] *Publishers' Circular* (1 March 1889) 215–17. See also Bannerman, *Struggle for Canadian Copyright* (n 11) ch 5.

[53] 52 Vict c 29. This and much of the correspondence that followed can be found in C-7783, *Correspondence on the Subject of the Law of Copyright in Canada* lxx.59 (1895).

[54] Seville, *Internationalisation* (n 4) 115–17.

protest, Canada refused to allow US citizens to register for Canadian copyright, on the grounds that the arrangement with the Americans was not an international copyright treaty. This was an embarrassment to the British Government, even though imperial copyright would still apply.[55]

Consideration of possible alternative legislative solutions continued, and the British Government began to contemplate conceding some sort of licensing scheme. The author Hall Caine travelled to Canada to discuss one draft bill, which did include a licensing scheme, although not an unlimited or compulsory one. This bill, again, was never passed. Further initiatives were attempted, but the problem remained intractable: the various interest groups were still a long way apart; the US still insisted on its manufacturing clause, and the constitutional questions of principle remained. No legislative action was taken in Canada regarding copyright until the 1900 Fisher Act, which offered further incentives for those with imperial copyright to licence publication in Canada.[56] But the Canadian House of Commons made it clear that its claim to exclusive jurisdiction on copyright remained firm.[57]

Fuel was poured on this fire by *Imperial Book Co v Black* (1905). The British publishers Adam & Charles Black sued the Imperial Book Co for importing reprints of their *Encyclopaedia Britannica* into Canada. Imperial alleged defects in A & C Black's registration of its imperial copyright. It also raised the old constitutional argument that, since the 1867 British North America Act, the Canadian Parliament had the authority to legislate for Canada regarding copyright, including the power to override earlier Imperial Acts. Previously, in *Smiles v Belford* (1876) the Toronto Court of Appeal had rejected these arguments. This time the matter reached the Supreme Court of Canada, which agreed that Black's registration was defective, and, more importantly, emphasised that they expressed no opinion one way or the other as to whether *Smiles v Belford* was rightly decided.[58] Matters concerning Canadian copyright thus remained unsettled.

3.7 The Berlin Revision of the Berne Convention

The 1908 Berlin revision of the Berne Convention brought significant changes; including the abolition of formalities, and the principle of a life plus 50-year term. Britain's relationship with her colonies was again tested by this initiative. A number of private bills had attempted to reform imperial copyright since the Royal Commission, but none had succeeded. The British Government had been unenthusiastic about these efforts, a major concern being the position of the colonies. The Board of Trade knew that any comprehensive legislation would involve repeal of the 1842 Copyright Act, which would inevitably raise constitutional questions regarding Britain's right to legislate for the self-governing colonies. The fear was that major legislative changes would conflict with Berne obligations, and undermine the arrangement with the US. The prospect of the Berlin conference in 1908 meant that these questions could no

---

[55] Ibid 118–20.
[56] 63 & 64 Vict c 25.
[57] Seville, *Internationalisation* (n 4) 121–35.
[58] *Imperial Book Co v Black* (1905) 35 SCR 488.

longer be avoided. The British Government agreed to send delegates, but, though in principle broadly supportive of the proposed changes, made no public commitment to implement them. The Colonial Office warned the Board of Trade privately that it would be impossible to avoid raising constitutional questions: although in September 1907 it wrote to the colonies to say that plans for comprehensive legislation had been abandoned for the present, and that only a restricted list of necessary amendments would be proceeded with.[59]

At the Berlin Conference the following month, the British delegates spoke of Great Britain's 'very serious difficulties' in connection with the subject of copyright, 'especially as regards harmonizing the interests of the mother country with those of the great self-Governing colonies.' Without resolution of these difficulties, the delegates explained, the British Government would not be able to implement any significant alterations in the Berne Convention.[60] Although broadly content with the outcome of the Berlin Conference, the British Government proceeded very cautiously. A Departmental Committee was appointed, chaired by Lord Gorrell, to advise on the legislation necessary to give effect to the changes. The Gorrell Committee's report was strongly in favour of ratification of the Berlin Act, and also expressed the view that 'so far as possible, there should be one law throughout the Empire'.[61] The support of the colonies was essential. The Board of Trade had from the outset envisaged an Imperial Copyright Conference to discuss matters, and this was organised for May 1910, in London.

The Imperial Conference was chaired by Sir Sydney Buxton, President of the Board of Trade. He set out the British Government's view that it was extremely important to achieve uniformity of legislation on international copyright throughout the British Empire, and, so far as possible, throughout the world. The Australian delegation had proposed a way through the constitutional question, which was that an Act covering all the essential aspects of Imperial copyright law should be passed by the Imperial Parliament, following consultation with the dominions.[62] Although that Act would be stated to extend to all the British possessions, every self-governing dominion would be free to opt out and make its own laws. This would, however, bring only local copyright, and the benefits of imperial and international copyright would be lost entirely. After considerable discussion, these proposals did eventually lead to a way forward. Canada objected to an Imperial Act applying to the self-governing dominions without the consent of their legislature. Canada was also unhappy with Article 6 of the Berlin Convention, which granted Union privileges to anyone publishing within the Union, even if their home state was not a signatory. This (if conceded) would allow American authors to obtain the extensive Berne privileges simply by publishing in Canada, while the US maintained a protectionist policy regarding its own national copyright. There was considerable sympathy for this dislike of Article 6: Buxton revealed that the Board

---

[59] Seville, *Internationalisation* (n 4) 136–37.
[60] Cd 4467, Miscellaneous No 2, Correspondence respecting the revised convention of Berne (1909) 3.
[61] Cd 4976, Report of the Committee on the Law of Copyright (1909). Seville, *Internationalisation* (n 4) 290–91.
[62] Very helpfully on the Australian position see Robert Burrell, 'Copyright Reform in the Early Twentieth Century: The View from Australia' (2006) 27 J Leg Hist 239.

of Trade had already considered ratifying the Berlin Convention subject to a reservation on this point. There was agreement on a life-plus term, but disagreement on the 50-year aspect of it. Concerns were expressed that this term was too long, and would leave the public vulnerable to high prices and lack of supply. Overall, the delegates showed a willingness to agree where possible, but also a mutual respect for different positions.[63]

In its recommendations, the *Memorandum of the Proceedings* set out a new framework for constitutional relations respecting copyright. It recommended that the Berlin Convention should be ratified by the Imperial Government on behalf of the Empire, and that reservations should be kept to a minimum. But no ratification was to be made on behalf of a self-governing dominion until its assent to that was received, and provision was to be made for each self-governing dominion's separate withdrawal. The Conference also recommended the passage of an Imperial Act providing for a uniform copyright law throughout the Empire. But again the Act was not to extend to a self-governing dominion without a declaration from its legislature, and subsequent withdrawal was to be provided for. A dominion was to be able to pass its own legislation 'substantially identical' to the Imperial Act, and still be treated as if it were a dominion to which the Act extended for the purposes of rights conferred by it. To address the Article 6 issue, it was also recommended that copyright should only be granted to authors who were British subjects or bona fide residents in the Empire (subject to extension to other countries by Order in Council). The resolution regarding term sought to guarantee the public's reasonable requirements regarding supply and price of copyright works.[64]

3.8 The 1911 Copyright Act

The 1911 Imperial Copyright Act was shaped in response to the Conference's resolutions. Although it achieved much, it could not achieve everything. One important difference was the proposed reservation from Article 6 of the Berlin Convention. Although the British Government had certainly intended to do as the Conference had agreed, British publishers and authors resisted this strategy, as likely to lead to the loss of American copyright. There was an attempt to negotiate a reservation solely for the dominions, since Canada was adamant that she could not adhere to the Berlin Convention otherwise, and that her denunciation of Berne would follow inevitably. But France and Germany objected strongly that such a reservation would infringe one of the original principles of the Union. The solution eventually adopted was a Protocol permitting the government of a Union country to restrict protection in the case of authors from non-Union countries which failed to protect the authors of that Union country 'in an adequate manner'.[65]

---

[63] Seville, *Internationalisation* (n 4) 139–41.
[64] Cd 5272, Imperial Copyright Conference, 1910: Memorandum of the Proceedings. Seville, *Internationalisation* (n 4) 141–42.
[65] This Additional Protocol was signed in Berne in March 1914. Canada was the only country ever to take advantage of this concession.

The 1911 Act came into force on 1 July 1912.[66] The colonies (other than the self-governing dominions), the protectorates and Cyprus could be treated as parts of the UK for the purposes of the Act.[67] The self-governing dominions were not covered by the Act unless a particular dominion's legislature had declared the Act to be in force there. Newfoundland, the Commonwealth of Australia and the Union of South Africa did adopt the 1911 Act.[68] Canada and New Zealand adopted local Acts on similar lines to the 1911 Imperial Act. The Secretary of State had the power to certify that a self-governing dominion's legislation granted British subjects resident elsewhere than in that dominion, or non-British subjects resident in parts of the dominion to which the Act extended, rights within that dominion which were substantially identical to those conferred by the 1911 Act. If this was done, so long as that legislation remained in force, the dominion would be treated as if it were a dominion to which the 1911 Act extended.[69] The New Zealand Act of 1913 satisfied these conditions, in conjunction with an Order of the Executive Council made under that Act on 27 March 2013. This was certified in that year. A Canadian Act satisfying these conditions was eventually passed in 1921, and this was certified in 1923.[70] The UK gave notice of Canada's accession to the Berne Union on 1 January 1924. Canada restricted protection in respect of US works under the terms of the 1914 Additional Protocol.[71]

The 1911 Act did consolidate copyright law within the British Empire to a significant extent. But at that same moment, imperial copyright law also acknowledged that it had to accommodate elements of difference. The way in which those freedoms were expressed in national laws still warrants investigation. Aspects of the 1911 Act can still be found in many contemporary national laws, but re-expressed within – and as only an element of – each legislative context. In consequence, the nature of its legacy is not easy to distil in brief form.

4. REALMS IN PROSPECT

As this chapter shows, much work has been done to unearth some of the histories of British colonial and imperial copyright. Yet their interest is such that more digging would seem likely to be rewarding. As just one example, India's relationship with imperial copyright raises weighty questions. Responding to the consultation regarding the Berne Convention, the Governor-General of India confirmed that India wished to enter the Berne Union, and also explained that India wished to retain the power to pass

---

[66] 1 & 2 Geo V c 46.
[67] The colonies were covered by s 25, the protectorates by s 28.
[68] Limited modifications and additions were permitted, solely to accommodate procedure, remedies, and local conditions: s 25(1). Newfoundland adopted the Act without modification. Certain modifications were made by Australia and South Africa. Notification of South Africa's accession to the Berlin Convention was given on 1 May 1920.
[69] s 25(2) and s 26(3).
[70] 11–12 Geo V c 24.
[71] In accordance with ss 13, 14, 27 of the 1921 Canadian Copyright Act. Sam Ricketson, *The Berne Convention for the Protection of Literary and Artistic Works: 1886–1985* (Kluwer 1987) 97–98.

local copyright legislation. The Governor-General acknowledged concerns that this might lead to anomalies, but expressed the view that India could be trusted to conform to the general principles of English legislation. He wished, nevertheless, to highlight 'peculiarities in connection with the copyright in Indian books which may require special treatment'.[72] By this he meant India's vernacular literature, and balancing its protection with facilitating access to it. Bently's excellent work in this area deserves further development.[73] Also significant is the fact that the change to the publication rule in the 1886 Act (publication anywhere in the dominions now giving imperial copyright) bolstered Macmillan's decision to launch a Colonial Library in that year, building on the firm's success in the education market in India. Sir Frederick Macmillan described it to Thomas Hardy as 'a kind of Colonial Tauchnitz Library', intended both to meet demand in India for cheap books and to keep out American reprints.[74] The interaction between the law and the book trade (of all sorts) in India could with benefit be further researched. The same is true of other colonies. *A Shifting Empire*, a welcome collection of pieces written to mark the centenary of the 1911 Imperial Act, offers enormously useful underpinning for this sort of research, and other tempting places to start.[75]

At a more general level, the British concern when implementing the Berne Convention to achieve, so far as possible, a single imperial copyright law has already been noted. Given the contemporary debates regarding harmonisation, it would perhaps be instructive to examine the assumptions that lay beneath that strong sense of pressure. Plainly, trade interests, competition, and political considerations of all kinds still affect policy making in the field of international copyright. In terms of local resentment of what can be seen as high-handed imposition of self-interested norms, modern parallels with colonial responses to imperial power can easily be drawn. But care must be taken in interpreting and applying these. International copyright law, then as now, expresses political compromise as well as principle. Looking from a broader perspective than that of simply copyright, Bently has noted the unplanned nature of British Colonial intellectual property law. In his valuable survey he also asks intriguing questions about the differences in the ways the various intellectual property rights developed.[76] Bently's own careful work underlines the importance of rigorous discipline when transporting the beguiling stories unfolded in this chapter to a post-imperial age. Colonial histories may well offer useful insights into the making of current international intellectual property norms. It is nevertheless important to remember that contemporary realms have their own geographies.

---

[72] Governor-General of India in Council to the Colonial Secretary, 19 June 1886: C-4606 Switzerland No 2 (1886) 16.

[73] Lionel Bently, 'Copyright, Translations, and Relations Between Britain and India in the Nineteenth and Early Twentieth Centuries' (2007) 82 Chi-Kent L Rev 1181.

[74] 31 May 1886, quoted in Priya Joshi, 'The Novel, the Colonial Library, and India' in Swapan Chakravorty and Abhijit Gupta (eds), *Print Areas: Book History in India* (Permanent Black 2004) 17, 24.

[75] Uma Suthersanen and Ysolde Gendreau (eds), *A Shifting Empire: 100 Years of the Copyright Act 1911* (Edward Elgar 2013).

[76] Lionel Bently, 'The "Extraordinary Multiplicity" of Intellectual Property Laws in the British Colonies in the Nineteenth Century' (2011) 12 Theo Inq L 161.

14. The public international law of copyright and related rights
Sam Ricketson

1. INTRODUCTION

Much of the historical scholarship concerned with copyright deals with developments at the national level. Such work is inevitably both rewarding and illuminating – knowledge of the past is always helpful in understanding the present, or at the very least explaining how we got here, and in providing pointers to possible future courses of action. But this historical perspective also has a wider international context that is helpful for the obtaining of a fuller understanding: even the most superficial account of national copyright laws will reveal the significant effect that international obligations have had upon the development of those laws and the broader policies underlying them.

The purpose of the present chapter is to provide a brief sketch of this wider horizon, and to alert readers to the wealth of historical materials and scholarship that can be drawn upon in reaching a workable understanding of the dimensions of international copyright protection and its interaction with national laws. It therefore begins with a short overview of the public international law landscape, in particular the gradual move from bilateralism to multilateralism, with some commentary on the way in which treaty obligations are to be interpreted and applied at the national level. It then moves to a consideration of the wide range of sources and other materials that are available for scholars working in this area, including the preparatory materials of revision conferences, international journals and commentaries, national government records, and the proceedings of relevant non-governmental international organizations. These, and other, materials give rise to a number of further research questions that would repay further investigation, and I end by listing some of the more intriguing of these.

Some of what is discussed in this chapter will be known, perhaps well known, to readers. But while we may be familiar with the main roads, we often pass the side roads and laneways without looking far down them. Much of the international copyright landscape is like that – well-known in outline but with the detail often quite hidden. The following account therefore aims to cast some light on these unknown areas and to highlight their utility to contemporary copyright scholars and policymakers.

2. A BRIEF SKETCH OF THE PUBLIC INTERNATIONAL LAW LANDSCAPE

Literary and artistic works, like birds, know no frontiers, particularly where common languages are used on both sides. It is notable that, while national laws on authors' rights outside the United Kingdom did not really develop until the end of the eighteenth century, it took less than 40 years before authors protected in one country became concerned about what was happening to their works across the border.[1] Works in English published in the UK were freely reprinted in the US and elsewhere; works in French had a similar circulation across continental Europe where French was the common language among the educated classes; while for German speakers, there was no 'Germany' at this stage, but just a collection of German states within which works in German could move with ease within the one linguistic pool.[2] This 'leakage' across borders was not limited to books, but extended to works of art, as well as to public performances of musical and dramatic works – as to the last, there were considerable differences between national laws as to what rights were actually protected, while protection against unauthorized performances occurring outside a composer's own country was very uncertain.[3]

The obvious solution to minimise these undesired spillover effects would be for the governments of the countries concerned to enter into agreements under which each undertakes to protect the works of other's authors. This presupposes, of course, that governments are so inclined, and this, in turn, is a socio-political question that will depend largely upon the relative economic importance of the interests concerned – in this case, authors, or more precisely, authors and their publishers, producers and other promoters – and the skill of their representatives in lobbying their respective governments to take action. In some countries, such as France, authors and artists had a central importance in the national psyche and governments were more inclined to act. In other instances, governments might well recognize the importance of their local creators but lacked the necessary heft to achieve an agreement for protection elsewhere.[4] Thus, for many years, the UK sought unsuccessfully to achieve an arrangement with the US for the protection of British authors in that country, but ran up against strong congressional resistance based largely, it seems, upon arguments that free access

---

[1] For a good general overview, see SP Ladas, *The International Protection of Literary and Artistic Property* (The MacMillan Company 1938) vol 1, ch 2; See further Sam Ricketson and Jane Ginsburg, *International Copyright and Neighbouring Rights: The Berne Convention and Beyond* (OUP 2006) ch 1; W Briggs, *The Law of International Copyright* (Stevens & Haynes 1906) ch 1, 2.

[2] See further Ladas (n 1) 23 ff; Briggs (n 1) ch 3. The situation in the German states is vividly illustrated in the allegorical copper plate of 1781 of Daniel Chodowiecki which is reproduced on the cover of Ronan Deazley, Martin Kretschmer and Lionel Bently (eds), *Privilege and Property: Essays on the History of Copyright* (OpenBook Publishers 2010). This was entitled 'Works of Darkness. A Contribution to the History of the Book Trade in German. Presented Allegorically for the Benefit of and as a Warning to All Honest Booksellers.' It shows unauthorized reprinters and original publishers as highwaymen and their victims while the Goddess of Justice sleeps nearby.

[3] See further Ladas (n 1) vol 1, 42–43.

[4] It would be mistaken to single out just France in this respect. Other countries, such as Italy, Belgium and Germany, were equally strong advocates for protection in particular cases where there was a strong national cultural tradition, as, for example, in the case of Italy and choreographic works: see further Ladas (n 1) vol 1, 220–22.

to works in English was necessary for the purposes of a rapidly developing country – an argument that has a peculiarly modern resonance.[5]

Accordingly, protection beyond national borders for literary and artistic works developed in a piecemeal and uneven way during the course of the nineteenth century. It focussed on bilateral agreements between individual states, with France being the main leader, followed by the UK, Italy and other principal European states.[6] By 1883 (the year of the first Berne diplomatic conference), there was a complex web of bilateral treaties in place that required careful study by lawyers seeking to advise their clients on what protection they might obtain abroad. The bases for these agreements varied considerably: from simple requirements to accord national treatment to agreements based on material reciprocity, and agreements falling somewhere in between. Not all covered the same subject matter, and, in many instances, compliance with formalities in both countries (registration, deposit of copies, etc) was necessary. In legal terms, protection of literary and artistic works outside one's own country therefore remained unpredictable or simply not available in important potential markets.

It was against this background that moves towards a multilateral agreement on authors' rights began. In this regard, it must be noted that multilateralism was a trend that only began to develop more generally in the second half of the nineteenth century, beginning with international arrangements in the areas of communications (posts and telegraphs), weights and measures, customs, railways and navigation, to be followed by agreements in relation to the treatment of prisoners of war and the conduct of war.[7] The protection of authors' rights, and likewise the rights of inventors and merchants, can be seen as part of this wider, internationally focussed, awareness, which was also reflected in the proliferation of 'universal exhibitions' that began with the Great Exhibition in London in 1851 and that were followed by a series of similar exhibitions in many of the major European and North American capitals.[8] While in the case of authors' and artists' rights there were broader arguments in favour of establishing some kind of 'universal law' of literary and artistic property,[9] these efforts soon became focussed on

---

[5] See further JJ Barnes, *Authors, Publishers and Politicians: The Quest for an Anglo-American Copyright Agreement 1815–1854* (Routledge & Kegan Paul 1974); and, for a more contemporary account, see Eaton S Drone, *A Treatise on the Law of Intellectual Property in Intellectual Productions in Great Britain and the United States* (Little, Brown and Company 1879) 92–96.

[6] See further Ricketson and Ginsburg (n 1) [1.29]–[1.41]; Ladas (n 1) vol 1, ch 3.

[7] For a useful review, see Paul Reinsch, 'International Unions and their Administration' [1907] 1 AJIL 579, 579.

[8] Between 1851 and 1900, there were at least 13 international or universal exhibitions held in the following cities (not all Old World): London (1851), Paris (1855), London (1862), Paris (1867), Vienna (1873), Philadelphia (1876), Paris (1878), Melbourne (1880), Barcelona (1888), Paris (1889), Chicago (1893), Brussels (1897), and Paris (1900): Bureau International des Expositions at <http://www.bie-paris.org/site/en/expos/about-expos/expo-categories/world-expos>. There were other 'international exhibitions' that were held during this period, although not included in this 'official' list: New York (1853), Porto (1865), Sydney (1879), Antwerp (1885), and Omaha (1898): see further, 'Five Men' (*New York World's Fair 1964/1965*) at <http://www.nywf64.com/building04.html>.

[9] Beginning with the famous Brussels literary and artistic congress held in 1858: see further Edouard Romberg, *Compte-rendu des travaux du congrès de la propriété littéraire et artistique*

practical outcomes that were spearheaded by authors' and artists' associations. In particular, the role of the International Literary and Artistic Association ('ALAI') was crucial, and it was out of the proceedings of this organisation that the first draft of a multilateral instrument emerged in 1882.[10] This was taken up by sympathetic elements in the Swiss Government which, in the following year, convoked the first of the diplomatic conferences that led finally to the adoption of the Berne Convention on the Protection of Literary and Artistic Works in 1886. From an initial text based primarily on national treatment, this has evolved through successive revisions to embody a solid corpus of basic norms of protection that each Berne Union country undertakes to apply to the authors (and their successors in title) of each other Union country, and which remain, even today, fully appropriate to the hard copy environment. The achievement here is considerable, although the issue of application in the digital networked environment has only been partially addressed with the adoption of the WIPO Copyright Treaty 1996 and the enforceability of Berne norms (historically a vexed issue) depends upon the mechanism of the WTO dispute settlement procedures applied through the TRIPS Agreement.

Multilateralism has not been confined to the adoption and subsequent evolution of the Berne Convention which is now an agreement with nearly universal membership. Perhaps largely forgotten today are the various Pan-American copyright conventions that were formulated in the early part of the twentieth century,[11] to say nothing of the Universal Copyright Convention that, for a significant period, played a critical role in providing a bridge between Berne Union countries and those retaining registration systems.[12] Multilateral agreements have also extended international protection in the area of related rights, beginning with the Rome Convention 1961[13] and continuing through to the WIPO Performers and Phonograms Convention in 1996 and the Beijing Audio-Visual Performers Treaty in 2012.

The ascendancy of multilateral treaty making has now been eroded to some extent by a return to bilateral and regional agreements, notably through free trade agreements that have extended protection in significant respects, most importantly with respect to matters of duration. Also increasingly important has been the influence of human rights obligations that arise under other international instruments adopted following the Second World War. There are profound social, economic and cultural factors that underpin and explain this long and interesting history of international copyright relations, but there are also challenging and important legal issues involved, in particular the role of treaties and their interpretation and application in national law.

(Flateau 1859); Alcide Darras, *Du droit des auteurs et des artistes dans les rapports internationaux* (Rousseau 1887) 518 ff.

[10] See further *Association littéraire et artistique internationale – Son histoire. Ses travaux* (1878–1889) (Bibliothèque Chaconac 1889) 2 ff; Ricketson and Ginsburg (n 1) [2.10].

[11] See further Ladas (n 1) vol 1, Part Third ('Inter-American Copyright Conventions').

[12] See further Arpad Bogsch, *The Law of Copyright under the Universal Copyright Convention* (3rd rev edn, Sijthoff, Leyden, and Bowker 1972); TR Kupferman and M Foner, *Universal Copyright Convention Analyzed* (Federal Legal Publications 1955); Ricketson and Ginsburg (n 1) [18.02]–[18.40].

[13] International Convention for the protection of Performers, Producers of Phonograms and Broadcasting Organisations 1961 (the 'Rome Convention').

292 *Research handbook on the history of copyright law*

Treaties are a fundamental component of what may be called the public international law of copyright, and this brings us, then, to a consideration of the sources and materials that are available to aid in the process of their interpretation and application. This is not just a matter of academic interest, but is of vital concern to national policy makers and legislators who are seeking to formulate national laws that conform with the relevant international requirements while giving effect to their own economic and social programmes.

3. TREATIES AND THEIR INTERPRETATION

Treaties, in fact, are the principal source of binding obligations under public international law, although over time it is possible that other sources, such as the decisions of WTO Panels and WIPO 'soft law' recommendations, will begin to emerge as further significant sources. But even these will have treaties as their starting point, and therefore treaties will be the focus of our discussion.

Historical materials are critical in the interpretation of international treaty provisions. In the most obvious instances of resolving issues of ambiguity, obscurity, absurdity or unreasonableness, recourse to such materials is specifically allowed under both Article 32 of the Vienna Convention on the Law of Treaties ('VCLT') and customary international law. But such recourse is also permitted, and indeed, desirable, to 'confirm' any interpretation that has been reached in relation to the 'primary task' of interpretation under Article 31, as well as being relevant to establishing the 'context' of the treaty as part of that primary task. Treaty interpretation is, in the understated words of the International Law Commission, 'to some extent an art, not an exact science',[14] and the meaning of treaty provisions will rarely be unambiguous and clear, following a simple reading of only the text of the provision in question. Treaty provisions, particularly in a multilateral instrument, invariably represent compromise positions that have been reached between states with frequently diverging interests and concerns, and often only after hard negotiation that is not directly reflected in the wording of the final text. While the latter may represent a consensus position, it will usually be the lowest common version that the states involved are prepared to accept. Understanding the 'context' of a treaty provision therefore involves looking at the instrument as a whole, as well as any accompanying and subsequent agreements, any subsequent state practice and the general rules of public international law, together with a wider consideration of other preparatory and background materials, in order to carry out the confirmatory and determinative roles envisaged in Article 32.

---

[14] International Law Commission, in commenting upon its proposed principles of interpretation in Articles 27 and 28, later Articles 31 and 32, of the Vienna Convention on the Law of Treaties, *United Nations Conference on the Law of Treaties: Official Records: Documents of the Conference*, A/CONF.39/11/Add.2, 38, [4]. See the United Nations Treaty Collection at <http://legal.un.org/diplomaticconferences/lawoftreaties-1969/vol/english/confdocs.pdf>

This is not the place to discuss in detail the various rules of treaty interpretation.[15] Rather, my purpose is to direct readers to the wealth of sources that are available to scholars and researchers in relation to copyright treaties, both old and new. Even in the case of the pre-1883 bilateral treaties, there is a useful body of commentary to be found in both French and English, principally directed at the poor practitioner seeking to advise a client on the complexities of obtaining protection for his or her work abroad. Thus, WA Copinger in his first edition[16] dealt at length with the difficulties involved in obtaining protection in overseas countries pursuant to the various bilateral treaties to which the UK was then party, while ES Drone in 1879 provided a detailed treatment of both UK and US laws.[17] Similar treatments are to be found in Scrutton's first text,[18] and in France in the commentary of Renault.[19] Valuable collections of bilateral treaties affecting France are those published by J Delalain in 1869 and C Lyon-Caen and P Delalain in 1889,[20] with a further and more general collection published by the Berne International Bureau in 1907.[21] While the vast majority of these treaties have now expired or have been superseded, they can sometimes provide interesting insights into the emergence of some of the provisions of the later multilateral agreements: one instance relates to the question of censorship and other public interest controls that cut across copyright owners' rights, another relates to the formulation of the national treatment obligation that was to find a central place in the Berne Act of 1886. In the case of the US, bilateral arrangements were, of course, to remain significant up until the time that country joined the Berne Convention in 1989.[22]

In the case of the multilateral treaties – the real focus of our concern – the wealth of material is enormous, and requires some further explication. A principal primary source

---

[15] For excellent treatments of this large topic, see R Gardiner, *Treaty Interpretation* (OUP 2008); Ian Sinclair, *The Vienna Convention on the Law of Treaties* (2nd edn, Manchester UP 1984); Anthony Aust, *Modern Treaty Law and Practice* (3rd edn, CUP 2013); A Orakhelashvili and S Williams (eds), *40 Years of the VCLT on the Law of Treaties* (British Institute of International and Comparative Law 2010).

[16] WA Copinger, *The Law of Copyright in Works of Literature and Art: Including that of the Drama, Music, Engraving, Sculpture, Painting, Photography and Ornamental and Useful Designs* (Stevens and Haynes 1870) ch 17, 18.

[17] Drone (n 5).

[18] Thomas E Scrutton, *The Laws of Copyright* (John Murray 1883) ch 11, 271–73; see also Sidney Jarrold, *A Handbook of English and Foreign Copyright in Literary and Dramatic Works* (Chatto and Windus 1881).

[19] Louis Renault, *De la propriété littéraire et artistique au point de vue international* (Extrait du Journal du droit international privée et de la jurisprudence comparée) (Marchal, Billard et Cie 1879).

[20] Jules Delalain, *Recueil des Conventions conclues par la France pour la reconnaissance de la propriété littéraire et artistique* (Université 1867); C Lyon Caen, and P Delalain, *Lois françaises et étrangères sur la propriété littéraire et artistique suivie des conventions internationales conclues par la France pour la protection des oeuvres de littérature et d'art* (Pichon 1889).

[21] International Copyright Office, *Recueil des conventions et traités concernant la propriété littéraire et artistique, publiés en français et dans les langues des pays contractants avec une introduction et des notices* (1904).

[22] In particular, the bilateral arrangement with Germany of 1892: see further, Ladas (n 1) vol 2, 836–49, in particular 844.

294 *Research handbook on the history of copyright law*

is to be found in the records of successive conferences of revision, followed by the monthly periodical publication (*Le Droit d'auteur/Copyright*) produced by the Berne International Office (now WIPO) between the years 1888–1994. Consideration should also be paid to the proceedings of relevant international and national non-governmental organisations, national government records, and to texts and other journals. All of these are grist to the mill of interpretation, and provide rich streams of gold to the researcher who follows them back over time. In the following sections, I therefore provide some comments on each of these principal sources.

4. SOURCES FOR RESEARCH

4.1 Conference Records

The starting point here is the records of the first diplomatic conferences at Berne 1884–1886 which adopted the Berne Convention,[23] and then the records of the successive conferences of revision that occurred in Paris (1896),[24] Berlin (1908),[25] Rome (1928),[26] Brussels (1948),[27] Stockholm (1967),[28] and Paris (1971).[29] Highly relevant also are the earlier proceedings of ALAI where the initiative for the adoption of a multilateral agreement began.[30] Unlike many international agreements, where much of the preparatory work and negotiation is unrecorded or squirrelled away in musty and disorganized files in national archives, the Berne Convention's life, like that of a first child, has been carefully and systematically documented. These records do not, of course, present a complete picture of all that happened at these conferences – here one must also look to national archives (which will clearly have a particular bias) and other sources. Nonetheless, they are extremely useful in describing what went on at each conference and what was ultimately decided. More importantly, they are of the

---

[23] See *Actes de la Conférence internationale pour la protection des Droits d'auteur réunie à Berne du 8 au 19 septembre 1884*, International Office, Berne (1884) ('*Actes 1884*'); *Actes de la 2me Conférence internationale pour la protection des oeuvres littéraires et artistiques réunie à Berne du 7 au 18 septembre 1885*, International Office, Berne (1885) ('*Actes 1885*') ; *Actes de la 3me Conférence internationale pour la protection des oeuvres littéraires et artistiques réunie à Berne du 6 au 9 septembre 1886*, International Office, Berne (1886) ('*Actes 1886*').

[24] *Actes de la Conférence de Paris de 1896*, International Office, Berne (1897) ('*Actes 1896*').

[25] *Actes de la Conférence de Berlin 1908*, International Office, Berne (1909) ('*Actes 1908*').

[26] *Actes de la Conférence réunie à Rome du 7 mai au 2 juin 1928*, International Office, Berne (1929) ('*Actes 1928*').

[27] *Documents de la Conférence réunie à Bruxelles du 5 au 26 juin 1948*, International Office, Berne (1951) ('*Documents 1948*').

[28] *Records of the Intellectual Property Conference of Stockholm, June 11 to July 14, 1967*, WIPO, Geneva (1971) ('*Records 1967*').

[29] *Records of the Paris Conference 1971 (Paris, 5–24 July 1971)*, WIPO, Geneva (1974) *Records of the Paris Conference 1971 (Paris, 5–24 July 1971)*, WIPO, Geneva (1974) ('*Records 1971*').

[30] *Association littéraire et artistique internationale* (n 10).

first importance as representing the 'preparatory work of the treaty' under Article 32 for the purposes of treaty interpretation under Article 31(1).

The principal reason for this extensive documentation is to be found in the efforts of the International Office set up under Article 16 of the Berne Act 1886, which also carried out the same functions for the Paris Union,[31] established three years earlier, and the two later Madrid agreements of 1891.[32] This was a small but dedicated secretariat,[33] which took seriously the functions allotted to it under paragraph 5 of the Closing Protocol to the Berne Act, including:

> The International Office will collect every kind of information relative to the protection of the rights of authors over their literary and artistic works. It will arrange and publish such information. It will undertake the study of questions of general interest concerning the Union, and, by the aid of documents placed at its disposal by the different Administrations, will edit a periodical publication in the French language on the questions which concern the purpose of the Union.
>
> ...
>
> The International Office will always hold itself at the disposal of members of the Union with a view to furnish them with any special information they may require relative to the protection of literary and artistic works.

Part of this information gathering and dissemination role included, from the start, the preparation of careful records of the diplomatic conferences that were at the heart of the Convention's regular revision process. While the records of the initial Berne conferences of 1884–1886 are mainly confined to the conference programme, the *procès-verbaux* of the conference debates, together with the relevant texts adopted at the end of the Conference, from the 1896 Conference on they assumed a much more informative format, drawn from the models adopted with the records of proceedings of the Paris and Madrid Conferences. With the advent of digitisation, these are now available online from WIPO and are readily accessible by researchers.[34] The records for the Berlin Revision Conference, one of the most significant in the development of the

---

[31] The Paris Convention for the Protection of Industrial Property 1883.

[32] Madrid Agreement Concerning the International Registration of Marks 1891; Madrid Agreement for the Repression of False or Deceptive Indications of Source on Goods 1891.

[33] For an account of the early years of the International Office or Bureau, see *1886–1896 Union internationale pour la protection des oeuvres littéraires et artistiques: sa fondation et son développement, Mémoire publié par le Bureau de l'Union* ('*Mémoire*'), Berne 1936, Seconde Partie, 99–110.

[34] This is in sharp contrast to the author's early experiences when working on a commentary in the mid-1980s where it was necessary to track down original hard copies that were not readily available in national libraries, even such as the British Library. The main and most reliable sources were the library of WIPO in Geneva, that of the Max-Planck-Institut in Munich, and the Library of Congress in Washington. Conservation rules however often made it difficult to obtain photocopies of the older of these records. All Berne conference records are now available at <ftp://ftp.wipo.int/pub/library/ebooks/Internationalconferences-recordsproceedings/>. English versions of the reports of these conferences were prepared by WIPO at the time of the centenary of the Berne Convention in 1986 and published in a centenary celebration volume, and are now available at <http://global.oup.com/booksites/content/9780198259466/>.

296 *Research handbook on the history of copyright law*

Berne Convention, provide a good example of the documentation available here, including the following:

- Circular letters of invitation to governments (of Union states and non-Union states alike) setting out the background to the revision.
- The conference programme of proposed amendments prepared jointly by the German Government and International Office, together with useful background commentary and reasons behind the proposals. It is possible to see here, as in later revision conferences, the hosting government having a significant effect on the shape of the final programme. By the time of the Brussels Conference the role of the International Offices appears to have been greater,[35] while the preparatory documents for the Stockholm Conference came out of extensive preliminary meetings that involved the wider membership of the Union (as witnessed by the work of the various committees that considered the development of the 'three step' test).[36] By this time, the convening of Committees of Experts and working groups was beginning to assume the form that we are now familiar with as part of WIPO's 'norm formulation' activities.
- Specific proposed amendments by various Union members. At the time of the Berlin revision, there were relatively few of these, but by the time of the Stockholm Conference these ran into the hundreds, either submitted before or during the conference.[37]
- A table of the different resolutions of congresses of the various international and national organizations concerned with literary and artistic matters during the period since the last revision of 1896.[38] The significance of this kind of table, grouped thematically and repeated in successive records up to the time of the Stockholm Conference, is that it provides a ready reference point to the interest group in

---

[35] See, for example, 'Les travaux préparatoires de la conférence de Bruxelles' [1933] Le Droit d'auteur ('DA') 73, 90, 97, 112, 121, prepared for the Brussels Revision Conference which was originally scheduled for 1936 (but did not take place until 1948). Note also that the International Office circulated preliminary documents before the Berlin Conference: International Bureau of the Union for the Protection of Literary and Artistic Works, *Conférence de Berlin – Documents préliminaires*, Berne (1907) (English translation made also by E Cutler KC and printed for private circulation by the UK Copyright Association).

[36] BIRPI, *General Report of the Swedish/BIRPI Study Group established at 1st June 1963*, Document DA/20/2 (1963 Study Group); BIRPI, *General Report of the Swedish/BIRPI Study Group established at 1st July 1964*, Document DA/22/2 (1964 Study Group); *Report of the Authors' Consultative Commission* (1963), Document DA 20/4 (Authors' Consultative Commission); *Report of the Sub-Committee charged with the study of sanctions and reciprocity in the Convention of Berne*, submitted to the 5th meeting of the Authors' Consultative Committee, 28 February and 1 March 1963; *Stockholm Conference Committee of Experts (November 1963), Report of the Debates*, Document DA/20/29 rev (1963 Committee of Experts); *Diplomatic Conference of Stockholm 1967, Committee of Governmental Experts (1965) Report of the Debates*, Document DA/22/33 (1965 Committee of Governmental Experts). See further the summary of the work of these committees in *Records 1967*, vol I, pp 79 and 111ff (Preparatory Document S/1 (Berne Convention).

[37] See *Records 1967*, vol 1, 603 ff.

[38] *Actes 1908*, 79–130.

question and the particular view that it was promoting and in relation to what issue. The role of ALAI is foremost here, as can be seen in a series of resolutions passed at successive congresses in relation to all aspects of the Convention, as well as proposals for extension of its protection (a notable example here being duration of protection, where ALAI congresses prior to 1908 strongly advocated adoption of a minimum term of the life of the author plus 50 years). In these early years of the Convention, the influence of the International Publishers Association can also be seen, along with those of some national groups, notably in Germany and France. The range of groups and interests represented becomes more varied in later sets of conference records, but they always provide a useful pointer to the issues that were agitating interested parties prior to each conference, and the concerned researcher can then trace these back further to the fuller records of those organizations (see further below). In addition, it is interesting to cross-reference the membership of these organizations with the membership of national delegations, where prominent members of national societies, with inevitable ties to ALAI, were frequently included (notably in the cases of Germany, Italy, Belgium and France).

- The summary minutes (*procès-verbaux*) of the sessions of the conference, reports of sub-committees and other memoranda prepared for delegates. Each of these sources can throw important light on particular decisions that were reached, as well containing the bones of what might be regarded today as 'agreed statements' which form part of the 'context' of the treaty finally adopted by the conference in question. These summaries and reports become more fulsome and detailed in later revisions, such as those of Rome, Brussels and Stockholm.

- A central feature of all the Berne revision conferences has been the report of the general reporter ('*rapporteur*') to the final plenary session of each conference.[39] These do not find a ready parallel in the case of the Paris Convention, where such reports were often at the level of bare summary with little more commentary, and it is therefore necessary to look at the reports of individual sub-committees where more detail is to be found. In the case of Berne, however, the general report plays a much more significant role, and the reporter was usually a practising or academic lawyer of some distinction, such as Louis Renault (France) at Berlin,[40] E Piolo Caselli (Italy) at Rome,[41] Marcel Plaisant

---

[39] In the case of the second Berne conference of 1885, there was also an extensive report that was prepared by a drafting committee for final approval by delegates: see *Actes 1885*, 39–59. For English translations of these, prepared by WIPO at the time of the centenary of Berne in 1986, see Ricketson and Ginsburg (n 1) Appendices.

[40] Renault (1843–1918) was a distinguished international lawyer who represented France at many significant international conferences and was involved in a number of important international arbitrations. He also chaired and presented a report on the proposals for the Paris Conference of 1896 which is useful in the interpretation of the amendments brought about by the Additional Act adopted at that Conference. See his obituary at [1918] DA 46–48.

[41] E Piola Casseli (1886–1943), President of the Chamber of the Court of Cassation and author of various texts on copyright and industrial property; also represented Italy at other international conferences, including the London Revision Conference of the Paris Convention in

(France) at Brussels,[42] and Svante Bergstrom (Sweden) at Stockholm.[43] Of these, the report of Renault at the Berlin Conference stands out, particularly as this was the Conference that saw the most substantial changes to the text of the Convention. These are elegantly and clearly explained by Renault, a highly experienced and respected international lawyer with a long involvement in matters relating to authors' rights. Also of some importance are the reports of important conference sub-committees, notably at the Rome and Brussels Conference, which do much to explain why particular initiatives may have stalled or been deferred or were the subject of hard fought compromise.[44] All these materials are important in providing background to the negotiations and final texts adopted, but more significantly are part of the 'context' in that they may record agreements between delegates as to certain matters not included or apparent in the text adopted (the practice of WIPO would now be to include them as annexed 'agreed statements' to the Convention text itself, as in the cases of the later WCT and WPPT). These reports may also contain the germs of a 'Berne acquis', as in the case of the minor reservations doctrine explained in rather sweeping terms by Plaisant in 1948[45] or on the scope for implied exceptions in relation to translations more cautiously outlined by Bergstrom in 1967.[46] In so far as one can find guidance on issues of originality, the report of Renault in 1908 is probably the best guide, in the absence of specific provisions in the Convention itself.[47] In other instances again, one may find an explanation for terminology in the text that is otherwise quite uncertain or misleading: a small but instructive example is to be seen in the case of Article 2*bis* adopted at the Rome Revision Conference where it becomes clear from the Report of Caselli that the reference to 'political speeches and speeches delivered in the course of legal proceedings' is really a reference to oral works in general, with a reservation to Union members as to whether protection would be accorded to such works.[48]

- Other useful materials are to be found in the conference records, including carefully compiled tables of information as to the state of accessions and

---

1934, and was closely involved in the drafting of the Italian Copyright Act 1941. See the glowing obituary of him at [1943] DA 82–3.

[42] Marcel Plaisant (1887–1958), a distinguished French lawyer and politician, and also member of the French resistance who was captured and tortured by the Gestapo during the Second World War: see his entry in French Wikipedia at <http://fr.wikipedia.org/wiki/Marcel_Plaisant>. He represented France at a number of copyright and industrial property conferences from the 1920s through to the 1940s: see his obituary at [1958] DA 77–8.

[43] Svante Bergstrom, a Professor at the University of Uppsala, who was also closely involved in the preparatory meetings leading up to the Conference.

[44] In the case of Rome, consider the sub-committee reports on the issues of moral rights, broadcasting and works of applied art: *Actes 1928*, 181, 183,190. In the case of the Brussels Conference, see *Documents 1948*, 111 ff.

[45] *Documents 1948*, 100–01.
[46] *Records 1967*, Vol 2, 1164, 1166.
[47] *Actes 1908*, 231–34, 264–65.
[48] *Actes 1928*, 195–96.

The public international law of copyright and related rights 299

applications of the Convention, reservations and other declarations made by states, as well as lists of bilateral treaties currently in force.
- A significant pointer to possible future action is also to be found in the various *'voeux'* or resolutions passed by successive revision conferences (though none were actually passed at Berlin). These frequently set the scene for amendments that would be adopted at the next revision.[49]
- Finally, the records are indexed in some detail, usually as to subject matter, Convention provision and delegate interventions, all of which makes it easier to pursue specific topics through a mass of otherwise irrelevant material. There can be no doubt that the International Office, which was in Berne until 1960, took great care in preparing these records as resources for Union members, present and intending. They provide an invaluable starting point for any investigation of issues arising under the Convention.

4.2 *Le Droit D'auteur/Copyright*

One of the other primary source delights for the scholar of international copyright is to be found in the pages of the journal, *Le Droit d'auteur/Copyright*, the publication of which was mandated in paragraph 5 of the Closing Protocol of the Berne Act 1886 quoted above. This began publication on a monthly basis in French in 1888, with an English version beginning in 1965. It was amalgamated with its sister journal *La Propriètè industrielle/Industrial Property* in 1995, and ceased to be published in this form in 1997 as WIPO moved to a more 'newsy' format in the *WIPO Magazine* combined with the use of online delivery of much of the documentation that had previously appeared in *Le Droit d'auteur/Copyright*. Almost until its end, the journal retained its character as an authoritative record and commentary on all things to do with Berne, together with continuous overviews of events and developments at the national level. In an age when communication was principally through the print media and the postal service, when reading the pages of *Le Droit d'auteur/Copyright* one receives the immediate impression of a continuing conversation between like-minded persons: on the one hand, the highly motivated staff of the International Office who initiated and/or compiled the information collected in each monthly issue, and, on the other, the interested readers in national offices and agencies, authors' and publishers' groups, collecting societies, universities and legal practitioners who supplied, in turn, their own contributions. It was, in truth and for most of its life, a learned journal which promoted the free exchange of a wide range of information and commentary on authors' rights. Unfortunately, perhaps, for the contemporary scholar, access to a complete run of the publication is not so easy, as few libraries apart from WIPO in Geneva and Max-Planck in Munich appear to hold a full set of the hard copy version. Microfiche versions, although not always easy to read and peruse, used to be available from WIPO, but may now be a thing of the past, although some scanned versions of significant articles and other items are available online at the WIPO website. Scanned (and downloadable) copies of the editions from 1888 to 1935 are also available online

---

[49] An example here is the *droit de suite* which was the subject of a resolution in 1928: *Actes 1928*, 349, and which was then adopted as Article 14*ter* in the Brussels Act 1948.

300 *Research handbook on the history of copyright law*

at the Bibliothèque Nationale de France,[50] and one can then usually fill the gaps for later years from the incomplete hard copy sets held in national libraries and individual scanned copies on the WIPO website. The path of the modern inquirer is therefore much easier than in the past, when hard copy versions of particular years or issues could be difficult to track down.

What, then, do these archival riches contain? The format and arrangement was based on those already established in the slightly older *La Propriété industrielle* (which began in 1885), with appropriate modifications, and was to remain largely unaltered throughout its existence, reflecting, no doubt, the orderly minds of its editors. The organization of the material is fully on display in the table of contents for the first year of publication (1888), and was essentially established in the first issue of January that year. Thus, it was divided into an 'Official Part' and a 'Non-Official Part', and this division was maintained until the last decade of the journal's publication.[51]

In 1888, this 'Official Part' consisted of the following: (a) articles and studies concerning the Convention; (b) 'diverse subjects', including statistics on the international publication of literary works; (c) 'communications' relating to the newly adopted convention, chiefly with the Swiss Government and between the Office and Union members; (d) texts of the Convention, bilateral treaties and national laws, including those recently adopted; (e) measures taken by Union members to implement the Convention within their own countries, including proposed legislative amendments; and (f) particular conventions of 'interest' to Union countries, including news of the prorogation of earlier bilateral agreements now overtaken by the Berne Convention.[52]

The 'Non-Official Part', as the name suggests, contained an even wider and more diverse range of material: (a) studies and 'various articles' ('articles divers'), on a range of topics, both legal and of more general interest; (b) an important section headed 'collaboration and correspondence' which was to develop into a regular series of reports from national authors on developments within their countries (Berne and non-Berne members alike), beginning in 1888 with Thorvald Solberg (US), Rosmini (Italy), Cattreux (Belgium) and Touchard (France), and to be followed by a number of distinguished contributors in the following decades, including Kohler (Germany), Darras, Huard and Pouillet (France) and Putnam (US);[53] (c) statistics of various kinds, such as the numbers of political science and legal publications appearing within particular periods and the numbers of public libraries in Europe; (d) case reports ('jurisprudence') from national courts and tribunals; and (e) 'various facts' ('faits divers'), including reports of the proceedings of international and national non-government organizations with an interest in authors' rights (ALAI being a regular subject here, but many others as well). The organization of these various groupings would vary somewhat over subsequent years, with some further interesting additions

---

[50] At <http://gallica.bnf.fr/ark:/12148/cb34465651m/date.r=Droit+d%27auteur.langEN>.

[51] The last year in which this was done was 1986; thereafter, however, the grouping of documents within the journal remains perfectly apt, e.g., 'Treaties', 'Studies', 'National Laws', etc.

[52] [1888] DA I–II.

[53] See Table of Contents 1888–1900, International Office, Berne, 1903, 28–29, available at <http://gallica.bnf.fr/ark:/12148/bpt6k5154933.image.langEN.r=Le%20Droit%20d'auteur>.

such as bibliographies (brief reviews of relevant works published in different countries) and 'necrologies' (obituaries) that provide a little more background on figures who are otherwise only known to us through the pages of the journal or the conference records. The journal is generally easy to follow, with good annual tables of contents, although there seems to be only one consolidated table for the first 13 years (1888–1900).

As a journal of record, *Le Droit d'auteur/Copyright* assumed growing significance as the place where all accessions, ratifications, reservations[54] and other declarations concerning the Convention were published, and in the more general annual reviews of the 'state of the Union' that begin to be published from 1930.[55] From a legal perspective, most interesting are the commentaries on the provisions of the Convention that were regularly published, either by officials of the International Office (anonymously[56]) or by outside commentators. More generally, the journal appears to have been open to as many differing perspectives as were available at the time, and included contributions from a number of distinguished national copyright lawyers, officials and scholars. The topics pursued were often ones touching on the borders of protection or discussing new areas of protection, for example, with respect to paying public domain, performing rights, moral rights and *droit de suite* – although it must also be said that there were fewer, if any, overtly anti-copyright and pro-user advocates than is the case today. In any event, in the later years of its publication, the contributions by the Office and its officials appear to have been reduced, and 'studies' by outsiders ceased after 1991, although the journal for that year still contained a significant number: six studies of a general character and 13 'letters' or correspondence from national contributors. Separate case notes or reports of national jurisprudence were also not published after 1953, but were a principal feature of national 'letters' up until 1991.[57] From 1992 to its last edition three years later, *Le Droit d'auteur/Copyright* was very much an 'official' journal of record and, in consequence, a rather dry and tedious publication. At that point, the 'conversation' between interested parties ceased, and moved into the other varied and emerging forums being adopted by WIPO, such as the Standing Committee on Copyright and Related Rights – indeed, it might be said that the conversation has become much more general now and has moved well beyond WIPO, with the advent of

---

[54] Clear information on the various reservations allowed under earlier texts of the Convention became necessary as these effectively created a series of 'sub-unions' between Union members, depending upon which reservations each had made and to what: see, for example, the list in [1925] DA 2.

[55] [1930] DA 2 ff.

[56] See, for example, those published after the Berlin Revision Conference: 'La Conférence de Berlin, ses travaux et ses résultats' [1909] DA 1, 19; 'La Convention de Berne revisée, du 13 novembre 1908', 'Classification des dispositions adoptées. Combinaison du droit interne et du droit conventionnel; source de droit des auteurs Unionists. Portée des engagements réciproques; le minimum de protection légale' [1909] DA 34, 45; 'Les oeuvres protégées. Commentaire des articles 4 et 15' [1910] DA 2; 'Commentaire de l'article 7: durée de la protection' [1910] DA 18, 29; 'Commentaire des articles 4, 5 et 6: personnes protégées; publication, pays d'origine' [1910] DA 59, 76, 93. It is likely that they were written by Dr Ernst Röthlisberger, vice-director of the office who subsequently became the director and died in office in early 1926. During the Second World War, the Office also published useful commentary on the effect of wartime conditions on the continued subsistence of protection under the Convention: see, for example, [1940] DA 5–8.

[57] But only cross-referenced separately for the assistance of readers until the mid-1980s.

302 *Research handbook on the history of copyright law*

the TRIPS Agreement, FTAs, the increasing engagement of other international organizations with an interest in copyright, and the emergence of new copyright industries and consumer and civil society groups, each with its own platform and constituency. What was once a vibrant and stimulating means of communication between a relatively closed audience of copyright enthusiasts disappears at this point, but remains an invaluable resource for those seeking entry points into what went before.

4.3 International and National Non-government Organizations and their Proceedings

Mention has already been made of the pointers to these sources that are to be found in the records of resolutions in revision conference records and in reports carried in *Le Droit d'auteur/Copyright*. The influence of some of these organizations in the development of the Convention will be well known, in particular the role of ALAI in preparing the first draft convention at its conference in 1882.[58] ALAI has continued to be a source of proposals for enhanced international protection of authors' rights and has had a continuing influence at all revision conferences and WIPO meetings, although this has now been significantly diluted by the presence and participation of so many other groups representing the copyright industries, consumer and civil society groups and others in the forums of WIPO and other international organizations with an interest in copyright. The simple point to be made here is that the contributions of these different groups to the development of international norms is often obscured in the state-to-state negotiations that follow successful lobbying and representation. For the researcher investigating the origins and evolution of particular norms, the records of these groups and their internal discussions may therefore prove fruitful, together with a study of their advocacy activities. In the case of ALAI, its annual proceedings and resolutions are readily available, and the same is true of other organizations such as the International Publishers Association and CISAC, but the range of organizations represented at recent diplomatic conferences is now large and varied.[59] In the case of the recent Marrakesh Treaty,[60] the advocacy of the World Blind Union and its relation to the African group of countries would, for example, make an interesting study of the development of new international norms and the political processes involved. A related area for investigation is the influence of other international intergovernmental organizations, which are now beginning to develop an interest in international intellectual property matters, particularly in the areas of trade and investment and human rights. While this interest and involvement is now a given, it is hardly new. In this regard, it is worth noting that the League of Nations was represented in an observer capacity at the Rome Revision Conference of 1928, along with the International Institute for Intellectual Co-operation (later absorbed into UNESCO after the Second World War). The work of the latter body during the 1930s, together with the International Institute of

---

[58] See further *Memoire* (n 33) 26–30.
[59] In the case of the 1996 Internet Treaties, see *Records of the Diplomatic Conference on Copyright and Related Rights, Geneva 1996* (WIPO 1999) vol 2, 870–881.
[60] Treaty to Facilitate Access to Published Works for Persons Who Are Blind, Visually Impaired or Otherwise Print Disabled, Marrakesh, 2012.

Rome for the Unification of Private Law (more usually known as UNIDROIT), did much to prepare the way for the adoption of neighbouring rights treaties after the Second World War and outside the forum of the Berne Convention.[61]

4.4 Texts and Other Journals

There is a wealth of contemporary commentary and reportage available on the background and development of the Berne Convention, which researchers will be familiar with from their own jurisdictions. Contemporary observations are always useful, and much of the early commentary on the Convention itself has the advantage of being written by individuals who actually participated in the proceedings in question, either as delegates (for example, Droz[62] of Switzerland, Bergne of the UK,[63] Wauwermans[64] and Borchgrave[65] of Belgium, Kohler of Germany,[66] and Baetzmann[67] and Raestad[68] of Norway) or as officials of the International Office, such as Röthlisberger.[69] However, there is a large number of other commentaries covering the first 50 years of the Convention that were published in French, German and English, as well as shorter notes and analyses in legal and arts-related journals, and some of the more significant of these sources are listed in the short bibliography at the end of this volume (in the case of the French texts, scanned and downloadable copies of many will be found online at the Bibliotèque nationale de France).[70] While authors' rights laws and treaties may have appeared to many people at the time to be a restricted and specialist

---

[61] See further Ricketson and Ginsburg (n 1) [19.05].
[62] Numa Droz, 'Conférence diplomatique de Berne dans le but de constituer une Union pour la protection des droits d'auteur' (1884) 11 JDIPJC (Clunet) 441; Numa Droz, 'Deuxième conférence diplomatique de Berne dans le but de constituer une Union pour la protection des oeuvres littéraires et artistiques' (1885) 12 JDIPJC (Clunet) 481; Numa Droz, 'Reponse aux observations du syndicat des sociétés littéraires et artistiques sur le projet de convention international relatif à la constitution d'une Union pour la protection des droits d'auteur' (1885) JDIPJC (Clunet) 163.
[63] HG Bergne, 'The International Copyright Union' (1887) 3 LQR 14.
[64] Paul Wauwermans, *La Convention de Berne (révisée à Berlin) pour la protection des oeuvres littéraires et artistiques* (Rivière ; Misch and Thron 1910); Paul Wauwermans, *Le droit des auteurs en Belgique* (Brussels 1894).
[65] Joseph Borchgrave, *Les Résultats de la Convention de Berlin et le Rapport de M Taillefer au Syndicat pour la Protection de la Properiété intellectuelle* (Bruylants 1909).
[66] Josef Kohler, *Die Immaterialgüter im internationalen Recht* (Duncker and Humblot 1896).
[67] Frederik Baetzmann, *Union internationale pour la protection des oeuvres littéraires et artistiques. Convention de Berne. Concordance des textes de 1883, 1884 et 1885* (Kugelmann 1889).
[68] Arnold Raestad, *La Convention de Berne révisée à Rome 1928 pour la protection de la littérature, de la musique, des arts figuratifs, de l'architecture, de l'art appliqué à l'industrie et des oeuvres de photographie et de cinématographie, contenant des dispositions relatives à la reproduction mécanique des sons, à la radiodiffusion et au droit de réimpression de la presse* (Editions internationales 1931).
[69] Ernst Röthlisberger, *Die Berner Übereinkunft zum Schutze von Werken der Literatur und Kunst und die Zusatzabkommen. Geschichtlich und rechtlich beleuchtet und kommentiert* (Francke 1906).
[70] <http://gallica.bnf.fr/?lang=EN>.

304   *Research handbook on the history of copyright law*

area of concern, it is amazing how far and wide interest in these matters extended among legal scholars, practitioners and government officials more generally, to say nothing of the recipients of the rights protected.

4.5   Government Records

These can be of considerable value in casting light on particular positions taken by delegations at conferences as well as indicating the difficulties faced by national governments in implementation of treaty obligations. As an extrinsic aid to interpretation for the purposes of Article 32 of the VCLT, they need to be treated with some caution as they will obviously reflect the particular attitudes of the state in question, but may still provide insights into those of other states at the conference. At the most superficial level, there will often be reports or commentaries in *Le Droit d'auteur/ Copyright* by national reporters that will provide pointers here, but the most obvious source will be the records of the government itself. What is available here will vary from country to country, and will be most readily accessible by scholars from those countries, but the examples of British and Australian records (those with which I am most familiar) will illustrate what kinds of material may be available. Thus, in the case of the British Government, many of the relevant documents for the Berne, Paris, and Berlin conferences, including instructions to delegates and their reports to government, were published as parliamentary papers.[71] Complemented by the files of the Board of Trade and Foreign Office available at the Public Records Office (now the National Archives), these reveal the diverging approaches towards entry into a multilateral copyright agreement that arose between the two responsible agencies of government. More importantly, they show that British involvement in the early Berne conferences was primarily because of the hope that the US Government would finally be prepared to join a multilateral copyright agreement after many years of congressional resistance to a bilateral treaty.[72] Subsequently, at the time of the Rome conference these records reveal an extraordinary contretemps between the UK (and Dominion Governments) and the Irish Free State as to the order of signature on the final instrument – a dispute that might have led the Irish delegation to veto its adoption. None of these subterranean

---

[71]   *Switzerland No 1 (1886), Correspondence respecting the Formation of an International Copyright Union*, Presented to both Houses of Parliament by Command of Her Majesty, January 1886, C-4606 (London 1886); *Switzerland No 2 (1886), Further Correspondence respecting the Formation of an International Copyright Union*, Presented to both Houses of Parliament by Command of Her Majesty, August 1886, C-4856 (London 1886); *Switzerland No 3 (1886), Further Correspondence respecting the formation of an International Copyright Union*, Presented to both Houses of Parliament by Command of Her Majesty, September 1886, C-4910 (London 1886); *Commercial No 6 (1897), Correspondence respecting the Copyright Conference at Paris*, Presented to both Houses of Parliament by Command of Her Majesty, August 1897, C-8441, HMSO (London 1897); *Miscellaneous No 2 (1909), Correspondence respecting the Revised Convention of Berne for the Protection of Literary and Artistic Works, signed at Berlin, November 13, 1908*, Presented to both Houses of Parliament by Command of His Majesty, February 1909, C-4467, HMSO (London 1909).

[72]   Ricketson and Ginsburg (n 1) [2.39]; and see also *Switzerland No 1 (1886), Correspondence respecting the Formation of an International Copyright Union*, Presented to both Houses of Parliament by Command of Her Majesty, January 1886, C-4606 (London 1886) 36.

manoeuvrings, however, finds expression or reference in the published proceedings of the conferences in question – indeed, in the case of the dispute at Rome it is possible that the other delegates might well have had difficulty in understanding what it was all about. Australian archival materials likewise cast considerable light on the thinking of a small and emerging country that was coming to international copyright relations for the first time at the Rome Conference of 1928 (the Australian delegate was a former dean of the Melbourne Law School and presented a detailed report to the Commonwealth Parliament on his return[73]). Other countries will provide similar interesting information: one wonders, for example, what were the precise instructions given to the delegates of such early Union members as France, Germany, Italy and Spain, whether there were competing government departments involved (as in the UK), and what were the submissions and papers received from interest groups, some of which were directly included on the delegations. Once again, a careful review of the pages of *Le Droit d'auteur/Copyright* may provide pointers as to what was going on in particular countries at particular times, but nothing there will be a substitute for further investigation of national records where the researcher has the appropriate language skills and access. Studies of these kinds of material might also provide a broader context for understanding, or even posing possible explanations for, some of the unanswered questions arising out of successive revision conferences (see further below).

4.6 National Legislation and Court Decisions

By way of conclusion, it is worth saying something about these, as they go directly to the issue of treaty implementation. It is one thing to form a view as to how a particular treaty provision is to be interpreted; it is quite another to carry that interpretation into effect, particularly where the provision in question allows for flexibility or differences in the way that this is to be done. In this regard, there are two broad scenarios to be considered: countries where treaties are capable of direct implementation (sometimes referred to as 'monist' legal systems where treaties can be self-executing); and those countries where some kind of legislative measure is required to implement treaty obligations ('dualist' legal systems).[74] Furthermore, there are only some provisions of the Berne Convention which are capable of direct implementation by a court in a monist system (Articles 6*bis* and 7 are good examples), while others may still require, or at least be supplemented by, some kind of implementing legislation (for example, those provisions relating to exceptions and the three-step test).

National laws have a limited but significant relevance in public international law. In one sense, what happens within a particular country stays there and does not move beyond its boundaries. In another sense, of course, there is significance if the national law fails to interpret and apply 'correctly' the treaty obligation in question, and, in the case of an international convention such as Berne, this clearly has an impact on those

---

[73] *Report of the Australian Delegate (Sir W Harrison Moore)*, presented to the Parliament of the Commonwealth of Australia and printed by Command, 31 August 1928, No 255.

[74] This is a very broad division, and three may be countries that will have a mixture of both monist and dualist elements: see generally David Sloss, 'Domestic Application of Treaties' in Duncan B Hollis (ed), *The Oxford Guide to Treaties* (OUP 2012) ch 15.

foreign authors claiming protection in that country under the Convention. For most of the Berne Convention's existence, this was a real problem as there was no effective means in public international law for the country of a prejudiced claimant to seek compliance on the part of a delinquent state.[75] The advent of the WTO and its dispute resolution procedures have now gone some way to redressing this gap. There is, however, a more positive sense in which national laws can influence and guide treaty interpretation and application. Notwithstanding that many of the substantive provisions of the Berne Convention are capable of direct implementation in monist legal systems, they still have language that is often open-ended and will permit of a range of nuances in interpretation – that is, they often set boundaries without providing clear prescription as to what falls within. Accordingly, there is usually considerable flexibility with which national laws can work. Whether this is through legislation or court decision, a body of important comparative material can be built up over time – in some instances, it is even possible that this may provide the basis for the emergence of a 'state practice' that will become binding on all states in treaty terms.[76]

In this regard, the issues of *Le Droit d'auteur/Copyright* provide an extraordinary resource for researchers. As noted above, from the very first year of publication (1888) this publication contained regular reports of relevant national court decisions as well as the texts of national legislation, present and pending. While legislation continues to be available on the WIPO website and regular comparative case notes appear in such other journals as IIC, RIDA and the EIPR, the range of material available in *Le Droit d'auteur/Copyright* should not be overlooked. A quick perusal of Stephen Ladas' authoritative treatise of 1938 reveals how much this kind of material enriches his discussion.

5. SOME RESEARCH QUESTIONS FOR THE FUTURE

Much of the public international law of copyright is like a series of icebergs, with some oddly shaped sections above sea level, but a great deal out of sight. The treatise writer in this area frequently has the feeling that he or she is simply skimming the surface in describing the bits of the iceberg in clear view, while doing his or her best to discern the underwater sections that can be seen from the surface but with a sneaking suspicion that this is hardly sufficient. Underwater exploration is clearly required, but can be time consuming and difficult. A common emotion for the general treatise writer (if they are to be allowed such indulgences) is to say, 'Oh, I wish I had time to investigate that question more fully – perhaps later, when I retire – but I hope I have got the broad outline correct'.

The metaphor of an iceberg should not be pushed too far – indeed, one might say there is a case for excluding metaphor entirely in any academic discussion. Nonetheless, it serves to highlight the need for more extensive exploration of the historical sources relating to the Berne Convention and other international treaties relating to copyright and related rights. Diving deeper into this material can provide insights into

---

[75] See further, Ricketson and Ginsburg (n 1) [17.80]–[17.92].
[76] As per Vienna Convention on the Law of Treaties 1969, Art 31(3)(b).

or explanations of issues that keep bubbling below the surface when only the bare text of a provision and its immediate origins is considered. Much of this anterior material may, of course, simply be interesting in itself in the sense of being curious or amusing, rather than of direct contemporary utility. Nonetheless, in the broader exercise of treaty interpretation it provides 'context' and evidence of the 'circumstances' of a treaty's conclusion for the purposes of Article 31 and 32 of the VCLT. With the passage of time, these matters are often overlooked or simply forgotten.

What, then, are some of the unanswered or only partly answered questions that would repay further historical research in this area? What follows is a short list that may be of assistance to readers. These suggestions may well mesh with, or follow on from, work that is already occurring at the national level and that will discussed in other chapters in the book. They may also overlap with or link into work that is being carried on in other disciplines, such as social, economic and cultural history, and suggest the fruitful opportunities that may exist for interdisciplinary research by legal scholars.

5.1 Philosophies of Copyright

There is a place for a detailed study of the history of the philosophies or ideas underlying the Berne Convention and other international copyright agreements. These are matters which general treatise writers must refer to by way of general background,[77] but there is a lot more here that remains to be teased out and explained. It might well be said that Berne is ultimately a pragmatic instrument that remains neutral on philosophical issues, but is this really correct? The trajectory of French thinking on authors' rights on the first ALAI draft convention and the first Berne draft is clear, but German legal thinking, coming from a different background, became important at later stages. Italian thinking was influential in the adoption of moral rights protection in 1928, but how did this relate to French and German conceptions of these rights? And why does the common law instrumentalist tradition represented from the start by the UK appear to have played so little part in the development of the Convention? Even without the US for Berne's first century, the UK was the dominant world economic and imperial power at the time of the formation of the Berne Union, and its delegates were sophisticated men who were well acquainted with European thinking and ideas.[78] Why, then, does the British contribution appear to be so small or simply reactive? Finding answers to these questions would cast light on many of the other questions listed below.

---

[77] Although it is noteworthy that Briggs has four chapters grouped under the general heading of 'The Theory of International Copyright' in Part II of his 1906 treatise, and Darras begins his 1887 treatise with a chapter on the theory of authors' and artists' rights of nearly 140 pages.

[78] These were Sir Francis Adams, British Ambassador to Berne, and Sir Henry Bergne (1842–1908), head of the treaties section of the Foreign Office but also an active member of the Society of Authors in the UK: see TH Sanderson, rev HCG Matthew, 'Bergne, Sir John Henry Gibbs (1842–1908), *Oxford Dictionary of National Biography* (OUP 2004) <http://www.oxforddnb.com.rp.nla.gov.au/view/article/30724>. Bergne served as the British delegate at the Berne, Paris and Berlin conferences.

5.2 Translation Rights, Exceptions and Developing Countries

The Development Agenda is now a central element in WIPO's programmes, but the issue of developing countries and their concerns is hardly a new one and would repay careful examination against the background of the early days of the Berne Convention. A number of developing countries were represented at the first Berne conferences – Haiti, Liberia, Tunisia, Costa Rica, Honduras and Paraguay – and Haiti and Tunisia were among the first group of members in 1887. While there may be a certain cynicism about the reality of these countries' involvement – Louis Renault of France, for example, represented Tunisia and several others were represented by locally based diplomats – Haiti's delegate, Louis-Joseph Janvier, was a French-educated medical doctor, journalist and diplomat, who ultimately became Haitian minister to London,[79] and who made a number of significant interventions in the conferences on behalf of his country's interests.[80] Limitations on translation rights and exceptions for such purposes as education and instruction were among the principal concerns of these countries, as well as of a number of other countries that were represented, such as Japan, Sweden and Norway. The history of reservations with respect to translation rights in the early years of the Convention gave rise to a series of bewildering sub-unions between Union members, and must reflect profoundly held national linguistic and educational policies. The same is true in more recent times with the moves to adopt the Stockholm Protocol that nearly split the Union in 1967. All these matters would repay closer investigation and have a clear resonance in contemporary discussions, if only to underline the truth of the observation in *Ecclesiastes 1:9*.[81]

5.3 No Registration Requirements

Linked to the introduction of the 'no formalities' rule in Article 5(2) in the Berlin Act 1908 is the question of why did this amendment so readily succeed? The assumption may be that national registration systems were falling into desuetude at the time, but is this correct? It is easy to see natural rights explanations underlying the abandonment of such systems in some continental jurisdictions, but how does this explain British readiness to remove registration requirements, particularly when to do so created an immediate barrier to US accession which did not come down until nearly 80 years later? Registration systems were also a feature of many Latin American countries, and meant that these remained outside the Berne Convention for many years, until the Universal Copyright Convention provided the necessary bridge to Berne countries without formalities. Important work has already been carried out in relation to these questions by Stef van Gompel,[82] particularly with respect to continental Europe, the

---

[79] See the brief Wikipedia entry for Janvier at <http://en.wikipedia.org/wiki/Louis-Joseph_Janvier>.
[80] See, in particular, at *Actes 1885*, 30–32 (concerning proposed Articles 8 and 9 on quotations from scientific articles).
[81] According to the King James Version: 'The thing that hath been, it *is that* which shall be; and that which is done *is* that which shall be done; and *there is* no new thing under the sun.'
[82] Stef van Gompel, *Formalities in Copyright Law: An Analysis of Their History, Rationales and Possible Future*, Information Law Series No 23 (Kluwer Law International 2011), in

UK and the US. But the issue of formalities continues to be a significant issue today in the context of the online exploitation of rights.

5.4 Duration of Protection

One of the intriguing features of the Berne Convention (and related agreements) is the way in which the life of the author plus 50 years term came to be adopted. No clear answer based on economic reasoning or empirical data is evident from the conference records, other than the need to have a harmonized term throughout the Union, a good answer, perhaps, on its own, but hardly a sufficient explanation of why the term should be 50 years *post mortem auctoris* rather than anything else, or why the term should be uniform across the board (with the exceptions of photographs and works of applied art). Again, the question arises: what was going on below the surface here?

5.5 Moral Rights and *Droit de Suite*

Both these provide the clearest instance of how conceptions of legal rights founded in the legislation and jurisprudence of only a few countries can enter into an international instrument and become ultimately accepted in other legal systems to which they are quite alien. In the case of moral rights, this journey has been well traced by Elizabeth Adeney in her major study,[83] but *droit de suite* provides an instance of a right that, on one analysis, is not even an authors' right at all but one based on the physical object itself – the painting, the sculpture, the original manuscript, and so on. Yet, there it is in Article 14*ter* of the Convention, albeit adumbrated only in general terms and made the subject of reciprocity – and it is now beginning to find a place in the laws of nearly half of the present Berne membership. How did this right, based initially on sentimental appeals for reward to long-suffering visual artists, find its way into the Convention and into its present position of growing acceptance in national laws?[84] There is a story here that requires a fuller telling.

---

particular ch 3. See also Stef van Gompel, 'Copyright Formalities and the Reasons for their Decline in Nineteenth Century Europe' in Ronan Deazley, Martin Kretschmer and Lionel Bently (eds), *Privilege and Property: Essays on the History of Copyright* (OpenBook Publishers 2010) 157.

[83] Elizabeth Adeney, *The Moral Rights of Authors and Performers: An International and Comparative Analysis* (OUP 2006). See also Stig Strömholm, *Le droit moral de l'auteur en droit allemand, français et scandinave avec un aperçu de l'évolution internationale* (Three Parts, Norstedt and Söners 1966, 1967 and 1973).

[84] There is an extensive literature already that has been spawned on *droit de suite*, but one influential figure is Albert Vaunois, a French lawyer, whose article calling for justice to artists was published in 1893 and is said to have led ultimately to the adoption of a *droit de suite* law in France in 1920. See further 'Du droit à la plus-value des oeuvres artistiques' [1914] *DA* 34, 57; J-L Duchemin, *Le Droit de Suite des Artistes* (1948) ('Duchemin'); François Hepp, 'Royalties from Works of the Fine Arts: Origin of the Concept of *Droit de Suite* in Copyright Law' (1959) 6 Bull Copyright Soc'y USA 91; Rita E Hauser, 'French *Droit de Suite*: The Problem of Protection for the Underprivileged Artist under the Copyright Law' (1959) 6 Bull Copyright Soc'y USA 94; J-L Duchemin, 'Droit de Suite' (1967–1968) 54–55 RIDA 369; Robert Plaisant, 'Droit de Suite' [1969] Copyright 157; JL Duchemin, 'Le Droit de Suite aux

5.6 New Technologies

The Berne Convention has been relatively swift to react to the emergence of new technologies that have both enhanced and threatened authors' rights, as well as bringing new claimants for protection in their wake. The provisions adopted in the Berlin Act 1908 dealt with these issues in relation to two technologies of recent provenance: sound recording and cinematography. In 1928, the same occurred in relation to public broadcasting, which had only become established after the end of the First World War. In the mid-1990s, although Berne no longer provided susceptible to ready revision, the formulation and adoption of the Internet Treaties (the WCT and WPPT) were startlingly swift international responses to the emergence of the networked environment. Each of these phenomena has involved major social, cultural and political upheavals, and the effectiveness and/or propriety of the treaty provisions adopted are obvious subjects for closer study (notably in the case of the last-mentioned). There are profound interests involved here: those of the new industries engaged in these activities, those of authors, and the wider public interest. The interplay of these interests at the international and national levels deserves fuller investigation, with the case of the recording industry and musical publishers perhaps providing the most striking subject.

5.7 Works on the Borderline and Neighbouring Rights

One of the intriguing issues for scholars of the Berne Convention has been the question of what falls within the magic circle of 'literary and artistic works'. While this appeared to be a relatively uncontentious issue at the outset – the various bilateral treaties provided a generally agreed starting point here – in subsequent revisions the admission of new entrants has frequently been contested. Some, such as architectural works and choreographic works, have entered the list without much difficulty. Others have had to pass through the fire and receive protection in stages, for example, photographic works, works of applied art, collections and compilations.[85] Others again have had the doors locked firmly against them, notably sound recordings, live performances and broadcasts. In each instance, the history of these developments may have much to offer current thinking, particularly as the protection of 'non-works' moved across to the adoption of separate treaties on what we now call 'neighbouring'

Artistes' (1969) 62 RIDA 78; Paul Katzenberger, 'The Droit de Suite in Copyright Law' [1973] 4 IIC 361; W Duchemin, 'Le Droit de Suite' (1974) 80 RIDA 4; W Nordemann 'The 1972 Amendment of the German Copyright Law' (1973) 4 IIC 179; E Ulmer, 'Le Droit de Suite et sa Réglementation dans la Convention de Berne' in *Hommage à Henri Desbois, études de propriété intellectuelle* (1974) 89; E Ulmer, 'The *"Droit de Suite"* in International Copyright Law' (1975) 6 IIC 12; W Nordemann, *'Droit de Suite'* in Art 14ter of the Berne Convention and in the Copyright Law of the Federal Republic of Germany' [1977] Copyright 342; US Copyright Office, Droit de Suite: The Artist's Resale Royalty (1992 Report), summarized at (1992) 16 Colum-VLA J L & Arts 318; S Perlmutter, Resale Royalties for Artists: An Analysis of the Register of Copyrights' Report (1992) 16 Colum-VLA J L & Arts 157; Liliane de Pierredon-Fawcett, *The Droit de Suite in Literary and Artistic Property: A Comparative Law Study* (L Marin-Valiquette tr, Center for Law and the Arts, Columbia University School of Law 1991).

[85] See generally Ricketson and Ginsburg (n 1) ch 8.

or 'related rights'. Once again, there is an interesting pre-history here that would repay investigation, including the efforts of the Berne International Office, the work of the International Institute of Intellectual Co-operation (a body linked to the League of Nations) and the advocacy of relevant interest groups, all of which led to the adoption of a draft treaty in Samaden, Switzerland, in 1939.[86] The 'Samaden project' was stillborn because of the advent of the Second World War, but remnants of it passed over to the first neighbouring rights treaty that was finally adopted in Rome in 1961, although, as we know, the work continues today.

5.8 Basis and Scope of Protection

Berne remains studiously silent on the important question of conditions for protection for literary and artistic works, although containing an intriguing hint of the need for 'intellectual creation' in the case of collections of works.[87] Why have these issues never been seriously debated in revision conferences? Do they simply fall into the category of the 'elephant in the room', with the unspoken assumption being that issues of originality as between the different legal traditions of Berne members are too difficult to deal with as part of the process of formulating new international norms? A related issue concerns the scope of the protection to be granted: it is only via the provisions of the TRIPS Agreement and the WCT that the issue of the idea-expression dichotomy is now addressed,[88] and the issue seems never to have seriously discussed in Berne revision conferences. Nonetheless, the inclusion of Article 2(8) of 'news of the day' and 'miscellaneous facts having the character of mere items of press information' is suggestive of something similar, albeit limited to the 'press', and would repay further investigation.

5.9 The Role of the International Office and WIPO

The role of the International Office and, later, WIPO, in the preparation of conference proceedings and publication of the monthly journal *Le Droit d'auteur/Copyright* has already been commented upon. The functions of the Office, of course, went beyond these matters, and the part that it (and WIPO) has played in the development of Berne and the related rights conventions would merit a separate study in itself, particularly in the early years. There is a broader sense in which the International Office is also important, as it was one of the early international organizations to be established under a multilateral treaty in the late nineteenth century (the secretariats of the Universal Postal Union and the International Telegraph Union were other early examples). The gradual transformation of the Berne International Office, combined with that of the Paris Union from the outset, into the World Intellectual Property Organization as a specialised United Nations agency is one that needs to be told (other than through

---

[86] For the commentary on the draft convention, largely drafted it seems, by Fritz Ostertag, the Director of the Berne Office, see [1940] *DA* 109, 12 and 138, and, for a note on the Samaden meeting, see [1940] DA 8.
[87] Stockholm Act of the Berne Convention, art 2(5).
[88] *TRIPS Agreement,* art 9(2), WCT, art 2.

'official histories' of which there are several that are highly factually informative but lacking, as might be expected, in critical self-evaluation[89]), and placed in the wider context of international organizations generally. It is a story of high professionalism and commitment, particularly on the part of its small but dedicated team of Swiss officials in the early years. It is also one of great achievement – in the case of the Berne Convention, the successive revisions that up to 1967 moved the level of protection assured ever upwards and, in the case of the Paris Convention, led to the adoption of major new treaties such as the Patent Cooperation Treaty and the Madrid Trademark Protocol. At the same time, it is a tale of monumental failure and barely avoided disaster in the case of both major Conventions, with the major split over developed countries in Berne that occurred at Stockholm in 1967 and the failure of the proposed Paris revision in the early 1980s. It is also a story of organizational crisis and regeneration, notably in recent years, and one in which individuals have frequently played a great part. From Numa Droz of Switzerland at the start, to successive directors such as Ernest Röthslisberger, Fritz Ostertag, Jacques Secretan, Georg Bodenhausen and Arpad Bogsch, the history of the organization and its personalities (to say nothing of some of the eminent delegates at various conferences as well as several of the influential commentators on the Convention[90]) would provide an interesting and vivid picture of the way the public international law of copyright (and industrial property) has reached its present shape.

6. CONCLUDING COMMENTS

The purpose of this chapter has been to provide a brief overview of the rich range of sources that are available for research into the history of the public international law of copyright and to suggest, by way of conclusion, some areas of uncertainty that would repay further and closer inquiry. Quite apart from the value of such work in providing the kind of insights that we anticipate from historical investigation generally, in the public international law sphere it has an immediate role and relevance in the task of treaty interpretation and implementation at the national level. In a real sense, when one undertakes the interpretation of a treaty provision, one is inevitably engaging in an exercise of historical research in which it is necessary to interrogate what was said, understood and intended by the parties concerned, as well appreciating the wider circumstances in which they were operating. Thus, history and treaty interpretation march hand in hand here, and cannot be separated from each other. There is much work here still to be done.

---

[89] See generally *Mémoire*,(n 33) *Seconde Partie* ('Le Bureau de l'Union'), 99–108; Arpad Bogsch, 'Special Issue for the Commemoration of the Berne Convention: The First Hundred Years of the Berne Convention for the Protection of Literary and Artistic Works' [1986] Copyright 291, 307; Arpad Bogsch, 'Brief History of the First 25 Years of the World Intellectual Property Organization' [1992] Copyright 247.

[90] It would be interesting to know, for example, something more about the backgrounds of Dr William Briggs, author of the first English-language treatise (1906), likewise, for Darras of France, a famous early commentator.

15. El Salvador and the internationalisation of copyright
*Jose Bellido**

1. INTRODUCTION

No history of copyright can ignore the role of El Salvador as a political experiment in the internationalisation of copyright.[1] El Salvador served as a crucial test in the attempt to bring Latin America into the international realm. Moreover, El Salvador was used as a catalyst to trigger international copyright. Ironically, its role as a conduit for internationalisation was played while lacking any domestic copyright law whatsoever. In attempting to construct this history, the chapter focuses on the mediating figure of the Salvadorian diplomat, the Colombian émigré and former Venezuelan representative José María Torres Caicedo (1830–1889).[2] Torres Caicedo took part in most of the

---

* Manuscript sources are from depositories and collections abbreviated as follows: ABR = Archivo Banco de la República, Biblioteca Luis Ángel Arango, (Bogotá, Colombia), AAEA = Archivo de la Asociación de Artistas y Escritores (Madrid, Spain), AI = Archives Issaverdens [private archives] (Paris, France), AG = Archivo Gutiérrez (Buenos Aires, Argentina), AGN = Archivo General de la Nación (Colombia), AMAE = Archivo del Ministerio de Asuntos Exteriores (Madrid, Spain), AN = Archives Nationales (Paris, France), NA = National Archives (Kew, United Kingdom), SB = Schweizerisches Bundesarchiv (Berne, Switzerland), CADN = Centre des Archives Diplomatiques de Nantes (Nantes, France), RSL = Royal Society of Literature Archives (London, United Kingdom) *Clunet* = Journal du Droit International. Thanks to Sandrine Mansour-Merien, Carlos Hernández, Paola Reaño, Silvia Amaya and Antoine Issaverdens for helping me with archival sources. Previous versions of this chapter were presented at workshops and conferences at the University of Cambridge (2009), Griffith University (2011) and CNRS Paris-Sorbonne (2013). In particular, thanks to Léonard Laborie, Lionel Bently, Céline Paillette, Kathy Bowrey, Isabella Alexander, and Tomás Gómez-Arostegui for their comments and suggestions.

[1] 'Torres-Caicedo, écrivain distingue et très apprécié comme diplomate. Il représente en France plusieurs Etat de l'Amérique du Sud, l'Uruguay, Salvador, etc … Il n'a pas été élu, parce qu'étant seul de son pays, il n'a pas cru devoir se donner sa voix. Nous pensons que l'assemblée voudra bien réparer cette erreur, en l'invitant à prendre au bureau. (Bravo! bravo!)' Société Des Gens De Lettres de France, *Congrès littéraire international de Paris 1878* (Imprimerie Charles Bot 1879) 31.

[2] '[H]e was subsequently appointed Secretary of the (Colombian) Legation to Paris and London, Financial Commissioner of Bolivia and Magdalena, Secretary of a Diplomatic Mission to Washington, and Chargé d'Affaires of Venezuela to France and Holland […] In 1872, however, he accepted the post of Chargé d'Affaires of the Republic of El Salvador'; see 'Obituary: Torres Caicedo' *The Times* (London, 28 September 1889) 6; Mauricio Villacorta, 'José María Torres Caicedo' *La Unión* (El Salvador, 16 November 1889) 1–2.

314 *Research handbook on the history of copyright law*

copyright-related discussions held in the late 1870s and the beginning of the 1880s.[3] He negotiated bilateral agreements and circulated drafts for multilateral treaties.[4] He intervened at informal gatherings and cocktails,[5] congresses and expositions.[6] Above all, he became the president of the most important copyright association at the time, the *Association Littéraire et Artistique Internationale* (ALAI), which he chaired from 1880 to 1885.[7] Torres Caicedo's biography shows us a life full of repetitive episodes, a life of consistent ministerial acts and appearances.[8] With his pencil-thin moustache, with his small, nervous body, there he was, always quoted in the relevant publications; he seemed to be everywhere.[9] He appeared publicly and corresponded privately. His interventions were recorded in the minutes of innumerable meetings.[10] Seemingly always prepared for the state of affairs, always dispatching, we find a man in action – a man immersed, indeed, in his favourite actions: speaking and writing. For some, he was no doubt a living example of man as a political animal. More importantly, he embodies something slightly different: a shift in the political choreography of international copyright. Precisely because of his role – the way he both exemplified this historical shift and was a part of it – it is interesting therefore to focus not only on his

---

[3] Société Des Gens De Lettres de France (n 2). At this congress he read a significant paper entitled 'La littérature de l' Amérique Latine'; see Emilio Carilla, 'José María Torres Caicedo: descubridor de la literatura argentina' (1989) 2 Thesaurus, 334; see also Sam Ricketson and Jane Ginsburg, *International Copyright and Neighbouring Rights: The Berne Convention and Beyond* (OUP 2008) 49. See also dossier 'Torres Caicedo' AN Fond Société des Gens de Lettres, 454 AP à 417.

[4] 'Draft model of an International Literary Convention proposed by His Excellency J.M. Torres Caicedo, Minister from San Salvador at the Courts of Paris and London, for consideration by a Conference of Authors and Representatives of Literary and Artistic Societies, to be held at Berne during the summer of 1883, under the auspices of the Helvetic Consideration', RSL 'Annual Report (1883)' 14.

[5] Banquet organised because of the military victory of El Salvador, 15 April 1885, reported in *La Correspondencia de España* (Madrid, 19 April 1885) 2; 'Banquet to Foreign Visitors' *The Times* (London, 13 June 1879) 10.

[6] See, for instance, the pamphlet he published on the occasion of the Paris Universal Exposition 1878 on El Salvador: Torres Caicedo and Laferrière, *Noticia Histórica y Estadística de la República de El Salvador* (Paris, 1878). See also *Diario Oficial* (San Salvador, 6 September 1878) 874.

[7] His participation at the ALAI Congress in London (1879) is reported in *Bulletin ALAI* (5 July 1879) 6.

[8] A cursory glance at the most representative sources such as the legal journal *Clunet*, *Bulletin ALAI* and the *Annuaire* of Industrial and Intellectual Property reveals his ubiquity. For his appointment and as the Secretary of the (Colombian) Legation to Paris and Great Britain, see 'Legación de los Estados Unidos de Colombia acerca de los gobiernos de Francia y Gran Bretaña; libro de correspondencia con el gobierno de Colombia y cónsules de la misma República' ABR Folios 1–175, vol. 2, Fondo Libros Raros y Manuscritos. His different diplomatic representations often caused confusion over his nationality, see 'Exterior' *La Unión* (El Salvador, 18 February 1890) 3.

[9] Leopoldo García Remón, 'Cartas de París', *Revista Contemporánea* (Madrid, 20 December 1886) 618–622.

[10] *Congrès littéraire international de Paris 1878; Conférence Internationale pour la protection de la Propriété Industrielle 1880;* etc.

desire to connect Latin America with the international realm but also on the role that El Salvador played as a catalyst for the internationalisation of copyright.

Representing 'Latin America' in the ALAI congresses or in any diplomatic negotiation – as Torres Caicedo did – was remarkable, to say the least. Latin America was not an official political entity but just an aspiration. An attempt to represent her internationally had obvious political implications.[11] Clearly, constraints of space here prevent us from entering into an extended discussion of the consequences of this non-existent diplomatic office. However, the particulars of Torres Caicedo's actions are significant. Because his job was that of a diplomat, the defining verb to attach to Torres Caicedo was not merely speaking or writing but something closer to the act of representation.[12] The way he managed the diplomatic tension between secrecy and publicity was the factor that made him particularly distinctive in international intellectual property politics. He constantly swung between representation and action, between inquiry and intervention. This privileged position can be seen in the extension of his plenipotentia. As has been observed by copyright historians, negotiations of intellectual property treaties have always been characterised by two features. First, negotiations tended to impose limits on the ability of diplomatic agents to act abroad.[13] That is why the invitations to both Paris and Berne diplomatic conventions highlighted that the project was not going to put nations under any obligations until signatures were ratified by the adherents' countries.[14] Second, negotiations were frequently held in secret. Torres Caicedo modified these ways of negotiating in order to make allies. First, he was able to act without any limitations – whether temporal or otherwise – to reach political compromises. Secondly, he announced the flexibility and the extensive scope of his plenipotentia to bind the nation he represented (El Salvador) on different occasions. Each of these aided intellectual property negotiations. For instance, in the negotiations leading to the Paris Convention for the Protection of Industrial Property (1883), he made it public not only that he was 'authorized to sign the project of the convention' but also that he could anticipate that 'the Salvadorian parliament was going to pass it'.[15] The same wide scope of his power to act and the announcement of his freedom to sign and to bind the country he was representing would also occur at the negotiation of the bilateral copyright treaties between France and El Salvador, and between Spain and El Salvador.[16]

---

[11] See further Jose Bellido, 'Copyright in Latin America. Experiences of the Making 1880–1910' (PhD, Birkbeck, University of London 2009).

[12] Caicedo has 'brilliantly represented the Republic in France, Belgium, Holland, England, Spain and Germany': Memoria de los Ramos de Relaciones Exteriores, Justicia y Culto por el señor Ministro Doctor don Salvador Gallegos, *Diario Oficial* (San Salvador, 18 February 1883) 1.

[13] Catherine Seville, *The Internationalisation of Copyright Law: Books, Buccaneers and the Black Flag in the Nineteenth Century* (CUP 1999) 66.

[14] See note 'pour le Ministre', Paris (23 May 1882) CADN, Sous-direction des affaires Commerciales, carton 9.

[15] Première Séance, Mardi 6 Mars 1883, Ministère des Affaires Etrangères. *Conférences Internationale pour la protection de la Propriété Industrielle* (Paris: Imprimerie Nationale) 22.

[16] Plenipotentiary, San Salvador (12 August 1879) AMAE Siglo XIX, TR 225, exp. 1.

2. EL SALVADOR AS A CATALYST FOR INTERNATIONALISATION

The role of El Salvador in the internationalisation of copyright is often neglected in standard copyright histories. However, as we shall explain below, the diplomatic intervention of El Salvador was key to the emergence of international copyright. The development of an international copyright discourse promoted by ALAI was sustained for several years prior to the Berne Convention (1886) thanks to the diplomatic impulse facilitated by El Salvador. The evidence for this claim is found in the bilateral copyright treaties signed by El Salvador and France in 1883, and a year later, between El Salvador and Spain.[17] Furthermore, this is also supported by the ongoing negotiations that took place that same year with Great Britain. All of these diplomatic interactions were inaugurated by Torres Caicedo representing that small Latin American country, and not by his European counterparts. The argument in this chapter is that these relations were strategically promoted by ALAI and not by El Salvador.

In order to make his diplomatic representations workable, Torres Caicedo converted the obstacle of the small country's lack of resources into its main resource. He developed an odd but brilliant tactic. He acted upon acts. Surprisingly Torres Caicedo became a representative who used representatives. He realised that professional people – from copyright experts to engineers – in Paris were eagerly interested in participating in world politics. Torres Caicedo nominated famous delegates to help him in the task of representing this 'petit' Latin American country in Europe. Conscious of the sensitive political move he was making, he reported quickly to the Salvadorian Foreign Office that he reserved the final act of signature to himself, but had delegated attendance at the negotiations to other people. This explains some of the mysterious signatures that appear on international conventions at the end of the nineteenth century (e.g. for El Salvador or Haiti). For instance, Torres Caicedo appointed a doctor in physics, the scientist Jules Raynaud (1842–88), as his deputy. That is why we see Raynaud listed, incongruously, as a Salvadorian representative participating in the negotiations of the 1872 international telegraph convention.[18] We can also see a second name entering into our narrative, another more important one for copyright scholars because it connects again the Latin American country with the international copyright association par excellence, ALAI. Jules Lermina, who became 'the first secretary general of the Association Littéraire International',[19] a key name in copyright historiography, was appointed second secretary of the Republic of El Salvador.[20] These two appointments

---

[17] 'Convenio entre España y El Salvador (1884)', AMAE, TR 225, exp 1 and the documents regarding this convention published in the *Bulletin AEA*, 1884. The official publication in El Salvador was *Diario Oficial* (San Salvador, 12 August 1884) 1.

[18] 'Memoria' (n 12) 1; See also *Colección de Tratados Internacionales firmados por la República de Costa Rica* (Tipografía Nacional 1901), 303. For a biographical note on Raynaud; see Andrew J Butrica, 'Baudot, Jean-Maurice Emile', in Fritz E Froehlich and Allen Kent (eds), *Froehlich/Kent Encyclopaedia of Telecommunications: Volume 2 – Batteries* (Marcel Dekker 1996) 31–33.

[19] Ricketson and Ginsburg (n 3) 51; see also 'The Literary Congress' *New York Times* (16 October 1892).

[20] Torres Caicedo to Marquis de Salisbury (5 March 1880) NA FO66/25.

are extraordinary examples of the use of diplomatic resources for cosmopolitan enterprises. Neither Lermina nor Raynaud knew much about El Salvador or Salvadorian politics. However, their appointments illustrate one key issue in the history of international copyright: El Salvador was used by Torres Caicedo and ALAI as an experiment to test the possibility of making copyright international.[21]

3. THE FRANCO-SALVADORIAN COPYRIGHT TREATY

Surprisingly, France made her first successful move in negotiating Latin American bilateral copyright agreements as a response to an invitation. Even more intriguing, it was not really a move: it was a response to a call made in Paris itself. When in October of 1879 WH Waddington, the French Minister of Foreign Affairs, received a letter from the Legation of El Salvador in Paris, he would certainly have been astonished to read that the tiniest country of Latin America was asking for an 'efficient legal remedy' to thoroughly secure the property of 'works of the intellect'.[22] At that point in history, reading about a country on the other side of the Atlantic not blessing but condemning piracy was something quite unforeseen. Because of that, it generated not only a personal but also a systemic surprise. Neither a programme nor a project for establishing Latin American copyright negotiations existed in France's Foreign Ministry until then. The institutional climate was one of reluctance or indifference due to the slowness of communications, ignorance of laws, difficulty of translations, and lack of interest when providing instructions. However, these problems faded at precisely this point. The route taken by that specific diplomatic letter was unusual. Such a bizarre transmission leads us to question whether that letter was expected or not and makes us doubt whether it actually came as a surprise. The letter arrived from a few blocks away with a recognisable signature: 'Torres Caicedo'. As we have seen, Torres Caicedo was a man of influence, well connected in Paris,[23] whose presidential position at ALAI had earned him renown amongst those interested in international copyright.[24]

The missive had been written a few days after the famous literary and artistic congress held in London (1879).[25] The event had been widely publicised. Reports of the 'comments' and 'decisions' articulated at the ALAI congress in London, and the

---

[21] Étienne Bricon, *Des droits auteurs dans les rapports internationaux* (Rousseau 1888) 128: ['En 1880, la France signait une convention littéraire avec la République du Salvador: c'est la gloire du Ministre de cet Etat, M. Torres Caicedo, d'avoir personnellement réalisé cette œuvre ui est vraiment une œuvre grande et originale'].

[22] Torres Caicedo to Waddington (22 October 1879) CADN, Sous-direction des affaires Commerciales, Amérique Centrale, carton 120. See also *Chronique du Journal général de l'Imprimerie et de la Librairie* (Paris, 26 March 1881) 53–60.

[23] Oswaldo Holguín Callo, 'Palma y Torres Caicedo: una amistad literaria' (1984) 30 Fénix 234.

[24] The President of El Salvador was appointed a member of the Comité d'Honneur of ALAI. See letter from Zaldívar to the President of ALAI (23 August 1879) *Bulletin ALAI* (Oct/Nov 1879) 8.

[25] Jean Cavalli, *La genèse de la convention de Berne sur La Protection Internationale des Œuvres de Littéraires et Artistiques* (Université de Lausanne 1986) 141–55.

year before in Paris, had obviously reached the ears of Waddington.[26] Such comments presented a critical diagnosis of the problem of international copyright piracy. The symptoms pointed to the management of his Foreign Ministry. Out of the statements issued at the 1878 ALAI Congress in Paris, there was one that highlighted a major institutional concern. It stated that France's Ministry of Foreign Affairs needed to review the copyright treaties which France had already arranged with other countries.[27] After such a declaration, a feeling of displeasure spread through French interdepartmental offices. It was as if these 'comments' had shaken the role of the Foreign Ministry by suggesting that the political space they were in charge of had somehow legitimated international piracy.

Waddington responded with a letter that was published in *Clunet*, the most important journal in international law at the time. He believed that there was enormous 'importance attached by this department to the defence of those interests' – namely, the protection of French copyright abroad.[28] He justified France's longstanding position by explaining that the Ministry had decided to cut copyright agreements from the typical clauses of commercial and friendship arrangements in favour of concluding stand-alone bilateral copyright treaties. Yet France did not have any bilateral or multilateral copyright treaty with any Latin American country. In other words, the importance his office attached to this problem was reflected in the new approach to developing distinct bilateral copyright treaties. He continued by giving diplomatic reasons to explain why he thought there were difficulties in reaching bilateral agreements. It was not a question of making piracy legitimate but of the eternal problem of compromise between diverging legal traditions. As a skilled diplomat, he finished his letter on a positive note by expressing the hope that working together (through public and private endeavours) was a possibility for improving the making of bilateral copyright treaties. Suggestions on 'particular points' were welcomed and associations such as ALAI were given the opportunity to collaborate with the Foreign Ministry. The door was opened for them to express which measures they believed could be improved. The objective was to join forces to enhance the 'intellectual value of this country'.[29]

Given these preoccupations, it is not surprising that one month later Waddington responded favourably to the invitation to treaty negotiations offered by El Salvador.[30] It was an opportunity too attractive to be missed. Engaging with this tiny country would enable him to prove how the task of negotiating distinct copyright treaties was among the priorities of the Ministry. It was the end of the year and in order positively to establish bilateral negotiations, he followed the standard routine.[31] His response

---

[26] Waddington to the Société des Gens de Lettres (28 June 1879) *Clunet* (1879), 465–66.
[27] Cavalli (n 25) 116–39.
[28] Waddington to the Société des Gens de Lettres (n 26) 465–66.
[29] On the general assembly of the *Cercle*, the role of the *syndicat* in coordinated action with the Foreign Office was reported. See 'Cercle de la Librairie. Assemblée Générale Annuelle du 7 mars 1884. Présidence de M. G. Hachette', *Chronique du Journal général de l'Imprimerie et de la Librairie* (Paris, March 1884) 48.
[30] Waddington to Torres Caicedo, (24 November 1879) CADN, Sous-direction des affaires Commerciales, Amérique Centrale, carton 120.
[31] See, generally, Jose Bellido, 'Latin American and Spanish Copyright Bilateral Agreements (1880–1904)' (2009) 12 JWIP 1.

included a request to examine Salvadorian copyright law.[32] This would normally have allowed for an observation period in order to find connections between the two copyright laws. Typically, two countries would agree to a period of three or four months during which diplomats could develop strategies to negotiate. Such a temporal gap was always crucial for developing ways to relate (and to negotiate that relationship). Unsurprisingly, many negotiations failed during the preliminary examination. Divergent traditions and manifest obstacles often foreclosed and paralysed further diplomatic moves. In this case, just a week after his request, Waddington received a new missive. It was again from Torres Caicedo, and it announced that El Salvador did not have any positive copyright law.[33] The letter revealed that this particular negotiation was of a different kind.[34] While the legislative void would normally have been a fundamental impediment in pursuing any bilateral negotiation in copyright, this was not the case now. Both parties were extremely interested in reaching an agreement, and a stream of correspondence was set in motion.

The insistence of Torres Caicedo's efforts can be perceived not only from his laudatory words on the subject of copyright in France, but also from his active investment in the Salvadorian case. As the holder of such a prominent position in ALAI, it seems that he wanted to achieve an exemplary treaty. A few days before, at ALAI, he had attached great importance to accomplishing one bilateral convention in less than one year.[35] Torres Caicedo's commitment to this objective can be measured in the rapidity of his communications with Waddington. His earnest responses were taking only six days, one week at the longest.[36] Such speed could have been interpreted as hiding a wide authority for political action. It was impossible that he could have managed in these brief periods of time to communicate with El Salvador, ask for instructions and then respond according to those instructions. In fact, he did not receive instructions from El Salvador before communicating with Waddington. Rather, he had already made public his extensive scope for action. Through the ALAI congresses and bulletins, Torres Caicedo had revealed the extent of his credentials, an unusual gesture in any strategic diplomacy.[37]

---

[32] Waddington to Torres Caicedo (n 30).

[33] '[…] répondant ainsi à la question qu'Elle me pose : qu'il n'existe encore aucune loi sur la matière', in letter from Torres Caicedo to Waddington (5 December 1879) CADN, Sous-direction des affaires Commerciales, Amérique Centrale, carton 120.

[34] This anomaly was commented on with curiosity by Alcide Darras, *Des Droits intellectuels. Du droit des auteurs des artistes dans les rapports internationaux* (Paris Rousseau 1887) 362–63, and Leon Poinsard, *Études de droit international conventionnel* (Librairie Cotillon 1894) 507.

[35] 'M. le président fait part au comité des démarches qu'il a faites auprès des différents gouvernements dans l'intérêt de la propriété littéraire, et compte pouvoir présenter au prochain Congrès des conventions littéraires de plusieurs pays de l'Amérique centrale': Proceedings of the ALAI Congress held in London (1879), session 1 October 1879, *Bulletin ALAI* (Oct/Nov 1879) 14.

[36] For instance, the letter from Waddington dated 24 November 1879 had a reply by Torres Caicedo dated 5 December 1879: CADN, Sous-direction des affaires Commerciales, Amérique Centrale, carton 120.

[37] 'Non seulement, M. le président Zaldivar fait à l'Association un don de cinq cents francs; mais, ce qui vaut mieux encore, il a donné pleins pouvoirs à M Torrès Caicedo pour conclure

After putting down that unusual letter, Waddington became extremely interested in the possibility of exploring a negotiation without the troubling examination of foreign legislation. To negotiate under such special conditions showed an unprecedented diplomatic flexibility. It involved the chance to explore a freedom to model a bilateral copyright treaty without constraints.[38] The Salvadorian negotiation was perhaps the simplest France could have ever faced in copyright.[39] It was modelled upon previous copyright treaties that France had signed with European countries.[40] In a few months, an agreement had been reached and approved by the respective chambers. The relationship between Salvador and France was formalised by an instrument signed on 9 June 1880. A few years later, Torres Caicedo recalled that easy process and conceived the negotiation as an opportunity to link up and incorporate the rest of Latin America within the realm of international copyright.[41] He imagined the treaty as an exemplary construction, as an example to be followed, to be 'imitated'.[42]

Paradoxically, his strategy was built on a significant vision that was embedded in a bizarre idealism. He believed that the example of the smallest country in Latin America could be extrapolated into the model for the rest of the region. In the history of copyright, the trajectory of the French-Salvadorian bilateral copyright treaty was quickly overshadowed by major developments in the international arena. The bilateral relationship then became a miniscule fact recorded as an anomalous event in copyright history. From a 'traité d'un libéralisme très avancé'[43] ('treaty of very advanced liberalism') the Salvadorian treaty turned into an atypical anecdote. In the early 1880s it was, however a significant success in a political laboratory that used El Salvador as an experiment and platform for the internationalisation of copyright. In fact, one of the notable features of the treaty was that it put forward the principle of national treatment.[44] Moreover, some aspects such as the assimilation of translation rights or the

---

avec la France des conventions qui garantiront pleinement la propriété littéraire dans toutes ses manifestations', in 'Procès-verbal de la séance plénière du 25 Octobre 1879. Présidence de Torrès Caicedo', *Bulletin ALAI* (Oct/Nov 1879) 16.

[38] The right of translation became a particularly interesting negotiating zone; it was a normative priority for Caicedo. Torres Caicedo wanted to assimilate the translation with the reproduction right. Letter from Torres Caicedo to Waddington (5 December 1879), CADN, Sous-direction des affaires Commerciales, Amérique Centrale, carton 120; letter from Torres Caicedo to Freycinet (1 January 1880) CADN, Sous-direction des affaires Commerciales, Amérique Centrale, carton 120.

[39] 'Chambre des Députes. Session de 1882', *Chronique du Journal général de l'Imprimerie et de la Librairie* (Paris, 11 February 1882) 21.

[40] Torres Caicedo requested the text of a few conventions (The Netherlands, Italy, Austria) and used them to draft the new treaty. See Letter from Torres Caicedo to Freycinet (1 Jan. 1880) CADN, Sous-direction des affaires Commerciales, Amérique Centrale, carton 120.

[41] Torres Caicedo to Núñez de Arce (22 June 1884) AAEA 'Correspondencia'.

[42] Torres Caicedo to Elduayen (Spanish Minister of Foreign Affairs) (26 June 1884) AMAE, TR225, Exp. 1.

[43] Bricon (n 21) 128.

[44] Article 1 Franco-Salvadorian copyright treaty (1880); CADN, Sous-direction des affaires Commerciales, Amérique Centrale, carton 120.

lack of copyright formalities revealed that this was not an ordinary bilateral agreement.[45] Here we can observe how the agreement was an attempt to find out about world politics and therefore to test the possibility of international copyright. Although El Salvador had not yet passed a special copyright law, this lack was not considered an obstacle to reach an international agreement.[46]

4. NEGOTIATIONS BETWEEN EL SALVADOR AND GREAT BRITAIN

After France, the next step was inevitably Britain. A few months after Earl Granville returned to the British Foreign Office in 1880, Torres Caicedo sent him a letter, now writing on behalf of El Salvador, reminding him of the friendship the two diplomats had enjoyed when Torres Caicedo was 'representing Colombia'.[47] Here we can observe an interesting feature: how Torres Caicedo shifted credentials and conceived diplomacy as a profession – and not a vocation – representing successively Venezuela, Colombia and El Salvador.[48] Now, as a Salvadorian diplomat and ALAI president, he started to focus on the negotiation of a copyright treaty between El Salvador and Great Britain. His first move was to send Granville a proposition, encapsulated in a sort of rhetorical question.[49] The Government of El Salvador, he explained, had authorised him to conclude a bilateral copyright treaty with Great Britain. He continued with the obvious question: would it be convenient for your nation to sign an agreement of this sort? Should any doubts still remain in Granville's mind, and in order to encourage diplomatic action, Torres Caicedo continued the letter with a mix of narcissistic satisfaction and negotiating tactics. He not only emphasised his diplomatic success but also reminded him of the copyright agreement he had just reached with Britain's neighbour, France.[50] It is clear that he thought this strategically chosen fact would best provoke the British desire, and therefore a response. He wrote, 'I have just signed a

---

[45] Ibid, art 4.
[46] Notwithstanding the principle of legal autonomy, the idea was that the convention served to fill the domestic lacuna before the copyright law was enacted. In this sense, the agreement was crucial since the material conditions and communication difficulties were perceived as more difficult aspects to overcome than doctrinal controversies, see Jose Bellido, 'The Editorial Quest for International Copyright – 1886–1896' (2014) Book History 380.
[47] Torres Caicedo to Earl Granville (1 May 1880) NA FO 66/25.
[48] His first diplomatic appointment was as secretary of the Colombian Legation in Paris; see decree by the president of Nueva Granada, Mariano Ospina (8 April 1857); AGN Ministerio de Relaciones Exteriores; tomo 274, folios 35–36; see also references to further appointments, Cecilio Acosta, 'El Dr. José María Torres Caicedo y Venezuela en París' *El Pasatiempo* (Caracas, 13 June 1878) 291–92.
[49] Torres Caicedo to Earl Granville (4 April 1881), NA FO66/26; see also Torres Caicedo (previously acting as Colombian diplomat) to Earl Granville (2 August 1870) [concerning the Panama Canal] in 'Legación de los Estados Unidos de Colombia cerca del gobierno de S.M.B. [manuscrito]; libro de correspondencia con el Foreign Office y varios en Inglaterra, 1868–1869' ABR, Fondo Libros Raros y Manuscritos, Folios 1–1705.
[50] 'Convention entre la France et le Salvador pour la garantie réciproque de la propriété des œuvres d'éprit et d'art', *Journal official de la République Française* (30 December 1880) 55–56.

bilateral copyright agreement with the Republic of France that is the most complete and developed treaty that has ever been signed yet'.[51] There was the usual self-confidence and sense of purpose in his writing, but the most surprising element of the letter was not his clear efforts to elicit a specific reply. On the contrary, the most interesting fact was that he seemed very well aware of the problems of bilateral reciprocity (or as Cornish once termed it, 'the canker of reciprocity').[52] Hence, his explicit emphasis on the rewards for Great Britain of signing a treaty in which 'for each Salvadorian book protected, hundreds of British ones would be protected'.[53] Such nationally self-effacing and ecumenical language, such constant appeal to international copyright justice was, to say the least, uncommon in the field of copyright politics.

With these profitable conditions on the table, it is no surprise that Granville penned a rapid reply.[54] Yet for a definitive position he had to request the Board of Trade to refer the draft to the Indian Colonial Office.[55] As Lionel Bently has already suggested the move towards internationalisation 'implicated British-colonial relations in interestingly conflicting ways'.[56] This was also the case here. Less than two weeks after Torres Caicedo sent the original dispatch, the whole British diplomatic machinery had been activated and promptly engaged in an epistolary exchange with El Salvador in order to reach a bilateral copyright agreement.[57] The Foreign Office was not alone in imagining a promising future for the negotiation; other British departments appeared equally optimistic. For instance, the Board of Trade had also begun negotiations, with a sympathetic approach.[58] And the colonial consultation had also happily (and rapidly) contributed to the British drafting process by including a rather ambiguous clause of applicability of the treaty 'to the colonies or foreign possessions of Her Britannic Majesty as far as the local laws of such colonies or foreign possessions may permit'.[59] This conditional inclusion was the colonial response in order to facilitate negotiations. However, the drafting ambiguity it represented already indicated an ongoing controversy that existed then around the interpretation and the interplay of British copyright between colonial and international regimes,[60] an ongoing controversy whose latest episode had concerned the interpretation of the Franco-British bilateral copyright

---

[51] Torres Caicedo to Earl Granville (n 49).
[52] William Cornish, 'The Canker of Reciprocity' (1988) EIPR 99.
[53] Torres Caicedo to Earl Granville (n 49).
[54] Earl Granville to Torres Caicedo (13 April 1881) NA FO66/26.
[55] Earl Granville to the Earl of Kimberley, 25 June 1881, NA FO66/26 [in order 'to inform Lord Granville whether there is any objection *from a colonial (Indian) point of v*iew, to the Draft being submitted to the Government of El Salvador in its present shape'] (my emphasis).
[56] Lionel Bently, 'The "Extraordinary Multiplicity" of Intellectual Property Laws in the British Colonies in the Nineteenth Century' (2011) 12 Theoretical Inquiries in Law 161, 192.
[57] Torres Caicedo to Earl Granville (3 May 1881) NA FO66/26.
[58] Board of Trade to Earl Granville (22 April 1881) NA FO66/26 ['In reply, I am to state for the information of Earl Granville that the Board of Trade are of the opinion that the proposal should be accepted, and that a Convention on the basis of existing international copyright conventions may be negotiated properly'].
[59] This was Article XIII of the draft, included for the 'sake of clarity': see note from the Foreign Office (9 July 1881) NA FO66/26.
[60] For more, see Seville, (n 13) 78–145; Bently, 'Extraordinary Multiplicity' (n 56).

treaty.⁶¹ Because this interpretative ambiguity arose again, the Foreign Office had to look for expert advice and contacted the well-known barrister and diplomat Julian Pauncefote (1828–1902) who recommended that flexible wording should be included.⁶² After that inclusion, the British Under-Secretary of State for India, Thomas Lawrence Seccombe (1812–1902) said that 'no objection' existed from the 'Indian point of view' to the proposed British–Salvadorian copyright agreement.⁶³

Internal clearance from Britain's diplomats looked promising and seemed to augur a quick deal. However, a significant drawback to this copyright negotiation occurred during the summer of 1881. It did not come from the British side. The scene of epistolary exchanges changed to a place to which Torres Caicedo had travelled on account of his weak health. He was now at the beautiful Cabourg Grand Hotel in Normandy. Torres Caicedo had begun to feel unwell and decided to take a rest from Paris. Though he broke from his everyday routine, he continued dispatching what he considered important and urgent business. One of those important pending issues was precisely the negotiation of the copyright agreement.⁶⁴ At the hotel, he received another letter from Granville.⁶⁵ The *envoi* contained two exemplars of a draft copyright convention between Great Britain and El Salvador.⁶⁶ The drafts had been framed upon the model of the convention recently concluded between Britain and Spain.⁶⁷ Immediately after receiving it, Torres Caicedo highlighted an issue that provoked a setback and an unexpected twist. Perhaps surprisingly to modern eyes, the problem was not that El Salvador wanted a more permissive agreement than the one proposed by Great Britain – one that would allow for some activities such as translation to be carried out without constituting a direct infringement. It was just the opposite. When Torres Caicedo stressed that El Salvador could not agree to the draft it was because, he said, El Salvador could not afford a convention that gave less protection to copyright than the Franco-Salvadorian copyright agreement recently signed.⁶⁸ While the Franco-Salvadorian copyright treaty (1880) had put forward an international agreement without copyright formalities, Great Britain was not so keen to pass an agreement without

---

⁶¹ Seville (n 13) 51–52; and Ronan Deazley, 'Commentary on International Copyright Act 1852' in *Primary Sources on Copyright (1450–1900)*, L Bently and M Kretschmer (eds) www.copyrighthistory.org.

⁶² Note from Julian Pauncefote to the Colonial Office (re: Salvador Copyright) (13 July 1881) NA FO66/26.

⁶³ Thomas Lawrence Seccombe, India Office, to the Foreign Office (20 July 1881) NA FO66/26.

⁶⁴ The reason of the delay was that the Board of Trade had to be consulted before submission of the draft to Torres Caicedo. See note from the Board of Trade to Earl Granville (21 June 1881) NA FO66/26 ['Draft may now be submitted. Draft sent to Torres Caicedo accordingly'].

⁶⁵ Earl Granville to Torres Caicedo (6 August 1881); and the reply from Torres Caicedo to Earl Granville (15 August 1881) NA FO66/26.

⁶⁶ Earl Granville to Torres Caicedo (ibid).

⁶⁷ Earl Granville to Torres Caicedo (ibid); see also the Board of Trade to Earl Granville (24 May 1881) NA FO66/26 ['the Copyright convention between this country and Spain, altered to the extent shown in the enclosed …'].

⁶⁸ Torres Caicedo to Earl Granville (21 November 1881) NA FO66/26.

formalities.[69] That it was Great Britain (and not El Salvador) that was uncomfortable with such a liberal regime seems counter-intuitive, more so if we take into account that the British publishing industry was obviously much more powerful than the Salvadorian.[70] Whereas the formal requirements of deposit and registration of a copyright work were obviously beneficial to 'a distant country such as El Salvador' – and that is precisely how the British negotiators saw it[71] – Torres Caicedo did not consider them so. The level of protection had to follow the previous agreement. Therefore he characterised the British proposal as a 'backward step on the already traced path'.[72] Surely this move was a common tactical exaggeration, intended to continue the negotiations and leave the door open to a new drafting. However, the excessive, unforeseen and rather surprising terms and conditions put forward by El Salvador were revealing. Torres Caicedo persisted in the idea of using the Franco-Salvadorian convention 'as a model',[73] particularly in the assimilation of translation rights.[74] And he proposed changes to the British draft.

The manoeuvre did not have the effect he expected. Despite the fact that some minor amendments were accepted,[75] Great Britain finally found the demands and aspirations of El Salvador impossible to meet.[76] This put an end to the negotiation.[77] Granville made his rationale abundantly clear to Torres Caicedo: 'It is with extreme regret that I have to state to you that the existing copyright laws of this country will not permit this Government to meet the wishes which the Government of El Salvador has expressed in the matter.'[78] It is more than ironic that the tiny country of El Salvador demanded less

---

[69] As Ricketson and Ginsburg have noted, 'a significant number of conventions, most notably those made by the UK, under which registration and deposit in the country where protection was claimed was necessary, at least in relation to some categories of works'. Ricketson and Ginsburg (n 3) 38.

[70] Ricketson and Ginsburg note how this issue (the gulf between what may be called the 'producing' nations – that is, nations such as the French, that were net exporters of literary and artistic products – and those nations, such as the Scandinavians (or El Salvador), which were 'users' – that is, net importers – of these products) affected the negotiations surrounding the 1884 Diplomatic Conference of 1884; ibid 67.

[71] For instance, note from the Board of Trade to Earl Granville (24 May 1881) NA FO66/26.

[72] Torres Caicedo to Earl Granville (21 November 1881) NA FO66/26.

[73] Ibid.

[74] Torres Caicedo to Earl Granville (14 November 1881) NA FO66/26 ['This legation therefore cannot possibly negotiate a literary convention with the Government of H B M unless on the bases which were adopted in making the convention between France and Salvador'].

[75] For instance, after the stubborn insistence of Torres Caicedo, the Under Secretary of State from the Foreign Office noted that 'having further considered the point now raised as to the insertion of a clause in the draft touching fair imitations and adaptations of dramatic works, the Board of Trade do not see any objection to meeting the wishes of the Salvadorian minister Torres Caicedo' (15 November 1881) NA FO66/26.

[76] Note from the Under-Secretary of State from the Foreign Office (1 December 1881) NA FO66/26 ['In reply, I am to state, for the information of the Earl of Granville, that the Board of Trade do not think that, in the circumstances stated, it would be desirable and indeed practicable to take any further steps in the negotiation'].

[77] Earl Granville to Torres Caicedo (8 December 1881) NA FO66/26.

[78] Ibid.

protection than the British Empire, that this developing country was more internationally copyright-ambitious than Great Britain. Surely for the underlying history of international copyright law, another dispatch is worthy of mention. A few weeks after the diplomatic failure, the British Foreign Office received the news that Jules Lermina was no longer secretary of the El Salvador Legation.[79] Lermina was the secretary of ALAI. That short note was further confirmation that these British-Salvadorian negotiations formed not only the bilateral treaty that never was, but were also part of a network of strategies between professionalism (ALAI) and officialism (diplomatic exchanges) which would shape international copyright for years to come.

5. THE SALVADORIAN–SPANISH COPYRIGHT TREATY

Torres Caicedo's breathless and political copyright negotiating skills were stunningly evidenced on another occasion, this time related to the negotiation of a bilateral treaty between El Salvador and Spain. Despite explicit and repetitive references in Spain throughout the nineteenth century to the 'urgent' necessity of establishing copyright relations,[80] Spain had not been able to sign an agreement with any Latin American country.[81] However, Spanish focus on Latin America in copyright matters was made practicable, once again, because of the instrumental and persistent role Torres Caicedo played in the negotiations. On 18 June 1883 he notified the Spanish Minister of Foreign Affairs, Antonio Aguilar y Ortega, Marquis of la Vega de Armijo (1824–1908) of the Salvadorian desire for a copyright bilateral treaty with Spain.[82] The letter referred to the earlier scenario, discussed above, of the Franco-Salvadorian copyright treaty as the platform from which negotiations could take place. Some distinctive ingredients however characterised this negotiation. While the previous arrangement with France could be described as a relatively surprising development in the field of international copyright, the Spanish-Salvadorian negotiation produced a particular type of historical experience which was perhaps even more astonishing. Taking into account that before independence in 1821 El Salvador had been a Spanish colony for many centuries, her

---

[79] Torres Caicedo to Earl Granville (29 December 1881) NA FO66/26.
[80] For instance, this necessity was highlighted in the debates held at the Spanish Senate when the text of the 1879 Spanish Copyright Bill was discussed. It was observed that, 'the most important [treaties] would be those to be made with the American Republics, making them recognize and respect the legitimate rights of our writers, composers and artists'. After that intervention, another Spanish Senator commented that '[…] of special importance would be conventions of this class with American States where Spanish is spoken: however you are aware of the many difficulties that had been opposed in America and that have never made us capable of achieving these literary property conventions'. *Diario de Sesiones, legislatura 1878. Asunto: proyecto de ley sobre propiedad intelectual* (1878) 1949.
[81] Although there was a previous copyright agreement between Guatemala and Spain (1864), this convention was never ratified. Bellido, 'Bilateral Agreements' (n 31); Manuel González Hontoria, *Los convenios de propiedad intelectual entre España y los países iberoamericanos* (Tomás Minuesa de los Ríos 1899); see also Torres Caicedo to Núñez de Arce (22 June 1884); AAEA 'Correspondencia'.
[82] Torres Caicedo to Marques de la Vega de Armijo (18 June 1883) AMAE, TR 225, exp 1.

desire now to reach an agreement as 'liberal' or generous (for the Europeans) as the one signed by France with her former metropolis was curious, to say the least.

In this sense, what interests us is that Torres Caicedo did not have to convince and persuade the Government of El Salvador but the Government of Spain. In fact, the Spaniards seemed reluctant at first to initiate negotiation because of the awkward itinerary in Torres Caicedo's letter. With some logic, they expected copyright treaty negotiations with El Salvador to have been initiated and to take place in Central America and not in Paris, where the letter came from.[83] However, despite the unusual opening of the negotiations, the bilateral relationship was particularly attractive to the Spanish. Torres Caicedo had made quite explicit what future benefits the treaty could bring to 'Spanish writers in El Salvador'.[84] As a result, two weeks after his invitation to negotiate, he received a positive response from the Spanish Minister of Foreign Affairs.[85] The negotiation was however affected by several factors. First, the summer break did not help. The break affected both parties. The negotiations on copyright coincided with the crucial contact Torres Caicedo had just made with the Swiss Federal Council for the organisation of international diplomatic conferences in Berne. So, multilateral and bilateral copyright negotiations inconveniently overlapped. Secondly, another difficulty emerged: the Minister with whom Torres Caicedo had established relations was suddenly replaced. This double twist threatened to upset Spanish-Salvadorian negotiations from the beginning. But here again we can see the exercise of skilful diplomatic tactics. Instead of waiting for the success or failure of the international enterprise, Torres Caicedo tried to navigate the diplomatic minefield in Spain by quickly sending a letter to the new Spanish Minister, Servando Ruiz Gómez (1821–1888). This letter summarised the ongoing negotiation between the two countries, copied a series of verbatim quotes of the compromise to negotiate achieved with the previous Spanish Minister, and included a draft of a convention.[86] No answer was forthcoming. Having failed to receive any feedback from the Spaniards, the interest he personally had in pursuing negotiation of the treaty in Europe also waned. He received a letter from El Salvador requesting him to freeze negotiations.[87]

However, his diplomatic efforts finally bore fruit. On 2 January 1884, Torres Caicedo sent a letter to the Spanish Minister saying that El Salvador was no longer interested in a copyright agreement in which Spain herself had shown no particular interest.[88] Then, a couple of months later, he notified the Spaniards that he was authorised again to

---

[83] Internal note from Florencio Iñigo to Marques de la Vega de Armijo (3 July 1883) AMAE, TR 225, exp 1.
[84] Torres Caicedo to Marques de la Vega de Armijo (18 June 1883) in AMAE TR 225, exp 1 ['Pero además obtendría un resultado práctico: el hacer respetar los derechos de los escritores españoles cuyas obras se reproducen sin que ellos, hasta ahora, hayan recibido indemnización alguna'].
[85] Marques de la Vega de Armijo to Torres Caicedo (9 July 1883) AMAE, TR 225, exp 1.
[86] Torres Caicedo to Servando Ruiz Gómez (19 November 1883) AMAE, TR 225, exp 1.
[87] Salvador Gallegos to Torres Caicedo (14 February 1884) AMAE, TR 225, exp. 1.
[88] Torres Caicedo to Servando Ruiz Gómez (2 January 1884) AMAE, TR 225, exp 1.

continue the negotiations.[89] This was not the only circumstance that transformed the state of affairs. Over a few months the conditions for a possible negotiation to reach a successful closure had changed. First, a new Spanish Minister of Foreign Affairs, José de Elduayen (1823–1898), had been appointed. It looked as if he was more inclined to sign the treaty. And the president of El Salvador, Rafael Zaldívar (1834–1903) had planned a trip to Europe.[90] For the Spaniards, the presence of Zaldívar in Europe offered a suitable occasion to sign the agreement. Ironically it was now in Spanish interests to negotiate with all due speed, and it was in the midst of this atmosphere of urgency that the treaty was signed.[91]

The text was almost identical to the Franco-Salvadorian treaty. For instance, it provided for an assimilation of translation rights,[92] national treatment and almost no copyright formalities.[93] The accelerated negotiation surely affected the drafting of the final version. So it is not surprising that language shortcomings made some expressions difficult to understand in Spanish.[94] Nevertheless, and despite this interpretative opacity, the importance of the Spanish-Salvadorian treaty (1884) went beyond its role of governing bilateral copyright relations between the two countries. The treaty became fundamental in the history of Spanish and Latin American copyright because it was used as a key means of communication for the Spanish Ministry of Foreign Affairs.[95] In fact, Spaniards strategically used the text of the bilateral treaty authored by Torres Caicedo as a springboard to initiate contacts with other Latin American countries.[96]

---

[89] Torres Caicedo to Elduayen (19 April 1884) in AMAE, TR 225, exp. 1 [Torres Caicedo received instructions to freeze negotiations but he insisted on continuing with them]; see also 'Europa' *Diario Oficial* (San Salvador, 18 March 1884) 275.

[90] Torres Caicedo reporting Zaldívar's visit to Europe to Granville (27 May 1884) NA FO66/30.

[91] Banquete en honor a Zaldívar, *El Globo* (23 June 1884) 2; 'En la Academia de la Lengua' *Diario Oficial* (El Salvador, 2 August 1884) 113.

[92] Salvadorian–Spanish Copyright Treaty [1884] Art 4, AMAE, TR 225, exp 1.

[93] Ibid, Art 2. This article required no formalities as long as the author could prove his right of property under the law of the country of origin. Ricketson and Ginsburg have traced this article to the Franco-Spanish Convention of 1880: Ricketson and Ginsburg (n 3) 37.

[94] The expression 'fragmentos enteros' (literally 'entire fragments') contained in Article 7 of the treaty was considered extremely obscure and grammatically incorrect. See Article 7 of the bilateral copyright treaty between Spain and El Salvador (1884) that is identical to Article 7 of the previous copyright treaty between France and El Salvador (1881). Some criticisms can be read in *Congreso Literario Hispano-Americano, Actas* (Ricardo Fe 1893) 543.

[95] The convention was attached as a 'model' to the Royal Order sent by the Spanish Government to her representatives in Latin America on 13 July 1891, Disp 29, AMAE TR317, exp 001.

[96] Bellido, 'Bilateral Agreements' (n 31); see also Hontoria (n 81) 9–15.

6. FROM PARIS TO BERNE

During Torres Caicedo's ALAI presidential tenure (1880–85), the first drafts of an international copyright convention were prepared.[97] This preparatory material was used to arrange a series of conferences that gave birth, in 1886, to the Berne Convention for the Protection of Literary and Artistic Property. Torres Caicedo first tried to convince France to convene a diplomatic conference on international copyright and after the reluctance of the French Government,[98] he persuaded the Helvetic confederation to host the well-known conferences during the summers of 1883–86.[99] As copyright historians have already noted, these conferences were crucial for the success of the Berne international copyright convention.[100] However, there is something of equal interest that frequently escapes historical accounts: the awkward similarity between the Paris Convention for Industrial Property (1883) and the Berne Convention three years later.[101] The signature of El Salvador surprisingly appears and disappears in the history of the conventions.[102] Nevertheless, one element remains: Torres Caicedo intervened in both of them,[103] using the political momentum generated after the Paris negotiation as a way to bring copyright to a multilateral framework.[104] He did so immediately after attending the signature of the Paris Convention for Industrial Property on 20 March 1883.[105] When the Swiss Federal Government expressed its wish to receive the bureaucratic institution resulting from that international agreement (the International

---

[97] Sam Ricketson, *The Berne Convention for the Protection of Literary and Artistic Works: 1886–1986* (Centre for Commercial Law Studies, Queen Mary 1987) 48–49.

[98] Ricketson and Ginsburg (n 3) 52.

[99] RSL 'Annual Report (1883)' 14.

[100] See, for instance, Eva Hemmungs Wirtén, 'A Diplomatic Salto Mortale: Translation Trouble in Berne, 1884–1886' (2011) 14 Book History, 88; Stef van Gompel, *Formalities in Copyright Law: An Analysis of their History, Rationales and Possible Future* (Kluwer Law International 2011) 135–36.

[101] See Yves Plasseraud and François Savignon, *Paris 1883: Genèse du droit unioniste des brevets* (Litec, Librairies Techniques 1983) and Beier, 'One Hundred Years of International Cooperation – The Role of the Paris Convention in the Past, Present and Future' (1994) 15 IIC 1–20.

[102] The anniversary of the entry into force of the Paris Convention did not select El Salvador in its history of the genesis of the convention. See 'Special Studies: One Hundredth Anniversary of the Entry into Force of the Paris Convention for the Protection of Industrial Property' (1984) Industrial Property 367; see also Arpad Bogsch, 'The First Hundred Years of the Paris Convention for the Protection of Industrial Property' (1983) Industrial Property 187.

[103] E.g., the invitation to Torres Caicedo (9 September 1880), CADN, Sous-direction des affaires Commerciales, carton 9; Letter from Légation et Consulat General de France au Centre-Amérique (7 June 1883) (saying that it was approved but not yet ratified) CADN, Sous-direction des affaires Commerciales, carton 11; also 'Acuerdos. Ministerio de Asuntos Exteriores' *Diario de La República, El Salvador* (12 October 1880) 234.

[104] Surely, the Paris model was based on the Postal Convention; see *Projet d'une Internationale pour la Protection de la Propriété Industrielle* (Arnous de Riviere 1879).

[105] The initial treaty signatories were 11: eight European (France, Belgium, Italy, Spain, the Netherlands, Portugal, Serbia, and Switzerland) and surprisingly three Latin American countries (Brazil, Guatemala, and *El Salvador*); see 'Relaciones Exteriores' *Diario Oficial* (El Salvador, 10 January 1883) 31.

Bureau of Industrial Property),[106] Torres Caicedo looked for the ALAI copyright annual congress to be hosted precisely there, in Berne. His subsequent gestures were significant. Not only had he already asked 'confidentially and unofficially' for the Swiss Federal Council to meet members of the famous copyright association (ALAI),[107] the association also 'suggested' Berne as the next venue for its 1883 Congress.[108] One year later, Torres Caicedo convinced the Federal Council to circulate the diplomatic invitation to the forthcoming 1884 diplomatic copyright conference.[109] Even more: the draft he prepared constituted the text on which the Berne diplomatic conferences were to work until 1886.[110] The interventions of Torres Caicedo reveal that it is not possible to characterise these conventions as being solely the result of European projects.[111] The subtle and profound interplay between an international professional association (ALAI) and its diplomatic and political experiment (El Salvador) under the common aegis of Torres Caicedo provide an excellent view of the complexity of the political and legal difficulties that emerged between Paris and Berne.

However, an element of contingency arises when we explore this curious enterprise, and that contingent twist could explain why the role of El Salvador in the internationalisation of copyright is still a blind spot in copyright historiography.[112] This political experiment culminated in a biographical disaster. As the decisive moment arrived, when all his strategic experience of official and unofficial files could have allowed Torres Caicedo to record his name and El Salvador in the history of copyright, when the Berne Convention was about to be signed, he did not attend the crucial meeting from which the convention originated.[113] To our surprise, and despite having initiated the series of conferences at Berne, he never arrived at the key meeting.[114] His absence is what makes this narrative particularly interesting. For someone so socially and politically connected, for someone so obsessed with credentials, it is astonishing

---

[106] Lardy to Arago (27 April 1883) CADN, Sous-direction des affaires Commerciales, carton 11; see also Ricketson and Ginsburg (n 3) 51–62.

[107] Kern (Swiss delegation in France) to Numa Droz (7 July 1882) SB E22 2377.

[108] Lucien Bastide, *L'Union de Berne de 1886 et la Protection Internationale des droits des Auteurs et des Artistes* (Giard 1890) 36; Seville (n 13) 60–65; Deazley, 'Commentary on International Copryright Act' (n 61).

[109] Note Conseil fédéral (3 December 1883), SB E22 2377.

[110] Draft model of an International Literary Convention proposed by His Excellency JM Torres Caicedo, Minister from San Salvador at the Courts of Paris and London, for consideration by a Conference of Authors and representatives of Literary and Artistic Societies to be held at Berne, during the summer of 1883, under the auspices of the Helvetic Confederation, 14–18, RSL 'Annual Report (1883)' 14.

[111] cf Ruth L Okediji, 'The International Relations of Intellectual Property: Narratives of Developing Country Participation in the Global Intellectual Property System' (2003) 7 Sing JICL 315.

[112] Another factor that surely contributed to this oblivion is the fact that the Salvadorian National Archives were completely destroyed by fire in 1889; see telegram from John Moffatt, San Salvador (21 November 1889) NA FO66/35.

[113] The political agitation in El Salvador and Torres Caicedo's ill-health could have been the causes why he missed that meeting; see letter to John Moffatt (14 March 1885) NA FO66/31.

[114] The surprise at his absence emerged because El Salvador had 'declared [herself] ready to be represented' as it is noted in Ricketson and Ginsburg (n 3) 58.

that he did not attend. It was 8 September 1884 and it seems as if his schedule short-circuited. It is not relevant that he was 'almost' there. He was not there.[115] Since this was the key moment for international copyright, his failure to attend was even more perplexing and unforeseen.[116] The consequences were clear, whatever the reason for his absence: his connection was suddenly off.[117] His importance in international copyright history would soon decrease, his image started fading away and his name fell into historical oblivion.[118] Unfortunately, the event he failed to attend became one of the most important meetings in copyright history, the vital step that would lead to the Berne Convention in 1886.[119] After so many years trying to make history, after so many treaty drafts and attempts to fulfil the ambitious dream of making copyright international,[120] he could not avoid what he always feared: to be forgotten. The classical lineal narrative of the stranger who came, failed and moved on is not even a sufficient description of this story. If ever there was a man to whom the traditional trajectory of rise and fall in international copyright diplomacy applies, it is José María Torres Caicedo, perhaps the first cosmopolitan copyright scholar.

7. CONCLUSION

It is worth mentioning a specific criticism levelled at characters such as Torres Caicedo. Such individuals were often accused of being on a singular quest for notoriety.[121] Of the accusations, one was particularly interesting. They were accused of creating 'fictitious' diplomatic missions to gain social and economic recognition in Europe. While the high-ranking position that Torres Caicedo achieved in ALAI, the appointments he made,[122] and his declarations through the ALAI congresses could give some

---

[115] Numa Droz to Torres Caicedo, saying that El Salvador had sent a letter accepting the invitation and highlighting that it was going to send a dispatch of the instructions to Torres Caicedo (9 October 1884) SB E22 2378.

[116] Torres Caicedo wrote to Numa Droz requesting an apology letter for not receiving the invitation to the conference despite having promoted the meetings at Berne: letter from Torres Caicedo to Numa Droz (11 October 1884), SB E22 2378; see also *Actes de la Conférence internationale pour la protection des droits d'auteur: réunie à Berne du 8 au 19 Septembre 1884* (Imprimerie K J Wyss 1884) 16.

[117] Certainly, the leading role was taken by Swiss diplomat Numa Droz as copyright historians often highlight: Ricketson and Ginsburg (n 3) 52 ['He (Droz) was to play a crucial role in the realization of the final convention'].

[118] For instance, his name disappears from among the former presidents (and he was one of them) in the *Bulletin de L'Association Littéraire et Artistique Internationale*, Decembre 1887.

[119] See Numa Droz 'Deuxième conférence diplomatique de Berne dans le but de constituer une Union pour la protection des œuvres littéraires et artistiques' (1885) *Clunet* 483.

[120] He was reported as the constant promoter of the copyright treaties in 'Banquete en honor a Zaldívar' *El Globo* (23 June 1884) 2.

[121] Santamaría (1870) 11, cited in Frédéric Martínez, *El nacionalismo cosmopolita. La referencia europea en la construcción nacional en Colombia, 1845–1900* (Instituto Francés de Estudios Andinos 2001) 228.

[122] The President of El Salvador, Rafael Zaldívar, was appointed as a member of the Comité d'Honneur of ALAI in August 1879; see *Bulletin ALAI* (Oct/Nov. 1879) 8.

El Salvador and the internationalisation of copyright 331

credit to such accusations,[123] it might be better to treat them with scepticism. Whether or not they had any substance, we will never know. What we certainly do know, however, and what deserves our attention, is that there exists an underlying and disturbing historical element in the internationalisation of copyright: the use of the Salvadorian diplomatic office by ALAI as a political experiment in the emergence of the international copyright discourse.[124] The purpose of this chapter has been to trace this experiment by looking at the role of the Salvadorian diplomat and ALAI president, Torres Caicedo. He actively and hastily initiated negotiations on behalf of El Salvador not only with France but also with Great Britain and Spain. Importantly, these negotiations were not isolated attempts to reach bilateral agreements, they were closely linked to and triggered by the international copyright project. Although Torres Caicedo failed to make a name in copyright historiography, the description of his unusual diplomatic moves still has a direct, immediate and powerful historical effect. His remarkable and strange career forces us to reflect upon the development of international copyright and the inherent problems embedded in political representation.

---

[123] Torres Caicedo was, however, individualised for this achievement. 'En 1880, la France signait une convention littéraire avec la Republique du Salvador; c'est la gloire du Ministre de cet État, M. Torres Caicedo, d'avoir personellement réalié cette oeuvre qui est uraiment une oeuvre grande et originale [...]' Bricon (n 21) 127.
[124] See n 37 above.

PART IV

NATIONAL PERSPECTIVES

16. United States copyright, 1672–1909
Oren Bracha

I. ORIGINS

When the American Copyright system was created in 1790 it was shaped by pre-existing institutions. There were two main antecedents. The first and most important was the British copyright tradition. Although British copyright law never applied in the American colonies, Americans were familiar with the 1710 Statute of Anne and some of the surrounding case law. The second source of influence was various colonial and state practices that were themselves local versions of the British institutions. These included sporadic colonial and state legislative grants of ad hoc exclusive printing rights and general copyright statutes legislated by the states in the 1780s. These were the building blocks out of which United States copyright would be assembled in 1790.

1. Colonial Precursors

The American British colonies that became the US had no systematic copyright protection. The British copyright regime under the 1710 Statute of Anne did not apply in the colonies; there was no local statutory copyright; and no known attempt to claim copyright under the common law was made. This is not surprising in light of the economic, social and political conditions in the colonies. The first colonial printing press arrived at Cambridge, Massachusetts in 1638.[1] The heavy involvement of Harvard College and the colony's authorities in its operation entailed both official sponsorship and supervision. Other colonies, where the printing press arrived in later times during the seventeenth and eighteenth centuries, developed their own combinations of support and restriction. Restrictions varied along a spectrum from a total ban, to a strict permit requirement for setting up a press, to licensing of content and post-publication sanctions. Encouragement could include official printer titles with various forms of patronage attached, a governmental commitment to purchasing printed works or even land grants to printers. In general, printing was treated as a dangerous threat to be tightly controlled but also as a public resource to be supported and utilized by the authorities.[2]

---

[1] George Parker Winship, *The Cambridge Press 1638–1692* (Southworth-Anthoensen Press 1945).
[2] Oren Bracha, 'Early American Printing Privileges: The Ambivalent Origins of Authors' Copyright in America' in Ronan Deazley, Martin Kretschmer and Lionel Bently (eds), *Privilege and Property: Essays on the History of Copyright* (OpenBook Publishers 2010) 89, 90–96.

In England, copyright emerged out of the Stationers' Company practice of allocating exclusive publishing rights among its members.[3] Nothing like the English book trade guild existed in the colonies even when a small and unorganized book trade gradually developed in some of them. Thus there was no institutional context where the equivalent of the stationers' copyright could arise. Moreover, there was hardly a pressing demand for exclusive publishing rights. In many cases the risk of competition either did not exist or was limited to the local market. An inter-colony market for books hardly existed due to the physical and economic barriers, but also because of cultural barriers. Much of what was printed in one colony – material such as governmental documents, religious texts or local histories – was of little relevance for the audience in other colonies. Given the small size of the book trade, when a concern of exclusivity did arise it could be ameliorated by means other than general legal rights. There were two main kinds of such mechanisms. One was a social norm in the trade against copying works published by others. The other consisted of more formal means, such as contractual arrangements among booksellers or offer on consignment by one bookseller or printer of materials published by another. The operation of these mechanisms in the colonial book trade is understudied, but there is some evidence that both kinds were used at least on some occasions.[4] These conditions persisted throughout the colonial period. Even in the second half of the eighteenth century when publishing centres began to emerge in places such as Boston or Philadelphia, these consisted of small concentrations of a handful of printers and booksellers.[5]

The only official exclusive publishing rights that did exist were in the form of sporadic, ad hoc, legislative grants. These grants were rudimentary versions of English royal printing patents that had been granted by the Crown since the early sixteenth century.[6] The colonial grant conferred on a publisher a limited-duration economic privilege to print or sell a text exclusively. The purpose was to encourage a specific publication project by reducing the risk associated with it. Like the printing patent, the colonial grant was an ad hoc, discretionary decision and not part of a general legal regime. Another line of similarity was the irrelevance of authorship. Colonial privileges were granted directly to publishers or printers and the texts involved, typically an official document of the colony, usually had no readily identifiable individual authors.

---

[3] Lyman R Patterson, *Copyright in Historical Perspective* (Vanderbilt University Press 1968) 42–77; John Feather, 'From Rights in Copies to Copyright: The Recognition of Authors' Rights in English Law and Practice in the Sixteenth and Seventeenth Centuries' in Martha Woodmansee and Peter Jaszi (eds), *The Construction of Authorship: Textual Appropriation in Law and Literature* (Duke University Press 1994) 191, 195–200.

[4] See John William Tebbel, *A History of Book Publishing in the United States* (RR Bowker Co 1972) vol 1, 42, 46; Helmut Lehmann-Haupt, *The Book in America: A History of the Making, and Selling of Books in the United States* (Bowker 1951) 99–100.

[5] Hugh Amory, 'The New England Book Trade, 1713–1790' in Hugh Amory and David D Hall (eds), *A History of the Book in America: The Colonial Book in the Atlantic World* (UNC Press 2007) vol 1, 199.

[6] On printing patents see Patterson (n 3) 78–113; John Feather, *Publishing, Piracy and Politics: An Historical Study of Copyright in Britain* (Mansell 1994) 10–14; Joseph Loewenstein, *The Author's Due: Printing and the Prehistory of Copyright* (University of Chicago Press 2002) 66–82.

It is unknown whether colonial legislatures modelled the printing privilege after the printing patent. The grant of these privileges was, however, part of the general pattern of colonial government. Printing privileges were indistinguishable in form and purpose from other exclusive privileges dispensed by colonial authorities in a variety of fields in order to encourage activities deemed to be economically or socially beneficial.[7]

The first known colonial printing privilege was the 1672 grant by the Massachusetts Bay General Court to John Usher. Usher was a merchant and a bookseller. By that time the colony's book trade had developed a rather fluid distinction between printers and booksellers. The latter, in addition to vending books, sometimes functioned as publishers. They would procure a text, hire a printer, cover other expenses and undertake the risk of a publishing project. Usher offered to the Massachusetts authorities to publish at his own expense the laws of the colony. In return for undertaking the risky enterprise, previously carried out by the authorities, Usher demanded exclusivity. The likely origin of this demand was Usher's distrust of his printer, Samuel Green, who was one of the two printers active in Boston at the time. Usher was probably concerned that Green would secretly make and sell extra copies of the publication, thereby undermining his market. The solution was an official legislative order from the Massachusetts General Court that specifically forbade any printer to make copies in addition to those ordered by Usher or any other person to reprint and sell the publication.[8] A year later, in response to another petition by Usher, another order issued forbidding anyone to print the laws of the colony. This time the prohibition was limited to seven years or the time when Usher sold all his copies.[9]

The occasional scholarly assertion that Usher's printing privilege was the only one granted in colonial times is incorrect.[10] The granting of exclusive publishing-related privileges was extremely sparse, but different variants of them were sometimes used. When in 1747 the North Carolina legislature decided to publish the local laws, James Davis was persuaded to relocate to the colony and was appointed official printer. Four 'Commissioners' were appointed for the purpose of revising and printing the laws. The Commissioners were given an exclusive right to print and sell the laws of the colony for five years, backed by penalties for unauthorized vending or importation.[11] Maryland used another arrangement. In 1700, in response to a petition for 'encouragement' by William Bladen, a law was passed mandating the printing of various official documents

---

[7] Bracha, 'Early American Printing Privileges' (n 2) 97.

[8] Nathaniel Bradstreet Shurtleff (ed), *Records of the Governor and Company of the Massachusetts Bay in New England, 1661–1674* (W White 1853–54) vol 4, 527. Available in Lionel Bently and Martin Kretschmer (eds), Primary Sources on Copyright (1450–1900) <http://copy.law.cam.ac.uk/record/us_1672>.

[9] Ibid 559.

[10] See eg Lehmann-Haupt (n 4) 99; Bruce W Bugbee, *The Genesis of American Patent and Copyright Law* (Public Affairs Press 1967) 106; Tebbel (n 4) 46.

[11] An Act for appointing Commissioners to Revise and Print the Laws of this Province, and for granting to his Majesty, for defraying the Charge thereof, a Duty of Wine, Rum and distilled Liquors, and Rice imported into this Province, § II, in *A Collection of all the Public Acts of Assembly, of the province of North-Carolina, now in force and use* (James Davis 1751) 242–45. Available in Primary Sources on Copyright (1450–1900) <http://copy.law.cam.ac.uk/record/us_1746>.

at set prices.[12] Another law of the same year authorized Bladen to print the laws of the colony and ordered the purchase of copies for a specified price.[13] Since Bladen was the only printer in the colony and unlicensed printing was prohibited, the upshot of these laws was an implicit exclusivity and an explicit subsidy. Similar arrangements were used in later years in Maryland and New York.[14] It is possible that further study of colonial sources will reveal similar cases of use of various publishing privileges by colonial authorities.

One grant of a printing privilege at the very end of the colonial period that never came into fruition marks the ideological change of the time. In 1770 William Billings who was working on a second edition of his popular *New England Psalm Singer* petitioned the Massachusetts House of Representatives for exclusive rights of selling the book for a limited time.[15] In 1772 Billings renewed his petition.[16] A bill giving Billings exclusive printing and selling rights in his book of tunes for seven years was passed by the House of Representatives and the Council.[17] The legislation was vetoed, however, by Governor Thomas Hutchinson and never went into force.[18] The episode marked a shift toward authorship. Colonial printing privileges were bestowed on publishers and were justified on the basis of the public benefit of the publishing project, not authorship. Billings's aborted privilege was the first attempt in America to grant exclusive rights to authors qua authors. The petition and the Bill reflected the transitional nature of the episode. Both contained traditional appeals to the value of supporting a publicly beneficial enterprise alongside new justifications focused on authorship and protection of the author's intellectual labor.[19] This anticipated the ideological and institutional developments that would soon take place in the new American states.

2. State Copyright

The central development related to copyright following independence was the rise of authorship both as an abstract ideological justification and as the underlying principle of actual legal measures. Until 1790 copyright-related developments took place on the state level. There were two parallel tracks for state copyright: individual legislative grants and the states' general copyright statutes.

---

[12] Lawrence C Wroth, *A History of Printing in Colonial Maryland, 1686–1776* (Typothetae of Baltimore 1922) 21.
[13] Ibid 23. Available in Primary Sources on Copyright (1450–1900), <http://copy.law.cam.ac.uk/record/us_1700>.
[14] Bracha, 'Early American Printing Privileges' (n 2) 100.
[15] *Journal of the Honorable House of Representatives* (Boston 1770) 143.
[16] Reproduced in Rollo G Silver, 'Prologue to Copyright in America: 1772' (1958) 11 Papers of the Bibliographical Society of the University of Virginia 259. Available in Primary Sources on Copyright (1450–1900) <http://copy.law.cam.ac.uk/record/us_1772a>.
[17] *Journal of the Honorable House of Representatives* (Boston 1772) 121, 124, 134. Reproduced in Silver (n 16).
[18] *Journal of the Honorable House of Representatives* (Boston 1772) 134.
[19] Bracha, 'Early American Printing Privileges' (n 2) 102–03.

Individual grants were a direct continuation of colonial printing privileges, but they also reflected some new important trends. In the 1780s the legislatures of several states issued individual printing privileges. Like colonial privileges, these were ad hoc measures that conferred on certain individuals tailored, limited-time exclusive rights for printing and selling specified texts. The main difference from colonial grants was the element of authorship. The typical grantees of state privileges were authors rather than publishers and authorship played an important role in justifying many of the grants.

Connecticut was particularly prolific in issuing individual printing privileges. Two grant petitions made in this state demonstrate the transitory nature of state privileges. In 1783 John Ledyard who participated in Captain James Cook's expedition petitioned the state legislature for a privilege in his account of the voyage. Ledyard's book was hardly a strong example of original authorship, as parts of it borrowed heavily from previous publications on Cook's voyages. The petition itself did not mention authorship as a justification for the grant. It emphasized instead the public benefits – specifically, those related to international commerce – that would flow from the publication and included also a plea for government patronage in the form of public employment. All of this made Ledyard's petition very similar to those by colonial publishers. A committee appointed by the Connecticut legislature to examine the petition concluded that Ledyard deserved exclusive rights, but instead of an individual privilege it recommended the passage of a general copyright statute.[20]

An earlier Connecticut privilege given to Andrew Law in 1781 is often referred to as the first author's copyright in America. In this case too, however, the grant reflected the transitory state of American copyright. Andrew Law, a music teacher, a composer and a shrewd business man, applied for a printing privilege in his book *Collection of the Best and Most Approved Tunes and Anthems for the Promotion of Psalmody*. Law's petition mentioned his investment in the project, concerns about piracy of the book and the need to protect and encourage 'works of Art.' The Connecticut legislature granted Law exclusive publishing and vending rights for five years. The rights applied to a list of tunes specifically mentioned in the grant.[21] Despite appearances, Law's grant was not exactly an author's copyright in the modern sense. Bibliographical research has shown that the book mentioned in the petition and in the Connecticut act probably never existed.[22] Law published the enumerated tunes in several distinct collections. As he explicitly admitted in his petition, he did not write the majority of these tunes. Law copied most of the tunes from English publications, from manuscripts he obtained from American composers and possibly from American publications. The privilege protected the specific tunes individually rather than the non-existent collection. In short, despite being bestowed on an authorial figure and justified in terms of authorship, Law's privilege was much closer to being a publisher's privilege.

---

[20] Ibid 110–13. Ledyard's petition is available in Primary Sources on Copyright (1450–1900) <http://copy.law.cam.ac.uk/record/us_1783>.

[21] Bracha, 'Early American Printing Privileges' (n 2) 105–06. Law's petition is available in Primary Sources on Copyright (1450–1900) <http://copy.law.cam.ac.uk/record/us_1781>. Law's grant is available ibid. <http://copy.law.cam.ac.uk/record/us_1781a>.

[22] I Lowens, 'Andrew Law and the Pirates' (1960) 13 J Am Musicological Soc'y 206, 210.

During the 1780s several other authors petitioned various state legislatures for individual privileges in their works. The lexicographer Noah Webster is most known for his journeys in search of legislative privileges for his textbook, but other authors too petitioned for and sometimes received such grants.[23] State grants continued to be issued after the states legislated general copyright statutes and even after the creation of the federal regime in 1790. Authors kept applying for individual privileges either because they did not qualify under the general regimes or because they hoped for better terms. The states' individual legislative grants were a transitory stage between legislative publishers' privileges and the new general regimes of authors' rights. Their significance was in the reorientation of exclusive printing rights toward authors, albeit in a gradual and ambivalent way. Similarly, the public rhetoric justifying the grants gradually came to be dominated by the ideas that rights were bestowed on authors as an encouragement for production or as a just reward for their intellectual labor. These developments anticipated and prepared the ground for modern, authorship-based copyright.

The second track for state protection of copyright was general copyright statutes legislated in the 1780s by all states except Delaware. Information about the local legislative processes is incomplete, but it appears that the statutes were typically passed after lobbying from literary figures and their supporters. The statutes were promoted on the basis of three arguments: the natural rights of authors, the social benefit of promoting learning and the national interest of the young republic in establishing its literary and cultural status among the leading civilized nations.[24] In January 1783 Connecticut passed the first American general copyright statute that was entitled 'An Act for the Encouragement of Literature and Genius.'[25] At the time petitions for individual privileges from Ledyard, Webster and others were pending before the state's legislature. According to Webster, the general act was 'obtained by the petition of several literary gentlemen in that state.'[26] In the following months Massachusetts and Maryland enacted their own statutes.

The difficulties of state copyright in the context of an emerging national market for books quickly became apparent. It was, however, doubtful whether the Continental Congress had power under the Articles of Confederation to legislate in the field. Thus the main goal of congressional lobbying at this stage was a general recommendation for state legislation. In 1783 the Continental Congress received 'sundry papers and memorials from different persons on the subject of literary property.'[27] The best known and probably most influential was the petition from Joel Barlow. The Connecticut poet wrote to Elias Boudinot, the president of the Continental Congress, and urged a recommendation to the states on the subject of copyright. He appealed to authors' natural property rights, the utilitarian interest in encouraging authorship and the need to

---

[23] Bugbee (n 10) 107, 124.

[24] Oren Bracha, 'Commentary on the Connecticut Copyright Statute 1783' in Primary Sources on Copyright (1450–1900) <http://copy.law.cam.ac.uk/cam/tools/request/showRecord?id=commentary_us_1783a>.

[25] *Acts and Laws of the State of Connecticut, in America* (Timothy Green 1784) 133.

[26] Noah Webster, 'Origin of the Copy-right Laws of the United States' in *A Collection of Papers on Political, Literary and Moral Subjects* (Webster & Clark 1843) 174.

[27] Worthington C Ford and others (eds), *Journals of the Continental Congress 1774–1789* (US Government Printing Office 1904–37) vol 24, 326.

establish the literary reputation of the new nation.[28] Following a favorable recommendation from an appointed committee on both natural rights and utilitarian grounds, Congress recommended to the states 'to secure to the authors or publishers of any new books, not hitherto printed' the copyright thereof for a minimal duration of two 14-year terms.[29] The resolution was not binding on the states but it probably helped to place the issue on their agendas. By April 1786 the number of states that passed general copyright statutes had risen to 12, with Delaware the only remaining holdout.

The states' statutes varied in their details, but they shared a close family resemblance. Some borrowed extensively from each other. All of the statutes were modeled closely after the 1710 British Statute of Anne that was frequently invoked in support of such legislation and whose text was accessible to Americans.[30] Each of the statutes created for the first time in America a general copyright regime under which copyright was universally available to anyone who met the statutory criteria. The original recipients of rights under all statutes were authors. All statutes except those of Virginia and South Carolina had preambles. The preambles contained various combinations of two justifications for copyright: the natural right of the author in the fruits of his labor, and the encouragement of learning for the benefit of the community. The encouragement of learning rationale was derived from the Statute of Anne. The natural rights rationale reflected more recent developments including the British literary property debate and the rise of authorship ideology. The statutes defined subject matter somewhat differently but all applied to books and various other printed materials. The statutes included many formalities as prerequisites for protection, the most common one being registration. Copyright's scope was limited to the exclusive right of printing and vending a text. All states limited the duration of copyright and a few adopted the Statute of Anne's 14-year term, once renewable. Remedies included forfeiture of infringing copies and various hybrids of penalties and statutory damages. Inspired by the Statute of Anne, four states required copyrighted books to be sold in sufficient numbers and five required reasonable prices for such books.[31]

Little is known about the actual practice of state copyright. It is possible that the statutes of Pennsylvania and Maryland never came into effect since their operation was suspended until all states legislated similar enactments, a condition that was never met due to Delaware refraining from doing so. It is unclear whether statutory copyright was used in practice in all relevant states, although a handful of records from some have been uncovered. In total there are fewer than 40 known copyright registrations prior to 1790 – a small fraction of the number of works published in the US during this period.[32] The general copyright statutes did not entirely supersede individual legislative privileges. Despite the existence of the state statutes, legislative privileges were

---

[28] *Papers of the Continental Congress, 1774–1789* (1783) vol 4, no 78, 369. Available in Primary Sources on Copyright (1450–1900) <http://copy.law.cam.ac.uk/record/us_1783b>.

[29] *Journals of the Continental Congress* (n 27) vol 24, 326–27.

[30] Oren Bracha, 'The Adventures of the Statute of Anne in the Land of Unlimited Possibilities: The Life of a Legal Transplant' (2010) 25 Berkeley Tech LJ 1427, 1444–50.

[31] Ibid. See also Francine Crawford, 'Pre-Constitutional Copyright Statutes' (1975) 23 Bull Copyright Soc'y 11, 14–35.

[32] George Thomas Tanselle, 'Copyright Records and the Bibliographer' (1969) 22 Studies in Bibliography 74, 83–84.

occasionally issued to specific individuals. The era of state statutes was very brief. The federal copyright regime of 1790 made state copyright unattractive. After its legislation, the local regimes that were not extensively used to begin with fell into disuse.

The main significance of the short-lived states' copyright statutes was not in creating a widely used, functioning copyright system, but in being landmarks, foreshadowing future developments. The texts of these statutes and the lobbying process preceding them provided an opportunity for the articulation of a new author-based copyright ideology in the US. Together with the individual legislative privileges the statutes were the main vehicles through which the new concept of authors' copyright and its two main rationales – natural rights and public utility – appeared for the first time in the US. The statutes also created an institutional precedent. Their legislation was the first time that a general copyright regime, as opposed to ad hoc privilege grants, was created in the US. The state statutes situated the Statute of Anne as the dominant framework for such a general copyright regime and familiarized state legislators, some of whom would be later involved in the creation of the federal regime, with its details. As a result, by the time that the US had set out to legislate a national copyright system the Statute of Anne was the natural template for it.

II. EARLY COPYRIGHT 1789–1840

The national copyright system of the US was born together with its new federal form of government. The US Constitution contained a specific clause empowering Congress to legislate in the area and in 1790 the new Congress exercised this power and passed the first copyright act. Despite some points of divergence, early American copyright was deeply immersed in its British origins. The 1790 Copyright Act followed closely the scheme of the Statute of Anne and subsequent amendments did not fundamentally change this framework. The US even experienced a local version of the British literary property debate over the existence and status of common law copyright. American copyright jurisprudence during this period reflected the traditional British concept of copyright. Under this framework copyright was the unique regulation of the book trade. True to its origins as the publisher's trade privilege, it was a narrow right to reproduce in print a protected text.

1. The Constitutional Clause

A major development in late eighteenth century American copyright was a shift from the state to the national level. The foundation of this shift was a clause in the US Constitution that explicitly granted Congress the power to legislate in the fields of patent and copyright. During the 1780s the shortcomings of local legal protection for writings and technological innovations in the context of an emerging national market and culture were becoming clear. Some famous cases made these difficulties vividly apparent. These cases included the efforts of Noah Webster to secure copyright in multiple states and the contests before state legislatures between John Fitch and his rival James Rumsey over protection for their steamboat inventions.[33] In preparation for the 1787 constitutional convention, James Madison identified 'the want of uniformity in the laws concerning naturalization & literary property,' as one of the weaknesses of the Articles of Confederation that needed to be remedied.[34] Madison and others later made similar observations. A national copyright and patent power, however, was hardly a top priority for the founders. Even Madison defined this subject as one of 'inferior moment.'[35] The issue was not mentioned in the early proposals for a national governance scheme presented to the convention by various states.[36] Nor was it mentioned in the first draft of the Constitution or in prior resolutions.[37] Copyright made its first known appearance almost three months after the convention began.

On 18 August 1787 James Madison and Charles Pinckney suggested various powers related to encouraging learning and technological innovation together with other proposed congressional powers. The proposed powers were recorded with no attribution or reasoning attached. Alongside the powers of protecting copyrights and patents, the list included the powers to establish a university and seminars, bestow premiums, and create public institutions, rewards and immunities for the promotion of agriculture, commerce trade and manufactures.[38] Not much is known about the process of forging the clause and the framers' underlying intent. There is even some uncertainty about the exact relevant powers suggested to the convention. It is known that the proposals were referred to the Committee on Detail where none survived in their original form. The committee recommended bestowing on Congress the power: 'To promote the progress of science and useful arts by securing for limited times to Authors and Inventors the exclusive rights to their respective writings and discoveries.'[39] This text was approved with no debate and became the Intellectual Property Clause of the Constitution.[40]

During Ratification, the Intellectual Property Clause attracted very little attention and debate. The most famous attempt to justify the clause was Madison's in the Federalist No. 43, where he wrote:

> The utility of this power will scarcely be questioned. The copyright of authors has been solemnly adjudged in Great Britain to be a right at Common Law. The right to useful inventions seems with equal reason to belong to the inventors. The public good fully coincides in both cases with the claims of individuals. The States cannot separately make effectual provision for either of the cases, and most of them anticipated the decision of this point by laws passed at the instance of Congress.[41]

---

[33] Bugbee (n 10) 128. See also Frank David Prager, 'The Steamboat Pioneers Before the Founding Fathers' (1955) 37 J Pat Off Soc'y 486.

[34] James Madison, 'Observations by J.M.' in *Documentary History of the Constitution of the United States of America 1786–1870* (1905) vol 4, 128.

[35] Ibid.

[36] Edward C Walterscheid, *The Nature of the Intellectual Property Clause: A Study in Historical Perspective* (WS Hein 2002) 81–82.

[37] Ibid 100.

[38] *Documentary History of the Constitution* (n 34) vol 1, 130–31.

[39] Max Farrand (ed), *The Records of the Federal Convention of 1787* (YUP 1911) vol 2, 505.

[40] US Const art I, s 8, cl 8.

[41] Benjamin F Wright (ed), *The Federalist No. 43* (1961) 309.

These arguments included various inconsistencies and obscurities. This is hardly surprising because the text was political rhetoric designed to justify the proposed Constitution and not a philosophical tract. The few other references to the clause during ratification mentioned the British precedent, the expected social benefits of protecting the rights of authors and inventors and the need for effective national rather than state measures in this area.[42] In March 1789, following ratification, the Intellectual Property Clause went into effect together with the rest of the Constitution.

Little is known about the interest group politics leading to the clause. There are various speculations about the involvement of specific persons with the creation of the clause, but there is no direct evidence on the subject.[43] More general public choice accounts of the Intellectual Property Clause are scarce and focused on explaining the shift of patent and copyright from the state to the national level, rather than the specific content of the clause. According to the main explanation in this vein, with the rise of a national market the value of national protection increased and the worth of state protection decreased, resulting in an overall support for a new national patent and copyright regime.[44]

While there is little information on the deliberative process that produced the clause, it is easier to reconstruct the intellectual and institutional background from which it emerged. There were three main relevant influences. First, many of the framers had legal education and were likely exposed to some degree to British practice and thought about patent and copyright. In line with the British tradition, the framers thought of patents and copyrights as exceptions to a general rule against monopolies justified by their service to the public good and limited by proper restrictions.[45] In a letter exchange shortly after the ratification of the Constitution Madison and Jefferson discussed the clause in exactly these terms.[46] Second, many of the framers were familiar with the patent and copyright practice of the states. By 1787 many of the states granted ad hoc legislative patents and copyrights and almost all of them legislated general copyright statutes. The majority of delegates to the constitutional convention were members of various branches of state governments, and it is likely that many of them had been exposed to those laws and practices. Third, many of the delegates were members of the Continental Congress. The Continental Congress never legislated in the area of patents and copyrights. It did receive, however, various petitions and issued a resolution on the subject. In light of this background, it is not surprising that the clause did not introduce any major novelty compared to existing patent and copyright practices. The concepts of authors, inventors, limited time monopolies and their use by government to encourage learning and technological innovation, were all familiar from the British and state

---

[42] Tyler T Ochoa and Mark Rose, 'The Anti-Monopoly Origins of the Patent and Copyright Clause' (2002) 84 J Pat & Trademark Office Soc'y 909, 924.
[43] See eg Irah Donner, 'The Copyright Clause of the U.S. Constitution: Why Did the Framers Include it With Unanimous Approval?' (1992) 36 Am J Legal Hist 361, 372; Prager, 'The Steamboat Pioneers' (n 33) 515–22; Walterscheid, *The Nature of the Intellectual Property Clause* (n 36) 96–97.
[44] Craig Allen Nard and Andrew Morriss, 'Constitutionalizing Patents: From Venice to Philadelphia' (2006) 2 Rev Law & Econ 223, 299–304.
[45] Ochoa and Rose (n 42) 925.
[46] Ibid 925–26.

context. The main innovation of the clause was the creation of a national power to legislate in this field.

In the centuries since it was created the Intellectual Property Clause became a central part of American intellectual property law. Despite the dearth of information about its creation, it attracted more scholarly attention than any other episode in the history of American copyright and patent. Similarly, the constitutional clause has played an important role in American intellectual property legal doctrine and in public and political debates in the field. Scholars and advocates tried to deduce binding meaning from the text or the procedural history of the clause. Some found support in the clause for strong intellectual property rights. The lack of known debate and dissent in either the convention or ratification over the clause was occasionally pointed to as evidence of general enthusiasm and consensus, although it is just as likely that it was an expression of lack of interest in a matter of 'inferior moment.'[47] Others have claimed that the text 'securing ... exclusive rights' in the clause indicates that the framers were motivated by a capacious understanding of patents and copyrights as based on pre-existing natural rights.[48] Even the absence of the words 'patent' and 'copyright' was used to claim that the framers intended to reject various restrictions and limitations that were routinely imposed on patent and copyright in their period.[49] In recent decades, it became more common for intellectual property skeptics to turn to the clause and interpret it as a source of restrictions on intellectual property rights. Thus for example, arguments attempting to cabin congressional expansion of intellectual property rights were based recently on both the 'limited times' and 'promote the progress' language of the clause.[50] In the case law the terms 'authors,' 'inventors,' and 'writings' were all used in different times to deduce threshold requirements for and limitations on copyright and patent rights.[51]

How did the clause, seen as relatively insignificant at the time of its creation, attain such a status? Reasons include the legitimacy-conferring status of the Constitution in the United States, the tendency in American legal culture to find answers to questions of legal meaning by trying to locate original meaning and the counter-majoritarian

---

[47] Walterscheid, *The Nature of the Intellectual Property Clause* (n 36) 80–81, 83.

[48] George Ramsey, 'The Historical Background of Patents' (1936) 18 J Pat Off Soc'y 7, 15–16; Frank David Prager, 'The Historic Background and Foundation of American Patent Law' (1961) 5 Am J Legal Hist 309, 318. For a critique of this claim see Walterscheid, *The Nature of the Intellectual Property Clause* (n 36) 212–20.

[49] Karl Fenning, 'The Origins of the Patent and Copyright Clause of the Constitution' (1929) 17 Geo LJ 109, 116.

[50] See eg Yochai Benkler, 'Constitutional Bounds of Database Protection: The Role of Judicial Review in the Creation and Definition of Private Rights in Information' (2000) 15 Berkeley Tech LJ 535; Malla Pollack, 'What Is Congress Supposed to Promote? Defining "Progress" in Article I, Section 8, Clause 8 of the U.S. Constitution, or Introducing the Progress Clause' (2002) 80 Neb L Rev 754; Dotan Oliar, 'Making Sense of the Intellectual Property Clause: Promotion of Progress as a Limitation on Congress's Intellectual Property Power' (2006) 94 Geo LJ 1771.

[51] See eg *Baker v Selden* 101 US 99, 105 (1879); *Trade Mark Cases* 100 US 82 (1879); *Sears, Roebuck & Co v Stiffel Co* 376 US 225, 230–31 (1964); *Graham v John Deere Co* 383 US 1, 5 (1966); *Bonito Boats, Inc v Thunder Craft Boats, Inc* 489 US 141, 146 (1989); *Feist Publ'ns, Inc v Rural Tel Serv Co* 499 US 340 (1991).

power of constitutional norms. Historically, the clause acquired its central status in a gradual process. Almost immediately after its creation there appeared attempts to use the clause as the basis for either expansion or restriction of intellectual property rights. Some argued hyperbolically that the Constitution created individual patent rights.[52] Others pointed out that the clause authorized Congress to encourage innovation only by granting patents and copyrights and not by other means such as financing a scientific expedition.[53] One recurring debate was whether the limited congressional power permitted patents to non-inventors who imported new technology, a practice that was common in England. The dominant view that emerged was that Congress could only grant patents to inventors and not patents of importation.[54]

Nineteenth century legal doctrine on the extent of the limitations laid on congressional power by the clause was not uniform. Some decisions declared a broad plenary power to Congress.[55] Others deduced from the clause limitations on congressional power, typically by interpreting existing law as consistent with such limitations.[56] After the Civil War, judicial reliance on the constitutional clause as support for delimiting the scope of copyright and patent intensified, especially in the copyright context.[57] The high watermark of the constitutionalization of copyright in this period was the Supreme Court's opinion in the *Trade-Mark Cases*.[58] The decision struck down as unconstitutional the first federal trademark statute. The Court rejected the Intellectual Property Clause as a source of congressional power to legislate in the field of trademarks because it found that 'the essential characteristics of a trade-mark' lacked the defining traits of inventions or authorial writings.[59] In the twentieth century this trend continued. The constitutional clause became a permanent part of both copyright and patent law, and some more elaborate doctrines related to it had appeared.[60] Courts' willingness to impose constitutional restrictions derived from the clause on congressional power had ebbed and flowed.[61] Regardless of these fluctuations, the constitutional layer remained an important part of American intellectual property law.

---

[52] Joseph Barnes, *Treatise on the Justice, Policy and Utility of Establishing an Effectual System for Promoting the Progress of Useful Arts by Assuring Property in the Products of Genius* (Francis Bailey 1792) 16.
[53] Linda Grant De Pauw, Charles Bangs Bickford and Helen E Vei (eds), *The Documentary History of the First Federal Congress of the United States* (Johns Hopkins University Press 1977) vol 10, 28–220.
[54] Edward C Walterscheid, *To Promote the Progress of Science and Useful Arts: American Patent Law and Administration, 1798–1836* (Rothman & Co 1998) 378–82.
[55] *McClurg v Kingsland* 42 US 202, 206 (1843).
[56] *Clayton v Stone* 5 F Cas 999, 1000 (SDNY 1829).
[57] See *Baker* (n 51) 105; *Burrow-Giles Lithographic Co v Sarony* 111 US 53, 56–59 (1883); *Higgins v Keuffel* 140 US 428, 430–31 (1891).
[58] 100 US 82 (1879).
[59] Ibid 93.
[60] See *Graham* (n 51); *Bonito Boats* (n 51); *Feist* (n 51).
[61] In some recent cases the Court adamantly rejected constitutional challenges to congressional legislative power in the field of copyright. See *Eldred v Ashcroft* 537 US 186 (2003); *Golan v Holder* 132 S Ct 873 (2012).

2. The 1790 Copyright Regime

Soon after the first federal Congress started its first session it was presented with various petitions for patent and copyright protection. The petitions were for individual legislative privileges rather than general enactments.[62] Petitioners, familiar with state practices, assumed that the Constitution conferred on Congress the powers to grant individual privileges previously exercised by the states and that it would exercise its power in this way. The initial response by Congress was favorable. At some point, however, it decided to forsake the individual privileges route and ordered a committee to prepare a bill for a general patent and copyright law.[63] There is no direct indication why this shift occurred. It is likely that one consideration was related to administrative feasibility. As soon became apparent from the continuing stream of petitions, the advantages of national protection attracted a large number of petitioners nationwide. Handling on an ad hoc basis this volume of petitions, several times the magnitude of those handled by state legislatures, would have been a heavy burden for a busy national legislature. Another possible consideration was British and state precedents. Many Americans were aware of the British Statute of Anne and the states' copyright statutes. Both formed an institutional precedent and a ready-made model with which to handle the demand for legislative protection. Whatever its reason, the decision to order the preparation of general legislation signified a crucial turn from ad hoc privileges to general copyright and patent regimes. In the future Congress would occasionally grant individual privileges or time extensions, but a general regime became the firm rule and ad hoc privileges the exception.

The legislation effort started with a joint patent-copyright bill.[64] The joint framework was more formal than substantive because the two fields were handled by separate parts of the bill. Subsequently the bill was split into separate copyright and patent bills. Representative Aedanus Burke reasoned that a copyright law could be legislated faster 'because it is almost as easy to ascertain literary as any other kind of property; whereas there is some difficulty in deciding upon improvements or inventions in the useful arts.'[65] As it happened, the 1790 Copyright Act was signed into law on 31 May 1790, a few weeks after its patent counterpart.[66]

The 1790 Copyright Act applied to any 'Map, Chart, Book or Books.' It extended protection to the authors of published works or to their assignees as well as to authors of unpublished and future works. Persons eligible for protection had to be citizens or residents of the US. The entitlement conferred was 'the sole right and liberty of printing, reprinting, publishing and vending such Map, Chart, Book or Books for the term of Fourteen years.' The right was renewable for another term of 14 years by a surviving author who followed a re-registration procedure six months before expiration.

---

[62] Bugbee (n 10) 133–37.
[63] *Journal of the House of Representatives*, 1st Cong, 1st Sess (20 Apr 1789) 18.
[64] See Walterscheid, *To Promote the Progress* (n 54) 87–105. No known copy of the bill H.R.10 has survived. A typescript of the bill is available in Primary Sources on Copyright (1450–1900) <http://copy.law.cam.ac.uk/record/us_1789c>.
[65] Annals of Congress, 1st Cong, 2nd Sess, 1080.
[66] Act of 31 May 1790, c 15, 1 Stat 124.

The Act also explicitly protected manuscripts against unauthorized printing or publication. Several formalities were imposed. Persons seeking protection were required to register the work with the clerks of the local federal District Courts. Owners were required to publish the registration record in public newspapers and deposit a copy of the work with the Secretary of State. Infringers were defined as any person who shall 'print, reprint, publish or import, or cause to be printed, reprinted, published or imported ... any copy or copies of such Map, Chart and Book or Books without the consent of the Author or the proprietor thereof,' as well as any person who 'knowing the same to be so printed, reprinted or imported, shall publish sell or expose to sale, or cause to be published, sold or exposed to sale any Copy of such Map, Chart, Book or Books.' Unlike modern copyright's strict liability standard, the sale entitlement required knowledge by the offender of the infringing character of the sold copy. Statutory remedies were very limited. Infringers were subject to forfeiture of all infringing copies. There was also a statutory penalty of 50 cents per sheet, to be divided between the 'Author or Proprietor ... who shall sue for the same' and the US. Those were the only remedies provided by the statute in regard to published works. There was no mention of damages or equitable relief. In regard to manuscripts the statute explicitly provided for damages. American courts, however, would soon follow their English counterparts and read the full array of remedies into the copyright regime. Although the early remedial practice of the lower courts in copyright cases is still shrouded in ambiguity, it seems clear that in the 1798 decision in *Morse v Reid* (the first reported American copyright decision) the court virtually ignored the statutory remedy.[67] It is not entirely clear whether the monetary relief it granted was the equitable remedy of disgorgement of defendant's profits or common law damages for plaintiff's lost profit, but it was not the statutory penalty. Later nineteenth century commentators flatly asserted the applicability of non-statutory remedies with little discussion or support.[68]

The 1790 Copyright Act was clearly modelled after the British 1710 Statute of Anne with which Americans were familiar. It is possible that the Statute of Anne influenced the 1790 Act indirectly through the texts of some of the state statutes. Yet the close similarity between the British and federal statutes on the level of structure, technical details and even specific text, suggests that the framers of the 1790 Act worked directly from a version of the Statute of Anne. The Statute of Anne was named 'An Act for the Encouragement of Learning, by Vesting the Copies of Printed Books in the Authors or Purchasers of such Copies, during the Times therein mentioned.' The title of the 1790 Act was 'An Act for the encouragement of learning, by securing the copies of maps, Charts, And books, to the authors and proprietors of such copies, during the times therein mentioned.' The 1790 Act dispensed with the preamble of the Statute of Anne but everything that followed was almost identical. Both statutes applied to existing, published works as well as to unpublished and future ones, although the Statute of Anne, unlike the American act, prescribed a longer term of 21 years for the first

---

[67] *Collections of the Massachusetts Historical Society* (1798) vol 5, 123. See John D Gordan, 'Morse v. Reid: The First Reported Federal Copyright Case' (1993) 11 LHR 21.

[68] Joseph Story, *Commentaries on Equity Jurisprudence as Administered in England and America* (2nd edn CC Little and J Brown 1839) vol 2, 210; George Ticknor Curtis, *A Treatise on the Law of Copyright* (CC Little and J Brown 1847) 313.

category. The statutes defined infringement in a very similar way. Unlike the Statute of Anne the American statute explicitly provided protection to manuscripts. In Britain manuscript protection was a judge-made law recognized in the 1741 decision *Pope v Curll* as an auxiliary to the statutory protection of published works.[69] The American drafters may have been aware of *Pope v Curll* or they may have been simply cognizant of the practical need for manuscript protection as a corollary to copyright in published works. Both Acts limited their remedies to forfeiture of infringing copies and a statutory penalty calculated on a per sheet basis to be divided between the plaintiff and the Crown or the US. The Statute of Anne probably contemplated qui tam actions by awarding half the sum of the statutory penalty 'to any Person or Persons that shall Sue for the same.' The early American copyright bill contained a similar arrangement that was dispensed with in the final act. The American Copyright Act followed the British statute in requiring registration and deposit of the protected work, although it modified and liberalized some of the technical details of these requirements. The Copyright Act also followed the Statute of Anne by setting a statutory term of 14 years and allowing a surviving author one renewal for an additional term of 14 years.[70]

The American version dispensed with some anachronistic features of the British statute. The Statute of Anne effectively commandeered the registration system of the Stationers' Company for purposes of general registration by any copyright owner. As a result, there was reason to expect that the Company's clerk might refuse to register copyright to non-members. For this reason the statute contained an alternative registration mechanism applicable in cases of refusal to register. The early American bill contained a similar provision that was deleted in the final version, probably when the drafters realized that it served no purpose under the different American circumstances. Similarly, the American Act did not contain any equivalent of the Statute of Anne's price control arrangement that applied to cases of unreasonable prices charged by the right owner. It is possible that Americans were less concerned about copyright leading to exorbitant prices than the early eighteenth century British drafters steeped in the period's English political thought about monopolies. Alternatively, Americans might have thought that the price control mechanism was never used in practice or simply worked with a version of the Statute of Anne that reflected the fact that the price-control provision was officially repealed in 1739.[71]

In short, the Statute of Anne served as both a general inspiration and a source of specific institutional arrangements for the 1790 Copyright Act. Despite the 80-year difference between them, the two enactments created very similar legal regimes. These regimes reflected copyright's transitory stage between its past as a publisher's economic privilege and its future as a general right based on the principle of authorial ownership of creative works. In this respect, the 1790 Copyright Act established at the national level the two innovations of the state statutes of the previous decade. It created a general regime of universal rights, rather than ad hoc privileges. It also placed authors, rather than publishers or printers, at the center of copyright. Authors were the formal, original recipients of copyright and all other entitlements were derivative of

---

[69] *Pope v Curll* (1741) 2 Atk 342.
[70] Bracha, 'The Adventures of the Statute of Anne' (n 30) 1453–55.
[71] Ibid 1455–56.

theirs. Similarly, the justifications of the regime and the discourse surrounding it were by this time firmly focused on authors as the creators of intellectual works. At the same time the new authorship-based regime of 1790 was still strongly grounded in traditional forms and concepts. In essence, the regime lifted the publisher's privilege, generalized it and conferred it upon authors.

In 1802 Congress amended the 1790 Act and added to it two significant features.[72] First, the notice formality was created. In addition to registration, deposit and newspaper publication, copyright owners were now required to include a copyright notice in the copies of their protected works. Second, the 1802 amendment added prints as a copyrightable subject matter. This was an important extension of copyright that had occurred in Britain much earlier with the Engravers' Copyright Act of 1735.[73] Even after this extension, however, copyright still remained limited to its traditional area of the realm of print.

There has been some research on the performance of the 1790 copyright regime in action, especially in its early years. We know relatively little on how the formal legal rules and procedures were translated into actual social practices such as publication arrangements, patterns of commercialization, or author-publisher relationships during this period. Studies of copyright registration records, however, recovered some interesting facts. One important finding is the small relative share of printed works that were registered and therefore protected by copyright. Out of more than 15 000 printed works published in the US between 1790 and 1800 less than 800 were copyrighted.[74] It is a plausible conjecture that the number of works whose protection was renewed after 14 years was even smaller. Entire categories of printed works like almanacs, sermons and newspapers, some of which were the staples of early American printers, are completely absent from the early registration records. This means that copyright was not only limited to the book trade, but also that it was relevant only to a small fraction of that trade's everyday business. Much of the development of print culture and democratic discourse in the early republic happened outside of the boundaries of copyright.

Another significant fact is the dominance of practical materials within early copyrighted works. Works of original literature or poetry constituted only a small fraction of registrations. Practical or utilitarian books such as textbooks, manuals or commercial directories were the most common.[75] Thus the most commonly copyrighted works had very little to do with the stereotypical image of original authorship in the romantic sense. Third, early copyright records reveal an interesting division of registrations between authors and proprietors. While authors could register copyright in

---

[72] Act of 29 Apr 1802, c 36, 2 Stat 171.
[73] Engraving Copyright Act 1735 (8 Geo II c 13).
[74] James Gilreath, 'American Literature, Public Policy, and the Copyright Laws before 1800' in *Federal Copyright Records, 1790–1800* (US Government Printing Office 1987) xxii. See also William J Maher, 'Copyright Term, Retrospective Extension, and the Copyright Law of 1790 in Historical Context' (2002) 49 J Copyright Soc'y USA 1021, 1027.
[75] See Jane C Ginsburg, 'Creation and Commercial Value: Copyright Protection of Works of Information' (1990) 90 Colum L Rev 1865, 1874; Meredith G McGill, 'Copyright in the Early Republic' in Robert A Gross and Marry Kelly (eds), *A History of the Book in America: An Extensive Republic: Print, Culture, and Society in the New Nation, 1790–1840* (UNC Press 2010) vol 2, 199.

their own works, proprietors were usually publishers or printers who registered works, presumably after the rights were assigned by the author. The relative share of registering proprietors was substantial from the start, but it steadily rose in the first decade.[76] This data points to a potential gap between copyright's ideology as authors' rights and its reality. In practice, right from the early days of the federal regime a substantial number of rights were registered, held and used by publishers. Assessing the exact financial and other effects of registration by proprietors would require a closer study than currently available of the exact assignment and compensation schemes between authors and publishers as well as their change over time.

3. The 1831 Copyright Act

The 1831 Copyright Act was the first major statutory reform of American copyright.[77] It was passed after extensive lobbying efforts led by Noah Webster. In September 1836 after he returned from England Webster wrote on the subject of copyright to Daniel Webster (no family relation) who was at the time a member of the House Judiciary Committee. He used natural property rights arguments that he might have picked up during his stay in England and asked that Daniel Webster's 'talents may be exerted in placing this species of property, on the same footing, as all other property, as to exclusive right & permanence of possession.' Specifically Webster wanted that the:

> legislature would come at once to the line of right & justice on this subject, & pass a new act, the preamble to which shall admit the principle that an author has, by common law, or natural justice, the sole & permanent right to make profits by his own labors, & that his heirs & assigns, shall enjoy the right, unclogged with conditions.[78]

Daniel Webster expressed some reservations about the philosophical basis of copyright, but promised to help and mentioned that his committee was already considering some changes of copyright law.[79] Despite continued lobbying including 'a petition signed by many respectable literary men,' progress was slow.[80] A bill submitted by the Judiciary Committee in 1828 and a revised version of it by Representative Gulian Verplanck did not advance.[81]

The turning point came in 1829 when in the words of Webster 'the Hon. Mr. Ellsworth, a member from Connecticut, was appointed one of the judiciary committee.'[82] Ellsworth, was, in fact, Webster's son-in-law and as such he had substantial interest in the value of the copyright of the aging lexicographer's newly completed dictionary. In December 1830, after some manoeuvring, he submitted a bill in the name

---

[76] Gilreath (n 74) xxiii.
[77] Act of 3 Feb 1831, 4 Stat 436.
[78] Available in Primary Sources on Copyright (1450–1900) <http://copy.law.cam.ac.uk/record/us_1826>.
[79] Noah Webster, *A Collection of Papers on Political, Literary, and Moral Subjects* (Webster and Clark 1843) 176–177.
[80] Ibid 177.
[81] *Journal of the House of Representatives,* 20th Cong, 1st Sess (21 Feb 1828) 324.
[82] Webster (n 79) 177.

of the committee accompanied by a detailed report on 'Copy-Right.'[83] The report stated three main objectives to the revision. The first was consolidating the 1790 Act with the 1802 Act that extended copyright to prints and ridding these statutes of 'provisions which are useless and burdensome.' The second purpose was acting upon the observation that 'the law of copy-right ought to extend to musical compositions, as does the English law.' The third purpose, described by the report as the chief one, was to 'enlarge the period for the enjoyment of copy-right.' The stated reason for this last purpose was 'to place authors in this country more nearly upon an equality with authors [i]n other countries.' This was premised on the assumption that the US was 'very far behind' other nations 'in encouraging science and literature, by securing the fruits of intellectual labor.' The report supported this claim with a comparative survey of the copyright laws of various European nations that was replete with errors. Reflecting this last purpose, the bill extended copyright's duration to an initial period of 28 years renewable for another 14 years by a surviving author or by a statutorily designated member of a deceased author's family. There is good evidence that the last feature was a direct response to a specific concern expressed by Webster.[84]

After the bill encountered difficulties Webster travelled to Washington and orchestrated one of the first congressional celebrity lobbying campaigns. The campaign included a successful lecture before the House of Representatives. Years later he wrote that it 'had no little effect in promoting the object of obtaining a law for securing copy-rights.'[85] The bill was passed by the House after some spirited debate and sailed through more smoothly in the Senate. It was signed into law in February 1831. Webster found that his presence in Washington was 'very useful and perhaps necessary to the accomplishment of the object.'[86]

The 1831 Copyright Act made several important changes to American copyright. First, it consolidated all existing subject matter categories – namely books, maps, charts, prints, and engravings – and added a new category of a 'musical composition.' The significance of adding this category and the specific reference to it in the committee report are enigmatic. The 1831 Copyright Act only protected printed sheet music against unauthorized reprints. There was little novelty in this. Despite some early doubts, sheet music had been protected against reprinting in England since its recognition as statutory subject matter in the 1777 decision *Bach v Longman*.[87] In the US, sheet music was among the earliest works copyrighted under the federal and the state statutes. Such subject matter was registered for protection on a regular basis. It is unclear what prompted the bill drafters to see a need for 'recognizing' copyright in music. Second, the new Act extended the initial term of copyright to 28 years and retained the 14-year period for the renewed term. Third, while previously the renewal right only accrued to a surviving author, now it could be also enjoyed by the widow or

---

[83] Available in Primary Sources on Copyright (1450–1900) <http://copy.law.cam.ac.uk/record/us_1830>
[84] David Micklethwait, *Noah Webster and the American Dictionary* (McFarland 2000) 216.
[85] Webster (n 79) 178.
[86] A letter from Noah Webster to William Chauncey Fowler, in Harry R Warfel (ed), *Letters of Noah Webster* (Library Publishers 1953) 424–25.
[87] (1777) 2 Cowp 623.

children of a deceased author. In addition the Act changed some other features of copyright. It lengthened the limitation period and removed the general requirement of newspaper publication of the registration in regard to new copyrights but retained it in regard to the renewal term. The Act also simplified the form of copyright notice and clarified that affixation of notice was a precondition for protection and that its absence could cause forfeiture. All the terms of the Act, including duration and renewal, applied both to new works and to existing works still under copyright.

4. The American Literary Property Debate

The 1834 case of *Wheaton v Peters* was the first copyright decision of the US Supreme Court.[88] Being a late version of the British literary property debate, the case involved fundamental questions about copyright law and its philosophical foundations. For the Supreme Court the litigation struck close to home. The parties were the reporter of the Supreme Court, Richard Peters Jr. and his predecessor Henry Wheaton. Both were tied in an array of professional and personal connections to some of the Court's Justices. The litigation originated in Peters's decision to republish in a condensed and cheaper series the decisions of the Supreme Court reported by the three previous reporters – Dallas, Cranch and Wheaton. After attempts to settle the affair amicably had failed, Wheaton and his publisher Robert Donaldson sued Peters and his publisher John Grigg.[89]

There were three main legal questions in the case. The first was whether the legal formalities in force at the time – registration, deposit of copies with the Secretary of State and a copyright notice published both in a newspaper and on the title page – were complied with by Wheaton and whether compliance was a precondition for a valid copyright. The second question was about the subject matter eligible for copyright protection. Could the reported opinions of the Supreme Court be protected by copyright? The parties' arguments on this question drew on competing accounts of the appropriate limits of private control of expression under the copyright laws. Wheaton's attorneys argued that the opinions were owned by the judges who produced them and that they transferred their rights to the reporter as a gift.[90] By contrast Peters's lawyers described the opinions as '*the law of the land*' and maintained that there could be no private property rights in such subject matter. They argued that 'the law cannot and ought not to be made the prisoner or the slave of any individual.'[91]

The third question that entailed theoretical inquiries about copyright's nature and philosophical underpinning was that of common law copyright. The practical impetus and the legal logic followed those of English booksellers who developed the argument of common law copyright in the eighteenth century. The argument was that copyright

---

[88] 33 US 591 (1834). See also *Report of the Copy-right Case of Wheaton v. Peters Decided in the Supreme Court of the United States* (J Van Norden 1834).
[89] See Craig Joyce, 'The Story of *Wheaton v Peters:* A Curious Chapter in the History of Judicature' in Jane C Ginsburg and Rochelle Cooper Dreyfuss (eds), *Intellectual Property Stories* (Foundation Press 2006) 42–49.
[90] *Report of the Copy-right Case of Wheaton v. Peters* (n 88) 71.
[91] Ibid 77.

was protected under the common law as a property right, independently of the statute. The upshot of this claim was that copyright was protected by common law and equitable remedies (in contrast to the statutory remedial penalties), irrespective of any statutory limitations. Unlike the limited statutory duration, this meant that the right was perpetual. More importantly for Wheaton, it also meant that common law copyright applied irrespective of compliance with any formal requirement imposed by statute such as notice or deposit. Some of the arguments on this third issue pertained to relatively technical legal questions, such as whether common law copyright was recognized in England at the relevant time and whether the English rule was adopted by Pennsylvania common law or federal common law if it existed. The question of common law property rights, however, necessarily raised more fundamental inquiries about property and intellectual property. To contemporaries the concept of common law rights meant much more than simply judge-made law. Common law rights were sharply distinguished from statutory law. While statutes were seen as political, the common law was pre-political. This meant that common law rights were derived from objective, 'natural' principles, while statutes were 'arbitrary' in the sense of reflecting subjective human policy judgments. Similarly, while statutory law was 'made' by legislatures, the common law was 'discovered' by judges who through the common law process of elaboration uncovered rules that were derived from pre-political, natural principles.[92] In the field of property this understanding meant that common law rights were assumed to reflect natural property rights. The debate thus turned on whether copyright could fit this mold, namely, whether there could exist natural property rights in intangibles.

The English literary property debate heavily influenced this aspect of the case. It supplied not just precedents, but philosophical and theoretical arguments about property in intangibles that framed the American discussion.[93] Both parties agreed that the question of common law copyright could only be answered by reference to a general theory of copyright. Both also agreed that the critical question was whether this general understanding of copyright could be reconciled with a natural rights theory of property.

Proponents of common law copyright relied on a reasoning that was first introduced in England by William Warburton almost a century earlier in his pamphlet on literary property.[94] They assumed that natural property rights were based on ownership of the fruits of one's labor and then equated intellectual labor and its product with physical labor and its product. The dissenting Justice Thompson described this argument like this: 'The great principle on which the author's right rests, is, that it is the fruit or production of his own labor, and that labor, by the faculties of the mind may establish a right of property as well as by the faculties of the body.'[95]

---

[92] Morton J Horwitz, *The Transformation of American Law 1780–1860* (HUP 1977) 4–9.
[93] On the British literary property debate, see Mark Rose, *Authors and Owners: The Invention of Copyright* (HUP 1993) 67–112; Brad Sherman and Lionel Bently, *The Making of Modern Intellectual Property Law: The British Experience, 1760–1911* (CUP 1999) 11–42.
[94] See William Warburton, *A Letter from an Author to a Member of Parliament Concerning Literary Property* (1747).
[95] *Report of the Copy-right Case of Wheaton v. Peters* (n 88) 110.

Opponents of common law copyright similarly relied on an argument developed by their English predecessors. Agreeing that the product of the mind was the result of labor, they maintained it lacked other essential characteristics of property. Specifically, because of its incorporeal nature, the alleged object of property was incapable of exclusive possession and did not have clear objective boundaries. One of Peters's attorneys explained that property depended on 'possession, and that of an adverse character, exclusive in its nature and pretensions' and that an intangible work could not be the subject of possession 'except of a subtle and imaginative character.'[96] In part, the argument was that publication necessarily threw out the work 'for public use.' Another strand of the argument, however, emphasized that an intangible object lacked any natural boundaries. As a result any limitation on its use was an 'artificial and therefore arbitrary rule,' the kind that was within the province of statutory law rather than that of pre-political common law.[97]

Wheaton's lawyers grounded their response to this objection in the distinction between ideas and expressions that appeared in the theoretical copyright debates in England and Germany in the previous century.[98] Those who objected to common law copyright, they argued, forgot 'that books are not made up of ideas alone, but are and necessarily must be, clothed in language, and embodied in a form which gives them individuality and identity that make them more distinguishable than any other personal property can be.'[99] Thus distinguishing between ideas and expression and limiting copyright's ownership claim to the latter served to justify the concept of intellectual property within the traditional framework of natural property rights.

The Supreme Court produced a split decision. The sharp substantive disagreements and the various personal aspects triggered by the case resulted in a tensed dynamics among the Justices that became apparent when the opinion was delivered.[100] In regard to the first legal question, the majority opinion written by Justice John McLean and joined by three others ruled that complying with the statutory formalities was necessary for a valid copyright, although it left the exact ruling somewhat ambiguous.[101] The second question of copyright in reported judicial opinions was the only one on which all the Justices were able to agree. The majority opinion disposed of this issue in one sentence ruling that 'no reporter has, or can have any copyright, in the written opinions delivered by this court.'[102] The dissenting Justice Henry Baldwin explained, however, that there could be no copyright in the judicial opinions but any supplementary materials by the reporter such as notes or summaries of the counsels' arguments could

---

[96] Ibid 79.
[97] Ibid.
[98] See Martha Woodmansee, 'The Genius and the Copyright: Economic and Legal Conditions of the Emergence of the "Author"' (1984) 17 Eighteenth Century Studies 425, 444–46; Sherman and Bently (n 93) 30–35.
[99] *Report of the Copy-right Case of Wheaton v. Peters* (n 88) 18.
[100] See Edward G White, *The Marshall Court and Cultural Change, 1815–1835* (Macmillan 1988) 408–24; Craig Joyce, 'The Rise of the Supreme Court Reporter: An Institutional Perspective on Marshall Court Ascendancy' (1985) 83 Mich L Rev 1291, 1382–84.
[101] *Wheaton* (n 88) 663–64. For a discussion of the ambiguity surrounding the ruling on the issue of formalities, see Joyce, 'The Story of *Wheaton v Peters*' (n 89) 68–69.
[102] *Wheaton* (n 88) 668.

be copyrighted.[103] Two years later in his *Commentaries on Equity Jurisprudence* Justice Joseph Story explained that this was indeed what the court had meant in its unanimous ruling on the subject.[104] On the third question of common law copyright the majority adopted the rule that by this time had become the conventional wisdom in England: common law copyright applied to unpublished works but published works could only be protected under the statutory scheme. The dissenting Justices Baldwin and Thompson sharply disagreed arguing that common law copyright equally applied to unpublished and published works.

Wheaton v Peters left important and lasting legacies in American copyright law. On the subject of ownership of official legal documents the principle outlined in the Supreme Court decision came to dominate American copyright law. On the federal level this principle eventually resulted in complete denial of copyright to US Government works.[105] In regard to state materials the rules that later consolidated were less conclusive, but copyright was still denied to materials embodying the law of the land as such.[106] Some earlier case law notwithstanding, *Wheaton v Peters* is also considered the origin of the American approach to formalities. This approach demanded strict adherence to all statutory requirements as a precondition for copyright in published works, subject to forfeiture of the right. Despite later liberalizations of the rule, this approach would endure well into the second half of the twentieth century.[107]

The most important legacy of the decision relates to the question of common law copyright and the underlying philosophical justification of copyright. *Wheaton v Peters* is commonly understood as a resounding rejection of the concept of copyright as a pre-political, natural right in favor of a utilitarian framework of copyright as a government-created grant in the service of the public interest.[108] This understanding is only partially accurate. The majority opinion, while analyzing copyright in terms of a state-granted monopoly and clearly not being sympathetic to the natural rights argument, was not exactly a model of clarity regarding the theoretical underpinning of copyright. More importantly, while the decision rejected post-publication common law copyright, it introduced for the first time in the US such rights in unpublished works. At the time there was a variety of competing views in Britain about the question of common law copyright in published works.[109] *Wheaton v Peters* declared a clear rule in the US under which common law copyright applied to unpublished works but dissolved after publication. The significance of adopting this rule was both practical and symbolic. Practically, the division between common law copyright in unpublished works and statutory copyright in published ones would dominate American copyright

---

[103] Ibid 698.

[104] Story (n 68) vol 2, 247–48.

[105] 17 USC s 105.

[106] L Ray Patterson and Craig Joyce, 'Monopolizing the Law: The Scope of Copyright Protection for Law Reports and Statutory Compilations' (1989) 36 UCLA L Rev 719.

[107] Stef Van Gompel, *Formalities in Copyright Law: An Analysis of their History, Rationales and Possible Futures* (Kluwer Law International 2011) 94–97.

[108] Patterson (n 3) 209; John Tehranian, 'Et Tu, Fair Use? The Triumph of Natural-Law Copyright' (2005) 38 UC Davis L Rev 465, 472–73.

[109] H Tomás Gómez-Arostegui, 'Copyright at Common Law in 1774' (2014) 47 Conn L Rev 1, 23–25, 41–45.

law until 1976. On the symbolic side, the narrative of copyright as originating in a common law natural property right retained some of its ideological power. For decades after *Wheaton v Peters* some would toy with the idea of obtaining court recognition for common law copyright in published works.[110] Gradually, the focus shifted elsewhere. Arguments about copyright as a natural property right that was abridged by the statutory scheme were used as general ideological justifications for various agendas other than common law copyright. Most commonly this narrative was used in arguments supporting recognition of international copyright.[111] Beginning in the mid-nineteenth century, American treatise writers also relied on the narrative of common law copyright as an absolute property right to justify a broad reading of the scope of statutory copyright.[112]

Another aspect of *Wheaton v Peters* reflected a traditional way of thinking about copyright that was about to change. The distinction between ideas and expression relied on by proponents of common law copyright in the case was different from the modern version that would appear later in the century. The claim that copyright ownership did not extend to ideas relied on the traditional premise that copyright's scope was limited to verbatim reproduction in print of a specific text. An absolute property in expression meant at this point a narrow-scope right that is perpetual and not encumbered by statutory formalities. This attempt to claim strong copyright was blocked by the Supreme Court's decision. By the late nineteenth century copyright would be expanded through a different route. Owning expression would come to mean general control of the market value of an intellectual work in all its possible concrete forms, a concept that extended well beyond the old right to reprint still assumed in *Wheaton v Peters*.

5. Early Copyright Jurisprudence

Our knowledge of the early American case law on copyright is very incomplete. Most copyright decisions during the first decades of the US were not reported. There are only a handful of reported cases prior to 1830 and many of the existing reports are extremely terse. Future research of original records from this period may uncover interesting findings. When the trickle of reported cases began to increase in the 1830s, English copyright case law, on which much of the developing American jurisprudence relied, was in a state of flux. This dynamism is reflected in the variety of approaches taken to the fundamental principles of copyright law in American case law during this period. Subject to this caveat, the dominant framework of American copyright roughly until 1850 was still heavily colored by traditional English copyright jurisprudence. Under this traditional jurisprudence, copyright was a hybrid between the new regime of authors' rights and the previous system of publishers' trade privileges. Since the 1710 Statute of Anne British copyright had become a general regime of authors' rights, but many of the specific institutional features of copyright still bore the mark of its origin

---

[110] Oren Bracha, 'The Statute of Anne: An American Mythology' (2010) 47 Houston L Rev 877, 900.
[111] Ibid 902–13.
[112] Ibid 913–16.

as a publisher's privilege. The same was true of American copyright during the first half century of its existence.

An important aspect of the transitory nature of early American copyright was its limited subject matter coverage. Historically, copyright as the unique privilege of the book trade applied only to printed texts. As late as 1897, although at this point the description was already an anachronism, the *Bouvier Law Dictionary* described the term copyright as limited to exclusive rights in a writing or a drawing 'which may be multiplied by the arts of printing in any of its branches.'[113] The coverage of British copyright law had broken beyond these boundaries with the 1798 Models and Busts Act, but in America copyright remained restricted to the product of the printing press for many more decades.[114] The 1790 Copyright Act covered maps, charts and books[115] and the 1802 extension to prints and engravings was well within copyright's traditional book trade domain.[116] Even the 1831 explicit addition of 'musical works' only protected sheet music against unauthorized reprints, which had already been the case from the earliest days of the regime.[117] This pattern was broken only with the 1856 statutory addition of photographs as copyrightable subject matter and a public performance right in dramatic compositions.[118] After this point, the process of transforming copyright into a universal field based on the principle of protecting all expressive works of authorship gradually unfolded over decades.

Similarly, the scope of early copyright was defined by the concept of reprinting a copy and as a result was very narrow. Although some judicial opinions from the 1830s began to go beyond it, early American case law was still heavily influenced by the traditional English rule that copyright only protected against verbatim reproduction and an additional narrow penumbra of evasive reproductions with trivial changes. Infringement was limited to a narrow area of close similarity and many secondary uses of works such as translations, abridgments and dramatizations were generally outside copyright's reach. Thus in a famous 1854 case, one court found a German translation of Harriet Beecher-Stowe's *Uncle Tom's Cabin* to be non-infringing because it was not a copy of the original.[119] By the same token, early copyright applied only to printed copies and did not cover non-textual reproductions. It would be only the 1856 addition of an exclusive right to publicly perform a dramatic work that would start a long process of statutory extensions and judicial reorientation of doctrine. This process would end up defining copyright's scope on a much higher level of abstraction as covering all substantial reproductions of the original work, irrespective of medium or format.

A different facet of the continued influence of copyright's origin as the publisher's trade privilege during the early period of authors' copyright was the lack of any rules

---

[113] John Bouvier, *Bouvier's Law Dictionary. A New Edition Thoroughly Revised and Brought up to Date* (Boston Book Co 1897) vol 1, 436.
[114] An Act for Encouraging the Art of Making New Models and Casts of Busts, and other things therein mentioned 1798 (38 Geo III c 71).
[115] s 1, 1 Stat 124.
[116] s 2, 2 Stat 171.
[117] s 1, 4 Stat 436.
[118] Act of 18 Aug 1856, c 170, 11 Stat 138.
[119] *Stowe v Thomas* 23 F Cas 201, 206–07 (CC ED Pa 1853).

for defining or identifying authorship. Early American copyright law bestowed copyright on authors and their assignees, but lacked any criteria for defining or limiting the concept of an author. In the absence of a statutory or judicial definition, an author was simply the person who created any text that could be printed. Relying on the constitutional decree that copyright's purpose is to promote the progress of 'science,' a few early decisions began to develop certain limitations on which works were properly within the ambit of copyright.[120] It was only in the last decades of the nineteenth century, however, that courts began to develop an elaborate requirement of originality that was explicitly founded on the concept of authorship.

III. THE MODERNIZATION OF COPYRIGHT 1840–1909

In between the fourth decade of the nineteenth century and the beginning of the twentieth century American copyright law underwent a gradual but extensive process of change. The outcome of this process was a system whose substance, procedures and underlying ideology contained most of the elements of modern copyright law. Many of the features traceable to the old publisher's privilege had faded away and copyright emerged as a universal field based on the abstract principle of owning expressive works of authorship. Underlying the legal change were two trends that often produced friction and even conflict. One trend was a greater recognition of individual authorship as the animating core principle of copyright. The other was the mounting commercial importance of copyright's control power over an ever-growing variety of commodified, intangible resources in the context of an emerging corporate market society. On the procedural side, the institutional origins of modern copyright appeared as the Library of Congress and the Copyright Office assumed responsibility for copyright's administration. Another important aspect of modern copyright – its internationalization – started to consolidate at the end of the century. Following a long struggle, the US began to extend copyright to some foreign works and made its first ambivalent steps toward joining an emerging system of international copyright.

1. Subject Matter

For the first half of the nineteenth century copyright was limited to the realm of print. It covered only books, maps, charts and as of 1802 prints. By the end of the century the coverage of copyright had expanded considerably through a series of statutory additions. The technical recognition of various new subject matter categories reflected and created a deep conceptual change. Gradually copyright ceased being the unique regulation of the book trade and came to be seen as applicable to any creative human expression.

The first extension of copyright beyond the realm of print happened in 1856 with the addition of a public performance right in dramatic compositions. Plays were protected as texts against reproduction in print from the beginning of the regime, but copyright in printed plays did not prevent unauthorized performance. Lobbying for a public

---

[120] *Clayton* (n 56); *Scoville v Toland* 21 F Cas 863 (CC D Ohio 1848).

performance right in dramatic works started in the 1840s and produced two failed bills. Finally, in 1856, after extensive lobbying by several playwrights, Congress added a public performance right for any 'dramatic composition, designed or suited for public representation.'[121] The new performance right meant that dramatic compositions became recognized as a category of protected subject matter distinct from their incarnation as printed texts. In 1865 Congress added photographs as copyrightable subject matter.[122] The conceptual and legal difficulties encountered by early attempts to enforce photographic copyright in the courts had been studied, but we know little about the process leading to the statutory recognition.[123] The 1870 Copyright Act added paintings; drawings; chromos, statues and artistic models or designs.[124] Sculptors and painters repeatedly tried to obtain copyright protection for their works at least since the 1820s. But it was only half a century later that the conventional wisdom in Congress became that 'an artist has as much right to the exclusive reproduction of his works as an author or engraver.'[125] The 1897 creation of a public performance entitlement in music had an effect similar to the earlier dramatic performance right.[126] Music, previously protected in its textual form only, became a fully recognized subject matter category.

The 1909 Copyright Act expanded and consolidated the extensions of the preceding half century. The Act contained a long list of specific categories of copyrightable subject matter, but it also mandated that copyright applied to 'all the writings of an author.'[127] At this point the incremental additions of specific categories of subject matter had crystalized into a new understanding of copyright as a general field based on the universal principle of protecting creative works of authorship. To a large extent, the process that transformed copyright from the book trade's regulation into a universal field was driven by new technologies for creation and exploitation of expression and the markets built around them. But there was also an ideological component. As the logic of copyright was gradually reconceived as based on an abstract principle of creative authorship, the extension of the law to new expressive areas came to be seen as natural and necessary.

2. Scope

During the same period when the coverage of copyright was extended to include new subject matter the scope of the right underwent a similar process of expansion and abstraction. Gradually copyright lost its traditional literal meaning as the right of

---

[121] 11 Stat 138, 139, s 1. See Oren Bracha, 'Commentary on the U.S. Copyright Act Amendment 1856' in Primary Sources on Copyright (1450–1900) <http://copy.law.cam.ac.uk/cam/tools/request/showRecord?id=commentary_us_1856>.
[122] Act of 3 Mar 1865, c 126, 13 Stat 540.
[123] See Jane Gaines, *Contested Culture: The Image, the Voice, and the Law* (UNC Press 1991) 52–65; Christine Haight Farley, 'The Lingering Effects of Copyright's Response to the Invention of Photography' (2004) 65 U Pitt L Rev 385.
[124] Act of 8 July 1870, s 86, 16 Stat 212.
[125] Congressional Globe, 41st Cong, 2nd Sess, 2854, 20 Apr 1870.
[126] Act of 6 Jan 1897, c 4, 29 Stat 694.
[127] Act of 4 Mar 1909, c 320, s 4, 35 Stat 1075–76.

making and selling verbatim, printed copies of the original. Several court decisions in the 1830s and 1840s, mostly written by Justice Joseph Story, abandoned the traditional view that copyright was limited to the making of verbatim copies and started to develop the modern approach, extending protection to higher levels of abstraction that encompass non-literal and structural similarities between works.[128]

Ironically the introduction into American law of the fair use doctrine – a doctrine that today is considered one of the main restrictions on copyright's scope – was part of this expansion process. The 1841 decision in the case of *Folsom v Marsh* that is considered the origin of the doctrine held that the use of extensive excerpts from the papers of George Washington in a semi-biographical work was infringing.[129] The decision laid the foundation for a dramatic reinterpretation of copyright's scope. Traditionally copyright was seen as limited to verbatim reproduction and an additional narrow penumbra of copying with merely colorable and evasive changes. This principle emphasized the element of new intellectual contribution by the copier and tended to immunize most derivative uses such as good faith abridgments and translations. The opinion of Justice Story cited the English precedents but subtly poured new content into the doctrine.[130] The base line was changed. Non-literal copying was now seen as infringing unless it was 'fair' – an inquiry that was based on a multitude of factors and accorded new prominence to the question of the copyright owner's market harm. There was no overnight change. The old concepts that defined copyright's scope narrowly and sheltered secondary uses of copyrighted works retained some viability. But the pre-Civil War decisions that introduced fair use and a more abstract concept of copyright's scope laid the foundation for future expansion.

After the Civil War the process of expansion and abstraction continued. Partly, it unfolded through legislation that upended the traditional relative immunity given to secondary uses of copyrighted works. The prominent example was the 1870 statutory extension of copyright's scope to cover translations and dramatizations of a protected work.[131] The more fundamental change happened, however, through judicial re-interpretation of the law. Once copyright was reconceived as applicable to a broad sphere of derivative uses of protected works, there was little need for statutory recognition of specific uses as infringing. Late nineteenth century decisions extended the scope of copyright infringement to new abstract levels of similarity. Some of these decisions dealt with the traditional print context, but others involved the new expressive areas brought within copyright's coverage.[132] One important new area where copyright's new subject matter coverage intersected with expanded scope was dramatic performances. The performance as an activity commonly seen as more than verbal was a context particularly ripe for abstracting the scope of copyright. Thus, some of the

---

[128] See *Gray v Russel* 10 F Cas 1035 (No 5,728) (CC D Mass 1839); *Folsom v Marsh* 9 F Cas 342 (CC D Mass 1841); *Emerson v Davies* 8 F Cas 615, 620 (CC D Mass 1845).
[129] *Folsom* (n 128).
[130] See Tehranian (n 108) 481–86; Oren Bracha, 'The Ideology of Authorship Revisited: Authors, Markets, and Liberal Values in Early American Copyright' (2008) 118 Yale LJ 186, 229–30; Mathew Sag, 'The Prehistory of Fair Use' (2011) 76 Brook L Rev 1371.
[131] s 86, 16 Stat 212.
[132] See eg *Lawrence v Dana* 15 F Cas 58; *Simms v Stanton* 75 F 6, 10 (CC ND Cal 1896); *Gilmore v Anderson* 38 F 846, 849 (SDNY 1889).

more innovative late nineteenth century decisions on copyright's scope involved dramatic performances.[133] The developing case law created and relied on a new underlying understanding of copyright. Instead of a narrow right to print a text, copyright was gradually reconceived as a general control of the market value of an intangible intellectual work that could take many concrete forms.[134]

As the old restrictions on copyright's scope were swept away, new legal doctrines for limiting the scope of copyright began to emerge. One was fair use. Building on the early pre-Civil War cases courts began to apply the fair use analysis – although not always using the term – to distinguish between permissible and infringing activities. Unlike the modern status of the doctrine as a formal defense, the fair use inquiry was incorporated into the analysis of infringement.[135] Another new category of boundary-drawing mechanisms was the distinction between ideas and expressions and related rules such as the denial of copyright protection to functional methods.[136] At the end of the nineteenth century and early in the twentieth century the idea/expression distinction started to play an increasingly important role in copyright's doctrine. The general principle that copyright extended only to expressions and did not protect ideas had existed at least since the eighteenth century literary property debate. In its early form, however, it was a merely theoretical principle rooted in copyright's traditional understanding as applicable only to the making of verbatim copies. In its later incarnation the idea/expression dichotomy became a doctrinal tool used by courts to regulate the appropriate outer limits of copyright that now extended well beyond the making of verbatim copies.

3. Entitlements

Parallel to the reinterpretation of copyright as covering higher levels of abstraction and broader spheres of similarity, the right was also extended beyond the realm of print. Traditionally one could only infringe copyright through reproduction in print. Beginning in the mid-nineteenth century, however, new entitlements were gradually added and expanded the owner's control power beyond this zone. The 1856 performance right in dramatic compositions was the first move in this direction.[137] Public performance rights in music arrived much later. Such rights were first proposed in 1844.[138] It was

---

[133] See eg *Daly v Palmer* 6 F Cas 1132 (SDNY 1868); *Daly v Webster* 56 F 483 (2nd Cir 1892); *Maxwell v Goodwin* 93 F 665 (CC ND Ill 1899). See generally Derek Miller, Judicial Criticism: Performance and Aesthetics in Anglo-American Copyright Law 1770–1911 (Unpublished Ph.D. Dissertation Stanford University 2013) 108–25.

[134] Bracha, 'The Ideology of Authorship Revisited' (n 130) 231–32.

[135] R Anthony Reese, 'The Story of *Folsom v. Marsh*: Distinguishing between Infringement and Legitimate Uses' in Ginsburg and Dreyfuss (eds), *Intellectual Property Stories* (n 89) 289.

[136] See Pamela Samuelson, 'The Story of *Baker v. Selden*: Sharpening the Distinction Between Authorship and Invention' in Ginsburg and Dreyfuss (ibid), 159–93; Bracha, 'The Ideology of Authorship Revisited' (n 130) 235–38.

[137] 11 Stat 138.

[138] Zvi S Rosen, 'The Twilight of the Opera Pirates: A Prehistory of the Exclusive Right of Public Performance for Musical Compositions' (2007) 24 Cardozo Arts & Ent LJ 1157, 1159–67.

only in 1897, however, that Congress amended the statute to add a musical public performance right.[139]

As with the scope of copyright, the changing principles of copyright that were developed in the case law proved as important as the piecemeal statutory interventions. In the second half of the nineteenth century commentators developed the idea that copyright allowed the owner to control all markets for exploitation of a copyrighted work with no regard to change of form or media.[140] But the case law did not reflect this principle. There was no general agreement that copyright covered all derivative markets or media of a protected work. It was not clear for example that a series of pictures or a motion picture based on a novel constituted an infringement of the copyright in it.[141] It was a widespread view that in the absence of a particular statutory extension such as the musical and dramatic performance rights, copyright only applied to reproduction in the same media as the original work. Courts only gradually accepted a general principle of derivative works. This first happened in the context of unpublished works where the widespread understanding of common law copyright as an absolute property right helped accept the principle of general control of an intellectual work irrespective of changes of media or market.[142] The acceptance of the same principle in regard to statutory copyright was more gradual. Thus in 1908 the Supreme Court could still rule that a reproduction of sheet music in the form of perforating rolls operating player pianos was not infringing because it was not 'multiplying copies of those sheets of music.'[143] Even when two years later the Court ruled that a motion picture adaptation of the novel *Ben Hur* was an infringement, it found it necessary to rely on circuitous reasoning that avoided describing the creation of the motion picture as direct infringement.[144] It was only in the following decades that the courts came to fully accept the principle previously developed in treatises and in the context of common law copyright under which copyright covered a broad swath of forms and markets derivative of the original.

Like subject matter, the abstraction of copyright's scope and the development of a general derivative works principle was driven by technological and economic developments. By the mid-nineteenth century economic and social conditions created a new national mass market for books. A growing and increasingly sophisticated publishing industry developed various techniques for cultivating and exploiting various niches of this market. In the context of many of these new techniques – such as translations, dramatizations and later motion picture adaptations – the extension of copyright held out the promise of control and increased profits. Other social and technological

---

[139] 29 Stat 694.
[140] Bracha, 'The Ideology of Authorship Revisited' (n 130) 230–31.
[141] Oren Bracha, 'How Did Film Become Property? Copyright and the Early Film Industry' in Brad Sherman and Leanne Wiseman (eds), *Copyright and the Challenges of the New* (Wolters Kluwer 2012) 170–71.
[142] See 'Authors' Rights before Publication – The Representation of Manuscript Plays' (1874–1875) 9 Am L Rev 236. See also Jessica Litman, 'The Invention of Common Law Play Right' (2010) 25 Berkeley Tech LJ 1381.
[143] *White-Smith Music Pub Co v Apollo Co* 209 US 1, 13 (1908).
[144] *Kalem Co v Harper Bros* 222 US 55 (1911). See Bracha, 'How did Film Become Property?' (n 141) 172–73.

developments opened up new areas where various forms of expression could be commercially exploited, including advertisement, a newly organized theatrical industry, photography, motion pictures and sound recording. The promise of higher profits through copyright control resulted in a pressure on both the legislature and the courts to extend copyright beyond the traditional realm of the book trade and to abstract its scope. Ideology too played a role in this process by smoothing the path of copyright's expansion. The new understanding of copyright as a general control of the market value of all the concrete forms of an intellectual work rationalized and naturalized the expansion and abstraction of the right.

4. Originality

Originality came to be seen as a fundamental element of copyright law in the last decades of the nineteenth century. Several pre-1850 decisions adamantly rejected suggestions that copyright's grounding in authorship required a high originality standard as a threshold requirement for copyright.[145] Other early decisions, while usually not using the term originality, did impose a threshold standard for copyright protection that may be seen as a quasi-originality requirement. Some cases distinguished between literary works and subject matter belonging to the realm of industry or commerce, limiting copyright to the former.[146] Under this rule the copyrightability of works such as price lists, product catalogs or even advertisements was questionable. Other cases denied copyright protection to subject matter seen as inappropriate or vulgar.[147] These decisions were based in part on the old English rule that denied copyright to seditious, libelous or blasphemous publications.[148] They were more commonly grounded, however, in the constitutional mandate of promotion of science.[149]

This field of copyright changed in the late nineteenth century in a paradoxical manner. Originality was newly articulated as an explicit and fundamental requirement for copyright protection inherent in the idea of authorship. A few decisions went further and construed originality as a constitutional requirement that defined the outer limits of the statutory regime.[150] Much of the development of the newly articulated originality requirement took place in the context of new technologies and industries built around them such as photography or the telegraph-age news industry.[151] At the same time that originality was elevated to new prominence, however, its practical significance was diminished. Prior precedents that drew boundaries based on the content or the commercial nature of the work declined and were replaced by judicial neutrality.[152] The

---

[145] *Gray* (n 128); *Emerson* (n 128); *Atwill v Ferrett* 2 F Cas 195 (CC SDNY 1846).
[146] *Clayton* (n 56); *Scoville* (n 120).
[147] *Martinetti v Maguire* 16 F Cas 920 (CC Cal 1867).
[148] Story (n 68) vol 2, 147–66; Eaton S Drone, *A Treatise on the Law of Property in Intellectual Productions in Great Britain and the United States* (Little, Brown 1879) 181–96.
[149] *Martinetti* (n 147) 922.
[150] See *Trade Mark Cases* (n 51); *Burrow-Giles* (n 57).
[151] See Farley (n 123); Robert Brauneis, 'The Transformation of Originality in the Progressive-Era Debate over Copyright in News' (2009) 27 Cardozo Arts & Ent LJ 321.
[152] See Bracha, 'The Ideology of Authorship Revisited' (n 130) 207–09.

1903 Supreme Court decision in *Bleistein v Donaldson Lithographic Company* became the canonic declaration of copyright's neutrality principle and marked the modern rise of the minimalist approach to originality.[153]

5. International Copyright

For most of the nineteenth century the US was a 'pirate nation' as far as copyright law was concerned. Despite repeated attempts and vociferous public campaigns, it adamantly refused to extend copyright protection to foreign authors. Attempts to obtain international copyright started in the late 1820s and continued in waves in successive decades. The arguments of both proponents and opponents remained remarkably constant throughout the decades of struggle. The growing size and value of the American book market, fueled by technological innovation and high literacy rates, progressively increased the stakes of the debate. Changes in the American publishing industry gradually reconfigured the relevant interests. Finally, in 1891, after numerous defeats, this shift of interests backed by an increasingly elaborate lobbying apparatus resulted in some recognition of international copyright. It was, however, a preliminary and ambivalent recognition.

The 1790 Copyright Act extended its protection only to authors who were American citizens or residents and explicitly permitted the importation and publication of foreign works.[154] This is hardly surprising. International copyright norms had not yet appeared at that point and the US, being a developing country highly dependent on importation of cultural goods, had a strong interest in facilitating the diffusion of affordable foreign works. Some grumbling about the lack of copyright protection for foreign works began to appear in the 1820s among certain American authors. Their argument, that would become a staple of the debate, was that American authors unfairly had to compete with cheap British works.[155] The alleged result was injustice to American authors and a chilling effect on the emergence of a vibrant, native literary culture.

In the 1830s several British publishers and authors took notice of the growing American market and started agitating for copyright protection.[156] They found some support from American authors, politicians and public figures. At this early stage American publishers were mostly opposed to international copyright, with the most notable exception being George Palmer Putnam. Putnam who supported international copyright on grounds of morality and the encouragement of native literature founded the American International Copyright Association in 1837.[157] In the same year petitions of British and American authors were submitted to Congress. They elaborated a long list of reasons supporting international copyright: the adverse effect on American authors and native culture, the inequitable lack of compensation to British authors,

---

[153] 188 US 239 (1903).
[154] ss 1, 5, 1 Stat 124–25.
[155] Catherine Seville, *The Internationalisation of Copyright Law: Books, Buccaneers and Black Flag in the Nineteenth Century* (CUP 2006) 157–59.
[156] Ibid 160; James J Barnes, *Authors, Publishers and Politicians: The Quest for an Anglo-American Copyright Agreement 1815–1854* (Ohio State University Press 1974) 60.
[157] Seville (n 155) 162.

damage to authorial reputation due to unauthorized publication of mutilated versions and the inconsistency with a general theory of property of copyright ownership limited by geographical boundaries. A select committee chaired by Senator Henry Clay drafted an international copyright bill and accompanied it with a report on the subject.[158] Despite some favorable responses, the Clay bill met stiff opposition. Opposing petitions were submitted on behalf of American publishers, typographers and other members of the book trade. In 1838 the Committee on Patents chaired by John Ruggles submitted a detailed report that discussed the conflicting arguments on the subject and expressed a strong opposition to the bill.[159] Three additional attempts by Clay to pass the bill in 1838, 1840 and 1842 were defeated.[160]

The next half century saw a long saga of further failed attempts to legislate international copyright. In 1849 John Jay (the grandson of the first Chief Justice of the US Supreme Court) initiated a new congressional petition backed by lobbying efforts that had never ripened into a bill.[161] A different route was tried in 1853 when Edward Everett the Secretary of State under President Fillmore signed a copyright treaty with Britain modeled after the Anglo-French treaty. Requiring only Senate ratification, the treaty held the promise of bypassing hostility in the House. Widespread opposition from the book trade, however, doomed the treaty and it was never ratified.[162] After sporadic activity in the 1850s, the next main effort arrived with the 1868 establishment of the American Copyright Association. The organization brought together American authors with several publishers supportive of international copyright. Probably with connection to this activity, Representative Baldwin chairing the Library Committee submitted to the House a new report recommending international copyright. The bill that accompanied the report did not advance.[163] During the 1870s there were several other failed bills as well as unsuccessful attempts to revive the treaty route.[164]

What explains the obstinate American resistance to international copyright in the face of relentless attempts to create it? The question is highlighted by the contrast with the field of patents where the US extended rights to foreign inventors early on and by the second half of the nineteenth century took a leading role in the creation of international norms.[165] Probably the most important factor was the balance of trade. In the relevant period the US was a net importer dependent on English books. The 1838 Ruggles report asked '[w]ho ever reads an American book?' and frankly concluded that the trade effects of international copyright 'would be for us on the wrong side of the ledger.'[166]

---

[158] Report with Senate Bill No 223, 24th Cong, 2nd Sess, 16 Feb 1837. Available in Primary Sources on Copyright (1450–1900) <http://copy.law.cam.ac.uk/record/us_1837a>.
[159] Report to Accompany Senate Bill No 32, 25th Cong, 2nd Sess, 25 June 1838. Available in Primary Sources on Copyright (1450–1900) <http://copy.law.cam.ac.uk/record/us_1838>.
[160] Seville (n 155) 161–62.
[161] Ibid 173–74.
[162] Ibid 180–84; Barnes (n 156) 216–62.
[163] Seville (n 155) 196.
[164] Ibid 199–206.
[165] B Zorina Khan, *The Democratization of Invention: Patents and Copyrights in American Economic Development, 1790–1920* (CUP 2005) 298.
[166] Report to Accompany Senate Bill No 32 (n 159) 4.

For similar reasons there were entrenched and powerful interests opposed to international copyright. Most American publishers were wary of losing to British publishers the lucrative market for reprints of English works and other book trade workers such as typographers and binders were similarly concerned in regard to book manufacturing. Ideology also played an important role. For much of the nineteenth century, the American book industry was pervaded by republican ideology that emphasized the ideal of accessible knowledge available to all on equal and affordable terms.[167] Cheap English reprints were seen not just as an economic opportunity but also as means for disseminating knowledge and enlightening all classes of the citizenry. Ruggles, an avid Jacksonian, referred in his report to the importance of cheap books for 'farmers, merchants and tradesmen' and observed: 'The multiplication of cheap editions of useful books, brought within the reach of all classes, serves to promote the general diffusion of knowledge and intelligence, on which depends so essentially the preservation and support of our institutions.'[168]

An important background of the resistance to international copyright was the fact that the lack of formal rights did not mean an absence of norms regulating the reprint of texts. In fact, publishing of foreign works was governed by a strong system of social norms known as the 'courtesy of trade.' Under this norm, observed by the big publishing houses, the first publisher to procure and print a text enjoyed de facto exclusivity. The informal system included dispute resolution methods and sanctions against a publisher who infringed the norm including public shaming and retaliation.[169] Not everybody observed the norm. The profit opportunity attracted smaller firms that produced cheap reprints in defiance of the courtesy of trade. Members of the more established firms regarded them as the 'cheap Ishmaelites of the trade.'[170] The result was a two-tier system. Large, respectable printing houses generally refrained from encroaching on each other's customary rights. These would usually pay British authors for the 'rights' of publishing their manuscripts, both out of a sense of honor and as means for getting a time advantage. Reprinters published unauthorized, often low-quality editions regardless of customary rights. Under this system the market was segmented. Reprinters defying the norm captured the demand for cheap lower-quality editions. Large publishing houses focused on higher quality editions, transferred some compensation to foreign authors and enjoyed relative exclusivity. Any remaining substitution effect from cheap reprints was moderated by first mover advantages to the big publishers derived both from their time lead and the fact that their editions were authorized by the author.[171]

While there is little doubt that American consumers of books benefited from the refusal to recognized international copyright, it was commonplace to assume, in line with the arguments of proponents of such a right, that two groups were adversely

---

[167] Meredith McGill, *American Literature and the Culture of Reprinting 1834–1853* (University of Pennsylvania Press 2003); Bracha, 'The Ideology of Authorship Revisited' (n 130) 243–45.

[168] Report to Accompany Senate Bill No 32 (n 159) 5.

[169] Robert Spoo, *Without Copyrights: Piracy, Publishing, and the Public Domain* (OUP 2013) 32–49.

[170] Ibid 50.

[171] Khan (n 165) 278–80.

affected: foreign and American authors. Recent empirical research sheds some doubt on this assumption. This research analyzes the data on book sales. It also considers the routes that were open to both British and American authors for monetizing their works in the American market and the degree of substitutionality between these two categories of works. Taking these considerations into account, it is far from clear that either British or American authors were greatly prejudiced by the lack of copyright protection during the relevant period.[172] Additional study of the available data and its interpretation may advance the debate and improve our understanding of the effects of the lack of international copyright in the American market for most of the nineteenth century.

The final push toward international copyright started with the establishment of the American Copyright League in 1882. The organization that claimed to represent all American authors and soon could boast a respectable membership rallied its members around the cause of international copyright. In the following years the Copyright League, soon to be renamed the American Authors League, supported two bills that offered unrestricted copyright to foreign authors. These bills met resistance from publishers and typographers and did not advance.[173] The turning point came in 1887 when the Authors League changed course and started cooperating with the American Publishers Copyright League that represented the major publishers. Under the new pragmatic approach both groups supported a bill promoted by Senator Jonathan Chace. A crucial compromise won support for the bill from the powerful typographical unions by agreeing to a requirement of typesetting in the US that would be known as the 'manufacturing clause.' It was only in 1891 following massive lobbying, some additional maneuvering and several amendments that a version of the bill originally introduced by Chace was finally passed into law.[174]

The copyright extended to foreign works by the Chace Act was limited in several respects. The most important limitation was a reciprocity requirement. The right was extended only to citizens of foreign countries that had been proclaimed by the President as offering American citizens copyright on substantially the same terms as its own citizens or as adhering to an international copyright agreement providing for reciprocity and open to the US. Belgium, France and Britain were the first nations to be proclaimed as meeting this condition and others were added in subsequent years.[175] The manufacturing clause of the act conditioned the right upon the work being printed from a type set or plates made in the US and prohibited the importation of foreign copies or plates. There was also a requirement of first or simultaneous publication in the US. This requirement together with the manufacturing clause created a substantial barrier to eligibility for works not written in English that later became the subject of complaints and reform attempts.[176] Foreign works also had to adhere to the strict formalities imposed by American law including notice, deposit and registration.

---

[172] Ibid 258–87.
[173] Seville (n 155) 218–24.
[174] Act of 3 Mar 1891, c 565, 26 Stat 1106.
[175] William F Patry, *Patry on Copyright* (Thomson Reuters 2010) s 23.4.
[176] Seville (n 155) 248.

Several factors, beyond the persistence of proponents and their efficient lobbying mechanism, explain how the longstanding resistance to international copyright was finally broken. In 1891 the US, while not yet the international powerhouse of cultural goods that it would become, was no longer completely dependent on foreign materials and gained a measure of self-confidence. The courtesy of trade system was undermined both by mounting fierce competition from reprinters and by new antitrust concerns, pushing big publishers to support the security and predictability offered by formal copyright.[177] The emphasis of republican ideology on egalitarian cheap access to knowledge was replaced by a more market-oriented version image of the book industry.[178] Perhaps most importantly, after repeated defeats the more pragmatic wing of proponents of international copyright gained the upper hand. This allowed for crucial compromises that accommodated the interests of big publishers and typographers thereby establishing a broad enough coalition.

The 1891 creation of copyright protection to foreign works was a hesitant and ambivalent first step by the US toward joining the international copyright system. While copyright was extended to foreign works, this protection came with special conditions and significant hurdles for those who wished to enjoy it. The US chose not to join the Berne Union created in 1886 because it regarded its version of copyright as too protectionist and foreign to the American tradition. For a century to come it would stand aloof from the more robust international copyright framework of the Berne Convention and its law would continue to pose significant hurdles to foreign works seeking protection.

6. Administration

In the last decades of the nineteenth century copyright administration was centralized and modernized. For 80 years the main officials responsible for copyright administration were the clerks of the federal District Courts. Under the 1790 Act registration and deposit of copies was made with these clerks.[179] The clerks transmitted the records and the copies deposited with them to the State Department. In 1859 the central power was transferred for a short period to the Patent Office under the Secretary of the Interior, but the District Courts clerks were still in charge of actual registration.[180] The decentralized nature of the system and lack of funds resulted in disorders in record keeping and maintenance of deposited copies.[181]

When Ainsworth Rand Spofford was appointed the Librarian of Congress in 1864 he set out to transform the Library of Congress into a national library.[182] An important aspect of this vision was centralization of copyright administration in the Library of Congress. This occurred with the 1870 Copyright Act. Under the Act all responsibility

---

[177] Spoo (n 169) 53–59.
[178] Bracha, 'The Ideology of Authorship Revisited' (n 130) 246.
[179] s 1, 1 Stat 124.
[180] Act of 5 Feb 1859, c 22, s 8, 1 Stat 380–81.
[181] PJ Federico, 'Copyrights in the Patent Office' (1939) 21 J Pat Off Soc'y 911, 913–17.
[182] Zvi S Rosen, 'Reimagining Bleistein: Copyright for Advertisements in Historical Perspective' (2012) 59 J Copyright Soc'y USA 347, 350.

for registration and administration of copyright matters was transferred to and centralized in the Library of Congress.[183] Some publishers and authors were opposed to the change whose main motivation was probably to enable the Library of Congress to build its collection through improved control of the deposit process.[184] The Act required the Patent Office and the District Courts clerks to transfer all previously made records and deposited books to the Library of Congress. As a result of staffing and funding problems as well as a surge in copyright registrations, the Library of Congress had difficulties cataloging the collection of deposited books and registering copyrights.[185] In 1897 Congress created a Copyright Department and the position of Register of Copyrights under the supervision of the Librarian of Congress.[186] This agency charged with 'all duties relating to copyright' would come to be known as the US Copyright Office. Thus by the end of the nineteenth century the institutional foundations for modern copyright administration were in place.

7. 1909 Copyright Act

The 1909 Copyright Act consolidated the changes of the preceding half century. It reflected the process of expansion and abstraction that copyright had undergone. The Act included a long list of subject matter categories, including the all-inclusive one of 'all the writings of an author.'[187] It also protected various entitlements extending well beyond reproduction in print, albeit in a somewhat fragmented manner.[188] Some crucial elements of copyright jurisprudence that were developed in the case law, such as the scope of the right or the idea/expression dichotomy, were untouched by the Act and left within the province of the courts. In other respects the Act still clung to traditional features of American copyright. It preserved the division between common law and statutory copyright with publication as the dividing line between them. Despite some liberalization, protection was still dependent on formalities under pain of forfeiture. The term of copyright was extended but remained within the traditional pattern. Unlike many European nations that had moved to terms extending beyond the author's life, the 1909 Act provided for two fixed terms of 28 years and preserved the renewal requirement.

Perhaps the most important modern aspect of the Act was the legislative process leading to it. As part of this process the Library of Congress held three conferences with participation of representatives of the major relevant industries and interests. The final result was a set of elaborate compromises between the various interest groups that reflected the balance of power among them as well as the absence of those interests who did not get a seat at the table.[189] This political economy pattern was established in the last stages of the international copyright struggle and it would come to characterize

---

[183] s 85, 16 Stat 212.
[184] Patry (n 175) s 1.33.
[185] Ibid.
[186] Act of 19 Feb 1897, c 265, 29 Stat 545.
[187] s 4, 35 Stat 1076.
[188] s 1, 35 Stat 1075–76.
[189] See Jessica D Litman, 'Copyright, Compromise, and Legislative History' (1987) 72 Cornell L Rev 857.

modern American copyright legislation. The combination of this legislative process with the new framework of copyright created a paradox. Copyright was now officially reconceived as a universal field based on a unifying principle of authorial ownership of creative expression. The new inclusiveness, however, brought within the ambit of copyright many industries operating in different social and economic circumstances. It also entailed clashes between various interest groups. The result was an intricate series of ad hoc compromises. The epitome of this pattern was section 1(e) of the Act[190] which reflected a compromise hammered out in the wake of a fierce struggle over the right to reproduce music in piano rolls.[191] The section introduced the new concept of a compulsory license, allowing others to reproduce mechanically a musical composition upon the payment of statutorily prescribed royalties to the copyright owner. The pattern of elaborate compromises reflected in context-specific statutory provisions would become a hallmark of American copyright. Paradoxically, the new universality of modern copyright resulted in unprecedented particularism.

The 1909 Copyright Act was the link connecting early and modern American copyright. It retained some of the traditional features of American copyright and failed to anticipate modern technologies, most importantly radio and television broadcast. Both in terms of substantive law and underlying legislative dynamics, however, the Act was the harbinger of modern copyright. It marked the end of an extended process in which American copyright had traveled a long way from its late eighteenth century origin as the publisher's trade right of reprinting a text.

---

[190] s 1(e), 35 Stat 1075.
[191] See Stuart Banner, *American Property: A History of How, Why and What We Own* (HUP 2011) 113–19.

17. 'Cabined, cribbed, confined, bound in': Copyright in the Australian colonies
*Catherine Bond**

I. INTRODUCTION

In an 1881 piece for colonial periodical *The Victorian Review*, lawyer John Finnamore employed the language of William Shakespeare's *Macbeth* to describe the pitiful state of Victorian and Imperial copyright law at the time, stating that it 'cabined, cribbed, confined, bound in' authors in the Australian colonies.[1] This comment, and Finnamore's *Victorian Review* piece more generally, are notable for three reasons. First, it is unusual that a lawyer would quote Shakespeare, but this reference, and others to Shakespeare's career in the piece,[2] indicates the broader symbolic and cultural arguments that Finnamore was attempting to advance in his article.

Second, Finnamore's account is one of only a handful of articles written before the twenty-first century to discuss or even mention colonial copyright law in Australia. Academic interest in the copyright laws of the Australian colonies is relatively recent, with the bulk of this work emerging over the previous decade.[3] To date, that scholarship has focused mainly on the role and influence of Imperial law, particularly the extent to which colonial legislatures and courts believed United Kingdom ('UK') copyright legislation, particularly the Copyright Act 1842 (UK),[4] applied locally, and, when local statutes were introduced by individual colonies from 1869 onwards, the influence that

---

* Many thanks to Kathy Bowrey for her comments on draft versions of this chapter. Earlier versions of this work were also presented, under different titles, at the 5th annual International Society for the History and Theory of Intellectual Property workshop at the Université Panthéon Assas (Paris 2) and Université Paris Diderot (Paris 7), 26–28 June 2013 and the Australasian Intellectual Property Academics Conference, Griffith University, 7–8 February 2014. This chapter has also been supported by an Australian Research Council Grant, DP140100172, and thanks to Jennifer Kwong for research assistance under that grant and Erin Kiley for proofreading. The quotation in the title to this chapter is from the play *Macbeth* by William Shakespeare, but was used to describe the colonial copyright situation in John Finnamore, 'Imperial Copyright Law, As Affecting the Colonies' [1881] The Victorian Review 712, 722.

[1] John Finnamore, 'Imperial Copyright Law, As Affecting the Colonies' [1881] The Victorian Review 712, 722.

[2] Ibid 712–13.

[3] Comments made by Kretschmer, Bently and Deazley on copyright historiography more generally also apply in the Australian context: 'During much of the twentieth century, "copyright" history ... was not thought of as a coherent, or even necessary field of inquiry. It was a pursuit of individual often rather isolated scholars, not an urgent contribution to knowledge.' See Martin Kretschmer, Lionel Bently and Ronan Deazley, 'The History of Copyright History (Revisited)' (2013) 5 WIPOJ 35, 35.

[4] (5 & 6 Vict c 45).

Imperial statutes had on the writing on those local laws. Depending on the category of creation, some scholars have argued that the legislation was essentially copied, with no consideration given to colonial interests, while others suggest that local legislatures did not feel bound by the black letter copyright law of Empire and deviated where necessary.

Third, Finnamore's suggestion that these laws 'cabined, cribbed, confined, bound in' colonial residents is also applicable to the interrelationship between local and Imperial law more broadly at that time. The complexities inherent in the operation of Imperial and colonial copyright law are symptomatic of the broader legal complications experienced by the colonies in the nineteenth century. Early concerns over the ability of the two colonies of Australia at the time, New South Wales and Van Diemen's Land (later renamed Tasmania),[5] to assert legislative independence and autonomy led to the introduction of the Australian Courts Act 1828 (UK).[6] This legislation sought to remove any doubts as to the application of British law to the two colonies: all British Acts in force on 25 July 1828, the date the statute received Royal Assent, would be held to apply to the colonies, though it was further provided that colonies were not bound by the operation of these statutes and could create laws appropriate to the local circumstances.[7] Yet, in the 1860s, a 'constitutional crisis' in the colony of South Australia again emphasised 'the major problems of the time on the relationship of British statutes to local law-making',[8] with one colonial judge of the Supreme Court of South Australia continuing to strike down local legislation arguably for no other reason than 'a disdain for many things colonial'.[9] In order to guarantee autonomy to colonial legislatures, the Colonial Laws Validity Act 1865 (Imp)[10] provided 'that colonial legislatures were only bound by British statutes which were directed to them and which therefore applied by paramount force'[11] and that only laws that were 'repugnant' to any British statute could be struck down.[12]

This chapter illustrates that colonial Australians were confined by the operation of Imperial and local laws of the time, and for a significant time bound to obey UK copyright without receiving any reciprocal protection for local creations.[13] However, when local legislatures introduced their own copyright statutes, they did not appear to

---

[5] See 'Order-in-Council changing name to Tasmania 21 July 1855 (UK)', Documenting A Democracy <http://foundingdocs.gov.au/item-did-78-aid-7-pid-68.html>.

[6] (9 Geo 4 c 83). See also Alex C Castles, *An Australian Legal History* (LawBookCo 1982) 124–30 and 'Australian Courts Act 1828', Documenting A Democracy <http://www.foundingdocs.gov.au/item-did-39.html>.

[7] Castles (n 6) 397. This in itself raises questions as to whether the Copyright Act 1842, introduced after 25 July 1828, or the Statute of Anne 1710 (UK) (8 Anne c 19), introduced prior to and in force at 25 July 1828, was actually the applicable statute in the colonies during the nineteenth century. Thanks to Kathy Bowrey for this point.

[8] Castles (n 6) 406.

[9] Ibid 407.

[10] (28 & 29 Vic c 63).

[11] Castles (n 6) 408.

[12] Colonial Laws Validity Act 1865 (Imp) (28 & 29 Vic c 63) ss 2 and 3.

[13] Finnamore made a similar point, noting that, 'to our direct disadvantage … we are forced to honour all British copyrights, without receiving any benefit in return'. See Finnamore (n 1) 716.

374 *Research handbook on the history of copyright law*

feel 'cabined' by their Imperial equivalents. Further, reference to newspapers indicates that colonial Australians were also bound by local cultural practices which emerged during this period and existed outside formal sources of law. Thus, a consideration of colonial copyright in a broader context of the interrelationship between legislation, reported case law and newspapers reveals a much more complex picture of formal and informal regulation than has been identified in much of the literature in this area to date.

This chapter first reviews the literature on colonial copyright in Australia, proposing reasons for the limited and late development of this field as an area of legal discourse. It suggests that a continued focus on particular types of creations and the use or omission of different sources, including legislation, case law and newspapers, has affected the conclusions made in this scholarship. In order to illustrate this finding, this chapter then uses a case study of the period 1868–69 to examine how colonial jurisdictions understood the impact of Imperial law and the influence that law had once local statutes were enacted, across multiple types of creations (literary, dramatic and artistic) and using multiple sources (legislation, case law and newspapers). The 1868–69 period has been selected for this chapter on account of the intersection of a number of legislative, jurisprudential and press-related issues that occurred across those two years. The chapter concludes with some brief reflections on the future of colonial copyright research and the broader role it may play in copyright discourse more generally.

II. COLONIAL COPYRIGHT AS AN AREA OF LEGAL RESEARCH

In one of the first considerations of historical Australasian IP undertaken by a legal scholar, Jeremy Finn commented that '[t]he history of [IP] is not, it may be said, a part of the mainstream of legal history; readers of either Castle's *Australian Legal History* or Kercher's more recent *An Unruly Child: A History of Law in Australia* will find no index entries for copyright, patents or designs'.[14] When the colonies joined together, 100 years earlier, to become states under one central government at the Federation of Australia, John Quick and Robert Randolph Garran, in their seminal constitutional text *The Annotated Constitution of the Australian Commonwealth*, did refer to those areas of law. They did this because of the inclusion of section 51(xviii) of the Australian Constitution granting power to the Federal Parliament to make laws with respect to 'Copyrights, patents of inventions and designs, and trade marks'.[15] Quick and Garran devoted a little over three pages of their tome to the 'copyrights' power, focusing on copyright law in the UK, United States of America (US) and Canada, with only a brief reference to any previous Australian developments in the area.[16] They simply noted

---

[14] Jeremy Finn, 'Particularism versus Uniformity: Factors Shaping the Development of Australasian Intellectual Property Law in the Nineteenth Century' (2000) 6 Aust J Leg Hist 113, 114.

[15] John Quick and Robert Randolph Garran, *The Annotated Constitution of the Australian Commonwealth* (first publ 1901, LexisNexis Butterworths 2002) 593–99.

[16] Ibid 593–96.

that, before Federation, '"Patents of Invention and Discovery" and "Copyright" were among the subjects which might be referred to the Federal Council, under the Act of 1885'.[17]

Quick and Garran's statement was correct: pursuant to section 15(i) of the Federal Council of Australasia Act 1885 (Imp),[18] the Federal Council was empowered to make laws for the regulation of patents and copyright, where two or more colonies referred the matter to the Council.[19] The Federal Council of Australasia had been created with the intention of bringing together the various colonies of Australia,[20] each represented by two individuals, with a view to creating united approaches to common issues faced by the colonies, such as quarantine and the immigration of criminals.[21] The body was plagued with problems from its inception,[22] and no colony ever referred the issue of patents or copyright to the Federal Council.

By the time of Federation, however, specific copyright statutes had been introduced in four of the six colonies of Australia – Victoria,[23] South Australia,[24] New South Wales,[25] and Western Australia.[26] The colonies of Queensland and Tasmania had also passed a number of statutes dealing with copyright, though these were not as comprehensive as those passed in their sister colonies.[27] In addition, about 20 cases involving copyright issues had been reported in the formal case reports of the applicable colony. Yet, noted lawyers of the time Quick[28] and Garran,[29] writing a text that would influence constitutional and legal debates in all areas of law for the foreseeable future, failed to mention any details of this legislative or jurisprudential development in *The Annotated Constitution of the Australian Commonwealth*.[30] It is perhaps not surprising then that, as Finn commented, 'the history of [IP] is not ... a

---

[17] Ibid 593.
[18] (48 & 49 Vict c 60).
[19] See Federal Council of Australasia Act 1885 (Imp) (48 & 49 Vict c 60) s 15(i).
[20] The 'colonies' were defined as Fiji, New Zealand, New South Wales, Queensland, Tasmania, Victoria, Western Australia and South Australia: see Federal Council of Australasia Act 1885 (48 & 49 Vict c 60) s 1.
[21] See John Williams, 'The Emergence of the Commonwealth Constitution' in HP Lee and George Winterton (eds), *Australian Constitutional Landmarks* (CUP 2003) 1, 9.
[22] Ibid.
[23] Copyright Act 1869 (33 Vict c 350); Copyright Act 1890 (Vic) (54 Vict c 1076).
[24] Copyright Act 1878 (SA) (41 & 42 Vict c 95).
[25] Copyright Act 1879 (NSW) (22 Vict c 20).
[26] See Copyright Act 1895 (WA) (59 Vict c 24).
[27] The Queensland statutes adopted the Imperial position: see Copyright Registration Act 1887 (Qld) (51 Vict c 2); Copyright (Fine Arts) Registration Act 1892 (Qld) (56 Vict c 6); Copyright Registration Act 1898 (Qld) (62 Vict c 13). The Tasmanian statute only introduced a limited regime of newspaper copyright: see Newspaper Copyright Act 1891 (Tas) (55 Vict c 49).
[28] See Michele Maslunka, 'Quick, Sir John (1852–1932)' (*Australian Dictionary of Biography*, first published 1988) <http://adb.anu.edu.au/biography/quick-sir-john-8140/text 14223>.
[29] See RS Parker, 'Garran, Sir Robert Randolph (1867–1957)' (*Australian Dictionary of Biography*, first published 1981) <http://adb.anu.edu.au/biography/garran-sir-robert-randolph-410>.
[30] In contrast, when discussing s 51(xxiv), which grants power to the Federal Parliament to make laws regarding '[t]he service and execution of the Commonwealth of the civil and criminal

376 *Research handbook on the history of copyright law*

part of the mainstream of legal history', given this early oversight, or purposeful omission, by Australia's leading legal scholars at that time.

Between Quick and Garran in 1901, and Finn's comment in 2000, discussion of copyright in the Australian colonies seems to have been largely left to humanities scholars and generally occurs in the context of a discussion on how copyright affected a specific colonial author or rights holder, or area of creation or trade.[31] One particular strand of this literature focuses on colonial author Marcus Clarke, an English-born author who immigrated to Australia and penned one of the seminal novels of the period, *His Natural Life*.[32] The book had been first published in serial form in 1872; it was revised and published in Victoria in a one-volume form in 1874 by local publisher George Robertson & Co; it was then published in a three-volume form by Richard Bentley and Son in the UK in 1875.[33] Clarke is of interest to literary scholars because, among other reasons, he was an outspoken copyright critic and died destitute, arguably as a result of the operation of copyright law at the time, an issue that will be discussed in greater detail below.[34] A handful of references have been made in pre-twenty-first century legal scholarship to either Clarke or colonial copyright, though without any sustained legal or other analysis.[35]

It was not until the immediate past decade that either colonial copyright history, or Australian copyright or intellectual property histories more generally, began to emerge as a field of legal discourse.[36] This emergence is likely attributable in part to the

---

process and the judgments of the courts of the States', Quick and Garran did make reference to the colonial position and relevant case law: see Quick and Garran (n 15) 613–18.

[31] See R Atkinson and R Fotheringham, 'Dramatic Copyright in Australia to 1912' (1987) 11 Australasian Drama Studies 47; Luke Trainor, 'Imperialism, Commerce and Copyright: Australia and New Zealand, 1870–1930' (1997) 21 Bibliographical Society of Australia and New Zealand Bulletin 199; Bronwyn Mason, *Negotiating the Pacific: George Coppin's Business Transactions with California (1864–1881)* (PhD Thesis, University of New South Wales 1999) 248–53.

[32] Brian Elliot, 'Clarke, Marcus Andrew Hislop (1846–1881)' (*Australian Dictionary of Biography*, first published 1969) <http://adb.anu.edu.au/biography/clarke-marcus-andrew-hislop-3225>.

[33] See Lurline Stuart, 'Introduction' in Marcus Clarke, *His Natural Life* (first publ 1874, Queensland UP 2001) xix, xxvii–xlviii.

[34] See Brian Elliott, *Marcus Clarke* (Clarendon 1958) 164–65; LT Hergenhan, 'English Publication of Australian Novels in the Nineteenth Century: The Case of *His Natural Life*' in Leon Cantrell (ed), *Bards, Bohemians, and Bookmen: Essays in Australian Literature* (Queensland UP 1976) 56, 60–62; PD Edwards, 'The English Publication of *His Natural Life*' (1982) 10 Australian Literary Studies 520, 520.

[35] See Staniforth Ricketson, *The Law of Intellectual Property* (Law Book Co 1984) paras 4.51–4.53; Sam Ricketson, 'Australia and International Copyright Protection' in MP Ellinghaus, AJ Bradbrook and AJ Duggan (eds), *The Emergence of Australian Law* (Butterworths 1989) 144, 146–51.

[36] See, for example, Robert Burrell, 'Copyright Reform in the Early Twentieth Century: the View from Australia' (2006) 27 J Legal Hist 239; Benedict Atkinson, *The True History of Copyright: The Australian Experience 1905–2005* (Sydney UP 2007); Andrew T Kenyon, Megan Richardson and Sam Ricketson (eds), *Landmarks in Australian Intellectual Property Law* (CUP 2009). In contrast to the generally piecemeal account of colonial copyright, Amanda Scardamaglia has taken a more cohesive approach to an explanation of colonial trade mark law,

increased digitisation of a variety of primary and secondary source materials that now make Australian legal history research significantly simpler and easier.[37] In 2008, the National Library of Australia ('NLA') commenced an ambitious project to digitise Australian newspapers, across cities, colonies, and time periods, and make these digitised copies freely available online.[38] Today, this digital library database, accessible through the NLA's Trove platform,[39] includes millions of digital newspaper articles, all freely accessible, from between 1803 and 1954. In addition, the Australasian Legal Information Institute ('AustLII') received two Australian Research Council grants, one in 2012 and a second for 2015, to fund the digitisation of historical colonial and state legal materials, including case law, legislation, and government gazettes.[40] Both resources were used in the completion of this chapter.[41]

For the most part, the topic of colonial copyright in legal literature has generally followed the pattern set by humanities scholars, focusing on individual authors or specific types of works or areas of trade.[42] Bently has examined the unusual colonial practice of protecting telegrams through copyright law.[43] Burrell took a more expanded approach in an exploration of the passing of the 1905 and 1912 Australian copyright

---

leading to the development of a rich discourse in this area. See Amanda Scardamaglia, 'The Colonial Trade Mark Regime: Parallel Rationales, Theories and Frameworks' (2011) 22 Kings LJ 259; Amanda Scardamaglia, 'Opening up the Australian Archives on Colonial Trade Mark Registrations' (2013) 23 AIPJ 222; Amanda Scardamaglia, *Colonial Australian Trade Mark Law: Narratives in Lawmaking, People, Power and Place* (Australian Scholarly Publishing 2015).

[37] But see Richard Fotheringham, 'Copyright Sources for Australian Drama and Film' (1986) 14 Archives and Manuscripts 144; Merilyn Minell, *A Nation's Imagination: Australia's Copyright Records, 1854–1968* (National Archives of Australia 2003).

[38] See Jennifer Foreshew, 'Devil in the Detail for Landmark National Library of Australia Project' (*The Australian*, 20 September 2011) <http://www.theaustralian.com.au/technology/devil-in-the-detail-for-landmark-national-library-of-australia-project/story-e6frgakx-1226141152015>.

[39] See 'Trove', <http://trove.nla.gov.au/>.

[40] See Australian Research Council Linkage Infrastructure, Equipment and Facilities (LIEF) Grant LE120100062, 'The Australasian Legal History Library'; Australian Research Council Linkage Infrastructure, Equipment and Facilities (LIEF) Grant, LE150100051, 'The Australasian Legal History Libraries: Stage II'.

[41] Ailwood and Sainsbury also acknowledge the use of Trove in both co-authored articles produced on literary colonial copyright: see Sarah Ailwood and Maree Sainsbury, 'Copyright Law, Readers and Authors in Colonial Australia' (2014) 14 J of the Association for the Study of Australian Literature 1; Sarah Ailwood and Maree Sainsbury, 'The Imperial Effect: Literary Copyright Law in Colonial Australia', *Law, Culture and the Humanities* <http://lch.sagepub.com/content/early/2014/05/27/1743872114533871.abstract>.

[42] In addition to the references in footnotes 43 to 47 below, see also Sam Ricketson, 'The Imperial Copyright Act 1911 in Australia' in Uma Suthersanen and Ysolde Gendreau (eds), *A Shifting Empire: 100 Years of the Copyright Act 1911* (Edward Elgar 2013) 52, 54–62.

[43] See Lionel Bently, 'Copyright and the Victorian Internet: Telegraphic Property Laws in Colonial Australia' (2004) 38 Loy LA L Rev 71; Lionel Bently, 'The Electric Telegraph and the Struggle over Copyright in News in Australia, Great Britain and India' in Brad Sherman and Leanne Wiseman (eds), *Copyright and the Challenge of the New* (Wolters Kluwer 2012) 43. See also Kathy Bowrey and Catherine Bond, 'Copyright and the Fourth Estate: Does Copyright Support a Sustainable and Reliable Public Domain of News?' [2009] 4 IPQ 399.

statutes, considering the colonial statutes as part of a broader legislative background.[44] In previous work I have attempted to answer some of the questions surrounding the colonial and Imperial copyright issues in Marcus Clarke's *His Natural Life*, as novel and play, in both colonial and post-Federation Australia.[45] In addition to providing a detailed account of the development of the technology and legal regulation of photography in the UK, Bowrey has also explored how the usefulness of photography in the colonies influenced the development of copyright in Victoria.[46] Most recently, Ailwood and Sainsbury considered how both Imperial legislation and locally developed colonial law influenced the availability of literature in pre-Federation Australia, utilising legislative materials and historical newspaper articles in an effort to create a fuller picture of the protection of literary copyright during this period.[47] Their work ultimately concludes that the 'colonies adopted an approach to copyright that was often contrary to the interests of their own authors and readers, in pursuit of a blind adherence to British imperial interests'.[48]

As noted above, the major theme explored in Australian colonial copyright literature to date is this concept of Imperial 'adherence' and influence: how did UK law influence the colonial statutes passed in Australia? Was this influence appropriate? Who did such adherence benefit? It is undeniable that Imperial law and policy had a significant influence on the colonial copyright laws passed in Victoria, South Australia, New South Wales, and Western Australia, as is evidenced by a cursory glance at any of those statutes. Yet, it is immediately clear from the opening page of the Copyright Act 1869 (Vic),[49] the first statute passed in the area of copyright by a colony in Australia, that the colonies were seeking to exercise their legislative autonomy under the Colonial Laws Validity Act and improving and refining what had been done previously in the UK. Here, Victoria was one of the first jurisdictions, internationally, to enact a consolidated piece of legislation that covered all copyright-protected creations.[50] Even jurisdictions that adopted copyright statutes long before any Australian colony did, such as New

---

[44] Burrell (n 36) 242–43. See also Lionel Bently, 'The "Extraordinary Multiplicity" of Intellectual Property Laws in the British Colonies in the Nineteenth Century' (2011) 12 Theo Inq L 161, 178–80.

[45] See Catherine Bond, '"Curse the Law!": Unravelling the Copyright Complexities in Marcus Clarke's *His Natural Life*' (2010) 15 MALR 452; Catherine Bond, '"The play goes on eternally": Copyright, Marcus Clarke's Heir's and His Natural Life as Play and Film – Part One' (2011) 23 IPJ 267; Catherine Bond, '"The play goes on eternally": Copyright, Marcus Clarke's Heirs and *His Natural Life* as Play and Film – Part Two' (2011) 24 IPJ 61.

[46] See Kathy Bowrey, '"The World Daguerreotyped: What a Spectacle!" Copyright Law, Photography and the Economic Mission of Empire' in Brad Sherman and Leanne Wiseman (eds), *Copyright and the Challenge of the New* (Wolters Kluwer 2012) 11; see also Catherine Bond, '"There's nothing worse than a muddle in all the world": Copyright Complexity and Law Reform in Australia' (2011) 34 UNSWLJ 1145, 1148–52.

[47] See Ailwood and Sainsbury, *Copyright Law* (n 41); Ailwood and Sainsbury, *Imperial Effect* (n 41).

[48] Ailwood and Sainsbury, *Imperial Effect* (n 41) 25.

[49] (33 Vict c 350).

[50] Ricketson (n 42) 55.

Zealand, maintained separate statutes for literary,[51] artistic,[52] and dramatic copyright,[53] as did the UK, until the introduction of the Copyright Act 1911 (Imp).[54]

Beyond these points of form, while UK law may have been heavily influential in some areas such as literary copyright,[55] an examination of the fuller picture of the law reveals that the relevant local legislatures were not always passively or slavishly copying existing statutes. There is evidence in the colonial statutes that these jurisdictions were making independent decisions designed to respond to a local requirement. As Bowrey notes, '[a] consideration of the debates surrounding the first Australian colonial copyright act in Victoria shows key political values were shared between the Mother country and colony, but UK law was not simply transplanted to new jurisdictions'.[56] This was particularly noteworthy in the area of artistic copyright, as will be discussed below.

Further, much of the recent colonial copyright literature focuses solely on legislation, with little discussion on case law that emerged in the colonies throughout the nineteenth century.[57] However, as noted above, the official case reports of a number of Australian colonies contain just approximately 20 decisions where copyright was at issue, both before and after the passing of any relevant copyright statute. For the most part, these decisions involved copyright in dramatic works and thus, in an examination of literary or artistic colonial copyright, these decisions are likely to remain unconsulted. Still, the issues that the judges were grappling with in these cases – for example, the ability of a licensee or assignee to sue in the jurisdiction of assignment or licence[58] – have broader ramifications for a construction and understanding of colonial case law today.

Maintaining too great an emphasis on black letter forms of law, whether legislation or reported case law, also has the capacity to obscure the usefulness and importance of one of the richest resources on copyright law and practices: colonial newspapers. As Ailwood and Sainsbury note, '[p]ublic debate in the Australian colonies throughout the

---

[51] Copyright Ordinance 1842 (NZ) (5 Vict c 18).
[52] The Fine Arts Copyright Act 1877 (NZ); The Photographic Copyright Act 1896 (NZ).
[53] The Fine Arts Copyright Act 1877 Amendment Act 1879 (NZ); The Dramatic Copyright Act 1903 (NZ).
[54] The colony of Queensland passed a trilogy of copyright statutes between 1880 and 1890, but these preserved the application of the existing UK statutes in that colony, while allowing local registration provisions: see Copyright Registration Act 1887 (Qld) (51 Vict c 2); Copyright (Fine Arts) Registration Act 1892 (Qld) (56 Vict c 6); Copyright Registration Act 1898 (Qld) (62 Vict c 13). For a discussion of the New Zealand position, see Geoff McLay, 'New Zealand and the Imperial Copyright tradition' in Uma Suthersanen and Ysolde Gendreau (eds), *A Shifting Empire: 100 Years of the Copyright Act 1911* (Edward Elgar 2013) 30.
[55] See Ailwood and Sainsbury, *Copyright Law* (n 41); Ailwood and Sainsbury, *Imperial Effect* (n 41).
[56] Bowrey (n 46) 32.
[57] The most comprehensive account of this case law to date can be found in Roslyn Atkinson and Richard Fotheringham, 'Dramatic Copyright in Australia to 1912' (originally published in (1987) 11 Australasian Drama Studies 47, revised and updated as of 11 September 2006) <http://espace.library.uq.edu.au/view/UQ:7887>.
[58] See *Coppin v Solomon* (1868) 2 SALR 83; *Holt v Woods* (1896) 17 LR (NSW) Eq 36.

nineteenth century reflects a high degree of interest in the nature of copyright',[59] a point that is repeatedly supported by entries on the issue in newspapers. The reason for this dedicated coverage was likely twofold: first, copyright involved both the regulation of cultural goods that many colonials would likely encounter on a daily basis, ensuring a personal connection between reader and report; and, second, copyright involved the regulation and worth of the 'genius' of the mind. Both prior to and after the passing of applicable copyright laws in the colonies of Australia, colonial newspapers would regularly print stories on copyright issues and injustices.[60] For the most part, recent literature, aided by the NLA's digitised newspaper collection, has recognised the importance of newspapers in considering colonial copyright, and the support, resistance, opinions and policy that can be garnered from these original sources.[61] The difficulty in utilising such resources lies in the prohibitive number of possibly relevant entries; a handful of entries are presented in the discussion below, but there may be more compelling and interesting coverage in newspapers yet to be consulted. Still, to adapt the quotation at the start of this chapter, scholars should not 'cabin, crib, confine or bind' themselves by focusing on the regulation of one type of creation, or one set of primary or secondary sources. This may mean that many colonial copyright legal and cultural practices not discussed here have been lost, or, perhaps more accurately, not yet found.

It is beyond the boundaries of this chapter to provide an all-encompassing, holistic account of nineteenth century copyright law in Australia. The remainder of this chapter, however, will endeavour to create a broad picture of the treatment of creations and copyright in the Australian colonies during the period 1868–69, using the sources highlighted above, and suggesting possible areas for further exploration through this immediate account. After a brief introduction, the next part illustrates that those in the Australian colonies appeared to believe that Imperial law applied in those jurisdictions to protect authors who published books in either the UK or the colonies, until the decision of the House of Lords in *Routledge v Low*[62] clarified that only the former was protected under the Copyright Act 1842. At the same time, in the area of dramatic works, informal practices were created through the use of colonial newspapers, operating to supplement the force of the black letter law. Further, when the Victorian legislature created a local copyright statute in 1869, it did so by combining aspects of various UK laws, but also deviating from this precedent in the area of artistic copyright. What emerges from this discussion is the existence of a complex web of formal and informal regulation, one that warrants greater examination beyond the time period and creations considered here.

---

[59] Ailwood and Sainsbury, *Copyright Law* (n 41) 1.
[60] The same may be said of newspapers today, where stories on intellectual property are regularly published.
[61] See Bowrey (n 46) 32; Ailwood and Sainsbury, *Copyright Law* (n 41); Ailwood and Sainsbury, *Imperial Effect* (n 41) 4, 22–24.
[62] (1868) LR 3 HL 100.

III. COPYRIGHT IN THE AUSTRALIAN COLONIES, 1868–69

On Saturday 10 July 1819 *The Sydney Gazette* printed the following item:

> BRITISH MUSEUM. From a late return made to the House of Commons, it appears, that the number of volumes received from Stationer's Hall by the British Museum, under the Copyright Act, from 1st January to 31st December, 1817, is as follows. 8 folios, 80 quartos, 761 octavos, and 287 duodecimos. Besides these, there have been delivered 222 articles of printed Music, in folio and quarto, the greatest number of which are single sheets.[63]

It is hard to imagine that this item was of any interest to any member of the colony of New South Wales: what relevance did numbers of deliveries of books and music to the British Museum, made under a British copyright statute, hold for the residents of that colony? Still, this extract appears to be the first time a colonial newspaper made more than a mere reference to copyright law, a practice that would continue throughout the nineteenth century. Some items would be of greater interest to colonial residents than others, as will be discussed below, but the subject of copyright would consistently appear in colonial newspapers from this point on.

For the most part, items on copyright published in colonial newspapers during this period focused on overseas developments, predominantly those occurring in London and the UK. As Ailwood and Sainsbury note, colonial newspapers published numerous items on the passage and development of the Copyright Act 1842.[64] It is arguable that such attention was paid to those debates on account of the fact colonial residents believed the protection afforded by that statute extended to those who published works within the colony of Australia. This is different to believing that UK statutes applied in the colonies, which was the correct (but much more limited) interpretation pursuant to the Colonial Validity Laws Act and case law at the time confirmed.[65] Rather, colonial residents appear to have been under the impression that, where a work was first published in that colony, it was protected throughout the Empire. Writing in 1881, Finnamore described the period after the introduction of the 1842 statute as follows:

> The Crown bound its colonies to recognise the rights of its subjects resident on the soil of England, Scotland, and Ireland, and the inference was that reciprocal rights were vested in Her Majesty's subjects in the colonies. There is not one expression in the act showing an intention to exclude the colonies from its benefits (…).[66]

In contrast, Ailwood and Sainsbury's research points to newspapers items that suggest, during the 1840s at least, the colonies realised copyright under the 1842 statute did not extend to them, with the accompanying proposal that colonial copyright statutes be

---

[63] *The Sydney Gazette and New South Wales Advertiser* (Sydney, 10 July 1819) 3 <http://nla.gov.au/nla.news-page494292>. *The Sydney Gazette* was the first newspaper to be published in the Australian colonies.
[64] Ailwood and Sainsbury, *Imperial Effect* (n 41) 14–16.
[65] See, eg, *Coppin v Solomon* (1868) 2 SALR 83, discussed in greater detail below. Later decisions also relied on other UK statutes: see eg *Fishburn Brothers v Adelaide Cyclorama Co Ltd* (1892) 25 SALR 20; *Holt v Woods* (1896) 17 LR (NSW) Eq 36.
[66] Finnamore (n 1) 714.

introduced during this period.[67] These recommendations are consistent with the fact that, as noted above, New Zealand introduced a literary copyright statute in 1842.[68] While Finnamore may have been writing during the nineteenth century, his recollection of the situation may have been incorrect.

Published alongside items on international and domestic legislative developments in copyright were comments on local and UK copyright matters, plus case reports of local and UK copyright decisions.[69] Interestingly, these comments and reports often concerned the same area: dramatic copyright. It is within this area that the development of both case law on colonial copyright matters, and a cultural practice of utilising newspapers to engage in copyright discourse, begun, during the 1868–69 period.

In September 1868, the *Bendigo Advertiser*, a local paper for a regional area that exploded during this period as a result of the Victorian Gold Rush,[70] published an item that was critical of an organisation called the Dramatic Authors' Society, for proposing legal action on the basis of a theatrical performance aimed at raising funds for charity.[71] The newspaper described the plays performed for the benefit as 'stock plays, frequently essayed by amateur actors, and so far no one has ever for a moment thought of questioning the legality of such performances'.[72] The piece went on to suggest that there had been some 'evil disposed person has been pulling the strings behind the scenes' for such threats of legal action to occur.[73]

That 'evil disposed person' was likely George Coppin, who was involved in numerous copyright matters in both his personal capacity and as colonial representative for the Dramatic Authors' Society, a UK organisation,[74] during this period. Coppin was well known throughout the Australian colonies: he had dabbled in the Gold Rush, worked as a comedian, been an elected member of the Victorian Legislative Council, and was manager of the Theatre Royal in Melbourne, Victoria.[75] As Bagot notes in his biography on Coppin, written in the 1960s:

> More important for Coppin's plans at this period was the acquisition of musical and dramatic performance rights for Australasia … In Dion Boucicault … he found a strong supporter, who

---

[67] See Ailwood and Sainsbury, *Copyright Law* (n 41) 3–4; Ailwood and Sainsbury, *Imperial Effect* (n 41) 4–10.

[68] See (n 51) and accompanying text; Ailwood and Sainsbury, *Imperial Effect* (n 41) 15.

[69] See 'Palace Court, July 24. Dramatic Copyright – *Moncrieff v. Williams*', *The Sydney Gazette and New South Wales Advertiser* (Sydney, 18 December 1839) 3 <http://nla.gov.au/nla.news-page498140>.

[70] For greater information, see 'Review of Bendigo History' <http://www.bendigohistory.com/review.shtml>.

[71] 'Interesting to Amateur Actors', *Bendigo Advertiser* (Bendigo, 12 September 1868) 3 <http://nla.gov.au/nla.news-page9030920>.

[72] Ibid.

[73] Ibid.

[74] For further discussion on the UK Dramatic Authors' Society, see Ronan Deazley, 'Commentary on *Dramatic Literary Property Act* 1833' in Lionel Bently and Martin Kretschmer (eds), *Primary Sources on Copyright (1450–1900)* <www.copyrighthistory.org>.

[75] See Sally O'Neill, 'Coppin, George Selth (1819–1906)' (*Australian Dictionary of Biography*, first published 1969) <http://adb.anu.edu.au/biography/coppin-george-selth-3260/text4935>.

readily agreed to place the acting rights of his popular plays, *The Octoroon, Colleen Bawn* and *Arrah-na-pogue*, in Coppin's hands. *Arrah-na-pogue* became the subject of the first of several law suits Coppin filed, shortly after his return to Australia, to test the validity of his copyright agency. The precedent established in this case by the Supreme Court of New South Wales, February 1866, in awarding a verdict for Coppin was followed by other colonial jurisdictions. ... Ten per cent of fees collected was a cheap rake-off for such a service. These negotiations resulted in Coppin's securing personal performing rights over a collection of fifty-two pieces of music and one hundred plays.[76]

Arrah-na-pogue, a romantic melodrama set in the context of the Irish rebellion, is also known as *Arrah of the Kiss* or *The Wicklow Wedding*. It was first performed at Dublin Theatre Royal in 1864, then in London and New York in 1865.[77] There was no formal case report made of the litigation that Bagot refers to, but references in a number of newspapers confirm that the Supreme Court of New South Wales did grant an injunction against the unauthorised performance of *Arrah-na-pogue* in Sydney in 1866.[78] However, Coppin does not appear to actually have been a party to the case before the Supreme Court. Rather, the newspaper accounts reveal that the issue in question was who had received permission to perform the play first: Barry Sullivan, and the Prince of Wales Theatre, who received permission from Boucicault directly, or a Mr Tolano, who had been given permission by Coppin, who in turn had previously been given permission by Boucicault.[79]

Two years later, in 1868 Coppin was involved in two copyright affairs: one that reached court and another that was essentially litigated before the public through *The Argus*, a Melbourne newspaper. In that year, Coppin launched an action in South Australia to enforce his right to produce *Arrah-na-pogue* in Australia and New Zealand.[80] In his judgment, Gwynne J noted that the issues of the case did 'not depend on the general law of copyright, but on the law applicable to rights of acting or performing dramatic pieces'.[81] Yet, regardless of the existence of the agreement between Coppin and Boucicault, Gwynne J found that as Coppin was a licensee, rather than an assignee, of the performing right in *Arrah-na-pogue*, he could not successfully pursue any legal action against any infringer.[82] It is noteworthy that, in *Coppin v Solomon*, Gwynne J applied two Imperial statutes, the Dramatic Literary Property Act 1833 (UK)[83] and the Copyright Act 1842, to the cause of action without considering whether this was appropriate in the local circumstances. Gwynne J did not refer to the Australian Courts Act or the Colonial Laws Validity Act at any point in his judgment.

---

[76] Alec Bagot, *Coppin the Great: Father of the Australian Theatre* (Melbourne UP 1965) 313.
[77] See 'Dion Boucicault Collections – Arrah-na-pogue' <http://www.kent.ac.uk/library/specialcollections/theatre/boucicault/plays/arrah-na-pogue.html>.
[78] *The Age* (Melbourne, 10 February 1866) 5 <http://nla.gov.au/nla.news-page18278691>; *The Argus* (Melbourne, 13 February 1866) 5 <http://nla.gov.au/nla.news-page215333>.
[79] *The Sydney Morning Herald* (Sydney, 9 March 1866) 2 <http://nla.gov.au/nla.news-page1471798>.
[80] *Coppin v Solomon* (1868) 2 SALR 83, 93.
[81] Ibid.
[82] Ibid 96–97.
[83] (3 & 4 Will c 15).

Later that year, Coppin pursued another theatrical producer, Gilbert Roberts, in an action that was played out through *The Argus*. On 3 October, in an item comprising most of a column, that newspaper reported that the Duke of Edinburgh Theatre in Melbourne was to reopen, with Roberts as producer and manager and two short pieces, and a lengthier production, *Maud's Perils*, to be staged.[84] However, a subsequent report in *The Argus* resulted in threats against the Duke of Edinburgh Theatre for unauthorised performances and an allegation that the Dramatic Authors' Society would pursue the theatre for a lack of a public theatre licence if it did not pay the 'appropriate' copyright licence fees. Thereafter, *The Argus* became both a battle site and courtroom for Coppin and Roberts, with the story and letters penned by the two main parties resembling arguments by counsel and court. Whenever a letter from one of the parties was published, it appeared under the headline 'Mr. Coppin and Mr. Roberts. To the Editor of the Argus', suggesting that the editor of *The Argus* newspaper, with the power to publish, was the judge and the public the jury in this case.[85]

It was Coppin who first approached *The Argus* when the story on the Duke of Edinburgh Theatre broke, providing a multi-column letter in defence of his involvement in the matter. He noted of his actions that '[a] licence from the Dramatic Authors' Society is uniform, and contains no exception in favour of one theatre over another. It gives "full power, authority and permission to represent the works of the Dramatic Authors' Society ..."'[86] Coppin also challenged a statement made by an *Argus* reporter concerning the validity of the power of the Dramatic Authors' Society agreements in the colony, noting that '[y]our reporter says that "it is now pretty well known that the enforcement of this claim could with difficulty be effected." I must really confess my ignorance, for I have never heard the applicability of the [UK] Dramatic Authors Act to the Australian colonies doubted by those competent to give an opinion'.[87]

Roberts responded immediately, with *The Argus* publishing his defence on 24 October 1868. Roberts stated that he had decided, after consulting with solicitors, not to enter into any agreement with the Dramatic Authors' Society, believing that he did not need this permission. As to the theatre licence, he further responded he did not know he needed one.[88] A second letter accompanied that by Roberts, in support of the theatre manager, stating that the fact that 'Mr. Roberts has been persecuted, and by Mr. Coppin, is well known'.[89] Given the circumstances – and the comments reported in the *Bendigo Advertiser* – it appears that there is some validity in the remarks of this individual.

Coppin then responded again, on 27 October. He denied the version of events presented by Roberts, and concluded his letter with, 'If he [Roberts] is under the

---

[84] 'The Duke of Edinburgh Theatre', *The Argus* (Melbourne, 3 October 1868) 5 <http://nla.gov.au/nla.news-page222750>.

[85] For a discussion on the significant role of newspapers more generally in the colonies, see Bowrey and Bond (n 43) 414–17.

[86] 'Mr. Coppin and Mr. Roberts. The Editor of the Argus', *The Argus* (Melbourne, 23 October 1868) 5 <http://nla.gov.au/nla.news-article5830610>.

[87] Ibid.

[88] 'Mr. Coppin and Mr. Roberts. To the Editor of the Argus', *The Argus* (Melbourne, 24 October 1868) 6 <http://nla.gov.au/nla.news-article5830695>.

[89] Ibid.

impression that the Dramatic Authors' Act does not extend to this colony, he has the undoubted right of declining to take out a licence'.[90] Roberts responded on 30 October, but the matter, at least for *The Argus*, appears to have ended there.[91] According to Bagot, as reported in Coppin's biography, the producer Walter Montgomery ended up paying a belated fee on behalf of the Duke of Edinburgh Theatre.[92]

At this point, it is worth noting a number of themes that emerge from this account. The discussion above illustrates how, at 1868, both formal and informal regulation appeared to be used in the colonies with respect to copyright. While UK legislation and case law applying that legislation operated to a certain extent, newspapers were also an important venue for copyright matters at this time. The editor of *The Argus* must have been delighted with the column space filled by the letters of Coppin and Roberts, providing each a forum for their legal and other opinions, with the public deciding whether to support Roberts and see his plays, or abide by what Coppin stated to be the law and boycott them all together. In addition, it is only by considering a number of areas of creation – in these instances, literary and dramatic works – that the truly complex picture of copyright at 1868 period begins to emerge. However, as the brief discussion on Finnamore's comments, and Ailwood and Sainsbury's research, indicates, there are still many unanswered questions, particularly as to the extent to which colonials believed they had rights in this area, or did indeed have rights, during this time.

It is noteworthy that the issues and cases discussed to date all involved works originally created in the UK. A piece published in *The Argus* in late 1868 arguably indicates why this was the case. The anonymous item argued:

> That the provisions of the various acts of the Imperial Parliament for securing to British authors and artists the copyright of their works should be strictly enforced in these colonies is only consonant with justice and equity. In this, as in the ordinary business of our daily lives, honesty is the best policy. ...
>
> It may be premature to speak of a distinctive literature and a distinctive school of art in Australia; but if these are objects desirable to be promoted and attained, we shall be doing our best to secure them by respecting the rights of British authors and artists, and by refraining from infringing either the spirit or the letter of the statutes passed for their protection by the Imperial Legislature.[93]

This suggests a pessimistic view of colonial culture and its perceived worthiness of copyright protection: colonial cultural creations at the time were seen to be lacking compared to the creations of British authors and artists, and subsequently were arguably not worthy of copyright protection. In reality, under the operation of the law,

---

[90] 'Mr. Coppin and Mr. Roberts. To the Editor of the Argus, *The Argus* (Melbourne, 27 October 1868) 6 <http://nla.gov.au/nla.news-article5830887>.

[91] 'Mr. Coppin and Mr. Roberts. To the Editor of the Argus', *The Argus* (Melbourne, 30 October 1868) 5 <http://nla.gov.au/nla.news-article5831228>.

[92] Bagot (n 76) 321.

[93] *The Argus* (Melbourne, 10 December 1868) 4–5 <http://nla.gov.au/nla.news-page223663> and <http://nla.gov.au/nla.news-page223665>. Ailwood and Sainsbury extract an item in *The Sydney Morning Herald* from 1842 that provides a similar sentiment: see Ailwood and Sainsbury, *Imperial Effect* (n 41) 14.

the belief that colonial creations were in some respects 'less worthy' than their Imperial counterparts was unintentionally reinforced by virtue of the operation of colonial and Imperial legislation.

This provides a useful transition to the decision of the House of Lords in *Routledge v Low*. That case concerned the protection of a book, *Haunted Hearts*, authored by an American who was temporarily resident in Canada, but first published in the UK. The court held that, in order to be protected under the Copyright Act 1842, the first publication of a book needed to occur in the UK, for protection to, in the words of section 29 of the Act, 'extend to the United Kingdom of Great Britain and Ireland, and to every Part of the British Dominions'.[94] As noted by Lord Cranworth:

> [The Act's] provisions appear to me to shew [sic] clearly that the privileges of authorship which the Act was intended to confer or regulate in respect to works first published in the *United Kingdom*, were meant to extend to all subjects of Her Majesty in whatever part of her dominions they might be resident ... [But] [t]hat Her Majesty's colonial subjects are, by the statute, deprived of rights they would otherwise have enjoyed, is plain (...).[95]

The implications of the findings of the House of Lords were far-reaching beyond the facts of the case; indeed, there was not one part of the colonies of the UK where the implications would not have been felt. The resultant effect of *Routledge v Low* in the colonies was two-fold. Where an author first published a book in his or her home colony, if that colony did not have a copyright statute in force then that book would not have copyright protection at all. In turn, where a colony did have, or subsequently enacted a copyright statute, that book would solely be protected within that colony, making that property, to quote Finnamore, 'comparatively valueless except in one small part of the world'.[96] For example, a book published in New Zealand would have been protected pursuant to the 1842 literary copyright statute of that jurisdiction, but the corollary was that the book was *only* protected in New Zealand and could legally be copied elsewhere. However, in the Australian colonies, where there were no copyright statutes in force at the time *Routledge v Low* was decided, there was no protection for books at all. Further, it appears that the decision was not limited to books, with arguably the same repercussions for artistic, dramatic and musical creations. Thus, while Coppin claimed that 'I have never heard the applicability of the [UK] Dramatic Authors Act to the Australian colonies doubted', as extracted above, that statute only operated to protect dramatic productions first performed in the UK. Coppin was, therefore, arguably on the privileged British, and legally enforceable, side of the operation of colonial copyright.

Writing in 1881, Finnamore described in the impact of *Routledge v Low* in terms arguably more dramatic than many of the copyright-protected plays of the time:

---

[94] See (1868) LR 3 HL 100, 110–11 (Lord Cairns); 112–13 (Lord Cranworth); 114 (Lord Chelmsford); 118 (Lord Westbury); 120 (Lord Colonsay).

[95] (1868) LR 3 HL 100, 113.

[96] Finnamore (n 1) 720–21. Both colonial and UK authors were further affected, however, by the lack of rights of dramatisation and translation during this period. See generally Bond, 'Play goes on – Part I' (n 45) 276–78.

[T]he Lord Chancellor, Lord Cairns, set fire to the mine, and blew the fortress into atoms which we imagined was so safe. No doubt he was quite right; but we, unfortunately, found ourselves all wrong. Many of us were so fast asleep, and most of us were so far away from the fortress, that we knew nothing of the explosion. Being now made aware of it, let the structure be rebuilt with better precautions as to its safety.[97]

By the next year the legislature of the colony of Victoria sought to introduce 'better precautions' in the area of copyright.

The first copyright statute to be introduced in one of the Australian colonies, the Victorian Copyright Act 1869, passed in the later part of that year. There was some debate as to whether such a law was needed at all. A newspaper report on the passage of the Copyright Protection Bill in *The Argus* noted that:

[T]he author and the artist are entitled to a fair measure of protection for their works, and the public have no other wish than that they should be protected. Let the bill be pushed on, then, that it may have the force of law before Parliament rises. Victoria will not be a very profitable field for the labour of the artist class for many years to come, even if their works were fully protected against piratical attack; and the least that the Legislature can do is to take care that their genius has some measure of fair play.[98]

As noted above, one of the major issues considered in previous literature on Australian colonial copyright is the influence of, or 'adherence' to, to use Ailwood and Sainsbury's term, Imperial statutes in this new legislation. While those authors have argued that the Imperial position was followed, even though this had a negative impact on local authors and readers,[99] Bowrey suggests that, as cited above, 'UK law was not simply transplanted to new jurisdictions'.[100] Further, as also highlighted earlier, the Victorian Act was an amalgamation of a number of UK copyright statutes, rather than separate items of legislation. This was one of the first times such a compilation had occurred.

The Act protected designs; literary, dramatic, musical productions and lectures; and fine arts, pursuant to the following terms.[101] Section 2, the interpretation provision of the Copyright Act 1869, defined the term 'copyright' exhaustively to 'mean the sole and exclusive right and liberty of making, printing, writing, drawing, painting, photographing or otherwise however multiplying copies of any matter, thing, or subject to which the said word is herein applied'.[102] It defined the term 'book' as 'every volume, part or division of a volume, newspaper, pamphlet, sheet of letterpress, sheet of music, map, chart, or plan, separately published'; 'dramatic or musical production' as 'every tragedy, comedy, play, opera, farce, or other scenic musical or dramatic piece, entertainment, or composition'; and provided definitions for the artistic creations of engravings, drawings and paintings, photographs and works of sculpture.[103]

---

[97] Finnamore (n 1) 714.
[98] *The Argus* (Melbourne, 2 September 1869) 4 <http://nla.gov.au/nla.news-page225431>.
[99] Ailwood and Sainsbury, *Imperial Effect* (n 41) 25.
[100] Bowrey (n 46) 32.
[101] To use the terms listed in the titles of each of the Parts of the Act: see Copyright Act 1869 (33 Vict c 350).
[102] Copyright Act 1869 (33 Vict c 350) s 2.
[103] Ibid.

For books, musical compositions and dramatic productions, copyright would subsist in any book published in the colony of Victoria, before or following the passing of that statute; in the case 'of any tragedy comedy play opera [or] farce', written either before or after the Act came into force, in the colony of Victoria, copyright would be the property of the author, and that author would have 'the sole liberty of representing or performing or causing or permitting to be represented or performed' that 'dramatic or musical production', at any place in Victoria. The length of copyright in published books was defined as the longer period of either life of the author plus seven years or 42 years.[104] Books, musical compositions and dramatic productions published or performed after the death of the author would receive protection for 42 years from that first publication or performance.[105] These definitions mirrored their Imperial counterparts. As noted above, such protection only extended to the borders of Victoria; it did not even go beyond the boundaries of that colony at this time and the subject matters it covered could be legally copied in other jurisdictions. Thus, as I have previously noted, 'copyright had the potential to be worth very little at this time. It conveyed an exclusive right under law within a particular colony; beyond that jurisdiction, any further economic gain was on the basis of whatever benefit an author or publisher could negotiate'.[106]

A number of significant changes were made, however, in the area of 'fine arts'. Under the Copyright Act 1869, the term of protection for artistic works first published in Victoria was significantly reduced when compared to the UK legislation.[107] In the UK, copyright protected photographs, paintings and drawings for the life of the author plus seven years.[108] Engravings were protected for 28 years,[109] while sculptures were protected for an initial 14 years, plus a second period of 14 years if the author was still alive at the end of that first term.[110] In contrast, in Victoria, copyright would subsist in 'such painting drawing work of sculpture and engraving' for 14 years, while photographs and associated negatives were protected for only three years.[111] Both Bowrey and I have previously hypothesised as to why such a change was introduced; the legislature was silent on its decision to make this amendment.[112] Given the provisions of the Colonial Laws Validity Act, it is interesting that there was no discussion of or challenge to these amendments on account of their 'repugnancy'. However, the fact that this term would only apply to those artistic creations first published in Victoria, and therefore did not affect the interests of UK artists more generally, suggests why no attention was paid to the 'repugnancy' issue.

---

[104] Ibid ss 14 and 29.
[105] Ibid.
[106] See Bond, 'Curse the Law' (n 45) 462.
[107] See Bond, 'Copyright Complexity' (n 46) 1150; Bently, 'Extraordinary Multiplicity' (n 44) 179; Bowrey (n 46) 32–33.
[108] See Fine Arts Copyright Act 1862 (25 & 26 Vict c 68) s 1.
[109] (7 Geo III c 38) (1766) s 7.
[110] (54 Geo III c 56) (1814) ss 2, 6.
[111] Copyright Act 1869 (Vic) (33 Vict c 350) s 36.
[112] See Bond, 'Copyright Complexity' (n 46) 1150; Bowrey (n 46) 32–33.

In addition, tucked at the end of the Victorian statute, the legislature included the following provision, also without comment, which Bowrey argues was included to encourage art education within the colony:[113]

> Provided also that notwithstanding the provisions of this Act it shall be lawful for any and all persons resident in Victoria to repeat imitate copy and otherwise multiply any painting drawing work of sculpture or photograph in or belonging to the Museum of Industry and Art the National Gallery or the Melbourne Library[.][114]

Both provisions were a significant deviation from existing UK legislation, creating a shorter duration of copyright and a public 'right' of reproduction of artistic creations held in public museums and galleries. Further, it is also worth noting that, when New South Wales introduced its own statute in 1879, a similar provision was included applying to paintings, etc in museums and libraries in that colony,[115] but South Australia and Western Australia did not include such provisions when introducing their local laws in 1878[116] and 1890[117] respectively. Victoria also included a similar section when it introduced a new copyright law in 1890.[118] As Bowrey notes more generally about colonial copyright, '[t]hese differences reflect the different priorities, character and aspirations of the various Australian colonies'.[119] Thus, even between the colonies, local decisions were made on what provisions to include or exclude, whether Imperial or otherwise, though a fuller discussion is beyond the boundaries of this chapter and worth a proper examination in its own right.

IV. CONCLUSION

John Finnamore was, to some extent, correct when he argued that Imperial and local laws 'cabined, cribbed, confined, bound in' authors in the Australian colonies. For a large part of the nineteenth century, the colonies were confined by the operation of Imperial laws that bound them to respect UK copyright without granting them reciprocal protection and left local creations without any formal legal recourse in the event of unauthorised reproduction. In addition, colonial Australians were also bound by local cultural practices that emerged and were publicised in newspapers, providing an informal avenue of regulation for any wrongdoings. However, while Imperial laws were undeniably influential, once the colonies begun to introduce domestic copyright legislation those legislatures did not feel confined to maintaining the status quo where there appeared to be a preferable alternative for that jurisdiction, at least in some areas.

While the colonies may have federated, and new statutes and technologies long surpassed those discussed in this chapter, the snippets discussed here, and the

---

113 Bowrey (n 46) 33–34. See also Bently, 'Extraordinary Multiplicity' (n 44) 179.
114 Copyright Act 1869 (33 Vict c 350) s 56.
115 Copyright Act 1879 (NSW) (22 Vict c 20) s 55.
116 See Copyright Act 1878 (SA) (41 & 42 Vict c 95).
117 See Copyright Act 1895 (WA) (59 Vict c 24).
118 Copyright Act 1890 (Vic) (54 Vict c 1076) s 57.
119 Bowrey (n 46) 32.

unanswered questions raised and conflicting answers suggested by scholars suggest that there is much work to be done here. Supported by a grant from the Australian Research Council, Kathy Bowrey and I are undertaking further research in this area, exploring copyright issues between 1868 to 1968 through the lens of a series of individual authors, artists, performers and producers.[120] Although to some extent limited by the 'individual', research from this project to date supports the findings presented in this chapter. Further, the issues highlighted here, from the role of newspapers to unusual jurisdictional choices in law-making, indicates that the use of emerging Australian colonial copyright literature should not be considered 'confined', to use a term of Finnamore's, or, more accurately, Shakespeare's, in its relevance and has much to offer the history of the field of copyright law more generally.

---

[120] See Australian Research Council Discovery Project DP140100172, 'Australian made: A history of Australian copyright law and creator success 1868–1968'.

18. Aspects of French literary property developments in the eighteenth (and nineteenth) centuries
*Frédéric Rideau**

1. INTRODUCTION

The general foundations of the French *droit d'auteur* system developed during the eighteenth century, but the principle of exclusivity originally stemmed from royal book privileges, a system which upheld exclusivity (*l'exclusif*, as Denis Diderot would put it) on book publication, for a limited time. The evolution from privileges to authors as proprietors[1] in their own right has been deeply debated, both in *droit d'auteur* and Anglo-American copyright systems. In this respect, the numerous sources directly available on the AHRC-funded Primary Sources on Copyright (1450–1900) website help contribute to objective comparisons.[2] The evolution that occurred showed strong convergences, in particular between France and England, from the time when property rights were roughly envisaged, until being clearly claimed in a more absolute way from the end of the seventeenth century. In other words, the exclusive right of reproduction was to be grounded upstream on the first step of labour leading to publication, that is, on the author's labour. It is also a well-known paradox (in France, but in England also), although eventually an easy one to explain, that the main supporters of literary property

---

* I am deeply grateful to Isabella Alexander and H Tomás Gómez-Arostegui for their numerous corrections, comments and help on earlier drafts of this chapter, which, besides, is partly based upon material developed for the AHRC-funded project: Primary Sources on Copyright (1450–1900).

[1] To borrow a phrase from Mark Rose. See Mark Rose, 'The Author as Proprietor: *Donaldson v. Becket* and the Genealogy of Modern Authorship' (1988) 23 Representations 51.

[2] Lionel Bently and Martin Kretschmer (eds), Primary Sources on Copyright (1450–1900) <http://www.copyrighthistory.org>. The official reasons for which these first privileges were granted were similar between printers and booksellers, and the very few authors who were applying for them. For an example of a privilege granted for two years to a renowned bookseller of the time, see 'Galliot Du Pré's privilege (1515)' in ibid. Galliot Du Pré was endowed with this royal protection so that he might be rewarded for his efforts, expenses, and the investments he had to make, in order to print this book. On Du Pré, see H-J Martin, 'Un éditeur juridique: Galliot Du Pré' in *Histoire de l'édition française* (Fayard 1990). For a general, exhaustive study of this particular period of book privileges, see the useful work of Elizabeth Armstrong, *Before Copyright: The French Book-Privilege System 1498–1526* (CUP 1990). See also the work of Laurent Pfister, 'Author and Work in the French Print Privileges System: Some Milestones' in Ronan Deazley, Martin Kretschmer and Lionel Bently (eds), *Privilege and Property, Essays on the History of Copyright* (OpenBook Publishers 2010) 115. The most detailed account of this whole period, and after, until 1957, can be found in the PhD thesis of the same author, 'L'auteur, propriétaire de son œuvre. La formation du droit d'auteur du XVIeme siècle à la loi de 1957' (PhD thesis, University of Strasbourg 1999).

theory were not the authors themselves but primarily the Parisian booksellers, at the expense of their provincial counterparts, who had been progressively neglected in the attribution of the royal favours and privileges.

The chief part of these new discussions focused therefore on the author, and his relation to his work as one line of argument which implied the respect of a natural right, absolute and potentially perpetual, arising from the specificity of the literary labour. The response to these views was to lay stress on a conditional prerogative or monopoly (as privileges had been since the beginning of the sixteenth century), granted temporarily and ultimately in the public interest of a society which had largely contributed to the final result.[3] Thus, the assertion of an author's attachment to a very peculiar, personally based type of property, the exclusivity of which had been originally linked to the trade organisation, can be understood as being congenitally afflicted by serious contradictions. For example, while authors had been cast aside from the literary market, how could a property claimed to be so uniquely personal remain at the same time so 'fully alienable'?[4] Even more, this 'nebulous' personalist path would persist in France during the nineteenth century, increasingly implying a retrograde and systematic view of a presumptuous author living in his garret, and sidelining the public interest. Thus it is possible to understand the completion of these 'meandering' developments from property to personality as emanating from extrinsic motivations, that is as a 'riposte' against the copyright systems.[5]

Nevertheless, this evolution, from the absolute monarchy era to the Third Republic, is overall more consistent than it may appear, except in the situation where the literary labour in question is assessed on principle as being utterly trivial, or, even, the role of natural law within the French legal modern developments as being incurably dubious. Indeed, as paradoxical and chaotic as it may appear, these historical aspects of literary property show certain permanent features which were anchored in the author's personal right rhetoric as early as the first half of the eighteenth century, and soon reinforced, as

---

[3] The so-called theory of social contract. See, for example, Pfister, 'Author and Work' (n 2) 131, which describes this theory as stating that 'every human production originates within the community of ideas upon which everyone can equally and freely draw for inspiration'. On public interest in copyright systems in particular, see Isabella Alexander, *Copyright Law and the Public Interest in the Nineteenth Century* (Hart Publishing 2010).

[4] Peter Baldwin, *The Copyright Wars, Three Centuries of Trans-Atlantic Battle* (Princeton UP 2014) 88. Baldwin also states that '[t]his first and most important insight was that personal property was either personal or it was property. It could not fully be both'. ibid 103.

[5] cf ibid 129: 'This Continental drift from property to personality was nebulous, meandering, and incomplete.' As to the riposte, it 'was elaborated only after', that is, after the confirmation of an 'Anglo-Saxon copyright', limited as a statutory monopoly, from *Donaldson v Becket* in 1774 in Britain, and *Wheaton v Peters* in 1834 in the United States. ibid 383. Although some legislators, as Thomas Noon Talfourd, bitterly regretted the outcome of the former great English decision: 'By this bare majority – against the strong opinion of the Chief Justice of England – was it decided that the Statute of Anne has substituted a short term in copyright for an estate in fee, and the rights of authors were delivered up to the mercy of succeeding Parliaments!,' in *Three Speeches delivered in the House of Commons in favour of a measure for an extension of Copyright* (London 1840) 9. For a compelling and recent re-evaluation of *Donaldson v Becket*, see H Tomás Gómez-Arostegui, 'Copyright at Common Law in 1774' (2014) 47 Conn L Rev 1.

we shall see in Part 2, in the second half of the century, by rather technical, and somehow rational, comparisons between the literary 'labour' process and an inventor's productions. Although this peculiarity was then difficult to define and to qualify legally speaking, individual property, from its enduring equivocal, but typical, shifts between political and juridical senses, simply offered primarily the most convenient path for delineating author's rights. Part 3 will recall that, in fact, the legal recognition of literary property, on these specific bases, compared to those underlying the protection of inventions, occurred well before 1793, during the *Ancien Régime* in 1777, and that, from this perspective, the two statutes, linked to their common natural right heritage, deserve to be closely connected to be analysed. The implementation of the very concise revolutionary literary and artistic property act of 1793 would prove complicated, but, as will be discussed in Part 4, still sufficiently open and flexible to allow judicial developments towards a broader range of authorial interests, without losing, for the judges who persisted to rely on the concept of property, a certain unity.

2. A PARADOXICAL PROPERTY

At the dawn of the eighteenth century, the Parisian booksellers, within the dominant *Communauté des libraires et imprimeurs de Paris,* felt compelled to secure their royal privileges, both as against their provincial counterparts and more generally to prevent any drastic changes in state policy. From 1720 onwards, the government had begun to grow impatient with Parisian monopolistic expectations, a fact that would be soon confirmed under Malesherbes' directorship of the book trade administration. It was during this time that Louis d'Héricourt, lawyer to the Parisian booksellers, expressly introduced a new strategy to protect his clients' interests, namely, that an author's labour was the main ground for literary property (Part 2.1). Other supporters of such a right, most notably Denis Diderot and Simon Nicolas Henri Linguet, would later adopt this argument against provincial booksellers who had challenged privileges (Part 2.2).

2.1 Louis d'Héricourt's Memorandum (1725–26)

At a time Antoine Furetière was defining, in his famous first full edition of the *Dictionnaire Universel,* that a privilege is 'a special private prerogative which a person benefits from with the exclusion of several others, and which he receives through the favour of his Sovereign', Parisian booksellers were already attempting to reconcile explicitly their royal monopolies with modern individualistic possessive grounds.[6] The premise of their demonstration was that printed books were supposed to be of two types: 'common' [*sortes communes*] and 'particular' [*sortes particulieres*]. Common

---

[6] Antoine Furetière, *Dictionnaire universel, contenant généralement tous les mots François tant vieux que modernes et les termes des sciences et des arts* (1st edn, Arnout and Reinier Leers 1690) vol 3, entry 'PRIVILEGE': 'Passedroit, grace, prerogative; avantage particulier dont jouit une personne à l'exclusion de plusieurs autres, & qui lui vient par le bienfait de son souverain.' This dictionary was published in Holland two years after its author's death.

books encompassed mostly ancient works (religious books, classics, etc). Particular books included:

> all the books which have been produced for the first time in this Kingdom by the individual industry of a bookseller or by the labour of an author [*l'industrie particulière d'un libraire ou par le travail d'un auteur*] who cedes to the former his work and his right, in some way which the two of them have agreed on together.[7]

This distinction implied consequences for the book privileges themselves. '[P]rivileges for books comprised under the category of "common sort" books [we]re favours which really can be regarded as exceptions from the common right/law [*des exceptions du droit commun*].'[8] On the other hand:

> privileges for particular sorts of books belong[ed] to those acts of beneficence which the King can avail himself of, in order to honour and reward the merit of those subjects of his who obtain them; [a]nd these benefactions which depend solely on him [the King], without affecting in any way the right of anyone else, are indeed so much the more favourable that they even ought to be perpetual.[9]

Thus, for the first time since book privileges were introduced, privileges for these 'sortes particulières', that is pertaining to books newly published, seemed to evolve from a grant *creating* exclusivity in its holder to an act *securing*, perhaps even perpetually, pre-existing rights to its recipients. The precise source of these purported rights was not yet fully determined at this time, however, because the protection of 'particular' books seemed to derive from both the author and the bookseller, making the labour of the former or the industry of the latter comparable and seemingly equivalent.[10] The author was not yet championed as the paramount figure. That step, a very important one, would occur a few decades later.

Louis d'Héricourt took it following a royal decree in April 1725, wherein the French government expressed its concern about abusive privileges.[11] Writing in a *mémoire*

---

[7] *Mémoire sur la contestation qui est entre les libraires de Paris et ceux de Lyon au sujet des privilèges et des Continuations que le Roy accorde pour l'impression des livres* (Paris ca 1690), Bibliothèque nationale de France, Mss Fr 22119, No 21, 2. For a reproduction and translation of this document, see 'Memorandum on the dispute between the Parisian and the provincial booksellers' (ca 1690), available at <http://www.copyrighthistory.org/record/f_1690s>.

[8] Ibid.

[9] Ibid.

[10] 'Il prouve en second lieu que les livres de nouvelle composition produits par le travail d'un auteur moderne ou par l'industrie d'un libraire sont d'autant plus de droit particulier, que personne autre que cet auteur ou libraire ne peut y pretendre aucune proprieté'. ibid 4.

[11] Pfister, 'Author and Work' (n 2) 128, believes this evolution can be illustrated by an *Arrêt du Conseil d'Etat portant règlement sur le fait de la librairie et imprimerie*, 10 April 1725, which was partly concerned by abusive privileges, which were said to be unacceptable, when privileges extensions were used to raise artificially prices on the market: '… et d'autres, ayant obtenu des renouvellements de privilèges pour des livres déjà imprimés, ne s'en sont servis que pour empêcher que d'autres libraires ne pussent obtenir des permissions'. Unfortunately for the provincial booksellers, even this piece of legislation did not bring any clarification as to the conditions allowing privileges to be renewed on books already published, in this perspective

aimed at the Keeper of the Seals Armenonville, Héricourt identified authors, probably for the first time in such an explicit way, as the central and original source of a natural property right:

> [A] Manuscript, in so far as it is not inimical to Religion, the Laws of the State, and the interests of private Individuals, is so much the property of its Author [*est en la personne de l'Auteur un bien qui lui est tellement propre*], that it is no more permissible to deprive him of it than it is to deprive him of money, goods, or even land; since, as we have observed, it is the fruit of his personal labour [*le fruit d'un travail qui lui est personnel*], which he must be at liberty to dispose of as he pleases …[12]

Scholars have argued that this decisive evolution can be linked to 'an emergent discourse concerning the creative individual', who was progressively able to emancipate himself from God in the process of creation, thus raising ultimately the question of his subjective literary originality.[13] At the time of this memorandum, the Lockean philosophy of property, and in particular drawing a comparison with land, was already perfectly suited to Héricourt's argument. Although Locke did not speak specifically in relation to intellectual labour, he did state that, of 'the products of the Earth useful to the Life of Man, [nine-tenths] are the effects of labour'.[14] It was therefore surely logical, in Héricourt's mind, that the property which an author could produce from his personal labour was, at least, as indisputable as a land cultivated following *occupatio* by a man 'being Master of himself, and Proprietor of his own Person, and the Actions

---

being not much more than a simple recall of the main book regulations of 28 February 1723, which were extended to the whole kingdom in March 1744 (full text available at <http://www.copyrighthistory.org/record/f_1725>). Malesherbes' policy between 1750 and 1763 would prove to be more worrying for the Parisian Book Corporation, as the provincial booksellers would later recall, in their most important memorandum, in 1776, from Gaultier (see infra, n 31).

[12] Louis d'Héricourt, 'Memorandum' (Paris 1725–26), Bibliothèque nationale de France: Mss Fr 22072, No 62, available at <http://www.copyrighthistory.org/record/f_1725b> 2–3.

[13] Pfister, 'Author and Work' (n 2) 129. Much has been written on the emergence of romanticism linked to possessive individualism, and the capacity to escape a mimetic view of art. Edward Young is often quoted to illustrate the maturity of this evolution during the eighteenth century:

> An *Imitator* shares his crown, if he has one, with the chosen object of his imitation; an *Original* enjoys an undivided applause. An *Original* may be said to be of a *vegetable* nature; it rises spontaneously from the vital root of genius; it *grows*, it is not *made*: *Imitations* are often a sort of *manufacture* wrought up by those *mechanics*, *art*, and *labour*, out of pre-existent materials not their own.

Edward Young, *Conjectures on Original Composition* (2nd edn, London 1759) 11–12. For general studies on this question, see, for example, Roland Mortier, *L'originalité, une nouvelle catégorie esthétique au siècle des Lumières* (Droz 1982); Tzetan Todorov, *Éloge de l'individu: Essai sur la peinture flamande* (Seuil 2004).

[14] John Locke, *Two Treatises of Government* (London 1690) 258–59, para 40. See also ibid 261, para 43: ''Tis Labour then which puts the greatest part of Value upon Land, without which it would scarcely be worth any thing'. On the deep influence of Locke in France and how it served individualistic interests in and against an 'absolute' monarchy, see Ross Hutchinson, *Locke in France: 1688–1734* (The Voltaire Foundation 1991).

or Labour of it'.[15] From this singular type of 'labour', derived naturally the author's freedom to dispose fully of what he produced. In other words, to Louis d'Héricourt, it meant that the author was the owner of his work perpetually, until he chose (or not) to transfer it.[16] About what was transferred, he used notably the word 'manuscript', which necessarily meant, according to book trade *usages*, the literary work itself.[17] In fact, Héricourt alternatively referred to this concept as *production littéraire* (literary production), *ouvrage* (which one can translate essentially as 'book'), and even, in a more modern way, the property of the *texte de l'ouvrage*.[18]

Finally, and most importantly, the introduction of this natural right in the literary market clarified the definition of book privileges already evoked in the 1690s. Traditional, temporary economic monopolies granted by virtue of royal sovereignty against the common law were now transformed into automatic measures to secure a pre-existing right. An 'authentic approval' [*approbation authentique*], as Héricourt put it, could no longer be interpreted solely as a sign of the King's generous discretionary protection for learned men and booksellers, but also, if not essentially, as an act of 'justice'.[19] This view threatened the royal prerogative, but not necessarily the public interest, according to Héricourt. Privileges, even those that were perpetual, indeed retained the virtue of stimulating authors and booksellers in their work 'for the glory of his Realm, and for the benefit of his people'.[20]

In introducing literary property as a natural right and redefining royal book privileges, Louis d'Héricourt's memorandum was fundamental. Thenceforth, the author became central to future arguments over the proper scope of exclusive rights in literary compositions. Other supporters of literary property would rely on his argumentation during the second half of the eighteenth century, including Diderot and Linguet. Those supporters, however, would now face a more organised opposition from the provincial

---

[15] Locke (n 14) 263, para 44.
[16] Héricourt (n 12) 6.
[17] The original manuscript constituted at the time, in contracts, the symbolic medium of the work. Concerning this evolution of its dematerialisation towards a more subtle conception of the literary work itself, see Frédéric Rideau, 'La formation du droit de la propriété littéraire en France et en Grande- Bretagne: une convergence oubliée' (Presses universitaires d'Aix-Marseille 2004) 307 ff ('du manuscrit original à l'œuvre').
[18] Héricourt (n 12) 2, 6.
[19] It is interesting to stress that this 'authentic approval', conceived as a privilege relegated as a prerogative only organised to secure the effectiveness of a pre-existent right, in other terms an additional protection, can be compared in spirit to the approach adopted by the London Booksellers to explain the relationship between the Statute of Anne and the literary property at Common law. In short, the statute was supposed to give an extra, direct protection, thanks to the penalties explicitly mentioned. On the first developments of this line of interpretation, see, for example *The Case of the Authors and Proprietors of Books* (1735), British Library, BM 816.m.12.(52).
[20] Héricourt (n 12) 4: 'parce que ces sortes de Privileges ne sont pas seulement des marques de sa bonté & de la Protection dont il honore les Sçavans & les Libraires, mais une justice qu'il leur rend pour les animer au travail pour la gloire de son Royaume, & l'utilité de son Peuple'. Besides, because these particular privileges, '*approbations authentiques*', were an act of justice, the King could not, in principle, withdraw them from their holder.

book trade and from proponents of public-interest goals, such as the lawyer Gaultier and Nicolas de Condorcet.

2.2 Literary Property in Debates

Diderot's famous *Lettre sur le commerce de la librairie* is often used to illustrate a continuous reinforced discourse towards the 'personalisation' of literary property, albeit a property that remained fully transferable. His letter on the book trade was written in 1763, probably following the request of the influential Parisian bookseller Le Breton, who was also a member of the Parisian book trade guild. The booksellers later submitted a slightly different version to the head of the royal book trade administration, M de Sartine. Diderot followed a Lockean path, deeply rooting literary property to the free individual, but he also appeared reluctant to use a direct analogy between literary works and other goods or laboured land. Consequently, the peculiar bond which purportedly united the author to his work seemed to be more enigmatic than ever:

> [W]hat can a man possess, if a product of the mind, the unique fruit of his education, his study, his efforts, his time, his research, his observation; if the finest hours, the finest moments of his life; if his own thoughts, the feelings of his heart, the most precious part of himself, that part which does not perish, that which immortalises him, cannot be said to belong to him? What comparison can there be between a man, the very substance of a man, his soul, and a field, a meadow, a tree or a vine which, at the beginning of time, nature offered equally to all men, and which the individual claimed for himself only by cultivation, the first legitimate means of possession? Who has more right than the author to use his goods by giving or selling them?[21]

This formulation would eventually be seen to be more consistent with the progress of ideas on subjective originality, which would explain, in Diderot's mind, his reluctance to accept a close comparison between all types of labour: although a substantial work was essential for both the author and the cultivator, in the way that it fixed their property in what was originally freely offered to all, only the latter's work remained objectively reproducible. Nonetheless, the gap between Diderot and Louis d'Héricourt must not be exaggerated. Indeed, the main question was to make the author's literary property so incontrovertible that its free disposal should consequently be absolute. Indeed, even Héricourt did not directly compare literary labour, which he did not define, to farmed land, but rather compared their juridical effects. In other words, it was already a property with a very specific subject matter – Linguet would use, a few

---

[21] Denis Diderot, *Lettre historique et politique adressée à un magistrat sur le commerce de la librairie*, Bibliothèque nationale de France, Mss Fr (Naf) 24232, No 3, full manuscript version also available at <http://www.copyrighthistory.org/record/f_1763> (manuscript numerotation from this database) 16. The Letter was edited in March 1764 by the Parisian guild under the title of *Représentations et observations en forme de mémoire sur l'état ancien et actuel de la librairie (…), présentées à M. de Sartine, Maître des requêtes, directeur général de la librairie et imprimerie, par les syndics et adjoints en charge*. Diderot had also a more direct relationship with Le Breton for the publishing of the Encyclopédie. For a more complete history of the *Letter*, see Jacques Proust, 'Pour servir à une édition critique de la lettre sur le commerce de la librairie' (1961) 3 Diderot Studies 321.

decades after, the term 'creation' (see below) – but nevertheless characterized by some ordinary technical consequences, that is, among others, as transferable as every other type of good, whether 'money, goods, or even land'.[22] As Diderot stressed, 'the author is master of his work, or nobody in society is the master of his possessions. The bookseller owns [a book] in the same way as it was owned by the author'.[23] It was precisely because the work was so personal to its author that he maintained his sovereign faculty to detach it from his person and to negotiate its transfer freely by contract with his bookseller. During the 1770s, lawyers like Joseph-Félicité Cochu would assert, in the same liberal way, that because the property in a work is 'more his [the author's] than a plot of land or a house which he might have bought, since he created it', the author's choice to use it as he wishes could not be limited by any political authority.[24]

Simon Nicolas Henri Linguet, a man of many talents (lawyer at the Parliament of Paris; man of letters; and journalist in England, where he chose to stay to launch his *Annales politiques, civiles et littéraires*), pursued a similar line of thought in the 1770s. In two connected memoranda, elaborated during the course of a dispute between his clients the Parisian booksellers and their provincial counterparts, he developed the argument initiated by Héricourt on the nature of literary property.[25] Like his predecessors, Linguet argued that the choice of property was an obvious one to illustrate the particular bond which united the author to his work:

> Certainly, if there is any property which is sacred and incontestable, it is that of an author over his work. This is not a type of property acquired, like others, by exchange, and whose possession, when formally scrutinized, can at times be cast into doubt or even annulled. The composition of a book of any kind is an act of genuine creation; a manuscript is part of the external substance the writer produces [*le manuscript est une partie de sa substance que l'écrivain produit au dehors*].[26]

---

[22] Héricourt (n 12) 2.

[23] Diderot, *Lettre historique* (n 21) 17.

[24] Joseph-Félicité Cochu, 'Requête au Roi' in Edouard Laboulaye and Georges Guiffrey (eds), *La propriété littéraire au XVIIIe siècle* (L Hachette & Co 1859) 217. Although the claim for such a property was compelling under an 'Absolute Monarchy', Cochu's formulation on literary property can be compared to the English developments, when, in *Millar v Taylor*, Aston J supported the same right at common law in the following terms: '[F]or, I confess, I do not know, nor can I comprehend any property more emphatically a man's own, nay, more incapable of being mistaken, than his literary works.' (1769) 4 Burr 2303, 2345.

[25] Simon Nicolas Henri Linguet, *Mémoire sur les propriétés et privilèges exclusifs de librairie* (1774), BnF Res-F-718-62, largely reused in 1777 and adapted to comment the last great piece of legislation passed in relation to the Book trade (30 August 1777 – see *infra*). We will use the latter version (and its pagination), from his *Annales politiques, civiles, et littéraires du XVIIIe siècle* (London 1777) vol 3, which is available at <http://www.copyrighthistory.org/record/f_1777b>. Linguet was fully aware of the English battle of booksellers: see in particular his report of the *Donaldson v Becket* decision, in his *Journal de Politique et de Littérature, contenant le principaux Evènemens de toutes les Cours; les Nouvelles de la République des Lettres, etc* (5 November 1774) vol 1, 75–76.

[26] Linguet, *Mémoire* (ibid) 31–32.

Although the manuscript was still symbolically used in a traditional way, this was probably the clearest formulation of the conception of a literary work as being able to bear (to put it in modern terms) the personality of its author. And, again, it inevitably followed that, because of the specific nature of this right of property, which cannot 'perish', it was fully transferable by contract between the author and his assignee.[27]

Simon Linguet's formulation is all the more interesting in that it also relied on a technical distinction between books and inventions (or discoveries). Thus, in the case of literary creation, only the writer would be allowed to modify it, from his own will and judgment. Indeed, since a literary work could not amount solely to a skill, a *savoir-faire* (even 'assembling an unknown machine'), a book of any kind remained 'such a noble object', notwithstanding its nature or merit, precisely because it sprung 'forth from the author's mind, as perfect as it can be'. In other words, it meant that 'if it is susceptible to a few degrees of improvement, it can only receive them from its father's hand', even if it could have been better in the eyes of the public.[28] Of course, it was only the form or expression of a literary work, with its hypothetical singularity, which was accordingly subject to such restrictions, leaving the ideas free to be used and debated. This essential distinction – idea/expression – was indeed, from the second half of the eighteenth century, clearly formulated in France, at the same time as it was in England.[29] The Parisian bookseller Charles-Guillaume Leclerc, for example, asserted that 'ideas, feelings which compose a book, the order in which the author display them, the manner in which he expresses them, are his'.[30]

Linguet's argument was irreconcilable with the traditional position defended by the Provincial booksellers. They also discussed the comparison between authors and inventors' labour, but did so in order to claim that such a distinction was an artificial

---

[27] Ibid 30. See also the lawyer Cochu, who argued similarly that the bookseller, as the transferee of the author and thus subrogated to all his rights, must enjoy them with the same intensity ('plénitude'). Cochu (n 24) 217.

[28] Linguet, (ibid) 24, who added that a book [*ouvrage*] stays necessarily as it was produced by its author: 'Il en reste nécessairement au point où la puissance qui lui a donné le jour, l'a laissé.'

[29] Francis Hargrave, for example, himself responding to the supposed resemblance or even identity between an inventor of a machine and the author of a book, stated that 'the principal distinction is, that in *one* case the claim really is to an appropriation of the *use* of *ideas*; but in the *other*, the claim leaves the use of the ideas *common* to the whole world'. Francis Hargrave, *An Argument in Defence of Literary Property* (London 1774) 36–37.

[30] Charles-Guillaume Leclerc (or Le Clerc), *Lettre à M. de Néville* (1778) in Laboulaye and Guiffrey (n 24) 407:

Mille autres ouvriers, mille autres artistes peuvent, par leur industrie, faire la même découverte que le privilégié; il n'a pas un droit exclusif à cette découverte; tous les autres ouvriers ou artistes y ont droit; le privilège qu'on lui accorde est donc une atteinte portée au droit des autres, au droit qu'ils ont par les lois de la nature de faire cette découverte, et de jouir des avantages qu'elle procure ... Il n'en est pas ainsi du privilège accordé à un auteur pour son ouvrage. Les idées, les sentiments qui entrent dans la composition d'un ouvrage, l'ordre dans lequel un auteur les expose, la manière dont il les exprime, sont à lui; nul autre que lui ne pouvait le produire tel qu'il est; l'auteur est donc non-seulement le seul propriétaire de cet ouvrage, mais encore on ne fait aucun tort à qui que ce soit, en lui accordant à perpétuité un privilège exclusif pour l'impression de son ouvrage ...

400 *Research handbook on the history of copyright law*

subtlety which legitimated abusive privileges. The lawyer Gaultier, acting for the booksellers of Lyon in 1776, stressed that 'the inventor of a machine, a new fabric, or whatever its kind, is not less the master, possessor of his invention, than the Author of his Book that he created, whatever the difference which can exist between the merit of the one or the other'. In fact, he added, there 'are even cases where the former would deserve a better privilege, because, frequently, to succeed, he was forced to do numerous expensive experiments'.[31] Regarding the assertion that the composition of a book of any kind 'is a genuine creation', he recalled that, the 'man of genius, who communicates his ideas to society, is only returning, in exchange, the product of those ideas that he has received from society'.[32] Since it was in the public's interest that the circulation of these ideas, belonging and useful to all, should be free, it was not so illogical that an invention or a book ought to remain fully available to be improved by anyone, even in cases where an inventor (or an author) did not choose to distribute it to the public.[33] Finally, Gaultier disagreed *a fortiori* with the idea of an incorporeal property, particularly following publication, and recalled that authors, as inventors, could only rely on royal grants.[34]

---

[31] Gaultier, *Mémoire à consulter pour les Libraires et Imprimeurs de Lyon, Rouen, Toulouse, Marseille et Nisme, concernant les privilèges de librairie et continuation d'iceux*, Bibliothèque nationale de France, Mss Fr 22073, No 144, 44, available at <http://www.copyrighthistory.org/record/f_1776>. Gaultier, although admitting that the composition of a book could be a 'genuine creation' [*véritable creation*], ibid 30, assimilates literary compositions to any 'inventions, techniques [recettes, meaning here procédé, word which is used further] or discoveries'. ibid 31. In fact, for the provincial booksellers, these literary productions are the only one to provoke controversies: 'les compositions littéraires sont les seules pour lesquelles on a excité ces controverses, & personne jusqu'à présent n'a pensé que ce fût faire un vol à l'inventeur de quelque objet, que de l'imiter ou copier, lorsque sans s'être muni d'un Privilege exclusif, il a rendu son invention publique par la vente ou autrement'. ibid 31, 32. The precise identity of Gaultier is unknown. This work was indeed simply signed 'Gaultier, Avocat'. The author might be Jean-François Gaultier de Biauzat, an active lawyer of Clermond-Ferrand and known in the region from the 1760s, and future deputy for the *Tiers État* in 1789. On this fundamental distinction, see also Abbot Pluquet (François-Adrien Pluquet)'s letters on the 1777 regulations and the book trade, Bibliothèque nationale de France, Mss Fr 22063, No 68, 68bis, 68ter, also available at <http://www.copyrighthistory.org/record/f_1778>, and in particular the *Seconde lettre à un ami, Sur les Affaires actuelles de la Librairie*, 11–12.

[32] Ibid 41.

[33] Ibid 32: 'A-t-on jamais taxé d'injustice les célebre Académiciens de l'Académie des Sciences de Paris, lorsque s'introduisant dans les atteliers des Arts, ils vont épier la marche & les procédés des plus habiles Maîtres; leur dérober, pour ainsi dire, leurs secrets, les divulguer ensuite & découvrir ces inventions au Public, afin que chacun, en les imitant, puisse travailler avec succès au profit général de la société. Quelqu'un oseroit-il les taxer d'avoir été par cette conduite, les instigateurs de ce que les Libraires appellent dans leur partie, un brigandage odieux?'

[34] Ibid 31:

Il est donc évident que le propriétaire d'un Manuscrit, qui en a vendu & distribué des copies au Public, sans avoir obtenu un Privilege exclusif du Gouvernement, n'est pas fondé à se plaindre, si ceux qui ont acheté ces copies, en font multiplier à leur gré les exemplaires; car il leur a communiqué par cette vente une propriété égale à la seule espece de propriété qu'il pouvoit avoir. C'est donc dans le seul Privilege exclusif accordé par le Gouvernement,

Gaultier's position was not unique. In his *Fragments sur la liberté de la Presse*, written in 1776 (but first published in the nineteenth century), Condorcet also appeared to be rather reluctant to give full attention to the distinctions made by supporters of literary property, although he agreed that book privileges encompassed the 'expressions' and 'phrases' used in a book, rather than the 'ideas' themselves.[35] Even if this distinction between ideas and their expression could lead to the protection of 'words', and even the 'author's name', it remained the case that the real value or utility of a book depended more on the ideas with which the author's name was associated, rather than on the choice of his 'pleasant expressions' [*tournures agréables*] to express them. Furthermore, he argued, protecting books simply led to them becoming more expensive in the market. True 'inventors' – those whose ideas or discoveries constituted the principal value of what he produced – were the ones deserving protection so as to protect the investment necessary to reach them. In other words, like Gaultier, Condorcet regarded the literary process, claimed to be so personal, as far less important than the communication of useful truths and discoveries in which the whole nation could potentially share. That being said, Condorcet recognized that even if 'the man of genius does not make books for money', without any material security or sufficient income, a writer could be forced to find an alternative gainful occupation, an outcome which could lead to negative effects for the public, for example by postponing the diffusion of useful ideas. Nevertheless, he argued that marketing books by 'subscription could easily replace, if not more, all the advantages [associated with privileges]'.[36]

The personal nature of literary property, claimed by Louis d'Héricourt and those who followed him was thus at the heart of the debate. There was, however, one serious problem with their characterisation of literary property as an inherently personal one, and that was the simultaneous insistence that it be fully transferable.[37] Interestingly, similar criticisms have been made by supporters of an 'Anglo-American' traditional philosophy of copyright. Peter Baldwin, for example, argues that the 'French' were at a dead end in the eighteenth century because they were '[t]hinking of literary works as conventional property'.[38] As Baldwin points out, Linguet 'granted the author an

---

> qu'existe le droit exclusif de multiplier & vendre les copies d'un Ouvrage, ensorte que la propriété d'un Manuscrit se communique par la vente ou cession des copies, tandis que la propriété du Privilège se conserve nonobstant cette vente. Il est bien nécessaire de distinguer ces deux sortes de propriété, si l'on veut s'entendre.

The same reluctance towards incorporeal property could be observed similarly in England, and the defence of its principle proved to be a complicated task, undertaken in the 1770, for example by William Enfield, in his *Observations on Literary Property* (1774).

[35] Nicolas de Condorcet, 'Fragments sur la liberté de la presse' (1776) in *Oeuvres* (Firmin Didot 1847) vol 2, 310–11, available at <http://www.copyrighthistory.org/record/f_1776a>.

[36] Ibid 310. The belief that men of letters did not write primarily for money, but for glory, was fully shared by Gaultier's clients: 'L'homme de génie qui entre dans la carriere pénible & honorable de la Littérature, peut avoir ces trois objets en vue; d'éclairer ses semblables, d'éterniser sa réputation, & même de retirer quelque salaire de ses travaux'. Gaultier (n 31) 46. In England, opponents of literary property at common law would use the same argument. See *Millar v Taylor* (1769) 4 Burr 2303, 2392 (Yates J).

[37] Eg Bernard Edelman, *Le sacre de l'auteur* (Le Seuil 2004) 251.

[38] Baldwin (n 4) 96.

aesthetic veto over changes, yet also insisted on full alienability to the publisher'.[39] This is why, he argues, that Linguet had 'posed the problem without solving it'.[40] But these apparent contradictions did not prevent authors from supporting property, as Diderot, who believed that this right could constitute a means of protecting all the proprietary interests of the author, at least in a better manner than subjecting it to an imposed public domain and its inevitable by-effects, in particular 'since honour is the most valuable portion of the benefits an author receives'.[41] Luneau de Boisjermain also supported very actively his absolute property rights as an author, above all the freedom to sell his own literary productions, despite the fight which ensued against the Parisian booksellers (see *infra*).

Such an individualist natural property, if fully recognised, would ultimately strengthen the Parisian booksellers' privileges, and Gaultier and Condorcet made a convincing point in supporting the so-called 'social contract' argument which supported fuller access of the Provincial booksellers to the book market. The way in which the message of the Enlightenment should best be disseminated was indeed the subject of an important debate during the second half of the eighteenth century which, despite sometimes opposite views, was moving irresistibly towards a common belief of the necessity of broader access of the public to instruction.[42] Malesherbes, head of the book trade and controller of the press from 1750, had clearly emphasised the benefits of reducing censorship in his *Mémoires sur la librairie*, not only for these idealistic reasons, but also for practical reasons, in particular its actual inefficiency.[43] He was also concerned with abusive guild rules, but at the same time was attentive to the authors' situation. Using terms that were certainly not trivial coming from a member of the royal government, he stated that an author should have 'the free disposal' of the 'fruits

---

[39] Ibid.
[40] Ibid. After stating that a group of proto-Kantian French Legal historians were supporting altogether a 'kind of sleeper right that will eventually blossom into the personalist connection between author and work' and calling this approach 'anachronistic', ibid 426 fn 20, Baldwin's condemnation of Linguet's incapacity to define, in 1774, a satisfying (juridical) solution to a 'problem' still debated today, despite doctrinal evolutions unknown to eighteenth century lawyers, is rather paradoxical.
[41] Diderot, *Lettre historique* (n 21) 23.
[42] On this issue we can rely on the interesting work of Roland Mortier, *Clartés et Ombres du siècle des Lumières* (Droz 1969), in particular, 'Esotérisme et Lumière, Un dilemme de la pensée du XVIIIe siècle', 60–103. Regarding the enlightenment of the masses, Voltaire's position was 'comparable neither to the scepticism of Fontenelle, nor to the enthusiasm of the encyclopaedists.' And while La Chalotais, mainly supported in this perspective by Voltaire, rejected the idea of an education system for the 'inferior' classes of society, Diderot, in his *Plan d'une Université pour le Gouvernement de Russie*, supported strongly the idea of an open university, to educate and civilize the whole nation, for he was convinced that 'education gives man some dignity …' (quoted by Mortier, ibid 84). ['L'instruction donne à l'homme de la dignité … Une université est une école dont la porte est ouverte indistinctement à tous les enfants d'une nation'].
[43] Guillaume-Chrétien de Lamoignon de Malesherbes, *Mémoires sur la librairie. Mémoire sur la liberté de la presse* (Imprimerie Nationale 1994). The *Mémoires sur la librairie* were written in 1758. Not surprisingly, Malesherbes would only recommend the total suppression of censorship in 1788, when his *Mémoire sur la liberté de la presse* was drafted.

of his genius' and consequently should be allowed to sell his own books because it was 'a natural right' of property. Echoing the formulation of Héricourt, Malesherbes stated that the right was even more legitimate than the one pertaining to land.[44]

Obviously, two viewpoints stood strong: a natural right of property, certainly enigmatic, but sufficiently convincing to be explicitly secured by legislation, even before the Revolution, but also, the concern for public utility, which, ultimately, would not be felt incompatible with this consecration.

3. THE LEGALISATION OF LITERARY PROPERTY

When discussing the recognition of literary property in France, an association should be drawn between the last book trade legislation of the *Ancien Régime*, namely the Decree of the King's Council of State of 30 August 1777 containing regulations on the duration of book trade privileges, and the famous Decree of the National Convention of 19–24 July 1793 regarding the property rights of authors to writings of all kinds, including composers of music, painters and illustrators. Both legislative interventions were concerned with literary property's recognition, although there has been a tendency among scholars to interpret the former as a very traditional *Ancien Régime* book trade policy, thereby reducing its significance. Nevertheless, the 1777 Decree clearly redefined book trade privileges and their nature pertaining to property, while the Act of July 1793 was passed to secure authors' rights, as will be discussed in the two sub-sections below. Part 3.1 addresses the 1777 Decree in the context of litigation that preceded it, and Part 3.2 then turns to the build up to the 1793 Act.

3.1 *'Une Propriété de Droit'*

While Parisian and Provincial booksellers were fighting about the duration of royal privileges, a few judicial cases before the King's courts, although not decisive, showed that the royal administration could also be concerned with the situation of authors (and their inheritance).

The case of the dramatic author Crébillon, which came before the King's Council of State on 27 March 1749,[45] has been interpreted as a recognition of the author's economic interests, or more ironically, according to Augustin-Charles Renouard, as an

---

[44] Ibid 161: 'Ce sont les auteurs, qui, suivant le droit naturel, devraient tirer tout le profit de leurs ouvrages, en ayant la faculté de les vendre eux-mêmes [...] Ne doit-on pas regarder les ouvrages d'un auteur, qui sont les fruits de son génie, comme lui appartenant encore à plus juste titre, et comme le bien dont il serait le plus convenable qu'il eût la libre disposition?' See Rideau, 'La formation' (n 17) 121. With the accession of Louis XVI to the throne in 1774, Malesherbes became part of his government, along with Turgot, until May 1776. He defended the King in 1792 and was guillotined in 1794.

[45] Arrest du Conseil d'Estat du Roy, en faveur du Sieur de Crébillon, Auteur de la tragédie de Catilina, Qui juge que les productions de l'Esprit ne sont point au rang des Effets Saisissables. Du 21 Mars 1749, Bibliothèque nationale de France: Mss Fr 22072, No 112, available at <http://www.copyrighthistory.org/record/f_1749>.

example of the indulgent treatment of men of letters.[46] The Court ruled that the fruits accruing from literary works were not seizable by Crébillon's creditors and should remain with Crébillon. The significance of this decision remains somewhat ambiguous because of the way Crébillon, in his argument during the case, focused on interests that went beyond his own property interests as author. His plea drew attention both to measures that were 'useful to the nation' and to the 'appreciable inconveniences' which the Monarchy might suffer in the absence of proper protection for the income of authors. If such practices were allowed to continue, Crébillon insisted, it would certainly have negative effects on the public itself, since authors would 'find themselves in the cruel position of not daring to bring to light their Works, often precious & interesting for the State'.[47]

The case can be compared to the dispute which pitted Jean de La Fontaine's granddaughters against the major Parisian booksellers, in which the former obtained the right to exploit themselves the '*Fables et Œuvres*' for 15 years, despite the book trade having held a monopoly on the Fables for 66 years. The Parisian booksellers objected to the registration of the 15-year royal permission thus granted. Before the State Private Royal Council, the lawyer Roussel, acting for La Fontaine's family, did not concentrate this time on the public interest, but instead focused on the direct family ties with the great fabulist, which implied that his work should belong to them 'naturally by right of inheritance' [*naturellement par droit d'hérédité*].[48] Was the court convinced by Roussel's plea, given that confirming the end to an old monopoly would in any event benefit the public? The fact remains that the judges found in favour of the La Fontaine granddaughters. But interestingly enough, the ruling seemed to favour an 'inheritance right' over publishing agreements concluded long ago with La Fontaine himself. At least, that is the way the Parisian book trade understood it, taking the ruling as a serious warning.

Subsequent rulings were to be no more reassuring for the trade. A few years before the decisive Decree of 1777, the author and editor Pierre-Joseph Luneau de Boisjermain, keen to defend what he saw as his personal authorial interest against the Parisian guild system, was determined not to relinquish his exclusive rights. Luneau arranged, in 1768, for several boxes of his works to be sent to five book traders in Paris, so that these in their turn could deliver them to booksellers in the provinces who were willing

---

[46] Indeed, according to Augustin-Charles Renouard, who was, in the nineteenth century, a major opponent of the concept of literary property: 'Un arrêt rendu par le conseil privé, le 21 mars 1749, au profit de Crébillon contre ses créanciers, offre un exemple remarquable des complaisances auxquelles on se croyait alors obligé envers les gens de lettres'. A-C Renouard, *Traité des droits d'auteur dans la littérature, les sciences et les beaux-arts* (Paris, Jules Renouard 1838–39) vol 1, 161. Marie-Claude Dock sees this ruling as an 'implicit recognition of literary property'. Marie-Claude Dock, *Contribution historique à l'étude des droits d'auteur* (LGDJ 1962) 119.

[47] Arrest du Conseil (n 45).

[48] Arrest du Conseil d'Etat privé du Roi, Qui déclare nulle l'opposition faite par les Libraires de Paris au privilège accordé par Sa Majesté aux demoiselles de la Fontaine; & enjoint aux Syndic & Adjoints d'enregistrer sans délai les privilége & permissions accordés par Sa Majesté. Du 14 Septembre 1761, Bibliothèque nationale de France: Mss Fr 22178, No 16, available at <http://www.copyrighthistory.org/record/f_1761>.

to sell his books. Luneau was consequently accused of meddling in the book trade and the Parisian booksellers secured a judicial order for the confiscation of his works. Represented by Linguet, Luneau founded his defence on authorial property. Later, a ruling in 1770 annuled the order of confiscation and brought to the fore, in an atmosphere of increasing tension between the Parisian and provincial guilds, the whole question of an author's ability to sell himself what he had produced.[49]

Although this judicial evolution seemed to reflect a growing attention to authors, even when their interests potentially clashed with those of the book trade, interpreting the true significance of these decisions is complicated by the King's justice system itself, that is the absence of motivation of its rulings. It was therefore difficult to foresee if or how the Monarchy would be ready to continue this evolution, as well as its possible impact on the book privileges system. In fact, it must be emphasised that a few years earlier, the Royal Declaration of December 1762 confirmed the traditional definition of privileges in relation to inventions, while trying to rationalise this field.[50] No property right had been discussed; instead, the declaration was mainly concerned with trade privileges [*Privilèges en fait de Commerce*] granted to encourage the inventor to pursue his experimentation.[51] The inventor's industry and labour were simply 'rewarded' if, following established criteria, they bore some novelty and were useful to the Realm. Thus, the 1762 provisions corresponded perfectly, in spirit, to the first privileges granted in the book trade during the first half of the sixteenth century and, not surprisingly, their duration was strictly limited so as not to establish 'a patrimonial inheritance' in place of what should only be a 'personal reward'. From this perspective, transfer of the privilege had to satisfy precise conditions, particularly concerning the inventor's family following his death, and as such was only possible if its members were able to continue exploiting the invention so that it could benefit the public.[52]

The Decree of 30 August 1777 departed from the Declaration of 1762 in a striking way.[53] Not only did the 1777 Decree secure authorial literary property, a '*propriété de droit*', to the author but, in doing so, it modified fundamentally the nature of book privileges.[54] The latter, stressed the preamble, was a 'favour which is founded in

---

[49] Pfister, 'Author and Work' (n 2) 132. On this case, and for more details on Linguet's argumentation, see also Pfister, 'L'auteur, propriétaire de son œuvre' (n 2) 326–40. The ruling is available at <http://www.copyrighthistory.org/record/f_1770>.

[50] See for example, Augustin-Charles Renouard, *Traité des brevets d'invention* (Paris, Guillaumin 2nd edn 1844) 85–86.

[51] Déclaration du Roy, concernant les Privilèges en fait de Commerce, Du 24 décembre 1762, Bibliothèque nationale de France: Mss Fr 22073, No 72, available at <http://www.copyrighthistory.org/record/f_1762>: 'Les Priviléges en fait de commerce, qui ont pour objet de récompenser l'industrie des Inventeurs, ou d'exciter celle qui languissoit dans une concurrence sans émulation …'.

[52] Ibid art 5. See also article 6 on the obligation and the necessity of having the invention exploited.

[53] Arrest du Conseil d'Etat du Roi, Portant Règlement sur la durée des Priviléges en Librairie. Du 30 août 1777, Bibliothèque nationale de France: Mss Fr 22073, No 146, available at <http://www.copyrighthistory.org/record/f_1777a>.

[54] The very fact that author's literary property was recognised has been discussed before: see for example Marie-Claude Dock, who claims that, although literary property was involved in

justice', but whose object is, 'when accorded to an author, to reward his labour, and when accorded to a bookseller, to guarantee the reimbursement of any advance and to indemnify him against costs incurred'. This careful distinction between the author's labour and the booksellers' industry carried obvious consequences pertaining to the privilege duration, notably 'that the author without doubt [*sans doute*] has a greater right to a more enduring [*plus étendue*] favour, while the bookseller may only expect the favour granted to him to be proportional to his total expenditure and to the size of his operation'. In fact, 'more enduring' constituted a compelling euphemism – article V secured an author's property rights in perpetuity. Fundamentally, such a duration implied that henceforth a book privilege complied with Héricourt's definition, that is, when granted to an author, it was a means to protect a pre-existing right (so long as the censorship requirements, as before, had been met).

Lastly, for the very first time, authors were also allowed to sell their own productions. This capacity, in itself symbolic in the face of a guild system which would prevail until the Revolution, would be confirmed in 1778.[55] However, the fact that the author's labour was explicitly distinguished from the labour deriving from publishing activities had some unexpected consequences when an author transfered a privilege to a bookseller. Indeed, for the latter, as for inventors following the 1762 Act, the royal grant seemed to retain its traditional character, since its maximum duration was drastically limited, that is, according to articles III and V, to the author's life, or ten years minimum. This reduction occurred solely in the situation that the right was transferred by the author [*par le fait seul de la cession*].[56] Ironically, if the argument developed more than 50 years earlier by

---

1777, the 1793 Act constituted in itself a 'considerable progress', but makes no further explanation. Dock (n 46) 157. Jean-Michel Ducomte went further, stating that the 'declaration of 1777' did not speak 'clearly' of property. Jean-Michel Ducomte, 'La Révolution Française et la propriété littéraire et artistique', in G Koubi (ed), *Propriété et Révolution* (CNRS Eds 1990) 120. Carla Hesse also explains that the recognition of the author's property in the 1777 decree was simply, by nature, a manifestation of an 'absolutist police state'. Carla Hesse, 'Enlightenment Epistemology and the Laws of Authorship in Revolutionary France, 1777–1793' (1990) 30 Representations 109, 113–14. Pfister suggests this is an incorrect interpretation of this legislation and quotes Miromesnil, the Keeper of the Seal, who wrote in a letter to the Académie française in 1778 that it appeared fair to him to 'consecrate in favour of men of letters a property on their intellectual production', and also 'to make them enjoy all the avantages able to encourage their talent'. Pfister, 'Author and Work' (n 2) 133–34. See also Laboulaye and Guiffrey (n 24) 627–28.

[55] See Arrêt du Conseil du 30 juillet 1778, in Laboulaye and Guiffrey (n 24) 363–66, available at <http://www.copyrighthistory.org/record/f_1778a>. As to property rights, a few years later, in 1786, the King would retain this same legal qualification for musical publications. Following Ballard's domination of the music publishing trade in the mid-16th century, the decree of the King's Council of 15 September 1786 was the first act of royal legislation under the *Ancien Régime* to cover music (available at the Archives nationales, AD 1075 and <http://www.copyrighthistory.org/record/f_1786>).

[56] Arrest du Conseil d'Etat du Roi (n 53) article 5:

TOUT Auteur qui obtiendra en son nom le privilége de son ouvrage, aura le droit de le vendre chez lui, sans qu'il puisse, sous aucun prétexte, vendre ou négocier d'autres livres; & jouira de son privilége, pour lui & ses hoirs, à perpétuité, pourvu qu'il ne le rétrocède à aucun Libraire; auquel cas la durée du privilége sera, par le fait seul de la cession, réduite à celle de la vie de l'Auteur.

Louis d'Héricourt was consecrated pertaining to the author's relation to his work, it was not, ultimately, in the favour of his usual assignees.

As one can imagine, the questionable purview of the 1777 Act was severely criticised. Linguet, for example, expressed difficulty in understanding its logic, and the new, if flexible, definition of book privileges it implied. As he emphasised, since 'a literary privilege is only a mark of recognition of pre-existing property rights, it cannot limit those rights'.[57] Given that literary property was secured as a perpetual right, deriving from the author's labour, and in this sense potentially different to all other privileges *en fait de commerce*, how, then, could these privileges become limited by the sole fact of their transfer with the literary work, since to enjoy his rights an author could either exercise them himself or choose freely to transfer them to a bookseller?[58] For the lawyer Cochu, the latter solution was obviously the best one, as many authors 'have neither the resources, nor the funds necessary to take care themselves of the edition and the sale of their works …'[59] Linguet thus finally concluded that:

> Literary property therefore becomes, by its very nature, according to the decree, a non-transferable entity; and a property which cannot be got rid of is nothing but a burden. This article, whilst appearing to respect the property rights of men of letters, in fact does them irreparable damage. It is precisely in concentrating these rights in their persons that it destroys them.[60]

Following numerous objections to the 1777 decree, Antoine-Louis Séguier, *Avocat général* (prosecutor) representing the King before the Paris Parliament, had the difficult task of justifying the new legislation.[61] He confirmed that 'for the first time', the legislation spoke of 'the right of authors', a 'property which seems so obvious, that it is allowed to the author to sell at home his work', a choice which 'derives from natural right'.[62] However, the author's 'sacred right of property', because of its peculiar nature, and the ease with which it could be copied, inevitably required that legislation secure it.[63] The general prosecutor emphasised that the 'restriction [the King] placed on the duration of the favour is not destructive of the property', as it concerned solely the means by which the latter was secured.[64] Needless to say that if Séguier was convinced

---

[57] Linguet, *Mémoire* (n 25) 30.
[58] Ibid 32.
[59] Cochu (n 24) 174–75. See also Linguet (ibid) 32, who wonders if the book trade has therefore become a 'shameful trade' [*négoce honteux*].
[60] Linguet (ibid) 37.
[61] Antoine-Louis Séguier's defence of the 1777 decrees (during the sessions of 10, 27, 31 August 1779), in particular on duration of book privileges, is to be found in 'Procès-Verbal de ce qui s'est passé au Parlement touchant les six arrêts du conseil Du 30 août 1777, concernant la Librairie, avec les Comptes rendus à leur sujet', in Laboulaye and Guiffrey (n 24) 463 ff, available at <http://www.copyrighthistory.org/record/f_1779>.
[62] Ibid 583.
[63] Ibid 589, because, with the author's publication, the public, in a way, becomes 'associated to this property'.
[64] Ibid 592: To the contrary, concerning the privilege granted to an author:

> Cette grâce est assurée à toujours dans la personne de l'auteur; elle n'est assurée que pour un temps certain dans la main du cessionnaire; c'est une modification de la grâce. Toutes les fois

by the peculiar nature of the author's labour, and the fact that it was not comparable to the booksellers' industry, he was probably aware that this argument, relying essentially on the new adaptable definition of book privileges, remained fragile. In fact, his conclusions even appeared embarrassed, as he praised, for the sake of public interest, the positive effects of free trade in books,[65] while recognising at the same time the fact that, in the same trade *usages*, the effects of the transfer of a manuscript (as the medium of the literary work) had long been the same as for other types of property, that is, as Diderot put it before, that the 'rights of the last owner [*propriétaire*] have been as sacred as the rights of the first'.[66]

From this perspective, the balance between private and general interests was certainly difficult to sustain on logical grounds. As Renouard later believed, it would have probably been easier for the royal administration to simply oppose these conflicting interests more explicitly.[67] Nevertheless, literary property's recognition seemed almost inevitable, particularly at a time when the guild system was stuck in nepotism, and under incessant attacks of more liberal 'economists', such as Vincent de Gournay, who had been supporting the suppression of its monopolies from the 1750s. Indeed, in March 1776 the Minister of Economy (Contrôleur général des Finances), Turgot, tried to abolish them on the ground of the natural freedom of each individual to fully benefit of the fruits of his labour.[68]

---

que le Roi accorde un privilège, il n'est pas question de la propriété en elle-même, il ne s'agit que de la manière d'assurer cette propriété. Le privilège en est le garant et la sauvegarde. Mais cette garantie, cette sauvegarde, peut durer plus ou moins, selon la volonté de celui qui s'oblige à la faire valoir. Encore une fois, le privilège est une grâce; elle est de justice pour l'auteur, et de libéralité pour le libraire.

[65] Ibid 593, stressing that extended 'monopolies' contributed to high prices: '… la facilité avec laquelle l'administration a accordé jusqu'à présent des continuations de privilège contribue à entretenir le prix exorbitant où le monopole des auteurs et des libraires …'.

[66] Ibid 594–95:

Nous ne pouvons cependant vous le dissimuler, l'usage a prévalu, et la véracité de notre ministère nous oblige d'avouer que la transmission de la propriété de la main de l'auteur dans celle de l'imprimeur ou du libraire, est au moins reconnue depuis le milieu du siècle dernier. Par une suite de cette propriété reconnue, les manuscrits sont devenus des effets commerçables, comme une terre, comme une rente, comme une maison; ils sont passés des pères aux enfants, avec le privilège qui en était l'accessoire; ils ont été donnés en dot, ils ont été vendus, cédés, transportés. Tel est depuis longtemps l'usage du commerce de la librairie, et les droits du dernier propriétaire ont été aussi sacrés que les droits des premiers.

[67] Renouard, *Traité des droits* (n 46) vol 1, 179, still in the light of his fight against literary property, and focusing on its traditional technical effects:

S'il ne s'était agi que de démontrer par des motifs de droit, et dans l'intérêt général, la nécessité de ne donner aux privilèges qu'une durée temporaire, les argumens n'auraient certainement pas manqués. […] Mais les arrêts, tout en cherchant, par le fait, à limiter les privilèges, avaient eu le tort de reconnaître en principe, au profit des auteurs, un droit de propriété perpétuelle. Il y avait contradiction manifeste entre le principe que l'on concédait, et le soin que l'on mettait à en éviter les conséquences. C'était rendre la défense des arrêts insoutenables en bonne logique.

[68] This piece of legislation was the Édit 'portant suppression des jurandes et communautés de commerce, arts et métiers' (Versailles, février 1776), with its famous natural rights argumentation:

The same difficulties in seeking an acceptable balance between divergent interests, while upholding natural property as a legal basis for the author's right, would also characterise the Revolutionary legislation of 1793, and continue throughout the nineteenth century.

3.2 The (Difficult) Path to the 1793 Act

The 1793 Act was enacted with little debate, and we know thus little about was said about the nature of literary property becoming limited to a short period after the author's death.[69] Nevertheless, two important bills, neither of which became law, preceded this act and offer some insight on the matter.

The first bill, which was supported by Emmanuel-Joseph Sieyès in his *projet* (and report) in January 1790,[70] is already well known. It is often quoted to suggest the influence of a strong social contract current – one that supports the idea of a utilitarian view of the public interest operating to the detriment of the author from whom the natural property right originated. For example, according to Carla Hesse, 'the revolutionaries explicitly intended to dethrone the absolute author, a creature of privilege, and recast him, not as a *private* individual (the absolute bourgeois), but rather as a *public* servant, as the model citizen'.[71] The notion that ideas were social rather than individual in origin is thus said to be very strong throughout the revolutionary period, and such a trend allegedly led to some practical consequences, notably drastic limitations in

---

Nous devons à tous nos sujets de leur assurer la jouissance pleine et entière de leurs droits; nous devons surtout cette protection à cette classe d'hommes qui, n'ayant de propriété que leur travail et leur industrie, ont d'autant plus le besoin et le droit d'employer dans toute leur étendue les seules ressources qu'ils aient pour subsister [...] Dieu en donnant à l'homme des besoins, en lui rendant nécessaire la ressource du travail, a fait, du droit de travailler, la propriété de tout homme ; et cette propriété est la première, la plus sacrée et la plus imprescriptible de toutes.

Turgot had to resign in May and his reform was lost. Even more than the pure physiocratic representative François Quesnay, Turgot tried to follow closely the conviction of Vincent de Gournay. On this, see for example Gournay's famous Éloge, written the year of his death (*Éloge de Vincent de Gournay*, 1759). Ironically, but not surprisingly, the book corporations, still for censorship reasons (along with a few other exceptions, such as guilds involved with pharmaceutical products), were not worried by the reform. Turgot's reform, although not implemented, would be closely revived during the Revolutionary era, in March–June 1791, with the 'Décret' of the Baron d'Allarde, on freedom of commerce and industry, and the 'Loi' Le Chapelier, which forbade explicitly all professional associations.

[69] As Renouard, *Traité des droits* (n 46) vol 1, 325, put it: 'On discutait peu à cette époque. Le décret fut adopté sans discussion après un bref rapport de M. Lakanal. Quoique ce décret n'établisse qu'un droit temporaire, le rapport se tait sur les motifs de la limitation de ce droit à une période de dix années après la mort de l'auteur'.

[70] Emmanuel-Joseph Sieyès, *Rapport de M. l'abbé Sieyès sur la liberté de la presse, et projet de loi contre les délits qui peuvent se commettre par la voie de l'impression, et par la publication des écrits et des gravures (1790)*, reprinted in in P-J-B Buchez and P-C Roux *Histoire parlementaire de la Révolution française* (Paris, Paulin 1834) vol 4, 273. The report is available, with translation, at <http://www.copyrighthistory.org/record/f_1790>.

[71] Hesse (n 54) 130.

copyright duration.[72] Sieyès' bill is in fact to be regarded in the light of Condorcet's *Fragments*, who is supposed to have even 'played a crucial role in drafting the National Assembly's first legislation to regulate the printing word'.[73]

The 1790 bill was indeed, chronologically, the first legislative effort which aimed to regulate the book market; symbolically it could therefore form a basis for subsequent legal developments until the passing of the 1793 Act. However, it must be stressed that Sieyès, in his report, was primarily concerned by the practical consequences of article 11 of the French Declaration of August 1789 on freedom of the press, and the chaotic multiplication of printed activities, sometimes counter-revolutionary in nature, in particular the point beyond which this freedom would eventually also 'become harmful to the rights of others'.[74] Literary property, again related to questions of press regulation in Sieyès' bill, only appeared in article 14.[75] Moreover, because, institutionally, everything, during the Revolution had to be legally reorganized – '[t]his present state of affairs is neither the old one, nor the new one' – the law, if passed, was not going to have any effect 'except during two years'.[76] Revealing as it was, Sieyès' bill was mainly conceived as a transitional measure.

This was not the case with the *projet* of François Hell, Deputy of the Bas-Rhin, which he submitted to the Constitutional Committee in September 1791. This can be seen as a counter-weight to that of Sieyès, and one which, at last, separated literary property from questions pertaining to press control.[77] It supported the notion that literary property, deriving from the author's labour, ought to be perpetually secured by law, even when the author transferred his right to a bookseller. This was obviously a radical position which, of course, had little chance of success, considering that even the 1777 legislation had organised limitations on duration in the public interest. Nevertheless, it is notable for enshrining literary property in such terms, using a syntax with which neither Louis d'Héricourt, Linguet, or, later, Joseph Lakanal would have been able to find any fault: 'Justice commands it because of all kinds of property the first is

---

[72] See also Pfister, 'Author and Work' (n 2) 136, who states that, Sieyès, by advocating a limited posthumous right, would be at the end followed in the two laws of January 1791 and July 1793, pieces of legislation 'nevertheless' grounded on property.

[73] Hesse (n 54) 119: 'In both form and content the proposal presented by Sieyès in 1790 bears a striking resemblance to the *Fragments sur la liberté de la presse* that Condorcet had composed in 1776'.

[74] Sieyès, *Rapport* (n 70) 274, who added that: 'La liberté de la presse, comme toutes les libertés, doit donc avoir ses bornes légales'.

[75] Ibid 283:

Le progrès des Lumières, et par consequent l'utilité publique se réunissent aux idées de justice distributive, pour exiger que la propriété d'un ouvrage soit assurée à l'auteur par la loi. En conséquence, toute personne convaincue d'avoir imprimé un livre pendant la vie d'un auteur, ou moins de dix ans après sa mort, sans son consentement exprès et par écrit, ou celui de ses ayans-cause, sera declaré contrefacteur.

[76] Ibid 278.

[77] *Rapport fait par M. Hell, Député du Bas-Rhin, sur la propriété des productions scientifiques ou littéraires* (Imprimerie nationale 1791), Bibliothèque nationale de France: LE29-1208, also available with translations at <http://www.copyrighthistory.org/record/f_1791a>.

that which one has in one's thoughts', a property which 'is inherent in the author to such an extent that without him it would not exist'.[78] The full recognition of literary property meant primarily that a writer would be able to reap the pecuniary profits of his books, but Hell seems also to have been convinced (although not the first to be so) that securing it to such an extent would allow, somehow, the protection of such personal interests as the author's honour, and, more precisely, the desire to prevent 'counterfeiters' from 'corrupting the purity & the literal sense of a work'.[79]

Hell also thought it necessary to distinguish again the 'spiritual' part of literary property, diffusing a 'light' which 'becomes the property of all' as soon as the book is published and made known to the world, from the 'material part', which 'ought to be preserved for the author' and his family.[80] The distinction between the 'spiritual' and 'material' elements of literary property helps one understand one of the best known parts (although frequently truncated by scholars) of another *projet*, this one advanced by Isaac-René-Guy Le Chapelier. A few months before Hell's *projet*, Le Chapelier had reported on a bill that would become the Dramatic Act of January 1791.[81] In his report, he introduced literary property as the 'most sacred', 'the most personal of all properties'. Following this introduction came the part so often truncated, namely the explanation that when a literary work is published, the writer has 'associated' the public with his property, or rather he has 'transferred it entirely to it'. Indeed, as the aim of an author is normally to publish his work (to benefit from it), the public, as soon as it welcomes the work, is associated, not just by nature but also spiritually as Hell would say, to all the 'beauties'[82] it contains. Yet, this transfer did not prevent the material aspect of this property from being secured, in particular against ancient monopolies aggressively defended by *La Comédie Française*, which Le Chapelier claimed had

---

[78] Ibid 5–6: 'Elle est tellement inhérente à l'auteur, que sans lui elle n'existeroit pas …'
[79] Ibid 5.
[80] Ibid 6: 'La partie matérielle au contraire est la véritable propriété qu'on doit conserver à l'auteur …'
[81] *Rapport fait par M. Le Chapelier, Au nom du Comité de Constitution, sur la Pétition des Auteurs dramatiques* (Imprimerie Nationale 1791), available with translations at <http://www.copyrighthistory.org/record/f_1791>. This led to the well-known Dramatic Act of 13–19 January 1791.
[82] Le Chapelier ibid 16. The famous extract, in the non-truncated version, after the first emphatic sentence concerning property, is the following:

La plus sacrée, la plus légitime, la plus inattaquable, & si je puis parler ainsi, la plus personnelle de toutes les propriétés, est l'ouvrage, fruit de la pensée d'un écrivain; cependant, c'est une propriété d'un genre tout différent des autres propriétés. Quand un auteur a livré son ouvrage au public, quand cet ouvrage est dans les mains de tout le monde, que tous les hommes instruits le connoissent, qu'ils se sont emparés des beautés qu'il contient, qu'ils ont confié à leur mémoire les traits les plus heureux; il semble que dès ce moment, l'écrivain a associé le public à sa propriété, ou plutôt la lui a transmise toute entière; cependant, comme il est extrêmement juste que les hommes qui cultivent le domaine de la pensée, tirent quelque fruit de leur travail, il faut que pendant toute leur vie & et quelques années après leur mort, personne ne puisse, sans leur consentement, disposer du produit de leur genie. Mais aussi, après le délai fixé, la propriété du public commence, & tout le monde doit pouvoir imprimer, publier les ouvrages qui ont contribué à éclairer l'esprit humain.

For a 'truncated' version, see for example Dock (n 46) 152.

caused authors to see 'their property leave their hands' through a sort of 'right of conquest' of grasping comedians.[83] However, Le Chapelier's law was far less radical than Hell's bill as the 'public's property', that is, the right for 'everyone' to print the author's book as he wished, began five years after author's death.[84] Although it seems hazardous to reduce categorically Le Chapelier's 'most sacred' property to unpublished works, this drastic limitation was certainly an efficient means of taking into consideration the public's interest.[85] Indeed, it seems that it was only the means of reaching the goal of public interest which varied, as even for Hell absolute property was supposed to create a great incentive fully consistent with the encouragement of a learning.[86] Because Le Chapelier's bill passed into law, Hell was inevitably forced to explain these limitations in duration as the peculiarities of the playwright property, that is, the fact that, then thought the deputies, 'the double revenue [accruing] from publication & performance needed to be set a limit'.[87]

Meanwhile, Stanislas de Boufflers produced a report dated 30 December 1790, supporting a bill to protect inventions, which would become law on 7 January 1791.[88] Although the law gave to inventors of machines, or discoverers of industrial processes, a property right secured by law, Boufflers' report largely focused on the primary interest of the French Nation against its competitors (in particular, England). This unprecedented consecration, but so explicitly contingent to the country's economic performances, seemed therefore vulnerable, and the property qualification would be soon temporarily disqualified in the law of 5 July 1844 (on 'brevets d'invention'). Moreover, a few years before, during the spring of 1839, Count Joseph-Marie Portalis, son of Jean-Étienne-Marie Portalis, one of the architects of the Code civil, brushed aside any common identity between authors and inventors' productions before the

---

[83] Ibid 18, relating to the risk, for some authors, to lose their rights on their work if its representations was not satisfactory enough, that is the fact that every play which did not produce 1500 *livres* in takings in winter and 1000 during the summer 'belonged to the comedians'. He added: 'Certes, il n'y aucune justice dans cette disposition réglementaire; car c'est faire dépendre une chose sacrée, la propriété, de la fantaisie, de la négligence, des manoeuvres de ceux qui ont intérêt à l'envahir.'

[84] Ibid 23.

[85] As to a 'sacred' and 'personal' property limited to unpublished works, we refer here to the landmark article of Jane Ginsburg, where she notes: 'But he said it respecting unpublished works'. Jane Ginsburg, 'A Tale of Two Copyrights: Literary Property in Revolutionary France and America' (1990) 64 Tul L R 991, 1006. In a way, Ginsburg's view shows that the fact that this famous passage of Le Chapelier was truncated was certainly counter-productive for those who wished primarily to defend author-centred conceptions, as the analysis shifted to the part truncated, rather than concentrating on the part which had been previously enthusiastically, but clumsily, highlighted. Obviously, this analysis focused, as is the case with Carla Hesse's analysis of Sieyès' report, on the evidence, not to say the domination, of an alleged public interest during the French Revolution.

[86] François Hell considered that 'the public interest' [*l'intérêt public*], as he put it, 'requires' [*sollicite*] to secure literary property, in relation to the protection of pecuniary, but also, as we have seen, non-pecuniary authors' interests. Hell (n 77) 5.

[87] Ibid 4 (note I). He added, in relation to general limitations in literary property duration: 'L'exemple des Anglois ne peut pas contre-balancer l'éternelle justice'.

[88] The text of the report and the Act that followed are available at <http://www.copyrighthistory.org/record/f_1790a>.

Chambre des Pairs (the second representative assembly of the *Monarchie de Juillet*), even claiming that there was no need to develop his point 'before such an assembly'.[89]

Finally, in the landmark Act of 19–24 July 1793, literary and artistic property was confirmed by the Deputy Joseph Lakanal in the emphatic tone of the revolutionary period. As before, the property right still bore the traces of some kind of personal peculiarity, but it was also, not surprisingly, limited in duration. Lakanal enthusiastically described in his report the property in 'works of genius':

> Of all properties, the most incontestable, the one whose increase is in no way injurious to republican equality and which gives no offence to liberty, is undeniably the property of works of genius [*c'est sans contredit celle des productions du génie*]; it is if anything surprising that it should have proved necessary to recognize this property and to secure its free exercise by a positive law, and that a great Revolution like ours should have been required to return us, in this as in so many other matters, to the simplest elements of common justice.[90]

Henceforth, statutes would be a means to secure literary property, rather than seeking protection by royal privilege. More importantly, this type of property, added Lakanal, could only be profitable to its original holder, that is the author, by means of publication. Thus, the notion of public property, to use Le Chapelier's words, was not to be misinterpreted by potential buccaneers [*corsaires*]:

> Since printing is the only means whereby the author may make useful exercise of his property, the fact of being printed alone cannot make an author's works public property, at least not in the way that the literary buccaneers understand; for if it were so, it follows that the author would be unable to make use of his property without losing it in the same moment.[91]

Following Lakanal's speech, seven articles were adopted without any discussion. Article 1 provided that 'Authors of writings of any kind [*en tout genre*]' shall have an exclusive right to their works, for a period, according to article 2, 'of ten years following the death of the author'. Article 6 required a deposit of two copies of the author's work at the National library, or the *Cabinet des Estampes*. This provision has been interpreted as supporting the utilitarian revolutionaries' goals mentioned earlier.

---

[89] Joseph-Marie Portalis, *Le Moniteur Universel* (May 1839) 774:

Messieurs, je crois qu'à cet égard il y aurait de grandes distinctions à établir entre les inventions d'un procédé chimique, mécanique, ou de fabrication, et les chefs-d'œuvre de nos grands poètes, les traités de haute philosophie, les grands ouvrages historiques et les recherches de profonde érudition; je crois qu'il y a quelque chose qui différencie singulièrement la position des auteurs de celle des personnes qui prennent des brevets d'invention, et je ne crois pas avoir besoin de développer cette pensée devant une assemblée comme celle-ci.

[90] Lakanal, *Le Moniteur Universel* (août 1793) 868 (see also, for the manuscript original version of the Act's purview, Archives nationales: BB/34/1/46): These sources are available, with translation at <http://www.copyrighthistory.org/record/f_1793>. It should be noted that Lakanal probably relied, for his report on a previous report written in February 1793 by the deputy (of Ardennes) Pierre-Charles-Louis Baudin. Rideau, 'La formation' (n 17) 261. In relation to the wording, 'incontestable', as we have seen, was also the very same term used by Linguet to characterised property (see *supra*).

[91] Ibid.

However, it was to be later interpreted by the judges as an enforcement requirement determining only the exercise of the right of property, and not its existence.[92]

In spite of the lack of debate surrounding it, this very concise legislation was to have exceptional longevity. It framed the nature of literary property throughout the nineteenth century. However, the same lack of discussion, in particular on the appropriate balance between promoting authors' rights and protecting the public interest, would exacerbate later debates on the proper duration of literary property. This occurred as soon as 1825, when a commission devoted to the question was established under the presidency of the Viscount Sosthène de La Rochefoucault.[93] The parliamentary initiatives for reform of literary property, especially between 1839 and 1841, would also be dominated by similar discussions until 1866 when the term of property was extended to 50 years after author's death.[94] Although some commentators have stressed the 'utilitarian' justifications during this legislative period, with Jane Ginsburg stating

---

[92] On these judicial decisions, see Eugène Pouillet, *Traité théorique et pratique de la propriété littéraire et artistique et du droit de représentation* (Marchal et Billard 1879) 354–55, who considered that article 6 was in itself sufficiently explicit ('those who fail to do so [ie, to proceed to the deposit] shall not have standing to bring legal proceedings against counterfeiters [*ne pourra être admis en justice pour la poursuite des contrefacteurs*]':

> Est-il possible d'exprimer plus clairement que, du dépôt, depend non pas la propriété de l'ouvrage, mais la recevabilité de l'action en contrefaçon? La preuve que la propriété de l'oeuvre ne saurait être attachée au dépôt, c'est qu'il y a des oeuvres, nous le verrons, dont le dépôt n'est pas et ne peut être exigé par la loi.

The question of deposit has been however debated by Jane Ginsburg, who sees this requirement in the 1793 Act, and in particular a *Cour de Cassation* ruling of 1834, although not decisive and followed by clearer decisions in 1844, 1863, 1866, as a supplementary proof of this strong utilitarian current within the revolutionary legislation. Ginsburg (n 85). See also, on the question of copyright formalities, including France, Stef van Gompel, 'Les formalités sont mortes, vive les formalités! Copyright Formalities and the Reasons for their Decline in Nineteenth Century Europe' in Deazley, Kretschmer and Bently (n 2) 157. From the same perspective, if the author's right really was an incontestable property, then it should be protected in the same way by all international agreements, an argument which was invoked by the critics of a natural property-based legal definition of author's rights. The gap was certainly complicated to fill throughout the nineteenth century between theoretical declarations on property and their international implementations, but some first progresses were however made for reasons of 'universal justice' with the Decree of 28 March 1852, which finally granted protection to the authors of works published abroad: see this legislation, with translations, at <http://www.copyrighthistory.org/record/f_1852>.

[93] The complete work of this commission is available at < http://www.copyrighthistory.org/record/f_1826>.

[94] We have seen before, from Portalis' interventions, the persistent comparison between literary works and inventions. The confrontation of Lamartine and Renouard is also symptomatic of the tensions between deputies during these debates. Responding to Lamartine and his convictions on literary's creation in the 1841 legislative sessions before the *Chambre des députés*, Renouard would have this famous flash of wit: 'Sans la Bible et Homère, sans Racine et Chateaubriand, aurions-nous M de Lamartine?' in *Le Moniteur Universel* (1841) 717, also available, with translations, at <http://www.copyrighthistory.org/record/f_1841>. Renouard's position seemed closer to Condorcet's convictions relating to the process of literary labour (ie, ideas being more important than what encompasses them).

that 'French revolutionary sources of copyright reveals that revolutionary legislators, courts, and advocates perceived literary property primarily as a means to advance public instruction',[95] the 1793 Act, along with the emphatic, yet typical, formulations of Lakanal's report, certainly left literary and artistic property sufficiently open not to be encompassed in a single rationale or objective. It is not therefore surprising, and certainly not *ex nihilo* (nor probably under, at this time, a Germanic influence on 'rights of personality') that Portalis still believed it useful to claim under its regime, in 1839, that what an author generates from 'his own substance' is property 'by nature, by essence, by the indivisibility of object and subject'.[96] In fact, he was consequently convinced that the transfer of the exclusive right of reproduction should not prevent the author from controlling the alterations of his work, a prerogative supposedly 'incommunicable, as his will, as well as his conscience'.[97] It was no more surprising that such a complex heritage would make it difficult for the judges to apply the revolutionary legislation.

4. A PERSONAL PROPERTY IN THE COURTS

'Sacred' and 'incontestable' as this property was said to be, the courts also had to apply it like any other property right in order to ensure at least that it complied, despite being limited in duration, with the usual technical consequences of a *droit réel*. This section will not focus precisely on the subject matter of protection or on the exact scope of the right of reproduction, but more on how, or whether, the judges translated in practical terms this 'personalist' perspective. Questions arose under the 1793 Act of how to define a literary and artistic work and how to set the threshold for protection. In the two sections that follow, are discussed the criteria for obtaining statutory protection (Part 4.1) and the first cases involving the protection of an author's non-pecuniary rights (Part 4.2).

4.1 Definition of a Literary and Artistic Work

Defining the threshold criteria which needed to be satisfied in order for an intellectual production to be protected was undoubtedly a complicated task for the judges, since, as we have seen, article 1 of the 1793 Act simply asserted that 'any kind' of literary or artistic work ought to be protected. The *Cour de Cassation* took an important first step on 2 December 1814, when it decided that compilations (a religious anthology) were

---

[95] Ginsburg (n 85) 1022.
[96] Portalis, *Le Moniteur Universel* (1839) 774: '… propriété par nature, par essence, par indivision, par indivisibilité de l'objet et du sujet'.
[97] Portalis, Chambre des Paris, 27 May 1839, *Archives Parlementaires*, t 124, 711, quoted by L Pfister, 'Particularismes nationaux et influences étrangères dans la construction du droit d'auteur français' in L Pfister and Y Mausen (eds), *La construction du droit d'auteur, Entre autarcie et dialogue* (Presses de la Faculté de droit et Sciences Politique de Montpellier 2013) 86, who also mentions, in relation to this 'inaliénable' part of property, Trolong and Pardessus, but in fact rightly doubts that the German influence from the end of the eighteenth century (Fichte in particular) had been at the time influential on its French supporters.

not to be excluded from the protection of the law if they could not be reduced to a bare quantitative *savoir faire*, a simple activity of 'research', or a form dictated by necessity. In other words, compilations were not excluded so long as the work revealed in its form 'conceptions' that were 'proper' to its author [*conceptions qui lui ont été propres*].[98] This decision, formulated under the influence of the famous prosecutor Merlin de Douai, was certainly able to retain at the same time an objective definition of novelty and a subjective definition of what the author produced. Arguing the case, Merlin had referred to compilations whose construction could resemble 'magnificent palaces', genuine 'creations' – terms and words which reflected the idea that authors' productions would be indisputably protected if they could demonstrate, somehow, the subjective part of the author's self.[99] Throughout the first half of the nineteenth century, the courts roughly applied the criteria of protection determined by the Court in 1814, until it became more explicitly subjective, especially from the second half of the nineteenth century onwards.

This evolution can be well illustrated by two important decisions. In 1857, the supreme judges of the *Cour de Cassation* decided, in a case dealing with artistic property, that 'however well-known the features of a commonplace article [*les traits d'un type commun*] may be, and in spite of the fact that tradition requires any copy to respect those features, this indispensable fidelity still leaves space for the talent of the artist, allowing him to create a work that bears a *special* character, and which becomes as such a property protected by law'.[100] This formulation has been understood as establishing a clear opposition between the 'banality of the subject' and the 'originality of the work'.[101]

The second ruling arrived in April 1861. Dealing this time with the protection of telegraphic news, the Court of Appeal of Bordeaux emphasised that the work had to bear 'in some way, the imprint of the personality' [*en quelque sorte, l'empreinte de sa personalité*] of its creator, a formulation which would later became symbolic of what subjective originality could convey.[102] In relation to photographic productions, the same expression would also be used by the Court of Paris in April 1862.[103] Although the

---

[98] *Leclerc v Villeprend and Brunet*, *Cour de Cassation*, 2 December 1814, Sirey 1812-1814.1.63, available, with translation, at < http://www.copyrighthistory.org/record/f_1814a>.

[99] Philippe-Antoine Merlin de Douai, *Répertoire universel et raisonné de jurisprudence* (Tarlier, 5th edn 1825) 277: 'Compiler de cette manière, ce n'est pas copier, c'est créer; c'est faire ce que ferait un architecte qui, après avoir démoli un édifice gothique, en emploierait tous les matériaux pour élever un superbe palais, un temple majestueux.'

[100] *Fontana v Public Attorney*, *Cour de Cassation*, 13 February 1857, Dalloz 1857.1.111. This case is available at <http://copyrighthistory.org/record/f_1857>.

[101] Pfister, 'L'auteur, propriétaire de son œuvre' (n 2) 571.

[102] *Havas, Bullier & Co. v Gounouilhou*, Court of Bordeaux, 22 April 1861 (and *Cour de Cassation*, 8 August 1861) Dalloz 1862.1.137. This case is available, with translations, at <http://copyrighthistory.org/record/f_1861>.

[103] *Betbéder et Schwalbé v Mayer and Pierson*, Court of Paris, 10 April 1862 (and *Cour de Cassation*, 28 November 1862), Dalloz 1863.1.53. These decisions are available, with translation at <http://www.copyrighthistory.org/record/f_1862:

Que leur perfection, indépendamment de l'habilité de la main, dépend en grande partie, dans la reproduction des paysages, du choix du point de vue, de la combinaison des effets de

word 'originality' was not used frequently at this stage, these expressions approved by the judges indicated that the 1793 Act would not protect all products of intellectual labour. Nevertheless, as works of all kinds could claim the protection of the law, without taking into 'account their merit or their importance', it meant that, so long as the threshold was deemed to be satisfied, at least theoretically, the author of *'la cuisinière bourgeoise'* would hold the same rights as 'Lamartine of Chateaubriand'.[104]

Indeed, despite the fact that literary works had formed the basis of the abovementioned legislative debates, in reality the courts had to deal with the scrawniest productions of the mind, such as almanacs, descriptive notices and commercial circulars; such works could not be excluded on principle.[105] Combined with a subjective threshold of protection, this heterogeneous character of the object of a property in judicial practices doubtless explains the numerous hesitations of the judges. This is so despite the notion stressed by Pouillet that the true value of a literary production had, again, to be only appraised by the public.[106]

4.2 The Protection of Non-pecuniary Rights

The formalisation of this subjective dimension, created within the French courts in search of judicial criteria for protection, was consubstantial with the protection of non-pecuniary rights; that is, while the emergence of 'moral rights' can be seen as the result of extrinsic influences, it is important to recognise the link between the repeated assumption of some kind of indivisibility characterising the bond between an author and his work, and the protection of non-pecuniary rights. As early as the first half of the nineteenth century, in fact very soon after the consecration of authorial property by the 1793 Act, the courts considered it legitimate to protect the extra-patrimonial interests in relation to the publication of a literary and artistic work, although the legal motivations for such decisions remained at the time primarily general, if not enigmatic. In June 1814, the *Tribunal civil de la Seine*, expressed the principle that, even after its transfer, a work should bear the name of its author, and should be published in 'the state in which it has been sold' [*dans l'état où il a été vendu*].[107] Other decisions

---

lumière et d'ombre, et, en outre, dans les portraits, de la pose du sujet, de l'agencement du costume et des accessoires, toutes choses abandonnées au sentiment artistique et qui donnent à l'oeuvre du photographe l'empreinte de sa personnalité.

[104] Eugène Pouillet, *Traité théorique et pratique de la propriété littéraire et artistique et du droit de représentation* (Imprimerie et librairie générale de jurisprudence, 2nd edn 1894) 38.

[105] In fact, even Renouard, *Traité des droits* (n 46) vol 2, 114, seemed to regret the judges' concern [*sollicitude*] for these trivial productions of the mind. He was in fact mentioning the same reality for the English copyright, by quoting Richard Godson, *A Practical Treatise on the Law of Patents for Inventions and of Copyright; with an Introductory Book on Monopolies, Illustrated with Notes on the Principal Cases* (London 1823).

[106] Pouillet, *Traité* (n 104) 42: 'le goût public juge ensuite du mérite de chacun, et classe bientôt les écrits parus d'après leur véritable valeur'.

[107] *Tribunal Civil de la Seine*, 17 March 1814, quoted in Pfister, 'Particularismes' (n 97) 88, and reported in Renouard, *Traité des droits* (n 46) vol 2, 332–33. The bibliography on this evolution is vast. Along with Stig Strömholm, *Le droit moral de l'auteur en droit allemand, français et scandinave, avec un aperçu de l'évolution internationale* (PA Norstedt et Söner

followed. For example, in 1828, the judges confirmed the right of disclosure, the work being unable to be seized and sold by creditors until its author chose to publish it.[108] Another significant decision is the famous Lacordaire's case, in 1845, in which the right of disclosure was tackled again by the court, reaching the same conclusion.[109] The judges of the *Tribunal Correctionnel de Lyon*, who condemned the unauthorised publication of l'abbé Lacordaire's speech against his will (soon followed by the Court of Appeal) stressed clearly that an author had a double interest in relation to his intellectual production. Along the pecuniary effects, pertaining to his 'moral personality and in the very interest of his doctrines', he must always retain 'the right of reviewing and correcting his work, to keep it under his surveillance, and to chose the time and the mode of publication'.[110] Although, as we have seen, this preoccupation was not new, judges themselves were henceforth clear, in appeal, on the absolute necessity for an author to protect himself 'against a dangerous alteration' of his work.[111]

The full recognition of authorial non-pecuniary rights under more explicit and assumed juridical bases would only be resolved by the most senior judges, at the very beginning of the twentieth century. Meanwhile, natural rights or Lockean property became framed, if not outshone, by a new set of doctrinal arguments coming from across the Rhine and deriving from a Kantian perspective on author's rights founded on personality rather than property. From the 1860s onwards monographs and articles by French jurists such as Alfred Bertauld and André Morillot probably contributed to the theoretical grounding of this evolution.[112] Morillot, in particular, sought to clearly

---

Förlag 1966) vol 1. See also G Michaelides-Noirot, *Le droit moral de l'auteur* (librairie Arthur Rousseau 1935), A-M El-Tanamly, *Du droit moral de l'auteur sur son œuvre littéraire et artistique* (Editions A Pédone 1943). On a comparison between the droit d'auteur and copyright system, see Y Gendreau, 'Genèse du droit moral dans les droits d'auteur français et anglais' (1988) 13 Revue de la Recherche Juridique, Droit Prospectif 41–59.

[108] *Veuve Vergne v créanciers Vergne*, Court of Paris, 11 January 1828, *Recueil général des lois et des arrêts* (Recueil Sirey), 1er série 1791–1830, 9e vol (1828–1830) 5, also available at <http://www.copyrighthistory.org/record/f_1828>. The musical work concerned in this case, a mass, had even been represented two times in a church.

[109] *Marie v Lacordaire*, Court of Lyon, 17 July 1845 (10 June, for the *Tribunal correctionnel de Lyon*), Dalloz, 1845.2.128, available at <http://www.copyrighthistory.org/record/f_1845>.

[110] Ibid 128:

Attendu, en effet, que, quel que soit le sujet traité, quelle que soit la forme primitive sous laquelle l'œuvre intellectuelle s'est produite, l'auteur a un double et légitime intérêt à conserver le droit exclusif d'éditer son ouvrage ou d'en céder la propriété; […] Qu'au point de vue de sa personnalité morale et dans l'intérêt même de ses doctrines, l'auteur doit toujours conserver le droit de revoir et de corriger son œuvre, d'en surveiller la fidèle reproduction, et de choisir le moment et le mode de sa publication …

[111] Ibid 129.

[112] See André Morillot, 'De la nature du droit d'auteur, considéré à un point de vue général', (1878) Revue critique de législation et de jurisprudence 111; André Morillot, 'De la personalité du droit de publication qui appartient à un auteur vivant' (1872–73) Revue critique de législation et de jurisprudence 29. Both are available, with a full translation for the former, at <http://www.copyrighthistory.org/>; Alfred Bertauld, *Question pratiques et doctrinales de Code Napoléon* (Imprimerie et Librairie générale de Jurisprudence, 1867). On this question, and the impact of this 'German' influence on French jurists at the end of the nineteenth century, such as

define the nature of the right accruing to the author by virtue of his creation. His basic premise was that 'the right of authorship may not be considered a form of property in the juridical sense of the term'.[113] Essentially concerned with property's most obvious technical consequences, it meant that 'the work [*l'oeuvre*] cannot be appropriated'.[114] Indeed, he asked, how could such a *droit réel* be reconciled with the fact that an artistic or literary creation 'may not exist outside of the intelligence which conceived it, and which alone may contemplate it beneath the physical characteristics it has been made to take on, by an entirely intellectual operation'.[115] Consequently, Morillot endeavoured to sustain, under the influence of the German jurist Rudolf Klostermann, a dualist approach to the author's right that strictly distinguished personal or extra-patrimonial authorial rights, inalienable by nature, and the purely economic transferable right of reproduction: 'While the first is entirely moral, the second is entirely pecuniary'.[116]

Yet, these doctrinal efforts still had to conform to the letter of the law, that is the 1793 Act. The legalisation of divorce, in 1884, would in particular urge the courts to deal again concretely with extra-patrimonial interests of the author. The question raised was whether literary and artistic property formed fully part of the joint estate that had to be divided between husband and wife when their separation occurred. Did this property entail no more than a sole economic exclusive right, and should be therefore fully included in the total estate to be divided, according to the contract of marriage? In the famous case involving the divorce of the musical composer, Charles Lecocq, the Court of Appeal of Paris, on 1 February 1900, relied on Lakanal's report to claim that the property consecrated in 1793 was a particular kind of property with a specific regime of laws.[117] Combining this approach with a negative interpretation of the Code Civil, which did not retain the author's rights in its classification of movable or real-estate goods, the judges decided that the 'property of these rights', among them the 'moral rights' [*droits moraux*] allowing the author to revise his work, could not fall into the joint estate of the spouse.[118] Indeed, the court found that to allow the contrary would lead to the most detrimental results, as a spouse or her beneficiaries would

---

Saleilles, Lyon-Caen, Darras, etc, see in particular the synthesis of Laurent Pfister, 'Particularismes' (n 97) 95–97. See also the commentary of Ambroise Colin, under the Lecocq's case of 1902 (infra, n 117).

[113] Morillot ibid 112.

[114] Ibid 114. And for Bertauld (n 112) 184: 'Ce droit [the author's right] ne dérive pas pour nous d'un prétendu droit de propriété que l'homme aurait sur lui-même. – L'homme, en effet, n'est pas tout à la fois homme et chose, sujet et objet, être actif et être passif, souverain et esclave, et le lien qu'il crée entre lui et la matière n'est pas à créer entre les diverses parties de lui-même.'

[115] Morillot, *De la nature* (n 112) 113.

[116] Ibid 127. Bertauld defended a 'monist' approach, the right of author being fully personal and inalienable, the pecuniary part being only incidental.

[117] *Cinquin v Lecocq, Cour de Cassation,* 25 June 1902 Dalloz Périodique, 1903.1.8: '... une propriété d'un genre tout à fait différent des autres propriétés'.

[118] *Cinquin v Lecocq,* ibid. The Court of Paris moreover stated that the general law of 9 March 1891 (on the rights of the surviving spouse) 'n'a pas d'avantage compris dans la communauté conjugale la propriété même de ces droits, bien que sa discussion au Parlement ait longuement porté sur la concordance de ses dispositions générales avec la loi particulière du 14 juill. 1866'. Dalloz Périodique, 1903.1.9.

become masters, against the author himself, of his 'most sacred' and his 'most personal' rights.[119] In doing so, it appears that the judges sought to reconcile the personal aspect, or at least the perception of it being derived from the revolutionary legislation, with a more Germanic influence, probably Bertauld's monist approach.[120]

Two years later, the prosecutor general Manuel Achille Baudoin appeared in the same case before the *Cour de Cassation*. Although he was ready to admit that the author's right 'is not a property in the ordinary sense', he was not prepared to state, as the judges on appeal had, that the right of the author was not transferable; that argument, in his view, would ostensibly be contrary to the 1793 Act and the article 1 letter in particular.[121] The supreme judges, in June 1902, thus overruled the earlier Lecocq decision, and laconically asserted that upon the dissolution of the joint estate, the total to be divided between the spouses had to include the 'monopoly of exploitation' [*monopole d'exploitation*] pertaining to the works published during the conjugal union, but that the pooling of this emolument could not derogate from the right of the author, which is 'inherent in his very personality [*inhérente à sa personnalité même*], to subsequently make some modifications to his creation or even to suppress it'.[122] André Morillot was involved in the case as a lawyer, and thus arguably influenced this 'dualist' solution,[123] knowing that, ultimately, the supreme judges remained legally concerned, in their decision, with the respect of the 1793 revolutionary act (and what they chose to interpret from it), that is the implementation of laws specific to literary property.[124]

---

[119] Ibid 9:

que la femme ou ses ayants cause deviendraient maîtres, contre l'auteur même, des droits les plus sacrés, les plus personnels, les plus difficiles à arracher raisonnablement à la volonté productive dont ils émanent, à la direction d'une intelligence dont ils sont comme la substance; – Que le compositeur dont les droits sur une partition même cédée ne sont pas contestés, ne pourrait plus remanier sa creation, l'embellir des gains d'un labeur continué ou d'un talent agrandi, la détruire au besoin, s'il la trouve inférieure à l'idéal vers lequel il se sent porté et élevé […].

[120] In this sense, see Pfister, 'Particularismes' (n 97) 99, who also stresses, nevertheless, this emphasis of the Court of Paris on the 'spirit of the revolutionary legislation'. The judges indeed considered that the solution adopted, the fact that the Lecocq's 'propriété des oeuvres musicales' could not fall in the joint estate, as principles 'ressortant des dispositions légales sur la matière, en leur texte et en leur esprit […]' (1903.1.9).

[121] Dalloz Périodique, 1903.1.10 and 12.

[122] Dalloz Périodique, 1903.1.14:

Attendu que des principes susénoncés il résulte que, lors de la dissolution de la société d'acquêts, la masse partageable doit, en l'absence d'une clause contraire du contrat de mariage, comprendre le monopole d'exploitation afférent aux oeuvres publiées par l'un ou l'autre des époux durant l'union conjugale, sans toutefois que la mise en commun de cet émolument puisse porter atteinte à la faculté de l'auteur, inhérente à sa personnalité même, de faire ultérieurement subir des modifications à sa creation ou même de la supprimer …

[123] In this sense, see Pfister, 'Particularismes' (n 97) 99.

[124] Certainly not without some hesitations, since in 1887, in a case relating to international copyright treaties, the supreme judges refused explicitly, although very temporarily, to describe author's right as a property: *Grus v Ricordi and Durdilly & Co, Cour de Cassation*, 25 July 1887, Dalloz Périodique 1888.1.5.

In the course of the next 50 years, the courts went on to develop a system of *droit moral* that secured the protection of first disclosure and integrity of the works in reliance on the 1793 Act. Eventually, the 1957 Act superseded the 1793 Act and, codifying its judicial implementation, provided in article 1 that the exclusive incorporeal property right encompassed not just pecuniary attributes but intellectual and moral attributes as well.[125]

5. CONCLUSION

Bearing in mind its heavy and ambiguous natural property rights heritage, it is understandable that the emergence of *droit moral* in France may appear as some kind of misgrowth, which, moreover, can be roughly explained as a sort of palliative tool introduced to compensate authors for the definitive loss of perpetual exclusivity.[126] Nonetheless, as this chapter has sought to emphasise, even before the German doctrine influenced French jurists in formulating a more explicit designation of authors' personal non-pecuniary interest, such personalisation was already consubstantial to legal discourses on literary property, which became in fact a powerful ally for those seeking expansive rights, although certainly a double-edged weapon.[127] Far from the medieval *'propriété-jouissance'* in which property was limited to its simple use under God, Nature or the King, by the time of the Revolution, property, within a whole legal system in transition, also bore thus an irreducible 'affective echo' [*résonance affective*], that highlighted, beyond its most obvious consequences as a *droit réel*, the 'fullness of the right of its holder' [*plénitude du droit du titulaire*].[128] This was particularly the case for the 'most incontestable' of all properties mentioned by Lakanal; but it also explains why, for example, the *Cour de Cassation* itself held in 1827 that families' patronymic 'is their exclusive property', even if, in precise legal terms, a patronymic name did not bear a *jus disponendi*.[129]

Ultimately, it seems actually that this evolution remains all the more open to criticism when the *droit moral* is viewed as an obstacle to people's immediate access to (popular) culture, with some, notably Americans, 'preferr[ing] happiness as a goal to

---

[125] Law of 11 March 1957 on literary and artistic property, art 1: 'L'auteur d'une œuvre de l'esprit jouit sur cette œuvre, du seul fait de sa création, d'un droit de propriété incorporelle exclusif et opposable à tous. Ce droit comporte des attributs d'ordre intellectuel et moral, ainsi que des attributs d'ordre patrimonial, qui sont déterminés par la présente loi.'

[126] See notably Baldwin (n 5) 103, who states, as one of his chief concerns, that from 'inherent contradictions of natural rights property had sprung the notion of moral rights'.

[127] Strömholm (n 107) 41.

[128] Anne-Marie Patault, *Introduction historique au droit des biens* (PUF Droit fondamental 1989) 235–37, who also speaks of the '*charge affective*' of the right of property. See also, for example, René Savatier, *Les métamorphoses économiques et sociales du droit privé d'aujourd'hui (Seconde Série): L'universalisme renouvelé des disciplines juridiques* (Paris, Dalloz 1959) 6: 'Le droit d'être pleinement propriétaire figurait ainsi parmi les Droits de l'Homme, comme garantie essentielle, et virtuellement égale pour tout homme, de sa liberté individuelle.'

[129] Sirey, 155. 2. 1827, quoted by Patault (n 128) 237.

pursue'.[130] Such an interpretation itself probably raises important further questions, which this chapter does not address. Nevertheless, it would be valuable to look beyond the allegedly traditional attachment of France (and Germany) for an elitist and exclusive 'high culture', not to mention the incestuous relationship between men of letters and the political power, to assess more precisely (and more widely than such emblematic and recurrent examples such as the John Huston's *Asphalt Jungle* colourisation case) the extent to which these specific non-pecuniary prerogatives are impeding the satisfaction of this noble goal.[131]

---

[130] Baldwin (n 5) 405. This vast goal, indeed explicit (but following Liberty) in the Declaration of Independence, is of course inversely supposed to explain the less tormented legal developments of the copyright system, until the growing Berne Convention began to alter its hypothetical purity. It reminds us incidentally that happiness was also mentioned in the 'Montagnarde' declaration of rights, within the Constitution of 24 June 1793!

[131] About the Asphalt Jungle's affair, see Baldwin (n 5) 1, 45, and from 47 (a paragraph entitled 'Colour as a sin'). On *Droit moral* before the courts, and especially the judicial regulation of its *post mortem auctoris* 'abuses', see, for example, André Lucas, Henri-Jacques Lucas and Agnès Lucas-Schloetter, *Traité de la propriété littéraire et artistique* (4th edn, Litec LexisNexis 2012) 542–51.

19. Codified anxieties: Literary copyright in mid-nineteenth century Spain
*Jose Bellido**

1. INTRODUCTION

Although there is a general consensus among historians that the 1847 Literary Copyright Act constituted the 'first copyright law in Spain',[1] there is a surprising lack of studies on what led up to such an important legislative event.[2] While this was the first law to 'extensively and clearly recognise copyright' in Spain,[3] yet to be adequately explored is the actual, and vast, transition from the ancient regime to liberalism that made the act possible.[4] Furthermore, relatively little is known about the political and legal framework that influenced the period between the enactment of the Spanish Civil Code, in 1844, and the drafting of a special copyright bill that was eventually submitted

---

*   Manuscript sources are from depositories and collections abbreviated as follows: AS = Archivo Senado (Madrid, Spain), ACE = Archivo de Consejo Estado (Madrid, Spain), AHN = Archivo Historicó Nacional (Madrid, Spain), CADN = Centre des Archives diplomatiques de Nantes (Nantes, France), NA = National Archives (Kew, United Kingdom), CLAR = Clarendon Papers, Bodleian Library (Oxford, United Kingdom), HOWD = Howden Papers, Bodleian Library (Oxford, United Kingdom). Thanks to Ramón Casas Vallés, Raquel Xalabarder, Lionel Bently, Martin Kretschmer, ALADDA and those who made possible the Spanish entry in the digital archive *Primary Sources on Copyright (1450–1900)*. Thanks also to Sandrine Mansour Merien, David Lobenstine, Isabella Alexander, Tomás Gómez-Arostegui and Cara Levey for comments on previous drafts.

[1] María Pilar Cámara Águila, 'La ley por la que se declara el derecho de propiedad a los autores y a los traductores de obras literarias, y establece las reglas oportunas para su protección, de 10 de junio de 1847' (1999) 2 Revista Pe i, 167, 167. See also JA Martínez Martín, *Vivir de la pluma. La profesionalización del escritor 1836–1936* (Marcial Pons 2009) 53; Juana Marco Molina, *La propiedad intelectual en la legislación española* (Marcial Pons 1995) 20; Juana Marco Molina, 'Bases históricas y filosóficas del derecho de autor' (1994) 47 Anuario de Derecho Civil 121, 140–45; Héctor S Ayllón Santiago, *El derecho de comunicación pública directa* (Editorial Reus 2011) 76.

[2] The full text of the Spanish Literary Copyright Act (1847) was published in the official bulletin (*Gaceta*) on 15 June 1847 and the legislative collection, *Colección legislativa de España, vol. 41* (Imprenta Nacional, 1849) 154. More accessible is the text published recently in the (1999) 2 Revista Pe i 187.

[3] Raquel Sánchez García 'La propiedad intelectual en la España contemporánea' (2002) 12 Hispania 993, 1000.

[4] For interesting references, see Javier García Martín, 'De la apropiación penal a la propiedad literaria: sobre los orígenes del derecho de propiedad intelectual en España (siglos XVIII–XIX)' (2000) 93 Revista de la Facultad de Derecho de la Universidad Complutense 105, 138. Molina, 'Bases históricas' (n 1) 136.

to the Senate in early February 1847.[5] This chapter is a modest attempt to highlight some of the circumstances that paved the way for such a legislative proposal, tracing the events that brought the Senate to this portentous moment. A discussion of the contingent factors leading to the bill's signing shows a number of interesting and distinguishing features of the political context in which the legislative draft was first written. For instance, it unveils the crucial intervention of the Royal Council, a group of advisers key to the Spanish Government,[6] who were involved in the discussions over the future regulation of copyright. Moreover, the historical account also shows how the framing of the Act was highly controversial and did not stop the emergence of dissenting voices such as the one formulated by the royal councillor and well-known Spanish codifier, Pedro Sáinz de Andino (1786–1863), who defended a very different and now forgotten vision of the nature and function of copyright.[7] Although the legislative enactment was an important milestone in Spanish copyright history, the focus on the law's emergence enables us to discuss a more interesting aspect of international copyright. With this approach it is possible to consider – as some scholars have already suggested – copyright history not merely as a 'history of laws'.[8] Rather, the history embraced here also involves the appreciation of domestic copyright politics and their relationship with international aspirations. The history of Spanish copyright in the mid-nineteenth century shows the varieties of national copyright narratives, and how they not only shaped but were also shaped by international copyright anxieties.[9] In fact, the history demonstrates how modern copyright in Spain emerged as a practical response to different anxieties about Spain's place in the world.[10]

---

[5] *Diario de las Sesiones de Cortes*. Senado, Appendix I (18), 20 February 1847, 221. Spain had a bicameral Parliament, composed of the Congress of Deputies (the lower house) and the Senate (the upper house).

[6] The advisory role was perhaps the most important function performed by the Royal Council. However, some commentators also highlight the importance of the Council in the configuration of the constitutional monarchy in Spain; see Alejandro Nieto, 'El Consejo Real como elemento de gobierno constitucional' (1977) 84 Revista de la Administración Pública 537, 546. The functions of the *Consejo Real* were established on 6 July 1845 (see Ley de 6 de julio de 1845, de organización y atribuciones del Consejo Real).

[7] A summary of his appointment as a royal councillor is found in Jesús Rubio, *Sáinz de Andino y la codificación mercantil* (Centro Superior de Investigaciones Científicas 1950) 54–55 and Juan Cruz Alli Aranguren, *Derecho, Estado y Administración en el pensamiento de Sáinz de Andino* (Universidad Pública de Navarra 2005) 183–84. For an interesting biography, see Fernando Toscano de Puelles, *Sáinz de Andino. Hacedor de Leyes* (Edit Excma Diputación Provincial de Cádiz 1987).

[8] Martin Kretschmer, Lionel Bently and Ronan Deazley, 'The History of Copyright History (Revisited)' (2013) 5 WIPOJ, 35, 36.

[9] Bently and Sherman have already noted the importance of bilateral treaties for the making of modern copyright in the UK, see Brad Sherman and Lionel Bently, *The Making of Modern Intellectual Property Law. The British Experience, 1760–1911* (CUP 1999) 111–28, 167–68.

[10] Similarly, in the British context, see Brad Sherman, 'Remembering and Forgetting: The Birth of Modern Copyright' (1995) 10 IPJ 1.

2. BILATERAL PRESSURE

By February 1845, there were rumours in the Madrid press that a copyright bill was circulating among different governmental departments in the Spanish capital.[11] However, the real media interest in copyright came later that year, on the last day of October, when the French Ambassador in Spain, Charles-Joseph, Comte de Bresson (1798–1847),[12] wrote a letter to the Spanish Secretary of State, Francisco Martínez de la Rosa (1787–1862).[13] Bresson requested a concrete international agreement, a treaty signed by France and Spain.[14] Although his letter was part of a much wider history of French policy in the defence of literary copyright,[15] it also had a very specific objective: to persuade Martínez de la Rosa, who was particularly interested in the issue, to sign a bilateral copyright treaty.[16] The final aim was to convince the Spanish Government of the need for a bilateral agreement, which could link the copyright interests of various nations of Europe.[17] Thus, with this initial diplomatic move, the

---

[11] *El Eco del Comercio*, 20 February 1845, 4; 'Gacetilla de la capital' *El Heraldo* (Madrid, 20 February 1845) 3. A first Commission was formed in 1840 by the following members: Martínez de la Rosa, Gil y Zárate and Bretón de los Herreros. The memorandum and a draft of a copyright bill were presented to the Parliament by Agustín de Armendáriz. See AHN Legajo 11329. Expediente 15, sección Consejos.

[12] Bresson has been described recently by RB Mowat as a 'very experienced and even brilliant diplomatist' in RB Mowat, 'The Near East and France' in Adolphus William Ward and George Peabody Gooch (eds), *The Cambridge History of British Foreign Policy, vol 2, 1815–1866* (CUP 2011) 195; see also David Thatcher Gies, *Theatre and Politics in Nineteenth-Century Spain. Juan de Grimaldi as Impresario and Government Agent* (CUP 1988) 169.

[13] Ministère des Affaires étrangères: instructions given to the Comte de Bresson, Paris (8 October 1845) CADN Madrid Ambassade, Carton B158 (1845–53).

[14] Comte de Bresson to Martínez de la Rosa, Madrid (31 October 1845) AHN Legajo 8477, Sección Estado.

[15] Pura Fernández, 'En torno a la edición fraudulenta de impresos españoles en Francia: la convención literaria hispano-francesa (1853)' in *Estudios de literatura española de los siglos XIX y XX (Homenaje a Juan María Díez Taboada)* (Instituto de Filología CSIC 1998) 200–09; Carlene A Adamson 'Boz as Tutor: The Reception of Dickens in Francophone Belgium' in Michael Hollington (ed), *The Reception of Charles Dickens in Europe* (Bloomsbury 2013) 257, 262. See also Victor Lefranc, *Rapport fait au nom de la Commission chargée d'examiner le projet de loi relatif à la convention conclue le 5 nov. 1850 entre la France et la Sardaigne, pour la protection des droits de la propriété littéraire et artistique contre la contrefaçon étrangère* (Impr de l'Assemblée nationale 1851); Adolphe Joanne, 'De la contrefaçon des œuvres littéraires et artistiques' *L'Illustration* (Paris, 28 December 1850).

[16] Earlier laws had been introduced that regulated copyright in dramatic works (1837) and Martínez de la Rosa was member of the legislative committee that was appointed to prepare those laws. Further, he had also presided over a study section on copyright in one of the most famous cultural institutions in Madrid, the Ateneo de Madrid ('Athenæum of Madrid'); see Rafael María de Labra, 'El Ateneo de Madrid' (1878) 59 Revista Contemporánea 85. There is an excellent account of this period in Lisa Surwillo, *The Stages of Property: Copyrighting Theatre in Spain* (University of Toronto Press 2007) 55–57; Margarita Llopis, 'Propiedad intelectual: antecedentes de la Ley de 1879' (1979) 29 Boletín de la Anabad 31, 34.

[17] It is significant that Muquardt's work on international copyright was timely translated into Spanish, see Charles Muquardt, *La propiedad literaria internacional, la falsificación de libros y la libertad de la imprenta* (Rivadeneyra 1852).

French anticipated a series of positions and legal strategies. In order to facilitate the drafting of the proposed agreement, and hence precipitate a response from the Spanish, a model was attached to the letter. To avoid any possible discrepancies, justifications and explanations were also provided. From the outset, the 'reciprocal' benefit – the respective protection of literary and artistic works in each country – was made clear.[18] The letter included a number of interesting references. The model attached was a bilateral agreement that, two years earlier, had been signed between France and Sardinia[19] and was complemented by a subsequent treaty signed in 1846.[20] The examples provided came from the Ministry of Foreign Affairs (*Ministère des Affaires étrangères*).[21] The underlying idea was to convince the Spanish that an arrangement 'would not damage either of the contracting parties', since – Bresson argued – 'the value attributed to Spanish books circulating in France was more or less equivalent to that of French books circulating in the Iberian peninsula'.[22] He also claimed that a bilateral agreement could standardise what was otherwise heterogeneous and varied. For example, the agreement could streamline the legal treatment currently given to each of the country's literary works.[23] Furthermore, translations made in either country would also be regulated.[24] In cases of infringement, judges would decide according to the respective laws, 'in the same way as if the violation had been committed to the detriment of a national literary work'.[25] In the face of such an explicit demand, and with the need for a diplomatic response, the Spanish Government began an internal inquiry to clarify the state of Spanish copyright law and to attempt an answer to the Comte de Bresson.[26]

---

[18] 'J'ai donc l'honneur de proposer au Gouvernement de la Majesté Catholique de négocier une convention qui garantisse réciproquement dans le deux Pays la propriété des œuvres d'esprit et d'art'. Bresson to Martínez de la Rosa, Madrid (31 October 1845) AHN Legajo 8477, Sección Estado.

[19] 'Première Convention conclue le 28 août 1843 pour garantir, en France en Sardaigne la propriété des œuvres littéraires et artistiques' *Bulletin des Lois*, IX, série no 1046; see also the reference to the bilateral treaty in *La Esperanza* (Madrid, 20 May 1845) 2.

[20] 'Deuxième Convention conclue le 22 avril 1846 pour garantir, en France en Sardaigne la propriété des œuvres littéraires et artistiques' *Bulletin des Lois*, IX, série no 1294.

[21] '[U]n arrangement de ce genre entre le Gouvernement du Roi et le gouvernement Espagnol, n'imposerait d'ailleurs aux contractants de sacrifice d'aucune espèce, car il résulte du tableau général du commerce de la France publie par l'administration de nos Douanes, pour l'année 1843' in Bresson to Martínez de la Rosa, Madrid (31 October 1845) AHN Legajo 8477, Sección Estado.

[22] '[Q]ue le valeur attribue aux livres Espagnols introduits en France correspond' in ibid.

[23] Article 1 Première Convention conclue le 28 août 1843 pour garantir, en France en Sardaigne la propriété des œuvres littéraires et artistiques *Bulletin des Lois*, IX, série no 1046.

[24] Ibid art 2.

[25] Première Convention ibid.

[26] On the central importance of techniques and artefacts such as files to govern and administer political and legal issues, see José Luis Rodríguez de Diego, 'Evolución histórica del expediente' (1988) Anuario de Historia del Derecho Español 475; Cornelia Vismann, *Files: Law and Media Technology* (Stanford UP 2008).

3. FROM THE FAILURE OF THE AGREEMENT TO THE ENACTMENT OF THE LAW

Over the next few months, a file was prepared at the Ministry of State, which was eventually sent 'along with a translated copy' to the Home Secretary and the Ministry of Education.[27] From there, it was passed to the Royal Council for review in February 1846.[28] When the file was sent to the Royal Council, a prominent member of the Ministry of Education, Antonio Gil de Zárate (1793–1861), highlighted a significant obstacle: even if the Spanish Government was willing to reach a bilateral agreement, they could not give an immediate response to the French Ambassador 'since Spain still lacked a literary copyright law'.[29]

Although there were some laws regulating the press,[30] and even a set of laws covering copyright over dramatic works, there was no general copyright act as such whatsoever.[31] That absence was a problem, according to the Royal Council, who recognised that Gil de Zárate had a 'well-founded concern'.[32] In fact, the lack was considered a hindrance that would inevitably condemn negotiations with 'foreign' countries to fail.[33] For the Royal Council, the basis of 'every agreement and contract' could be nothing other than a specific copyright law.[34] It was essential to 'secure, first and foremost, copyright in our own country' in order to then attempt to 'extend it through treaties'.[35] After realising the normative deficit, which the Royal Council believed was a legal weakness, the Home Secretary decided to include a draft of a copyright bill in the file that was sent to the Royal Council, to be dealt with 'as quickly as possible'.[36]

The urgency of the matter was rapidly apparent. By the time the Royal Council received the file, it was already the summer vacation, and the legislative draft would

---

[27] 'Nota de Gil de Zárate 28 de julio de 1846' ACE G-045-012.
[28] 'Minuta de remisión del expediente al Consejo de 1 de agosto de 1846' ACE G-045-012.
[29] 'Nota de Gil de Zárate (n 27).
[30] See generally Fernando Cendán Pazos, *Historia del derecho español de prensa e imprenta (1502–1966)* (Editora nacional 1974). In particular, the Council considered the press regulations that had been declared in force by the Royal Decree of 4 January 1834. For an interesting study of these specific regulations, see José Eugenio de Eguizábal, *Apuntes para una historia de la legislación española sobre imprenta* (Imprenta de la Revista de Legislación 1873) 174–78.
[31] See generally Surwillo (n 16).
[32] Dictamen. Consejo Real. Sección de Gobernación. Madrid 10 de Noviembre 1846, ACE G-045-01.
[33] Dictamen. Consejo Real. Sección de Gobernación. Madrid 10 de Noviembre 1846, ACE G-045-012.
[34] Ibid.
[35] Ibid.
[36] 'Nota del Ministro de Gobernación al Vicepresidente del Consejo Real. Madrid 1 de agosto de 1846' and 'Proyecto de ley sobre propiedad literaria remitida a informe del Consejo por Real Orden de 1 de agosto de 1846' ACE G-045-012. And this news was suddenly leaked to the press, see 'Propiedad literaria' *El clamor público* (Madrid, 20 August 1846) 4; El *Popular* (Madrid, 19 August 1846) 4.

have to be submitted prior to Parliament's next session, which started in September.[37] Some of Madrid's press expressed concern that the issue would ultimately come to a bureaucratic halt with the Royal Council.[38] That was not the case this time. On this occasion, the Council members overcame their long-earned reputation for slowing down legislative developments. The matter was dealt with and a legal opinion was issued. After receiving the original bilateral treaty request to which the draft of the copyright bill had been added, the Royal Council met on a number of occasions.[39] It is perhaps worth pointing out here that the Council was a Francophone body,[40] comprised of counsellors described by some historians as 'former political émigrés to the north of the Pyrenees'. In other words, the Royal Council was made up of counsellors who felt 'a deep admiration for the French Government'.[41] Although the Council was characterised by such a particular ethos, it was nevertheless very difficult to reach a consensus among more than two dozen politicians of varied political tendencies, a group that included such diverse and complex personalities as Pedro Sáinz de Andino, Alberto Baldrich, Marquis of Vallgornera (1786–1864), and Antonio de los Ríos Rosas (1812–73).[42]

In November 1846, the Council began to draw up a report, divided into two sections. The first part, which would end up being the most substantial, focused on the domestic legislation. The second part dealt with the original request – and the reason for which the file was passed to the Council: the possibility of a bilateral copyright agreement between France and Spain. Regarding the bill, the Council proposed 'some useful and necessary changes' to the Home Secretary's proposed draft.[43] According to the report, the Council's changes would 'strengthen' and 'consolidate copyright of intellectual works'.[44] It also included other changes aimed to harmonise the rights of authors and owners in an attempt to balance private and public interests. The aim was to guarantee the alignment of these interests while ensuring the protection of the country's literary industry.[45] Although recent academic studies have suggested that debates surrounding the 1847 law did not include a thorough discussion of the nature of intellectual property

---

[37] 'Nota del Ministro de Gobernación al Vicepresidente del Consejo Real. Madrid 1 de agosto de 1846' ACE G-045-012.

[38] 'Propiedad literaria' *El clamor público* (Madrid, 1 September 1846) 4.

[39] Sesión del 29 y 30 de septiembre de 1846, ACE G-045-012.

[40] Jordana de Pozas notes the similarities between the French and the Spanish institutions, for instance, regarding the number of members appointed, see Luis Jordana de Pozas, *El Consejo de Estado Español y las Influencias Francesas a lo largo de su evolución* (Publicaciones del Consejo de Estado 1953) 23.

[41] Ibid 22.

[42] For biographical sketches, see Eduard de Balle 'L'Albert de Baldrich, un vallenc capdavanter de la cultura' (1982) 1 Quaderns de Vilaniu [Valls] 5; Juan del Nido y Segalerva, *Historia política y parlamentaria de Antonio de los Ríos Rosas* (Congreso de los Diputados 1913); Consuelo Martínez-Sicluna, 'La defensa de la legalidad y de las instituciones: Antonio de los Ríos Rosas' (2006) Revista Foro 85.

[43] 'Borrador de Dictamen. Consejo Real. Sección de Gobernación. Dirigido al Excmo Sr Vicepresidente del Consejo Real, 30 October 1846' ACE G-045-012.

[44] Dictamen. Consejo Real. Sección de Gobernación. Madrid (10 November 1846) ACE G-045-012.

[45] Ibid.

in general or copyright in particular,[46] the truth is that there was a deliberative study on this very matter within the Royal Council. The Royal Council considered 'mental' or 'intellectual works' to be the primary focus of the law.[47] In order to standardise the aforementioned interests, it considered the need to establish copyright restrictions as a fundamental part of the law. There is more: the Council drew attention to a term that would end up becoming a trendy word in our own day: 'intellectual capital'.[48] The Council's report guided the Parliament by distinguishing literary copyright from other types of property, such as industrial property. More significantly, the Council's report was also an attempt to crystallise a modern definition of copyright in Spain. Indeed, it advised new wording in multiple instances so that the resulting legislation would be more abstract and forward looking. For instance, 'print' was replaced with 'reproduce'. And the Council recommended a technologically neutral definition of 'copy' in order to remain relevant to not-yet-developed technologies. Finally, the Council also suggested a gradual standardisation of the different methods of acquiring literary copyright. In sum, the Royal Council's recommendations reveal a surprisingly advanced understanding of copyright with which the Council is not often credited; we can see from their recommendations the emergence of modern copyright arising a few months before what many historians consider the birth of modern copyright in Spain.[49]

In contrast to the Council's careful attention to a future domestic copyright legislation, the fate of the request for a bilateral agreement with France was remarkably different. The Council's main focus was the legislative draft, which took priority in their response. The report began with references to the draft, positioning domestic copyright law as if it were the most important issue, and then later went so far as to disregard the agreement with France. According to the Council, discarding such an agreement was a necessary and logical step, for it was not 'wise to advise the signing of treaties'.[50] If a bilateral treaty with France was signed, 'it might impose on the country [Spain] a significant hardship and a serious problem without adequate compensation'.[51] In the Council's comments we can see how its members were aware that any deliberation over the legal status of translations and other imported works should be in the hands of the nation's legislative body. The Council warned of the risks for the development of Spain's economy and literature if the country pursued international agreements without first having a domestic copyright law. This explains the Council's stress on the possible damage that could arise from the signing of a treaty with France, and the report's primary focus on the need for domestic legislation. The logic of the situation and the contingency of the moment placed national legislation on the immediate political horizon; the possibility of a bilateral treaty was left for a more appropriate occasion. However, it is possible to find a link between domestic legislation

---

[46] Molina, 'Bases históricas' (n 1) 142.
[47] Dictamen. Consejo Real. Sección de Gobernación. Madrid (10 November 1846) ACE G-045-012.
[48] See, for instance, David J Teece, *Managing Intellectual Capital* (Clarendon Press 2000).
[49] For a comprehensive analysis of the emergence of 'modern' copyright in Britain, see Sherman and Bently (n 9).
[50] Dictamen. Consejo Real. Sección de Gobernación. Madrid (10 November 1846) ACE G-045-012.
[51] Ibid.

and international relations. This link crystallised in the increased attention given to the international dimension of copyright by Spanish legislative and executive authorities. Moreover, as we look further we see that the domestic law was already haunted by the need to embrace an international copyright dimension. In this sense, the law was burdened by the urge to connect national and international copyright. If a bilateral relationship presupposed the existence of a national law, making reference to such agreements in the proposed law itself would make things easier. This is how the Council appears to have understood the situation and they recommended the inclusion of a specific article that established the terms and attempted to determine the parameters of the bilateral treaties, even though no such treaties yet existed. We can fully appreciate this by looking at subsequent events. Five years after the promulgation of the Literary Copyright Act (1847), the same institution, the Royal Council, issued a radically different report, now favourable to a bilateral treaty.[52]

The Royal Council submitted its report in January 1847, just a few days after a new government was elected.[53] Almost all of the Council's recommendations were incorporated into the draft presented to the Senate by the Minister of Commerce, Education and Public Works. We can see the Council's additional influence, beyond the report itself, in the fact that several royal councillors, such as the Marquis of Vallgornera and the Marquis of Falcés, were also politicians who actively participated in the Senate's discussions of the copyright bill.[54] Bearing in mind that the Council was a Francophone institution, and that the bill from which the proposal came was shaped most directly by its members, it is no coincidence to find textual influences and echoes between French and Spanish copyright laws, as a number of copyright historians have already pointed out.[55] Furthermore, it is no coincidence that copyright was limited, following 'the doctrine accepted by the main European countries'.[56] At least some members of the Parliament argued that it was convenient for Spain to imitate the legislation and practices of other countries.[57] Despite being inspired by French law, the Marquis of Falcés also indicated that the Parliament had taken into account Russia, Germany and 'other countries where literary and artistic property was recognised'.[58]

---

[52] Dictamen. Consejo Real. Sección de Gobernación. Madrid (1 May 1952) ACE G-045-012.
[53] This government was led by Carlos Martínez de Irujo, Duke of Sotomayor and Marquis of Casa Irujo y McKean (1802–55).
[54] 'Cortes' *El Espectador* (Madrid, 11 March 1847) 3, 'Proyecto de Propiedad Literaria' *El Heraldo* (Madrid, 11 March 1847) 1.
[55] María Pilar Cámara Águila (n 1). See also generally Molina, 'Bases históricas' (n 1).
[56] Dictamen. Consejo Real. Sección de Gobernación. Madrid (10 November 1846) ACE G-045-012.
[57] Speech by Tarancón at the Senate (11 March 1847), Mariano Vergara, *Legislación de la Propiedad Literaria en España* (Librería de Moya y Plaza 1864) 17.
[58] Speech by Marquis of Falcés at the Senate (11 March 1847), Vergara (n 57) 32.

4. THE MAKING OF THE LAW

In order to promote the bill, the proponents of literary copyright formulated their arguments in a very creative way. One of the most remarkable speeches was given by one of the bill's promoters, Roca de Togores, Marquis de Molins: he used a sort of environmental imagery to describe literary copyright, casting the work as a 'plant'.[59] The analogy developed a particular vision of property in which the fruits benefited the whole society, but the benefit was so great that the one providing the seed should be specially rewarded and given a property right.[60] In addition to that notable speech, other politicians also helped imagine different ways to construct the concept of property in copyright. Especially significant in this regard was the suggestion that the duration of copyright should be calculated from the moment that the book was written and not from the death of the author. Tactically, the proponents of literary copyright delivered speeches in both the Congress and the Senate claiming that the property at stake was not 'really' property but just 'fictitious property'.[61] This definition of literary copyright as a legal fiction was repeated throughout the parliamentary discussions by different speakers.[62] No doubt the description was repeatedly used because it was quite handy, not only for evaluating the peculiarity of the property in question, but also for justifying the specific textual choices made in the bill. Likewise, it is not surprising that the argument continued with the idea of literary copyright as a balancing mechanism between the interests of the author and the public.[63] Parliamentary support was secured by using utilitarian justifications. This formula may sound familiar to contemporary copyright scholars. It was just the right time to say that 'the more encouraging rewards given, the greater the number of works published'.[64]

The law was passed by both the Senate and the Congress and was finally sanctioned by the Queen in June 1847. The resulting Act itself featured several unusual aspects. Although the concept of the 'work' in copyright was not fully developed, parliamentary discussions had already exhibited more abstract definitions of the intangible property than the text used in the final version of the law. It seems that despite, and possibly because, modern copyright in Spain was as yet not fully crystallised,[65] the law perceived the relevant material worthy of protection in a very curious manner. This can be appreciated if we look at the first section of the law that aimed to protect authors of

---

[59] Roca de Togores, speech to the Senate (11 March 1847), Vergara (n 57) 23.

[60] For a thought-provoking reflection on the controversial role of environmental concepts in contemporary discussions of intellectual property, see Mario Biagioli, 'Nature and the Commons: The Vegetable Roots of Intellectual Property', in Jean-Paul Gaudillière, Daniel J Kevles, Hans-Jörg Rheinberger (eds), *Living Properties: Making Properties and Controlling Ownership in the History of Biology* (Max Planck Institute for the History of Science 2009) 241.

[61] Gómez de la Serna, speech to the Congress (17 April 1847) in *Diario Sesiones de las Cortes*, Congreso de los Diputados, 1402.

[62] Ondovilla, speech to the Senate (10 March 1847), Vergara (n 57) 10; see also 'Cortes' *El Espectador* (Madrid, 11 March 1847) 3 [García Goyena].

[63] Ayllón Santiago (n 1) 76.

[64] García Goyena, speech to the Senate (10 March 1847), Vergara (n 57) 11–12.

[65] Roca de Togores, speech to the Senate (10 March 1847), Vergara (n 57) 23.

original 'writings'.[66] Here we can observe how the law was a hybrid between old and modern copyright conceptions. While the explicit reference to 'writings' instead of 'works' seemed to imply a material understanding of the intangible property, the law was made somehow abstract in different ways, for instance, by introducing the concept of originality. The link was difficult and the awkward early appearance of the adjective 'original' made some politicians uncomfortable; several senators requested its deletion.[67] Nevertheless, and following the standard set up by literary copyright, other authors' works were assimilated within the law, such as the authors of translations,[68] maps, musical works, dramatic works,[69] sculptures and paintings.[70] By extending the concept of literary copyright, established from the beginning of the Act, to encompass a much larger group of people, the law provided an avenue for becoming an author and a possibility for the emergence of the idea of copyright in a 'work'. Furthermore, there was another feature that shows how the structure of the Spanish law had shifted to a 'modern' way of understanding copyright. The standard duration of the property was settled in the following manner: 50 years *after the death of the author*.[71] Post-mortem copyright of 50 years was considered sufficient time to cover two generations. More interestingly, the policy was deemed appropriate to enable the close relatives to benefit from an author's work posthumously.[72]

Since the law was already haunted by an international anxiety, translations attracted special attention. The impulse was to include translations in the same phrase as original writings and not to state them separately in another provision of the law. A great deal of parliamentary discussion had already concentrated on how to regulate translations. And considerable insight was offered into the complex task of translating. Not only were translations explicitly authorised in the law, they were also fully recognised as mechanisms through which an object of property and its legal subject were legitimately produced.[73] They were – as we have just mentioned – assimilated to original writings. The special care, even the obsession, with protecting translations was made even clearer when we look at the nuanced regulation they received. In particular, the law offered different legal treatment based on the language from which the translation was made. And distinctions proliferated. The term granted to translations of works from living languages was significantly shorter than the one given to translations from dead languages.[74] On the one hand, the need to enhance competition in the marketplace was

---

[66] Article 1 Spanish Literary Copyright Act (1847).
[67] Ondovilla, speech to the Senate (11 March 1847), Vergara (n 57) 27.
[68] Article 3 paras 1 and 2 Spanish Literary Copyright Act (1847).
[69] Article 16 Spanish Literary Copyright Act (1847).
[70] Article 3 para 5 Spanish Literary Copyright Act (1847).
[71] For a detailed analysis in a more general context, see Sam Ricketson, 'The Copyright Term' (1992) 23 IIC 753; see also the discussion concerning the copyright term established in the Berne Convention (1886) in Sam Ricketson and Jane Ginsburg, *International Copyright and Neighbouring Rights: The Berne Convention and Beyond* (2nd edn, OUP 2006) 530–31.
[72] Roca de Togores, speech to the Senate (10 March 1847), Vergara (n 57) 23–24.
[73] José Vicente y Caravantes, 'Sobre la Propiedad Intelectual' in Florencio García Goyena, *Febrero o Librería de Jueces, Abogados y Escribanos*, vol 1 (Imprenta y Librería de Gaspar y Roig 1852) 222–23.
[74] Article 3 para 1 and 4 para 2 Spanish Literary Copyright Act (1847).

the main rationale for limiting the property over translations from living languages such as French or English. But it also flowed, on the other hand, from an understanding that translating from some languages, such as French, was an easy job.[75] 'Even a child can do it,' said one speaker in the Senate.[76] At the same time, the law established more distinctions on the regulation of translations. It also began to focus on the form in which the translation could be made. In so doing, it categorised translations in prose and verse differently, providing a system of varying durations for copyright in translations. In that sense, the regulation of translations was intimately related to the question of how long their copyright should last. While the general copyright term of life plus 50 years applied to translations in verse and translations in prose from dead languages, the law imposed a reduced term to translations in prose from living languages, limiting them to life plus 25 years.[77] The line of reasoning behind this regulation seems to have been that the task of translating verse was considered to be more difficult than translating prose.[78]

Despite such detailed regulation on translations, there was nevertheless a remarkable legal silence. No reference was made to the possibility of translating from Spanish to Catalan and Basque (Euskera) or vice versa. The issue was however raised at the Congress. When the deputy for Barcelona, Tomás Illa y Balaguer (?–1869), asked for a clarification on this point,[79] he was quickly answered that these 'dialects' were comprised within the Spanish language.[80] As the linguistic distinction opened a knotty political issue, the deputies did not continue the discussion. Nevertheless, a quick glance at the parliamentary debates shows how some specific translations were particularly disturbing for Spanish politicians. One of the main frustrations for them concerned translations and reprints of Spanish works made in France. Their concern was not that they were made in France but that they were distributed in the so-called *provincias de ultramar* (overseas provinces) and in Spain's former colonies.[81] However, the Parliament appeared impotent in regulating that market.[82] Even though it seemed an unreachable political objective, the Parliament discussed possible ways to make a statement for the Spanish Government, and a very timid reference was drafted and

---

[75] And when the distinction was made, there was a discursive 're-entry' of originality. For instance, it was possible to hear that underlying that distinction between translations from live and dead languages there was a difference between 'original' and 'non-original' translations. See Burgos' speech to the Senate (11 March 1847), Vergara (n 57) 30. See also Vicente y Caravantes (n 73) 220–23.

[76] Barrio Ayuso, speech to the Senate (11 March 1847), Vergara (n 57) 29.

[77] For a criticism of these distinctions, see Manuel Danvila y Collado, *La Propiedad Intelectual* (Imprenta de la Correspondencia de España 1882) 370.

[78] Burgos, speech to the Senate (11 March 1847). Vergara (n 57) 30.

[79] Illa y Balaguer, speech to the Congress (17 April 1847), Vergara (n 57) 114.

[80] Arrazola, response to Illa y Balaguer at the Congress (17 April 1847), Vergara (n 57) 115.

[81] Vázquez Queipo, speech to the Congress (17 April 1847), Vergara (n 57) 133; see also Manuel González Hontoria, *Los convenios de propiedad intelectual entre España y los países ibero-americanos* (Tomás Minuesa de los Ríos 1899).

[82] Pastor Díaz' speech to the Congress (17 April 1847), Vergara (n 57) 133.

included in the law. It was not a request but a declaration of aspirations for the government to 'try' bilateral copyright agreements.[83]

Another interesting feature of the law was the possibility of literary extracts becoming legitimate works. According to section 11 of the Act, extracts could be authorised based upon their merits and importance. In a procedure that could be regarded as an expropriation, it was for the government (and not for the courts) to authorise the publication of extracts on a case-by-case basis after hearing experts and interested actors. If the extract received copyright protection, the author of the work being extracted had a right to be compensated; the amount of such compensation decided by the government on a declaration of public utility.[84]

The law also established a legal deposit.[85] Deposit and protection came together in a provision that required the publisher or the author to deliver two copies of the work, prior to publication, to the National Library and to the Ministry of Education in order to gain protection.[86] No section of the law caused more interpretative nightmares than this one. This can be observed by the numerous attempts to clarify and to provide instruction that took place between 1847 and 1857. And that happened partially because soon after the enactment of the law, rules suddenly transformed the deposit obligation into a sort of copyright registry.[87] Receipts were given, indexes were produced and book entries were organised. Regulations for the creation of provincial registries in order to cover the entire Spanish territory were also issued. While these efforts to create a sort of copyright registry at the National Library in Madrid seem to have had some initially reasonable results, the first steps – which obliged civil governors to report back the index produced and the works registered – were more problematic. Troubling questions were specially raised in relation to artistic works, and this was because the wording of article 5 of the law referred to artistic 'works' instead of 'writings'.[88] This term created a concern among artists who wondered about the type of obligation being imposed on them. Fearing for the loss of protection, the obvious questions the artists asked were the following: how should artists perform that obligation? Where artistic works should be deposited?[89] In 1850, the sculptor Sabino Medina y Peñar (1812–88) presented a petition for clarification about whether artistic works were precluded from the legal deposit requirement. Instead of an exemption, the answer he received was a set of specific deposit rules for artistic works.[90] Depending on the specific category of artistic work, a form of deposit was specified. For instance, deposit rules for sculptures were fulfilled with the delivery of the mould cavity. If the mould was too big to be deposited, a rigorous and sufficient drawing of the work in a minor scale could be used as a substitute. Engravings and cuttings also required

---

[83] Article 26 Spanish Literary Copyright Act (1847); see also the discussion 'Cortes-Senado' *El Español* (Madrid, 12 March 1847) 1.
[84] Article 11 Spanish Literary Copyright Act (1847).
[85] Manuel Danvila y Collado (n 77) 367.
[86] Article 13 Spanish Literary Copyright Act (1847).
[87] See the description of the copyright registry in the circular (12 August 1853) published in *El Clamor Público* (Madrid, 24 August 1852) 2.
[88] *El Áncora,* (Barcelona, 7 April 1850) 78.
[89] Ibid.
[90] *La España* (Madrid, 4 April 1850) 2.

Literary copyright in mid-nineteenth century Spain 435

registration, with the copies to be delivered being the most expensive ones. To make things more complicated, the deposit was not to be made to the National Library and the Ministry of Education but to the National Museum and the Academy of Arts.[91]

The enactment of the law also raised other even more practical issues and legal technicalities that had to be considered. One of the most difficult problems was the effect the law would have on those who had already acquired exclusive deals in relation to their material. If the law – as the legislators thought – was creating a new type of subjective right given to authors, the transitional solution was to create a retroactive provision.[92] Although the transitional clause drafted and sanctioned seemed clear, thus making the property return to the authors on the expiration of any contract or privilege granted whatsoever, some commentators thought otherwise. They interpreted it as a *tabula rasa* and without retroactive effects. Their attempts to interpret the law in such straightforward manner failed. A few years later, a petition to declare dramatic works in the public domain was bluntly rejected.[93] Not only was the retroactive effect a difficult issue to be regulated, the way in which the retroactive effect worked and the effect it had on the making of the public domain would continuously re-emerge in Spain as the most stubbornly persistent copyright issue throughout the nineteenth century.[94]

5. A DISSENTING VOICE

One of the politicians absent from the Senate's discussions of the law was a well-known Spanish jurist of the era: Pedro Sáinz de Andino, a member of the Royal Council. Owing to a twist of fate, Sáinz de Andino was not able to attend the parliamentary debates: he was sworn in as a senator just days after his new colleagues had approved the bill in the Senate and sent it to the Congress.[95] He would undoubtedly have participated in the debates if he had been appointed earlier because he had a very specific view of the nature of literary copyright. He had already made his opinion clear at an earlier stage. In the report sent in January 1847 by the Royal Council to the Spanish Government, his dissenting opinion stood out. While the Council first recommended, and then the Parliament agreed, to codify copyright as limited property, Sáinz de Andino argued that copyright should be declared perpetual. Although the copyright term that both the Royal Council and the Parliament established was the longest in Europe, he could not find any reason to justify such a restriction. For him, property was the 'basis on which society rests' and he could not see there to be any

---

[91] 'Royal order of March 22 1850 clarifying article 17 of Spanish Literary Copyright Act (1857) (*Real Orden de 22 de Marzo aclarando el artículo 13 de la ley de 10 de Junio de 1847 sobre propiedad literaria*)' in Luis de Ansorena, *Tratado de la Propiedad Intelectual en España* (Sáenz de Jubera Hermanos 1894; republ 1911) 49–51.
[92] Article 28 Spanish Literary Copyright Act (1847).
[93] Petition lodged by Javier Paulino to the *Gobernador Civil* (Valencia, Oct 1858) AHN Legajo 11390. Expediente 63, sección Consejos.
[94] See Jose Bellido, Raquel Xalabarder and Ramón Casas Vallés (2011) 'Commentary on Spanish Copyright Law (1879)' in L Bently and M Kretschmer (eds), *Primary Sources on Copyright (1450–1900)*, <www.copyrighthistory.org>.
[95] 'Nombramiento de Senadores' *La Esperanza* (Madrid, 17 March 1847) 4.

'difference in origin or in quality' between literary and real property. The rejection of differences did not mean a lack of recognition, since in Sáinz de Andino's opinion the intangible character of literary property 'of course' had to be recognised. In other words, his view was that the only aspect that needed to be solemnly declared was the right to those objects that were 'rigorously abstract'.[96]

However, and more importantly, any domestic regulation over these intangible properties should not be triggered by an international anxiety. There was not any rush. Sáinz de Andino continued to make both his aesthetic and legal distance to the Council's report very clear, pointing out that 'copyright does not fall upon ideas, but rather the benefit that the author might derive from the exclusive right to his publication'.[97] His dissenting voice insisted on labour as the main feature upon which copyright was justified. He highlighted the link between labour and property to show that it might be a case of mental or intellectual labour, but labour above all. The legal subject that emerged in Sáinz de Andino's view was thus a specific figure who legitimated copyright: the author as labourer. And thus, he continued, 'if there is a common original identity in the causes of real and literary copyright, why should not their effects be the same?'[98] With this argument he found himself in a distant position to that of the Council's majority, which considered that the 'mental' or 'intellectual' character of the property enabled copyright to be classified as a different legal category.[99]

Perhaps even more interesting is another of Sáinz de Andino's atypical reflections about copyright. He did not consider the moment of creation of a work as the main reason for the existence of literary copyright. Rather, he specifically linked it to the moment of its publication. It is therefore not a surprise that he located the legal benefit in the *use* made of the property. Thus we understand why Sáinz de Andino focused on the *use* of the property rather than on its *substance*. The *use* was so significant that – he thought – it should not be left unregulated and therefore he emphasised the need for a legislative intervention to regulate how a piece of intellectual labour was exploited.[100] Sáinz de Andino argued that any responsible legislation had to introduce 'the necessary requirements to clearly establish the conditions upon which literary copyright was considered abandoned for not having been used and as a result, enabling the property to form part of the public domain'.[101] If one of the main functions of the Royal Council was – according to Sáinz de Andino – to preserve and protect the public interest, he criticised the Council's report for its vagueness regarding the contours of the public domain, a criticism that would also accompany the modern system of copyright that emerged in the late nineteenth century.[102] What his dissenting opinion also reveals is how fractured and polyvalent these early debates about national copyright laws really

---

[96] Andino's dissenting opinion (2 January 1847) ACE G-045-012.
[97] Ibid.
[98] Ibid.
[99] Ibid.
[100] Ibid.
[101] Ibid.
[102] Ibid.

were – in contrast to the simplified vision of copyright law that we get when we only look at the history after the internationalisation of copyright.

6. THE RISE OF BILATERALISM

In 1847, one speaker at the Spanish Senate, Manuel Joaquín Tarancón y Morón (1782–1862), had imagined a future free from bilateral copyright agreements altogether.[103] Despite the fact that the Literary Copyright Act contemplated a desire for international agreements,[104] he could not foresee the possibility of stitching together the copyright laws of different countries.[105] In his view, the variety of legislation produced insurmountable obstacles. One decade later, Spain had signed not only one but two bilateral copyright agreements.[106] The senator's pessimism proved totally wrong; the difficulties were overcome. And this was accomplished in many different ways. In fact, a 'complex web of bilateral agreements' was formed throughout the nineteenth century.[107] Retrospectively, we may now perceive different patterns of bilateralism in the decades following the Spanish law. These patterns correspond with different waves of diplomatic negotiations; the first could loosely be concentrated on the 1840s and 1850s, and the second surely began in the 1880s.[108] Of all the considerable differences among them, perhaps the most interesting one refers to the way in which negotiations were seen. By the 1880s the content of the negotiations themselves (and not just the treaties that emerged as a result) was much more visible in newspapers and legal journals, such as *Bibliographie de la France*, *Clunet* and *Le Droit d'Auteur*.[109] It is also clear that the negotiations were conducted by a new group of people – an emerging set of international and professional actors such as ALAI (*Association Littéraire et Artistique Internationale*).[110] In other words, new institutional projects for international copyright perspectives had arisen.[111] Nonetheless, what the negotiation of all bilateral copyright agreements offered was a direct challenge to political predictions. The

---

[103] Speech by Tarancón at the Senate (11 March 1847), Vergara (n 57) 19.
[104] Article 26 Literary Copyright Act (1847).
[105] Similarly, see *Apuntes sobre la Propiedad Literaria en respuesta al artículo inserto en la Gazeta de Madrid* (Imprenta de J Ferrer de Orga 1838) 4.
[106] Franco-Spanish Copyright Agreement (1853) and Anglo-Spanish Copyright Agreement (1857).
[107] Isabella Alexander, *Copyright and the Public Interest in the Nineteenth Century* (Hart Publishing 2010) 142.
[108] Catherine Seville, *The Internationalisation of Copyright Law: Books, Buccaneers and the Black Flag in the Nineteenth Century* (CUP 2006) 49–50. See also Jose Bellido, *Copyright in Latin America: Experiences of the Making (1880–1910)* (PhD thesis, Birkbeck, University of London 2009) ch 4; José Miguel Rodríguez Tapia, 'Centenario de la Unión de Berna: 1886–1986. Precedentes históricos' (1986) Anuario de Derecho Civil 885.
[109] For a detailed account of the internationalisation and the influence of these journals, see Jose Bellido, 'The Editorial Quest for International Copyright (1886–1896)' (2014) 17 Book History 380.
[110] See Jose Bellido, 'El Salvador and the Internationalisation of Copyright' (in this volume).
[111] 'The rise of interest groups and the interplay of domestic and international copyright' in Alexander (n 107) 147–53.

success or failure of negotiations was not only dependent on an assessment of the compatibility of the two countries' laws but mainly on the control of different contingent factors, especially the time at which the negotiations were introduced and the way in which they were handled. For instance, it is not a surprise that the Anglo-Spanish bilateral copyright negotiations were triggered after the Franco-Spanish bilateral agreement was concluded in 1853.[112] While the negotiation of the treaty between Spain and the UK was thwarted for three years, it was finally signed in 1857.[113]

Although bilateral agreements in the mid-nineteenth century are often seen as a chaotic process,[114] the growth of bilateralism can also be understood as a network of agreements that emerged in a cascade following a series of diplomatic strategies. To a certain extent, we could say that political connections became the main feature behind the signature of the Spanish and French copyright treaty in 1853. That, at least, was the view of a privileged observer, John Hobart Caradoc, Lord Howden (1799–1873), British Minister at Madrid.[115] According to him, such an arrangement was so advantageous to the French that it constituted an 'undeniable proof' of their influence in Spanish politics.[116] As mentioned above, the institution that had paved the way for a bilateral agreement, by recommending a domestic copyright law to precede it, was also considered a Francophone political body, the Royal Council.

In Lord Howden's account, such influential persuasion had been manifested in two different ways. First, the perseverance of French ambassadors and secondly, the 'decorations' distributed by the French among politicians and literary men in order to persuade them. The Franco-Spanish bilateral copyright treaty was signed in December 1853 and ratified in early January 1854.[117] The bilateral copyright treaty and the diplomatic skills developed by the French had also immediately grabbed the attention of Lord Howden. Such recognition should not surprise us, as the Spanish press had been commenting on and criticising the negotiations for many months before the treaty was signed.[118] And for many days, attacks on the treaty covered the front pages and featured in the editorial comments of newspapers such as *La España* and *El Clamor*

---

[112] A general overview is given by Pura Fernández (n 15) 200–09.

[113] *La Época* (Madrid, 26 May 1857) 3. For an analysis of the copyright formalities in these agreements, see Stef van Gompel, *Formalities in Copyright Law: An Analysis of Their History, Rationales and Possible Future*, (Kluwer Law International 2011) 121–24.

[114] See generally Seville (n 108).

[115] On the British Legation and Howden, see Frances Erskine Inglis, *The attaché in Madrid; Or, Sketches of The Court Of Isabella II* (Appleton and Company 1856) 90–96.

[116] Lord Howden, Madrid to the Earl of Clarendon (16 March 1854) CLAR, Ms.CLAR dep. C. 20.

[117] 'Convenio celebrado entre España y Francia para asegurar recíprocamente en dichos Estados el ejercicio del derecho de propiedad literaria y artística, firmado en Madrid á 15 de Noviembre de 1853' in *Documentos internacionales del reinado de doña Isabel II: desde 1842 a 1968* (Imprenta de Miguel Ginesta 1869) 80–83. See also *Gaceta de Madrid* (Madrid, 26 January 1854) 1; Vergara (n 57) 85.

[118] Ironical remarks of the 'great' treaty in *La Época* (Madrid, 24 January 1854) 2; and direct attacks to 'the real disaster of the copyright treaty' in *La Época* (Madrid, 1 February 1854) 2; *El Áncora* (Barcelona, 5 February 1854), 7; see also *Gaceta de Madrid* (Madrid, 23 February 1854) 1.

Público.[119] In February 1854, Howden's dispatch to the British Foreign Secretary, GWF. Villiers, 4th Earl of Clarendon (1800–70), enclosed the French-Spanish copyright treaty.[120] If France had obtained a favourable copyright treaty with Spain, the existing political inertia could allow Britain to sign a similar one. More precisely, if the French had used influence, the key issue was to concentrate on diplomatic form and manner. Spain could not refuse to sign a similar treaty with the UK: such a refusal would be discourteous. Lord Howden was a bit more cautious than the Foreign Office since he had witnessed how the press had attacked 'without mercy' the previous negotiations.[121] Nonetheless, his view was that the only way of avoiding press coverage that could jeopardise the negotiations was to broker 'a like convention' as quickly as possible.[122] In so doing, Howden was then convinced that the enterprise would succeed 'one way or another' for he had the support of the literary establishment in Spain.[123] What he could not have suspected was that his confidential communications with the Earl of Clarendon and the instructions conveyed thereof had been intercepted by the Spanish intelligence system.[124] The confidential dispatch between London and Madrid was leaked in London and translated and read in Madrid.[125] So when Lord Howden wrote to propose a 'nearly identical convention', such a move was already expected by the Spaniards.[126] As a result, the initial steps taken by the British diplomat in Madrid were not as simple and easy as his Foreign Office had first envisaged.

Nevertheless, another negotiating opportunity immediately arose. The Spanish heads of the government suddenly changed during the summer of 1854.[127] As soon as the new Spanish Minister of Foreign Affairs took office, Howden informed him of the British desire 'to conclude a similar' copyright treaty to the one Spain had signed with the French.[128] Not only did he insist on the idea of a 'like convention' and a 'speedy agreement',[129] he also tried to convince the newcomer that his predecessor in office had

---

[119] Front-page and editorial comments in *El Clamor Público* (Madrid, 27 January 1854) 1; front-page and editorial comments in *La España* (Madrid, 27 January, 31 January 1854).

[120] The reply to that dispatch was Earl of Clarendon, to Lord Howden (9 March 1854) AHC Legajo 8480, Tratados, Negociaciones, Inglaterra, 1857.

[121] Lord Howden, Madrid to the Earl of Clarendon (16 March 1854) CLAR, Ms.CLAR dep. C. 20.

[122] Lord Howden to Pacheco y Gutiérrez (19 August 1854) NA FO72/845.

[123] Lord Howden, Madrid to the Earl of Clarendon (25 May 1854) CLAR Ms.CLAR dep C. 20.

[124] 'Instrucciones recibidas por Lord Howden sobre la negociación de un convenio de propiedad literaria' AHN Legajo 8480, Exp 141, Tratados, Negociaciones, Inglaterra, año 1857.

[125] The confidential dispatch also included copies of the Anglo-French Copyright Treaty 1851.

[126] Lord Howden to Calderón de la Barca (16 May 1854) AHN Legajo 8480, Exp 141, Tratados, Negociaciones, Inglaterra, año 1857.

[127] An account is given in Victor Gordon Kiernan, *The Revolution of 1854 in Spanish History* (OUP 1966) 67–81.

[128] Lord Howden, Madrid, to Pacheco y Gutiérrez (19 August 1854) NA FO72/845.

[129] The beginning of the dispatch was also remarkable. Howden directly referred to the French-Spanish copyright treaty (1853). 'A convention on Literary Property having been concluded between the Country and France [...]' Lord Howden, Madrid, to Pacheco y Gutiérrez (19 August 1854) NA FO72/845.

agreed to everything and that it was just a matter of routine to sign the treaty. But again, the strategy did not work as smoothly as he had hoped; the response of the Spanish Minister was reluctant, to say the least. Obstacles and difficulties arose. For instance, the Spanish Minister suggested that reciprocity was impossible to achieve because the two systems created 'unequal rights'.[130] After this second drawback, there was an avalanche of correspondence in which Spain appeared to be particularly disinclined to sign an agreement. However, Howden remained determined and for more than two years he continued his particular crusade.[131] Two projects had become the main concerns of his political agenda: the copyright treaty and the postal convention.[132] A few weeks before he was removed from his post, he signed both of them.[133]

Although bilateral negotiations, especially when involving parties from countries using different languages, were often filled with discussions on the protection to be afforded to translations, this part of the negotiation did not manifest any particular difficulties. A similar treatment to the Franco-Spanish copyright treaty (1853) was accorded.[134] As a matter of fact, it was similar but not identical. Whereas the copyright treaty signed by the Spaniards with the French had established a ten-year duration rule, the translation right now agreed with the British comprised five years.[135] Bilateral copyright protection was also associated with formalities. Foreign authors were given three months after publication in Spain or the UK to register their works and translations in the Stationers' Hall and the Spanish Ministry of Public Works respectively.[136] Yet another final rule was also carefully negotiated: the period of time for the treaty. Limiting the duration was particularly important for the Marquis of Pidal, who was reported to be 'anxious' to sign in order to avoid the opposition of the press. And a short period was also beneficial for both countries in case things did not develop as expected. As countries did not want to compromise the future form of their international relations, the duration of the treaty was restricted to six years.[137]

---

[130] Pacheco y Gutiérrez, Madrid, to Lord Howden (16 October 1854) NA FO72/846.

[131] 'I take the liberty of calling to the remembrance of Your Excellency that some time ago a Convention for the Protection of Literary Property in both Countries was almost upon the point of being satisfactorily concluded between England and Spain', Lord Howden, to Juan de Zavala y de la Puente (4 February 1856) AHN Legajo 8480, Exp. 141, Tratados, Negociaciones, Inglaterra, año 1857.

[132] Lord Howden, Madrid to the Earl of Clarendon (25 March 1856) CLAR Ms.CLAR dep C 58.

[133] 'Convenio sobre obras literarias y artísticas entre España, la Gran Bretaña é Irlanda, firmado en Madrid á 7 de Julio de 1857' in *Documentos internacionales del reinado de doña Isabel II: desde 1842 a 1968* (Madrid: Imprenta de Miguel Ginesta 1869) 128–31. The official publication was *Gaceta de Madrid* (29 September 1857). Convention between Her Majesty and the Queen of Spain (Signed at Madrid, July 7, 1857) (1857–78) 60 *British Parliamentary Papers* 261.

[134] Manuel Danvila y Collado, *La Propiedad Intelectual* (Imprenta de la Correspondencia de España 1882) 170.

[135] Article 4 Bilateral Copyright Convention between Spain and UK (1857).

[136] Article 8 ibid.

[137] Article 13 ibid.

The agreement on the duration of copyright to be enjoyed in each country was the most disputed point during the negotiations.[138] Spanish copyright, as we have seen, had recently established a property rule of 50-year protection after the death of the author.[139] By contrast, English copyright had a different copyright duration system organised around the publication of the work and not the death of the author; the outcome was a more limited copyright term. It is no surprise then that the British opted for their national interpretation as the rule of duration. In that sense, British authors were going to achieve more protection than the Spaniards. It seems an elementary point, but the difference became important. In defining reciprocity, the negotiating parties were indeed radically disagreeing. According to the Spaniards, reciprocity meant a fresh term of copyright adopted for both in the treaty by looking at the minimum standard,[140] that is, equal to the term which the British law accorded to a Spanish author in the UK.[141] The British saw reciprocity in a different manner. What they meant by the term was not 'equitable' but 'legal' reciprocity: the principle was to give British authors the same reward and protection as the Spanish copyright law awarded to its own authors.[142] The divergence was so striking that it constituted a deadlock, a barrier at which the negotiations stopped during 1855 and 1856.[143] In January 1857, Howden took new steps to renew the negotiations.[144] He was then reported to be 'with hope' that the Spanish Government would give up on this issue.[145] For a few months he continued displaying diplomatic skills by convincing the Spanish Minister of Foreign Affairs, the Marquis of Pidal (1799–1865), of the importance of the treaty.[146] This was the final and decisive attempt and the Spanish Government eventually conceded.[147] The clause relating to the duration of copyright was signed according to the British draft.[148]

---

[138] A commission was appointed in Spain to study the proposal. The commission was formed by a book seller (Rivadeneyra); a minister and writer (Eugenio de Ochoa) and presided over by a writer and politician (Martínez de la Rosa). Report written by Albistur, July 15, 1854, AHN Legajo 8480, Exp. 141, Tratados, Negociaciones, Inglaterra, año 1857.

[139] Article 2, Spanish Literary Copyright Act (1847).

[140] 'The treaty between Spain and France had stipulated for a fixed and equal period of protection in each country' wrote Howden in 'Instrucciones recibidas por Lord Howden sobre la negociación de un convenio de propiedad literaria', AHN Legajo 8480, Exp 141, Tratados, Negociaciones, Inglaterra, año 1857.

[141] Pacheco y Gutiérrez, Madrid, to Lord Howden (16 October 1854) NA FO72/846.

[142] Lord Howden to Claudio Antón de Luzuriaga (24 December 1854) AHN Legajo 8480, Exp 141, Tratados, Negociaciones, Inglaterra, año 1857.

[143] 'Her Majesty's Government [...] reluctantly finds itself unable to accept the proposition'. Lord Howden, Madrid to Claudio Antón de Luzuriaga (18 May 1855) AHN Legajo 8480, Exp 141, Tratados, Negociaciones, Inglaterra, año 1857. See also Lord Howden, Madrid to Marquis de Pidal (22 December 1856) AHN Legajo 8480, Exp 141, Tratados, Negociaciones, Inglaterra, año 1857.

[144] Howden to Clarendon (7 January 1857) NA FO72/913; Vergara (n 57) 85.

[145] Clarendon to Sir James Emerson Tennent (Board of Trade) (5 June 1856) NA FO72/907.

[146] Pidal to Howden (21 January 1857) NA FO72/913.

[147] Telegram from Howden to Clarendon (29 May 1857) NA FO72/916.

[148] Article 1 Bilateral Copyright Convention between Spain and UK (1857).

7. CONCLUSION

Receiving a request to negotiate a bilateral copyright agreement set in motion the Spanish legislative machinery. It was a result of this external communication that the passing of a national law was viewed as something both urgent and inevitable. It is not a coincidence, therefore, that the 1847 law emerged in the same decade in which France, England and Austria had also passed their new laws and that the network of bilateral agreements emerged after these enactments. If there is a characteristic that defined the emergence of modern copyright in Spain, it is precisely this sense of law as the result of an external agitation. In examining the 1847 Spanish copyright law's birth and aftermath, it is possible to trace the interplay between bilateral negotiations and domestic politics. For instance, the drafting of the domestic legislation was crucially determined by the contribution of the Royal Council, a key state mechanism in the run up to the parliamentary discussion. As a counterpoint to the Royal Council's report, we have also shed light on the dissenting voice of Pedro Sáinz de Andino, who, paradoxically, was cautious and prudent in the face of such codifying anxiety. Although the Literary Copyright Act (1847) marks, for most contemporary historians, the genesis of modern copyright law in Spain, its reading and value changed throughout the nineteenth century. That sense of value, of course, also depended on who was doing the reading. Those who participated and promoted the law, not surprisingly, considered it to be extremely valuable.[149] Those lawyers involved in the writing of legal history also praised its momentum. But a different and interesting category of reader emerged in the nineteenth century as an effect of the interplay between domestic laws and bilateral negotiations. It seems that those who were commenting on Spain's law by examining foreign copyright laws had more criticisms to offer. An appendix to the well-known treatise *Febrero*, written by José Vicente y Caravantes (1820–80) in 1852, exemplifies this particular outward-looking tendency. His account was a typical, and an enjoyable, exercise – comparing Spain's 1847 Act with other laws such as the 1842 British Copyright Act and the 1846 Austrian Copyright Law – and it was indeed critical.[150] If we continue to look at additional scholarship about the Spanish Literary Copyright Act, we find a similar equation. The more internationally curious the reader was, the more critical he became.[151] The international perspective fostered the need for legislative reform. Our law was 'scientifically useless', one student claimed when defending his doctoral thesis.[152] 'How many defects can we find in it?' asked another copyright scholar.[153] And the answer was obviously 'many', because the law was now perceived as 'faulty, nonsensical, and full of absurdities'.[154]

If we consider the possible influence that international relations had on the crystallisation of copyright law in Spain, there is a remarkable point to be made

---

[149] Mariano Roca de Togores, *Bretón de los Herreros: recuerdos de su vida y de sus obras* (Tello 1883) 392.
[150] José Vicente y Caravantes (n 3) 220–23.
[151] Manuel Danvila y Collado (n 77) 370–71.
[152] Vergara (n 57) 81–82.
[153] Ansorena (n 91) 39.
[154] Ibid.

regarding nineteenth century history of bilateral negotiations and domestic enactments. Bilateral requests not only offered more nuanced responses, acknowledging the different stages of development of the economies and legal cultures of the different treaty-making states, they also facilitated the emergence of a particular perspective to assess and compare domestic legislations. In so doing, bilateralism offered opportunities for lawyers and politicians alike to look internationally in order to shape and/or criticise their domestic realm. Although such foreign influence was not completely decisive in the future of Spanish copyright, it became a driving force that precipitated and triggered the development of most ensuing domestic legislation. That impact on Spanish copyright was not just a question of legislative models, but a more provocative and pervasive effect: the possibility of developing a comparative perspective to cater for her own domestic anxieties.

Bibliography

The materials in this bibliography are generally limited to secondary sources that are works of history, with the exception of the section on the Company of Stationers and the Berne Convention, both of which list a number of primary sources.

Readers should also consult the various records and associated commentaries on the following website: L Bently and M Kretschmer, Primary Sources on Copyright (1450–1900), www.copyrighthistory.org. The national webpages are listed below under their national editors.

1. COPYRIGHT HISTORIOGRAPHY

Birnhack M, 'Copyright Pioneers' (2013) 5 WIPOJ 118

Bowrey K, 'Don't Fence Me In. The Many Histories of Copyright' (SJD, University of Sydney 1994)

Bowrey K, 'Who's Writing Copyright's History?' (1996) 18 EIPR 322

Bowrey K, 'Who's Painting Copyright's History?' in D McClean and K Schubert (eds), *Dear Images Art, Copyright and Culture* (Ridinghouse 2002) 257

Bowrey K and Fowell N, 'Digging Up Fragments and Building IP Franchises' (2009) 31 Sydney L Rev 185

Bracha O, 'Copyright History as History of Technology' (2013) 5 WIPOJ 45

Cornish WR, 'The Copyright History of What Must-Have-Been' in G Roussel and others (eds), *Mélanges Victor Nabhan* (Editions Yvon Blais 2004) 61

Deazley R, *Rethinking Copyright: History, Theory, Language* (Edward Elgar 2006)

Feather J, 'The Significance of Copyright History for Publishing History and Historians' in R Deazley, M Kretschmer and L Bently (eds), *Privilege and Property: Essays on the History of Copyright* (OpenBook Publishers 2010) 359

Hughes J, 'Copyright and Incomplete Historiographies: Of Piracy, Propertization, and Thomas Jefferson' (2006) 79 S Cal L Rev 993

Johns A, 'Language, Practice, and History' in L Bently, J Davis and JC Ginsburg (eds), *Copyright and Piracy: An Interdisciplinary Critique* (CUP 2010) 44

Kretschmer M, Bently L and Deazley R, 'The History of Copyright History (Revisited)' (2013) 5 WIPOJ 35

2. HISTORIES OF BRITISH COPYRIGHT LAW

2.1 General Surveys and Monographs

2.1.1 Primarily English law
Alexander I, *Copyright Law and the Public Interest in the Nineteenth Century* (Hart Publishing 2010)
Birrell A, *Seven Lectures on the Law and History of Copyright in Books* (London, Cassell & Co 1899)
Bracha O, 'Owning Ideas: A History of Anglo-American Intellectual Property' (SJD, Harvard Law School 2005)
Brodowski JH, 'Literary Piracy in England from the Restoration to the Early Eighteenth Century' (DLS, Columbia University 1973)
Cornish W, 'Part Five: Personality Rights and Intellectual Property' in W Cornish and others (eds), *The Oxford History of the Laws of England, Volume XIII 1820–1914: Fields of Development* (OUP 2010) 907
Deazley R, *On the Origin of the Right to Copy* (Hart Publishing 2004)
Deazley R, *Rethinking Copyright: History, Theory, Language* (Edward Elgar 2006)
Deazley R (ed), United Kingdom, Primary Sources on Copyright (1450–1900), www.copyrighthistory.org
Feather J, *Publishing, Piracy and Politics: An Historical Study of Copyright in Britain* (Mansell 1994)
Kaplan B, *An Unhurried View of Copyright* (Columbia UP 1967) ch 1
Loewenstein J, *The Author's Due: Printing and the Prehistory of Copyright* (Chicago UP 2002)
Lowndes JJ, *An Historical Sketch of the Law of Copyright* (2nd edn 1842)
Patterson LR, *Copyright in Historical Perspective* (Vanderbilt UP 1968)
Ransom H, *The First Copyright Statute* (U of Texas Press 1956)
Rose M, *Authors and Owners: The Invention of Copyright* (Harvard UP 1993)
Seville C, *Literary Copyright Reform in Early Victorian England* (CUP 1999)
Sherman B and Bently L, *The Making of Modern Intellectual Property Law: The British Experience, 1760–1911* (CUP 1999)

2.1.2 Primarily Scottish law
Couper WJ, 'Copyright in Scotland before 1709' (1931) 9 Records of the Glasgow Bibliographical Society 42
MacQueen HL, 'Intellectual Property and the Common Law in Scotland c1700–c1850' in CW Ng, L Bently and G D'Agostino (eds), *The Common Law of Intellectual Property* (Hart Publishing 2010) 21
Mann AJ, 'Book Commerce, Litigation and Art of Monopoly: The Case of Agnes Campbell, Royal Printer, 1676–1712' (1998) 18 Scottish Econ and Social Hist 132
Mann AJ, *The Scottish Book Trade 1500–1720* (Tuckwell Press 2000) ch 4
Mann AJ, 'Scottish Copyright Before the Statute of 1710' (2000) Jur Rev 11
Mann AJ, '"Some Property is Theft": Copyright Law and Illegal Activity in Early Modern Scotland' in R Myers, M Harris and G Mandelbrote (eds), *Against the Law:*

Crime, Sharp Practice and the Control of Print (Oak Knoll Press and British Library 2004) 31

Mann AJ, '"A Mongrel of Early Modern Copyright": Scotland in European Perspective' in R Deazley, M Kretschmer and L Bently (eds), *Privilege and Property: Essay on the History of Copyright* (OpenBook Publishers 2010) 65

McDougall W, 'Copyright Litigation in the Court of Session, 1738–1749 and the Rise of the Scottish Book Trade' (1988) 5 Transactions Edinburgh Bibliographical Society 2

McDougall W, 'Copyright and Scottishness' in SW Brown and W McDougall (eds), *The Edinburgh History of the Book in Scotland* (EUP 2012) vol 2, 23

Tompson RS, 'Scottish Judges and the Birth of British Copyright' (1992) Jur Rev 18

2.2 The Company of Stationers

2.2.1 Transcriptions of records and indices

Arber E (ed), *A Transcript of the Registers of the Company of Stationers 1554–1640 AD* (1875–94)

Eyre GEB (ed), *A Transcript of the Registers of the Company of Stationers from 1640–1708 A.D.* (1913–14)

Greg WW and Boswell E (eds), *Records of the Court of the Stationers' Company 1576 to 1602 from Register B* (Bibliographical Society 1930)

Greg WW (ed), *A Companion to Arber, Being a Calendar of Documents in Edward Arber's Transcript* (Clarendon Press 1967)

Jackson WA (ed), *Records of the Court of the Stationers' Company 1602 to 1640* (Bibliographical Society 1957)

Kassler M, *Music Entries at Stationers' Hall 1710–1818* (Ashgate 2004)

McKenzie DF and Bell M, *A Chronology and Calendar of Documents Relating to the London Book Trade 1641–1700* (OUP 2005)

Shell A and Emblow A, *Index to the Court Books of the Stationers' Company 1679–1717* (OUP & Bibliographical Society 2007)

Williams WP, *Index to the Stationers' Register 1640–1708* (McGilvery 1980)

2.2.2 Secondary sources

Bell M, 'Entrance in the Stationers' Register' (1994) 6th ser, 16 The Library 50

Blagden C, 'The English Stock of the Stationers' Company: An Account of its Origins' (1955) 6th ser, 10 The Library 163

Blagden C, 'Charter Trouble' (1957) 6 Book Collector 369

Blagden C, 'The Stationers' Company in the Civil War Period' (1958) 5th ser, 13 The Library 1

Blagden C, *The Stationers' Company: A History 1403–1959* (George Allen & Unwin 1960)

Blayney PWM, 'The Publication of Playbooks' in JD Cox and DS Kastan (eds), *A New History of Early English Drama* (Columbia UP 1997) 383

Blayney PWM, *The Stationers' Company Before the Charter 1403–1557* (Company of Stationers 2003)

Blayney PWM, *The Stationers' Company and the Printers of London, 1501–1557* (CUP 2013)
Epstein SR, 'Craft Guilds in the Pre-Modern Economy: A Discussion' (2008) 61 Econ Hist Rev 155
Gadd I, '"Being like a field": Corporate Identity in the Stationers' Company 1557–1684' (DPhil, University of Oxford 1999)
Gadd I, 'The Press and the London Book Trade' in I Gadd (ed), *The History of Oxford University Press, Volume I: Beginnings to 1780* (OUP 2013)
Gadd I and Wallis P, 'Reaching Beyond the City Wall: London Guilds and National Regulation, 1500–1700' in SR Epstein and M Prak (eds), *Guilds, Innovation and the European Economy 1400–1800* (CUP 2008)
Kemp G and McElligott J (eds), *Censorship and the Press, 1580–1720* (Pickering & Chatto 2009)
Mandelbrote G, 'Richard Bentley's Copies: The Ownership of Copyrights in the Late 17th Century' in A Hunt, G Mandelbrote and A Shell (eds), *The Book Trade and its Customers 1450–1900: Historical Essays for Robin Myers* (St Paul's Bibliographies 1997)
McKitterick D, *A History of Cambridge University Press – Volume I: Printing and the Book Trade in Cambridge 1534–1698* (CUP 1992)
Myers R, *The Stationers' Company Archive 1554–1984* (St Paul's Bibliographies 1990)
Myers R (ed), *The Stationers' Company: A History of the Later Years, 1800–2000* (Worshipful Company of Stationers and Newspaper Makers 2001)
Pollard G, 'The Company of Stationers before 1557' (1937) 4th ser, 18 The Library 1
Pollard G, 'The Early Constitution of the Stationers' Company' (1937) 4th ser, 18 The Library 235
Sisson CJ, 'The Laws of Elizabethan Copyright: the Stationers' View' (1960) 5th ser, 15 The Library 8
Treadwell M, '1695–1995: Some Tercentenary Thoughts on the Freedoms of the Press' (1996) 7 Harvard Library Bulletin 3
Treadwell M, 'The Stationers and the Printing Acts at the End of the Seventeenth Century' in J Barnard, DF McKenzie and M Bell (eds), *The Cambridge History of the Book in Britain: Volume IV 1557–1695* (CUP 2002) 755

2.3 Printing Privileges

Baker JH, 'English Law Books and Legal Publishing' in J Barnard, DF McKenzie and M Bell (eds), *The Cambridge History of the Book in Britain: Volume IV 1557–1695* (CUP 2002) 474
Baloch TA, 'Law Booksellers and Printers as Agents of Unchange' (2007) 66 CLJ 389
Blagden C, 'Thomas Carnan and the Almanack Monopoly' (1969) 14 Studies in Bibliography 23
Curtin RS, 'The "Capricious Privilege": Rethinking the Origins of Copyright Under the Tudor Regime' (2012) 59 J Copyright Society USA 391
Curtin RS, 'Hackers and Humanists: Transactions and the Evolution of Copyright' (2013) 54 IDEA 105

Ferguson MG, 'A History of English Book Trade Privileges During the Reign of Henry VIII' (DPhil, University of Oxford 2001)

Ferguson MG, '"In Recompense of his Labours and Inuencyon": Early Sixteenth-Century Book Trade Privileges and the Birth of Literary Property in England' (2004) 13 Transactions of the Cambridge Bibliographical Society 14

Hunt A, 'Book Trade Patents, 1603–1640' in A Hunt, G Mandelbrote and A Shell (eds), *The Book Trade and its Customers 1450–1900: Historical Essays for Robin Myers* (St Paul's Bibliographies 1997) 27

Mace NA, 'The History of the Grammar Patent, 1547–1620' (1993) 87 Papers of the Bibliographical Society of America 419

Mace NA, 'The History of the Grammar Patent from 1620 to 1800 and the Forms of Lily's Latin Grammar' (2006) 100 Papers of the Bibliographical Society of America 177

Nash NF, 'English Licenses to Print and Grants of Copyright in the 1640s' (1982) 6th ser, 4 The Library 174

Rogers S, 'The Use of Royal Licenses for Printing in England, 1695–1760' (2000) 7th ser, 1 The Library 133

2.4 Copyright at Common Law

Abrams HA, 'The Historic Foundation of American Copyright Law: Exploding the Myth of Common Law Copyright' (1983) 29 Wayne L Rev 1119

Abrams HA, 'The Persistent Myth of Perpetual Common Law Copyright: A Preliminary Response to H. Tomás Gómez-Arostegui' in E Cooper and R Deazley (eds), *What is the Point of Copyright History?* (CREATe 2016)

Bracha O, 'A Page of History: Remarks on "Copyright at Common Law in 1774" by H. Tomás Gómez-Arostegui' in E Cooper and R Deazley (eds), *What is the Point of Copyright History?* (CREATe 2016)

Cornish WR, 'The Author's Surrogate: The Genesis of British Copyright' in K O'Donovan and GR Rubin (eds), *Human Rights and Legal History* (OUP 2000) 254

Deazley R, 'The Myth of Copyright at Common Law' (2003) 62 CLJ 106

Deazley R, 'Re-Reading Donaldson (1774) in the Twenty-First Century and Why it Matters' [2003] EIPR 270

Deazley R, *On the Origin of the Right to Copy* (Hart Publishing 2004)

Deazley R, *Rethinking Copyright: History, Theory, Language* (Edward Elgar 2006)

Elliott JE, 'Conjecturing the Common in English Common Law: *Donaldson v. Beckett* and the Rhetoric of Ancient Right' (2006) 42 Modern Language Studies 431

Gómez-Arostegui HT, 'Copyright at Common Law in 1774' (2014) 47 Conn L Rev 1

Gómez-Arostegui HT, 'A Reply to my Colleagues Regarding *Donaldson v Becket*' in E Cooper and R Deazley (eds), *What is the Point of Copyright History?* (CREATe 2016)

MacQueen H, 'Ae Fond Kiss: A Private Matter' in A Burrows, D Johnston and R Zimmermann (eds), *Judge and Jurist: Essays in Memory of Lord Rodger of Earlsferry* (OUP 2013) 473

MacQueen H, 'The War of the Booksellers: Natural Law, Equity, and Literary Property in Eighteenth-Century Scotland' (2014) 35 J Leg Hist 231

O'Melinn LS, 'The Recording Industry v. James Madison, aka "Publius": The Inversion of Culture and Copyright' (2011) 35 Seattle Univ L Rev 75

Phillips J, 'Legal Outrage and Established Guile' [1981] 10 EIPR 295

Rose M, 'The Author as Proprietor: *Donaldson v. Becket* and the Genealogy of Modern Authorship' (1988) 23 Representations 51

Rose M, '*Donaldson* and the Muse of History' in E Cooper and R Deazley (eds), *What is the Point of Copyright History?* (CREATe 2016)

Seville C, '*Millar v Taylor* (1769): Landmark and Beacon. Still' in S Douglas, R Hickey and E Waring, *Landmark Cases in Property Law* (Hart Publishing 2015) 54

Walters G, 'The Booksellers in 1759 and 1774: The Battle for Literary Property' (1974) 5th ser, 29 The Library 287

Whicher JF, 'The Ghost of *Donaldson v. Beckett*: An Inquiry into the Constitutional Distribution of Powers over the Law of Literary Property in the United States' (pts 1 & 2) (1961–62) 9 Bull Copyright Society USA 102, 194

2.5 Subject Matter (Factual Works, Music, Engravings, Photographs, Obscene Works, etc)

Alexander I, '"Manacles Upon Science": Re-Evaluating Copyright in Informational Works in Light of 18th Century Case Law' (2014) 38 MULR 1

Alexander I, 'The Legal Journey of *Paterson's Roads*' (2014) 67 Imago Mundi 12

Alexander JR, 'Evil Angel Eulogy: Reflections on the Passing of the Obscenity Defences in Copyright' (2013) 20 J Intell Prop L 209

Allen-Russell AV, '"For Instruments Not Intended": The Second J C Bach Lawsuit' (2002) 83 Music & Letters 3

Bellido J and Bowrey K, 'From the Author to the Proprietor: Newspaper Copyright and *The Times* (1842–1956)' (2014) 6 JML 180

Bently L, 'The Electric Telegraph and the Struggle over Copyright in News in Australia, Great Britain and India' in B Sherman and L Wiseman (eds), *Copyright and the Challenge of the New* (Wolters Kluwer 2013) 43

Bowrey K, 'Copyright, Photography and Computer Works – The Fiction of an Original Expression' (1995) 18 UNSW LJ 278

Bowrey K, '"The World Daguerreotyped – What a Spectacle!" Copyright Law, Photography and the Economic Mission of Empire' in B Sherman and L Wiseman (eds), *Copyright and the Challenge of the New* (Wolters Kluwer 2013) 11

Carroll MW, 'The Struggle for Music Copyright' (2005) 57 Fla L Rev 907

Cooper E, 'Art, Photography, Copyright: A History of Photographic Copyright 1850–1911' (PhD, University of Cambridge 2011)

Deazley R, 'Struggling with Authority: The Photograph in British Legal History' (2003) 27 History of Photography 236

Deazley R, 'Breaking the Mould? The Radical Nature of the Fine Arts Copyright Bill 1862' in R Deazley, M Kretschmer and L Bently (eds), *Privilege and Property: Essays on the History of Copyright* (OpenBook Publishers 2010) 289

Deazley R, 'Photography, Copyright and the South Kensington Experiment' [2010] IPQ 293

Hunter D, 'Music Copyright in Britain to 1800' (1986) 67 Music & Letters 269

Hunter D, 'Copyright Protection for Engravings and Maps in Eighteenth-Century Britain' (1987) 6th ser, 7 The Library 128

Lauriat B, 'Charles Reade's Role in the Drama of Victorian Dramatic Copyright' (2009) 33 Colum J L & Arts 1

Lockhart W, 'Trial by Ear: Legal Attitudes to Keyboard Arrangement in Nineteenth-Century Britain' (2012) 93 Music & Letters 191

Mace NA, 'Haydn and the London Music Sellers: Forster v. Longman & Broderip' (1996) 77 Music & Letters 527

Mace NA, 'Litigating the *Musical Magazine*: The Definition of British Music Copyright in the 1780s' (1999) 2 Book History 122

Mace NA, 'Charles Rennett and the London Music-Sellers in the 1780s: Testing the Ownership of Reversionary Copyrights' (2004) 129 J of the Royal Musical Association 1

Mace NA, 'The Market for Music in the Late Eighteenth Century and the Entry Books of the Stationers' Company' (2009) 7th ser, 10 The Library 157

McCauley A, '"Merely Mechanical": On the Origins of Photographic Copyright in France and Great Britain' (2008) 31 Art History 57

Milhous J and Hume RD, 'Librettist versus Composer: The Property Rights to Arne's *Henry and Emma* and *Don Saverio*' (1997) 122 J of the Royal Musical Association 52

Phillips J, 'Copyright in Obscene Works: Some British and American Problems' (1977) 6 Anglo-American L Rev 138

Phillips J, 'Prince Albert and the Etchings' [1984] 12 EIPR 344

Rabin RJ and Zohn S, 'Arne, Handel, Walsh, and Music as Intellectual Property: Two Eighteenth-Century Lawsuits' (1995) 120 J of the Royal Musical Association 112

Rose M, 'Technology in 1735: The Engraver's Act' (2005) 21 The Information Society 63

Saunders D, 'Copyright, Obscenity and Literary History' (1990) 57 English Literary Hist 431

Scherer FM, 'The Emergence of Musical Copyright in Europe From 1709 to 1850' (2008) 5 Rev of Economic Research on Copyright Issues 3

Slauter W, 'Understanding the Lack of Copyright for Journalism in Eighteenth-Century Britain' (2013) 16 Book History 34

Small J, 'J C Bach Goes to Law' (1985) 126 Musical Times 526

Small J, 'The Development of Music Copyright' in M Kassler (ed), *The Music Trade in Georgian England* (Ashgate 2011) 233

2.6 Infringement and Fair Dealing

Alexander I, 'All Change for the Digital Economy: Copyright and Business Models in the Early Eighteenth Century' (2010) 25 Berkeley Tech LJ 1351

Alexander I, '"Manacles Upon Science": Re-Evaluating Copyright in Informational Works in Light of 18th Century Case Law' (2014) 38 MULR 1

Bowrey K, 'On Clarifying the Role of Originality and Fair Use in Nineteenth Century UK Jurisprudence: Appreciating the "humble grey which emerges as the result of long controversy'" in CW Ng, L Bently and G D'Agostino (eds), *The Common Law of Intellectual Property* (Hart Publishing 2010) 45

Deazley R, 'The Statute of Anne and the Great Abridgment Swindle' (2010) 47 Hous L R 793

De Zwart M, 'A Historical Analysis of the Birth of Fair Dealing and Fair Use: Lessons for the Digital Age' [2007] IPQ 60

Howell J, 'Eighteenth Century Abridgments of *Robinson Crusoe*' (2014) 15 The Library (7th ser) 292

Sag M, 'The Prehistory of Fair Use' (2010) 76 Brook L Rev 1371

Sims A, 'Appellations of Piracy: Fair Dealing's Prehistory' [2011] 1 IPQ 3

2.7 Remedies and Court Procedure

Bottomley S, 'Patent Cases in the Court of Chancery, 1714–58' (2014) 35 J Legal Hist 27

Bottomley S, *The British Patent System During the Industrial Revolution, 1700–1852* (CUP 2014)

Bryson WH, *The Equity Side of the Exchequer* (CUP 1975)

Bryson WH (ed), *Cases Concerning Equity and the Courts of Equity 1550–1660* (Selden Society 2001)

Deazley R, *On the Origin of the Right to Copy* (Hart Publishing 2004)

Gómez-Arostegui HT, 'What History Teaches Us About Copyright Injunctions and the Inadequate-Remedy-at-Law Requirement' (2008) 81 S Cal L Rev 1197

Gómez-Arostegui HT, 'Prospective Compensation in Lieu of a Final Injunction in Patent and Copyright Cases' (2010) 78 Fordham L Rev 1661

Gómez-Arostegui HT, 'The Untold Story of the First Copyright Suit Under the Statute of Anne in 1710' (2010) 25 Berkeley Tech LJ 1247

Gómez-Arostegui HT, 'What History Teaches Us About US Copyright Law and Statutory Damages' (2013) 5 WIPOJ 76

Horwitz H, *A Guide to Chancery Equity Records and Proceedings 1600–1800* (2nd edn, HMSO 1998)

Jones WJ, *The Elizabethan Court of Chancery* (Clarendon Press 1967)

Macnair MRT, *The Law of Proof in Early Modern Equity* (Duncker and Humblot 1999)

Yale DEC (ed), *Lord Nottingham's Chancery Cases* (Selden Society 1957 & 1961)

Yale DEC (ed), *Lord Nottingham's 'Manual of Chancery Practice' and 'Prolegomena of Chancery and Equity'* (Wm W Gaunt & Sons 1986)

2.8 Miscellaneous

Adams S, 'Intellectual Property Cases in Lord Mansfield's Court Notebooks' (1987) 8 J Legal Hist 18

Alexander I, 'Criminalising Copyright: A Story of Publishers, Pirates and Pieces of Eight' (2007) 66 CLJ 625

Alexander I, 'The Lord Chancellor, the Poets and the Courtesan: Public Morality and Copyright Law in the early Nineteenth Century' in A Lewis, P Brand and P Mitchell (eds), *Law in the City* (Four Courts Press 2007)

Alexander I, 'All Change for the Digital Economy: Copyright and Business Models in the Early Eighteenth Century' (2010) 25 Berkeley Tech LJ 1351

Alexander I, '"Neither Bolt nor Chain, Iron Safe nor Private Watchman, Can Prevent the Theft of Words": The Birth of the Performing Right in Britain' in R Deazley, M Kretschmer and L Bently (eds), *Privilege and Property: Essays on the History of Copyright* (OpenBook Publishers 2010) 321

Alexander I, 'The Genius and the Labourer: Authorship in Eighteenth- and Nineteenth-Century Copyright Law' in L Bently, J Davis and JC Ginsburg (eds), *Copyright and Piracy: An Interdisciplinary Critique* (CUP 2010) 300

Bald RC, 'Early Copyright Litigation and Its Bibliographical Interest' in *The Bibliographical Society of America* 1904–79 (1980) 172

Barrington Partridge RC, *The History of the Legal Deposit of Books: Throughout the British Empire* (Library Association 1938)

Bently L, 'Art and the Making of Modern Copyright Law' in D McClean and K Schubert (eds), *Dear Images: Art, Copyright and Culture* (Ridinghouse 2002) 331

Bently L, 'Copyright, Translations, and Relations Between Britain and India in the Nineteenth and Early Twentieth Centuries' (2007) 82 Chi-Kent L Rev 1181

Bently L, 'R. v the Author: From Death Penalty to Community Service' (2008) 32 Colum J L & Arts 1

Bently L, 'Introduction to Part I: The History of Copyright' in L Bently, U Suthersanen and P Torremans (eds), *Global Copyright* (Edward Elgar 2010) 7

Bently L and Ginsburg JC, '"The Sole Right … Shall Return to the Authors": Anglo-American Authors' Reversion Rights from the Statute of Anne to Contemporary U.S. Copyright' (2010) 25 Berkeley Tech LJ 1475

Bond RP, 'The Pirate and the *Tatler*' (1963) 5th ser, 18 The Library 257

Brennan DJ, 'The Root of Title to Copyright in Works' [2015] IPQ 289

Collins AS, 'Some Aspects of Copyright from 1700 to 1780' (1926) 4th ser, 7 The Library 67

Cooper E, 'Copyright and Mass Social Authorship: A Case Study of the Making of the Oxford English Dictionary' [2015] Social and Legal Studies 1

Cornish W, 'The Statute of Anne 1709–10: Its Historical Setting' in L Bently, U Suthersanen and P Torremans (eds), *Global Copyright* (Edward Elgar 2010) 14

Deazley R, 'The Life of an Author: Samuel Egerton Brydges and the *Copyright Act 1814*' (2006) 23 Georgia St Univ L Rev 809

Deazley R, 'What's New About the Statute of Anne? *Or* Six Observations in Search of an Act' in L Bently, U Suthersanen and P Torremans (eds), *Global Copyright* (Edward Elgar 2010) 26

Feather J, 'The Book Trade in Politics: The Making of the Copyright Act of 1710' (1980) 8 Publishing Hist 19

Feather J, 'The Publishers and the Pirates: British Copyright Law in Theory and Practise, 1710–1775' (1987) 22 Publishing Hist 5

Feather J, 'Authors, Publishers and Politicians: The History of Copyright and the Book Trade' (1988) 12 EIPR 377

Feather J, 'From Rights in Copies to Copyright: The Recognition of Authors' Rights in English Law and Practice in the Sixteenth and Seventeenth Centuries' in M

Woodmansee and P Jaszi (eds), *The Construction of Authorship: Textual Appropriation in Law and Literature* (Duke UP 1994)

Ford LR, 'Prerogative, Nationalized: The Social Formation of Intellectual Property' (2015) 97 J Patent and Trademark Office Society 270

Gaba JM, 'Copyrighting Shakespeare: Jacob Tonson, Eighteenth Century English Copyright, and the Birth of Shakespeare Scholarship' (2011) 19 J Intell Prop L 21

Ginsburg JC, '"Une Chose Publique"? The Author's Domain and the Public Domain in Early British, French and US Copyright Law' (2006) 65 CLJ 636

Gómez-Arostegui HT, 'The Untold Story of the First Copyright Suit Under the Statute of Anne in 1710' (2010) 25 Berkeley Tech LJ 1247

Judge EF, 'Kidnapped and Counterfeit Characters: Eighteenth-Century Fan Fiction, Copyright Law, and the Custody of Fictional Characters' in R McGinnis (ed), *Originality and Intellectual Property in French and English Enlightenment* (Routledge 2009) 22

Kirschbaum L, 'Authors' Copyright in England before 1640' (1946) 40 Papers of the Bibliographical Society of America 43

Kirschbaum L, *Shakespeare and the Stationers* (Ohio State UP 1955)

Lauriat B, 'The 1878 Royal Commission on Copyright: Understanding an Attempt at Victorian Copyright Reform' (PhD, University of Oxford 2013)

Lauriat B, 'Revisiting the Royal Commission on Copyright' (2014) 17 JWIP 47

Lauriat B, 'Free Trade in Books: The 1878 Royal Commission on Copyright' (2014) 61 J Copyright Society USA 635

Leeming M, 'Hawkesworth's *Voyages*: The First "Australian" Copyright Litigation' (2014) 9 Aust J Leg Hist 159

Nichol DW, 'On the Use of "Copy" and "Copyright": A Scriblerian Coinage?' (1990) 6th ser, 12 The Library 110

Oldham J, *The Mansfield Manuscripts and the Growth of English Law in the Eighteenth Century* (North Carolina UP 1992) vol 1

Oldham J, *English Common Law in the Age of Mansfield* (North Carolina UP 2004)

Pollard AW, 'Some Notes on the History of English Copyright' (1922) 4th ser, 3 The Library 97

Raven J, 'Booksellers in Court: Approaches to the Legal History of Copyright in England Before 1842' (2012–13) 104 Law Library J 115

Richardson M and Thomas J, *Fashioning Intellectual Property: Exhibition, Advertising and the Press 1789–1918* (CUP 2012)

Rogers P, 'The Case of Pope v. Curll' (1972) 5th ser, 27 The Library 326

Rose M, 'The Author in Court: *Pope v. Curll* (1741)' in M Woodmansee and P Jaszi (eds), *The Construction of Authorship: Textual Appropriation in Law and Literature* (Duke UP 1994) 211

Rose M, 'The Statute of Anne and Authors' Rights: *Pope v. Curll* (1741)' in L Bently, U Suthersanen and P Torremans (eds), *Global Copyright* (Edward Elgar 2010) 70

Rose M, 'The Public Sphere and the Emergence of Copyright: Areopagitica, the Stationers' Company, and the Statute of Anne' in R Deazley, M Kretschmer and L Bently (eds), *Privilege and Property, Essays on the History of Copyright* (OpenBook Publishers 2010) 67

Ross T, 'Copyright and the Invention of Tradition' (1992) 26 Eighteenth-Century Studies 1
Saunders D, 'Purposes or Principle? Early Copyright and the Court of Chancery' [1993] 15 EIPR 452
Seville C, 'Authors as Copyright Campaigners: Mark Twain's Legacy' (2008) 55 J Copyright Society USA 283
Seville C, 'The Statute of Anne: Rhetoric and Reception in the Nineteenth Century' (2010) 47 Hous L Rev 819
Sherman, B, 'Remembering and Forgetting: The Birth of Modern Copyright Law' (1995) 10 IPJ 1
Stern S, 'Tom Jones and the Economies of Copyright' (1997) 9 Eighteenth-Century Fiction 429
Stern S, 'Copyright, Originality, and the Public Domain in Eighteenth-Century England' in R McGinnis (ed), *Originality and Intellectual Property in French and English Enlightenment* (Routledge 2009) 69
Stern S, 'From Author's Right to Property Right' (2012) 62 U Toronto LJ 29
Stern S, '"Room for One More": The Metaphorics of Physical Space in the Eighteenth-Century Copyright Debate' (2012) 24 Law and Literature 113
Stern S, 'Speech and Property in *David Simple*' (2013) 79 English Literary Hist 623
Suarez MF, 'To What Degree Did the Statute of Anne (8 Anne, c. 19, [1709]) Affect Commercial Practices in Eighteenth-Century England?' in L Bently, U Suthersanen and P Torremans (eds), *Global Copyright* (Edward Elgar 2010) 54
Sutherland JR, '"Polly" Among the Pirates' (1942) 37 Mod Lang Rev 291
van Gompel S, 'Copyright Formalities and the Reasons for their Decline in Nineteenth Century Europe' in R Deazley, M Kretschmer and L Bently (eds), *Privilege and Property: Essays on the History of Copyright* (OpenBook Publishers 2010) 157
van Gompel S, *Formalities in Copyright Law: An Analysis of Their History, Rationales and Possible Future* (Wolters Kluwer 2011)
Zimmerman DL, 'The Statute of Anne and its Progeny: Variations Without a Theme' (2010) 47 Hous L Rev 965

3. INTERNATIONAL HISTORIES OF COPYRIGHT LAW

3.1 United States

Abrams HA, 'The Historic Foundation of American Copyright Law: Exploding the Myth of Common Law Copyright' (1983) 29 Wayne L Rev 1119
Bracha O, 'Owning Ideas: A History of Anglo-American Intellectual Property' (SJD, Harvard Law School 2005)
Bracha O, 'The Ideology of Authorship Revisited: Authors, Markets, and Liberal Values in Early American Copyright' (2008) 118 Yale LJ 186
Bracha O, 'Early American Printing Privileges: The Ambivalent Origins of Authors' Copyright in America' in R Deazley, M Kretschmer and L Bently (eds), *Privilege and Property: Essays on the History of Copyright* (OpenBook Publishers 2010) 89

Bracha O, 'The Adventures of the Statute of Anne in the Land of Unlimited Possibilities: The Life of a Legal Transplant' (2010) 25 Berkeley Tech LJ 1427

Bracha O, 'The Statute of Anne: An American Mythology' (2010) 47 Houston L Rev 877

Bracha O, 'How Did Film Become Property? Copyright and the Early Film Industry' in B Sherman and L Wiseman (eds), *Copyright and the Challenge of the New* (Wolters Kluwer 2012) 170

Bracha O (ed), United States, Primary Sources on Copyright (1450–1900), www.copyrighthistory.org

Brauneis R, 'The Transformation of Originality in the Progressive-Era Debate over Copyright in News' (2009) 27 Cardozo Arts & Ent LJ 321

Bugbee BW, *Genesis of American Patent and Copyright Law* (Public Affairs 1967)

Crawford F, 'Pre-Constitutional Copyright Statutes' (1975) 23 Bull Copyright Society USA 11

Donner I, 'The Copyright Clause of the U.S. Constitution: Why Did the Framers Include it With Unanimous Approval?' (1992) 36 Am J Legal Hist 361

Federico PJ, 'Copyrights in the Patent Office' (1939) 21 J Pat Off Soc'y 911

Fenning K, 'The Origins of the Patent and Copyright Clause of the Constitution' (1929) 17 Geo LJ 109

Gilreath J, 'American Literature, Public Policy, and the Copyright Laws before 1800' in J Gilreath (ed), *Federal Copyright Records, 1790–1800* (US Government Printing Office 1987) xxii

Ginsburg JC, 'A Tale of Two Copyrights: Literary Property in Revolutionary France and America' (1990) 64 Tul L Rev 991

Ginsburg JC, '"Une Chose Publique"? The Author's Domain and the Public Domain in Early British, French and US Copyright Law' (2006) 65 CLJ 636

Gordan JD, '*Morse v. Reid*: The First Reported Federal Copyright Case' (1993) 11 LHR 21

Gordon W, 'The Core of Copyright: Authors, Not Publishers' (2014) 52 Hous L Rev 213

Joyce C, '"A Curious Chapter in the History of Judicature": *Wheaton v. Peters* and the Rest of the Story (of Copyright in the New Republic)' (2005) 42 Hous L Rev 325

Khan BZ, *The Democratization of Invention: Patents and Copyrights in American Economic Development, 1790–1920* (CUP 2005)

Litman J, 'The Invention of Common Law Play Right' (2010) 25 Berkeley Tech LJ 1381

Maher WJ, 'Copyright Term, Retrospective Extension, and the Copyright Law of 1790 in Historical Context' (2002) 49 J Copyright Society USA 1021

McGill MG, 'Copyright in the Early Republic' in RA Gross and M Kelly (eds), *A History of the Book in America: An Extensive Republic: Print, Culture, and Society in the New Nation, 1790–1840* (UNC Press 2010)

Miller D, *Judicial Criticism: Performance and Aesthetics in Anglo-American Copyright Law 1770–1911* (PhD, Stanford University 2013)

Ochoa TT and Rose M, 'The Anti-Monopoly Origins of the Patent and Copyright Clause' (2002) 49 J Copyright Society USA 675

O'Connor SM, 'The Overlooked French Influence on the Intellectual Property Clause' (2015) 82 U Chicago L Rev 733

Oliar D, 'Making Sense of the Intellectual Property Clause: Promotion of Progress as a Limitation on Congress's Intellectual Property Power' (2006) 94 Geo LJ 1771

Oliar D, 'The (Constitutional) Convention on IP: A New Reading' (2009) 57 UCLA L Rev 421

Patterson LR and Joyce C, 'Copyright in 1791: An Essay Concerning the Founders' View of the Copyright Power Granted to Congress in Article I, Section 8, Clause 8 of the U.S. Constitution' (2003) 52 Emory LJ 909

Rosen ZS, 'The Twilight of the Opera Pirates: A Prehistory of the Exclusive Right of Public Performance for Musical Compositions' (2007) 24 Cardozo Arts & Ent LJ 1157

Rosen ZS, 'Reimagining Bleistein: Copyright for Advertisements in Historical Perspective' (2012) 59 J Copyright Society USA 347

Silver RG, 'Prologue to Copyright in America: 1772' (1958) 11 Papers of the Bibliographical Society of the University of Virginia 259

Tanselle GT, 'Copyright Records and the Bibliographer' (1969) 22 Studies in Bibliography 74

Walterscheid EC, 'Authors and Their Writings' (2001) 49 J Copyright Society USA 729

Walterscheid EC, *The Nature of the Intellectual Property Clause: A Study in Historical Perspective* (Hein 2002)

Walterscheid EC, 'The Preambular Argument: The Dubious Premise of *Eldred v. Ashcroft*' (2004) 44 IDEA 331

Walterscheid EC, 'Understanding the Copyright Act of 1790: The Issue of Common Law Copyright in America and the Modern Interpretation of the Copyright Power' (2006) 53 J Copyright Society USA 313

3.2 Australia

Ailwood S and Sainsbury M, 'Copyright Law, Readers and Authors in Colonial Australia' (2014) 14 J of the Association for the Study of Australian Literature

Ailwood S and Sainsbury M, 'The Imperial Effect: Literary Copyright Law in Colonial Australia' in *Law, Culture and the Humanities* (2014)

Atkinson B, *The True History of Copyright: The Australian Experience 1905–2005* (Sydney UP 2007)

Atkinson B, 'Australia's Copyright History' in B Fitzgerald and B Atkinson, *Copyright Future Copyright Freedom* (Sydney UP 2011) 29

Atkinson R and Fotheringham R, 'Dramatic Copyright in Australia to 1912' (1987) 11 Australasian Drama Studies 47

Bently L, 'Copyright and the Victorian Internet: Telegraphic Property Laws in Colonial Australia' (2004) 38 Loy LA L Rev 71

Bently L, 'The "Extraordinary Multiplicity" of Intellectual Property Laws in the British Colonies in the Nineteenth Century' (2011) 12 Theo Inq L 161

Bently L, 'The Electric Telegraph and the Struggle over Copyright in News in Australia, Great Britain and India' in B Sherman and L Wiseman (eds), *Copyright and the Challenge of the New* (Wolters Kluwer 2013) 43

Bond C, 'For the Term of his Natural Life ... Plus Seventy Years: Mapping Australia's Public Domain' (PhD, University of New South Wales 2010)

Bond C, '"Curse the Law!": Unravelling the Copyright Complexities in Marcus Clarke's *His Natural Life*' (2010) 15 MALR 452

Bond C, '"The play goes on eternally": Copyright, Marcus Clarke's Heir's and *His Natural Life* as Play and Film – Part One' (2011) 23 IPJ 267

Bond C, '"The play goes on eternally": Copyright, Marcus Clarke's Heirs and *His Natural Life* as Play and Film – Part Two' (2011) 24 IPJ 61

Bond C, '"There's nothing worse than a muddle in all the world": Copyright Complexity and Law Reform in Australia' (2011) 34 UNSWLJ 1145

Burrell R, 'Copyright Reform in the Early Twentieth Century: The View from Australia' (2006) 27 J Leg Hist 239

Finn J, 'Particularism versus Uniformity: Factors Shaping the Development of Australasian Intellectual Property Law in the Nineteenth Century' (2000) 6 Aust J Leg Hist 113

Kenyon AT, Richardson M and Ricketson S (eds), *Landmarks in Australian Intellectual Property Law* (CUP 2009)

Minell M, *A Nation's Imagination: Australia's Copyright Records, 1854–1968* (National Archives of Australia 2003)

Ricketson S, 'The Imperial Copyright Act 1911 in Australia' in U Suthersanen and Y Gendreau (eds), *A Shifting Empire: 100 Years of the Copyright Act 1911* (Edward Elgar 2013)

Trainor L, 'Imperialism, Commerce and Copyright: Australia and New Zealand, 1870–1930' (1997) 21 Bibliographical Society of Australia and New Zealand Bulletin 199

3.3 France

Armstrong E, *Before Copyright, The French Book-Privilege System, 1498–1526* (CUP 1990)

Barber G, 'French Royal Decrees Concerning the Book Trade, 1700–1789' (1966) 3 Australasian J French Studies 312

Ginsburg JC, 'A Tale of Two Copyrights: Literary Property in Revolutionary France and America' (1990) 64 Tul L Rev 991

Ginsburg JC, '"Une Chose Publique"? The Author's Domain and the Public Domain in Early British, French and US Copyright Law' (2006) 65 CLJ 636

Pfister L, 'L'auteur, propriétaire de son œuvre. La formation du droit d'auteur du XVIeme siècle à la loi de 1957' (PhD, University of Strasbourg 1999)

Pfister L, 'Author and Work in the French Print Privileges System: Some Milestones' in R Deazley, M Kretschmer and L Bently (eds), *Privilege and Property, Essays on the History of Copyright* (OpenBook Publishers 2010) 115

Rideau F, *La formation du droit de la propriété littéraire en France et en Grande-Bretagne: une convergence oubliée* (Presses Universitaires d'Aix-Marseille 2004)

Rideau F, 'Nineteenth Century Controversies Relating to the Protection of Artistic Property in France' in R Deazley, M Kretschmer and L Bently (eds), *Privilege and Property: Essays on the History of Copyright* (OpenBook Publishers 2010) 241

Rideau F (ed), France, Primary Sources on Copyright (1450–1900), www.copyrighthistory.org

Scott K, 'Maps, Views and Ornament: Visualising Property in Art and Law: The Case of Pre-Modern France' in R Deazley, M Kretschmer and L Bently (eds), *Privilege and Property: Essays on the History of Copyright* (OpenBook Publishers 2010) 255

3.4 Spain

Ayllón Santiago HS, *El derecho de comunicación pública directa* (Editorial Reus 2011)

Bellido J, 'Latin American and Spanish Copyright Bilateral Agreements (1880–1904)' (2009) 12 JWIP 1

Bellido J (ed), Spain, Primary Sources on Copyright (1450–1900), www.copyrighthistory.org

Bouza Álvarez F, *Dásele licencia y privilegio: Don Quijote y la aprobación de libros en el Siglo de Oro* (Akal 2012)

Cámara Águila MP, 'La ley por la que se declara el derecho de propiedad a los autores y a los traductores de obras literarias, y establece las reglas oportunas para su protección, de 10 de junio de 1847' (1999) 2 Revista Pe i 167

Cendan Pazos F, *Historia del Derecho Español de Prensa e Imprenta (1502–1966)* (Editora nacional 1974)

Chartier R, *El Orden de los Libros: Lectores, Autores, Bibliotecas en Europa entre los Siglos XIV y XVIII* (Gedisa 2000)

Fernández P, 'En torno a la edición fraudulenta de impresos españoles en Francia: la convención literaria hispano-francesa (1853)' in *Estudios de literatura española de los siglos XIX y XX (homenaje a Juan María Díez Taboada)* (Instituto de Filología CSIC 1998) 200

García Martín J, 'De la apropiación penal a la propiedad literaria: sobre los orígenes del derecho de propiedad intelectual en España (siglos XVIII–XIX)' (2000) 93 Revista de la Facultad de Derecho de la Universidad Complutense 105

González Hontoria M, *Los convenios de propiedad intelectual entre España y los países ibero-americanos* (Minuesa de los Ríos 1899)

Llopis M, 'Propiedad intelectual: antecedentes de la Ley de 1879' (1979) 29 Boletín de la Anabad 31

Martínez Martín JA, *Vivir de la pluma. La profesionalización del escritor 1836–1936* (Marcial Pons 2009)

Molina JM, 'Bases históricas y filosóficas del derecho de autor' (1994) 47 Anuario de Derecho Civil 121

Molina JM, *La propiedad intelectual en la legislación española* (Marcial Pons 1995)

Sánchez García R, 'La Propiedad Intelectual en la España Contemporánea' (2002) 62 Hispania 993

Surwillo L, *The Stages of Property: Copyrighting Theatre in Spain* (U of Toronto Press 2007)

3.5 Italy

3.5.1 History of the book in 16th-century Italy, particularly in Rome
Barberi F, *Per una storia del libro: profili, note, ricerche* (1981)
Barberi F, *Paolo Manuzio e la stamperia del popolo romano 1561–1570 con documenti inediti* (Rome, Gela reprints 1985)
Edit 16, Istituto Centrale per il catalogo unico delle biblioteche italiane e per le informazioni bibliografiche – Laboratorio per la bibliografia retrospettiva, http://edit16.iccu.sbn.it/web_iccu/imain.htm
Farenga P (ed), *Editori ed edizioni a Roma nel Rinascimento* (Rome 2005)
Grendler P, *The Roman Inquisition and the Venetian Press, 1540–1605* (1977)
Kostylo J (ed), Italy, Primary Sources on Copyright (1450–1900), www.copyrighthistory.org
Masetti Zannini L, *Stampatori e librai a Roma nella seconda metá del Cinquecento* (1980)
Menato M, Sandal E and Zappella G, *Dizionario dei tipografi e degli editori Italiani: il Cinquecento A–F* (Bibliografica edn 1998)
Nuovo A, *Commercio librario nell'Italia del Rinascimento* (1998)
Nuovo A and Coppens C, *I Giolito e la stampa nell'Italia del XVI secolo* (2005)
Nuovo A and Sandal E, *Il libro nell' Italia del rinascimento* (1998)
Ridolfi R, 'Nuovi contribute sulle stamperie papali di Paolo III' (1948) 50 La Bibliofilia 183
Santoro M, *Storia del libro italiano: Libro e società in Italia dal Quattrocento al Nuovo Millennio* (2nd edn 2008)
Santoro M (ed), *La Stampa in Italia nel Cinquecento: Atti del convegno Roma 17–21 Ottobre 1989* (1992)
Veneziani P (ed), *Il libro italiano del Cinquecento: produzione e commercio* (1989)

3.5.2 Works concerning, excerpting or listing papal printing privileges
Ascarelli F, *Annali tipografici di Giacomo Mazzocchi* (1961)
Barberi F, 'Le edizioni romane di Francesco Minizio Calvo' in *Miscellanea di scritti di bibliografia ed erudizione in memoria di Luigi Ferrari* (1952) 57
Blasio MG, *Cum Gratia et Privilegio Programmi editoriali e politica pontefìcia Roma 1478–1527* (1988)
Blasio MG, 'Privilegi e licenze di stampa a Roma fra Quattro e Cinquecento' (1988) 90 La Bibliofilia 147
Bury M, 'Infringing Privileges and Copying in Rome c. 1600' (2005) 22 Print Q 133
Ceresa M, *Una stamperia nella Roma del primo seicento: annali tipografici di Guglielmo Facciotti ed eredi (1592–1640)* (2000)
Fontana P, 'Inizi della proprietà letteraria nello stato pontefìcio: Saggio di documenti dell'Archivio Vaticano' (1929–30) 3 Accademie e biblioteche d'Italia 204
Ginsburg JC, 'Proto-Property in Literary and Artistic Works: Sixteenth-Century Papal Printing Privileges' (2013) 36 Colum J L & Arts 345
Leicht PS, 'L'Editore veneziano Michele Tramezzino ed i suoi privilegi' in *Miscellanea di scritti di bibliografia ed erudizione in memoria di Luigi Ferrari* (1952) 357
Leuschner E, 'The Papal Printing Privilege' (1998) 15 Print Q 359

Lincoln E, *The Invention of the Italian Renaissance Printmaker* (2000)
Panzer GW, *Annales Typographici ab anno MDI* (1800) vol 8, 245
Pon L, 'Prints and Privileges: Regulating the Image in 16th-Century Italy' (1998) Harv Univ Art Museums Bull no 6 40
Romani V, 'Luoghi editoriali in Roma e nello Stato della Chiesa' in M Santoro (ed), *La Stampa in Italia nel Cinquecento* (1990) 516
Simonsohn S, *The Apostolic See and the Jews* (1988)
Tinto A, *Annali tipografici dei Tramezzino* (1968)
Tschudi VP, 'Ancient Rome in the Age of Copyright: The Privilegio and Printed Reconstructions' (2012) 25 Acta ad Archaeologiam et Artium Historiam Pertinentia 177 (2012)
Vichi AMG, *Annali della Stamperia del Popolo Romano* (1959)
Witcombe CLCE, 'Christopher Plantin's Papal Privileges, Documents in the Vatican Archives' (1991) 69 De Gulden Passer 133
Witcombe CLCE, 'Herrera's Papal Privilegio for the Escorial Prints' (1992) 9 Print Q 177
Witcombe CLCE, *Copyright in the Renaissance: Prints and the Privilegio in Sixteenth-century Venice and Rome* (2003)
Witcombe CLCE, *Print Publishing in Sixteenth Century Rome* (2008)

3.6 International Law

3.6.1 Primary sources and commentaries on the Berne Convention

Association littéraire et artistique internationale, *Avant-projet de révision de la Convention d'Union de Berne* (1907)
Association littéraire et artistique internationale – Son histoire. Ses travaux (1878–1889) (Bibliothèque Chaconac 1889)
Baetzmann F, *Union internationale pour la protection des oeuvres littéraires et artistiques. Convention de Berne. Concordance des textes de 1883, 1884 et 1885* (Kugelmann 1889)
Bastide L, *L'Union de Berne de 1886 et la protection internationale des droits des auteurs et des artistes suivie du texte de l'avant-projet de la Conférence de Berne de 1883, de la Convention définitive du 9 septembre 1886, de la loi espagnole du 9 jan 1879 sur la propriété intellectuelle et la loi belge du 22 mars 1886 sur le droit d'auteur* (Giard 1890)
Baum A, *The Brussels Conference for the Revision of the Berne Convention* (Library of Congress 1949) (trans by W Strauss from [1949] *GRUR* 1)
Beguin G, *La Clause juridictionnelle du nouvel art 27bis de la Convention de Berne pour la protection des oeuvres littéraires et artistiques*, extract from (1949) 6 Annuaire suisse du droit international 282 (Ed polygraphiques 1950)
BIRPI, *Le cinéma dans la Convention de Berne. The cinema in the Berne Convention* (BIRPI 1960)
Bodenhausen GHC, *Guide to the Application of the Paris Convention for the Protection of Industrial Property* (BIRPI 1968)
Bodenhausen GHC, *Developing Countries and International Copyright* (Address at New Delhi, 23 October 1973) (WIPO 1973)

Bolla P, *The Berne Convention for the Protection of Literary and Artistic Works in the text revised at Brussels* (Library of Congress 1949)

Borchgrave J, *Les Résultats de la Convention de Berlin et le Rapport de M Taillefer au Syndicat pour la Protection de la Properiété intellectuelle* (Bruylants 1909)

Boutet M and Plaisant R, *Régime International du droit d'auteur. La Convention de Berne, révisée à Bruxelles* (Juris-Classeurs, Libraire de la Cour de cassation 1950)

Bricon E, *Des droits d'auteur dans les rapports internationaux* (Rousseau 1888)

Carmichael VCH, *The Paris International Literary Congress* (1878)

Carotti F, *Le Projet de Convention pour l'Union Générale Littéraire et Artistique. Considérations dediées à Mm les Délégues des Gouvernements Adhérents à la Conférence de Berne (8 septembre 1884)* (Civelli 1884)

Clunet E, *Étude sur la Convention d'Union internationale pour la protection des oeuvres littéraires et artistiques* (Marchal and Billard 1887)

Constant C, *Union internationale pour la protection des oeuvres littéraires et artistiques. Convention de Berne du 9 septembre 1886 et Acte Additionnel de Paris du 4 mai 1896. Textes et documents, publiés avec quelques observations* (Agence générale 1897)

Constant C, *Protection internationale des oeuvres artistiques* (Société des artistes françaises 1914)

Coppetiers de Gibson D, *La Conférence diplomatique du droit d'auteur (Bruxelles 5–26 juin 1948)* (Goemaere 1948)

Copyright Association (UK), *The Articles of the International Copyright Union* (Longmans, Green and Co 1887)

Darras A, *Du droit des auteurs et des artistes dans les rapports internationaux* (Rousseau 1887)

Darras A, *Rapport sur la deuxième Conférence réunie à Berne par l'Association littéraire et artistique international* (Pichon 1890)

Deàk F, *Report on the Status of International Copyright Protection and on the Brussels Meeting of the Committee of Experts*, Committee for the Study of Copyright, Sub-committee of the American National Committee of International Intellectual Co-operation (Columbia UP 1938)

Desbois H, Françon A and Kerever A, *Les conventions internationales du droit d'auteur et des droits voisins* (Dalloz 1976)

Desjeux X, *La protection des auxiliaires de la création littéraire et artistique selon la Convention de Rome du 26 octobre 1961* (Pichon and Durand-Auzias 1966)

Dittrich R, *Die Stockholmer Fassung der Berner Übereinkunft*, Internationale Gesellschaft für Urheberrecht, Schriftenreihe, Band 40 Berlin-Frankfurt/Main (1968)

Droz N, 'Deuxième conférence diplomatique de Berne dans le but de constituer une Union pour la protection des œuvres littéraires et artistiques' (1885) *Clunet* p 483

Droz N, 'Réponse aux observations du syndicat des sociétés littéraires et artistiques sur le projet de convention internationale relatif à la constitution d'une Union pour la protection des droits d'auteur' (1885) *Clunet* pp 163–64

Fleischmann A, *Die Berner Übereinkunft zum Schutze des Urheberrechts*, extract from (1888) *Unsere Zeit – Deutsche Revue der Gegenwart* 314, Brockhaus, Leipzig (1888)

Fliniaux C, *Essai sur les droits des auteurs étrangers en France et des auteurs françaises en pays étrangers* (Thorin 1879)

Goldbaum W, *Berner Übereinkunft zum Schutze von Werken der Literatur und Kunst, vom 2 juni 1928* (Stilke 1928)

Goldbaum W, *Verfall und Auflösung der sogenannten Berner Union und Übereinkunft zum Schutz von Werken der Literatur und Kunst* (Vahlen 1959)

Grunebaum-Ballin P, *Le droit moral des auteurs et des artistes. Commentaire d'un projet des textes sur le droit moral à insérer dans la Convention de Berne revisée, suivi des textes proposes* (Imprimerie du Palais 1928)

Hachette L, *Modifications apportées à la Convention de Berne de 1913 à 1931. Rapport présenté à la IXme Session du Congrès des éditeurs à Paris* (Cercle de la librairie 1931)

Hoffman W, *Die Berner Übereinkunft zum Schutze von Werken der Literatur und Kunst vom 9 September 1886, revidiert in Berlin am 13 November 1908 und in Rom am 2 Juni 1928* (Springer 1935)

Huard G, *Etude sur les modifications apportées à la Convention de Berne par la Conférence réunie à Paris, du 15 avril au 1er mai 1896*, extract from *Bulletin de la Société de législation compare* (Pichon 1897)

Institut de Droit international, *Révision de la Convention de Berne du 9 Septembre 1886 créant une Union internationale pour la protection des oeuvres littéraires et artistiques. Conclusions présentées au nom de la commission par Mm Roguin rapporteur et Renault co-rapporteur* (1895)

International Institute of Intellectual Co-operation, *La Protection internationale du droit d'auteur* (Fontenay 1928)

Janlet V, *De la Protection des oeuvres de la pensée. Créations littéraires* (Moens 1888)

Junker C, *Die Berner Konvention zum Schutze der Werken der Literatur und Kunst und Österreich-Ungarn* (Hölder 1900)

Kohler J, *Die Immaterialgüter im internationalen Recht* (Duncker and Humblot 1896)

Kohler J, *Urheberrecht an Schriftwerken und Verlagsrecht* (Enke 1906–07)

Kupferman TR and Foner M, *Universal Copyright Convention Analyzed* (Federal Legal Publications 1955)

de Lavigne AG, *Les Conventions Internationales pour la protection de la propriété littéraire et artistique et des droits de l'auteur* (Larose et Forcel 1891)

Lavollée R, *Propriété littéraire et la Convention de Berne*, extract from *Journal des économistes*, 15 mars 1887 (Guillaumin 1887)

Lermina J, *Convention de Berne, Unification des Législations, Historique de l'Association littéraire et artistique internationale* (Baer 1906)

Majoros F, *Les arrangements bilatéraux en matière de droit d'auteur* (Pedone 1971)

Malaplate L, *Le Droit d'auteur, sa protection dans les rapports franco-étrangers* (Sirey 1931)

Marwitz R, *Die Berner Übereinkunft und die Römische Konferenz. Text, Übersetzungen und Erläuterungen* (Vahlen 1928)

Masouyé C, (trans W Wallace), *Guide to the Berne Convention for the Protection of Literary and Artistic Works* (WIPO 1978)

Masouyé C, *Guide to the Rome Convention and to the Phonograms Convention* (WIPO 1981)

Moynier G, *Les bureaux internationaux des unions universelles* (Cherbuliez 1892)

Nordemann W, Vinck K, and Hertin PW, *Internationales Urheberrecht und Leistungsschutzrecht der deutschaprachigen Länder unter Berücksichtigung auch der Staaten der Europäischen Gemeinschaft, Kommentar* (Werner 1977). Also published in French under the title of *Droit d'auteur international et droits voisins. Commentaire* (trans by J Tournier) (Bruylant 1983)

Orelli AD, *La Conférence internationale pour la protection des droits d'auteur réunie à Berne du 8 au 19 septembre 1884* (Murquardt 1884)

Orelli AD, *La deuxième Conférence internationale pour la protection des oeuvres littéraires et artistiques réunie à Berne du 7 au 18 septembre 1885*, no publisher given (1885), also published in [1886] *Revue de droit international* 37

Peter F-W, *Das Stockholmer Protokoll für die Entwicklungsländer. Gefahr für das internationale Urheberrecht* (Börsenverein des Deutschen Buchhandels 1970)

Petit A, *Étude sur la Convention de Berlin de 1908 pour la protection des oeuvres littéraires et artistiques. Le point de vue littéraire* (Jardin 1911)

Plaisant M and Pichot O, *La Conférence de Rome: Commentaire pratique de la nouvelle Convention pour la protection internationale de la propriété littéraire et artistique* (Recueil Sirey 1934)

Poinsard L, *Études de droit international conventionnel*, Première série. Transports, Transmissions, Relations Economiques Internationales, Propriété Intellectuelle (Pichon 1894)

Poinsard L, *Les Unions et ententes internationales* (2nd edn, Baumgart 1901)

Poinsard L, *La propriété artistique et littéraire et la Conférence de Berlin* (1910), extract from *Annales des Sciences Politiques, Revue bimestrielle*, January 1910 (Alcan 1910)

Potu E, *La Convention de Berne pour la protection des oeuvres littéraires et artistiques. Revisée à Berlin le 13 novembre 1908, et la Protocol additionnel de Berne du 20 mars 1914* (Rousseau 1914)

Pouillet E, *Traité théorique et pratique de la propriété littéraire et artistique et du droit de représentation* (2nd edn, Marchal and Billard 1894)

Pouillet E, *Traité théorique et pratique des dessins et modèles* (5th edn, Marchal and Godde 1911)

'Publisher, A', *Copyright, National and International, with some remarks on the Position of Authors and Publishers* (Sampson Low, Marston, Searle and Rivington 1887)

Putnam GH, *International Copyright Considered in Some of its Relations to Ethics and Political Economy* (Putnams 1879)

Putnam GH, *The Question of Copyright* (2nd edn, Putnams 1896)

Putnam GH, *Memories of a Publisher 1865–1915* (Putnams 1915)

Raestad A, *La Convention de Berne révisée à Rome 1928 pour la protection de la littérature, de la musique, des arts figuratifs, de l'architecture, de l'art appliqué à l'industrie et des oeuvres de photographie et de cinématographie, contenant des dispositions relatives à la reproduction mécanique des sons, à la radiodiffusion et au droit de réimpression de la presse* (Editions internationales 1931)

Regensteiner L, *Schutz des Urhebers eines literarischen Werkes gegen Bearbeitung seines Werkes nach deutschem Recht und nach der revidierten Berner Konvention* (Himmer 1913)

Rehbinder M and Larese W (eds), *Die Berner Übereinkunft und die Schweitz* (Stampfli 1986)

Renault L, *De la propriété littéraire et artistique au point de vue international* (1879)

Report of the United States Observer Delegation to the International Conference for the Revision of the Berne Convention... held in Brussels, Washington (1949)

Rivière L, *La Protection internationale des oeuvres littéraires et artistiques, Etude de législation comparée* (Fontemoing 1897)

Roeber G (ed), *Die Pariser Revisionen der Übereinkünfte zum internationalen Urheberrecht* (Schweitzer 1975)

Röthlisberger E, *Schriftstellerische Postulate zur Revision der Berner Konvention vom 9 September 1886* (Heymanns 1893)

Röthlisberger E, *Préparation de la seconde Conférence diplomatique de révision de la Convention de Berne. Le Colloque de Berlin (novembre 1905)* (1905)

Röthlisberger E, *Die Berner Übereinkunft zum Schutze von Werken der Literatur und Kunst und die Zusatzabkommen. Geschichtlich und rechtlich beleuchtet und kommentiert* (Francke 1906)

Röthlisberger E, *Der interne und internationale Schutz des Urheberrechts in den Ländern des Erdballs* (4th edn, Leipzig 1931, by C Hillig and G Greuner)

Ruffini F, *De la protection internationale des droits sur les oeuvres littéraires et artistiques* (Extrait du Recueil des Cours, Hachette 1927)

Saenger A, *Verhältnis der Berner Konvention zum innerstaatlichen Urheberrecht* (Vlg für Recht und Gesellschaft 1940)

Schulze E, *The forthcoming Stockholm Revision Conference 1967* (also in German and French), Internationale Gesellschaft für Urheberrecht, Schriftenreihe, Band 36 (Vahlen 1964)

Schulze E, *Intellectual Property Conference of Stockholm 1967* (also in German and French), Internationale Gesellschaft für Urheberrecht, Schriftenreihe, Band 39 (Vahlen 1967)

Schulze E, *Revision of the International Copyright* (also in French and German), Internationale Gesellschaft für Urheberrecht, Schriftenreihe, Band 46 (Vahlen 1971)

Sidjanski D and Castanos S, *Droit d'auteur ou copyright. Les rapports entre les différents systèmes en vigueur* (Rouge 1954)

Solberg T, *Report on the Berlin Conference of 1908* (US Copyright Office 1908)

Solberg T, *The Development of International Copyright Relations between the United States and Foreign Countries* (1933)

Soldan C, *L'Union internationale pour la protection des oeuvres littéraires et artistiques. Commentaire de la Convention de Berne du 9 Septembre, 1886* (Thorin 1888), also in (1887) *Revue générale du droit, de la legislation et de la jurisprudence en France et à l'étrangère*, 392–424, 493–520

Strömholm S, *Le droit moral de l'auteur en droit allemand, français et scandinave avec un aperçu de l'évolution internationale*, (Three Parts) (Norstedt and Söners 1966, 1967 and 1973)

L'Union internationale pour la protection des oeuvres littéraires et artistiques. Sa fondation et son développement 1886–1936. Mémoire (Bureau de l'Union 1936)

Vaunois A, *Note sur la Convention de Berne de 1886 relative aux oeuvres littéraires et artistiques (Texte révisée à Berlin en 1908)*, Association des inventeurs et artistes industriels (1908)

Vaunois A, *Protection internationale des oeuvres littéraires et artistiques d'après la Convention d'Union de Berne révisée signée à Berlin le 13 novembre 1908* (2nd edn, Guyonnard 1910)

Wauwermans P, *Le droit des auteurs en Belgique* (1894)

Wauwermans P, *La Convention de Berne (révisée à Berlin) pour la protection des oeuvres littéraires et artistiques* (Rivière 1910)

Wood GS, *Preliminary Observations upon and Arguments against the Amendments to the Berne Convention of 1886 proposed by the Italian Government in conjunction with the Office of the International Union for the Protection of Literary and Artistic Works, with general suggestions for revisions of that convention along different lines* (Mechanical Music Industry of Great Britain 1927)

3.6.2 Secondary sources

Adeney E, *The Moral Rights of Authors and Performers: An International and Comparative Analysis* (OUP 2006)

Bannerman S, *The Struggle for Canadian Copyright: Imperialism to Internationalism, 1842–1971* (UBC Press 2013)

Bannerman S, *International Copyright and Access to Knowledge* (CUP 2016)

Bappert W and Wager E, *Internationales Urheberrecht, Kommentar* (Beck, Munich and Berlin 1956)

Bappert W, Maunz T and Schricker G, *Verlagsrecht, Kommentar zum Gesetz über das Verlagsrecht vom 19.6.1901* (2nd edn, Beck Munich 1984)

Barker RE, *Copyright: The New International Conventions* (Publisher's Association 1971)

Barnes JJ, *Authors, Publishers and Politicians: The Quest for an Anglo-American Copyright Agreement, 1815–1854* (Routledge & Kegan Paul 1974)

Beier F-K, 'One Hundred Years of International Cooperation – The Role of the Paris Convention in the Past, Present and Future' (1984) 15 International Review of Industrial Property and Copyright Law 1

Bellido J, 'Colonial copyright extensions: Spain at the Berne Convention' (2011) 58 J Copyright Society USA 243

Bellido J, 'Copyright in Latin America. Experiences of the Making 1880–1910' (PhD, Birkbeck, University of London 2009)

Bellido J, 'Latin American and Spanish Copyright Bilateral Agreements (1880–1904)' (2009) 12 JWIP 1

Bellido J, 'Montevideo vs Berne: The Rise of an Interpretation in International Copyright' (2011) 229 Revue Internationale du Droit d'Auteur 1

Bellido J, 'The Editorial Quest for International Copyright (1886–1896)' (2014) 17 Book History 380

Bently L and Sherman B, 'Great Britain and the Signing of the Berne Convention in 1886' (2001) 48 J Copyright Society USA 311

Bogsch A, *The Law of Copyright under the Universal Copyright Convention* (3rd rev edn, Sijthoff, Leyden and Bowker 1972)

Bogsch A, 'The First Hundred Years of the Paris Convention for the Protection of Industrial Property' (July/August 1983) *Industrial Property* 187

Bogsch A, 'Special Issue for the Commemoration of the Berne Convention: The First Hundred Years of the Berne Convention for the Protection of Literary and Artistic Works' [1986] Copyright 291

Bogsch A, 'Brief History of the First 25 Years of the World Intellectual Property Organization' [1992] Copyright 247

Boguslavsky M, *The USSR and International Copyright Protection* (trans from Russian) (Progress Publishers 1979)

Boytha G, *Reciprocity in International Copyright Law* (Hungarian Branch of the International Law Association 1968)

Boytha G, *Interrelationship of Conventions on Copyright and Neighbouring Rights* (Hungarian Academy of Sciences 1983)

Burke P, *The Law of International Copyright between England and France in Literature, the Drama, Music and the Fine Arts* (Sampson Low 1852)

Cavalli J, *La genèse de la convention de Berne sur La Protection Internationale des Œuvres de Littéraires et Artistiques* (Université de Lausanne 1986)

Dock MC, *Etude sur le droit d'auteur* (Pichon and Durand-Auzias 1963)

Duchemin J-L, *Le droit de suite des artistes* (Recueil Sirey 1948)

Hemmungs Wirtén E, 'A Diplomatic Salto Mortale: Translation Trouble in Berne, 1884–1886' (2001) 14 Book History 88

Jarrold S, *A Handbook of English and Foreign Copyright in Literary and Dramatic Works* (Chatto and Windus 1881)

Kase JR, *Copyright Thought in Continental Europe: Its Development, Legal Theories and Philosophy; a Selected and Annotated Bibliography* (Rothman 1967)

Ladas SP, *The International Protection of Literary and Artistic Property* (The MacMillan Company 1938)

Ladas SP, *Patents, Trademarks, and Related Rights: National and International Protection* (Harvard UP 1975)

Masouyé C, 'The Role of ALAI in the Development of International Copyright Law' (1978) 14 Copyright 120

Moyse P-E, 'Canadian Colonial Copyright: The Colony Strikes Back' in Ysolde Gendreau (ed), *An Emerging Intellectual Property Paradigm, Perspectives from Canada* (Edward Elgar 2008) 107

Moyse P-E, 'Colonial Copyright Redux: 1709 v. 1832', in L Bently, U Suthersanen and P Torremans (eds), *Global Copyright* (Edward Elgar 2010) 144

Nowell-Smith S, *International Copyright Law and the Publisher in the Reign of Queen Victoria* (Clarendon Press 1968)

Ricketson S, *The Berne Convention for the Protection of Literary and Artistic Works: 1886–1985* (Kluwer 1987)

Ricketson S and Ginsburg JC, *International Copyright and Neighbouring Rights: The Berne Convention and Beyond* (2nd edn, OUP 2006)

Rodríguez Tapia JM, 'Centenario de la Unión de Berna: 1886–1986. Precedentes históricos' (1986) Anuario de Derecho Civil 885

Seville C, *The Internationalisation of Copyright Law: Books, Buccaneers, and the Black Flag in the Nineteenth Century* (CUP 2006)

Seville C, 'Edward Bulwer Lytton Dreams of Copyright: "It might make me a rich man"' in F O'Gorman, *Victorian Literature and Finance* (OUP 2007) 55

Seville C, 'The Principles of International Intellectual Property Protection: From Paris to Marrakesh' (2013) 5 WIPOJ 95

4. WORKS EXPLORING AUTHORSHIP OR THE TRADE

Amory H and Hall DD (eds), *A History of the Book in America: The Colonial Book in the Atlantic World* (UNC Press 2007)

Amory H, '"De Facto Copyright"? Fielding's Works in Partnership, 1769–1821' (1984) 17 Eighteenth-Century Studies 449

Astbury R, 'The Renewal of the Licensing Act in 1693 and its Lapse in 1695' (1978) 5th ser, 33 The Library 296

Baines P and Rogers P, *Edmund Curll, Bookseller* (OUP 2007)

Baldwin P, *The Copyright Wars, Three Centuries of Trans-Atlantic Battle* (Princeton UP 2014)

Belanger T, 'Booksellers' Sales of Copyright: Aspects of the London Book Trade 1718–1768' (PhD, Columbia University 1970)

Belanger T, 'Booksellers' Trade Sales, 1718–1768' (1975) 5th ser, 30 The Library 281

Belanger T, 'Tonson, Wellington and the Shakespeare Copyrights' in *Studies in the Book Trade: In Honour of Graham Pollard* (Oxford Bibliographical Society 1975) 195

Belanger T, 'Publishers and Writers in Eighteenth-Century England' in I Rivers (ed), *Books and their Readers in Eighteenth-Century England* (Leicester UP 1982) 5

Bell M, 'Women in the English Book Trade 1557–1700' (1996) 6 Leipziger Jahrbuch zur Buchgeschichte 13

Black J, *The English Press in the Eighteenth Century* (U of Pennsylvania Press 1987)

Blayney PWM, *The Bookshops in Paul's Cross Churchyard* (Bibliographical Society 1990)

Bonnell TF, *The Most Disreputable Trade: Publishing the Classics of English Poetry 1765–1810* (OUP 2008)

Brown GS, *Literary Sociability and Literary Property in France, 1775–1793* (Ashgate 2006)

Brown HF, *The Venetian Printing Press* (reprint 1969) (1891)

Collins AS, *Authorship in the Days of Johnson* (Routledge & Kegan Paul 1927)

Coombe RJ, *The Cultural Life of Intellectual Properties: Authorship, Appropriation, and the Law* (Duke UP 1998)

Crist T, 'Government Control of the Press after the Expiration of the Printing Act in 1679' (1979) 5 Publishing History 49

Dawson NM, 'The Death Throes of the Licensing Act and the "Funeral Pomp" of Queen Mary II, 1695' (2005) 26 J Legal Hist 119

Dawson R, *The French Booktrade and the 'Permission Simple' of 1777: Copyright and Public Domain* (Voltaire Foundation 1992)

Dickson R and Edmond JP, *Annals of Scottish Printing: From the Introduction of the Art in 1507 to the Beginning of the Seventeenth Century* (Macmillan & Bowes 1890)

Dugas D-J, 'The London Book Trade in 1709 (Part One)' (2001) 95 Papers of the Bibliographical Society of America 31

Dugas D-J, 'The London Book Trade in 1709 (Part Two)' (2001) 95 Papers of the Bibliographical Society of America 157

Dunstan V, 'Book Ownership in late Eighteenth-century Scotland: a Local Case Study of Dumfriesshire Inventories' (2012) 91 Scottish Historical Review 265

Eisenstein EL, *The Printing Press as an Agent of Change* (CUP 1979)

Eisenstein EL, *The Printing Revolution in Early Modern Europe* (2nd edn, CUP 2005)

Feather J, *A History of British Publishing* (2nd edn, Routledge 2006)

Febvre L and Martin H-J, *The Coming of the Book: The Impact of Printing, 1450–1800* (D Gerrard trans, NLB 1976)

Feltes NN, *Modes of Production of Victorian Novels* (U Chicago Press 1986)

Feltes NN, *Literary Capital and the Late Victorian Novel* (U Wisconsin Press 1993)

Foucault M, 'What is an Author?' (James Venit tr) (1975) 42 Partisan Rev 603

Foxon D, *Pope and the Early Eighteenth-Century Book Trade* (Clarendon Press 1991)

Girdham J, *English Opera in Late Eighteenth-Century London. Stephen Storace at Drury Lane* (OUP 1997)

Greene J, *The Trouble with Ownership: Literary Property and Authorial Liability in England, 1660–1730* (U of Pennsylvania Press 2005)

Gregg WW, *Some Aspects and Problems of London Publishing Between 1550 and 1650* (Clarendon Press 1956)

Griffin D, *Literary Patronage in England 1650–1800* (CUP 1996)

Griffin D, *Authorship in the Long Eighteenth Century* (U of Delaware Press 2014)

Hamm Jr RB, 'Walker v. Tonson in the Court of Public Opinion' (2012) 75 Huntington Library Quarterly 95

Handover PM, *Printing in London from 1476 to Modern Times* (Harvard UP 1960)

Harvey DJ, *The Law Emprynted and Englysshed: The Printing Press as an Agent of Change in Law and Legal Culture 1475–1642* (Hart Publishing 2015)

Hellinga L, *William Caxton and Early Printing in England* (British Library 2010)

Jaszi P, 'Toward a Theory of Copyright: The Metamorphoses of "Authorship"' (1991) 40 Duke LJ 455

Jaszi P, 'Is There Such a Thing as Postmodern Copyright?' in M Biagioli, P Jaszi and M Woodmansee (eds), *Making and Unmaking Intellectual Property: Creative Production in Legal and Cultural Perspective* (U Chicago P 2011) 413

Jaszi P and Woodmansee M, 'The Ethical Reaches of Authorship' (1996) 95 South Atlantic Quarterly 953

Johns A, *The Nature of the Book* (Chicago UP 1998)

Johns A, *Piracy: The Intellectual Property Wars from Gutenberg to Gates* (Chicago UP 2010)

Judge CB, *Elizabethan Book-Pirates* (Harvard UP 1934)

Kewes P, *Authorship and Appropriation: Writing for the Stage in England 1660–1710* (OUP 1998)

Kewes P, *Plagiarism in Early Modern England* (Palgrave 2003)

Lehmann-Haupt H, *The Book in America: A History of the Making, and Selling of Books in the United States* (Bowker 1951)

Mazzeo TJ, *Plagiarism and Literary Property in the Romantic Period* (U of Pennsylvania Press 2007)

McDougall W, 'Gavin Hamilton, John Balfour and Patrick Neill: A Study of Publishing in Edinburgh in the 18th Century' (PhD, University of Edinburgh 1974)

Mcfarlane R, *Original Copy: Plagiarism and Originality in Nineteenth-Century Literature* (OUP 2007)

McGill M, *American Literature and the Culture of Reprinting 1834–1853* (U of Pennsylvania Press 2003)

McKitterick D, *Print, Manuscript and the Search for Order 1450–1830* (CUP 2003)

Parkinson JA, 'Pirates and Publishers' (1972) 58 Performing Right Journal 20

Paschall G, *A History of Printing in North Carolina* (Edwards & Broughton 1946)

Pettegree A, *The Book in the Renaissance* (Yale UP 2010)

Plant M, *The English Book Trade: An Economic History of the Making and Sale of Books* (2nd edn, George Allen & Unwin 1965)

Pottinger DT, *The French Book Trade in the Ancien Régime 1500–1791* (Harvard UP 1958)

Price C, Milhous J and Hume RD, *Italian Opera in Late Eighteenth-Century London* (OUP 1995)

Putnam GH, *Authors and Their Public in Ancient Times: A Sketch of Literary Conditions and of the Relations With the Public of Literary Producers, From the Earliest Times to the Invention of Printing* (GP Putnam's Sons 1894)

Raven J, *Judging New Wealth: Popular Publishing and Responses to Commerce in England, 1750–1800* (Clarendon Press 1992)

Raven J, *The Business of Books: Booksellers and the English Book Trade 1450–1850* (Yale UP 2007)

Raven J, *Bookscape: Geographies of Printing and Publishing before 1800* (British Library 2014)

Raven J, *Publishing Business in Eighteenth-Century England* (Boydell Press 2014)

Rogers P and Baines P, 'Edmund Curll, Citizen and Liveryman: Politics and the Book Trade' (2007) 62 Publishing History 5

St Clair W, *The Reading Nation in the Romantic Period* (CUP 2004)

St Clair W, 'Metaphors of Intellectual Property' in R Deazley, M Kretschmer and L Bently (eds), *Privilege and Property: Essays on the History of Copyright* (OpenBook Publishers 2010) 369

Saunders D, *Authorship and Copyright* (Routledge 1992)

Saunders D, 'Dropping the Subject: An Argument for a Positive History of Authorship and the Law of Copyright' in Sherman B and Strowel A (eds), *Of Authors and Origins: Essays on Copyright Law* (Clarendon Press 1994) 93

Sher RB, 'Corporatism and Consensus in the Late Eighteenth-Century Book Trade: The Edinburgh Booksellers' Society in Comparative Perspective' (1998) 1 Book History 32

Sher RB, *The Enlightenment and the Book: Scottish Authors and their Publishers in Eighteenth-Century Britain, Ireland, and America* (Chicago UP 2006)

Sherman B and Strowel A (eds), *Of Authors and Origins: Essays on Copyright Law* (Clarendon Press 1994)

Simpson P, 'Literary Piracy in the Elizabethan Age' (1947) New ser, 1 Oxford Bibliographical Society Publications 1

Spoo R, *Without Copyrights: Piracy, Publishing, and the Public Domain* (OUP 2013)

Stevenson S and Morrison-Low AD, *Scottish Photography: The First Thirty Years* (National Museums Scotland 2015)

Tebbel JW, *A History of Book Publishing in the United States* (RR Bowker Co 1972)

Thomas I, *The History of Printing in America* (J Munsell 1874)

Townsley MRM, *Reading the Scottish Enlightenment: Books and their Readers in Provincial Scotland, 1750–1820* (Brill 2010)

Treadwell M, 'London Printers and Printing Houses in 1705' (1980) 7 Publishing History 5

Woodmansee M, 'The Genius and the Copyright: Economic and Legal Conditions of the Emergence of the "Author"' (1984) 17 Eighteenth Century Studies 425

Woodmansee M, 'On the Author Effect: Recovering Collectivity' (1992) 10 Cardozo Arts & Ent LJ 279

Woodmansee M, *The Author, Art and the Market: Rereading the History of Aesthetics* (Columbia UP 1994)

Woodmansee M, 'The Cultural Work of Copyright: Legislating Authorship in Britain 1837–1842' in A Sarat and TR Kearns (eds), *Law in the Domains of Culture* (Michigan UP 1998)

Woodmansee M and Jaszi P (eds), *The Construction of Authorship: Textual Appropriation in Law and Literature* (Duke UP 1994)

Woodmansee M and Jaszi P, 'The Law of Texts' (1995) 57 College English 769

Wroth LC, *A History of Printing in Colonial Maryland, 1686–1776* (Typothetae of Baltimore 1922)

Yeo R, *Encyclopaedic Visions: Scientific Dictionaries and Enlightenment Culture* (CUP 2001)

Zachs W, *The First John Murray and the Late 18th Century London Book Trade* (OUP 1998)

Index

Abrams, Howard 20, 21, 47
abridgements 178, 179–80, 183, 187–9
abstraction thesis 43–5
Adeney, Elizabeth 309
Ailwood, Sarah 378, 379–80, 381–2, 387
Alexander, Isabella 24, 209
Alexander v Mackenzie (1847) (Scotland) 136
American Authors League 368
American International Copyright Association 365
American Publishers' Copyright League 15–16
Arnold, Sir Richard 12
art
   artistic copyright *see* artistic copyright
   artists' indifference towards audiences 29–30
   associationist aesthetics theory 35–6
   fine art as a coherent category 29
   function of 35–6
artistic copyright 3, 158–73
   Copyright Act (1911) 168
   engraving 160–63
   infringement 172
   painting 164–5
   photography 165–8
   privileges for images in France 159–60
   registration and ownership 170–72
   sculpture 163–4
   term and qualification 169–70
Austen v Cave (1739) 177
Australia 3
   artistic copyright 168
   colonies, copyright in *see* Australian colonies, copyright in
   copyright history, use of 8
   definition of copyright 176
   federation of 374
   legal distinctiveness 187
   photographic copyright 166
   precedent 187
Australian colonies, copyright in 372–90
   application of British law to colonies 373
   case law 379
   colonial newspapers 379–80, 381, 382
   dramatic copyright 362–5

   emergence of colonial copyright history as field of legal discourse 376–7
   first copyright statute in a colony 387–8
   formal and informal regulation on copyright 385
   Imperial 'adherence' and influence, exploration of 378–9, 387
   pessimistic view of colonial culture 385–6
   role and influence of Imperial law 372–3
   Routledge v Low, impact of 386–7
   see also British colonial and imperial copyright
authorship
   abstraction thesis 43–5
   Berne Convention *see* Berne Convention (1886)
   collaborative production, and 70, 76
   construction of authorship 30–33
   definition of 53
   derivative nature of creative work 53–4, 54–8
   development of 28, 31–2
   foundation of Anglo copyright, as 50
   international copyright, authorial entitlement in 62–3, 64, 70
   literary property extended to letters 40
   Locke 48–50, 51
   modern invention of 30
   natural law, ideas belonging to 30
   natural right to own creation 38
   prior right to literary property 37–8
   proprietor, author as 37–42
   'romantic' authors *see* 'romantic' authors
   theories of 30, 31–2
   traditional culture, and 70–71

Bach v Longman & Lukey (1777) 3, 140, 144–5, 156, 352
Bagehot, Walter: *The English Constitution* 13, 14
Baldwin, Peter 401–2
Bankton, Lord 120–21, 126, 127, 132
   Institute 125
Baskett v Parsons (1718) 221–2, 225
Battle of the Booksellers 18, 97, 123–4

471

cheap reprints of registered works as cause 123
legal action by London booksellers 124–7
remedies, different approach of English and Scottish judges to 124–6
reasons for 126–7
Beckford v Hood (1798) 135, 224–5
Beijing Audio-Visual Performers Treaty (2012) 291
Bell, George Joseph 122, 136
Commentaries 123, 134–5
Principles of the Laws of Scotland 98, 123
Bently, Lionel 175
artistic copyright 162, 165, 168, 173
bilateral copyright treaties 164, 165
painting 164
colonial copyright 287, 322, 377
Dear Images 164
Privilege and Property: Essays on the History of Copyright 12
The Common Law of Intellectual Property 167–8
The Making of Modern Intellectual Property Law 11, 164
Statute of Anne 174
Bergk, Johann Adam: *Die Kunst, Bücher zu lesen* (The Art of Reading Books) 33–4, 35
Berne Convention (1886) 53, 62, 173, 182, 303
basis of protection 311
Berlin Revision (1908) 182, 183, 270, 283–5
British colonial copyright, and 281–3, 287
Berlin Revisions 283–5
Canada 281–3
membership of value to colonies 281–2
UK signing for colonies and possessions 270, 281
compliance 306
conference records 294–9
derivative works 251–2
developing countries 308
droit de suite 309
duration of protection 309
implementation of provisions 305, 306
International Office, role of 311–12
moral rights 309
neighbouring and related rights 310–11
new technologies 310
no registration requirements 308–9
obligations 291
origins 63–4, 269, 291, 328–30

purpose 64
scope of protection 311
WIPO, role of 311–12
Berne International Office 293, 294, 295, 311
Berne Convention, role regarding 311–12
Bertauld, Alfred 418
Birrell, Augustine 13–14, 16, 17, 22, 190–91
Black v Murray (1870) (Scotland) 136
Blackstone, William 14–15, 16, 21, 44
Commentaries on the Laws of England 37, 38, 4
Blackwell v Harper (1740) 219–20, 222–3, 224, 225
Blayney, Peter 82–3, 83–4, 85, 86
Bleistein v Donaldson Lithographic Company (1903) (US) 365
Boisjermain, Luneau de 402
book privileges 30–31
England *see under* Stationers' Company in England before 1710
France *see* French literary property developments in 18th and 19th centuries
Germany 30–32
Scotland *see* Scotland: copyright law before 1710
Vatican *see* Papal printing privileges in 16th century
Boosey v Whight (1900) 181
Boswell, James 55, 57, 129
Bowker, Richard R 21
Bowrey, Kathy 11, 158
colonial copyright 378, 379, 387, 389
infringement 185, 186, 187
photography 166, 167, 378
The World Daguerreotyped: What a Spectacle 167, 168
Boyle, James 12
Bracha, Oren 186
Bramwell v Halcomb (1863) 179
Bray, Samuel 195–6
British colonial and imperial copyright 3, 268–87, 372–3
Berne Convention 281–3
Berne Convention, Berlin Revision of 283–5
copyright and foreign reprints: overview 268–70
constitutional questions in Britain's relationship with colonies 260–70
difficulties in enforcing rules 269
foreign piracy of English books 268
introduction of British system of international copyright 269

mass market for books, emergence of 269
Copyright Act 1842 and its impact on the colonies 270–73
Copyright Act (1911) 285–6
copyright in Dominion of Canada 275–9
early British Copyright Acts and their coverage 270
Foreign Reprints Act 1874, towards 273–5
India 286–7
Royal Commission on Copyright and Colonial Issues 279–81
see also Australian colonies, copyright in
Brussels Congress on Literary and Artistic Property (1858) 63
Bulun Bulun v R & T Textiles (1998) 71–7
Bürger, Gottfried August: *Lenore* 33, 35
Burnet v Chetwood (1720) 177
Burrell, Robert 184, 377–8
Bury, Michael 256–7
Butler, Joseph 46

Cadell and Davies v Robertson (1804) (Scot) 135–6, 137
Cadell and Davies v Stewart (1804) (Scot) 133–4, 137
Caird v Sime (1885) (Scot) 136
Canada
   American book trade, and 282–3
   Berne Convention, and 281–3, 285
      Berlin Revision, and 284–5
   book market 270–73, 273–5
   Copyright Act 1842, impact of 270–73
   Copyright Act (1911) 286
   copyright in Canada 275–9
   foreign reprints 269, 273–5
Carnan v Paterson (1786) 209
Cary v Kearsley (1802) 191
censorship 25, 39
   privileges not part of mechanism of censorship 84
   Scotland 99, 100
Chambers, Ephraim: *Cyclopaedia* 191–2
Cinquin v Lecocq (1902) (France) 419–20
Ciolino, Dane 12
Clarke, Marcus: *His Natural Life* 376, 378
Coleridge, Samuel Taylor 32, 35–6
   genius 54
   On the Principles of Genial Criticism Concerning the Fine Arts 35
   Wordsworth, collaboration with 59–60, 61
collaborative and collective production 70, 76

colonies and dominions *see* Australian colonies, copyright in; British colonial and imperial
common law copyright 13, 17–21, 22, 174
   Donaldson v Becket establishing nature/purpose of copyright 18–21
   natural rights 21, 22, 25, 354
   right to divulge 13
   Statute of Anne, and 13, 17–21
      common law right superseded 18, 20–21, 36
   whether common law recognised literary property 17
   whether common law right had existed 19, 20–21
   whether copyright a property right or statutory privilege 17–18, 25
Company of Stationers *see* Stationers' Company in England before 1710
Condorcet, Nicolas de 397, 401, 402, 410
   Fragments 410
Copinger, WA 20, 181
   Copinger and Skone James on Copyright 13, 293
copyright law in Scotland *see* Scotland: copyright law before 1710
Cornish, William 175, 176
   Oxford History of the Laws of England 176
Craig, Sir Thomas: *Jus Feudale* 98
customary international law 292

D'Agostino, Guiseppina: *The Common Law of Intellectual Property* 167–8
Davis, Bertram 56
Deazley, Ronan 13, 20, 21, 23, 24, 42, 168
   abridgements 188
   Brydges and legal deposit debates 193
   disgorgement 220
   engraving 160–61
   History of Photography 165–6
   painting 165
   photography 165–6, 167
   Primary Sources on Copyright History 1, 160–61, 163
   Privilege and Property: Essays on the History of Copyright 12, 165
   Rethinking Copyright 11
   sculpture 163
definition of copyright 176
Defoe, Daniel 48, 106, 188
   A Book is the Author's Property, 'tis the Child of his Invention 39, 40

An Essay on the Regulation of the Press
    94–5
derivative nature of creative work 53–4, 54–8
    borrowing sermons 55–6
    ghostwriting 56–7
developing countries 70
    translation rights, exceptions, and 308
Dicey, Edward 25
Diderot, Denis 391, 396, 397–8, 402
    Lettre sur le commerce de la librairie 397
disgorgement of profits 3, 220–27
    earliest disgorgement order 220–21
    legal basis for award 222–5
    process for assessing profits 225–7
    process for obtaining profits 225
    standard for obtaining profits 225
Dodsley v MacFarquhar (1775) (Scot) 132–3, 137
Donaldson v Becket (1774) 13, 17, 18–21, 23, 27–8, 42–3, 49, 96, 128–9, 131, 145, 174, 178, 215
Donelson, Erin 12
Drone, ES 292
Duke of Queensberry v Shebbeare (1758) 134

Edelman, Bernard 166
El Salvador and internationalisation of copyright 3, 313–31
    Britain and El Salvador, negotiations between 321–5
    El Salvador as catalyst for internationalisation 316–17
    Franco-Salvadorian Copyright Treaty 317–21
    José María Torres Caicedo, role of 313–16
    ALAI, and 314, 315, 317, 321, 328
    international copyright convention, preparation for 328–30
    treaty negotiations 317, 319–27
    Paris-Berne, from 328–30
    Salvadorian-Spanish Copyright Treaty 315, 325–7
engraving 160–63
Enlightenment philosophy 193
Enquiry Into the Origin and Nature of Literary Property 7–8, 13, 14
Epstein, Larry 85–6
equitable infringement remedies before 1800 195–234
    disgorgement of profits 3, 220–27
    earliest disgorgement order 220–21
    legal basis for award 222–5
    process for assessing profits 225–7

    process for obtaining profits 225
    standard for obtaining profits 225
    injunctions *see* injunctions
Erskine, John 126, 127, 132
expansion of copyright 69–70
expert opinion in copyright cases 77

fair use/fair dealing 178–9, 180, 182, 184–7, 190
    abridgements/fair abridgement principle 178, 179–80, 183, 187–8, 189
    comment 180
    corrective to authorial bias of law 77
    criticism 179, 180
    illustration 179, 180
    quotation 178–9, 180
    rebalancing rights in interests of artistic freedom 77
    review 180
    Royal Commission on Copyright 182
    United States 12, 184, 186–7
Farrer, Sir Thomas 20, 22, 25, 26, 278, 280
Fichte, Johann Gottlieb 30, 31–2, 39
Finn, Jeremy 375, 375–6
Finnamore, John 381, 382, 386–7, 389, 390
Folsom v March (1841) (US) 186, 187, 361
Fontana v Public Attorney (1857) (France) 416
Foucault, Michel 28, 30
France 3, 100
    authors and artists, importance of 290
    Berne Convention 307
    bilateral agreements 290
    Code of Intellectual Property 238
    copyright as incorporeal right 238
    Franco-Salvadorian Copyright Treaty 316, 317–21
    Franco-Spanish bilateral copyright treaty 425, 438–9
    French Declaration (1789) 410
    literary property *see* French literary property developments in 18th and 19th centuries
    photographic copyright 166
    privileges for images 159–60
French literary property developments in 18th and 19th centuries 391–422
    booksellers supporting literary property 391–2
    Boufflers' report 412
    Decree of 30 August 1777, effects of 405–7
    foundations of *droit d'auteur*, development of 391

Hell's bill supporting literary property 410–11, 412
introduction of 1793 Act 413–14
later debates on duration of literary property 414
Le Chapelier's bill for the Dramatic Act of 1791 411–12
literary property in debates 397–403
　Condorcet's arguments against protecting books 401
　Diderot's personalisation of literary property 397–8
　Gaultier's rejection of idea of incorporeal property 400–401
　Linguet's concept of literary work bearing author's personality 398–9
　personal nature of literary property at heart of debate 401
　social contract/public utility argument 402–3
　transferability of personal property 401–2
Louis d'Héricourt's Memorandum (1725–26) 393–7, 401
　authors as central/original source of natural property right 394–6
　book privileges granted as act of 'justice' 396
　booksellers securing royal privileges 393–4
　common and particular books 393–4
　opposition to supporters of literary property 396–7
personal property in the courts 415–21
　definition of literary and artistic work 415–17
　droit moral, development of 421
　protection of non-pecuniary rights 417–21
royal book privileges, principle of exclusivity stemming from 391
Sieyès bill to regulate book market 409–10
utilitarian justifications 414–15
Frosio, Giancarlo 17
Furetière, Antoine: *Dictionnaire Universel* 393

Gahagan v Cooper (1811) 164
Garran, Robert Randolph: *The Annotated Constitution of the Australian Commonwealth* 374–6
Gaultier de Biauzat, Jean-François 397, 400–401, 402
　Fragments sur la liberté de la Presse 401
Gay v Walker (1729) 220–21, 222, 223, 225

genius
　individual origination/innovation 54, 55, 62
　nature of 31, 32
　gendered nature of 34–5
Germany
　aesthetic thinkers 28–36
　book publishing industry 30–31
　book privileges 30–31
　　need to improve material conditions of authors and publishers 31–2
　concept of authorship, development of 32
　ideas belonging to the public, concept of 30
Gill, Stephen 60
Ginsburg, Jane 185, 414–15
ghostwriting 56–7
Gladstone, William 272, 273, 277
Golan v Holder (2012) (US) 9
Gómez-Arostegui, Tomás 19, 20–21, 175
Gompel, Steph van 308–9
Gordon, Wendy 24
Gorell Committee 183, 284
Gournay, Vincent de 408
Graves' Case (1868–69) 167
Gyles v Wilcox (1740) 178, 186, 188, 213–14

Hale, Sir Matthew: *Pleas of the Crown* 178
Hargrave, Francis: *Argument in Defence of Literary Property* 37, 38–9, 42
Hargraves, Matthew: *Candidates for Fame* 162
Havas, Bullier & Co. v Gounouilhou (1861) (France) 416–17
Hawkins, John 56
Haydn, Joseph 153
Héricourt, Louis d' 393–7, 398, 401, 403, 406–7, 410
Hesse, Carla 409
Hills v Lee (1681) 214, 217–18, 218–19
Hinton v Donaldson (1773) (Scotland) 15, 18, 119, 126, 128–32, 135–6, 137
Hirst, Paul 166
Hitch v Langley (1739) 177
Hogarth, William 160, 161–2
Hogg v Scott (1874) 180
Hollingshead, John 193
Hoock, Holger 163
Horne v Baker (1709) 223–4
Howden Lord 438–41
Howell, Jordan 188, 189
Hughes, Justin 12–13, 166
Hugo, Victor 63, 64
Hume, David 122, 137
Hunter, David 160

Huston, John: *Asphalt Jungle* 422

IceTV v Nine Network (2009) (Aus) 9, 23
Imperial Book Co v Black (1905) (Can) 283
infringement in 18th and 19th century Britain 3, 174–94
  abridgements/fair abridgement principle 178, 179–180, 183, 187–9
  book trade practice 186, 187–8, 189
  cinematographic film, reproduction on 181
  different approaches to infringement 181–2
  fair dealing 184–7
    public interest concerns 185–6
  fair use 178–9, 180, 182, 184, 186–7, 190
  substantial taking, threshold of 179
  transformative technologies 181
  translations 180–81
  works of information 190, 191–3
  see also equitable infringement remedies before 1800
injunctions 3, 196–220
  categories of injunctions 197–214
    injunctions granted at hearing 210–14
    injunctions until answer 197–207
    injunctions until hearing 207–10
  earliest injunctions 196–7
  injunctions granted at hearing 210–14
  injunctions until answer 197–207
  merits required 215–20
    final injunction, for 217–20
    interlocutory injunction, for 215–17
intellectual property
  alleged newness of term 13
  development of 16–17
international copyright 15–16, 64, 164
  authorial entitlement in 62–3, 64
  British system of international copyright 63, 269, 281
  Berne Convention *see* Berne Convention (1886)
  public international law *see* public international law of copyright and related rights
  traditional culture 70
  US 365–9
  see also British colonial and imperial copyright
International Law Commission 292
International Literary and Artistic Association (ALAI) 64, 291, 294, 297, 302, 307
  El Salvador as experiment to make copyright international 317–19, 325, 329–30
  promoting international copyright discourse 316
  Torres Caicedo as President 314, 315, 317, 321, 328
International Publishers Association 297, 302

Jaszi, Peter 53, 62–3, 64, 70
Jefferson, Thomas 12
Johns, Adrian (*Piracy*) 1, 11
  Brydges and legal deposit debates 193
Johnson, Samuel 55–8
  collaborative and collective work 55–6, 58
  Dictionary of the English Language 55
  ghostwriting 56–7
  Life of Pope 56
  Lives of the Poets 55–6
  The Plays of William Shakespeare 55

Kames, Lord: 126–7, 131
  Principles of Equity 126–7, 131
Kant, Immanuel 418
  Critique of Judgment 33, 35
Kaplan, Benjamin: *An Unhurried View of Copyright* 7, 10, 11
Karno v Pathé Frères (1908) 181
Kenrick, William 174–5
Kernan, Alvin 57–8
Klostermann, Rudolf 419
Kretschmer, Martin: *Privilege and Property: Essays on the History of Copyright* 12

La Roche, Sophie von: *Fräulein von Sternheim* 34–5
labour
  authorial labour 185
  converting good into private property through labour 37–8
  differentiation of 'authoring' from ordinary literary labour 55–6
  incentivisation of creative labour 23, 24
  labour theory of property 44, 45, 394
  natural rights arising from labour 392–3
Ladas, Stephen 306
Latour v Bland (1818) 149
Latour v Weller (1818) 149
Lauriat, Barbara 193–4
Le Droit d'auteur/Copyright 299–302, 304, 305, 306, 311
League of Nations 302, 311
Leeming, Mark 190
legal positivism 44
Linguet, Simon 393, 396, 397–8, 401–2, 405, 407, 410

Annales politiques, civiles et littéraires 398
literary property in Scotland *see* Scotland: literary property in 18th and 19th centuries
Lobban, Michael 40, 175
Locke, John 27, 44, 93–4
   Essay on Human Understanding 44, 46, 48, 50
   importance of consciousness 46–7
   poetry 47–8
   properties of Locke's self 45–6
   property of Locke's text 46–50, 51
   Thoughts Concerning Education 47
   Two Treatises on Government 37–8, 39, 40, 45
Lucasfilm v Ainsworth (2011) 8–9
Lytton, Edward Bulwer 193

McCaulay, Anne 165
Macaulay, Lord 12, 278, 279
   Lays of Ancient Rome 277, 278
Madrid Trademark Protocol 312
Malesherbes, Guillaume-Chrétien de Lamoignon de 402–3
   Mémoires sur la librairie 402
Marie v Lacordaire (1845) (France) 418
May, Christopher 23
   Intellectual Property Rights: A Critical History 16–17
Midwinter v Hamilton (1748) (Scotland) 124–7
Millar v Taylor (1769) 17, 18, 19, 21, 38, 128, 130, 178, 215, 216–17, 225
Milsom, SFC 189–90
Milton, John 39, 49
   Paradise Lost 204
Molyneux, William 48–9
monopolies
   lawful monopolies granted for public good 121
   privileges as temporary commercial monopolies 84
   Stationers' Company monopoly, breaking 23
More, John Shank 122–3
Morillot, André 418–19, 420
Moritz, Karl Philipp: *Towards a Unification of all the Fine Arts and Letters under the Concept of Self-Sufficiency* 29–30
Morse v Reid (1798) (US) 348
music copyright 3, 139–57
   Bach v Longman 144–5
   compositions first printed on Continent, status of 154–5
   compositions written by foreign composers, status of 153–4
   music as intellectual property 139
   musical adaptations, status of 151–3
   registration of musical works with Stationers' Company 146
   royal privileges granting exclusive rights 140–41
   Statute of Anne, seeking to apply 141–3

nature of copyright 28
Netanel, Neil 24
'new matter' doctrine 251–2
Ng, Catherine: *The Common Law of Intellectual Property* 167–8
Nikolaus-Peifer, Karl 22–3
Nottage v Jackson (1882–83) 166

originality
   individual genius/originality, focus on 54
   Literary Copyright Act (1847), concept of originality 432
   and modernization of copyright 364–5

painting 164–5
Papal printing privileges 3, 237–67
   adaptations and translations/derivative work 249–53
      artists' images, exclusive rights in 252–3
      'new matter' doctrine 251–2
      privilege extending over derivative works 249–51
   authorship, privileges grounded in 238, 239, 263–6
   exclusive rights granted as a 'special grace' 239
   justifications for privileges 259–67
   remedies and enforcement 256–8
      confiscation of infringing matter 256
      excommunication 247, 254, 256
      fines 256
   revocation of privileges 266–7
   rights protected 246–53
      adaptations and translations 249–53
      duration 248
      geographic scope 246–7
      Papal privileges as multiterritorial 246–7
      reproduction, sale and importation 248–9
      territorial nature of exclusive rights in works of authorship 246
Paris Convention (1883) 315

Patent Cooperation Treaty 312
Patterson, Lyman Ray 23
  Copyright in Historical Perspective 11
Patry, William 184
photography 165–8
piracy 1–2, 39
  alleged newness of term 13
  expansion of notion of 32
  foreign piracy of English books 268
  Stationers' Company, and 89–90
plagiarism 17
poetry
  English Romantic poets 32, 35–6
  Locke 47–8
  nature and function of 33
  unpublished works, protection as 135–6
  value of poetry and its reception 35
  Wordsworth's concept of 60–61
Pope v Curll (1741) 40, 41, 134, 210, 349
Primary Sources on Copyright (1450–1900)
  digital archive 1
printing rights and privileges
  Scotland *see* Scotland: copyright law before 1710
  UK *see under* Stationers' Company in England before 1710
  Vatican *see* Papal printing privileges
'propertization' of copyright 12–13
proto-property in literary and artistic works *see* Papal printing privileges
public international law of copyright and related rights 288–312
  sources for research 294–306
    conference records 294–9
    government records 304–5
    Le Droit d'auteur/Copyright 299–302, 304, 305, 306, 311
    international and national NGOs and their proceedings 302–3
    national legislation and court decisions 305–6
    texts and other journals 303–4
  treaties and their interpretation 292–4
    context of a treaty 292
    customary international law 292
    interpretation, use of historical materials 292
    multilateral treaties 293–4
    principal source of binding obligations 292
    sources, use of 292
Purday, Charles Henry 19–20
Puri, W 184

purposes of copyright 21–5, 64
  authors' rights, protecting 22, 23, 24
  owners of books, protecting 22
  printers and booksellers, protecting 22–3
  public interest, promoting 23–4
  publishers, protecting 23, 61
  recognition of natural rights 24
  regulatory void, filling 96–7
  trade and commodification 23
Putnam, George Haven 15–16

Quesnel, Francois: *Map of Paris* 159
Quick, John: *The Annotated Constitution of the Australian Commonwealth* 374–6

Rahmatian, Andreas 21
Reade, Charles 193–4
reading
  act of 32
  educational purposes 34
remedies
  different approach of English and Scottish judges to 124–6
  England *see* equitable infringement remedies before 1800
  Scotland 123–7
  US 195–6
  Vatican 256–8
Renault, Louis 293, 297–8, 308
Renouard, Charles-Augustin 403–4, 408
Richardson, Megan 175
Ricketson, Sam 63
'right of paternity' 265–6
Ringer, Barbara 238
Rogers v Koon (1992) (US) 64–71, 77
'romantic' authors 52–77
  before 'authorship' 54–8
    collaborative and collective work 55–6, 58
    Samuel Johnson 55–8
  international copyright legislation, UK 63
  romantic authorship 58–61
    Wordsworth 58–61
  romantic values in legal decision-making 64–77
    Bulun Bulun 71–7
    Rogers v Koon 64–71, 77
Rome Convention (1961) 291
Rose, Mark 21, 44, 51, 161–2
  Authors and Owners 27, 37–42
  engraving 161–2
  oversimplification of authorship debate/role of philosophy 27–8, 39, 41–3, 44–5

proprietors, authors as 37–42, 44–5, 46
　determining distinctiveness of work by identity occupying it 38–9
　literary property extended to letters 40
　natural right to own creation 38
　prior right to literary property 37–8
Routledge v Low (1868) 276, 277, 380, 386–7
Roworth v Wilkes (1807) 179
Royal Academy of Arts 162
　artistic copyright 170, 171–2
　　infringement 172
　　sculpture 163, 168
Royal Commission on Copyright and Colonial Issues (1878) 12, 22, 26, 193, 279–81
　artistic copyright 170, 171, 182
　colonial copyright 279–81
　fair use 182
　infringement 182
　Report 19
　witnesses 19–20, 279, 280
Royal Council (Spain) 424, 427–9, 430, 435, 436, 438, 442

Sag, Michael 186
Sainsbury, Maree 378, 379–80, 381–2, 387
Saint Bonaventure 55
St Clair, William 188
Sáinz de Andino, Pedro 424, 435–7
Salinger, J D
　Catcher in the Rye 77
Saunders, David 23
Sayre v Moore (1785) 191
Schiller, Johann Christoph Friedrich 35
　Aesthetic Letters 33
Scotland: copyright law before 1710 2, 96–117
　adherence of authors and printers to copyright regime 115–17
　　James Kirkwood's grammar 115–16
　　legal agreements: printing Stair's *Institutions of the Laws of Scotland* 116–17
　　Scottish books entering English market 96–7
　　The Works of Sir David Lindsay 115
　legal tradition 97–9
　　Civilian/European influences 97, 120, 131
　　Hart's case 98–9
　　limits placed on copyright protection 98
　　property requiring physical form 98
　　'reasonableness' test 98
　　Roman law, influence of 97–8, 119, 131
　　Scots law grounded on social law and 'evident utility' 98
　printing patent and litigation 112–15
　　book trade disputes 113–14
　　almanacs 114–15
　　Bibles 114
　　Crown's 'printing patent' as most significant patent 112
　　proprietorial view of copyright before 1710 112–13
　　religious publishing 114
Scotland: literary property in 18th and 19th centuries 119–38
　Copyright Act 1911 136–7
　copyright and patents as 'exclusive privileges' 120–22
　copyright and patents as incorporeal rights 122
　copyright and patents as part of law of real rights or property 121, 122
　copyright and patent rights as heritable 122–3
　Hinton v Donaldson 128–32
　literary property and equitable remedies 123–7
　　Battle of the Booksellers *see* Battle of the Booksellers
　Statute of Anne, 1707 Union, and 119–20
　unpublished works 132–6
　　poetry 135–6
　　private correspondence 132–4
Scott, Katie 159–60
　Privilege and Property 159–60
Scott, Sir Walter 136, 137
Scrutton, TE 171–2
　infringement 181–2
　The Laws of Copyright 19, 292
sculpture 163–4
Sell, Susan 23
　Intellectual Property Rights: A Critical History 16–17
Seville, Catherine 22, 25, 193
Sher, Richard 2
Sherman, Brad 175
　bilateral copyright treaties 164, 165
　The Making of Modern Intellectual Property Law 11, 164
Sims, Alexandra 186, 187–8
Smiles v Bedford (1876) (Can) 283
Smith, Adam 85, 121, 122
Snow, Ned 12
Society of Artists 162
Society of Social Science 171

soft law 292
Spain 4, 100
  Anglo-Spanish bilateral copyright agreement 438
  literary copyright *see* Spain: literary copyright on mid-19th century
  Salvadorian-Spanish Copyright Treaty 315, 325–7
  Spanish Civil Code 423
Spain: literary copyright in mid-19th century 423–43
  advantages of bilateral treaty 426
  bilateralism 425-6, 437–42
  French request for copyright treaty 425
    Anglo-Spanish bilateral copyright treaty 439–42
    Franco-Spanish bilateral copyright treaty 438–9
    visibility of negotiations 437–8
  Literary Copyright Act (1847) 431–5
    duration of protection 432
    first copyright Act, as 423, 432
    law as hybrid between old and modern copyright conception 431–2
    legal deposits, requirement for 434–5
    literary extracts becoming legitimate works 434
    retroactive effect, consequences of 435
    translations 432–4
Stair, Viscount 125, 131
  Institutions of the Laws of Scotland 98, 116
Stationers' Company 1710 2, 22, 23, 38, 49, 81–95, 99–102, 105, 107, 111, 112, 146, 153, 336, 349
  incorporation of Stationers' Company 85–6
  membership 81–2
  monopolies 101
  nature of 81
  origins 81
  printing and privileges: book trade 1553 81–5, 99
    content of books regulated through pre-publication licensing 84
    Crown's interest/privileges 83–4
    generic privileges 84
    overlapping of privileges 84–5, 86
    privileges granted by placard 84
    privileges granted under great seal 84
    privileges protecting right to print by royal grants 83
  privileges, copies and 1710 Act 92–5
  privileges under Mary's reign 85–6, 87–8
  Scottish publications entered 123

Stationers' Register 81, 88–92, 107
  commercial value of a 'copy' 91
  importance of 91
  learning and encouragement of authors 91–2
  market for 'copies', development of 91
  permissions to publish 89
  piracy 89–90
  protecting publishing rights, as model for 90
  Statute of Anne, and 23, 81
Stationers v Carnan (1775) 141, 145
Statute of Anne (1710) 1, 3, 4, 28, 37, 61, 119, 139, 189, 335
  abridgements 188
  author's copyright 22
    author-figure indistinct 61
    statutory right, copyright as 174
  author's nascent right already existing 40
  Enlightenment philosophy, and 193
  colonies, and 335
  enacted 2
  infringement 3, 69, 124, 176–8, 184
  interpretation 126–7, 131–2
  legal effects of 17–21
  limitation on copyright 37
  modern significance 25
  music 140, 141–3
  purposes of 22
    authors' rights, protecting 22, 23, 24
    printers and booksellers, protecting 22–3
    public interest, promoting 23–4
    publishers, protecting 23, 61
    recognition of natural rights 24
    regulatory void, filling 96–7
    trade and commodification 23
    trade regulation statute, as 23
  scope 96, 119, 270, 335
  Union of 1707, and 119–20
  US legislation, and 347, 348–9
Statute of Monopolies 101, 121
Stern, Simon 23
Story, Justice Joseph 361
  Commentaries on Equity Jurisprudence 356
strict liability 12

Tagg, John: *The Burden of Representation* 166
Talfourd, Thomas Noon 62, 179, 269
Thomas, Julian 175
Tonson v Collins (1761) 14, 18, 38
Tonson v Baker (1710) 176–7
Tonson v Walker (1739) 96, 204

Torres Caicedo, José María *see under* El Salvador and internationalisation of copyright
Trade-Mark Cases (1879) (US) 346
traditional culture 70–71
　Bulun Bulun 71–7
treaties 292–4
　context of a treaty 292
　customary international law 292
　interpretation, use of historical materials 292
　multilateral treaties 293–4
　principal source of binding obligations 292
　sources, use of 292
Trevelyan, Sir Charles 278, 279
TRIPS Agreement 291, 311
Trollope, Anthony 193
　Ralph the Heir 194
Tschudi, Victor Plahte 256
Twain, Mark 24

UNESCO 302–3
UNIDROIT 302–3
United Kingdom
　Anglo-Spanish bilateral copyright treaty 438–42
　artistic copyright *see* artistic copyright
　Berne Convention 307
　　colonial copyright *see under* Berne Convention
　　see also Australian colonies, copyright in; British colonial and imperial copyright
　definition of copyright 176
　El Salvador copyright agreement negotiations 321–5
　English Romantic poets 32, 35–6
　　see also individual poets
　infringement *see* infringement in 18th and 19th century Britain
　infringement remedies *see* equitable infringement remedies before 1800
　music copyright *see* music copyright in late 18th and early 19th century Britain
　'particular' copyrights: England and Scotland 99–103
　Scotland
　　copyright law *see* Scotland: copyright law before 1710
　　literary property *see* Scotland: literary property in 18th and 19th centuries
　Stationers' Company *see* Stationers' Company in England before 1710

Statute of Anne *see* Statute of Anne (1710)
UK authors in US, protection for 289–90
United States
　Berne Convention 293, 307, 308
　Canadian book copyright, and 282–3
　Constitution 24, 342
　copyright 1672–1909 *see* United States copyright 1672–1909
　copyright history, use of 9
　definition of copyright 176
　early English law, importance of 187
　fair use 12, 184, 186–7
　infringement, remedies for 195–6
　'new matter' doctrine 251–2
　photographic copyright 166
　purpose of copyright 24
　Register of Copyright 14
　UK authors in US, protection for 289–90
United States copyright 1672–1909 3, 335–71
　early copyright 1789–1840 342–59
　　American literary property debate 353–7
　　constitutional clause 342–6
　　Copyright Act 1790, regime under 347–51
　　Copyright Act (1831) 351–3
　　early copyright jurisprudence 357–9
　modernization of copyright 359–71
　　administration 369–70
　　Copyright Act (1909) 370–71
　　entitlements 362–4
　　international copyright 365–9
　　scope 360–62
　　subject matter 359–60
　origins 335–42
　　colonial printing privileges/grants 336–8
　　colonial precursors 335–8
　　copyright, state 338–42
　state copyright 338–42
　　general copyright statutes 340–42
　　individual grants 339–40
Universal Copyright Convention 291, 308

Vaidyanathan, Siva 9, 24
Vatican printing privileges *see* Papal printing privileges in 16th century
Vaver, David 188
Vertue, George 162
Vienna Convention on the Law of Treaties 292–3
　interpretation 292, 304, 307

Walter v Lane (1900) 186
Watson, James: *History of the Art of Printing* 110

Watson, the younger v Freebairn, Baskett and Campbell (1713–18) (Scotland) 113
Wellington v Levi (1709) 208–9
Wheaton v Peters (1834) 353–7
Whitaker v Hime (1815) 156
Whittingham v Wooler (1817) 218
Wieland, Christoph Martin 34
Winfield, Percy 21
 The Chief Sources of Legal History 10
WIPO *see* World Intellectual Property Organization (WIPO)
Wolfe v Payne (1547) 197, 221–2
women writers
 excluded from status of genius 34–5
Woodmansee, Martha: *The Author, Art and his Market* 28–37, 42, 44, 51
 contribution to history of ideas, as 28–9
 'Aesthetic Autonomy as a Weapon in Cultural Politics': Schiller's *Aesthetic Letters* 33
 'Aesthetics and the Policing of Reading': strategies for improving art of reading 33–4
 'Engendering Art': gendered nature of genius 34–5
 'Genius and Copyright'; construction of authorship 30–33
 'Interests of Disinterestedness: modern theorisation of art 29–30
 'Uses of Kant in England' influence of aesthetics on Wordsworth and Coleridge 35–6

Wordsworth, William 32, 35–6
 copyright reform, supporting 62
 'Daffodils' 58–9
  Dorothy Wordsworth's role 58
 efforts to secure perpetual copyright 36
 Essay 36, 54
 genius/individual origination 54, 55
 Lyrical Ballads 35, 54
  collaboration with Coleridge 59–60, 61
 poetry, nature of 60–61
 romantic author, as 58–61
World Intellectual Property Organisation (WIPO) 299, 302, 306
 Berne Convention, role regarding 311–12
 conference records 295
 Development Agenda 308
 soft law recommendations 292
 WIPO Performers and Phonograms Convention (1996) 292, 298, 310
 World Copyright Treaty (1996) 291, 298, 310, 311
World Trade Organisation 306
Wyatt v Barnard (1814) 181

Yeo, Richard 191
Young, Edward: *Conjectures on Original Composition* 30, 31, 38, 54

Zwart, Melissa de 184–5